1989

The collapse of the Berlin Wall has come to represent the entry of an isolated region onto the global stage. On the contrary, this study argues that Communist states had in fact long been shapers of an interconnecting world, with 1989 instead marking a choice by local elites about the form that globalisation should take. Published to coincide with the thirtieth anniversary of the 1989 revolutions, this work draws on material from local archives to international institutions to explore the place of Eastern Europe in the emergence, since the 1970s, of a new world order that combined neoliberal economics and liberal democracy with increasingly bordered civilizational, racial, and religious identities. An original and wide-ranging history, it explores the importance of the region's links to the West, East Asia, Africa, and Latin America in this global transformation, reclaiming the era's other visions such as socialist democracy and authoritarian modernization that had been lost in triumphalist histories of market liberalism.

JAMES MARK is Professor of History at the University of Exeter. He is the author of *The Unfinished Revolution: Making Sense of the Communist Past in Central-Eastern Europe* (2010), which was nominated for the Longman History Today Book Prize 2011 and selected as one of the 'best books of 2011' by *Foreign Affairs*. He is co-author of *Europe's 1968: Voices of Revolt* (2013) and co-editor of *Secret Agents and the Memory of Everyday Collaboration in Communist Eastern Europe* (2017) and *Alternative Globalizations: Eastern Europe and the Postcolonial World* (2020).

BOGDAN C. IACOB is Associate Researcher in the Department of History at the University of Exeter. He is editor of the special issue 'State Socialist Experts in Transnational Perspective: East European Circulation of Knowledge during the Cold War', published in *East Central Europe* (2018), and co-editor of *Ideological Storms: Intellectuals, Dictators, and the Totalitarian Temptation* (2019) with Vladimir Tismaneanu.

TOBIAS RUPPRECHT is Lecturer in Latin American and Caribbean History at the University of Exeter. He is the author of *Soviet Internationalism after Stalin: Interaction and Exchange between the USSR and Latin America during the Cold War* (2015).

LJUBICA SPASKOVSKA is Lecturer in European History at the University of Exeter. She is the author of *The Last Yugoslav Generation: The Rethinking of Youth Politics and Cultures in Late Socialism* (2017).

NEW APPROACHES TO EUROPEAN HISTORY

Series editors

T. C. W. BLANNING, *Sidney Sussex College, Cambridge*
BRENDAN SIMMS, *Peterhouse, Cambridge*

New Approaches to European History is an important textbook series, which provides concise but authoritative surveys of major themes and problems in European history since the Renaissance. Written at a level and length accessible to advanced school students and undergraduates, each book in the series addresses topics or themes that students of European history encounter daily: the series embraces both some of the more 'traditional' subjects of study and those cultural and social issues to which increasing numbers of school and college courses are devoted. A particular effort is made to consider the wider international implications of the subject under scrutiny.

To aid the student reader, scholarly apparatus and annotation is light, but each work has full supplementary bibliographies and notes for further reading: where appropriate, chronologies, maps, diagrams, and other illustrative material are also provided.

For a complete list of titles published in the series, please see:
www.cambridge.org/newapproaches

1989

A Global History of Eastern Europe

James Mark
University of Exeter

Bogdan C. Iacob
University of Exeter

Tobias Rupprecht
University of Exeter

Ljubica Spaskovska
University of Exeter

CAMBRIDGE
UNIVERSITY PRESS

CAMBRIDGE
UNIVERSITY PRESS

University Printing House, Cambridge CB2 8BS, United Kingdom

One Liberty Plaza, 20th Floor, New York, NY 10006, USA

477 Williamstown Road, Port Melbourne, VIC 3207, Australia

314–321, 3rd Floor, Plot 3, Splendor Forum, Jasola District Centre, New Delhi – 110025, India

79 Anson Road, #06–04/06, Singapore 079906

Cambridge University Press is part of the University of Cambridge.

It furthers the University's mission by disseminating knowledge in the pursuit of education, learning, and research at the highest international levels of excellence.

www.cambridge.org
Information on this title: www.cambridge.org/9781108427005
DOI: 10.1017/9781108576703

© James Mark, Bogdan C. Iacob, Tobias Rupprecht and Ljubica Spaskovska 2019

First published 2019

Printed in the United Kingdom by TJ International Ltd. Padstow Cornwall

A catalogue record for this publication is available from the British Library.

ISBN 978-1-108-42700-5 Hardback
ISBN 978-1-108-44714-0 Paperback

Cambridge University Press has no responsibility for the persistence or accuracy of URLs for external or third-party internet websites referred to in this publication and does not guarantee that any content on such websites is, or will remain, accurate or appropriate.

Table of Contents

Acknowledgements

We wish to thank the Leverhulme Trust, which generously supported the research for this book as part of the project '*1989 after 1989: Rethinking the Fall of State Socialism in Global Perspective*'. It funded the time required for research and writing for three of the authors, James Mark, Ljubica Spaskovska, and Bogdan C. Iacob as well as the work of Wu Biyu and Alesia Kananchuk who assisted with some research. The book is the product of collaborative writing and research, and of equal effort from the four authors. We would also like to thank Ned Richardson-Little, who climbed the foothills with us, before leaving to ascend other peaks. For careful reading and comments on earlier drafts as well as for providing intellectual companionship, we wish to express our gratitude to a good number of our academic colleagues, amongst them Catherine Baker, Cornel Ban, Florian Bieber, Susan Bayly, Nelly Bekus, Eric Burton, Aron Buzogány, Kim Christiaens, Guillem Colom-Montero, Gregor Feindt, Zoltán Ginelli, Raluca Grosescu, Frank Hadler, Konrad Jarausch, Robert Kindler, Michal Kopeček, Albert Manke, Angela Romano, Chris Saunders, Christina Schwenkel, Quinn Slobodian, Lars Fredrik Stöcker, Balázs Trencsényi, Joanna Wawryniak and Felix Wemheuer. We are thankful to the three anonymous Cambridge University Press reviewers for their insightful comments and suggestions. We are especially grateful to the '1989 after 1989' project co-ordinators Natalie Taylor and Alison Tytherleigh, whose support has been invaluable. We also wish to thank our proofreader, Martin Thom, whose sterling efforts have hidden the occasional awkwardness of our phrasings and done much to refine our text.

Introduction

The most powerful images of the end of state socialism in Eastern Europe – broadcast around the world – showed cheering East and West German citizens dismantling the Berlin Wall. Due to a series of lucky coincidences and failures in communication, the heavily fortified border had been breached first during the night of 9 November 1989. TV stations all around the world showed the images of *Mauerspechte* ('wall woodpeckers'), who were chipping away openings in the Wall that had stood as a symbol of dictatorship and a divided Europe for twenty-eight years.[1] Within two months Communist rule would collapse across Eastern Europe, and then, in 1991, in the Soviet Union, too. The enduring power of these images, particularly in the Western media, derived from the fact that they appeared to provide a powerful illustration of the ways in which we have come to understand the transition in formerly socialist Eastern Europe.[2] First of all, the Wall itself stood for the isolation of the region, shut off from a world society and economy; such isolated socialist polities apparently could no longer survive in an increasingly globalised and interconnected world. Second, the cheerful crowds who dismantled the Wall seemed by their existence to prove that European peoples had been captured by an Eastern tyrannical system that was alien to their nature; their hopes of joining and catching up with the West seemed to embody a supposedly eternal desire for freedom and prosperity. Third, the cameras' focus on ordinary people as agents of historical change hid a far less marketable truth about 1989: contrary to public perceptions in the West, it was mainly reforming Communist elites,

---

[1] On the series of accidents, see Mary Elise Sarotte, *Collapse* (New York: Basic Books, 2014), xix.

[2] On the absence of Berlin Wall images in Eastern Europe and their popularity in the West, see James Mark, Anna Saunders, Muriel Blaive, Adam Hudek, and Stanislaw Tyszka, '1989 after 1989: Remembering the End of State Socialism in East-Central Europe', in Michal Kopeček and Piotr Wciślik (eds.), *Thinking through Transition: Liberal Democracy, Authoritarian Pasts, and Intellectual History in East Central Europe after 1989* (Budapest: Central European University Press, 2015), 495–96.

rather than popular revolt, that had played the pivotal role in shepherding many countries of the region to a new world.[3] Last, and perhaps most importantly, such imagery stood as an easy visual shorthand for a much wider intellectual apparatus that made sense of the transformations of 1989 through the lenses of Western liberalism: here was a region, they seemed to say, that was shifting from immobility to mobility, passivity to activity, the old to the modern, obsolete planning to the market, and inertia to development.[4] Eastern Europe's transformation underpinned and nurtured ideas about the superiority of the Western liberal model: '1989' confirmed to many that the dynamic mix of liberal democracy, free markets, and Western-led globalisation would be the future of modern statehood.

Such stories were not just Western mythologies propagated to sustain a particular post–Cold War identity renewed by a sense of victory over Communism and the inevitability of the triumph of its own political and economic models. In the first fifteen years after the end of Communism, many Eastern European elites were happy to align themselves with such narratives, too. Although there was remarkably little positive commemoration of 1989 in the region itself, such readings of the past were often performed on a pan-European or wider stage: they were intended to prove the commitment of Eastern European states to a new post–Cold War Western-dominated order and its values, as they endeavoured to integrate into the European Union and NATO.[5] This commitment also provided them with a sense of their region's new global importance: they were the ones who had brought Communism to a close, had liberated themselves from the Soviet 'Evil Empire', and now had a moral obligation to support a Western-led world. Understanding the promotion or armed imposition of market democracy in other authoritarian contexts as part of a wave that included their own experience of liberation from a centrally planned dictatorship, many Eastern European post-socialist governments – alongside former dissidents from Adam Michnik in Poland to Václav Havel in the Czech Republic and Liu Xiaobo in China – supported the US-led invasion of Iraq in 2003. Other important figures of Eastern Europe's transition took on roles as advisors in the so-called

---

[3] For this thesis, see Stephen Kotkin, *Uncivil Society: 1989 and the Implosion of the Communist Establishment* (New York: Modern Library, 2009).

[4] Christina Schwenkel, 'Rethinking Asian Mobilities. Socialist Migration and Post-Socialist Repatriation of Vietnamese Contract Workers in East Germany', *Critical Asian Studies*, 46/2 (2014), 240–41.

[5] On the absence of commemoration, see James Mark, *The Unfinished Revolution. Making Sense of the Communist Past in Central-Eastern Europe* (New Haven, CT: Yale University Press, 2010), chap. 1.

Colour Revolutions from Ukraine and the Balkans to Central Asia or as consultants on how to do democratic transitions during the Arab Spring in 2011.[6]

This dominant liberal narrative, which downplayed the particularity of the historical conjuncture that had enabled the revolutions of 1989, has now come under attack. The notion of Eastern Europe as a region that is naturally converging on a form of Western liberalism at home and is advocating its values abroad was increasingly questioned from the beginning of the 2010s.[7] Right-wing populist governments across Eastern Europe have turned against the liberal interpretation of '1989': they drastically cut funding for institutions charged with preserving the democratic values of 1989, such as the European Solidarity Center in Gdańsk.[8] Some of the heroes of 1989, including such once luminous figures as the former Solidarność leader and Polish president Lech Wałęsa, have been rebranded as traitors to the nation for having compromised with the former Communist elites. Revisionist histories of 1989 suggest it was not a revolution at all but rather an opportunity captured by socialists whose grip on the state was not loosened until twenty years after the notional collapse.[9]

As the liberal narrative of 1989 faces head winds, so too does the notion of Eastern Europe's inevitable Westernisation. Under Vladimir Putin, from the early 2000s, Russia increasingly rejected the idea of being an ordinary nation-state in a 'common European home', preferring rather to reclaim a great power status between Europe and Asia. In the 2010s this notion of civilizational separateness spread to those countries that had initially integrated themselves westwards through joining the European Union. Whilst liberal forces still championed their region's attachment to what they encode as Western progressive cultural values, an ever-strengthening populism from the right and the left defined itself against a morally dissolute West and looked to Moscow and Beijing for

---

[6] Leszek Balcerowicz, 'Economic Reform. Lessons for Post-Saddam Iraq from Post-Soviet Europe' (American Enterprise Institute working paper, 24 March 2005); 'Ein "Balcerowicz-Plan" für den irakischen Wiederaufbau. Was der Irak von Polen lernen kann', *Neue Zürcher Zeitung*, 14 June 2005.
[7] Ivan Krastev, '3 Versions of Europe Are Collapsing at the Same Time', *Foreign Policy*, 10 July 2018.
[8] See www.gdansk.pl/wiadomosci/darowizny-dla-europosjkiego-centrum-solidarnosci-jest-juz-numer-konta,a,136983#.XFGai2w5bzc.facebook.
[9] See, e.g., Rudolf Tőkés, *A harmadik magyar köztársaság születése* (The Birth of the Third Hungarian Republic) (Budapest: L'Harmattan, 2015). Tőkés argues that 1989 was captured by 'socialist lawyers' and that real 'moral reparation' for the nation did not happen in Hungary until 2011 with the passing of a new 'Fundamental Law'.

new political, financial, and economic support.[10] After Viktor Orbán, once an iconic liberal figure of Hungary's 1989, was re-elected prime minister in 2014, he all but disregarded the twenty-fifth anniversary of the end of state socialism. Instead, in a series of programmatic speeches he declared that the 'Western financial crisis' had been a more pivotal turning point than 1989, posited his 'illiberal democracy' against despised 'European values', and aligned himself with Singapore, China, India, Turkey, and Vladimir Putin's Russia.[11] Across Central Europe right-wing populist governments began to challenge the dependency on Western investment and transnational capitalism of the first decades of the post-Communist order.[12] For those in the Balkans who had not been admitted to the European Union, the performance of desiring Europe whilst being kept in a state of 'ambivalent liminality' had begun to wear thin.[13]

This anti-liberal shift was not confined to Eastern Europe but could be observed in many regions that negotiated the transition from authoritarianism to multiparty democracy between the late 1970s and early 1990s: in Southern Europe, such radical political parties as Syriza in Greece and Podemos in Spain have developed fundamental critiques of the transition as the source of later political corruption and economic inequality; a younger leftist generation in South Africa turned away from the ruling party, the African National Congress, and its celebration of the negotiated South African transition; right-wing populists such as Brazilian president Jair Bolsonaro reject their countries' liberal cultures of transition and openly celebrate military dictatorship; parts of the left in the Philippines have critiqued the unfinished nature of the pre-1986 struggle to topple Ferdinand Marcos's dictatorship and how it paved the way for

---

[10] On this crisis, see Ivan Krastev, *After Europe* (Philadelphia: University of Pennsylvania Press, 2017); Ziemowit Szczerek, 'New Separatisms: Or What Could Happen If the West Disappeared from Eastern Europe?', *New Eastern Europe*, 3/4 (2018), http://neweasterneurope.eu/2018/04/26/new-separatisms-happen-west-disappeared-eastern-europe/.

[11] 'Viktor Orbán's Speech at the XXV. Bálványos Free Summer University and Youth Camp, 26th July, 2014, Băile Tuşnad (Tusnádfürdő)', *Budapest Beacon*, https://budapestbeacon.com/full-text-of-viktor-orbans-speech-at-baile-tusnad-tusnadfurdo-of-26-july-2014/.

[12] Vera Šćepanović and Dorothee Bohle, 'The Institutional Embeddedness of Transnational Corporations: Dependent Capitalism in Central and Eastern Europe', in Andreas Nölke and Christian May (eds.), *Handbook of the International Political Economy of the Corporation* (Northampton, MA: Edward Elgar, 2018), 152–166.

[13] Christoffer Kølvraa, 'Limits of Attraction: The EU's Eastern Border and the European Neighbourhood Policy', *East European Politics and Societies and Cultures*, 31/1 (2017), 11–25.

the revival of authoritarianism under President Rodrigo Duterte from 2016.[14]

The collapse of a consensus is often a fortuitous moment for historians. It enables new questions to be asked and previously calcified versions of events to be challenged and rethought. No longer are the events of 1989 only precursors of the present. After a generation they can be analysed in their own right and as a very particular historical conjuncture. '1989' represented the highpoint in a faith in a liberal vision that came to be challenged both in Eastern Europe and in the world more broadly. Without the sense of inevitable convergence, the story of 1989 now appears as a very specific moment in the region's history, chronologically bracketed on either side by movements – whether Communists or today's populists – whose leaders were resistant to, or at least deeply sceptical towards, certain types of integration with the West. Moreover, this divergence sheds light on other aspects of these years of transition that have got lost in the too easy celebration of a liberal breakthrough. Just beneath the surface, other forms of transformation, populist, authoritarian, or radical socialist, were widely articulated in the transition period but erased from the liberal script in the aftermath. A reconsideration of the historically contingent assemblage that triumphed around 1989 also highlights the existence of alternative but forgotten political geographies: Eastern European elites looked to Asia and Latin America as they did to the West in making sense of their late twentieth-century transformations. A global history of 1989 needs to explain how these alternative visions were closed down but must also address their persistence in some Eastern European political cultures. These ideas, forged in the decade of crisis that preceded the collapse of Communism, returned to inform aspects of the illiberal populist moment in the region in the 2010s.

Going Global

The notion that it was a 'wind of change' blowing in from the West that swept away stale Eastern dictatorships dominated both popular images and scholarly frameworks of the Communist era in Eastern Europe. It was not only the West German rock group the Scorpions but also US president Bill Clinton who were drawn to this metaphor: 'If we learn anything from the collapse of the Berlin Wall and the fall of the

---

[14] Kostis Kornetis, 'Introduction: The End of a Parable? Unsettling the Transitology Model in the Age of Crisis', *Historein*, 15/1 (2015), 5–12; Lisandro E. Claudio, 'Memories of the Anti-Marcos Movement: The Left and the Mnemonic Dynamics of the Post-Authoritarian Philippines', *South East Asia Research*, 18/1 (2010), 33–66.

governments in Eastern Europe', he asserted in a speech given to announce the establishment of the North American Free Trade Agreement (NAFTA) in 1993, 'even a totally controlled society cannot resist the winds of change that economics and technology and information flow have imposed in this world of ours'.[15] Historical frameworks to understand the transformation of Eastern Europe were established at a high point in the faith in a Western-led globalisation – studies often concentrated on those integrative processes that acted as precursors to a world dominated by the West.

Although histories of the Eastern European transformation are usually not very global in outlook, they nevertheless rely implicitly on frameworks derived from a very Western-centric version of global history: Eastern Europe commonly came to be viewed as a victim and as a passive recipient of Western 'medicine' for its ailments, a cure that enabled the region to abandon its isolation and engage with the one true globalisation. According to one US intellectual, 1989 represented 'removing a temporary roadblock to globalization, ending traditional colonialism, and permitting Eastern Europe to enter post-history'.[16] The prominent German left-liberal public intellectual Jürgen Habermas spoke of the 'rectifying' or 'catching up' revolutions of 1989, which represented the idea that, as sociologist Talcott Parsons had put it, 'the great civilisations of the world would converge towards the institutional and cultural configurations of Western society'.[17] So-called transitologists normalised a convergence on the values of Western economy and politics[18];

---

[15] President William J. Clinton, 'Remarks at the Signing Ceremony for the Supplemental Agreements to the North American Free Trade Agreement' (14 September 1993). The German rock group the Scorpions' 'Wind of Change' was the soundtrack to German reunification. Others have argued that, despite its seemingly apolitical content, the Swedish pop band Roxette's 'Listen to Your Heart' was *the* song of 1989, as it was used in some of the first post-Communist election campaigns – including by Havel's Civic Forum and Viktor Orbán's FIDESZ: Joshua Clover, *1989: Bob Dylan Didn't Have This to Sing About* (Berkeley: University of California Press, 2009), 108–9.

[16] Gale Stokes, 'Purposes of the Past', in Vladimir Tismaneanu and Bogdan C. Iacob (eds.), *The End and the Beginning: The Revolutions of 1989 and the Resurgence of History* (Budapest: Central European University Press, 2012), 35–54, 52.

[17] Talcott Parsons, quoted in Gareth Dale, *Between State Capitalism and Globalisation. The Collapse of the East German Economy* (Bern: Peter Lang, 2004), 9–10; Jürgen Habermas, 'What Does Socialism Mean Today? The Rectifying Revolution and the Need for New Thinking on the Left', *New Left Review*, 183 (1990), 3–21.

[18] Guillermo O'Donnell and Philippe Schmitter (eds.), *Transitions from Authoritarianism: Comparative Perspectives* (Baltimore: Johns Hopkins University Press, 1986); Juan Linz and Alfred Stepan, *Democratic Transitions and Consolidation: Eastern Europe, Southern Europe and Latin America* (Baltimore: Johns Hopkins University Press, 1996); Kathryn Stoner and Michael McFaul (eds.), *Transitions to Democracy: A Comparative Perspective* (Baltimore: Johns Hopkins University Press, 2013).

postcolonial scholars suggested that Eastern Europeans had internalised a 'Western gaze' through which they constructed their own backwardness and peripherality;[19] leftist economists took this further, arguing that Eastern Europe had been turned into the West's 'Third World' so it could become the object of economic transformation by international institutions.[20] This was a unidirectional imagination in the tradition of 1950s' modernization theory: non-Western 'peripheries' had shown themselves to be unworthy of their own history and would inevitably recognise their destiny to become 'like us'.

The idea of Western capitalism as the sole engine of modernity has left us with a distorted view of socialist states as inward-looking, isolated, and cut off from global trends until the transition to capitalism in the 1990s.[21] There are many manifestations of this. Seen through Western liberal eyes, only those aspects that appear to be missing from their conceptions of an authentic globalisation tend to be noted, such as Eastern European limitations on mobility and lower levels of transnational economic integration. Post-Communist historians from the region most commonly sought to revive the anti-Communist *national* story and displayed scant desire to write their twentieth century into histories of globalisation.[22] The division between post-Communist and postcolonial scholars has meant that there has been, until recently, little interest in bringing together stories of a wider socialist world.[23] The gradual economic integration of late socialism has been addressed, but usually in an account that has stressed how the region was a victim of such processes. This is another 'rest to the West' story: only after 1989 does the region enter a true (i.e., Western-led) globalised world.[24] In this sense such accounts essentialise the region's home in the West and provide a

---

[19] Lucy Mayblin, Aneta Piekut, and Gill Valentine, '"Other" Posts in "Other" Places: Poland through a Postcolonial Lens?', *Sociology*, 50/1 (2016), 70.

[20] Andre Gunder Frank, 'Nothing New in the East: No New World Order', *Social Justice*, 19/1 (1992), 34–59.

[21] For an account along these lines, see André Steiner, 'The Globalisation Process and the Eastern Bloc Countries in the 1970s and 1980s', *European Review of History*, 21/2 (2014), 165–81.

[22] Histories of globalisation in Eastern Europe usually start in 1989. See, for example, Katalin Fábián (ed.), *Globalization. Perspectives from Central and Eastern Europe* (Bingley: Emerald, 2007).

[23] On this divide, see Sharad Chari and Katherine Verdery, 'Thinking between the Posts. Postcolonialism, Postsocialism, and Ethnography after the Cold War', *Comparative Studies in Society and History*, 51/1 (2009), 6–34, 16.

[24] The study of globalisation in Eastern Europe, or nascent 'Global East studies', usually start only after 1989.

relatively unproblematic story of convergence with a Western liberalism according to which it was 'liberated' in 1989.[25]

In this book we contend that a very different view of the history of the Eastern half of the continent is needed. Eastern Europe not only has long been globally interconnected, but also has been, for two hundred years, a 'swing region'. Its very identity as a meaningfully distinct area has always been shaped by a sense of its in-betweenness; it has self-defined both with, and against, the West.[26] Various postwar experts, and in particular economists, believed that Communism could produce a future for the region free from dependency on the West, in alliance with anti-imperialist forces across the globe; in the late twentieth century, the idea that the region belonged in a liberal West came back; populists have in the 2010s once again questioned the region's relationship to an imagined 'liberal West' and sought new alliances with China, Russia, and the Middle East. We also have to recognise the heterogeneity of this in-betweenness: Yugoslavia as part of the Non-Aligned Movement always viewed itself as between East and West, whereas other states found their Western-ness only later in the Cold War. None of these positions were absolute: Eastern Europeans have always contested these geopolitical and geocultural regional positionings of their elites. Anti-Communists argued that Communist regimes had stolen their region from the West in the name of a barbaric Eastern Bolshevism in the early Cold War, whereas many leftists argued against an uncritical embrace of a Western orientation of the region in 1989. Yet the question of where the region belonged in the world was constantly raised. From this perspective, 1989 was not the attainment of an inevitable destiny in the West but part of a much longer-term argument about Eastern Europe's place in the world, one that is still ongoing.

The region's engagement with the world during the Communist period was not a type of globalisation immediately recognisable to the

---

[25] For a criticism of this focus on the West in the 1980s and the Soviet turn to East Asia, see Chris Miller, *The Struggle to Save the Soviet Economy : Mikhail Gorbachev and the Collapse of the USSR* (Chapel Hill: University of North Carolina Press, 2016), 20–23.

[26] See the approach adopted in Balázs Trencsényi, Maciej Janowski, Monika Baár, Maria Falina, Michal Kopeček, 'Introduction', in Trencsényi, Janowski, Baár, Falina, and Kopeček, *A History of Modern Political Thought in East Central Europe. Volume I: Negotiating Modernity in the 'Long Nineteenth Century'* (Oxford: Oxford University Press, 2018), esp. 3–5; Katherine Lebow, Małgorzata Mazurek, and Joanna Wawrzyniak, 'Making Modern Social Science: The Global Imagination in East Central and Southeastern Europe after Versailles', *Contemporary European History*, 28/2 (2019), 137–42; Manuela Boatcă, 'Semi-peripheries in the World-System: Reflecting Eastern European and Latin American Experiences', *Journal of World-Systems Research*, 12/2 (2006), 321–46.

West; mobility was limited, and Communist states often eschewed multilateral cooperation. Nevertheless, to differing degrees Eastern European states had already opened up to trade and engaged in developmental and cultural exchanges with the states that had decolonised in the Global South, within a broader socialist world, and out towards the West long before 1989.[27] For a time there was thus a commitment to building an alternative world order based on a common anti-imperialist solidarity that would protect the region from political or economic subordination to the West. Yet, tentatively, from the late 1960s, with the relaxation of tensions between East and West, reflected in the so-called Helsinki Process, gradual integration occurred economically and culturally. Over the last two decades of the Communist system, the region's in-betweenness prompted important questions: Was it to ally with a non-Western alternative form of global modernity, or rather integrate into Western globalism? Was a fealty to both systems possible, or was the world converging towards one global system? The answer given differed from country to country, from political group to political group, and within society at large. Nevertheless, increasingly, alternative global visions were hollowed out from within.

Adopting this perspective, we argue that 1989 was less the beginning of the region's globalisation than a confirmation of a choice about the form of globalisation that the region would take, based on a process of partial, often contradictory, and sometimes reversed attempts at realignment that had started from the 1960s. It provided finality to the process of hollowing out an alternative form of global interconnectedness based on anti-imperialist geographies. These shifts were more commonly remarked on by those from outside the region, some of whom viewed them as a moment of loss: some African and Caribbean leftists, for instance, saw the end of state socialism as the reconstitution of a white colonial Europe that marked a definitive end to an era of high decolonisation. In this view the Iron Curtain had not been lifted in 1989 but displaced southwards along the Mediterranean, dividing Europe from Africa. Some non-European anti-imperialists understood 1989 as a story of deglobalisation through which Eastern Europe had sought a civilizational realignment to a white world and the racialized privileges this would afford them. They could point to the fact that since the dismantling of the inner-European fortified border, over a thousand kilometres of new walls

---

[27] James Mark, Artemy Kalinovsky, and Steffi Marung, 'Introduction – Alternative Globalizations: Eastern Europe and the Postcolonial World', in Mark, Kalinovsky, and Marung (eds.), *Alternative Globalizations: Eastern Europe and the Postcolonial World* (Bloomington: Indiana University Press, 2020).

and fences have been used by EU countries to redraw the boundaries of an expanded Europe.[28]

Eastern European reformers, by contrast, did not note a racialised reorientation or the new forms of bordering that this realignment implied; they saw it rather as a return to a normal path towards modern global civilisation.[29] Against the background of economic crisis in the 1980s in Eastern Europe, this became a compelling script that served to normalise a particular vision of Western development based on liberal democracy, the smaller state, and a market economy, which later appeared to be the only plausible route to success. They abandoned all belief in the possibility of an alternative global modernity and presented their course as a journey to normality. Even Communist leaders themselves saw the West as the natural destiny for Eastern Europe by the late 1980s: the Soviet leader Mikhail Gorbachev announced that the Soviet Union had now decided to 'enter world civilisation', while Jerzy Urban, the Communist spokesman for the military ruler of Poland, General Wojciech Jaruzelski, admitted in 1989 that 'the superiority of Western civilization had become obvious for everybody'.[30] There were also critics, whose voices have been lost in histories of 1989: they feared that an uncritical Westernisation would lead to economic re-peripheralisation, high social costs, an end to profitable international trade, the undermining of hard-won social, economic, and gender-based rights, and the marginalisation of labour. We will tell their stories too.

The Long Transition and the Making of Transitional Elites in Global Perspective

Eastern Europe's realignment to dominant Western economic and political norms generated remarkably little critique at the time. The reorientation of its elites from state socialism to liberal capitalism happened astonishingly quickly considering that they had based their legitimacy on

---

[28] Ainhoa Ruiz Benedicto and Pere Brunet, 'Building Walls: Fear and Securitization in the European Union' (2018) www.tni.org/files/publication-downloads/building_walls_-_full_report_-_english.pdf.

[29] On 'race' as an absent category in Eastern European studies, see Catherine Baker, *Race and the Yugoslav Region: Postsocialist, Post-conflict, Postcolonial?* (Manchester: Manchester University Press, 2018), esp. the introduction; Anikó Imre, 'Whiteness in Post-socialist Eastern Europe: The Time of the Gypsies, the End of Race', in Alfred J. Lopez (ed.), *Postcolonial Whiteness: A Critical Reader on Race and Empire* (Albany: State University of New York Press, 2005), 79–80.

[30] Georges Mink et Jean-Charles Szurek, *La grande conversion: Le destin des communistes en Europe de l'Est* (Paris: Seuil, 1999), 88.

a rhetoric of anti-capitalism, anti-imperialism, and anti-Westernism.[31] It was also striking that the huge dislocations produced by this transformation were widely tolerated by the population at large – to the surprise, in fact, of many international institutions who provided policy advice regarding the implementation of this new economic order. This lack of resistance is still more striking if we venture a comparison with other world regions undertaking similar transformations: in Africa and Latin America one found significant opposition to the deregulated capitalism of the so-called 'Washington Consensus'.[32] To explain the rapid embedding of this new compact in Eastern Europe, our book considers the ways in which the region itself was an active producer of its own global realignment. This was not a region isolated and in stasis, simply waiting to be rescued; rather, a long revolution from within occurring within late socialist societies was in large part responsible for the new political, cultural, and economic consensus that emerged and could be implemented once Soviet control was withdrawn.

Who were the actors that produced this transformation? In the immediate aftermath of the revolutions, histories focussed on heroic dissidents who combated the system from below, dragging the region 'back to Europe'.[33] Yet in most countries that experienced this transformation, 1989 was initially referred to not as a revolution but rather as a turn (*Wende*, a coinage of the GDR leader Egon Krenz) or a system change (*rendszerváltás* in Hungarian).[34] This choice of terminology speaks an important truth: 1989 was in many countries marked by an elite-guided transition. In Hungary and Poland Communist elites and parts of the opposition helped usher in multiparty democracy at roundtable talks; in Czechoslovakia and the GDR they relinquished power following a minimum of social pressure. Only in Romania was a violent revolution necessary to remove a dictator from power.[35]

---

[31] Nikolay R. Karkova and Zhivka Valiavicharska, 'Rethinking East-European Socialism: Notes toward an Anticapitalist Decolonial Methodology', *Interventions*, 20/6 (2018), 785–813.

[32] G. K. Helleiner, *The IMF and Africa in the 1980s: Essays in International Finance* (Princeton, NJ: Princeton University, 1983).

[33] See, e.g., Barbara Falk, *Dilemmas of Dissidence in East-Central Europe: Citizen Intellectuals and Philosopher Kings* (Budapest: Central European University Press, 2003).

[34] German dissidents always disliked *Wende* and spoke of the *friedliche Revolution* ('peaceful revolution'). The latter term eventually superseded the former.

[35] Kotkin, *Uncivil Society*. For a critique, see Konrad H. Jarausch, 'People Power? Towards a Historical Explanation of 1989', in Vladimir Tismaneanu and Bogdan C. Iacob (eds.), *The Revolutions of 1989 and the Resurgence of History* (Budapest: Central European University Press, 2012), 109–25.

At the centre of this book is the global history of the incremental, stuttering formation of what would in 1989 become 'transitional elites'. By the late 1980s the liberal-left leadership of the trade union Solidarność in Poland, liberal economists in the late socialist administration in Czechoslovakia, or second- and third-tier party members in Romania were ready to take on such roles. These new elite networks were often made up of both reforming Communists and former members of oppositions, and in some cases it became difficult to draw a firm line between them: the leading dissidents counted among their ranks many disillusioned intellectuals or members of purged establishment elites. Expert groups, mainly economists and lawyers, who often straddled the divide between Communist functionary and dissident thinker, led the process of remaking economies and constitutions. These emerging networks played the crucial role in initiating the processes of realignment towards the norms of global capitalism, liberal democracy, and European culture that would accelerate in 1989.[36] Many other oppositional forces – from peace movements to the radical right – were excluded. Other expert groups who provided powerful oppositional critiques 'from below' of both the social crisis of late socialism and the deleterious social effects of capitalist change – most notably sociologists – were also kept far from power.[37]

Where scholarship *did* embrace the role of these new elites in transition, it often accused them of betraying or capturing a popular democratic revolution in the name of a capitalism dominated by ex-Communists and their 'liberal hirelings'. The fact that former representatives of the party-state had been left in a dominant economic position in 1989 was seen by some as the original sin of the new Eastern Europe.[38] From their perspective the transition process had failed to enforce a clear break in economic ownership around 1989, which had in turn led to the ineffective functioning of the market, social inequalities, and corruption. The

---

[36] For this perspective, see Michal Kopeček (ed.), *Expertní kořeny postsocialismu: Československo sedmdesátých až devadesátých let* (Prague: Argo, 2019).

[37] On the sidelining of late socialist sociology with the loss of faith in the late 1970s in the scientific management of culture, and elite dislike of expert culture's capacity to record alienation rather than produce consent, see Adela Hîncu, 'Managing Culture, Locating Consent: The Sociology of Mass Culture in Socialist Romania, 1960s–1970s', *Revista Română De Sociologie*, 1–2 (2017), 12–13.

[38] This position received its fullest academic expression in the work of sociologist Jadwiga Staniszkis, who presented the early 1980s as the most important moment of transition, when Communist apparatchiks began to exchange their political power for economic status, beginning a process of appropriating state enterprises and transforming them into semiprivate companies. Jadwiga Staniszkis, *The Dynamics of the Breakthrough in Eastern Europe* (Berkeley: University of California Press, 1991) and Staniszkis, '"Political Capitalism" in Poland', *East European Politics and Societies*, 5/1 (1991), 127–141.

political instrumentalisation of such narratives by populist movements and governments has sometimes discouraged research into the actual role of elites in the history of the region's realignment. But we do not need to agree with such narratives of an ostensible 'treasonous elite' to acknowledge the crucial role of political and intellectual elites in the long-term transition to liberal capitalism in Eastern Europe.

In this process of self-reorientation, Eastern European Communist elites and oppositions, although shaped by their own national transformations and struggles, interacted with broader global developments. Many of the ideas that came to dominate in the late twentieth century – market capitalism, liberal democracy, self-determination, and regional integration – circulated in Eastern Europe too. Its elites were neither simply agents nor recipients of these changes of the late Cold War; they were part of networks and international institutions through which these ideas were created and remade. Yet for years analyses not only downplayed Eastern Europeans' agency in the history of their own transformation but also showed little interest in analysing the active role the region had played within a global history of the market, of democracy, and of the civilisational transformations of the late twentieth century.[39] If we take global historians' critique of 'West to the rest' framings seriously, then it is important not only to examine changes to so-called (semi-)peripheries as local manifestations of major global transformations but also to discuss their active role in shaping them.

The upper strata of late socialist polities had been more exposed than any others to global currents. Often in conversations within new networks and ideological currents abroad, they responded to the crisis in both socialist development and the global economy in the 1970s and 1980s.[40] Over the course of the 1960s East-West networks, enabled by the policy of peaceful coexistence, had led to proliferating exchanges between economists, urban planners, and many other expert groups. These exchanges served to nurture a new technocratic generation, particularly on the western fringes of socialist Europe, whose values increasingly spanned the Iron Curtain. Trade and production networks and internationally engaged socialist enterprises crossed the ideological divide too. Indebtedness resulting from an excessive

---

[39] On this need to give a 'Global East' agency, see Martin Müller, 'In Search of the Global East: Thinking between North and South', *Geopolitics* (2018), www.tandfonline.com/doi/full/10.1080/14650045.2018.1477757.

[40] Johanna Bockman, *Markets in the Name of Socialism. The Left-Wing Origins of Neoliberalism* (Stanford, CA: Stanford University Press, 2011); Michal Kopeček, 'From Scientific Social Management to Neoliberal Governmentality? Czechoslovak Sociology and Social Research on the Way from Authoritarianism to Liberal Democracy, 1969–1989', *Stan Rzeczy*, 13 (2017), 171–96.

borrowing of petrodollars in the mid-1970s and the rise of interest rates on commercial bank loans had brought several Eastern European states into close engagement with Western banks and other financial institutions. Evolving communication with Western elites helped break down many of the oppositions that had sustained political distance.

We also propose a less Eurocentric account of the region's Westernisation. Too often the role of the West in the transition has been overplayed to the detriment of other global connections that shaped Eastern Europe before and after 1989. The failure to remember earlier linkages with the Global South may have been in part because of their association with a socialist internationalism demonised after 1989. Yet they were indeed important. The global interconnectedness of socialist culture, at the level of everyday interactions and elite contacts, had been to a large extent a result of the global processes unleashed by postwar decolonisation.[41] While many socialist elites had, by the late 1970s, abandoned a loyalty to an anti-imperialist struggle, the legacy of these internationalist cultures of expertise and politics endured. This ensured that regional responses to the rise of new forms of globalisation in the 1980s were informed by a very broad sense of international currents and long-standing networks that went well beyond Europe or North America. Even if we conceptualise 1989 as a reorientation to the West, the route to imagining this reintegration both for elites and oppositions passed through many other world regions.

In dominant understandings of 1989, the norms of a deregulated global market capitalism – later dubbed 'neoliberalism' – had been produced in an Anglo-American world and exported into Eastern Europe when Communism collapsed: in such a historical imaginary, Western economists such as Jeffrey Sachs played key roles as the travelling experts arriving to convert unbelievers on the fringes of Western civilisation. Although it has become fashionable to see 'semi-peripheries' such as Eastern Europe as 'experimental zones' for Western neoliberals,[42] we suggest a rather more multidirectional history of economic ideas and practises. Notions of deregulation, market efficiency, privatisation, shrinking the state, individualising economic responsibility, and structural adjustment of the national economy developed on the world's peripheries alongside their construction within the Anglo-American

---

[41] James Mark and Péter Apor, 'Socialism Goes Global: Decolonisation and the Making of a New Culture of Internationalism in Socialist Hungary, 1956–1989', *Journal of Modern History*, 87/4 (2015), 891.

[42] On Eastern Europe as a testing ground for neoliberalism, see Peter Gowan, 'Neo-liberal Theory and Practice for Eastern Europe', *New Left Review*, 213/1 (1995), 3–60; Naomi Klein, *The Shock Doctrine. The Rise of Disaster Capitalism* (London: Penguin, 2007), 169.

sphere, where their advocates questioned a postwar consensus on welfare capitalism and Keynesian trade cycle policies. Eastern European reformist economists too focussed on developing the socialist market and shared many assumptions with Western neoliberals about competition, markets, and discipline. These were often developed as much in collaboration with countries thought to occupy similar 'semi-peripheral' positions in the global economy to Eastern Europe's, such as the East Asian and Latin American states, as they were through East-West links or inspiration from Thatcherism or Reaganomics.[43]

Even if some Western economists and institutions did see Eastern Europe as a potential 'laboratory' for their ideas, their Eastern counterparts did not need the West to become 'more West than the West'. In Chapter 1 we show how Eastern European economists in the 1990s were often more radical in their prescriptions and ignored pleas for restraint from Western-dominated institutions. Neoliberal advocates in Western Europe, at the same time, used the Easterners' reforms as arguments for transforming Western economies that were still based, as they saw it, on an earlier social democratic consensus, which had not yet been overcome. Indeed, the East's own rapid transformation had some impact on the development of economies elsewhere: this Eastern acceleration eventually led to the development of low wage sectors in Western European economies too.[44]

There is still a tendency to view the economic transformation of Eastern Europe as a 'West to the rest' history, and this for a number of reasons: first of all because reformers in Eastern Europe often instrumentalised the advice of Western institutions as a cover for their own reforms, as if to intimate that these latter were a necessary part of re-joining 'Western civilisation'; second because Eastern Europe's transition was narrated in exactly this way by powerful Western governments as they continued to pressurise countries in the Global South in the 1990s. Western liberals and neoconservatives were quick to recognise the power of the collapse of Communism as a global 'teaching moment'.

---

[43] Duccio Basosi, 'An Economic Lens on Global Transformations. The Foreign Debt Crisis of the 1980s in the Soviet Bloc and Latin America', in Piotr H. Kosicki and Kyrill Kunakhovich (eds.), *The Legacy of 1989: Continuity and Discontinuity in a Quarter-Century of Global Revolution* (forthcoming); Bockman, *Markets in the Name of Socialism*. The economic rise of East Asia was often of interest to socialist reformers from Moscow as much as the emergence of an economically integrated Western Europe. Miller, *Struggle to Save the Soviet Economy*, 23–27.

[44] Philipp Ther, *Die neue Ordnung auf dem alten Kontinent. Eine Geschichte des neoliberalen Europa* (Berlin: Suhrkamp, 2014); Anders Åslund and Simeon Djankov, *The Great Rebirth. Lessons from the Victory of Capitalism over Communism* (Washington, DC: Peterson Institute for International Economics, 2014).

The developments in Eastern Europe, a region formerly committed to anti-Westernism, could now be employed to emplot the inexorable nature of the Washington Consensus and naturalise the congruence between the market and liberal democracy. It became a powerful story that was used by Western governments and financial institutions to justify new forms of political conditionality, economic reform, or debt restructuring in Africa – as we explore in Chapter 5.[45]

Eastern Europe's political transformation was also part of a much broader 'third wave' of democratisation that had swept through Southern Europe, Latin America, and parts of East Asia, stopping short in China, before crossing the Iron Curtain and then reaching out, stutteringly, into Africa. The central story in many of these shifts was one of the deradicalisation of the left: Communists accepted multiparty democracy and negotiated settlements in transitions in Southern Europe in the late 1970s; radical anti-imperialist movements often made their peace with liberal parliamentarianism in the 1980s; and the African National Congress (ANC) accommodated itself with a negotiated end to apartheid and truth commissions in the 1990s. Eastern Europe was no exception: here the settlements were in large part the work of reformers in Communist parties who consented to pluralist solutions, initially still within the framework of state socialism, until that quickly spun out of their control and shattered their dominance.

It was far from clear before 1989 itself that sufficient sections of Communist parties would embrace multiparty democracy. Nevertheless, new discussions about pluralism, democracy, and rights – which laid foundations for the eventual settlement – were shaped by these broader transformations of the international left. A common language of Marxist revisionism was forged during the 1960s in both the East and West of the continent to democratise Communism. It provided the basis for the Eastern European party elites' rapprochement with a deradicalised left in Southern and Western Europe. Gorbachev, for instance, developed relationships with Southern European Eurocommunists who had embraced parliamentary democracy, along with Western social democrats. Whilst he did not initially intend to dismantle the Communist party's monopoly on power, these changes on the left helped reinvigorate discussions on the limits of pluralism at home and inspire the Soviet leader's rather utopian vision of a Common European Home through which, he hoped, countries would freely choose a more democratic

---

[45] On the ideas about neoliberalism that circulated between peripheries and came to South Africa in the early 1990s, see Nelson Mandela and Mandla Langa, *Dare Not Linger: The Presidential Years* (London: Macmillan, 2017), 75–76.

socialism. Increasingly strident Western claims from the late 1970s that Communist states were not bearers of true rights – which were civic and individual rather than socioeconomic and collective – forced Communist hardliners onto the back foot and opened out space for reformers to reignite discussions on the socialist rule of law and on the necessity of democracy for economic development. Pluralism was of course not embraced by many: the more conservative wings of the ruling parties presciently feared the resulting loss of control.

Instead, a new template for survival was available to reformists: nego-tiated transition, which had first been pioneered in post-Francoist Spain in the mid-1970s as *consenso* ('consensus'), and then extended to Latin America during the end of military dictatorships from the mid-1980s. For the party top echelons it was attractive because it helped them envision a life beyond one-party rule. For the opposition it was a way of breaking a cycle of resistance and repression between themselves and regime hardliners. Moreover, as Eastern European Communists became more and more Europeanised and distanced themselves from radical Third Worldism, violence in the name of progress became coded as a political practice of less civilised regimes outside the continent. Reproducing the violence of the suppression of the Tiananmen Square protests in China became for almost all parties an untenable solution for a European setting.[46] In the one country that required revolution, Romania, opponents viewed the regime's use of violence in a vain attempt to retain control as reminiscent of a Third World dictatorship.

Oppositions – whilst usually less globally connected than their country's elites – were nevertheless part of these broader shifts over the meaning of democratisation. Most of them had not been liberal democrats *in nuce* in the 1970s; even in the 1980s only a minority were supporters of what in 1989 emerged as a liberal consensus on political-civic rights, multiparty systems, free elections, and the free market. Some conservative, national-ist, and leftist dissenters rejected liberalism altogether. Yet for that crucial section of the opposition who engaged in negotiated settlements to exit Communism, their gradual creeping towards liberal democracy not only was a response to their failures to reform socialism but also catalysed through contacts beyond the region itself. From the early 1980s some saw themselves as part of a world movement towards democratisation and helped produce, through their revival of the notion of totalitarianism, a political imaginary that defined the democratic wave of the 1970s to the 1990s: a world ordered not by earlier notions of right and left or fascism

---

[46] Quinn Slobodian, 'China Is Not Far! Alternative Internationalism and the Tiananmen Square Massacre in East Germany's 1989', in Mark et al., *Alternative Globalizations*.

and anti-fascism but rather by making the opposition between dictatorship (of whatever hue) and democracy the lynchpin of contemporary visions of governance. Such a stance was heavily supported by democracy-promotion institutions such as US-funded National Endowment for Democracy and the Soros Fund, which helped bring oppositions and reformers in socialist countries into contact with anti-dictatorial movements in Latin America and South Africa.

After 1989 former dissidents took their message of democratisation and peaceful change into other East European countries and occasionally to Latin American, African, and Middle Eastern states that had yet to set out on the path to liberal democracy. They became coproducers of global visions about non-radical, inter-elite negotiated transitions from authoritarianism. Together with post-Communist Eastern European politicians and Western democracy-promotion agencies, they would play leading roles in international movements against authoritarian regimes, assisting the Colour Revolutions in formerly socialist countries from the post-Soviet and former Yugoslav spaces to Iraq and Libya – as well as promoting political change in still-socialist Cuba and Vietnam. The impact of these endeavours varied: they helped speed the processes of bringing the worldviews of the African and Latin American left to the liberal democratic centre – while simultaneously providing a masterclass for the still ruling East Asian Communist elites on how not to enact political transformation.

1989 was also an important chapter in the global history of decolonisation and self-determination. On one hand it represented a Westernising civilizational realignment of a region following the exhaustion of the processes of postwar global decolonisation. Earlier Communist claims that Eastern Europe was part of a broader anti-colonial world that had fought for freedom and thrown off fascist-imperialist occupation no longer had any purchase. Liberal democracy and market capitalism were seen as representing a high Western modernity that Eastern Europeans aspired to join. The idea of a return to Europe, or the West more broadly, was often presented as the rallying cry of the dissident against an Eastern Bolshevism and an unwanted socialist internationalism – but in fact was shared by many reforming Communists in the 1980s. In this sense 1989 marked the end of a process of building a wider rejection of an anti-colonial internationalism that had previously animated Eastern European politics. From the mid-1970s onwards more and more states instead looked to the reconstitution of Europe as the space in which their political life should naturally find a home. And no longer was this a concept of Europe derived from the values of the decolonisation era. As we explore in Chapter 3 there had been competing visions of what the continent should be after the end of Empire: some envisioned a much less bordered Europe in a world of equal civilisations. From the 1970s, however, many amongst both elites and oppositions championed through the Helsinki Process a high European civilisation that was defined in opposition to Africa in the South and the Islamic world in the East. Over a decade before Samuel Huntington wrote his *Clash of Civilizations*, actors were engaged in cultural political work in which putative civilizational spaces were produced in relation to revivals of the threatening racial or religious other. We should also remember that 1989 was the year during which the persecution of Bulgarian Muslims was at its height and when migrant workers from non-European socialist countries such as Cuba, Vietnam, and Mozambique were forced to return home.

On the other hand, the effects of anti-colonialism did not disappear from the region in 1989. In this sense the end of European state socialism was part of a broader global history of the forging of the meaning of self-determination – one moment in a longer, interconnected global chain of 'end of empire' stories. The processes that led to the withdrawal of Soviet control in Eastern Europe and the collapse of the Soviet, Yugoslav, and Czechoslovak federations in the region were not only paralleled by processes of self-determination elsewhere but also entangled with them. In the 1960s, inspired by anti-colonial nationalisms across the world, Communist states had presented themselves as part of an expanding anti-colonial world and as protectors of their nations from Western imperialism; opposition movements as well as republics in socialist federations also invoked parallels with Afro-Asian movements to criticise the Soviets as occupiers in Europe or to push for greater autonomy. The swing away from the Global South in the 1970s challenged the primacy of this political language. To some degree it survived, albeit now shorn of the earlier leftist claims to collective self-determination or justice in the global economy. Self-determination had been appropriated by the political right, now articulated as narrower national struggles. For some Eastern European conservative opposition movements, the liberation of the nation was placed above all. Others combined it with what was becoming known as the 'transition' paradigm: true independence could be achieved only with the guarantee of civic rights, a market economy, and a realignment to the West. As Yugoslavia was breaking up, claims for the self-determination of republics were no longer internationalist – but rather built around the defence of a narrow definition of the nation or of a Christian Europe against Islam.

The history of late twentieth- and early twenty-first-century processes of Europeanisation played down Eastern European agency: certainly, the idea that the region was simply being incorporated into already established Western European structures and values was an integral part of the identity of the European Union (EU) in the 1990s and 2000s.[47] Yet Europe in its most recent manifestation – an East-West unification project, and strictly bordered from the South – is better understood as a coproduction between both sides of the continent from the late Cold War. Just as the East had once sought out the Third World, the European Community (EC) had early in its life experimented with the idea of 'Eurafrica': Western Europe, facing a divided continent, looked southwards, bringing former African colonies into a close economic and political partnership.[48] Both projects declined in parallel with the emergence of European détente in the 1970s. This process was initiated in large part from the East, where states played key roles in establishing the Helsinki Process. Then from the early 1980s the region's dissenting intellectuals successfully promoted the idea of Central Europe to international audiences: this imaginary captured the idea that part of the bloc was a 'captured West'. The symbolic reclaiming of a high Europeanness, distanced from the values of socialist internationalism and 'Eastern Bolshevism', provided a crucial ideological underpinning for visions of post–Cold War Euro-Atlantic integration, confirming the viability of an eastwards extension of the European project into a culturally and politically unthreatening space after 1989. Their vision also contributed to a broader re-imagining of Europe as a more culturally and politically distinct civilisation – or, as critics would later call it, 'fortress Europe'.

A Global History of the Other '1989s'

The extraordinary convergence of marketisation, democratisation, self-determination, and Westernisation that 1989 came to represent was anything but inevitable. Right up until the actual collapse of European state socialism, other historical paths were possible and often seemed much more likely to contemporaries in East and West. The crises of socialist societies and economies in the 1970s and 1980s were very real and certainly required fundamental change, but what that change constituted was an open question. The West was in economic crisis, too, in the late 1970s, and governments reacted by curtailing the power of trade

---

[47] Kim Christiaens, James Mark, and José M. Faraldo, 'Entangled Transitions: Eastern and Southern European Convergence or Alternative Europes? 1960s–2000s', *Contemporary European History*, 26/4 (2017), 577–99.

[48] Peo Hansen and Stefan Jonsson, *Eurafrica: the Untold History of European Integration and Colonialism* (London: Bloomsbury Academic, 2015).

unions and an increasing accommodation with an international rule-based system that protected global markets from national democratic control.[49] Eastern Europe was part of this turn: early in the 1980s some economists in Hungary, Poland, and Czechoslovakia argued that deregulation, privatisation, and opening up to world markets were necessary to create modern efficient economies – and could be undertaken effectively by nominally Communist one-party dictatorships.[50] Many dissident groups of altogether different persuasions did not initially call for liberal democracy, either: the ten-million-strong Polish trade union Solidarność, the largest oppositional movement in the Eastern Bloc, was wedded to incremental reform and the leftist-minded protection of workers' rights, rather than a fully fledged multiparty system. And many nationalist anti-Communists envisioned returns to interwar authoritarian statehood rather than a Westernisation of their countries.

Even in 1989 itself, a development towards Western democracy and radical market economy was seldom considered a natural convergence. Western observers, such as the British-German liberal Ralf Dahrendorf, were not convinced that economic and democratic reform could realistically be attempted at one and the same time in Eastern Europe.[51] Western governments, fearing instability, were on the fence about how to support such transformations. In the months around the collapse of Communist rule, many possible versions of democracy circulated: a wide variety of human rights, anti-militaristic, religious, and ecological groups had mobilised in the years leading up to 1989. Some dissidents rejected outright marketisation as fundamentally undemocratic and advocated self-management of socialist economies combined with greater democratisation right until the collapse.[52]

'Freedom', 'rights', 'democracy', 'national renewal', 'prosperity', and 'Europe' had different meanings for different people around 1989.

---

[49] David Harvey, *A Brief History of Neoliberalism* (New York: Oxford University Press, 2005).

[50] For this approach, see János Mátyás Kovács and Violetta Zentai, 'Prologue', in Kovács and Zentai (eds.), *Capitalism from Outside? Economic Cultures in Eastern Europe after 1989* (Budapest: Central European University Press, 2012), 3–7. On regional economists' role in transnational debates since the 1960s, see Bockman, *Markets in the Name of Socialism*.

[51] Ralf Dahrendorf, *Reflections on the Revolution in Europe: In a Letter Intended to Have Been Sent to a Gentleman in Warsaw, 1990* (London: Chatto & Windus, 1990).

[52] See leading Polish dissident Bronisław Geremek, interviewed in *Libération* (Paris), 16 December 1986, 27; Iván Szelényi, 'Eastern Europe in an Epoch of Transition: Toward a Socialist Mixed Economy?', in Victor Nee and David Stark (eds.), *Remaking the Economic Institutions of Socialism: China and Eastern Europe* (Stanford, CA: Stanford University Press, 1989), 208–32; Ljubica Spaskovska, *The Last Yugoslav Generation: The Rethinking of Youth Politics and Cultures in Late Socialism* (Manchester: Manchester University Press, 2017), chaps. 3 and 4.

Groups such as Poland's Wolność i Pokój ('Freedom and Peace'), East Germany's Für unser Land ('For Our Land'), and Czechoslovakia's Nezavisla mirova sdruzeni ('Independent Peace Association') uttered radical demands for direct democracy. Conservative and ethno-populist movements such as Polityka Polska ('Polish Politics') and Ruch Młodej Polski ('Young Poland movement') held ambivalent views about liberal democracy and linked the language of human rights to discourses of national and Catholic renewal.[53] Many reforming elites were well aware of the numerous directions change could follow and sought therefore to limit political participation of such alternatives from below.[54] In 1989 in Poland, for instance, during the negotiations between Solidarność and the Polish United Workers' Party, conservative voices were sidelined, while more radical groups such as Solidarność Walcząca ('Fighting Solidarity') boycotted the semi-free elections in June that year in protest at the compromise with the Communists. This eventually fuelled a sense of alienation amongst those in Eastern Europe who felt excluded from this pact of the elites in 1989. Right-wing populists such as Jarosław Kaczyński and Viktor Orbán later skilfully used these resentments as springboards for their political careers.

The End of the '1989' Era?

The alternative political, economic, and cultural visions that were closed down in the name of a liberal market transition came back to haunt post-socialism. Already by the mid-1990s a right-wing critique had emerged in Eastern Europe that accused reform Communists and the liberal opposition of enacting a transition from above that had robbed 'the people' of their own revolution.[55] In Russia too attacks against uncritical Westernisation proliferated across the political spectrum and a new consensus formed around returning the country to its status as a great Eurasian power, now in a multipolar post-Western world. Only in the late 2000s did critiques become widespread in Eastern Europe. Now that a significant number of the former socialist states had joined the European Union there was no need for local elites to hide their doubts about Westernisation: moreover, against the background of anger about the effects of the 2008 global economic crisis, earlier, sporadic critiques

---

[53] Balázs Trencsényi et al., *Political Thought in East Central Europe. Volume II: Negotiating Modernity in the 'Short Twentieth Century' and Beyond Part II: 1968–2018* (Oxford: Oxford University Press, 2018), 145, 153–54.

[54] On radical alternatives, see Padraic Kenney, *A Carnival of Revolution. Central Europe 1989* (Princeton, NJ: Princeton University Press, 2002), 299.

[55] Mark, *Unfinished Revolution*, chap. 1.

within these societies turned into concerted full-frontal attacks on 1989 and the liberal economics and politics that it had ushered in. Populist nationalists and left radicals pilloried the political figures of the transition period as traitors and revived debates that had been side-lined in the 1990s. As the previously assumed link between Westernisation, democratisation, and prosperity began to lose its appeal,[56] so a (mainly younger) New Left developed in the region, which drew on the Marxist, anti-authoritarian, and socialist traditions of 1968 and 1989 in order to critique the selfishness and social instability that neoliberalism had brought.[57] Others looked for inspiration to Chinese or East Asian authoritarian-capitalist models of development now that, in their view, a 'European model' had failed – just as their predecessors had done in the late 1980s when they were considering a transition under the guidance of the Communist party.

By the mid-2010s populists of both the right and left also rejected the civilizational script that had underpinned 1989, namely that the West was the model to aspire to. Against the fear of demographic decline following large-scale Eastern European emigration to Western Europe from the 2000s and the wave of refugees from the Middle East and North Africa from 2015, such politicians presented themselves not only as saviours of their nations from ethnic disappearance but also as defenders of a 'true Europe' that Western liberalism had abandoned. Aligned with similar populist movements in Western Europe and North America, they attacked the values of liberal cosmopolitanism that 1989, for them, represented. The pan-Western liberal script that employed the end of state socialism as its legitimating moment of global victory came under attack, too: the belief that 1989 could be reproduced across the world had been gradually undermined with the limited success of the Colour Revolutions and the chaos and violent conflict that followed the Iraq War and the Arab Spring. Significant voices in Eastern Europe once again returned their region to a state of in-betweenness, allied to the West, but also increasingly critical of such integration and searching for

---

[56] On the New Left in South-Eastern Europe and the former Yugoslavia, see Igor Štiks and Srećko Horvat (eds.), *Welcome to the Desert of Post-socialism: Radical Politics after Yugoslavia* (London: Verso, 2015); Igor Štiks and Krunoslav Stojaković, 'Southeastern Europe's New Left', *Rosa Luxemburg Stiftung*, February 2019, www.rosalux.de/en/publikation/id/39943/#_ftn1. See also the LeftEast Platform (www.criticatac.ro/lefteast/about/), which brought together left-wing voices from the former socialist space as well as global actors. In a veiled reference to pre-1989 traditions, this internationalist project aims 'to constitute an alternative to the way we see the region but also to the type of intellectual production historically associated to this part of the world'.

[57] Marci Shore, *The Taste of Ashes. The Afterlife of Totalitarianism in Eastern Europe* (New York: Random House, 2013), 237–38.

alternatives. Officials in Moscow or Beijing encouraged this resurgent sense of distinctiveness by offering economic, political, and cultural alignments such as Eurasianism or the Belt and Road Initiative that challenged the continent's geography purportedly built around the EU centre. But the legacies of 1989 did not die. As we explore in Chapter 6, protest movements against such new populisms, illiberal authoritarianism, cultural divergence from the West, or political corruption often invoked the practices and memories of the transition period. 1989 may be marginalised or ostracised in mainstream politics, but it is still recalled as a powerful symbol of an aspiration for Eastern Europe's future.

1. Globalisation

On 15 October 1989 the Cracovian Catholic philosopher and political activist Mirosław Dzielski, who had been talked about as possible first post-Communist Polish prime minister in the turbulent summer before, died young from an aggressive cancer during a trip to the United States. With him departed the popular memory of what was then called the 'Polish Pinochet' variant of transition from socialism.[1] While the Polish 'democratic revolution' and its heroic defeat of state socialism eventually captured the world's imagination in 1989, this type of authoritarian transformation had actually seemed far more probable in the preceding years. Like many other Eastern European intellectuals, Dzielski had been searching from the mid-1970s for ways out of the ever more obvious economic and moral crisis of socialist societies. Yet the power of the Communist parties, with their firm support from Moscow, seemed inalterable. Intellectuals and economists also harboured doubts about the maturity of their populace to handle Western-style democracy and resist the temptations of populist nationalism. Dzielski and many like-minded figures in Poland, Hungary, Czechoslovakia, and the Soviet Union thus suggested an authoritarian capitalist path to fix their countries' problems without dismantling their one-party regimes.

---

[1] On Franco and Pinochet as models, see Mirosław Dzielski, 'Potrzeba twórczego antykomunizmu', *13 Grudnia*, 11 (1987), 7; Adam Michnik, *Letters from Freedom. Post–Cold War Realities and Perspectives* (Berkeley: University of California Press, 1998), 99; Tobias Rupprecht, 'Formula Pinochet. Chilean Lessons for Russian Liberal Reformers during the Soviet Collapse, 1970–2000', *Journal of Contemporary History*, 51/1 (2016), 165–86; Miklós Mitrovits, 'From the Idea of Self-Management to Capitalism. The Characteristics of the Polish Transformation Process', *Debatte. Journal of Contemporary Central and Eastern Europe*, 18/2 (2010), 163–84; Karel Půlpán, *Economic Development of Spain as Inspiration for the Czech Republic* (Stockholm: Institute of Economic Studies, 2001); Piotr Wciślik, 'Political Languages of Anti-Solidarity: Mirosław Dzielski and the Differentia Specifica of Polish Neo-Liberalism', in *Proceedings of the 16th International Conference on the History of Concepts, Bilbao, 29–31 August 2013*, 170–76, http://dx.doi.org/10.1387/conf.hcg2013.2.

The inspiration for an integration into capitalist world markets under the guidance of an authoritarian, nominally Communist regime came partly from the West. The writings of Friedrich Hayek were widely read amongst reform-oriented economists in Eastern Europe. The Austrian-British neoliberal economist had argued from the 1940s that socialist economics, no matter how well meaning, would always eventually lead to totalitarian dictatorship and that a liberal dictator would be preferable to a democratic government lacking commitment to economic liberalism.[2] Dzielski had enthusiastically echoed Hayek in several underground publications from the late 1970s: 'All true supporters of freedom will cherish the liberty of enterprise, the mobility, the regional self-government and the legal safeguards provided by such an [authoritarian capitalist] government', he wrote in a 1985 samizdat essay, 'with democratisation, we can wait for better times'.[3]

Dzielski did however regard other elements of the 'West' as a problematic influence. In the view of economically liberal reformers like him, leading figures of the political opposition, the idealistic dissidents, were under the influence of Western social democracy and, like Western social democrats, he thought, clueless about the economy. The Polish trade union Solidarność (Solidarity), ten million strong in the early 1980s and the largest oppositional movement in Eastern Europe, was for him a case in point: their support for the Miners' Strike in the United Kingdom betrayed their anti-liberal economic leanings, as did their criticism of the military ruler of Poland General Jaruzelski, who for them apparently got on too well with the British conservative prime minister Margaret Thatcher. Before the democratic revolution of 1989, many Western observers shared Dzielski's scepticism regarding expanded popular participation in politics and visions of a non-authoritarian socialism. At a discussion organised by the International Monetary Fund (IMF) in Washington in 1981, US bankers holding Polish debt or looking to invest concurred. Martial Law, introduced in 1981 in an attempt to crush growing opposition, was for them not a wholly negative phenomenon: the stability provided by the re-established centralised control of the state was preferable to Solidarność's lofty ideas about workers' self-management.[4]

---

[2] Friedrich Hayek, *The Road to Serfdom* (London: Routledge, 1944); Bruce Caldwell and Leonidas Montes, 'Friedrich Hayek and His Visits to Chile', *Journal of Austrian Economics*, 28/3 (2015), 261–309.

[3] Mirosław Dzielski, *Duch nadchodzącego czasu, 1–2* (Wrocław: Wektory, 1985), 5.

[4] 'Summary Discussion of Polish Economic Situation and Prospects For Economic Reform' (at the Wilson Center in September 1981), IMF-EUR Divisions Country Desk Files-Poland-913-Economic Reform since 1980–1984-box 38–3, 1–5.

In Dzielski's vision, too, Martial Law was not a tragedy but an opportunity: all Polish economic liberals needed to do was to convince Jaruzelski to deregulate the economy – as the Chilean dictator Augusto Pinochet had done a couple of years earlier.[5] Economically successful development dictatorships in the Global South thus provided inspiration for possible elite-guided transitions in Eastern Europe to capitalism without bothersome and potentially counterproductive democratic procedures. Poland was not alone in this fascination with strong leaders in sunglasses and crisp uniforms. Similar ideas of learning from authoritarian models circulated in most parts of the Eastern Bloc in the 1980s: both Yuri Andropov and Mikhail Gorbachev paid close heed to Deng Xiaoping's reforms and sent observers to learn from China.[6] And Hungarian economists and reform Communists alike saw military-ruled South Korea as one of their role models on how to combine one-party dictatorship with economic success.[7] After the revolutions of 1989, Eastern Europe would quickly become the region that illustrated the natural equivalence between democratisation and marketisation – the proof that China failed to provide after the crushing of the Tiananmen Square protest. Yet until very late in the day in Eastern Europe, market reform and gradual integration into the global economy did not necessarily mean democratisation. A state capitalist model with an authoritarian leadership, such as eventually prevailed in China and Vietnam, seemed much more likely at the time in Eastern Europe, too.

The interest in authoritarian models from the Global South before 1989 also demonstrated that, contrary to a popular notion of a culturally and economically isolated socialist camp, Eastern European socialist societies were not cut off from the wider world. Long before the fall of the Berlin Wall, the region's elites had become deeply engaged with global economics. The story that is often told of 1989 as a Western takeover of a passive and parochial region that had to yield to the forces of Westernisation and, as it became known in the 1990s, 'globalisation', is a fragmentary and misleading one. In fact, local elites and experts were already globally engaged from the 1960s, albeit around the idea of two world economies and the victory of the anti-imperialist socialist one over the capitalist. The changes in 1989 were not Eastern Europe's entry into globalisation, but rather its elites' realignment with a specific

---

[5] Mirosław Dzielski, 'How to Perpetuate Power in People's Poland?' in *Merkuryusz Krakowski i Światowy* (Samizdat, 1980).
[6] Chris Miller, *The Struggle to Save the Soviet Economy* (Chapel Hill: University of North Carolina Press, 2017), 2.
[7] Stephen Kotkin, *Uncivil Society. 1989 and the Implosion of the Communist Establishment* (New York: Random House, 2009), 33.

Western-facing capitalist form. This journey was however not always by way of the West. Reformers also often looked to Latin America and East Asia as they rethought their place in the world. The westernmost countries of socialist Europe, Hungary, Poland, and Yugoslavia, had been the most advanced in this global outlook; but reformers in more isolated societies such as the Soviet Union likewise drew on the global connections and international experience that they had gathered before the transformation of their systems.

Following the end of Communist one-party regimes in 1989, Eastern European states – at varying speeds – privatised their economies, deregulated their labour markets, set prices free, and opened up to international trade and foreign investments. This process happened suprisingly quickly considering that these were countries that had hitherto seemed like monolithic Communist dictatorships whose legitimacy rested on a rhetoric of anti-capitalism, anti-imperialism, and anti-Westernism. Within a decade a variety of capitalisms replaced a system that had claimed to be their antagonistic alternative. This process was particularly rapid in those countries that had had the most extensive links with the outside world and that had experimented most intensively with economic reforms during the socialist period: Poland was the trailblazer for the capitalist revolution of 1989; Hungary and the Baltic states soon followed suit.

This integration into a capitalist globalisation occurred with astonishingly little resistance from old elites or societies. This was especially striking in the light of the high levels of labour unrest across the region in the 1980s. Surveys in the early 1990s noted the survival of 'socialist values' (in a study on the young Yugoslav generation published in 1990, for example, 53 per cent of the respondents declared support for 'socialism as theory'[8]) and a scepticism towards privatisation and foreign investment, but the economic and social disruption caused by transition did not come under organised attack.[9] Labour unions were weak, faced a collapsing membership and an inability to expand into new capitalist workplaces, and were easily demonised through their association with the Communist era.[10] Compared with other world regions, however, capitalist restructuring faced only marginal critique. The trenchant criticism of the neoliberal Washington Consensus, and of novel forms of so-

---

[8] S. Mihailović et al., *Deca krize: Omladina Jugoslavije krajem osamdesetih* (Beograd: Institut društvenih nauka/Centar za politikološka istraživanja i javno mnenje, 1990).

[9] Jan Drahokoupil, *Globalisation and the State in Central and Eastern Europe* (London: Routledge, 2009), 97.

[10] David Ost, 'The Consequences of Postcommunism. Trade Unions in Eastern Europe's Future', *East European Politics and Societies*, 23/1 (2009), 14–19.

called neocolonialism, which had already established itself within the left in Southern Europe, Africa, and Latin America, had little purchase in the East of Europe. This changed only in the late 1990s, with the rise of anti-globalisation movements, and then again after the 2008 financial crisis.

If we are to understand the speed with which Eastern Europe's economic transformation happened, we need to consider how local attitudes had changed long before the arrival of Western advisors. The national economies created after 1989 were not built from scratch or imported wholesale from the West. It was decisions of Eastern European elites, who were aware of the economic crisis and the need for fundamental reform in their countries, that led to the final abandonment of alternative non-Western-centric forms of global integration. Rather than being the sudden importation of entirely foreign concepts, the decision to adopt market capitalism and a western-facing globalisation was the culmination of many ongoing changes in expert cultures and thinking as part of an exchange with a wider world during late socialism.

From Socialist Internationalism to Capitalist Globalisation

The widespread view that 1989 marked the end of the East's economic self-isolation and the import of Western globalism was vividly illustrated in Wolfgang Becker's 2003 *Ostalgie* comedy *Good Bye Lenin!* The protagonist is a dedicated East German socialist who lives in the isolation of her small apartment, barred from leaving her sickbed. In it her son Alex has created the illusion of the ongoing existence of her beloved GDR. She finds out about the fall of the Berlin Wall only when, in a famous scene towards the end of the film, she eventually leaves her apartment and sees Western cars and large IKEA advertisements in her street. The internationally popular film was an emotionally touching portrayal of the hardships of East Germans during the transition period, but its depiction of globalisation was misleading in two respects. First, the view of a world insulated behind barbed wire obfuscated a much longer history of Eastern Europe's global integration. Volkswagen and IKEA had actually crossed the Iron Curtain as early as the beginning of the 1970s. The West German car company and the Swedish furniture manufacturer had discovered the socialist world and its well-trained workforce as a group of low-wage countries, located conveniently near to their markets. That some of the labour for IKEA was provided by political prisoners in the GDR was just as easily overlooked. By the time Lenin bid farewell to East Berlin in 1989, the GDR and several other Eastern European socialist states on the western fringes of the Eastern Bloc had in fact long been integrated into global capitalist commodity chains.[11]

Second, globalisation had not always meant Westernisation. Eastern Europe looked beyond the continent just as it looked to its Western neighbours. Alongside offering cheap labour for Western companies, the GDR exported its economic expertise and industry across the world. It built, for instance, the infrastructure for the expansion of Vietnam's coffee industry, putting the Asian country on the path to becoming the world's second largest coffee exporter – although only after the demise of the socialist state that had helped develop it.[12] In the 1980s the Berlin-based nationally owned enterprise VEB Funkwerk Köpenick constructed one of the world's first mobile phone infrastructures, in Mexico, where the governor in Toluca de Lerdo proudly boasted of a car phone 'made in the GDR'. The technology was then exported to Algeria, Madagascar, Yemen, and Mozambique. Nevertheless, it was never installed at home: the East German secret police objected to means of communication that would have escaped their surveillance.[13] The collapse of Communist-ruled polities thus did not represent the entry of Eastern Europe into a global economy. 1989 should be understood as the culmination of an engagement with what was called an 'interdependent' world economy that Communist elites had themselves encouraged. It was also a choice about the form that such globalisation should take. Alongside an acceleration of westwards integration, 1989 also often marked an end to, or rapid shrinking of, cooperation with the Global South. This 'de-globalising' moment of 1989 would only be questioned over twenty-five years after the end of Communism, when China became an increasingly important economic partner for the region.

Contrary to the prevailing view of an isolated and idiosyncratic socialist Eastern Europe, the region had actually followed many global economic trends in the twentieth century: a long phase of economic nationalism since the Great Depression had ended in the 1950s, in Eastern Europe as in other world regions. From the 1950s, world trade picked up pace again and reached pre-1914 levels by the mid-1970s.[14] In parallel with

---

[11] Tobias Wunschik, *Knastware für den Klassenfeind. Häftlingsarbeit in der DDR, der Ost-West Handel und die Staatssicherheit 1970–1989* (Vandenhoeck & Ruprecht, 2014); 'Ikea ließ auch in Kubas Gefängnissen produzieren', *Frankfurter Allgemeine Zeitung*, 2 May 2012.

[12] Bernd Schaefer, 'Socialist Modernisation in Vietnam: The East German Approach, 1976–1989', in Quinn Slobodian (ed.), *Comrades of Color: East Germany in the Cold War World* (New York: Berghahn, 2015), 108.

[13] 'Telefontechnik. Ein Handy für die DDR', *Mitteldeutsche Zeitung*, 1 April 2011.

[14] Guillaume Daudin, Matthias Morys, and Kevin O'Rourke, 'Europe and Globalisation 1870–1914', in Stephen N. Broadberry and Kevin H. O'Rourke (eds.), *Unifying the*

the West, if more cautiously, Eastern European states opened up to world trade from the 1960s – with the export of technical expertise and the import of raw materials and selected manufactured products. Global integration had not always meant Westernisation, as the West had partly shut out Eastern European states: Cold War economic blockades, embargoes, and sanctions had restricted their participation in international trade. In 1947 the United States had imposed new controls on business with socialist states. In 1950 all NATO countries, except Iceland, also imposed similar restrictions with their so-called Co-Com lists. By 1951 the US Mutual Defence Assistance Control Act forbad economic, financial, and military assistance to countries that exported strategic material to Eastern European states.[15] Their exclusion from Western European markets was exacerbated with the construction of a protectionist European Community in the late 1950s.[16] Moreover, many experts in Eastern Europe saw advantages in delinking from the West: their region's economic underdevelopment was in part blamed on an advanced West that had confined large parts of the East to a rural hinterland. Too much opening up to Western European capitalism, some feared, would result in a re-peripheralisation of the East.

Given this separation from the West, it was rather the rapid acceleration of decolonisation in the late 1950s that gave Eastern European states new trading and investment opportunities. Following the economic isolationism of the Stalinist period, Eastern Europe nursed hopes of developing an anti-imperialist world economy in which their region would play a central role, helping them to escape their former subservient position as a low-wage hinterland to the West.[17] Contrary to our notions today, some of its elites saw socialism as a promoter of global free trade and Western capitalism, with its sanctions and high tariffs for agrarian products, as neocolonial protectionism.[18] The Soviet Union even

European Experience: An Economic History of Modern Europe (Cambridge: Cambridge University Press, 2010), 5-29.

[15] Paul Luif, 'Embargoes in East-West Trade and the European Neutrals: The Case of Austria', *Current Research on Peace and Violence*, 7/4 (1984), 221–22.

[16] The only exception was the GDR: the Treaty of Rome did not challenge the idea, embodied in Germany's postwar Basic Law, that intra-German trade between the FRG and GDR was 'domestic trade'. Thus they had much better access to Western markets than any other Eastern European state.

[17] James Mark and Yakov Feygin, 'The Soviet Union, Eastern Europe and Alternative Visions of a Global Economy 1950s–1980s', in James Mark, Artemy Kalinovsky, and Steffi Marung (eds.), *Alternative Globalizations: Eastern Europe and the Postcolonial World* (Bloomington: Indiana University Press, 2020).

[18] Johanna Bockman, 'Socialist Globalisation against Capitalist Neocolonialism: The Economic Ideas behind the New International Economic Order', *Humanity*, 6/1 (2015), 109–28.

abolished custom duties on all products imported from developing countries in January 1965.[19] From the late 1960s, in response to a fear of an end to cheap Soviet oil, smaller Eastern European states were encouraged to look to the Middle East and Africa for energy and raw material supplies. Some socialist companies were active on the global stage: about fifty large socially or state-owned multinational companies were active around the world in the mid-1970s, mostly in the raw material sector, such as Yugoslavia's huge 'socialist multinational', Energoinvest.[20]

Alongside this opening up to the South, Eastern Europe still looked to collaborate with the West – with vastly varying degrees of access. This happened first in Yugoslavia: ousted from the socialist bloc by Stalin in 1948, its self-positioning between East and West enabled it to develop trade links with both Western Europe and partners in the Non-Aligned Movement. The first major engagements were through industrial cooperation – licensing agreements and joint production. As early as the 1950s the Yugoslav manufacturer Zastava had signed licence contracts with Fiat and IVECO and produced cars and lorries, alongside weaponry, for the world market. Under the brand name Yugo, cars were even exported to the United States in the 1980s (Bruce Willis was not entirely convinced by its quality when he chased his opponent in one in the 1995 film sequel to *Die Hard*). Some Yugoslav companies, such as the electronics manufacturing corporation Iskra, established their own subsidiaries in the West.[21] Yugoslavia became an observer in the Organisation for European Economic Co-operation in 1955, a full member in the Economic and Development Review Committee of its successor OECD, and a member of GATT in 1966, diversified its foreign trade with fellow NAM states, and was, from 1968, the first socialist state to have diplomatic and institutional links with the EC. These liberalising economic reforms opened up the country to the West, with an end to party control over the economy even being envisaged: subsidies were cut, inefficient companies were shut down, productivity was increased,

---

[19] 'Statement by the Union of Soviet Socialist Republics Concerning Prospects for the Development of the USSR's Trade and Economic Cooperation with the Developing Countries', in *Proceedings of the United Nations Conference on Trade and Development* (UNCTAD, 1972), 410.

[20] Jozef Wilczynski, *The Multinationals and East-West Relations: Towards Transideological Collaboration* (Boulder, CO: Westview, 1976), 138.

[21] Harry Trend, '"Iskra" of Yugoslavia Establishes Subsidiaries in West Germany and the United States', Radio Free Europe Research, 11 May 1967, HU OSA (Open Society Archivum) 300–8–3–9978.

control over the expanding foreign trade was given to all worker-run companies, and foreign direct investment was allowed.[22]

For most in the Eastern Bloc, such engagement took off only from the late 1960s. West Germany had set the framework: the policy of 'Ostpolitik', and the recognition of Eastern European borders, would enable it to gradually repair industrial linkages and markets that had been lost since the war – a move that laid the foundations for the rapid expansion of German ownership in the region after 1989. These first steps towards an economic reintegration of Eastern Europe with the capitalist West were harshly criticised by Third World socialists such as Fidel Castro, who blamed the 'so-called Yugoslav communists' for this 'promotion of bourgeois-liberal policy' in Eastern Europe and thanked the Soviet Union for having curtailed such experiments in Czechoslovakia with an invasion.[23] But before long the Soviets warmed to Western capitalists as well: as early as 1971 an elite group of West German industrialists was invited to Siberia to inspect its riches. Upon their return to Moscow, Soviet premier Alexei Kosygin was reported to have declared to them in a toast, 'Gentlemen, you have seen the great possibilities. Please help yourselves'.[24] In 1972 Kosygin and many other leading Soviet statesmen received John D. Rockefeller, who opened a branch of his bank on Moscow's Karl Marx Square.[25] In 1973 General-Secretary Leonid Brezhnev declared in a speech in Kiev that he sought the expansion of large-scale and long-term economic collaboration with both socialist and capitalist countries.[26] From 1974 Soviet citizens could buy Pepsi Cola produced on licence by Soviet government-run bottling factories in exchange for an exclusive right for Pepsi to market Stolichnaya vodka in the West.[27] By 1975, about one-half of the Soviet passenger car production were in fact Fiats, manufactured and sold under a coproduction agreement as Zhigulis – and re-exported to the West as the affordable Lada.

The Soviet Union itself had also started supplying Western Europe with oil and gas in exchange for hard currency by the mid-1970s.

---

[22] Ivan Obadic, 'A Troubled Relationship: Yugoslavia and the European Economic Community in Détente', *European Review of History*, 21/2 (2014), 329–48.

[23] Fidel Castro, 'Comments on Czechoslovakia – Speech 24 August 1968', https://marxists .org/history/cuba/archive/castro/1968/08/24.html.

[24] Wilczynski, *Multinationals*, 20.   [25] Ibid., 21.

[26] Harold Berman, 'Joint Ventures between United States Firms and Soviet Economic Organizations', *Maryland Journal of International Law* 1 (1976), 141.

[27] Norman Girvan, 'Economic Nationalists v. Multinational Corporations: Revolutionary or Evolutionary Change?', in Carl Widstrand (ed.), *Multinational Firms in Africa* (Dakar/ Uppsala: African Institute for Economic Development and Planning/Scandinavian Institute of African Studies, 1975), 36.

Western elites agreed in part because the invasion of Czechoslovakia had convinced them that the Soviets would be better managed through economic cooperation rather than confrontation.[28] Western companies, in return, built pipelines, factories, and airports in the Soviet Union. From the early 1980s Western institutions and firms diverted significant investment from the Global South into Eastern Europe. As one prominent West German development specialist noted in 1989, 'banks and private investors had long ago turned their sights away from the "Third World", from the misery of black Africa and the debt problems of Latin America. This process started long before the "European House" became a palpable attraction and long before the economic opportunities in Central and Eastern Europe became apparent'.[29] The hidden integration of Europe had taken off well before 1989.

Eastern Bloc and Western European enterprises had also begun to collaborate in the Global South.[30] The first tentative steps were taken by Czechoslovak and Romanian firms from the early 1970s, which collaborated with West German businesses in the Middle East and Africa.[31] Czechoslovak enterprises used Belgian companies to sell their products to consumers in Central Africa.[32] In the early 1980s the Hungarian enterprise Vegyépszer helped construct Pepsi plants in Baghdad, and the GDR used cheap Chinese labour to build Iraqi railway lines.[33] The GDR, Yugoslavia, and Romania were more closely economically linked with Western capitalist states than with their Comecon partners in the 1960s and 1970s. And détente also opened up markets in Eastern Europe for East Asian business in the 1970s and 1980s. The Japanese Kajima Corporation built East Berlin's version of a World Trade Centre in 1976: located near the central Friedrichstraße train station,

---

[28] Per Högselius, *Red Gas: Russia and the Origins of European Energy Dependence* (New York: Palgrave Macmillan, 2013), 218–19.

[29] Volkmar Köhler, 'European House or Third World: Are We Forgetting Development Policy?' in Üner Kirdar (ed.), *Change: Threat or Opportunity for Human Progress*, vol. 1 (New York: United Nations Publications, 1992), 213.

[30] A total of 226 so-called 'tripartite' projects took place between 1965 and 1979: Patrick Gutman, 'Tripartite Industrial Cooperation and Third Countries', in Christopher T. Saunders (ed.), *East-West-South: Economic Interactions between Three Worlds* (London: Macmillan, 1981), 337. Western companies themselves could both leverage the benefit of a socialist partner to undermine ideological reservations of Third World partners and lower the cost of bids through the use of cheaper Eastern Bloc labour.

[31] Sara Lorenzini, 'Comecon and the South in the Years of Détente: A Study on East–South Economic Relations', *European Review of History*, 21/2 (2014), 183–99, 187. The social democratic Friedrich Ebert Foundation was at the forefront of this. Sara Lorenzini, 'Globalising Ostpolitik', *Cold War History*, 9/2 (2009), 223–42.

[32] Jan Záhořík, 'Czechoslovakia and Congo/Zaire under Mobutu, 1965–1980', *Canadian Journal of History*, 52/2 (2017), 311.

[33] *Hungarian Exporter*, 3 March 1983.

the Internationales Handelszentrum, it was to support trade with non-socialist countries, and did so quite successfully. In the year of its opening companies from twenty-six Western countries rented offices there with hard currency, eighteen from Japan alone. Just as in the case of the People's Republic of China, the GDR increasingly imported technology from Japan to revive its economy, and just like China, it financed these imports with hard currency credits.[34] Japan was keen to expand contacts in the socialist world, even forgoing Western embargoes, until Toshiba's export of submarine engines to the Soviet Union became public and Japan ended all secret trade connections with Comecon states. From the mid-1970s South Korea engaged in a so-called *Nordpolitik*, aiming to woo East European states away from their northern rival. By 1983 this was paying economic dividends, as Hungary and the GDR started developing trading links, which would lay the foundations for significant South Korean investment in the region from 1988 onwards.[35]

Different paths were taken within the socialist world in respect to foreign trade in the 1970s, and these choices later shaped the form of the various countries' transitions to capitalism: the Soviet Union, Albania, and Mongolia maintained their state monopoly of foreign trade; Yugoslavia had long abolished it, and China and Vietnam gradually dismantled it from the 1980s to the late 1990s. Bulgaria introduced producer unions for foreign trade operations together with Western companies in the early 1970s; from the mid-1980s these were also allowed within the country.[36] Hungary passed new legislation in the 1970s in order to attract more foreign direct investments: this would lay the foundations for it to become the largest per capita recipient of foreign direct investment in Eastern Europe in the 1990s.[37] Poland, Czechoslovakia, and the GDR technically still maintained the state monopoly, but large government enterprises and joint-stock companies

[34] Lothar Heinke, 'Hochhaus in Berlin Mitte. World Trade Center der DDR', *Tagesspiegel*, 28 October 2014.

[35] Balázs Szalontai, 'The Path to the Establishment of Hungarian-South Korean Diplomatic Relations: The Soviet Bloc and the Republic of Korea, 1964–1987', *Cold War International History Project Bulletin*, 14/15 (2010), 87–103.

[36] Jerzy Jakubowski, *Przedsiebiorstwa w Handlu Miedzynarodowym. Problematyka prawna* (Warsaw, 1970).

[37] Adam Török and Agnes Györffy, 'Ungarn in der Vorreiterrolle', in Jutta Günther and Dagmara Jajeśniak-Quast (eds.), *Willkommene Investoren oder nationaler Ausverkauf? Ausländische Direktinvestitionen in Ostmitteleuropa im 20. Jahrhundert* (Berlin: Berliner Wissenschafts-Verlag, 2006), 253–74; Besnik Pula, *Globalization Under and After Socialism: The Evolution of Transnational Capital in Central and Eastern Europe* (Stanford, CA: Stanford University Press, 2018), chap. 4.

were now permitted, and even encouraged, to handle their own international transactions. Over a hundred such foreign trade organisations existed in Poland in the 1970s, and even more in Czechoslovakia.[38]

This accelerated opening up in the early 1970s was, from an Eastern perspective, partly a result of declining returns on their model of extensive growth. Expanding inputs rather than increasing productivity to develop the economy had led to very high rates of growth in the first postwar decades but did not turn out to be a sustainable approach to economic development. The exhaustion of this model occurred against the background of socialist states promising to 'catch up' with the West, abandoning political repression and basing claims to legitimacy on rising standards of living.[39] From the 1960s, this race became defined as a competition over living standards and private consumption. Yet the socialist elites struggled to formulate policies that would allow them to keep up according to these criteria. It was this imperative, economists argued, that necessitated technology transfer and learning from the West. Modernised industries would be able to provide a modern consumerism with private flats, cars, and holidays as well as competitive export goods. The latter could generate hard currency that was to be used to pay off the debts incurred in obtaining said technology. Moreover, states realised that they lacked the know-how in modern business practices such as deterritorialised production, and they were lagging far behind in the digitisation of production and products.

As in the West, commentators from the East spoke from the mid-1970s of an increasingly 'interdependent' world economy that cut across political blocs. Soviet economists acknowledged in 1976 that 'in the contemporary world, the progress of each country is inseparable from its participation in the global exchange of material and spiritual values, reflecting an interdependence of all countries ... A mass of visible and invisible threads links the economic development of separate countries with those changes that take place in the world economy'.[40] In the first years of this increased economic exchange such attempts of bloc states to integrate themselves into the international division of labour were not

---

[38] K. Grzybowski, 'Socialist Countries in GATT', *American Journal of Comparative Law*, 4 (1980), 544–47.

[39] Paulina Bren and Mary Neuburger, 'Introduction', in Bren and Neuburger (eds.), *Communism Unwrapped. Consumption in Cold War Eastern Europe* (New York: Oxford University Press, 2012), 12–13; György Péteri, 'Introduction', in Péteri (ed.), *Imagining the West in Eastern Europe and the Soviet Union* (Pittsburgh: University of Pittsburgh Press, 2010), 8–12.

[40] Nikolaj Shmelev, 'Ekonomicheskie sviazi Vostok-Zapad', *Institut Ekonomiki Mirovoi Sotsialisticheskoj Sistemy*, 12–13, 14 (1976).

seen as ideologically problematic. Majority ownership lay with the Eastern partner, and such collaborations would be confined to limited industrial spaces, closed off from the rest of socialist society. States would not go beyond bilateral agreements, and there would be no large-scale opening of domestic markets to Western goods. And, crucially, the ownership structure and redistribution of wealth under socialism, it was claimed, undermined any superficial similarities in economic aims, or arguments about ideological convergence between East and West.[41]

Some were not so sure that this race with the West and the tentative integration it required would not have longer-term consequences for the future of an alternative political project. Not only radical Third World socialists like Castro but also the New Left in both Eastern and Western Europe argued that the Soviet Bloc appeared to be giving up on an alternative global system and its values.[42] The French radical André Gorz suggested that socialist consumerism was becoming simply a tardy and tawdry imitation of the Western one, and he questioned why such countries were abandoning collective solutions to consumption. Why, he wondered, were individual washing machines being placed in Czechoslovak homes and private motoring encouraged in the Soviet Union?[43] Others asked whether integration, marketisation, the increasingly dominant position of technocrats in both East and West, common obsessions with the technological revolution across the Iron Curtain, and a turn towards planning within capitalist systems did in fact represent a real convergence. Researchers at Institutes of Global Economy in the East, employing the world systems approach, argued that a 'one world' economy was being established in part through the reintegration of Eastern Europe and asked whether the region could resist being re-peripheralised as a hinterland for Western industry as a result. Others were unsure whether this could be achieved without seriously undermining socialist states' control over their own economies, and whether they would eventually fall prey to capitalists.[44] Beijing concurred with these New Left critiques, claiming that Eastern Europe's seemingly all-too-easy accommodation with the capitalist world for the sake of technology imports

---

[41] The press across the bloc between the late 1960s and early 1970s is full of arguments against convergence: see, e.g., 'Pravda Denies that Economic Reform Rejects Socialism', 16 September 1969, HU-OSA 300–40–2 Box 108.

[42] For a contemporary critique, see Sándor Ausch, *Theory and Practice of CMEA Cooperation* (Budapest: Akadémiai Kiadó, 1972).

[43] André Gorz, *Le socialisme difficile* (Paris: Seuil, 1967), 126–7.

[44] Andre Gunder Frank, *Crisis: In the World Economy* (New York: Holmes and Meier, 1980); see also his 'Long Live Transideological Enterprise! The Socialist Economies in the Capitalist International Division of Labor and West-East-South Economic Relations', *Review (Fernand Braudel Center)*, 1/1 (1977), 91–140.

could only be at the expense of commitment to an alternative world order.

Debt and Ideological Reorientation

The increasing economic integration of socialist Eastern Europe with the capitalist West gained momentum during a time of dramatic global economic and financial changes. By abolishing the gold standard in 1971, the United States dismantled the global financial order in place since the Second World War, which had pegged the US dollar to other convertible currencies.[45] The end of the so-called Bretton Woods system meant the beginning of a new era in international economic relations marked by deregulation and market volatility. This was a shift towards finance capitalism and was part of an overall freeing of capital markets in the 1970s and 1980s. The accumulation of national debts would in the long run also significantly increase the power of the IMF and the World Bank. In these institutions Western influence was significantly stronger than in the UN and its agencies, which were based on a one-state-one-vote principle. Finance capitalism now played a much larger role in globalisation, and several Eastern European states got drawn into it long before the political changes of 1989.

In the West, a widespread sense of crisis in the 1970s was exacerbated when the Arab members of OPEC, a cartel of oil-exporting countries in the Global South, decided to embargo countries that supported Israel in the 1973 Yom Kippur War. As an immediate result world market prices for crude oil quadrupled; in industrial states that depended on the import of oil, panic crept in. Eastern Bloc states, initially, seemed to profit from the crisis: higher world market prices for oil meant that the oil-exporting Soviet Union was suddenly awash with hard currency. Eastern European states such as the GDR, which resold cheap Soviet oil and refined oil products on the world market, benefitted too. Even more importantly, the oil-exporting Arab states, swamped with more capital than they could spend, stashed these enormous sums in international banks, which in turn were looking for investments and offered credits at low interest rates.

In order to satisfy domestic consumer demand, and with a view to modernising their industries to be competitive on the world market, Eastern European states started to borrow the so-called 'petrodollars' that had flowed out of energy-producing states at low rates of interest.

---

[45] Douglas I. Irwin, 'The Nixon Shock after Forty Years: The Import Surcharge Revisited', *World Trade Review*, 12/1 (2013), 29–56.

The contrast here with China is instructive. Its globalizing turn in the late 1970s came at a propitious moment, when Western economies were weak, and international capital was looking for new areas to invest in. Moreover, it had large overseas ethnic communities who were willing to invest back home. China was thus not fettered by the type of debt that gave Western-dominated financial institutions leverage. Moreover, in Eastern Europe the expected payback from this debt-laden investment never occurred. Unlike other 'semi-peripheries' such as the 'East Asian Tigers', which successfully integrated into the world economy in the same period, many Eastern Bloc countries were unable to develop large competitive state-supported enterprises. There were many reasons for this. Managerial elites lacked incentives to export as they could earn greater profits on the domestic market with its regulated prices. Moreover, whereas the 'Tigers' were given access to the US market, bloc countries faced protectionism from the neighbouring EC. Unable to export in sufficient volume – and in fact facing major pressures to import to satisfy consumer demand – bloc states were not able to earn or hold on to hard currency from the West and developed very serious imbalances in trade.[46]

Through the 1970s and 1980s many Eastern Europe countries increasingly resorted to borrowing money to maintain standards of living necessary to secure the Communist parties' short-term legitimacy. With the spiralling costs of raw materials and rising interest rates in the late 1970s, countries from Hungary to Bulgaria became ever more mired in debt. When the United States drastically raised the Federal Funds Rate to curb domestic inflation, the Polish government soon after had to announce that it was no longer able to fulfil its obligations to international creditors.[47] In the Yugoslav federation banks and companies based in the individual republics had been able to borrow abroad without the consent of the Yugoslav National Bank or the federal government,

---

[46] Anders Åslund, *How Capitalism Was Built. The Transformation of Central and Eastern Europe, Russia, the Caucasus, and Central Asia* (Cambridge: Cambridge University Press, 2013), 102.

[47] Debts in Eastern Europe rose from 20 to 200 billion US dollars from 1971 to 1979; Adam Fabry, 'The Origins of Neoliberalism in Late "Socialist" Hungary. The Case of the Financial Research Institute and "Turnabout and Reform"', *Capital & Class*, 42/1 (2017), 12–17. Of Hungary's 20-billion-dollar debt, only 4–5 billion was invested in increasing productivity: Ivan T. Berend, 'Global Financial Architecture and East Central Europe Before and After 1989', in Ulf Engel, Frank Hadler, and Matthias Middell (eds.), *1989 in a Global Perspective* (Leipzig: Leipziger Universitätsverlag, 2015), 56–57; Stephen Kotkin, 'The Kiss of Debt. The East Bloc Goes Borrowing', in Niall Ferguson et al. (eds.), *Shock of the Global. The 1970s in Perspective* (Cambridge, MA: Harvard University Press, 2010), 80–93.

adding to tensions between the national republics. This increasing indebtedness also reshaped the country's position in the world economy: Yugoslavia drew closer to the West and further from the South.[48] This debt crisis occurred not only in Eastern Europe but also across Africa and Latin America, and significantly reduced the economic and political independence of socialist and developing countries. Most debtor countries in Eastern Europe, the Middle East, Africa, and Latin America now depended on further loans from Western-dominated institutions like the IMF. As a consequence, they prioritised the payment of hard currency to their Western creditors over the fulfilment of their obligations to each other. In 1989, many Eastern Bloc states would be owed huge sums: the Soviet Union alone was owed 150 – 160 billion dollars by sixty-one countries, making it a net creditor, but without much hope of ever seeing again most of the money it had furnished around the Global South. Iraq's substantial debts to Eastern Europe would eventually be paid off only with the oil proceeds extracted after the US-led invasion in 2003.[49]

This turn of the socialist and developing world to the West had a corrosive effect on the earlier solidarity-type values, which had underpinned these world regions' attempts at an alternative globalisation. Socialist states outside Europe were viewed less and less as the object of Eastern Europe's developmental support.[50] In the 1980s far more emphasis was placed on profitability and payment in hard currency instead. Large sums were earnt from arms exports from the Eastern Bloc to Africa, which were partly used to pay off their debts to the West. Workers from Vietnam, Cuba, and Mozambique began arriving in

---

[48] Mark Mazower termed this the 'real new international economic order': *Governing the World: The History of an Idea, 1815 to the Present* (New York: Penguin, 2013), chap. 12; Susan Woodward, *Balkan Tragedy. Chaos and Dissolution after the Cold War* (Washington, DC: Brookings Institute, 1995), especially chap. 3; Momčilo Cemović, *Zašto, kako i koliko smo se zadužili? Kreditni odnosi Jugoslavije sa inostranstvom* (Beograd: Institut za unapređenje robnog prometa, 1985). See also Human Development Report 1990 (New York: United Nations Development Programme, 1990).

[49] Saddam's fall in 2003 revealed that Iraq owed 130 billion dollars. The Soviet Union had owed approximately 40 billion roubles, or half of the amount owed to it. The largest debtors were Cuba, Mongolia, Vietnam, India, Syria, Afghanistan, Yemen Republic, Iraq, Ethiopia, North Korea, Algeria, Angola, Egypt, Libya, and Nicaragua, each owing well in excess of 1 billion dollars to the Soviet Union. Johanna Bockman, 'The 1980s Debt Crisis Revisited: The Second and Third Worlds as Creditors' (manuscript).

[50] For an early account of this shift, see László Csaba, *Eastern Europe in the World Economy* (Cambridge: Cambridge University Press, 1990), 127–29. Pál Germuska, 'Failed Eastern Integration and a Partly Successful Opening Up to the West: The Economic Re-orientation of Hungary during the 1970s', *European Review of History*, 21/2 (2014), 278. In all, 226 firms had arranged joint ventures across the Iron Curtain by 1976, but only 7 per cent in third markets. HU OSA 300–2–5-Box 49.

Eastern Europe in large numbers at the behest of states that wished to 'export their unemployment' and to gain high-quality training for parts of their labour force in a developed socialist Europe. In the 1960s and 1970s such Third World incomers had been supported by Eastern Bloc states keen to express their solidarity-based generosity. By the 1980s Eastern European states used migrant labourers, who were cheaper to employ and enjoyed fewer social rights, to address labour shortages and develop profitable hard-currency-earning export sectors.[51] The practice continued after the end of state socialism with the use of North Korean labour in remote parts of Siberia and in Eastern Europe.[52] Although Eastern Bloc states still objected to international institutions' reluctance to relieve Africa of its debts in the 1980s, their complaints were increasingly muted, as these states also owed significant sums to the bloc. Only socialist Yugoslavia and Romania continued criticising structural North-South inequalities in the world economy to the end: at the 1989 Belgrade Summit of the Non-Aligned Movement, Yugoslav elites called for the writing off of debt for the least developed countries.[53]

Overall, debt brought Eastern Europe closer to the West. As the Soviet Union started reducing its oil exports to socialist allies in the late 1970s, Eastern European obligations to international creditors rose tenfold. By the collapse Hungary had the third highest per capita debt in the world. Several East European states were barred from further access to cheap private credits and thus lobbied international institutions for support, which in turn drew them further into the world of western capitalism. To stave off financial collapse in early 1982, Hungary joined the IMF. In this sense debt operated as a 'school for capitalism': Hungarian national banks in particular, which managed loans from both Western and Middle Eastern sources, had become well versed in the workings of Western finance long before 1989.[54] The need for hard currency reoriented these countries westwards in other ways too. Many used international tourism. Yugoslavia had abolished visas in 1967, and, by 1989, hard currency

---

[51] See Alena Alamgir and Christina Schwenkel, 'From Socialist Assistance to National Self-Interest: Vietnamese Labor Migration Into CMEA Countries', in Mark et al., *Alternative Globalizations*; James Mark and Bálint Tolmár, 'From Heroes Square to the Textile Factory: Encountering Cuba in Socialist Hungary 1959–1990' (forthcoming).

[52] See https://edition.cnn.com/2011/12/15/world/asia/north-korean-labor-camps-in-siberia/index.html; www.telegraph.co.uk/news/2016/05/31/polish-firms-employing-north-korean-slave-labourers-benefit-from/.

[53] Final Document – Declaration, 9th Summit Conference of Heads of State or Government of the Non-Aligned Movement, Belgrade, 4–7 September 1989, 87–90.

[54] Attila Mong, *Kádár hitele. A magyar államadósság története 1956–1990* (Budapest: Libri, 2012), 152.

revenue from visitors amounted to 2.5 billion dollars per year. Yugoslavia also allowed its nationals to be guest workers earning hard currency in Western Europe, their money transfers eventually contributing almost 20 per cent of their country's GDP.[55]

Nevertheless, the turn towards the West was not inevitable. Several socialist states actually managed to avoid the indebtedness that put pressure on bloc solidarity. Czechoslovakia had abandoned a cautious liberalisation of the economy after the crushing of the Prague Spring in 1968. The new leaders took the view that loans were not necessary to update production, and they continued to rely on their once highly developed industries from the interwar period. The Romanian dictator Ceaușescu decided to pay back all his country's debts to the IMF in order to avoid any foreign interference and thus removed Romania from the reach of international finance in the 1980s – with disastrous consequences as social welfare collapsed.[56] Such was also the case in China, where, by contrast with Eastern Europe, the Communist Party had never had to secure its political legitimacy by borrowing money for public consumption and indeed became a creditor to the IMF for much of the 1980s. At that time, many Eastern European states continued to rely on the Soviet Union – both for energy supplies and for loans. Soviet leaders tolerated these associations with Western financial institutions because they could serve to reduce their own economically unsustainable obligations to Eastern European partners. But they still feared the role of the IMF as conduit for Western political interests and thus took care to set a limit to Western flirtations in Prague and Budapest.[57]

One should avoid concluding that the necessary consequences of foreign debt and economic underperformance were the dismantling of socialism and the turn to Western liberal capitalism. The GDR might have survived on loans and credits from the West in the 1980s, but even while economically struggling it was not yet bankrupt and indeed had

---

[55] The number of registered tourists peaked at 20 million per year in the late 1980s (40 per cent of which were foreigners); Igor Duda, 'Adriatic for All: Summer Holidays in Croatia', in Breda Luthar and Maruša Pušnik (eds.), *Remembering Utopia: The Culture of Everyday Life in Socialist Yugoslavia* (Washington, DC: New Academia Publishing, 2010), 290; Karin Taylor and Hannes Grandits, 'Tourism and the Making of Socialist Yugoslavia', in Karin Taylor and Hannes Grandits (eds.), *Yugoslavia's Sunny Side: A History of Tourism in Socialism (1950s–1980s)* (Budapest: Central European University Press, 2010), 11.

[56] Cornel Ban, 'Sovereign Debt, Austerity, and Regime Change. The Case of Nicolae Ceaușescu's Romania', *East European Politics and Societies*, 26/4 (2012), 743–76.

[57] Suvi Kansikas, 'Acknowledging Economic Realities. The CMEA policy Change vis-à-vis the European Community 1970–3', *European Review of History*, 21/2 (2014), 311–28.

lower foreign debt rates than West Germany.[58] And other Communist states such as Cuba and North Korea were economically much worse off – and did not collapse. The fact that Communist parties gave up on their monopoly over power was a political decision best explained through their elites' sense of exhaustion with their own project rather than a decision narrowly defined by economic necessity.

Abandoning Alternative Trade

Central to the story of 1989 was Eastern European alienation from the increasingly radical economic projects of the Global South. In the mid-1970s the so-called 'Group of 77' (G77) states called for a 'New International Economic Order', which asserted a right to development, advocated regulating capital flows so as not to reproduce the injustices of colonialism, and urged international institutions to engineer a global redistribution of wealth from North to South.[59] Amongst Eastern European nations, only Romania and Yugoslavia – one a 'renegade' member of the Eastern Bloc and the other a non-aligned state outside the Soviet sphere of influence – were members of the G77. Whilst professing their ideological sympathies rhetorically, most bloc states criticised the scheme as excessively utopian or feared that it undermined attempts to extract energy or raw materials from the South. As a consequence, many Third World countries resolved to cease differentiating ideologically between the socialist and capitalist states of the northern hemisphere; for them, the fundamental division in the world was now between an underdeveloped 'Global South' and an industrialised 'Global North', which held on to its structural advantages in the world economy.

Although there had always been battles over the extent to which socialism and solidarity should determine trade preferences,[60] it was much clearer by the 1970s that many Eastern European states were relinquishing an approach based on political sympathies. In 1977 the Hungarian Central Committee officially abandoned their country's prioritisation of trade with socialist-oriented countries.[61] New technocratic arguments presented Western capitalism as less of a threat and Western companies as potential partners to help fix economies in the East. Even so, the extent of Eastern European involvement in capitalist foreign

---

[58] Jan Dams, 'Die DDR war in Wahrheit gar nicht pleite', *Die Welt*, 7 November 2014.

[59] Nils Gilman, 'The New International Economic Order: A Reintroduction', *Humanity*, 6/1 (Spring 2015), 2–4.

[60] Poland had delivered coal to Spain, helping to break a strike of coal miners against the Francoist regime as early as 1963.

[61] Germuska, 'Failed Eastern Integration', 278.

trade, often kept secret from their own populations, displayed an ever-greater cynicism. Many bloc countries re-established economic connections with Franco's Spain in the early 1970s – leading to severe criticism from the Spanish Communist party.[62] The Soviet Union imported much of its grain from the military dictators in Argentina.[63] The GDR, while publicly condemning Pinochet as a puppet of international capitalism and imperialism, secretly expanded its trade volume with the Chilean dictatorship in the 1970s.[64] In the 1980s, when its socialist allies in Mozambique could no longer service the credits that they were given to buy East German products, the GDR demanded a share of their black coal, which it immediately sold on the world market before the ships reached the Baltic Sea. Contract workers from Mozambique had to work off their state's debts to East Berlin like modern indentured labourers in the GDR. Despite having cut official ties with South Africa after the 1960 Sharpeville Massacre of black demonstrators, the Soviet Union continued to process its diamonds with the South African mining company De Beers. And Eastern Bloc countries supplied arms and military electronics to the apartheid regime in the 1980s.[65]

In the last decade of socialism in Eastern Europe, enterprises were offered opportunities to do business with far less state interference. In June 1987 a new Soviet law on state enterprises gave managers of some large companies, as in Yugoslavia, autonomy to directly conduct business with foreign partners and allowed for joint ventures with international companies on Soviet territory. A month later Czechoslovakia introduced similar legislation and Bulgaria created free-trade zones for global companies.[66] This variety of global economic contacts provided socialist elites with expertise about the benefits of international trade, and they made for a culture of internationally linked economics beyond

[62] RFE Hungarian Situation Report, 22 September 1970.
[63] Stella Krepp, 'A View from the South. The Falklands/Malvinas and Latin America', *Journal of Transatlantic Studies*, 15/4 (2017), 348–65, 357; Augusto Varas (eds.), *Soviet–Latin American relations in the 1980s* (Boulder, CO: Westview, 1987).
[64] Georg Dufner, 'Chile als Partner, Exempel und Prüfstein. Deutsch-deutsche Außenpolitik und Systemkonkurrenz in Lateinamerika', *Vierteljahreshefte für Zeitgeschichte*, 4 (2013), 513–49.
[65] Hennie van Vuuren, *Apartheid, Guns and Money – A Tale of Profit* (Johannesburg: Jacana Media, 2017), 269–71; Paul Betts, James Mark, Idesbald Goddeeris, and Kim Christiaens, 'Race, Socialism and Solidarity: Anti-Apartheid in Eastern Europe', in Robert Skinner and Anna Konieczna (eds.), *A Global History of Anti-Apartheid. 'Forward to Freedom' in South Africa* (Cham: Palgrave Macmillan, 2019), 153–54, 174–75.
[66] UNCTAD Division for Trade with Socialist Countries, 'Developments in Economic and Foreign Trade Management Systems in the Socialist Countries of Eastern Europe', 9 December 1987, ARR40 1929 065 Box 546.

ideological frontiers. Moreover, the well-rehearsed pragmatism that some of its political and economic elites displayed when it came to trading with alleged ideological enemies in part explains the ease with which a rapid reorientation was possible after 1989. Many successful post-Communist professional biographies were rooted in this late Cold War globalisation: Sándor Demján, who became one of the richest men in post-socialist Hungary, began his business with his country's covert openings to South Korea in the 1970s; Ovidiu Muşetescu, the director of one of Romania's most successful companies in the Global South building shipping yards, Contrasimex, after 1989 became a prominent businessman and minister of privatisation in the social-democratic government that negotiated Romania's accession to the EU.

The West Is Not the Enemy: Reinterpreting Peripheralisation and Backwardness

In the last decades of the Cold War the advantages of Westernisation increasingly appeared to outweigh the potential pitfalls for many Eastern European elites. Since the nineteenth century the question of escaping peripheralisation and backwardness on the European continent had been key for Eastern European development. Communism itself was in its early years underpinned by the assumption that the nations in this region had to be wary of the West and that only through autarkic development could they catch up and escape their historic role as its economic hinterland.[67] The consensus around Western integration by the late 1980s, by contrast, was based on the remarkable absence of a fear of re-peripheralisation. Such critiques would return to the mainstream only in the 2010s.[68]

One can partly trace this to the effects of the deep economic crisis that beset the region in the 1980s: the alternatives to Westernisation appeared worse. In spite of the borrowing incurred to raise technological inputs, most countries were held back by central planning and export regulations. Productivity failed to rise and many countries were unable to create effective export industries that could earn hard currency to pay it back.[69] Moreover, with increased economic cooperation, Eastern European states were most susceptible to changes in the global economy:

---

[67] On the limits of this aspiration for autarchy, see Pula, *Globalization*, chap. 2.
[68] Vera Šćepanović and Dorothee Bohle, 'The Institutional Embeddedness of Transnational Corporations: Dependent Capitalism in Central and Eastern Europe', in Andreas Nölke and Christian May (eds.), *Handbook of the International Political Economy of the Corporation* (Northampton, MA: Edward Elgar, 2018), 152–166.
[69] Pula, *Globalization*, chap. 4.

'The effects of economic developments in capitalist countries are now an integral part of the production process in socialist national economies', the Hungarian economist Gabriella Izik-Hedri warned her East German colleagues, who had invited her in 1981 to share the experience of market socialism in Hungary. 'This means that disturbances in capitalist production processes lead automatically to disturbances in socialist production processes'.[70] Enterprises' greater autonomy could be disruptive too: from the 1980s, Yugoslav companies could trade freely with foreign partners – which in combination with the shortage of capital in the country created frequent deficits of basic goods. In 1979, for instance, the supply of fresh milk to Belgrade collapsed because the only existing licenced agro-industrial company decided to export its milk to Greece, where it could sell at much higher prices.[71]

Living standards were now lower in Eastern Europe than Southern Europe and parts of East Asia – more meaningful reference points than a much more developed Western Europe. Spain had had a place in the world economy akin to that of Poland, and roughly the same GDP in the 1950s. By the late 1980s the Spanish economy was four times as big as Poland's, where mass protests were held against the dramatic lack of consumer goods.[72] Even in relatively rich countries of the Eastern Bloc such as the GDR, the consumer situation worsened significantly in the 1980s after the Soviet Union had curtailed its subsidies. Coffee and bananas became rare goods – material for many notorious jokes in West and East alike. Deepening poverty amongst the elderly forced the regime to allow everyone over the age of sixty-five to emigrate to the West, undermining claims to represent a more just economic system. Western media and family contacts kept most East Germans informed about everyday life, culture, and living standards in the West. The resulting sense of deprivation was exacerbated in large part because the provision of a Western-inspired individualist consumerism had been promoted as the future – and as a plank of regimes' legitimacy – since the early 1960s. This policy in effect served to further glorify the seemingly abundant Western capitalist consumer world in the 1980s, whilst making it ever clearer that Eastern European states could not compete on this terrain.

---

[70] Inhaltlicher Bericht über Vortrag und Diskussion mit Professor G. Izik-Hedri am 15 Dezember 1981 am IPW / Bericht über ein Gespräch von Genossin Prof. Izik-Hedri beim Forschungsinstitut des Ministeriums für Außenhandel am 16 Dezember 1981, Bundesarchiv BArch DC 204/61.

[71] 'Jugoslawien: "Es gibt keinen zweiten Tito". Das gescheiterte Werk des großen Partisanenführers aus dem Zweiten Weltkrieg', Der Spiegel, 21 January 1980.

[72] Jeffrey Sachs, The End of Poverty. Economic Possibilities of Our Time (New York: Penguin, 2006), 116.

Yet it is important to note that there were economic crises in other socialist states outside Europe that did not lead to calls for greater Western integration or, eventually, the collapse of their Communist systems. In Eastern Europe many political and economic elites shaped and mobilised the meaning of such crises to rethink questions of peripherality, backwardness, and started – tentatively at first – to turn them into civilisational questions.

This was not true everywhere. For elites and experts in Romania and Yugoslavia, the only two countries in the region that had backed the radical New International Economic Order, the roots of the economic crisis were still predominantly located in the structural inequality of the global economy which further Westernisation would only entrench. Romania's leader Ceauşescu sought to break the hold of Western banks, promising to pay off all loans, and re-adopting an autarkic model of development. Even those who opposed him from within the party often remained apprehensive about the IMF. Silviu Brucan, a champion of market socialism, declared structural adjustment a new form of Western neocolonialism.[73] Romanian economists continued to argue that Western policies fuelled the global crisis of the early 1980s by imposing 'a unique therapy' regardless of national characteristics, which created debt and in fact impeded attempts at reform.[74]

Yet elsewhere in the bloc new arguments were being made that ended the equation of Westernisation with a renewed peripheralisation of the region. Weaknesses in national economies could no longer be blamed only on external global forces or Western imperialism; rather, change had to come through disciplining local economies, reforming political institutions, and creating 'human capital' from within. The insistence of the IMF that the crises of the 1980s were the result of local failures of governance and were best addressed in national frameworks became more and more influential, particularly in those bloc countries that joined it. In their institutional view individual national economies could be disciplined towards economic efficiency, with little thought given to the relation between these containers in the context of a broader global economy. For them, the market was the effective disciplinary mechanism for the reformation of human behaviour within states.

By the late 1980s the idea that 'culture mattered' became popular, both in the West and in the East: some development theorists now

---

[73] Silviu Brucan, *World Socialism at the Crossroads* (New York: Praeger, 1987) and his *Piaţă şi democraţie* (Bucureşti: Editura ştiintifică, 1990).
[74] Costin Murgescu, 'Criza economică mondială: Concept, dimensiuni, implicaţii', in Murgescu (ed.), *Criza economică mondială* (Bucureşti: Editura ştiintifică, 1986), 12.

claimed that underdevelopment was a 'state of mind'.[75] It thus became fashionable to assume that long-term backwardness had been the fault of long-held and unreformed regional mentalities – which could now be disciplined through exposure to the free market. Just before he became Polish prime minister, Zbigniew Messner put it thus in 1985: 'For our country to become more efficient, the psychology of the people – inherited from the 1970s – must also change. The population must become more willing to work, to save and to be less wasteful'.[76] Already he was identifying IMF-led reform as having the potential to fulfil the country's true civilisational status: 'One must realise that Poland is a "medium-developed" country whose position in the world is not as high as was assured by the propaganda of the 1970s, yet not so low so as to categorise us with the "fourth world". The international financial circles have a much brighter picture of Poland than of many other debtor countries because of our potential and of our level of education. The most difficult problem is, thus, to realistically assess our potential'.[77]

In this context, the fear that integration into Western Europe would lead to a peripheralisation of the region similar to that of the pre-Communist era was much weaker. There emerged, amongst economists and geographers, most notably in Poland, the idea of a possible 'new geography' for Europe of equal nations devoid of sharp hierarchies.[78] Those experts who had focussed on global cores and peripheries in the 1970s began to present evidence that former peripheries could catch up. Institutes of World Economy became fascinated with how other formerly marginal areas, with structural similarities to Eastern Europe, had now successfully integrated into the Western capitalist system. Experts pointed, variously, to the success of the East Asian periphery that had developed markets in the West and created powerful export industries, or the recent advance of Spain from autarky to successful integration into the Western European economy.[79] Policy advice was developed around

---

[75] Lawrence E. Harrison, *Underdevelopment Is a State of Mind: The Latin American Case* (Cambridge, MA: Center for International Affairs, Harvard University and University Press of America, 1985).

[76] 'Summary of Messner's Interview "In What Condition Is Poland" in Office Memorandum, 24 May 1985, EUR Divisions Country/Country Desk Files, Poland-911-Economic Reform, 1981–1987, Box 38–2, 3.

[77] Ibid., 2.

[78] Tomasz Zarycki, 'De-spatialisation and the Europeanisation of Late Communist Imaginary: The Intellectual Trajectory of Polish Geographer Antoni Kukliński' (paper presented at Revolution from Within: Experts, Managers and Technocrats in the Long Transformation of 1989, Jena, June 2018); Anna Sosnowska, *Zrozumieć zacofanie. Spory historyków o Europę Wschodnią, 1947–1994* (Warszawa: Trio, 2004).

[79] On the potential for Eastern Europe to follow Mediterranean Europe and quickly catch up, see James Mark, '"The Spanish Analogy": Imagining the Future in State Socialist

high skilled education, the nurturing of 'human capital', and the construction of large-scale export industries to this end.[80]

This was a world in which Westernisation did not appear to necessitate being confined as a less developed hinterland. Yet, not all were sure that this would be the case in the late 1980s. The UN Economic Commission for Europe feared that the debt that hung over some Eastern European countries would ensure they were denied agency even after extensive reform.[81] At a debate between economists from Algeria, Yugoslavia, and Hungary organised by the Centre National d'Études et d'Analyses pour la Planification (CENEAP), the Algerian economists present criticised their counterparts in Hungary and Poland for failing to consider the relevance of long-term hierarchies in the world economy, and their own possible re-marginalisation, when accepting new Western prescriptions for economic development.[82] Some experts recognised this danger, particularly those of an older generation trained in global economics who had engaged with questions of world systems and North-South trade: István Dobozi of the Institute of World Economy in Budapest argued in 1988 that Western integration could result in Eastern Europe becoming an 'impoverished global South'.[83] Andrei Kortunov, a reformer at the Institute of the U.S.A. and Canada in Moscow, feared in the autumn of 1989 that the new Central European governments could find themselves consumed by the West and wholly on the West's terms – and proposed that they should keep Comecon and the Warsaw Pact to ensure they retained influence in their negotiations surrounding their integration into West European structures and institutions.[84]

Nevertheless, Eastern Europe took the Westernising plunge. The EC swiftly funded new programmes such as PHARE (Poland and Hungary: Assistance for Restructuring their Economies) that embodied the

Hungary, 1948–1989', *Contemporary European History*, 26/4 (2017), 600–620; Antoni Kukliński, 'The Geography of New Europe', *GeoJournal*, 30/4 (August 1993), 459–60.

[80] Ivan T. Berend, *History in My Life: A Memoir of Three Eras* (Budapest: Central European University Press, 2009), 138–39.

[81] Gert Rosenthal, 'Report on the ECLAC/ECE Dialogue on Economic Policy in Latin America, the Caribbean and the Countries in Transition in Central and Eastern Europe', 2 April 1991, UNOG-G-ECE Box 011 ECLA 121, 1–9.

[82] Telegramă nr. 011409, 29 July 1989, MAE [Ministerul Afacerilor Externe]-Algeria 27/1989, 135.

[83] István Dobozi, 'Patterns, Factors and Prospects of East-South Economic Relations', in Pawel Bożyk (ed.), *Global Challenges and East European Responses* (Warsaw: Polish Scientific Publishers, 1988) [book issued by the United Nations University], 327.

[84] Jacques Lévesque, *The Enigma of 1989: The USSR and the Liberation of Eastern Europe* (Berkeley: University of California Press, 1997), 244.

utopian hope in the 'end of geography': a growing field of regional science funded by this programme argued for a new Europe of interconnected sub-regions that could each flourish through successful management. With eventual membership of the European club, substantial economic catch-up in a manner that avoided the re-peripheralisation of the East seemed viable.[85] But even after 1989, doubts remained: some Hungarian and Polish economists argued that small Eastern European states should resist an uncritical integration into the European Union: it would be better to follow the lead of the independent East Asian Tigers, specialise in certain sectors, and resist stagnation as peripheral, low-value locations in the newly emerging 'global factory'.[86] Following the invitation in 1993 to Central and Eastern European countries to embark upon the process of EU accession, such voices became marginal – until the 2010s, when the outsourcing and 'nearsourcing' of Western European industry and services to a well-educated, culturally familiar region with a still significantly lower labour cost returned in debates over cycles of dependency to the mainstream – both on the left and on the right.[87]

Less the beginning of Eastern Europe's globalisation, 1989 marked a weakening of alternative forms of non-Western trade and development projects for Eastern Europe. This shift was not preordained: economic links had expanded outside Europe in the 1980s. Yugoslav companies successfully built new markets in the Middle East and Soviet Union in the 1980s, commerce grew significantly between Eastern Europe and Africa from the 1970s, and the arms and energy trade between the Soviet

---

[85] Frank Schimmelfennig and Ulrich Sedelmeier, *The Politics of European Union Enlargement: Theoretical Approaches* (London: Routledge, 2005), 160.

[86] See, e.g. Maciej Perczyński, 'Global Determinants of East-South Relations', in Bożyk (ed.), *Global Challenges*, 313. In Hungary, the economist Sándor Kopátsy was the most vocal advocate of this position: e.g. 'Új világrend felé. Vissza és előre ötven évet', *Társadalmi Szemle*, 5 (1992), 13–23; 'A magyar privatizácio sajátos vonásai', *Mozgó Világ*, 1 (1993), 23–28. For accounts of the South Korean model as inspiration for the Polish transformation, see, e.g., Aleksandra Jasińska-Kania, 'National Stereotypes and Economic Cooperation: Images of Korea in Poland' (paper presented at 'Korean and Korean Business Interests in Central Europe and CIS Countries', Seoul National University, August 1997), 10. She notes that in 1991 the Balcerowicz reforms were criticised for following the Argentinian rather than South Korean model.

[87] On 'nearsourcing' in Eastern Europe, see Jamie Peck, *Offshore: Exploring the Worlds of Global Outsourcing* (Oxford: Oxford University Press, 2017), 20, 145. On the revival of dependency, see Vera Šćepanović and Dorothee Bohle, 'The Institutional Embeddedness of Transnational Corporations: Dependent Capitalism in Central and Eastern Europe', in Andreas Nölke and Christian May (eds.), *Handbook of the International Political Economy of the Corporation* (Northampton, MA: Edward Elgar, 2018), 152–66.

Union and the developing world grew exponentially.[88] Following 1989, many projects ground to a halt. Developmental workers became individualised private contractors. Large industrial enterprises that had underpinned this engagement were no longer viewed by Western investors as viable global players and were split up into their constituent parts. In other cases, most notably the car industry, Western collaborations enabled the continuation of market share in the Global South. Before 1989, Dacia had been a Romanian-French joint venture with Renault providing the engines and design; it would be bought outright by Renault in 1999 and significantly modernised, with some of its models directed at Africa, Asia, and South America; its most significant market remained Western Europe, however.[89] Some links did remain, particularly in the arms industry, which had prospered in late socialism and continued to do so after 1989: Omnipol in Czechoslovakia and Serbia's Zastava Arms as well as many Russian producers of ordnance continued to export successfully, both to former partners in Africa and to the Middle East, including the Iraqi and Afghan security forces.[90] According to a study of the Belgian NGO Conflict Armament Research, 97 per cent of the weaponry used by the Islamist terrorist group ISIS in Iraq and Syria between 2014 and 2017 had its origins in Russia, Eastern Europe, and China.[91]

The Choice of 'Neoliberal' Globalisation

If, in economic terms, the changes of 1989 were the result of decisions by local elites to reorient, why then did they choose the 'neoliberal' path? A popular argument invokes the economic zeitgeist. The Communist states of Central and Eastern Europe collapsed at a moment of high faith

---

[88] Mark Kramer, 'The Decline in Soviet Arms Transfers to the Third World, 1986–1991', in Artemy Kalinovsky and Sergey Radchenko (eds.), *The End of the Cold War and The Third World: New Perspectives on Regional Conflict* (Abingdon: Routledge, 2011), 56–57. On East Germany, see Klaus Storkmann, *Geheime Solidarität: Militärbeziehungen und Militärhilfen der DDR in die 'Dritte Welt'* (Berlin: Christoph Links, 2012). In the 1970s and 1980s, Soviet bloc countries also compensated for their relative weakness with a focus on supplying arms, military and intelligence training, and energy products to the Global South. Ruben Berrios, 'The Political Economy of East-South Relations', *Journal of Peace Research*, 20/3 (1983), 240–41.

[89] 'Dacia a făcut profit mai mare în 2012, din vânzări mai mici cu 8%', *Wall-Street*, www.wall-street.ro/articol/Auto/147366/dacia-a-facut-profit-mai-mare-in-2012-din-vanzari-mai-mici-cu-8.html.

[90] 'Inside Serbia's Booming Arms Industry', *Radio Free Europe*, www.rferl.org/a/24998852.html; 'Ask Not from Whom the AK-47s Flow', *Economist*, www.economist.com/europe/2016/04/16/ask-not-from-whom-the-ak-47s-flow.

[91] 'Weapons of the Islamic State', Conflict Armament Research, www.conflictarm.com/reports/weapons-of-the-islamic-state/.

in the efficiency of privatisation and shrinking the state. Margaret Thatcher and Ronald Reagan had recently successfully deregulated their national economies, and international financial organisations had been propagating the so-called 'Washington Consensus' to developing countries in the 1980s. The fact that many Western economic advisors, often sent by the IMF or the World Bank after 1989, flocked to Eastern Europe while it radically liberalised its economy has led many to believe that this was a Western-imposed process. But these advisors often found that their local partners had more radical ideas on how to deregulate and privatise national economies than they had themselves. In contrast with Latin America or Africa, many Eastern European governments needed no pressure from international organisations to adjust their economies. Many former Communist elites and oppositional figures seemed to agree on the necessity of budget cuts and destatisation, and levels of public resistance to these reforms were low.

An explanation for this surprising consensus in 1989 and the ensuing quick transition to capitalism requires an understanding of how Eastern European politics and societies had already undergone changes that laid the ground for that consensus. There was an increasing acknowledgement of the underperformance of socialist economies, and consequently a search for alternative models. Western social democracy was seen to be in crisis, too. Thatcherism in the United Kingdom and variants of state capitalism in the Global South, however, represented successful economic reform paths, often with an authoritarian bent. A pre-1989 consensus on the necessity of radical economic reform was also possible because it was not in and of itself oppositional: many proponents of market socialism were Communist Party elites or technocrats in state administrations. Moreover, it had the potential to benefit directly some members of the former Communist political elite.

In the years before the political collapse, in Hungary, Poland, Bulgaria, and elsewhere, state managers had spontaneously taken control of their enterprises, and turned them into private companies – often in suspicious circumstances.[92] Bureaucrats in education, the military, and the Communist Youth had already appropriated the assets of the institutions they controlled.[93] There are many examples across the region of former youth

---

[92] Eric Hanley, 'Cadre Capitalism in Hungary and Poland. Property Accumulation among Communist-Era Elites', *East European Politics and Societies*, 14/1 (1999), 143–78; Venelin I. Ganev, *Preying on the State. The Transformation of Bulgaria after 1989* (Ithaca, NY: Cornell University Press, 2007), 50–55, 57; Jadwiga Staniszkis, *The Dynamics of Breakthrough in Eastern Europe* (Berkeley: University of California Press, 1991).

[93] Steven Lee Solnick, *Stealing the State: Control and Collapse in Soviet Institutions* (Cambridge, MA: Harvard University Press, 1998).

functionaries – well-placed institutionally and generationally – whose networks survived and propelled them to great wealth. In Croatia, the former president of the Socialist youth organisation Goran Radman became Microsoft's director for South-Eastern Europe and a close associate of Bill Gates.[94] And Mikhail Khodorkovsky began his rise to become post-Soviet Russia's richest man with multiple small businesses as a local Komsomol leader in the late 1980s.

Contrary to a popular view of the socialist world as isolated and parochial, Eastern European economic elites after 1989 tended to have experience of the world abroad, and global economic knowledge that they had acquired in the 1970s and 1980s. In the final two decades of state socialism Communist leaders had had to react to global financial and economic crises – and just like their Western counterparts increasingly relied on the expertise of economists. Drawing on the networks built through socialist globalisation and taking lessons from global shocks, some economists, in exchange with colleagues and international organisations, developed Eastern European variants of marketisation and global integration from the 1970s – which were not usually linked to democratisation. Liberal economic ideas and practices were not just imported from the West, or imposed by Western advisors, from 1989, but emerged within small circles of Eastern European economists from the 1970s, in the responses of domestic political and economic elites to the economic malaise of the planned economy.[95] They were not able to implement these ideas during the rule of their Communist Parties, but successfully lobbied for their ideas in and after 1989.

Economic research institutes and university economics departments had been expanding since the early 1960s in much of the socialist world. They had produced an increasing number of excellent economists, often with a background in mathematics and quantitative analysis, which they expertly used to provide themselves with distance from contemporary ideological demands. Some of them were allowed to study abroad, in particular at universities in the United Kingdom and United States, whilst others participated in a 'technocratic internationalism' at the UN and its agencies.[96] Within their own restricted circles, such economists in

[94] 'Sekretari SKOJ-a u boljoj budućnosti' (The Secretaries of SKOJ in a Better Future), *Nacional*, http://arhiva.nacional.hr/clanak/52777/sekretari-skoj-a-u-boljoj-buducnosti; Ljubica Spaskovska 'The "Children of Crisis". Making Sense of (Post)socialism and the End of Yugoslavia', *East European Politics and Societies and Cultures*, 31/3 (2017), 504.

[95] Fabry, 'Origins of Neoliberalism', 3.

[96] Michel Christian, Sandrine Kott, and Ondrej Matejka (eds.), *Planning in Cold War Europe. Competition, Cooperation, Circulations (1950s–1970s)* (Berlin: De Gruyter Oldenbourg, 2018).

Eastern Europe from the 1970s amassed considerable knowledge of current global economic theory and were very much aware of the economic deficits in their own countries and conditions in other parts of the world. All Western and international economic literature was available in libraries to select small circles of academics even in ostensibly sealed-off societies like the Soviet Union's. Long before 1989, liberal economic ideas had been widely shared by restricted numbers of economists in the socialist world.[97] In unofficial, but not openly dissident, groups, through samizdat that circulated ideas from Warsaw to Novosibirsk, young pro-market economists had been discussing possible economic reforms in most Eastern European states long before 1989.

Markets were not an entirely novel concept to many Eastern Europeans in 1989. Many consumer goods were available only on the black market. And necessary for the survival of dysfunctional command economies was what Soviet liberal critics of socialism in their samizdat publications of the 1970s and 1980s had called a 'bureaucratic market'. They argued that markets already existed in the Soviet Union because industrial managers, who could not rely on plans and allocations from Gosplan, had to organise their raw materials and supplies in horizontal networks without state interference.[98] In other states, market elements were always officially tolerated: small enterprises were never nationalised in much of Eastern Europe; agriculture remained largely private in Poland, whilst a large part of housing was in private hands in the GDR. And in some socialist states, market forces were officially used to make socialism more effective. Hungary had introduced a state-backed market socialism after 1968, whilst Yugoslavia propagated a market-based worker self-management socialism. Those who knew how to profit from these market elements under socialism were often those who, after 1989, easily accommodated with a more radical marketisation.

The economic ideas that eventually dominated reforms after 1989 had not only come from the West directly, but had been circulating in between socialist states, and between states with a similar level of development and a similar position in the global economy. In more isolated

[97] János Mátyás Kovács and Violetta Zentai, 'Prologue', in Mátyás Kovács and Zentai (eds.), *Capitalism from Outside? Economic Cultures in Eastern Europe after 1989* (Budapest: Central European University Press, 2012), 3–7. On regional economists' role in transnational debates since the 1960s, see Johanna Bockman, *Markets in the Name of Socialism. The Left-Wing Origins of Neoliberalism* (Stanford, CA: Stanford University Press, 2011).

[98] Vitaly Nayshul, 'Bjurokraticheskiy *rynok*. Skrytye prava i ekonomicheskaja reforma', *Nezavisimaya gazeta*, 26 September 1991.

countries like the Soviet Union and China, it was mostly Eastern European economists that spread ideas on market reforms. In particular Hungarian and Yugoslav economists were able to promote their ideas of markets across and behind the Iron Curtain.[99] The future Russian reformer Yegor Gaidar had his first contacts with liberal economic theory when he read Adam Smith and Paul Samuelson while living in Belgrade around 1970.[100] A particularly important role in the spread of economic ideas within the socialist world was played by the Hungarian János Kornai. An early critic of state planning, he had been barred from leaving Hungary for many years after the 1956 Hungarian Uprising but turned into a global traveller and a transmitter of economic ideas between the East and the West in the 1970s and 1980s. He occupied parallel positions at the Hungarian Academy of Science and at Harvard University, had an intimate knowledge of economic conditions in the socialist world, and from the early 1980s formed close links with economists such as Gaidar in the Soviet Union, Wu Jinglian in China, and Balcerowicz in Poland.[101] His 1980 book *The Economics of Shortage* probably did more to discredit economic planning amongst economists in the socialist world than all Western advisors and IMF representatives put together after 1989. Its Russian translation circulated in the Soviet samizdat, then in the later Gorbachev years officially sold seventy thousand copies. In China, a 'Kornai fever' (*Ke'ernai re*) erupted in the mid-1980s: his critique of investment shortage, state paternalism, and enterprise inefficiency resonated powerfully with reform circles clustered around the general secretary of the CCP Zhao Ziyang.[102] Kornai's book sold over a hundred thousand copies after his visit in 1985 and was the best-selling Chinese nonfiction book of the year.[103]

---

[99] Johanna Bockman, 'The Long Road to 1989. Neoclassical Economics, Alternative Socialisms, and the Advent of Neoliberalism', *Radical History Review*, 112 (2012), 9–42; Johanna Bockman, 'Scientific Community in a Divided World. Economists, Planning, and Research Priority during the Cold War', *Comparative Studies in Society and History*, 50 (2008), 581–613. János Mátyás Kovács, 'Importing Spiritual Capital. East-West Encounters and Capitalist Cultures in Eastern Europe after 1989', in Peter Berger and Gordon Redding (eds.), *The Hidden Form of Capital. Spiritual Influences in Societal Progress* (London: Anthem Press, 2010), 133–69.

[100] Yegor Gaidar, *Days of Defeat and Victory* (Seattle: University of Washington Press, 1999), 16–18.

[101] János Kornai, *The Road to a Free Economy. Shifting From a Socialist System* (New York: Norton, 1990).

[102] Julian Gewirtz, *Unlikely Partners. Chinese Reformers, Western Economists, and the Making of Global China* (Cambridge, MA: Harvard University Press, 2017), 160.

[103] János Kornai, *By Force of Thought. Irregular Memoirs of an Intellectual Journey* (Cambridge, MA: MIT Press, 2006), 247.

Authoritarian Transformations?

Marketisation pre-1989 was imagined within the existing political frame-work. Some proponents of market socialism envisioned a combination of vertical political power with deregulated markets out of conviction. Other, more technocratically minded ones, did so out of necessity because they assumed that questioning seemingly unalterable power structures would endanger their careers, or that more democracy might thwart their reform plans. Either way, before 1989, marketisation and global integration were not necessarily linked with liberal democracy. Dzielski's ideas of a 'Polish Pinochet' noted above were shared by Club Dziekania, a group of liberal economists in the 1980s who had the support of the Catholic Church and were tolerated by the Communist government with the intention of isolating the Solidarność opposition movement. The fascination with economically successful anti-Communist dictators from the Global South was not limited to Poland, however. When Károly Grósz became the prime minister of Hungary in 1987, he looked to the authoritarian model of integration into the world economy exemplified by Park Chung Hee's South Korea. In Bulgaria, the decades-long Communist Party boss Todor Zhivkov, in a conversa-tion with the visiting Bavarian prime minister Franz-Josef Strauß, sug-gested a similar path of development for his country. The Communist Party might keep political power but relinquish some control over economic questions, allowing joint ventures with Western companies that would be free to hire and fire and pay as much as they saw fit. International Bulgarian networks and labour could be used for common projects with the West in the Global South. Zhivkov even declared his interest in bringing a Communist-led but economically liberalised Bul-garia into the European Economic Community.[104]

For those reform-oriented elites in socialist countries who wished to maintain the absolute power of the Communist Party while liberalising the economy, Asian socialism had become an even more obvious point of reference. In the early 1980s, the Soviet leader Andropov promoted several Soviet Sinologists to high-ranking positions as political advisors, to keep the Soviet leadership informed about China's market reforms.[105] China's embrace of entrepreneurship, marketisation, and openness to world trade was a key moment in the erosion of faith in the Soviet model

---

[104] Franz-Josef Strauß, *Die Erinnerungen* (Berlin: Siedler, 1989), 484–86.
[105] N. Leonov, E. Fediakova, and J. Fermandois, 'El general Nikolai Leonov en el CEP', *Estudios Públicos*, 73 (1999), 65–102, 78.

of planning.[106] While Gorbachev was a true believer in a reformed type of socialism, he too bore in mind the Chinese reforms enacted under Deng. Before the Tiananmen massacre, Soviet reformers saw in Deng's programme an example of the kind of reforms that could be instigated from above to stimulate economic growth: if Gorbachev failed with his attempts to decollectivise Soviet agriculture and decentralise Soviet industry, it was not for want of trying. What defeated Gorbachev was the massive resistance of the influential managerial elite.

After Tiananmen China remained a source of inspiration, but now for Soviet conservative elites, who were increasingly concerned with maintaining the absolute power of the Communist Party. Vietnam provided some guidance as well: initially with some inspiration from Moscow, reformers in Hanoi had followed a model involving a convertible currency and the gradual introduction of elements of a market economy.[107] Vietnam had gradually raised state-controlled prices then swiftly introduced market prices in order to avoid inflation – all implemented and controlled by the Communist government. 'Indisputably, [it] gives a very concrete example … also for other countries, including the USSR, which are trying to change their model of economic development', recommended an economist from the Economic Institute at the Soviet Academy of Science.[108]

Beyond the socialist world, it was particularly Latin America that served as a source of both inspiration and cautionary tales. As early as the 1960s Eastern European economists had come to see the region as occupying a structurally similar position in the 'semi-periphery' of the world economy, and facing similar domestic issues connected to the dismantling of autarkic development. By the 1980s it was the region's early uptake of neoliberal reforms that was of the greatest interest. Some of this influence came via Western advisors: Jeffrey Sachs had written a book outlining some Peruvian economic reforms and had managed to save Bolivia from hyperinflation in the mid-1980s – Polish government officials, who had learned of his feats in South America, approached him in 1989 and asked him to use this experience to guide their transition to capitalism. And the 1982 'plan chileno', a technocratic management plan by the military government to deal with a grave debt crisis by placating

---

[106] Ibid., 48, 51; Odd Arne Westad, 'Conclusion', in George Lawson et al. (eds.), *The Global 1989. Continuity and Change in World Politics* (Cambridge: Cambridge University Press, 2010), 273; Miller, *Struggle*, 20–23.

[107] Tuong Vu, *Vietnam's Communist Revolution. The Power and Limits of Ideology* (New York: Cambridge University Press, 2017), 245–48.

[108] E. Bogatova, 'V'etnamskaja model' dviženija k konvertiruemosti nacional'noj valjuty', *Voprosy Ekonomiki*, 9 (1990), 69–75.

international lenders, now shaped the IMF's stance on Eastern Europe.[109] Many of its economists looked to the cases of inflation control and deregulation in Chile, Bolivia, and Mexico in the 1980s as they addressed post-1989 Eastern Europe.[110]

Some influential Eastern Europeans had had their own experience of Latin America and had drawn their own conclusions as to what worked: the economist Lajos Bokros had studied in Panama in the 1970s and written his dissertation on economic policies in Central America – as Hungarian finance minister in the 1990s, he implemented the so-called 'Bokros Package', a set of harsh and unpopular austerity measures, which Bokros later also recommended as advisor to several post-Soviet republics and Romania. Influential Hungarian economists advised their government to replicate the Mexican *maquiladora* (low cost, tariff-free assembly plants) system to attract investments from the West.[111] Kornai gleaned insights from the literature on the end of military dictatorship in Latin America.[112] Poland's post-1989 finance minister Balcerowicz, too, had closely studied the successes and failures of Latin American financial stabilisation programmes of the 1980s – and it was from Latin America, not the West, that he drew the conclusion that the gradual setting free of prices did not work and that shock therapy was needed.[113]

In a yearlong series, 'The Latin American Experience – At the Service of Russia', Russian experts on Latin America discussed in 1993 the fundamental questions that Russia faced and the parallels and lessons

---

[109] Karin Fischer, 'The Influence of Neoliberals in Chile before, during, and after Pinochet', in Dieter Plehwe and Philip Mirowski (eds.), *The Road from Mont Pèlerin. The Making of the Neoliberal Thought Collective* (Cambridge, MA: Harvard University Press), 331–32.

[110] On this fascination with Latin American transition as a model, see Duccio Basosi, 'An Economic Lens on Global Transformations. The Foreign Debt Crisis of the 1980s in the Soviet Bloc and Latin America', in Piotr H. Kosicki and Kyrill Kunakhovich (eds.), *The Legacy of 1989. Continuity and Discontinuity in a Quarter-Century of Global Revolution* (forthcoming); David E. Hoffman, *The Oligarchs. Wealth and Power in the New Russia* (New York: Public Affairs, 2002), 198; Werner Baer and Joseph Love, 'Introduction', in Baer and Love (eds.), *Liberalisation and Its Consequences. A Comparative Perspective on Latin America and Eastern Europe* (Cheltenham: Elgar, 2000), 4; Adam Przeworski, *Democracy and the Market. Political and Economic Reforms in Eastern Europe and Latin America* (Cambridge: Cambridge University Press, 1991), 191–92.

[111] Baer and Love, 'Introduction', 4; Przeworski, *Democracy and the Market*, 191–92; Ther, *Die neue Ordnung*, 51.

[112] János Kornai, *By Force of Thought. Irregular Memoirs of an Intellectual Journey* (Cambridge, MA: MIT Press, 2006), 345.

[113] Jeffrey Sachs, *Poland's Jump to the Market Economy* (Cambridge, MA: MIT Press, 1993), 45; Leszek Balcerowicz, *Socialism, Capitalism and Transformation* (Budapest: Central European University Press, 1996), 357.

to be learned from the Americas. What was to be done with a domestic industry and an underdeveloped agriculture that was not competitive on the world market? What role should the state still play in the economy? How can a transformation from authoritarianism to pluralism and an economic and political global integration pass off successfully? Some pointed out that Russia and Latin America were connected through a self-perception of being 'almost European', and through their attempts at imitating Europe with radical means, nationalist as well as socialist. 'Ahead of us lies an underdeveloped, imitative capitalism of the Latin American type', elaborated one scholar, and added the warning: 'we should consider not only its successes but also its disorders'.[114] Returning exiles after 1989 fuelled what for a while became a craze about everything Latin American. Stanisław Tyminski, who had become a millionaire in Peru in the 1980s, ran – unsuccessfully – on a pro-business platform for the Polish presidency in 1990. Others celebrated the Latin American abandonment of structuralist economics and suggested emulating it in Eastern Europe. The tycoon Harry Männil, who had made his fortune in Venezuela, returned to his native Estonia in the late 1980s. As economic advisor to several Estonian prime ministers in the early 1990s, he warned against an emulation of the Swedish social democracy and recommended Pinochet's Chile as role model instead.

Transformation from Within

As part of their selective opening up to the world from the 1960s, many socialist countries had been experimenting with modern management techniques, which were imported from the West, with a view not to abolish socialism, but to render it more efficient. The Soviet-Ukrainian economist Evsei Liberman had developed models to introduce competition within a planned economy in the 1960s. While his ideas resulted in some experimenting in Soviet factories, they were soon shelved in the Soviet Union – with the notable exception of Estonia. And they continued to influence economic practice throughout Eastern Europe. Dzhermen Gvishiani, a nationally and internationally well-connected Soviet academician, wrote books on US management techniques and industrial administration in the 1960s and the 1970s.[115] An expert culture developed in Czechoslovakia from the 1970s, centred around

---

[114] 'Opyt Latinskoj Ameriki – na sluzhbu Rossii', *Latinskaja Amerika*, 7 – 12 (1993).
[115] D. Gvishiani, *Organisation and Management. A Sociological Analysis of Western Theories* (Moscow: Progress, 1972).

institutions for so-called *prognostika* – social forecasting and management.[116] This culture of technocratic optimising, with its focus on efficiency and rationality, was increasingly common in many socialist countries. Most technocrats within socialist administrations and the managers of socialist enterprises struggled considerably less than the population at large to adapt to capitalism in 1989 and were often the ones who were developing neoliberal ideas behind the scenes. Public servants in the Hungarian Ministry of Finance, for example, had already accepted some tenets of radical economic reform during late socialism – and were at the forefront of economic reforms after 1989.[117] In countries where no such counter-elite had developed – Bulgaria, Romania, Slovakia, Ukraine, Moldova – radical economic reforms were much slower to arrive.[118]

During the transition of 1989, economists who had been part of the socialist establishment played a crucial but – compared to the more visible civil rights activists – rather inconspicuous role. Andrey Lukanov, an economist who in the early 1970s had worked for the United Nations in Geneva and had held several posts in the upper echelons of the bureaucracy in socialist Bulgaria, played an essential part in the round-table discussions that negotiated the main democratic reforms and the transition to market economy in Bulgaria. After 1989, he was twice prime minister of the country. In Poland Leszek Balcerowicz, who had studied economics in the United States in the 1970s and in the United Kingdom and West Germany in the 1980s and had remained a party member until 1981, became an economic advisor to the Polish opposition in Solidarność and an advocate of marketisation in the 1980s. He would become the domestic architect of shock therapy in Poland after 1989. What were in the 1980s called 'Gdańsk liberals' would produce a Polish prime minister, Jan Bielecki, and a minister for privatisation, Janusz Lewandowski. Václav Klaus, who had studied in Italy and the United States in the 1970s and worked at the Czechoslovak state bank and Academy of Sciences, came to the political fore in 1989. A longtime

[116] Vítězslav Sommer, 'Forecasting the Post-socialist Future: Prognostika in Late Socialist Czechoslovakia, 1970–1989', in Jenny Andersson and Eglė Rindzevičiūtė (eds.), *The Struggle for the Long-Term in Transnational Science and Politics: Forging the Future* (New York: Routledge, 2015), 144–68; Michal Kopeček, 'From Scientific Social Management to Neoliberal Governmentality? Czechoslovak Sociology and Social Research on the Way from Authoritarianism to Liberal Democracy, 1969–1989', *Stan Rzeczy*, 13 (2017), 188–90.

[117] Fabry, 'Origins of Neoliberalism'.

[118] For Bulgaria, see Ganev, *Preying on the State*, 30, 71–72; for Romania, see Cornel Ban, *Ruling Ideas: How Global Neoliberalism Goes Local* (Oxford: Oxford University Press, 2016), 75–89.

admirer of Hayek, Thatcher, and Reagan, he became finance minister and later prime minister for most of the 1990s and from this position acted as one of the most effective supporters in the region for a 'market without adjectives'. In the Soviet Union a group of young academic economists from elite academic institutions, mostly Communist Party members with no inclination to political dissent, had spent the 1980s reading Kornai, Hayek, and Friedman and on weekend trips to their dachas would debate ways of marketizing the dysfunctional Soviet economy. This group included Yegor Gaidar, the first post-Soviet Russian finance minister, and Anatoly Chubais, Boris Yeltsin's leading economic advisor throughout the 1990s. As opposed to the majority of the Russian population, they had no problem adapting to or pushing for a deregulated capitalism.

If Western-dominated international organisations like the IMF played an important role in the transition of socialist economies, it was not so much via the oft-criticised 'Marriott Brigades' of Western advisors who flocked to the newly opened luxury hotels across Eastern Europe after 1989. It was often radical local reformists like Klaus or Gaidar who invited them to their countries – often less for actual economic advice than for the purposes of obtaining political cover for their already existing plans. The IMF, still, had an important impact on the processes of economic transformation, but the dynamics were rather different to that which is often remembered. It was socialist states themselves that had sought to join the organisation long before 1989. Local elites called on its expertise to legitimise their own projects, aspiring to see them endorsed by a civilised, modern international institution. After asking the pope for his approval, the socialist Polish foreign minister had applied for IMF membership in 1981, a request initially declined on account of the recent imposition of Martial Law. But even members of Solidarność sent requests to the organisation asking to be accepted, 'as a vehicle to build a better country'.[119] Poland was eventually admitted in 1986, joining several other socialist states that had become members even earlier, such as Romania (1972), Vietnam (1975), China (1980), Hungary (1982), and Mozambique (1984). Even North Korea and the Soviet Union had inquired in the 1980s about the conditions governing membership of the IMF. The IMF in its turn had showed a willingness to accept socialist states into their ranks even though the latter did not always meet its membership criteria.

---

[119] Harold James, *International Monetary Cooperation since Bretton Woods* (Oxford: Oxford University Press, 1996), iv.

IMF membership provided economists from centrally planned countries with courses on banking supervision, payments and settlement mechanisms, and economic and monetary analysis; the legal department assisted with draft legislation; the fiscal department advised on tax policy custom administration, treasury systems, budgetary accounting, public expenditure management, and social security.[120] It was a school of capitalist economics that connected socialist elites to international economic debates via an institution that itself was being taken over by a Western-dominated neoliberal elite from the early 1980s. High levels of debt in Eastern Europe seemed to give the lenders leverage to apply conditionality and structural adjustment programmes to countries that needed that debt 'rescheduled'.[121] But while Hungary, Poland, and Bulgaria were indeed mired in debt, other former socialist countries were not – and made similar decisions internally. Radical economic reforms grew out of a local consensus, whereas international institutions often warned local economists of their excessive zeal as they expected high levels of social resistance – which never came. Western liberals and social democrats, too, usually advocated more moderate and gradual approaches. Ralf Dahrendorf warned against a wholesale application of 'casino capitalism'.[122] And such Spanish socialists as Felipe González and José Luis Zapatero from early 1989 frequently put it to their Eastern counterparts that they needed to develop an 'alternative socialist transition'.[123] They emphasised that reformed Communist parties in Eastern Europe should steer their countries away from the full force of the market and pay attention to the maintenance of the welfare state and social equality. To no avail.

During the transitions around 1989 it was local political and economic elites, 'neoliberalised' as much as the IMF was, that pushed for deregulation and global integration. 'Western influence on the transition is much exaggerated', recalled Gaidar, 'they had no idea about how to undertake a transition'.[124] Chilean advisors, Chicago-trained former members of Pinochet's governments who were popular guests across Eastern Europe after 1989, often found that their hosts were more prone than they themselves to ignore the social costs of their planned reforms. The neoliberal zeitgeist, it seemed, had long affected Eastern European

[120] Ibid., 576.   [121] Kotkin, 'Kiss of Debt'.

[122] Ralf Dahrendorf, 'Straddling Theory and Practice', 4 April 1989, http://globetrotter .berkeley.edu/conversations/Elberg/Dahrendorf/dahrendorf0.html.

[123] Mark, 'Spanish Analogy'.

[124] Paul Dragoş Aligică and Anthony John Evans, *The Neoliberal Revolution in Eastern Europe. Economic Ideas in the Transition from Communism* (Cheltenham: Edward Elgar, 2009), 155.

elites before the advent of foreign advisors. Neoliberal ideas on how to transform the economy were there already amongst small circles of economic and political elites in most socialist countries. They had developed these ideas in communication amongst colleagues in other socialist countries, in exchange with colleagues in the West and with international organisations. As Dzielski's visions of a 'Polish Pinochet' show, these ideas on a capitalist transformation were not necessarily linked with democratisation.

The authoritarian capitalist variant, considered a more probable outcome of economic reform in the 1980s, was no longer seen as relevant by most liberals by the end of the decade. The end of Soviet support fundamentally weakened local Communist parties and thus opened up possibilities of other political alliances for economic reformers. While a democratised type of socialism seemed an attractive path to some intellectuals and parts of the population in Eastern Europe, it offered no economic model. The new democratic rulers thus opted voluntarily for rapid marketisation, which economists immediately suggested to them was the only viable model for Poland, Hungary, Czechoslovakia, and post-Soviet Russia. The view that free markets and democracy necessarily go together was, however, a post-1989 construction, not a view held by many before. Many of those neoliberal reformers who presented themselves as champions of democracy after 1989 were very late proselytes: in the 1980s they envisioned deregulated economies under the authoritarian rule of the Communist Party. In those countries where the party had lost its influence, these visions soon disappeared and were conveniently forgotten. But where Communist parties remained powerful, some liberal opponents revived Hayek's preferences for the liberal dictator against illiberal democracy.

This longing for an anti-Communist dictator continued through the 1990s in post-Soviet Russia, where the re-created and still powerful Russian Communist Party threatened to block or reverse liberal economic reforms. Some former dissidents and Russian nationalists pleaded for an 'authoritarian path' to overcome a party-controlled totalitarianism and catch up with Western economic and intellectual development, before only then, when the initial economic dislocation had subsided, introducing democratic institutions.[125] In 1994 Dmitrij Travin, a young economist in Yeltsin's team of advisors, demanded an 'Authoritarian Break for the Red Wheel', adopting Solzhenitsyn's vehicular metaphor

---

[125] From 1988 to the early 1990s, Andranik Migranyan, a prominent historian at the Moscow Institute of World Economy, argued this: A. Migranjan, 'Avtoritarizm – mechta dlja nas', *Latinskaja Amerika*, 1 (1990), 44–50.

to describe the unstoppable Communist regime. 'History teaches us', Travin explained, 'that most radical economic reforms, if not all, are not implemented by democratic rulers, but by autocrats', citing Franco's Spain and Syngman Rhee's South Korea in the 1960s, military-ruled Brazil from 1964, and Turkey after the 1980 military coup d'état as role models for Russia as 'examples of successful national economies that would not have come into being without authoritarian leadership'.[126] Faced with a possible return of the Communist Party to power, nationalists and economic liberals outdid each other in their praise for the Communist-slayer Pinochet, who during his retirement in Santiago de Chile received many admiring visitors from Russia. In late 1993 Saint Petersburg's deputy mayor Vladimir Putin told a delegation of German industrialists that a Chilean-style liberal authoritarianism may be necessary to fend off enemies of the ongoing economic reform.[127]

In Eastern European countries to the west of Russia, liberals faced less resistance from former Communists. A key concern of the technocratic transitional elite here was the eclipse of an ill-defined but still pervasive attachment to a 'third way' between capitalism and socialism. Václav Klaus, the first democratically elected leader of the Czech Republic, put his views on this option pithily: 'the third way leads to the "Third World"'.[128] His influential 'Club of Young Economists' had been founded in 1968, less in opposition to Communist authoritarianism than to the Prague Spring reform socialist Third Way – ideas that he continued to fight after 1989. János Kornai, too, warned against any concessions to this demand in his 1990 book *The Road to a Free Economy*: 'the basic idea of market socialism simply fizzled out. Yugoslavia, Hungary, China, the Soviet Union, and Poland bear witness to its fiasco'.[129] Gdańsk liberals in Poland, wary of reform socialist ideas within Solidarność, agreed. Balcerowicz later recalled that 'with Poland's newly gained freedom to shape her institutions, I believed, we were no longer condemned to search for a kind of "third way" solution'.[130]

Although all economists eventually embraced democratisation, they nevertheless often hoped to work in a technocratic space beyond it, which

---

[126] Dmitrij Travin, 'Avtoritarnyj tormoz dlja "krasnogo kolesa"', *Zvezda*, 6 (1994), 125–135.

[127] 'St. Petersburger Politiker will die Diktatur. Pinochet als Vorbild', *Neues Deutschland*, 31 December 1993.

[128] Václav Klaus, speech at the World Economic Forum, Davos, January 1990.

[129] János Kornai, *The Road to a Free Economy. Shifting from a Socialist System* (New York: Norton, 1990), 58.

[130] Mario I. Bléjer and Fabrizio Coricelli, *The Making of Economic Reform in Eastern Europe: Conversations with Leading Reformers in Poland, Hungary, and the Czech Republic* (Cheltenham: Edward Elgar, 1995), 45.

would allow them to make their reforms irreversible. This was partly the result of the emergence of a more authoritarian managerialism in the 1980s in many countries in Eastern Europe, which had delegitimised sciences of society and had bolstered the sense that experts had the right and obligation to impose from above.[131] Even the leader of Polish shock therapy Balcerowicz admitted that such reforms were much harder under democratic conditions and that such fundamental reform had – history showed – been more effectively carried out under dictatorial conditions. He conceded that democracy was important for human dignity but nevertheless did not think that it could provide a useful input into economic reforms: 'popular disillusionment with reform should not be taken as a yardstick by which to judge … and not as a reason to condemn it'.[132] When addressing domestic and international audiences, the transitional elites presented their neoliberalism-inspired economic reforms as a return to normality – not only in economics, but more broadly as a civilisational choice. Radical deregulation was sold as a civilising mission, which brought Eastern Europe back to the West and distanced the region from the Global South with its failed anti-imperialist statist economics.

The notion of liberal economics as a return to normality did not mean that all countries had to choose the exact same path. While all of them opted for liberal capitalism, and none for authoritarian capitalism or democratic socialism, most Eastern European technocrats around 1989 concurred that each country should follow its own path to capitalism and work out its exact forms locally. Poland had been the first country to undertake economic reforms, still under the Communist government. By early 1989 small independent businesses had been created, there was reduced control over central allocation, and price deregulation began. As macroeconomic chaos and soaring inflation hit the country, the new semi-democratically elected government opted for radical steps and a 'stabilisation package' that set all prices free in January 1990. While GDP and real wages initially declined and levels of unemployment rose, these reforms, in combination with mass privatisation from 1993, made Poland the fastest growing economy in Europe in the 1990s. Polish liberal elites then actively spread the 'Polish model' across Eastern Europe – especially in Lithuania, Belarus, and Ukraine, regions that had once belonged to the Polish-Lithuanian Commonwealth.

---

[131] Adela Hîncu, 'Managing Culture, Locating Consent: The Sociology of Mass Culture in Socialist Romania, 1960s–1970s', *Revista Română de Sociologie*, 1–2 (2017), 12–13.
[132] Leszek Balcerowicz, *Post-Communist Transition. Some Lessons* (London: Institute of Economic Affairs, 2002), 18.

The East German economic transition was a particular case because soon after the entire state ceased to exist. The Treuhand commission quickly privatised the assets of the East German economy, and the reunited Germany dismissed many former Communist elites. The currency union at an exchange rate of 1:1 was meant to create purchasing power parity and avoid mass migration from the East to the West after the fall of the Wall. A disastrous side effect was that East German companies could no longer afford to pay their workers' wages, and their low productivity and quality of products meant that many of them were unable to compete in a free economy. Much East German industry went bust. An expansive German welfare state ensured that most East Germans in the 1990s were economically better off than before – but many were unemployed or degraded to jobs with lower social prestige, with devastating cultural and moral consequences.

In Czechoslovakia a federal assembly elected the former dissident Václav Havel president, who acted as figurehead of the country's transition to democracy. Economic policies, however, were defined by Václav Klaus, first as finance minister, then as prime minister. Klaus stood for a mix of small entrepreneurialism and nationalism. Under his leadership the Czech Republic underwent the most radical deregulation and privatisation programme in Eastern Europe, in part because it had been the least reform-oriented pre-1989 economy: there had existed almost no private sector, prices had been nearly completely controlled, and 60 per cent of Czechoslovak trade was with other socialist countries. After the radical turnaround of the 1990s, the Czech Republic even came to hold a critical view of the European Community as a new form of state dirigisme. This radicalism of Czech liberal reforms was matched only by Estonia's, where the young president Mart Laar was inspired to undertake his economic reforms by what was by his own account the only book on economics he ever read: Milton Friedman's *Free to Choose*. By the mid-1990s the IMF used the lessons of what they saw as regional 'success stories' and turned them into the basis for establishing criteria of conditionality for those regional laggards that had not adopted neoliberal policies and struggled to attract foreign direct investment.

The levels of social resistance against these often painful radical economic reforms were conspicuously low across the region. Traditions of authoritarian political culture and political passivity go some way to explaining this acceptance of the elites' reorientation. In no state socialist countries, with the notable exception of Poland and Yugoslavia, did notions of a civil society exist outside tiny circles of urban intellectuals. But labour unrest was rampant across Eastern Europe in the 1980s – and then very sporadic in the years after 1989. Even when it did occur it had little long-term effect: the Mazowsze branch of Polish Solidarność spear-headed the country-wide protest wave in spring 1993 against the neoliberal cuts on social and economy rights that brought down the government of Prime Minister Hanna Suchocka and paved the way for the ex-Communists' return to political power. But even the ex-Communist-led Alliance of the Democratic Left persevered with the neoliberal policies of previous Solidarność-backed administrations.[133]

As labour unions were weak, faced a collapsing membership and were unable to expand into the new capitalist workplaces, economic liberals could easily demonise these institutional bases for resistance through their association with the Communist era, while they co-opted the more liberal wing of the left into their new governments. This would later be portrayed as betrayal by the more conservative anti-Communist wing of Solidarność and lay the foundation of the political careers of the populist Kaczyński brothers and their Law and Justice Party. But in the early 1990s anti-Communist sentiments and high expectations from a Western-style consumerism – an aspiration that had been stoked for the last three decades of the Communist era – gave many a firm faith in, and initial patience with, the capitalist transition. Indeed, 'market populists' also developed the habit of blaming external actors to distract criticism from local elites. While neoliberal reformers saw international institutions such as the IMF as appropriate discipliners of Eastern European societies, they could also use them as bogeymen for some of the hardships of transition.[134]

The idea of a democratic socialist transition was confined to Yugoslavia. There was little resistance to the first wave of privatisations under its last prime minister, Ante Marković, as these privatisations were seen as directly benefitting the workers, who obtained shares in companies, in line with the traditions of Yugoslav self-management.[135] But for many Eastern Europeans in 1989 everything that smacked of socialism was discredited through its association with a repressive political system and a

---

[133] David Ost, *Defeat of Solidarity. Anger and Politics in Postcommunist Europe* (Ithaca, NY: Cornell University Press, 2006), 50–51; and Grzegorz Ekiert and Jan Kubik, *Rebellious Civil Society: Popular Protest and Democratic Consolidation in Poland, 1989–1993* (Ann Arbor: University of Michigan Press, 2001), 146–48.

[134] For complaints about IMF insistence on low budget deficits and its impact on spending, see, e.g., 'Antall Interviewed on Current Issues', 31 May 1993, FBIS-EEU-93–104, 16.

[135] Anna Calori, 'Making Transition, Remaking Workers. Market and Privatisation Reforms in Bosnia and Herzegovina: The Case of Energoinvest (1988–2008)' (PhD thesis, University of Exeter, 2019), esp. chap. 1; Kathrin Jurkat, '"I'm Both a Worker and a Shareholder". Workers' Narratives and Property Transformations, Continuity and Change in Post-socialist Bosnia and Serbia', *Südosteuropa*, 4 (2017), 654–78.

malfunctioning national economy. Reform Communists stood no chance in the first free elections: 1968 hero Alexander Dubček's attempt to run for president in Czechoslovakia in 1989 met with fierce resistance from the Civic Forum. The catastrophic economic failure of perestroika made market socialism distinctly unpopular in the Soviet Union. Yet Gorbachev's mix of socialism and markets granted rights only to some enterprises and stuck to artificially low domestic prices for some goods. This created enormous economic imbalances and privileges for well-connected old elites who made fortunes. Gorbachev's political fate was sealed when, after returning from his forced exile during the August 1991 putsch, he publicly announced that he would now introduce proper socialism.

Not all Eastern European states immediately introduced radical economic reforms in 1989. In countries that lacked a neoliberalism-friendly technocratic elite and a liberal democratic opposition under socialism, radical economic reforms faced higher degrees of resistance. This came mostly from elites, but they occasionally mobilised opposition in the street as well. The first post-independence Slovakian government under Vladimír Mečiar' encouraged opposition to neoliberalism as an essentially foreign imposition, in order to bolster its credentials as protector of the nation. In the Soviet Union conservative reformers around Prime Minister Nikolay Ryzhkov envisioned a much slower and only partial marketisation of the Soviet economy. They nudged Gorbachev to reject a proposal, inspired by the Polish reforms, to privatise the Soviet economy in five hundred days. This caused many disappointed liberals to abandon Gorbachev and support the new power centre around Boris Yeltsin. With the disintegration of the Soviet Union after the August 1991 putsch, more radical liberals such as Gaidar and Chubais began to exert influence over the economic policies of Russia under its new president Yeltsin. But the newly founded Communist Party of Russia, with the support of Russian nationalists, vilifying the liberal reformers as traitors to the motherland and agents of US imperialism, blocked a large part of their reform plans from the Supreme Soviet until Yeltsin disbanded and shelled it during the Constitutional Crisis in October 1993.

In Romania and Bulgaria the domestic bases for a rapid economic rupture during transition did not exist either. The first transitional governments consisted of former Communists who fought to retain workers' social protections in the face of external pressure and used a populist-conservative-nationalist narrative of Western colonisation that could still mobilise significant constituencies. The Senate president Alexandru Bârlădeanu, who during the 1960s had been the Romanian Communist

Party's representative at the CMEA and Romania's chief negotiator during its articulation of an autonomous economic position within the socialist camp, now responded to IMF and World Bank conditionality in the same way as he had dealt with Soviet plans of integration within the CMEA: both were forms of economic interference in domestic affairs that curbed Romania's sovereignty.[136] The attempts of the liberal wing of the government to set prices free and cut public spending met with fierce resistance. In what was called the fourth 'mineriad', Romanian coal miners in September 1991 took to the streets of Bucharest, where they looted newly opened supermarkets and beat up World Bank advisors at the Intercontinental Hotel – whereupon several international organisations withdrew their delegations from Romania.[137]

In Bulgaria too there was an early attempt at the introduction of neoliberal reforms. After the elections of October 1991, the right-wing Union of Democratic Forces was able to form, with the support of the representatives of the Turkish minority, the first non-Communist government. The new prime minister Philip Dimitrov pursued an ambitious programme of reform that generated significant opposition from the trade unions as well as its coalition colleagues. In less than a year he lost power under pressure from the street and Parliament alike. These early neoliberal attempts in Romania and Bulgaria had a demonstration effect in the second half of the 1990s: when centre-right coalitions returned to power, they radicalised their economic programmes, so as to catch up with states that had already successfully implemented fundamental economic reforms. In 1996 the Romanian government implemented a programme designed by the IMF and the cheerleader for Polish shock therapy, Leszek Balcerowicz.[138]

These momentous instances of resistance notwithstanding, Eastern Europe's capitalist turn proceeded unexpectedly quickly. In the long run, privatisation also occurred in Russia, Slovakia, Romania, and Bulgaria. The various speeds of the various reforms and the different extents of the resistance they faced suggest that the rapid changes in and

---

[136] Cornel Ban, 'Neoliberalism in Translation. Economic Ideas and Reforms in Spain and Romania' (PhD diss., University of Maryland College Park, 2011), 360–62; Bogdan Murgescu, *România și Europa. Acumularea decalajelor economice (1500–2010)* (București: Polirom, 2010), 465–70.

[137] Romulus Caplescu, 'O Ialtă economică', *Adevărul*, 3 October 1991, 8; Dumitru Tinu, 'Cealaltă față a medaliei', *Adevărul*, 2 October 1991, 1; 'Agenția France Presse: Principala explicație – Decăderea economică', *Adevărul*, 1 October 1991, 1.

[138] Ban, *Ruling Ideas*, 86. Also see Bogdan C. Iacob, 'Transition to What and Whose Democracy? 1990 in Bulgaria and Romania', in Joachim von Puttkamer and Włodzimierz Borodziej (eds.), *The Year 1990 in Central and Eastern Europe* (London: Routledge, 2019), 117–141.

after 1989 can be understood only by taking into consideration forms of proto-capitalist reforms and global cooperation in the decades before. By the late 1990s opposition to the idea of radical economic transformation was limited to a marginal anti-globalisation left across Eastern Europe. One of them, the Russian trade unionist Boris Kagarlitsky, complained, 'We were promised capitalism and we have got it. The ordinary people and the hordes of leaders all envisaged the rich displays of the best Paris shops, forgetting about the half-starved unemployed of Lima and Sao Paulo. The plane has taken off and a section of the public still believes it will land in Paris or Stockholm. But, in fact, the course has been set for Brazil, or even Nigeria, since this airline and this make of plane do not fly to the West at all. True, some will achieve their aim and live in Moscow as if it were Paris – but at the expense of those who will live as in South America or Africa'.[139]

Conclusion

1989 was not the beginning of Eastern Europe's globalisation imposed from the West. Rather, it marked the decision of local elites to embrace a liberal version of it and finally abandon visions of an alternative non-Western-centric global integration. This decision was not inevitable. The inefficiency of socialist economics per se did not necessarily mean reorientation: the perseverance of the Cuban and North Korean planned economies after 1989 demonstrated that economic planning was indeed still 'viable' as long as the political will was there to uphold it with repression and as long as living standards elsewhere were not taken as yardsticks. And marketisation may well have happened anyway under authoritarian regimes, just as in China and Vietnam.

To properly understand the mostly elite-guided transitions of the European socialist states, we need to consider their increasing interconnectedness with the outside world long before 1989. Knowledge of capitalist modes of production did not have to be built up from scratch in much of Eastern Europe in 1989, which partly explains the swift reorientation of some of its elites once Soviet imperial control had vanished. Yet initially global economic integration had been seen as an opportunity to advance their countries' socialist economic development in times of crisis and stagnation, to raise living standards in response to heightened popular expectations, and thus to lend political legitimacy to Communist governments. Such an integration in fact left bloc states

---

[139] Boris Kagarlitsky, *The Disintegration of the Monolith* (London: Verso, 1992), ix.

more exposed to shocks in the world economy, particularly as many had taken out high loans to update their industries: debt would ultimately be the vehicle through which alternative projects of global interconnectedness would be hollowed out. Nevertheless, it was also the internationalism of socialist elites, forged through decolonisation and détente, that eventually gave them the tools to think through new economic visions and forms of integration into the broader global economy. Often these were radical but not necessarily modelled on Western market democracy: new forms of neoliberal economics were attractive in part because a powerful strand of contemporary international opinion held that these were best implemented by authoritarian one party systems. Just as China from the late 1970s had looked to the East Asian Tigers or Japan as models of transformation with strong state control, so too would Eastern European reformers. Russian and Polish economists admired Pinochet's Chile, and the Hungarian 'Korea Boys' looked to Seoul's authoritarian miracle or Franco's modernisation of Spain, just as much as they took lessons from Thatcherism or Reaganomics – in part because through them they also saw the possibility of their own one-party state surviving. Yet by the late 1980s dictatorship was viewed more and more as a obstacle to economic development. Moreover, as elements within the nomenklatura leveraged their political assets to gain control over parts of the economic sphere, the prospect of democratisation began to appear less threatening.

The origins of Eastern Europe's economic transformation preceded the formal transition to a market economy and parliamentary democracy. Post-Communist capitalism had some of its roots in the global economic integration of the socialist world, in the expert cultures of late socialism, its market rationality, and its hierarchical forms of management. Those states with a socialist-era tradition of attracting foreign direct investments and working with transnational corporations could build on these links, giving them a head start in the transition to capitalism. This was not path dependent, however, and political decisions still mattered. Those states that opened up most actively to the global economy after 1989 fared best in their economic development, whether they followed a radical 'neoliberal' deregulation programme (such as Estonia and the Czech Republic, the poster children of libertarian think tanks) or a more corporative development (such as Slovenia). This transition was often painful. Many had underestimated the threat that East Asian goods would pose in the 1990s in the West as competition, a crucial component of the experience of deindustrialisation in Eastern Europe in the 1990s. The long-term economic effects included booming cities and declining countrysides, higher levels of unemployment, demographic decline, and devastating cultural effects on some who saw their familiar world disintegrate. While living standards and consumption rates rose in general in the 1990s, some profited considerably more than others, who sometimes developed a sense of being sold out to the West, cheated, or left behind. Moreover, the top-down nature of the transition, with its toleration of nomenklatura privatisation and transitional amnesties – themselves legacies of the 1980s authoritarian approach to marketisation – stoked a widespread feeling of betrayal enacted by a coalition of old Communist elites and detached rich urban liberals. This would later fuel the populist revival.

Criticism of the transition now often draws on late socialist arguments about dependency that were taken up again after the financial crisis of 2008. Now right-wing populists consider the quandaries presented by the dominant role played by Western-led transnational capitalism and its role in suppressing their own national enterprises, whilst considering what a new 'national capitalism' might look like. And the West no longer automatically appears as the most attractive economic system: the fact that Poland and Hungary eventually looked to non-Western, non-liberal models for inspiration in the 2010s was also a delayed effect of these global entanglements of the socialist period. Victor Orbán has declared Hungary's affinity with Russia and China; and in Warsaw in 2012 the Forum 16+1 brought together all former socialist Eastern European states (except the GDR) with socialist China. Alternative forms of globalisation seemed defunct in 1989; yet they were partly revived, in a new ideological garb, thirty years later.

2.   Democratisation

On 4 June 1989, even as Poland held its first partly free parliamentary elections, tanks rolled into Tiananmen Square and violently ended the democratic movement in China. This event took place three weeks after the departure of the Soviet leader Mikhail Gorbachev from Beijing. His presence had brought unprecedented numbers of protesters to the streets of the capital, some of whom held posters celebrating the Soviet leader, in Chinese and Russian, as 'Ambassador of Democracy'. For once Russia was seen as an inspiration for political transformation. Interpretations of the nature of the demonstrators' demands, however, varied considerably across the world. Many Chinese and Western leftists saw Gorbachev's popularity as an expression of a desire for democratic socialism. In the United States the dominant view was that the demonstrations were an uprising against Communist rule: according to Secretary of State James Baker, the Chinese people were seeking 'the values of the West'.[1] Eastern European political and intellectual elites were for their part divided. Party leaders in Romania, the GDR, Czechoslovakia, Bulgaria, and Albania openly supported the Chinese hardliners, who violently persecuted and killed thousands of ringleaders and bystanders in the aftermath of the clearing of Tiananmen Square. The Soviet and Yugoslav governments declared the events a domestic issue; in Hungary and Poland, however, the crackdown was condemned in the press and in public gatherings.[2] Several representatives in Beijing of non-aligned states intimated that the protests had been fuelled by foreign meddling in Chinese affairs and interpreted the events as a global Western offensive

---

[1] Jeffrey Engel, '1989: An Introduction to an International History', in Jeffrey Engel (ed.), *The Fall of the Berlin Wall: The Revolutionary Legacy of 1989* (Oxford: Oxford University Press, 2012), 17.

[2] Péter Vámos, 'The Tiananmen Square "Incident" in China and the East Central European Revolutions', in Wolfgang Mueller, Michael Gehler, and Arnold Suppan (eds.), *The Revolutions of 1989: A Handbook* (Vienna: Austrian Academy of Sciences Press, 2015), 93–111.

against socialism.[3] Some diplomats from Arab countries, at the same time, sided with the demonstrators, arguing that they had turned violent only after the repression.[4]

The Tiananmen Square protests and the Chinese Communist regime's bloody crackdown occurred during a summer of widespread political turmoil. Multiple notions of democracy – socialist, direct, liberal – were competing, each based on a claim to shape a changing global order. After the events in Beijing, Eastern Europe's experiences were granted a privileged role in the narration of world history. Its grasp of both market economy and liberal democracy became, for many Western elites, an ideal illustration of the natural convergence of such a combination across the world. Liberal democracies, however, did not become the rule in the three decades after 1989. Of roughly 1.6 billion people who lived under socialist regimes in the late 1980s, only a minority came to be governed by governments that were liberal democratic. Rather than following a natural path of history, Eastern Europe's democratisation was an exception that calls for explanation.

The international celebration of Eastern Europe's democratic transformation soon came to mask the presence of many other, earlier programmes for the region's future. Although new ideas about socialist legality, civic participation, and human rights had developed over the 1970s and 1980s, and set the stage for such for a turn, there was scant commitment to *liberal* democracy amongst either elites or oppositions until very late in the day. Some – on both sides of the barricades – were attracted by the authoritarian modernisations to be found in Latin America, Spain, and East Asia. Many dissidents were for a long time advocates of the development of social and economic rights, and of socialist or direct democracy, as against its multiparty parliamentary variant. The use of force for regime survival remained until the end an option for power holders – most notoriously in Romania, but the method was considered and sparingly applied in Bulgaria, the GDR, Czechoslovakia, and Albania too.

To understand the triumph of a specific form of negotiated peaceful transition to liberal democracy is also therefore to explain the defeat of the other political possibilities articulated in Eastern Europe during the last decade and a half of the Cold War. Reformist elites from within Communist parties and oppositionist groupings played pre-eminent

---

[3] Telegramă nr. 015983, 10.06.1989/09:00, 1 and Telegramă nr. 015990, 13.06.1989, 1 in MAE-China, Situația internă volum II, 213/1989.

[4] Telegramă nr. 016019, 20.06.1989, in MAE-China, Situația internă volum II, 213/1989, 1–2.

roles in enabling the peaceful transfer of power and the embedding of liberal democratic politics around 1989. Many groups came to re-imagine the meaning of democracy and the possibilities for their own participation in it. This extended well beyond the region. Eastern Europe's liberal democratisation occurred at the high point of many international shifts that underpinned a powerful far-reaching liberal democratic consensus. As many radicals across the world were giving up on violent revolution and accommodating themselves to peaceful transition and multiparty democracy, liberals and conservatives were shifting the international debate over rights from its previous focus on economic and social justice to the struggle for civil-political rights against 'totalitarian states'. Political liberalism, in conjunction with market economy, was increasingly viewed as vital for long-term economic development.

And yet it was not long before this form of democratisation was questioned. Internationally, the Eastern European model of systemic change – peaceful, elite-led, and negotiated – was soon celebrated as part of the expansion of a Western-led liberal order at the end of the Cold War. A new, globally circulating paradigm of transition, whose influence extended from Latin America to Eastern Europe and Southern Africa in the service of embedding market economy, met a receptive audience in many countries in the region, where reforming elites and dissidents reached for models of political demobilisation, fearing their own societies' capacity for unbridled populism, violence, or nationalism after forty years of dictatorship. But at home this transition model was quickly accused of being distant, discouraging popular participation and mobilisation from below, excluding the right wing, or marginalising imaginaries linked to social rights, collectivist-egalitarian values, or populist and nationalist projects. Its critics saw 1989 less as a celebratory carnival of revolution than as an elite-disciplining project that some of them dubbed 'low intensity democracy'.[5] Such a path to change in Eastern Europe resulted in demobilisation among the broader strata of the population in the longer term; sections of now 'transitional societies' argued that they had been excluded from significant decision-making processes.[6] This would later fuel beliefs in 1989 as a betrayal and became the foundation upon which some political forces would reject

[5] Barry Gills, Joel Rocamora, and Richard Wilson (eds.), *Low Intensity Democracy: Political Power in the New World Order* (London: Pluto Press, 1994).
[6] István Rév, *Retroactive Justice: Prehistory of Post-Communism* (Stanford, CA: Stanford University Press, 2005), 30. In his formulation, '[Communism's] strange death fooled the people one more time by denying them the experience of their sovereignty. Communism killed itself instead of letting the people do it themselves'.

the settlement as a legitimate foundational moment for Eastern Europe's journey away from Communism.[7]

Reforming Elites

With the exception of Belarus and Yugoslavia, democratic settlements prevailed in the entire former socialist Europe during the late 1980s and early 1990s. At the heart of these changes were reforming Communists.[8] In Poland General Jaruzelski had been responsible for the crushing of Solidarność in 1981; by 1988 he was prepared to engage in negotiations with its representatives, an essential step for regime change. Around the same time in Hungary the discussions between the reform wing of the Hungarian Socialist Workers' Party and the local opposition paved the way to the creation of political parties and democratic pluralism. Growing numbers of Eastern European Communists themselves came to embrace, tolerate, or reluctantly accept peaceful, democratic change. By 1989 many were questioning the viability of state socialism, envisioning their countries' futures as part of a broader European community that transcended the Iron Curtain and envisaging a life for themselves beyond a one-party system and socialist scarcity. Where such a pre-1989 consensus was lacking, the transition turned violent: over eleven hundred Romanians died during the violent toppling of their Communist leaders.

In the early 1970s the traditional claims of Communist elites that they were part of an expanding global system and an important bulwark against reactionary imperialism had not yet become entirely implausible. Outside Europe since the late 1950s, decolonisation had brought socialist or non-capitalist projects to countries in Africa and Asia. Elites often noted the renewed importance of anti-imperial solidarity given the ever-widening presence of right-wing authoritarianism in Latin America, Africa, and Southern Europe. Where such regimes were in a state of decay – as at the end of the Franco and Salazar regimes – it was still possible to believe that state socialism might take root. Even the US secretary of state Henry Kissinger believed that the Portuguese 'Carnation Revolution' in spring 1974 might re-enact the Russian Revolution.[9] In a speech given in September that year, Hungary's leader János Kádár still expressed confidence that just as socialists would eventually oust Augusto

---

[7] James Mark, *The Unfinished Revolution. Making Sense of the Communist Past in Central-Eastern Europe* (New Haven, CT: Yale University Press, 2010), 30.

[8] Stephen Kotkin, *Uncivil Society. 1989 and the Implosion of the Communist Establishment* (New York: Random House, 2009).

[9] Samuel Huntington, *The Third Wave: Democratization in the Late Twentieth Century* (Norman: University of Oklahoma Press, 1993), 4–5.

Pinochet in Chile, so too their comrades would overthrow dictatorships on the Iberian Peninsula and seize power.[10]

Yet by the end of the decade this worldview had been significantly eroded. Communist leaders became increasingly sceptical as to whether the world was really going their way. Many Eastern European regimes became ever more distanced from progressive experiments in the Global South, which had in some cases turned to radical authoritarianism, and in others declared allegiance to a campaign for the radical redistribution of wealth from North to South, the so-called New International Economic Order. It was also becoming plain that state socialism was unlikely to spread within Europe: in the Southern European transitions the Spanish Eurocommunists broke with the Soviet and Portuguese traditions of popular workers' democracy and embraced the liberal democratic multiparty system. By the late 1970s the idea of Europe itself was firmly associated with liberal democracy and with the 'politics of moderation'.[11]

It was now increasingly difficult for the East to portray the West simply as the enemy. In the early 1970s West German leaders abandoned confrontation, reached out to the East, and promised to guarantee previously contested borders with Poland. With the fear of Western revanchism much diminished, the claims that Communist regimes were protectors of the nation from Western imperialism lost its meaning.[12] Links between Eastern and Western European economies increased, too: Poland and Hungary began to privilege export to Western European markets and to engage in joint ventures. Elites now formulated their narratives of progress, development, peace, and technology transfer within pan-European frameworks.[13] Claims that Eastern Bloc countries were threatened by a predatory Western imperialism were losing credence.

Against this backdrop, reform-oriented Communist elites began to question the axiomatic superiority of their own form of democracy. This questioning had in fact begun much earlier, as socialist polities sought to

---

[10] János Kádár, *A fejlett szocialista társadalom építésének utján* (Budapest: Kossuth, 1975), 14–15.

[11] On the lesson of Portugal as a turn to moderate solutions, see Kenneth Maxwell, 'Portugal's Revolution of the Carnations, 1974–75', in Adam Roberts and Timothy Garton-Ash (eds.), *Civil Resistance and Power Politics* (Oxford: Oxford University Press, 2009), 161.

[12] This was particularly the case in Poland. See also Charles Maier, 'What Have We Learned', in *Contemporary European History*, 18/3 (2009), 261.

[13] Angela Romano and Federico Romero, 'European Socialist Regimes Facing Globalisation and European Co-operation: Dilemmas and Responses: Introduction', *European Review of History*, 21/2 (2014), 160–62.

come to terms with the mass violence inflicted upon their own citizens during the Stalinist period. In response, reformers had attempted to place rule by law at the heart of their party-states and of life under socialism. This too had inspired projects of democratizing socialism in Hungary (1956), Poland (1956 and 1968), and Czechoslovakia (1968), which despite their defeat, remained crucial reference points for reformist thinking in the following decades.[14] In the 1970s Communist states faced new challenges to their understandings of democracy from the global arena, as the meaning of human rights became the lynchpin of new struggles between the Global South and Western conservatives.[15] In what many actors from the Global South perceived as a defeat, a Western-led international initiative (led by countries such as the United States and the Netherlands) was under way at the United Nations and beyond that challenged the primacy of struggles for collective rights against imperialism and racism and for self-determination and economic sovereignty, replacing them with more individualistic conceptions focussed on protecting the citizen from dictatorship, political repression, and restrictions on mobility.[16] Western governments now effectively employed the language of individual human rights to promote democratisation and attack political oppression in the Eastern Bloc.[17] This was a major challenge to states that claimed to be the bearers of what they considered the most important types of rights – to employment, welfare, equality, and self-determination.

Over the course of the 1980s bloc elites thus tried to re-assert their role as the protectors of such 'true rights' – whilst also endeavouring, in limited ways, to embed those civic rights which their critics accused them of crushing. Such initiatives were certainly initially aimed not at the establishment of Western-style democracy but rather at the re-invigoration of its socialist variant. Nevertheless, they served to reinforce principles of legality, civic rights, and, in places, political pluralism. Whilst this by no means invariably resulted in a liberal constitutional order, the process generated within Communist parties various debates about democratisation and what contemporaries called 'the socialist rule

[14] Silvio Pons, *The Global Revolution. A History of International Communism 1917–1991* (Oxford: Oxford University Press, 2014), 210–18.

[15] Joseph Slaughter, 'Hijacking Human Rights: Neoliberalism, the New Historiography, and the End of the Third World', *Human Rights Quarterly*, 40/4 (2018), 735–75.

[16] Jan Eckel and Samuel Moyn (eds.), *The Breakthrough of Human Rights in the 1970s* (Philadelphia: University of Pennsylvania Press, 2014); Akira Iriye, Petra Goedde, and William Hitchcock, *The Human Rights Revolution: An International History* (Oxford: Oxford University Press, 2012).

[17] Barbara Keys, *Reclaiming American Virtue: The Human Rights Revolution of the 1970s* (Cambridge, MA: Harvard University Press, 2014).

of law'.[18] Such re-formulations of legal cultures steadily delegitimised hardliners and facilitated reformists' accommodation to political pluralism – the ideological bedrock for the negotiated settlement between regime representatives and the opposition as this late socialist rights project collapsed.[19]

The most ambitious bid within Eastern Europe to redefine rights was the attempt to craft a 'Socialist Declaration of Human Rights', as a response not only to Western rights offensives but also to the 'African Charter of Human Rights and People's Rights' and the 'Universal Islamic Declaration of Human Rights', both of which were drafted in 1981. It was initiated in 1982 by the Socialist Unity Party (SED) in the German Democratic Republic and its chief ideologist Kurt Hager (famed for his rejection of perestroika) but evolved into a collective initiative within the Warsaw Pact. The document was supposed to underline the globality of socialist countries' achievements in terms of ensuring equality, welfare, employment, as well as anti-imperialist solidarity. Ultimately, the declaration could neither garner agreement between Eastern European states nor galvanise a global socialist-led debate about rights; its fate further confirmed the exhaustion of socialist, revolutionary internationalism.[20]

Yet by the mid- to late 1980s several delegations working on this declaration moved beyond simply refuting 'capitalist propaganda' and towards ideas of reforming socialism by broadening its legally grounded freedoms.[21] Negotiations over this document enabled reformers to push at the limits of human rights in Eastern Europe. The Hungarians pondered introducing 'liberal rights within the socialist system'; the Poles argued for 'legal mechanisms for citizens to question the state', while Czechoslovaks wanted to include 'rights to personal property' and warned against idealizing really existing socialism. In April 1989, the committee of Eastern Bloc experts issued their report, which remained unpublished but circulated across the region. It rejected the idea that 'the problem of human rights had "automatically" been solved in a

---

[18] Michal Kopeček, 'The Socialist Conception of Human Rights and Its Dissident Critique. East Central Europe 1960s–1980s', *East Central Europe* 46/2–3 (2019), 13.

[19] Ned Richardson-Little, 'Human Rights as Myth and History: Between the Revolutions of 1989 and the Arab Spring', *Journal of Contemporary Central and Eastern Europe*, 23/2–3 (2015), 15.

[20] Silvio Pons and Michele di Donato, 'Reform Communism', in Juliane Fürst, Silvio Pons, and Mark Selden (eds.), *The Cambridge History of Communism. Volume 3: Endgames? Late Communism in Global Perspective, 1968 to the Present* (Cambridge: Cambridge University Press, 2017), 179–80.

[21] Ned Richardson Little, 'The Failure of the Socialist Declaration of Human Rights: Ideology, Legitimacy, and Elite Defection at the End of State Socialism, 1981–1991', *East Central Europe* 46/2–3 (2019), 8–11.

qualitatively superior way' under socialism. And it underlined the 'undervaluation of personal and political rights versus economic, social and cultural rights and the undervaluation of the legal guarantees of personal rights of the citizen against state and society'.[22] The re-imagining of human rights in the East had evolved into the full recognition of the crisis of values in the socialist world.

Such a challenge was not taken necessarily to imply the unviability of the democratisation of state socialism. In the Soviet Union Mikhail Gorbachev embraced 'the socialist rule of law', in order to strengthen the legal and constitutional basis of perestroika and to modernise the party-state by bringing it nearer increasingly dominant international democratic norms.[23] Unlike previous Soviet leaders, and echoing the new approaches in Eastern Europe, he did not consider the realisation of human rights under socialism to be a given. In this he had in part been inspired by Southern European Communist parties, which had become reconciled with the liberal state from the early 1970s.[24] In Spain the Communists participated in the consensual negotiated transition and achieved an accommodation with the multiparty system that had emerged after the death of the country's authoritarian leader General Franco; in Italy the Communist Party entered into a political alliance with the Christian Democrats (1976). These parties, dubbed Eurocommunists, defined themselves against the ideological rigidity and authoritarianism of the Eastern Bloc, but nevertheless provided important new arguments about pluralism that would eventually be taken up by these countries' reforming elites.[25]

Gorbachev turned his full attention to Italian Eurocommunism in 1987 just as he embarked on perestroika and adopted new thinking in his foreign policy.[26] Although he did not aim at an emulation of the

---

[22] Little, 'Failure', 21.

[23] At the Malta summit in December 1989, Gorbachev told US president George Bush, 'Why are democracy, transparency and the market "Western" values? ... They are also ours [and] they are universal values'. Quoted in Jacques Lévesque, *The Enigma of 1989: The USSR and the Liberation of Eastern Europe* (Berkeley: University of California Press, 1997), 211.

[24] See the famous declaration by the head of the PCI in February 1976: www.nytimes.com/1976/02/28/archives/italian-red-takes-independent-line-at-soviet-parley-berlinguer.html.

[25] Cezar Stanciu, 'Nicolae Ceauşescu and the Origins of Eurocommunism', *Communist and Post-Communist Studies*, 48/1 (2015), 83–95; Vernon Aspaturian, Jiri Valenta, and David Burke (eds.), *Eurocommunism between East and West* (Bloomington: Indiana University Press, 1980); Pons and di Donato, 'Reform Communism', 190.

[26] Silvio Pons, 'Western Communists, Mikhail Gorbachev and the 1989 Revolutions', *Contemporary European History*, 18/3 (2009), 354. Members of the PCI tried to find interlocutors in Eastern Europe for their vision of the new, democratic left. Their representatives' meetings with Tadeusz Mazowiecki and Alexander Dubček did not amount to anything (259).

liberal democratic system, Eurocommunists provided the inspiration for a renewal of socialism based on popular support and directed against conservative forces in the CPSU. Gorbachev's thinking evolved from acknowledging socialist pluralism in the draft report for the celebration of the seventieth anniversary of the Bolshevik Revolution in 1987 to the acceptance of political pluralism the year after. The Nineteenth Conference of the CPSU created a new legislature, the Congress of People's Deputies, and introduced multiple-candidate lists for elections. In February 1990 Gorbachev proposed the removal of the passage on the Communist Party's 'leading role' from the Soviet Constitution.[27]

The turn of ruling parties in Poland and Hungary towards political pluralism in 1988 and their engagement in roundtable talks with opposition forces was presented to Soviet citizens as a necessary constitutional reworking for the survival of socialism. In 1988 the state newspaper *Izvestiia* proudly announced that the negotiations in Poland were 'a death knell to the myth that socialism cannot be reformed'.[28] Similarly, in June 1989, when the Hungarian Communists published their programme of democratic socialism, the official CPSU daily *Pravda* declared that this was a platform for 'a law-based State, a multiparty parliamentary system, and a market economy based on the decisive role of social property'.[29] For a short time Gorbachev's embrace of the socialist rule of law seemed to be vindicated by developments in Poland and Hungary, which appeared to prove the viability of a pluralist socialist system that maintained the leading role of the party.

In the end reforming elites, first in Poland and Hungary and then elsewhere, did dismantle state socialism in negotiated transitions. Reformers within Eastern European parties also came to terms with the idea of political pluralism by finding inspiration in Western social-democratic models of governance – although right until the end they wished to restrict such pluralism to options within the existing socialist system. Gyula Horn, the Hungarian Communist minister of foreign affairs in 1989–1990 and prime minister between 1994 and 1998, noted that he had learnt about political pluralism and market economy through links with Western European social democracy, most notably in Germany, France, Spain, and England.[30] The Spanish Socialist Workers' Party under Felipe González became a close partner for a number of

---

[27] Archie Brown, 'Did Gorbachev as General Secretary Become a Social Democrat?', *Europe-Asia Studies*, 65/2 (2013), 205.
[28] Lévesque, *Enigma of 1989*, 115.   [29] Ibid., 136.
[30] Georges Mink and Jean-Charles Szurek, *La grande conversion: Le destin des communistes en Europe de l'Est* (Paris: Seuil, 1999), 62.

reform leaders. The attraction of Spain lay in providing a clearly successful model of how a left-wing politician might steer a peripheral European country to a stable pluralist democracy and a 'return to Europe'. Gorbachev's close friendship with González may have played a crucial role in the development of his political thinking from Leninism to pluralist socialism. In their conversations González extolled the virtues of parliamentarianism and the free market in the consolidation of socialism and openly criticised Lenin for his lack of humanism, his suppression of legality, and his responsibility for the world's division into hostile camps.[31] Gorbachev considered, but never implemented, splitting up the CPSU in order to create a social democratic party that might engineer transition as the Spanish socialists had done.[32] In turn, in 1989, González helped end the 1947 ban of the Socialist International which forbade collaboration between Social Democrats and Eastern European Communists, helping eventually to transform Communist parties and their successors into 'normal' political actors in the consolidation of democracy.[33]

Neither Gorbachev nor the Communist elites in Eastern Europe expected to completely lose political control during the transition processes that they supported. The reform Communists accepted pluralism only as a stopgap solution to the growing international and domestic pressure for reform. Aleksander Kwaśniewski, participant at the roundtables on the side of the Polish United Workers' Party (PUWP), and later Poland's president between 1995 and 2005, recalled that in the aftermath of the massive strikes in 1988 the party's strategy was to satisfy some demands of the society while maintaining its main principles: 'It was enough to move furniture around, even throw some of it, without giving up on the walls'.[34] Prime Minister Mieczysław Rakowski presumed that once power had been divided the public would blame the opposition for the country's economic plight. In Hungary, the leading reformer Imre Pozsgay remained confident about the party's ability to carry the country on a socialist path. He lambasted critics of negotiations with the opposition for their 'lack of imagination in the possibilities of socialism'[35] and

---

[31] Robert English, 'Ideas and the End of the Cold War: Rethinking Intellectual and Political Change', in Silvio Pons and Federico Romero (eds.), *Reinterpreting the End of the Cold War: Issues, Interpretations, Periodisations* (London: Frank Cass, 2005), 126.

[32] Brown, 'Gorbachev', 210.

[33] 'Declaration of Principles', XVIII Congress of the Socialist International, 20–22 June 1989, www.socialistinternational.org/viewArticle.cfm?ArticlePageID=984.

[34] Quoted in Mink and Szurek, *La grande conversion*, 42.

[35] 'Interview with PPF Secretary General Imre Pozsgay by Henrik Havas', 24.09.1987, FBIS-EEU-87–190, 35.

expected to be appointed president in 1990, following a similar move in Poland where General Jaruzelski was given this office.[36]

Opposition from the Local to the Global and Back

In the context of a changing international environment characterised by growing rapprochement between the East and the West in Europe, ideological deradicalisation, as well as economic crisis, party elites played a central role in opening new avenues for engineering democratisation. However, peaceful change in 1989 required an additional factor: opposition forces. The largest and most influential movement was the left-leaning Polish trade union Solidarność; at its peak in 1981, it had over ten million members and was by far the greatest organised challenge to the authority of any regime in the socialist bloc. Other influential but much smaller groups existed in Czechoslovakia – such as Charta 77 – and in Hungary – such as the Beszélő circle – along with initiatives advocating environmentalism, peace, and human rights. Others were conservative, nationalistic, and religious movements such as Polityka Polska, which saw the Catholic Church as a space for civic resistance, and ethno-populist writers who focused on the spectre of ethnic disappearance of Hungarians outside of the country's borders.[37]

Opposition movements were crucial in a number of ways. First of all, they helped support a roundtable settlement out of dictatorship. Despite fears in many countries that violence would erupt, only Romania succumbed to it. The fact that Nicolae Ceaușescu had prevented any organised opposition was crucial: clinging on to power, and without partners to effect negotiated change, a bloody revolution resulted. Second, across the region – to varying degrees – the opposition helped create political cultures that supported a turn to a Western form of democracy. Yet there was no guarantee of this: up until the last years of the regime, many forms of opposition were not liberal democratic or even prepared to mount any kind of political challenge against regimes that they considered to be unchallengeable. Moreover during the transition there were those rightist oppositionists, most notably in Poland, who rejected peaceful democratic settlement. Nevertheless, by 1989 significant opposition forces came to embrace individual civic rights, democratic elections, parliamentary rule, and the liberalisation of

---

[36] Lévesque, *Enigma of 1989*, 134–35.
[37] Balázs Trencsényi et al., *Political Thought in East Central Europe. Volume II: Negotiating Modernity in the 'Short Twentieth Century' and Beyond Part II: 1968–2018* (Oxford: Oxford University Press, 2018), 153–154, 162.

economy – minimal common denominators for the coexistence of various ideological camps among its ranks,[38] while also learning to negotiate with the power holders whom they opposed. Their practices and attitudes were reshaped by broader sets of currents of the late Cold War: new ideas of transformation founded on political settlements developed in Latin America and Southern Europe; discourses on totalitarianism, dictatorship, and democracy circulated among opposition movements globally and underpinned newly revived commitments to liberal democracy as the only alternative to dictatorships – whether of a left- or right-wing hue. Whilst opposition movements are often imagined as heroic forces that led their countries to liberal democracy, many had not in fact been wedded to this political form and their conversion to it came very late.

Histories of dissidence usually commence their narratives in the late 1970s at a moment when many oppositionists were discovering the importance of political and civic freedoms: political principles that would constitute the foundation for their embrace of a liberal consensus after 1989. Yet many such movements in fact had their origins in the student movements of the 1960s in a very different ideological context. Many of those who would go on to populate the higher ranks of dissident movements had not rejected socialism per se but sought rather to articulate a democratic socialism based on Marxist humanism and socialist legality, which they distinguished from the official, dogmatic interpretation of socialist classics.[39] The opposition's embeddedness in socialist discourse came from its strong links with local ruling parties. At the University of Warsaw in the mid-1960s student circles criticised the system for having betrayed left-wing ideals. They formed a group called the 'Commandos', which played a crucial role in the protests of March 1968 – a turning point in the coagulation of anti-regime opposition in Poland. They relied heavily on symbols related to the condemnation of the Vietnam War and US support for military dictatorships. Across the region anti-party mobilisation was inspired by anti-imperialist solidarities with left-wing and anti-colonial movements.[40] The 'Commandos' comprised individuals who would later become prominent Polish dissidents: Adam Michnik,

---

[38] Jerzy Szacki, *Liberalism after Communism* (Budapest: Central European University Press, 1996), 73–117.

[39] Vladimir Tismaneanu, *The Devil in History: Communism, Fascism, and Some Lessons of the Twentieth Century* (Berkeley: University of California Press, 2012), 132–41.

[40] James Mark, Péter Apor, Radina Vučetić, and Piotr Osęka, '"We Are with You, Vietnam": Transnational Solidarities in Socialist Hungary, Poland and Yugoslavia', *Journal of Contemporary History*, 50/3 (2015), 439–64; James Mark and Péter Apor, 'Socialism Goes Global: Decolonisation and the Making of a New Culture of Internationalism in Socialist Hungary, 1956–1989', *Journal of Modern History*, 87/4 (2015), 852–91.

Jan Lityński, or Barbara Toruńczyk.[41] The dissident movements that emerged in the late 1970s – such as the Workers' Defence Committee (Komitet Obrony Robotników, KOR), a precursor to Solidarność in Poland, or Charta 77 in Czechoslovakia – counted among their ranks many disillusioned intellectuals or members of purged establishment elites.[42]

In the late 1960s opposition groups in general envisaged not a final collapse to state socialism but rather a gradual convergence between Eastern Europe, which appeared to be liberalising, and the West, which seemed to be moving towards greater state planning. Student activists in Budapest or Warsaw rejected both 'really existing socialism' and capitalism, seeing themselves as a part of a common struggle, along with the Western New Left, against the alienating effects of modern industrial society.[43] When the Soviet dissident and future Nobel Peace Prize recipient Andrei Sakharov published his seminal manifesto *Thoughts on Progress, Coexistence and Intellectual Freedom* (1968), he argued that this convergence would 'transcend the political and social malaise of the West and the East'.[44] As belief in the possibility of reform ebbed away from the late 1960s to the mid-1970s – at varying paces in different bloc countries – the notion of convergence collapsed and 1968 was constructed in dissident memory as the last moment when such a vision of reformism was conceivable – such hopes returned only in the second half of the 1980s once Gorbachev launched perestroika.[45] Even in the late 1970s some dissidents were still suspicious of Western parliamentarianism as they viewed it as alienating routinised politics that was incapable of truly recognising societal interests.[46] Radicals such as Jacek Kuroń and intellectuals around KOR in Poland, as well as Czechoslovak dissidents, for instance Petr Uhl, insisted on balancing party pluralism with the

---

[41] Péter Apor and James Mark, 'Solidarity: Homefront, Closeness, Need', in James Mark and Paul Betts (eds.), *Socialism Goes Global: Cold War Connections between the 'Second' and 'Third Worlds'*, vol. 1 (Oxford: Oxford University Press, forthcoming), 15–17.

[42] Kopeček, 'Socialist Conception', 5.

[43] Jeffrey Isaac, 'The Meanings of 1989', *Social Research*, 63/2 (1996), 318.

[44] Mark Bradley, 'Human Rights and Communism', in Silvio Pons and Stephen Smith (eds.), *The Cambridge History of Communism. Volume 1: World Revolution and Socialism in One Country 1917–1941* (Cambridge: Cambridge University Press, 2017), 168.

[45] Péter Apor and James Mark, 'Mobilizing Generation: The Idea of 1968 in Hungary', in Anna von der Goltz (ed.), *'Talkin' 'bout my generation': Conflicts of Generation Building and Europe's '1968'* (Göttingen: Wallstein Verlag, 2011), 110–13.

[46] Alan Renwick, 'Anti-political or Just Anti-communist? Varieties of Dissidence in East-Central Europe and Their Implications for the Development of Political Society', *East European Politics and Societies*, 20/2 (2006), 304–7.

devolution of decision making so that it would permit the broader political participation of the citizenry.[47]

The majority of oppositionists were never prepared to contest the right to rule of Communist parties. This reflected the failures of reform socialism at home: the movements that challenged the policies of the ruling elites had been met with force – either through internal repression, as in Yugoslavia (1966) and Poland (1968), or through Soviet intervention, as in Czechoslovakia (1968). The founders of Solidarność came from a generation that knew, following the suppression of workers' strikes in Poland in 1970 and 1976, that little could be achieved through direct confrontation with the state. In many cases oppositions thus sought to criticise the regime by claiming that the regime did not live up to its ideals: Solidarność was founded as a trade union defending the rights to work and welfare, which Communist states themselves professed to nurture.[48] Catholic social doctrine also played an important role within the movement, which greatly benefited from the support it received from the Polish Pope John Paul II, especially after his visit to the country in 1979. The language that brought together secular-liberal and more religiously inclined groups within Solidarność was that of human rights.[49] Moreover, the trade union – like many other opposition movements – sought to limit its activism so that it did not directly challenge political power. Nevertheless, in Poland in December 1981 this self-limiting approach was ultimately met with violence by the power holders: threatened by the spread of the movement, the Communist state imposed Martial Law. The trade union did not regain its standing until the late 1980s.

The impossibility of contesting Communist parties' rule consolidated opposition around single-issue mobilisation. New activists from a younger generation – often a decade or more junior to Solidarność's leaders – challenged dictatorial regimes in new ways. Unlike their older counterparts, who had combined more general critiques of the regime with a focus on sociopolitical problems such as poverty, inequality, and minority issues, this new wave rather emphasised conscientious objection to military service, pollution, environmental destruction, and, after the accident at Chernobyl, the threat of nuclear power.[50] The two

---

[47] Jacek Kuroń and Krystyna Aytoun, 'Reflections on a Program of Action', *Polish Review*, 22/3 (1977), 51–69; Petr Uhl, 'The Alternative Community as Revolutionary Avant-Garde', in Václav Havel et al., *The Power of the Powerless: Citizens against the State in Central-Eastern Europe* (London: Routledge, 2015), 188–97.

[48] Kopeček, 'Socialist Conception', 11–13.

[49] Trencsényi et al., *Political Thought*, 99–100.

[50] Padraic Kenney, *A Carnival of Revolution: Central Europe 1989* (Princeton, NJ: Princeton University Press, 2002), 13–14 and Trencsényi et al., *Political Thought*, 166, 171.

generations came together in some areas, particularly through those peace movements that questioned their Communist elites' claims truly to represent the 'struggle for peace', which had been a central tenet of their regimes' internationalist campaigns. Freedom and Peace, founded in Poland in 1984,[51] was particularly influential, inspiring and establishing connections with other similar Eastern European groups, such as the Peace Group Dialogue (Hungary), the Initiative for Peace and Human Rights (GDR), and the Peace Movement Working Group (Slovenia).[52] Charta 77 issued the Prague Appeal (1985), which called for the dissolution of NATO and the Warsaw Pact, the withdrawal of foreign troops, and the creation of a united Europe. Such movements reached across the Iron Curtain, working with Western organisations such as European Nuclear Disarmament to advocate the creation of a demilitarised, non-aligned continent through the promotion of human rights, pacifism, and environmentalism. This brought Eastern European oppositionists into realms of foreign policy that until then had been successfully monopolised by their regimes.[53]

Before the 1980s no Eastern European opposition represented a hidden liberal democratic thread, biding its time within socialist states. Rather these were groups that had been shaped by, and usually worked within, the ideological framework of the regime. Then this situation changed: movements began to see that calls for social reform and greater welfare rights were no longer enough – political pluralism and civic-political rights had become essential for overcoming state socialism's underdevelopment. This rereading is most striking in the programme that Solidarność adopted at its first congress in 1981. The document premised the defence of socioeconomic rights on the realisation of basic civic-political ones that were guaranteed by the trade union's independent existence.[54] In this Eastern European movements were indirectly becoming contributors to, and shaped by, a broader global shift in the language of rights: away from social and welfare rights towards the protection of the individual in the face of the overbearing state.

The Journey to Liberal Democracy

By the late 1970s many oppositional forces began to fight for autonomous social spaces in which they could develop programmes that might

---

[51] *Polish Independent Press Review*, no. 3, 13 April 1987, HU OSA 300–55–9 Box 1, 9–10.
[52] Kenney, *Carnival*, 123–44.
[53] Kacper Szulecki, 'Heretical Geopolitics of Central Europe. Dissidents Intellectuals and an Alternative European Order', *Geoforum*, 65 (2015), 25–36.
[54] Kopeček, 'Socialist Conception', 12.

peacefully push power holders into retreat and reform. Although tentative and not aligned to a liberal democratic agenda at this time, these baby steps would end up laying important foundations for negotiations for a future democratic system a decade later.[55] By the late 1980s influential leaders of opposition movements were adopting the idea of a peaceful, inter-elite, negotiated, deradicalised transformation from within. This idea, which was already termed 'transition' in the West, would set their countries on a journey from autocracy to pluralism. Yet it was a particular version of transformation that was eventually adopted in the years following 1989 – one that rejected the participatory and engaged politics of the early dissident movements, instead prioritising the deradicalisation and depoliticisation of society in the name of establishing a stable transition to a new market order. Some oppositional movements not only were reacting to the failures of reformed socialism domestically but also came to see themselves by 1989 as part of a broader anti-autocratic front that stretched from their supporters in the West to Latin America to Southern Africa – within which they both contributed to and were shaped by new globally circulating languages and practices of political transformation.

The shift towards civic and political rights – and eventually to an embrace of liberal democracy in the early 1990s – was in part due to a change in perception of the nature of the Communist state. Political abuses came to the forefront of political critique, and party-states were increasingly represented as totalitarian. In Bulgaria the most important instance of dissent was the publication in 1981 of *Fascism* by Zhelyu Zhelev – who would become the future president of the country between 1990 and 1997. His historical study of totalizing parties that create a state within a state was a thinly veiled attack on the socialist regime. The book resonated with both anti-Communist critics and party members from the interwar period who took it as a progressive critique of Todor Zhivkov's autocracy.[56] Domestically, the re-conceptualisation of Communism as totalitarianism was the outcome of the failures to reform and democratise state socialism from the late 1960s. It expressed dissidents' attempts to reinterpret the sources of party-states' resilience and their means of social control, and to counter claims of reforming elites in the 1980s that their systems would eventually be capable of incorporating pluralism while

---

[55] Jacques Rupnik, 'Totalitarianism Revisited', in John Keane (ed.), *Civil Society and the State: European Perspectives* (London: Verso, 1988), 55–58.

[56] Zhivka Valiavicharska, 'How the Concept of Totalitarianism Appeared in Late Socialist Bulgaria: The Birth and Life of Zheliu Zhelev's Book *Fascism*', *Kritika: Explorations in Russian and Eurasian History*, 15/2 (2014), 303–34.

maintain the party's leading role. The term 'totalitarianism', which had taken off in the 1940s and 1950s as a way to condemn Communist and fascist states that employed terror and purges, was now retooled to make sense of the evolution of the machineries of power that normalised Communist everyday domination. It was a condemnation of the subjugation of society by means of what the Slovak dissident Milan Šimečka called 'civilised violence'.[57]

The Eastern European opposition's promotion of the idea of Communism as totalitarianism also emerged out of fears from the late 1970s that their struggle was being abandoned abroad. They saw Western governments' cooperation with socialist states in the name of détente and the promotion of liberalisation from within as a sell-out – a position seemingly confirmed by Western European social democratic parties' failures to unambiguously criticise the imposition of Martial Law in Poland in the early 1980s.[58] It seemed that among Western politicians and left-wing intellectual circles the idea of struggling for civil rights in the face of totalitarian power was fading. Indeed, in the Federal Republic of Germany trade union mobilisation in support of Poland's Solidarność was limited and the local peace movement accused Eastern European oppositions of neglecting social and economic rights and merely extolling the 'bourgeois understanding of human rights prevalent in Western democracies'.[59]

Yet elsewhere the idea of a struggle against totalitarianism was a powerful argument that could be mobilised to gain support on an international stage. In France, where the Communist movement had remained powerful longer than anywhere else in Western Europe, a disenchantment with really existing socialism was cemented by the publication of Aleksandr Solzhenitsyn's account of the brutality of Soviet political prisons in *The Gulag Archipelago*, which, in the words of Georges Nivat, one of his translators, 'broke us'.[60] Many former French leftists' disillusionment with the 'Third World' struggle was replaced by a

---

[57] Rupnik, 'Totalitarianism Revisited', 271–77.
[58] Piers Ludlow (ed.), *European Integration and the Cold War: Ostpolitik–Westpolitik, 1965–1973* (London: Routledge, 2007).
[59] Robert Brier, 'Poland's Solidarity as a Contested Symbol of the Cold War: Transatlantic Debates after the Polish Crisis', in Kiran Patel and Kenneth Weisbrode (eds.), *European Integration and the Atlantic Community in the 1980s* (Cambridge: Cambridge University Press, 2013), 102.
[60] Robert Horvath, '"The Solzhenitsyn Effect": East European Dissidents and the Demise of the Revolutionary Privilege', *Human Rights Quarterly*, 29/4 (2007), 907; Michael Scott Christofferson, *French Intellectuals against the Left* (New York: Berghahn Books, 2004); Jan Plamper, 'Foucault's Gulag', *Kritika: Explorations in Russian and Eurasian History*, 3/2 (2002), 255–80.

fascination with the anti-Soviet, anti-totalitarian (and sometimes Catholic) opposition in the 'Second World'.[61] Leftist intellectuals and trade unions, which had previously acknowledged the Soviets as an international ideological avant-garde and a legitimate alternative to the capitalist West, increasingly saw their fascination with Soviet modernity undermined by the political rights that it breached.[62] In the early 1980s countless campaigns expressed solidarity with individuals and groups suffering from repression and organised mass protests against Poland's Martial Law.

The idea of totalitarianism also allowed opposition movements to present themselves as a part of a new international anti-dictatorial front extending from Latin America to East Asia to Europe that transcended Cold War bipolarism. Through tours of Latin America, the leaders of Solidarność's international committee forged alliances with both right-wing oppositional movements such as in Nicaragua and those left-wing fighters against military regimes such as Augusto Pinochet's in Chile.[63] Solidarność's leaders often used these ecumenical embraces to demonstrate that they had outgrown the previously dominant left versus right division of the Cold War; rather, they supported struggles against all kinds of authoritarianism, whatever its political hue. An instance of this global opposition was the proclamation 'Solidarity with Chile', written by US and Chilean intellectuals: it was signed in 1987 by Czechoslovak, Polish, Hungarian, and Yugoslav dissidents. Its introduction epitomised the new trans-regional anti-totalitarian ethos of the times: 'We express our support to all liberation and social justice movements of the world, regardless if they are in South Africa, Poland, Turkey, or USSR'.[64] Still, these connections often did not come naturally, because many of the movements in the Global South were Marxist and backed by state

---

[61] James Mark and Anna von der Goltz, 'Encounters', in Robert Gildea, James Mark, and Anette Warring (eds.), *Europe's 1968: Voices of Revolt* (Oxford: Oxford University Press, 2013), 155–59.

[62] Robert Brier, 'Broadening the Cultural History of the Cold War: The Emergence of the Polish Workers' Defence Committee and the Rise of Human Rights', *Journal of Cold War Studies*, 15/4 (2013), 120.

[63] Kim Christiaens and Idesbald Goddeeris, 'Competing Solidarities? Solidarność and the Global South during the 1980s', in James Mark, Steffi Marung, and Artemy M. Kalinovsky (eds.), *Alternative Globalizations: Eastern Europe and the Postcolonial World* (Bloomington: Indiana University Press, 2020), 1–20.

[64] 'Společné prohlášení k situaci v Chile', *Informace o Chartě 77*, 10/7 (1987), 24–25, www.vons.cz/data/pdf/infoch/INFOCH_07_1987.pdf.

socialist regimes. Often such actors criticised Eastern Europeans' liberal and right-wing supporters in the West.[65]

Around the same time a new paradigm of theorizing the transformation from dictatorship to democracy was articulated: the transition template. It originated among social scientists from Latin America, most of whom were former Marxists and social democrats who had supported anti-imperialist and anti-authoritarian struggles of the 1970s.[66] Latin American structuralist scholars of dependency such as Fernando Henrique Cardoso and Guillermo O'Donnell played a leading role in the initial conceptualising of 'transition'. They began to imagine change not through violent insurrection but in modelling how pacts with parts of the bureaucratic authoritarian elite might be sufficient to nudge them towards democratisation.[67] This theoretical blueprint would be embraced by conservative and liberal organisations in the United States alongside elites from Latin America, South Africa, and Eastern Europe who by late 1980s moved away from left-wing, socialist-centred visions to inter-elite, negotiated, peaceful, and non-radical forms of change. The 'transition paradigm' signalled a re-interpretation of democracy itself: a move away from visions of working-class, broad-based participation in politics mixed with welfare principles, from radical economic distribution and collectivist self-determination.[68] This conceptual narrowing reflected the burgeoning global imaginary centred on individual political rights, and constitutionalism. It also assigned a new role to democratising elites: they embraced – then disciplined their societies accordingly – the goal of breaking peacefully with dictatorship, fearing a return to radicalism, nationalism and even violence as their authoritarian states crumbled.

US policymakers took up this paradigm too: it provided them with the necessary language of change that could be disseminated through democracy promotion.[69] The imposition of Martial Law in Poland in

---

[65] Kim Christiaens, 'Europe at the Crossroads of Three Worlds: Alternative Histories and Connections of European Solidarity with the Third World, 1950s–80s', *European Review of History: Revue européenne d'histoire*, 24/6 (2017), 947.

[66] Nicolas Guilhot, *The Democracy Makers: Human Rights and International Order* (New York: Columbia University Press, 2005), 165.

[67] Jeremy Adelman and Margarita Fajardo, 'Between Capitalism and Democracy: A Study in the Political Economy of Ideas in Latin America, 1968–1980', *Latin American Research Review*, 51/3 (2016), 3–22; Paige Arthur, 'How "Transitions" Reshaped Human Rights: A Conceptual History of Transitional Justice', *Human Rights Quarterly*, 31/2 (2009), 346.

[68] Greg Grandin, 'The Instruction of Great Catastrophe: Truth Commissions, National History, and State Formation in Argentina, Chile, and Guatemala', *American Historical Review*, 110/1 (2005), 46–47.

[69] Thomas Carothers, *Aiding Democracy Abroad: The Learning Curve* (Washington, DC: Carnegie Endowment for International Peace, 1999), 94.

1981 was a trigger for the renewal of US engagement with such programmes. During his address before the British Parliament on 8 June 1982, Ronald Reagan spoke of the struggles of Poland's Solidarność and anti-Communist movements in El Salvador as he announced his 'Project Democracy'.[70] A year later, a bipartisan bill in the US Congress created the National Endowment for Democracy (NED), which soon lent its support to the financially struggling Solidarność. Through the NED the Polish underground was paid around three hundred thousand dollars per year from 1983 to 1988, with an additional one million dollars per year from Congress in 1988 and 1989.[71] This trend continued after the end of socialism: up until 1994 Poland received the largest portion of US assistance in Eastern Europe.

These initiatives were funded by the United States but were also part of newly circulating norms about transformation that were promoted by a new class of interlocutors across Eastern Europe, Latin America, and Southern Africa who feared that the collapse of authoritarianism would usher in violence or unbridled populism. This international vision of change was about deradicalisation in general, and bringing left-minded intellectuals to the political centre in particular. An influential actor in this dynamic was the Hungarian American billionaire George Soros. Alongside supporting moderates who from the mid-1980s sought a negotiated transition in South Africa, he began to construct a similar network in Eastern Europe, launching his first Open Society Fund in Hungary in 1984, before extending by the end of the decade to Poland, Czechoslovakia, Bulgaria, and the Soviet Union – and then officially in 1993 to South Africa.[72] Institutions such as the New School for Social Research in New York or the Institute for Human Sciences in Vienna, created in 1983 by the Polish philosopher Krzysztof Michalski, were hubs for articulating narratives about the role of 'civil society' in dismantling 'totalitarianism' and founding Western-style political regimes.[73]

Support for the NED only grew amongst US elites in the second half of the 1980s, reflecting a shift away from assistance to anti-Communist authoritarians to the active endorsement of peaceful, stable liberal

---

[70] Brier, 'Poland's Solidarity', 87.
[71] Gregory Domber, 'The AFL-CIO, The Reagan Administration and Solidarność', *Polish Review*, 52/3 (2007), 304.
[72] Daniel Bessner, 'The Globalist: George Soros after the Open Society', *N+1*, 18 June 2018, https://nplusonemag.com/online-only/online-only/the-globalist/.
[73] The New School's journal *Social Research* consistently published Eastern European intellectuals. In 1988, 1990, and 1991 the periodical had several special issues on reforms in the socialist camp and the transformation of these societies as well as of their economies and politics. See *Social Research*, 55/1 (1988), 57/2 (1990), and 58/4 (1991).

processes of transformation. This 'transition paradigm' appeared to be able to demobilise and deradicalise the left much more effectively than autocrats had managed in the past. Carl Greshman, the NED president, declared that his institution was 'a means of addressing a fundamental problem in U.S. foreign policy that became acute in the late 1970s with the downfall of the Shah and Somoza … the failure or absence of democratic reform helped make it possible for radical anti-American movements to supplant pro-American governments. As a result, many concluded that the U.S. should nurture democratic alternatives to authoritarianism that would be better able to withstand the challenges of the radical left'.[74] In 1987 the NED organised the Challenges of Democracy conference, which gathered together Western academics, Eastern European exiles who represented opposition movements, and think tanks from Latin America, the Caribbean, Africa, and East Asia. The event articulated the idea that the United States needed to get behind internal forces that sought to encourage the peaceful promotion of democracy.[75] Exiled oppositionists often acted as liaisons between dissidence at home and institutions such as the NED. The crackdown against reform socialism in 1968 as well as frequent expulsions of dissidents since the 1970s had created a politicised exile community that kept opposition in Eastern Europe internationally visible and linked with other anti-authoritarian movements.[76] Since the mid-1980s such groups were firmly associated with the activity of democracy promotion organisations. The Committee in Support of Solidarity from New York coordinated the NED's financial support to Solidarność;[77] exiled dissidents figured prominently in international conferences to disseminate the Western idea of negotiated, non-radical change from within.[78] The Eastern European interlocutors of these institutions were exactly the actors that US elites hoped would be attracted to the 'transition template': intellectuals (often left-leaning) who were willing to accommodate with liberal internationalism.[79] Organisations such as Soros's Open

---

[74] Christopher Bright, 'Neither Dictatorships nor Double Standards: The Reagan Administration's Approach to Human Rights', *World Affairs*, 153/2 (1990), 71.

[75] Dorin Tudoran, 'Farmecul discret al democrației', *Agora*, 1/2 (1988), 2.

[76] Trencsényi et al., *Political Thought*, 75.   [77] Domber, 'AFL-CIO', 288n39.

[78] See also the NED-funded 'Will Communist States Survive? The View from Within' (New York, 1987). Highly prominent exiled dissents from Eastern Europe as well as Cuba and Nicaragua participated along with important neoconservative American intellectuals. Vladimir Tismăneanu, 'Despre neoconservatorism', 25 September 2009, https://tismaneanu.wordpress.com/2009/09/25/.

[79] Nicolas Guilhot, 'A Network of Influential Friendships: The Fondation Pour Une Entraide Intellectuelle Européenne and East–West Cultural Dialogue, 1957–1991', *Minerva*, 44 (2006), 379–409. Guilhot argues that the success of the Soros-funded

Society Fund (later Open Society Foundations), the Ford Foundation, the NED, the German Marshall Fund of the United States, the Rockefeller Foundation, and the Aspen Institute provided forums from the late 1980s to the early 1990s to help an emerging transnational 'transition-minded' elite develop a common language around transformation in the aftermath of dictatorship.[80] Considering the fragility of the new democratic polities, their primary concerns were the protection of the settlement achieved through inter-elite negotiation, the exclusion or disciplining of the excessively radical, and the creation of a climate conducive to market reforms.

By 1989 parts of opposition movements had altered their ideological outlook. For instance, important Solidarność intellectuals who would take part in the roundtables had moved away their earlier focus on socio-economic rights and towards liberalism. While many of the trade union leaders maintained their socialist views, it was not they who collaborated with the reformists within the PUWP in the negotiations to end one-party rule. Indeed, these discussions excluded even minimal popular input on policies deemed to bring about, at breakneck speed, the new capitalist, democratic order.[81] In 1991 one critic underlined the gap between the intelligentsia and the workers, accusing the Parliament (dominated by Solidarność) and the government of Tadeusz Mazowiecki (created after the first semi-free elections) of 'neglect[ing] to communicate with society'.[82] Former leftists joined forces with economic liberals. By 1988 Radio Free Europe reported that the core of Solidarność's economic reform programme had swung in favour of 'the idea of an individual's right to private property'. The NED's support for Solidarność played a crucial role in entrenching the trade union's sympathy for US president Ronald Reagan.[83] Some of its prominent representatives thereby came to embrace liberal and neoconservative policies

Central European University can be explained also by its connection with East-West intellectual circulations and origins in the democracy-promotion programs of the late Cold War and early 1990s. Nicolas Guilhot, 'Une vocation philanthropique: George Soros, les sciences sociales et la régulation du marché mondial', *Actes de la recherche en sciences sociales*, 151–152/1 (2004), 36–48.

[80] For details on conferences such as 'State Crimes: Punishment or Pardon' (New York, 1988), 'Justice in Times of Transition' (Salzburg, 1992), and 'Dealing with the Past' (Cape Town, 1994), see Renée Jeffery, *Transitions to Democracy: Amnesties, Accountability, and Human Rights* (Philadelphia: University of Pennsylvania Press, 2014), 59–68 and 85–89 and Arthur, 'How "Transitions"', 325.

[81] David Ost, *Defeat of Solidarity. Anger and Politics in Postcommunist Europe* (Ithaca, NY: Cornell University Press, 2006), 180–81.

[82] Wiktor Osiatynski, 'Revolutions in Eastern Europe', *University of Chicago Law Review*, 58/2 (1991), 857.

[83] Kenney, *Carnival*, 119.

emphasizing individual rights, limited democracy, and the dominant role of the market in the economy. Intellectuals within the movement were fond of such liberal and neoliberal economists as Milton Friedman, Guy Sorman, and Friedrich Hayek.[84] According to later leftist critiques, this transformation marked the moment when the vision of Solidarność as an economically and democratically inclusive movement was defeated.[85]

The idea of a peaceful negotiated settlement as the most appropriate process to enable change also had origins abroad. Polish dissidents had first come to learn important lessons about the value of political negotiation from the democratic transformation in Southern Europe. In Poland, for example, Spain's *consenso* model following the death of Franco was important for an emerging dissident movement in the mid-1970s. Adam Michnik, a left-liberal strategist within Solidarność, termed the Spanish approach the 'New Evolutionism', and saw its policy of negotiation as a way out of Poland's political impasse.[86] This fascination fell away in the early 1980s, as Martial Law rendered such compromise impossible. In 1984, the samizdat journal *KOS* concluded that Poland had now gone the Chilean way where political forces could not find a middle ground and the reformists ('calculating democrats') were defeated by hardliners.[87] This interest in the Spanish form of negotiation returned in the late 1980s as a model for pacted transition and was then embraced in 1989–90 with Tadeusz Mazowiecki's first post-Communist government, which wished avoid revenge and to draw a 'thick line under the past' – just as Spain had attempted to do.[88]

Such a far-reaching compromise did not go uncontested. By 1989 the politics of consensus and historical compromise prevailed in Central Europe, but they concealed political polarisations that threatened to undermine a precarious unity.[89] The language of anti-totalitarianism had stoked morally indignant nationalist movements that viewed their

---

[84] *Polish Independent Press Review*, no. 3, 6 April 1988, HU OSA 300–55–9 Box 1, 11.

[85] Ost, *Defeat of Solidarity*, 37–59.

[86] Adam Michnik, *Letters From Prison and Other Essays* (Berkeley: University of California Press, 1985), 143.

[87] RAD Polish Underground Extracts no. 13/1984, HU OSA 300–55–9 Box 2, 3–6.

[88] Dominik Trutowski, 'Poland and Spain "Entangled". Political Learning in Transitions to Democracy' (paper presented at 'Entangled Transitions: Between Eastern and Southern Europe 1960s–2014', University of Leuven, 2014). See also the importance of Gandhi and Luther King on Adam Michnik in Jeffrey Stout, 'Between Secularism and Theocracy. King, Michnik, and the American Culture Wars', in Piotr Kosicki and Kyrill Kunakhovich (eds.), *The Legacy of 1989: Continuity and Discontinuity in a Quarter-Century of Global Revolution* (forthcoming).

[89] Michal Kopeček, 'Human Rights Facing a National Past. Dissident "Civic Patriotism" and the Return of History in East Central Europe, 1968–1989', *Geschichte und Gesellschaft*, 38/4, (2012), 591.

countries as victims of Soviet imperialism whose suffering was being ignored. From the mid-1980s tensions among centrist, populist, conservative, or radically democratic groups within national opposition movements were growing sharper, anticipating the ideological cleavages of post-socialism. Across Eastern Europe the actors who created the consensus of the 1990s were not without challengers, especially from the nationalist right, some of whom contested the need for liberal democracy.[90] Solidarność's strategies of peaceful resistance after the Martial Law and dialogue with the authorities once the regime adopted a series of amnesties were sharply criticised by groups such as Fighting Solidarity, the Independent Students' Association, or the Federation of Fighting Youth. These organisations often employed nationalist programmes of self-determination and advocated mass public demonstrations as the proper means of defeating the regime. They even boycotted the first semi-free elections in June 1989 because they allegedly undermined 'the nation's sovereignty' and compromised the opposition by integrating it into an undefeated Communist political order.[91] Negotiated change in Eastern Europe narrowed down other political options out of fear of radicalism, ranging from direct democracy to nationalism. This was facilitated by the adoption of a global model of elite-based negotiated change coproduced in Latin America, North America, Southern Europe, and Southern Africa – with the help of democracy promotion organisations.[92] Yet some opposition forces were already questioning the legitimacy of negotiated change, a loose thread that populists would later pull in order to unravel the myth of 1989 as democratic revolution.

Alternatives to '1989': Authoritarianism and Violence

Despite all these new ideas about democratisation, a peaceful pluralistic settlement was in no way assured. The socialist camp had a long history of crushed hopes of democratisation – from Berlin (1953), Hungary (1956), and Czechoslovakia (1968) to Martial Law in Poland. Right up until the late 1980s even certain reformist elites saw authoritarian modernisation as a way out of economic crisis, whilst hardliners toyed with the violent suppression of mounting protests. Yet in the end only Romania succumbed to violence; after the revolution some of

---

[90] Trencsényi et al., *Political Thought*, 137–38, 153, 163, 182.
[91] *Polish Independent Press Review*, no. 7, 7 November 1989, HU OSA 300–55–9 Box 1, 9–11.
[92] Ashley Lavelle, *The Death of Social Democracy. Political Consequences in the 21st Century* (Aldershot: Ashgate, 2008).

Ceauşescu's successors continued to be fascinated with modernisation engineered by semi-dictatorial means. Over the course of the late 1980s shifts across the world increasingly removed the powerful arguments that had underpinned these options. It is striking just how international political reference points had become for both Communists and opposition: they debated the lessons of General Franco's regime in Spain and Pinochet's modernisation, the applicability of the Chinese model, and the South Korean path of authoritarian capitalism. Looking outwards to make sense of their own region's trajectory, the collapse of other authoritarian projects in Latin America and parts of East Asia in the mid- to late 1980s helped to delegitimise this alternative solution to systemic crisis, whilst the violence that accompanied the Chinese suppression of reform rendered a similar option more and more untenable in Eastern Europe.

Authoritarian Models at the Semi-periphery

Even in the mid-1980s reformist elites, and even some among the opposition, were still convinced that their systemic crises could be addressed through authoritarian methods – as we saw in Chapter 1.[93] Franco's modernisation of Spain and Pinochet's economic reforms, although the product of reactionary politics, could still be viewed as a guide for a one-party state undertaking extensive marketisation and opening out to the global economy. The Soviets even embraced some military juntas of Latin America both because they developed (cautiously) critical stances towards the United States and because some of them shared a belief in land reform and the nationalisation of banks or natural resources – and hence were praised as defenders of sovereignty.[94] Nor was there significant pressure from international organisations to democratise: the IMF remained ambivalent about the type of political organisation that would best ensure market reform. And the EC well into the late 1970s remained more concerned about stability and growth than about democratisation and was often supportive of the policies of industrial growth and 'expert

---

[93] James Mark, '"The Spanish Analogy": Imagining the Future in State Socialist Hungary 1948–1989', *Contemporary European History*, 26/4 (2017), 600–601.
[94] Tobias Rupprecht, 'Formula Pinochet: Chilean Lessons for Russian Liberal Reformers during the Soviet Collapse, 1970–2000', *Journal of Contemporary History*, 51/1 (2016), 170.

societies' in Eastern Europe, Portugal's Estado Novo, and Spain in the last decade of Franco's rule.[95]

Yet by the mid- to late 1980s the international environment was shifting. Around this moment the EC embraced democracy and human rights as structuring concepts of its mission, developing this new institutional identity in response to its role shepherding Southern Europe towards stable multiparty systems.[96] Moreover, authoritarian modernisation projects in countries that had been of great interest to reformers were now collapsing: in South Korea democratisation was triggered by mass protests in June 1987, but it was controlled by insiders who had concluded that dictatorship could not sustain long-term development;[97] in Chile General Pinochet lost a 1988 referendum and consented to the return of pluralism as parts of the political and economic elites now considered his dictatorship a roadblock to continuous growth.[98] In Eastern Europe the collapse of these regimes in countries seen as in a structurally similar position – 'semi-peripheries' in the world economy – was used to ask the question of whether, in the end, dictatorship always held back economic progress. For reform-minded economic experts such as two deputy directors of the Central Committee Department of International Relations in Hungary, the experience of South Korea, Taiwan, or Chile showed that an efficient economy could operate for a while under dictatorial circumstances. However, they insisted that 'after a certain point the absence of democracy acts as an economic brake'. Only peaceful democratisation such as that which occurred in Spain would ensure continued domestic growth.[99]

---

[95] Birgit Aschmann, 'The Reliable Ally. Germany Supports Spain's European Integration Efforts 1957–1967', *Journal of European Integration History*, 7/1 (2011), 37–51; Laurel Miller, Jeffrey Martini, Stephen Larrabee, Angel Rabasa, Stephanie Pezard, Julie Taylor, and Tewodaj Mengistu, *Democratisation in the Arab World: Prospects and Lessons from Around the Globe* (Santa Monica, CA: Rand Corporation, 2012), 156.

[96] Kim Christiaens, James Mark, and José Faraldo, 'Entangled Transitions: Eastern and Southern European Convergence or Alternative Europes? 1960s–2000s', *Contemporary European History*, 26/4 (2017), 590–91.

[97] Carl Saxer, 'Democratic Transition and Institutional Crafting: The South Korean Case', *Democratisation*, 10/2 (2003), 45–64.

[98] Mary Helen Spooner, *The General's Slow Retreat: Chile after Pinochet* (Berkeley: University of California Press, 2011).

[99] Imre Szokai and Csaba Rabajdi, 'The Changing Hungarian Social Model: A Change in the Orientation of Hungarian Foreign Policy?', *Magyar Nemzet*, 18 March 1989 in FBIS-EEU-89-061, 30. For some Franco remained a model during post-socialism. In Romania, xenophobic politician Corneliu Vadim Tudor, one of the most prominent promotors of Nicolae Ceaușescu's personality cult before 1989, compared 'his leader' with the Spanish dictator: 'Why does Franco have the right to a mausoleum and why do the Spanish people and even King Juan Carlos recognise that, leaving aside his dictatorial style, Franco never betrayed its country, just as Ceaușescu never betrayed

The democratisation in South Korea in particular weakened groups in Warsaw, Budapest, and Prague who had focussed on the East Asian Tigers, and especially Seoul, as models of successful authoritarian modernisation. Alexander Dubček, former leader of the 1968 Prague Spring, argued that the transformation taking place in Seoul illustrated how necessary democracy was for development and should be taken as a model for the region's transformation.[100] Others came to the opposite conclusion. In Romania, even opponents of Ceauşescu's despotism nevertheless argued that rapid economic change would continue to require authoritarian methods. Silviu Brucan, one of the leaders of the post-revolutionary National Salvation Front, still invoked South Korea *before* democratisation. For him, Romania was not ready for full political liberalisation and had to be steered in this direction over the longer term.[101] Nevertheless, once right-wing dictatorships had begun to turn towards managed pluralism, leaders across the socialist bloc witnessed the reality of *ancien régime* elites surviving into new systems and not being punished. It appeared increasingly plausible they might manage to survive in the Soviet Union, Hungary, and Poland and even in isolated party circles in Bulgaria and Romania.[102]

The collapse of such regimes across the world's semi-peripheries further reinforced reformers' sense of a culturally or economically familiar world turning towards liberal democracy, and the viability of negotiated settlements. Soviet experts referred to the collapse of dictatorship in Latin America as the 'Europeanisation' of its politics – betokening a global shift away from authoritarianism towards moderation, and a further confirmation of the growing strength of social democratic Western modernity.[103] Despite their support for radical socialist projects such as the Sandinistas in Nicaragua, in many other cases they tended rather to emphasise the need for compromise and the deradicalisation of the left as such military regimes collapsed: in December 1986 *Pravda* warned against violent revolution in Latin America for it could turn from 'midwife to the gravedigger of history ... The nuclear age demands of revolutionary forces the most serious consideration of decisions over armed

his'. Quoted in Raluca Grosescu, *Les communistes dans l'après communisme: Trajectoires de conversion politique de la nomenklatura roumaine après 1989* (Paris: Michel Houdiard Éditeur, 2012), 281–82.

[100] 'Dubček Regards South Korea as Development Model', *Yonhap*, 22 March 1990, FBIS-EEU-90-056, 18.

[101] Silviu Brucan, *Generaţia irosită* (Bucureşti: Editurile Univers & Calistrat Hogaş, 1992), 256.

[102] Ion Iliescu, *Revoluţie şi reformă* (Bucureşti: Editura Enciclopedică, 1994), 184.

[103] Jerry Hough, 'The Evolving Soviet Debate on Latin America', *Latin American Research Review*, 16/1 (1981), 137.

struggle and the definitive rejection of ... leftist extremism'.[104] Gorbachev supported the Central American Peace Accords (1987), when the presidents of Costa Rica, El Salvador, Honduras, Guatemala, and Nicaragua agreed to end regional civil wars and pursue democratisation and free elections.[105]

In the end these transformations were instrumentalised by reformers to stress the need for both elites and societies to commit to responsible political transformation – and not entertain fantasies of violent revolutionary transformation. For this reason, reforming elites and dissidents began to embrace those former leftist radicals who now advocated 'responsible' political change.[106] For instance Nelson Mandela was promoted as a figure to emulate, defined against the radical wings of the African National Congress, as the moderate, politically responsible figure, ready to negotiate, and as the 'voice of wisdom'. The Nelson Mandela seventieth birthday concert at Wembley on 11 June 1988 was widely screened in Eastern Europe.[107] South Korea's democratisation, which had been beset by significant violence and social conflict, was highlighted as a warning about excessive division. In Hungary, as multiparty democracy looked ever more likely by late 1988, Korea's June Democracy Movement was invoked by reform Communists. Gyula Horn, Hungary's last Communist-era minister for foreign affairs, and later post-Communist prime minister, spoke on a morning TV discussion show about South Korea in February 1989: he explored the ways in which violence had been controlled and emphasised the need for a stabilising 'middle strata' whose responsible participation in transformation had prevented it from turning into 'anarchy' – a clear appeal to Hungarians themselves to not revive the conflicts of the past.[108] Hungarian Communist reformers liked to use such international reference points to legitimise themselves as the handmaidens of responsible transformation to a civilised democratic future. In November 1988 they had

---

[104] Rodolfo Cruz, 'New Directions in Soviet Policy towards Latin America', *Journal of Latin American Studies*, 21/1 (1989), 11.

[105] Roger Hamburg, 'Soviet Foreign Policy toward Different Audiences and with Conflicting Premises: The Case of Nicaragua', *Conflict Quarterly*, 9/1 (Winter 1989), 10–11.

[106] For such a dissident voice: Miklós Szabó, 'Egy tilalommal kevesebb, vagy egy elvtelenséggel több?', *Beszélő*, 2/2 (1990), http://beszelo.c3.hu/print/2868.

[107] Paul Betts, James Mark, Idesbald Goddeeris, and Kim Christiaens, 'Race, Socialism and Solidarity: Anti-Apartheid in Eastern Europe', in Robert Skinner and Anna Konieczna (eds.), *Global History of Anti-apartheid: Forward to Freedom in South Africa* (New York: Palgrave, 2019), 175–6.

[108] 'Gyula Horn Interview on "Reggeli Párbeszéd"', RFE, Hungarian Monitoring, 1 February 1989, HU OSA 300–40–1 Box 894.

chosen Madrid – with its echoes of the 'consenso', the Spanish pacted transition – to announce the end of their one-party rule.[109] Fifteen days after the fall of the Berlin Wall, Roh Tae-woo, a former general under the dictatorship and now the democratically elected South Korean president – appeared at the Hungarian parliament flanked by the reformers Nyers and Pozsgay: following a clearly agreed script, he referred to them as 'pioneers of change'.[110]

China and the Dilemma of Violence

Whilst Eastern European reformers viewed Latin America, Southern Europe, and South Korea as spaces that were either culturally familiar or faced similar economic issues, and hence were influential when they democratised, China was seen in a different light: a cautionary tale about what not to do; first by hardliners who did not approve of Beijing's market reform, then by a wider spectrum within Communist parties, who resisted recourse to mass violence as a means to ensure socialism's survival. Representations of China in 1989 also bore the weight of orientalising impulses that had resurfaced since the Sino-Soviet split: despite its socialism, it was still a region where a barbarous politics might easily resurface. China thus appeared to have less and less relevance to a European sphere where détente had embedded a peaceful, moderated form of political action. Even those hardliners who were tempted to impose a Chinese solution invoked ideas of civilisational difference as they revealed their reluctance to open fire.

Until the mid-1980s the Chinese leadership, who had embarked in 1978 on market-oriented transformation and introduced changes to the political power holders' style of wielding power,[111] looked to Eastern Europe for ideas of economic reform.[112] Deng Xiaoping sought inspiration there for new methods to quell opposition; his greatest obsession was Poland, particularly the handling of Solidarność. Its legalisation in

---

[109] James Mark, '"The Spanish Analogy"', 617.
[110] 'No Tae-u Addresses Parliament', *Budapest Domestic Service*, 23 November 1989 in FBIS-EEU-89–230, 78; 'Kölcsönösen előnyös együttműködés távlatai a tárgyalásokon', *Magyar Hírlap*, 23 November 1989.
[111] Vámos, 'Tiananmen Square', 96–98.
[112] Péter Vámos, 'A Hungarian Model for China? Sino-Hungarian Relations in the Era of Economic Reforms, 1979–89', *Cold War History*, 3/18 (2018), 361–78.

1980 was seen by the Chinese leadership as endangering the leading role of the party.[113] Deng endorsed Martial Law and sent police units to Poland for anti-riot training.[114] After 1981 the Chinese leadership provided extensive economic and political support to Jaruzelski's regime, thinking thus to pre-empt Solidarność's rebirth and control spillover back home.[115] Compared to a new technocratic generation emerging in Eastern Europe, Deng Xiaoping and his older colleagues, a cohort that had fought in the civil war, saw violence as the necessary re-enactment of past revolutionary struggles to defend the socialist order.[116] Growing openness in the Soviet Union, Hungary, and Poland accentuated the fears of the leadership in Beijing, who also, unlike their counterparts in the bloc, were not disposed to emulate left-wing democratic models.[117] After Gorbachev's ascent to power, Deng distanced himself from the Soviet reforms. Fears of Gorbachev's influence were countered with campaigns against 'bourgeois liberalisation' and censorship of coverage of the Soviet Union and reformist countries in Eastern Europe.[118]

Whilst China would later become a model after the 2000s for some in Eastern Europe, Chinese politics in this earlier period was more commonly viewed as a warning. From 1987 the country experienced turbulence similar to that in Eastern Europe: student demonstrations, high inflation, growing social inequalities generated by market reforms, and a bank crisis took China to the brink.[119] Witnessing such instability and emboldened by Gorbachev's perestroika and new thinking, Eastern European reformers preferred more gradual, pragmatic departures from planning and one-party rule. Hardliners rather saw the troubles in Beijing as a cautionary tale against excessive reformism. When the GDR leadership attempted a rapprochement with China in order to find

---

[113] Jeanne Wilson, '"The Polish Lesson"': China and Poland 1980–1990', *Studies in Comparative Communism*, 23/3–4 (1990), 261, 266.

[114] Jean-Philipp Béja, 'China and the End of Socialism in Europe: A Godsend for Beijing Communists', in Jacques Rupnik (ed.), *1989 as a Political World Event: Democracy, Europe and the New International System in the Age of Globalisation* (New York: Routledge, 2013), 214–15.

[115] Margaret Gnoinska, '"Socialist Friends Should Help Each Other in Crises": Sino-Polish Relations within the Cold War Dynamics, 1980–1987', *Cold War History*, 17/2 (2017), 153.

[116] Bruce Gilley, 'Deng Xiaoping and His Successors', in William Joseph (ed.), *Politics in China: An Introduction* (Oxford: Oxford University Press, 2010), 119–47.

[117] Martin Dimitrov, 'Understanding Communist Collapse and Resilience', in Martin Dimitrov (ed.), *Why Communism Did Not Collapse: Understanding Authoritarian Regime Resilience in Asia and Europe* (Cambridge: Cambridge University Press, 2013), 20–24.

[118] Vladislav Zubok, 'The Soviet Union and China in the 1980s: Reconciliation and Divorce', *Cold War History*, 17/2 (2017), 130–31.

[119] Ibid., 136.

new markets for industrial goods, its experts stressed that Deng underestimated the dangers of market reforms and cooperation with what they still considered the imperialist camp.[120] In February 1989 a worried Czechoslovak ambassador in Beijing cabled back to Prague that capitalist policies had generated dysfunctions within Chinese society.[121] On 19 May, a day before the government in Beijing officially declared Martial Law, the Romanian ambassador reported that Chinese reforms were resulting in the underdevelopment of broad swathes of the country, growing inequality, and worsening social conditions for intellectuals, youth, and women, together with uncontrolled prices, inflation, and stagnation.[122]

Before the crackdown against protesters in and around Tiananmen Square, a residual orientalism and fears of political instability made most elites doubt the applicability of Chinese reforms to their own countries. Gorbachev was not impressed by the Chinese pro-Gorbachev democracy movement. During his visit to Beijing on 15 May, he told his entourage, 'Some of you present here have promoted the idea of taking the Chinese road. We saw today where this road leads. I do not want Red Square to look like Tiananmen Square'.[123] The use of lethal force in China consolidated his belief in liberalisation as premise for economic development in order to forestall socialism's collapse and to counter a conservative push back to his reforms. He employed democratisation as a source of legitimacy because, unlike in China, there was limited support for his reforms in the party and amongst powerful industrial and agricultural interest groups.[124] China also strengthened the Soviet leader's belief in the nonviability of military intervention in Eastern Europe or the use of force in the Soviet Union. He had tackled the question of repression before 4 June. In April 1989 riot troops had killed twenty demonstrators demanding independence in Tbilisi. These events convinced Gorbachev that the 'use of force is excluded. We excluded it in foreign policy, thus it is even more inadmissible against our own peoples'.[125] There were,

---

[120] Zhong Zhong Chen, 'Defying Moscow: East German-Chinese Relations during the Andropov-Chernenko Interregnum, 1982–1985', *Cold War History*, 14/2 (2014), 273.

[121] Telegramă nr. 015638, 24 February 1989, MAE-China: Situația internă volum I, 212/ 1989, 2.

[122] Telegramă nr. 015894, 19 May 1989, MAE-China, Situația internă volum I, 212/1989, 2–4.

[123] Quoted in Zubok, 'Soviet Union and China', 139.

[124] Chris Miller, *The Struggle to Save the Soviet Economy: Mikhail Gorbachev and the Collapse of the USSR* (Chapel Hill: University of North Carolina Press, 2016), 52–54, 180–82.

[125] William Taubman and Svetlana Savranskaya, 'If a Wall Fell in Berlin and Moscow Hardly Noticed, Would It Still Make a Noise?', in Jeffrey Engel (ed.), *The Fall of the Berlin Wall: The Revolutionary Legacy of 1989* (Oxford: Oxford University Press, 2012), 76.

however, later instances of state violence in the Soviet Union. In January 1991 conservatives within the CPSU, the KGB, and several generals sanctioned military intervention in Lithuania, Latvia, and Estonia, where mass movements led to freely elected governments. After declarations of independence from Moscow, sixteen demonstrators in Vilnius and four in Riga were killed. This crackdown failed, however, to trigger a violent response from the crowds; it enabled Gorbachev finally to eliminate military action as a potential response to the unravelling of the Soviet Union (see Chapter 4).[126] In contrast to Deng, Gorbachev persevered with liberalising the regime and trying to find a peaceful settlement with centrifugal forces within the Soviet Union; along the way he took state socialism beyond the point of no return.

In Poland and Hungary the failures of socialist governance that the violence of Tiananmen Square represented were used by reformists to bolster their arguments for so-called roundtable settlements – a series of negotiations with representatives of the opposition with the aim of reaching a common ground for democratic reform.[127] The Polish prime minister Mieczysław Rakowski remarked in April 1989 that unrest in China could be avoided only through such discussions.[128] Warsaw's ambassador in Beijing rejected comparisons between the 'the peaceful, nonviolent and humanitarian' use of Martial Law in Poland and its 'harsh, unpopular' implementation in China.[129] The two elites would adopt very different solutions to the crisis socialism: between February and early April the PUWP leadership initiated the roundtables with Solidarność that ended really existing socialism in Poland and thus helped to forge the model later implemented in Hungary, East Germany, and Bulgaria.

Negotiated, peaceful change took hold also because of fears about escalating violence. In Hungary, on 16 June 1989 the reburial of Imre Nagy, the leader of the local anti-Soviet revolution in 1956, brought thousands of people to the streets of Budapest. The event provoked trepidation, among party elites and the opposition alike, about the possibility of a return to the massive destruction that had wreaked havoc in the country just over thirty years before.[130] The reform Communist Imre

---

[126] Archie Brown, *The Gorbachev Factor* (Oxford: Oxford University Press, 1995), 562.
[127] Vámos, 'Tiananmen Square', 109.
[128] Mieczysław Rakowski, *Dzienniki polityczne 1987–1990* (Warszawa: ISKRY, 2005), 419.
[129] Telegramă nr. 016003, 16.06.1989/10:30, MAE-China, Situația internă volum II, 213/1989, 1–2.
[130] The procession was organized by the opposition, but four leading members of the Hungarian Socialist Workers' Party came to pay tribute. They were introduced to the crowd by the governmental titles out of fear that public mention of the party would trigger a violent reaction from the crowd. Henry Kamm, 'Hungarian Who Led '56 Revolt Is Buried as a Hero', *New York Times*, 17 June 1989, www.nytimes.com/1989/

Pozsgay, referring to the possibility of repression against Chinese demonstrators, proclaimed that 'weapons are powerless if they are used against [the] people's will'.[131] Though tragically not borne out by events in China, the prediction nevertheless affirmed the Hungarian elites' vision of political change: in the summer and autumn of 1989, the Hungarian Socialist Workers' Party and the opposition engaged in discussions that led to the creation of a multiparty system, effectively ending the Communist regime in the country.

Nevertheless, Deng's decision to crush the protests had shown that democratisation could be rolled back. Regimes in Romania, Bulgaria, the GDR, and Czechoslovakia expressed their support for the CPC's determination to effect a bloody crackdown. Even if these hardliners were tempted to follow the Chinese example, with the exception of Romania's Nicolae Ceaușescu, they were not prepared to follow through. When the Chinese deputy prime minister Yao Yilin went to East Berlin on 7 October 1989, the general secretary Erich Honecker assured him that the SED would 'never give up the leading roles of the working class and of the communist party'.[132] Up until 9 October the SED had employed violence against protesters, but when push came to shove its leadership found that holding the line against mass protests was more difficult than they imagined. Not wishing to be responsible for the use of lethal force, the SED's top ranks deferred to local party and security officials to implement the crackdown without issuing a clear mandate to shoot protesters. Militia units were undermanned and refused to quell demonstrations; police suffered from low morale and chose not to confront crowds; senior military officials were unwilling to do the party's dirty work. Local elites feared that violence would catalyse regime collapse. Leipzig party secretary Kurt Meyer recollected his conviction at the time that 'if blood had been spilled, socialism would have been swept away. We couldn't accept that'.[133] Once Honecker's plans for an East German Tiananmen collapsed, Egon Krenz, the youngest member of the Politburo, took advantage and toppled him as head of the SED.[134] He too was

---

06/17/world/hungarian-who-led-56-revolt-is-buried-as-a-hero.html; István Rév, 'Parallel Autopsies', *Representations* 49 (Winter 1995), 15–39.

[131] 'Interview with Imre Pozsgay', *Frakfurter Rundschau*, 3 June 1989, FBIS-EEU-89–106, 10.

[132] Quoted in Zhong Zhong Chen, 'Defying Moscow, Engaging Beijing: The German Democratic Republic's Relations with the People's Republic of China, 1980–1989' (PhD diss., London School of Economics, 2014), 208.

[133] Steven Pfaff, *Exit-Voice Dynamics and the Collapse of East Germany: The Crisis of Leninism and the Revolution of 1989* (Durham, NC: Duke University Press, 2006), 184–85.

[134] Mary Elise Sarotte, *1989: The Struggle to Create Post–Cold War Europe* (Princeton, NJ: Princeton University Press, 2014), 20.

a conservative, but his legitimacy had been built on rejecting violence. He faced tremendous pressure from mass protests: between 9 October and the fall of the Berlin Wall on 9 November, four million people took to the streets. During late 1989 and early 1990, the SED leadership was forced into a series of roundtables that set the stage for the regime's democratisation and speedy disappearance.

In Czechoslovakia officials sought to emulate the Chinese solution, but feared the repercussions of deadly force. After an initial crackdown in Prague, Prime Minister Ladislav Adamec decided that the escalation of violence provoked more resistance and undermined the power of the party at home and damaged its reputation abroad: 'Signed international treaties dealing with human rights cannot be taken lightly'.[135] Considering violence beyond the pale of civilised European politics, and with growing popular pressure, the Czechoslovak party leadership resigned. In early December 1989 Adamec negotiated with the opposition about a pluralist government. As Gorbachev refused to intervene to prop up crumbling regimes in Eastern Europe, it was the compromise in Poland and Hungary, rather than the Chinese decision to shoot, that was eventually emulated in East Germany, Czechoslovakia, and Bulgaria. Party leaders who engaged in dialogue acquired the necessary credibility to serve as negotiating partners and broker a reform programme.

Chinese repression of the democracy movement was a touchstone for the Eastern European opposition in 1989 too. They were still facing the threat of mass violence from regimes under siege that still had large military forces and security apparatuses under their control. While non-violence was a principle for the peace movement, avoiding provocations that might set off a similar massacre as in China became a pressing imperative. In East Germany citizens wrote letters to the central government characterizing the repression in China as 'fascist barbarism'. Others argued that the crackdown in Tiananmen Square showed that socialism had lost its moral high ground. The 6 June 1989 issue of the dissident publication *Umweltblätter* ('environmental sheets') shows that such protest again the Chinese government was not necessarily a championing of Western liberalism: 'We take our distance from the human rights shrieking of Western politicians ... We declare solidarity with the Chinese population and students because we have the same opponent:

---

[135] Quoted in Rosemary Foot, 'The Cold War and Human Rights', in Melvyn Leffler and Odd Arne Westad (eds.), *The Cambridge History of the Cold War. Volume III Endings* (Cambridge: Cambridge University Press, 2010), 463.

governments who take their sinecures on the backs, and against the will, of the population'.[136]

The Romanian Lesson

Romania was the only Eastern European socialist country where the end of the regime was the result of a violent revolution – over eleven hundred people were killed. Here roundtables were not an option: compared with Poland, Hungary, and Czechoslovakia, there was no organised opposition that could become a negotiating partner with the Communist leadership.[137] Within the party there was limited, hesitant criticism, which was effectively stifled; there was little that might compare to the rise of reformers within the PUWP and the HWSP.[138] In contrast to most surrounding countries, Ceauşescu and his Politburo still considered violence a legitimate tool for regime survival. Unlike the hardliners in the GDR, Ceauşescu elicited enough compliance from the army, police, local party officials, and the secret police (Securitate) to repress the protests. Only days before his execution Ceauşescu met a Chinese envoy, who shared the experience of crushing public demonstrations.[139] For him, the compromises his reform-minded comrades were making in Poland and Hungary enabled Western imperialist encroachments on a region that had previously stood firm. He saw himself as being among the last revolutionaries to hold the line against such attacks; commenting on the changes taking place in Budapest in the summer of 1989, he proclaimed before his politburo, 'The defence of socialism is the duty of all communists! Everywhere socialism is in danger, we must defend it! This is the reality!'[140]

Even with the collapse of Ceauşescu's regime in late December 1989, violence continued to be seen as a viable tactic. Power was swiftly seized by the National Salvation Front (NSF), a catch-all post-revolutionary organisation that was controlled by second- or third-tier members of the former Communist party; their ambivalence towards political pluralism meant

---

[136] Quinn Slobodian, 'China Is Not Far! Alternative Internationalism and the Tiananmen Square Massacre in East Germany's 1989', in Mark et al., *Alternative Globalizations*, 7 and 12.

[137] Cristina Petrescu, *From Robin Hood to Don Quixote: Resistance and Dissent in Communist Romania* (Bucureşti: Editura Enciclopedică, 2013).

[138] Vladimir Tismaneanu, *Stalinism for All Seasons: A Political History of Romanian Communism* (Berkeley: University of California Press, 2003), 227–30.

[139] Sergey Radchenko, *Unwanted Visionaries: The Soviet Failure in Asia at the End of the Cold War* (Oxford: Oxford University Press, 2014), 181.

[140] 'Stenograma şedinţei Comitetului Politic al CC al PCR, 17.06.1989', ANIC [Arhivele Naţionale Istorice Centrale], CC al PCR, Cancelarie, 47/1989, 8 verso.

that the few dissidents who had joined the Front's top echelons resigned in January 1990. The NSF saw the public broadcast of Ceauşescu's violent execution as a necessary tactic to legitimise this new but still authoritarian order.[141] The parallels that contemporaries drew suggested a mind-set that continued to be rooted in the violent conflicts of an earlier era of anti-imperialist struggle: the NSF leader and future president of the country Ion Iliescu was advised to execute Ceauşescu in order not 'to end up like Allende [the Chilean head of state who died during Pinochet's coup d'état]'.[142] For the following two years the NSF was prepared to use violence against those political and civic organisations that criticised its monopoly of power. It endorsed in 1990 and 1991 several visits to Bucharest of coal miners from the Jiu Valley, who attacked and killed anti-government protesters while vandalizing parts of the city.[143] The NSF also stoked ethnic conflict in Transylvania, where a large Hungarian minority lived.[144] Dominating the political landscape and media, the NSF and its main successor party won the 1990 and 1992 elections; only in 1996 did Romania elect its first government that was not made up predominantly from successor parties of the former Communist one, marking the first peaceful transition of power.

Like in China, the violence in Romania reinforced the move to pluralism elsewhere. The Bulgarian response stood out: here political change had begun much later, in November 1989, long after elites in Budapest or Warsaw had already begun to dismantle their regimes. The decision to shoot was considered by those who had ousted the longtime Communist leader Todor Zhivkov. When crowds surrounded the parliament in mid-December, the newly appointed Communist general secretary Petar Mladenov – who only two months earlier had resigned as foreign minister to protest police violence against environmental activists – remarked that 'it is better for the tanks to come'.[145] Cooler heads prevailed and the elites led by the economist Andrey Lukanov, who admired the Chinese reforms but not their propensity to resort to violence, opted for a round-table with opposition groups. Romania acted as a salutary warning of the dangers of a crackdown against protesters. Bulgarian Communists

[141] Grosescu, *Les communistes*, 139, 147, 167–68.
[142] Richard Andrew Hall, 'Theories of Collective Action and Revolution: Evidence from the Romanian Transition of December 1989', *Europe-Asia Studies*, 52/6 (2000), 1088–1089.
[143] Alin Rus, *Mineriadele: Între manipulare politică şi solidaritate muncitorească* (Bucureşti: Curtea Veche, 2007).
[144] Tom Gallagher, *Theft of a Nation: Romania since Communism* (London: Hurst, 2006), 84–88.
[145] Vesselin Dimitrov, *Bulgaria: The Uneven Transition* (London: Routledge, 2008), 46.

admitted that they feared meeting a gruesome end akin to Ceaușescu's. Reflecting on recent events some four months later, during the talks with the opposition, Aleksander Lilov, the chairman of the BCP's Supreme Council, stated that there were only two options for exiting one-party rule: 'that of Romania or [that of] Hungary, bloodshed and pogroms or reforms'.[146]

By 1989 Communist leaders had begun to see violence as uncivilised and outside the framework of European politics. Late socialist legal cultures, alongside visions of rational, efficient states, were antitheses of the turmoil and arbitrariness presupposed by the massive use of force. The political transformations in areas that socialist experts imagined to be similar – such as Southern Europe or Latin America – were perceived as instructive because of similar concerns as states pursuing modernisation and flirting with representative democracy. Solidarities based on shared European cultural traditions narrowed geopolitical distances. In contrast, the turmoil in China was seen as the distant operation of the less developed socialist other and the CPC's decision to opt for violence as beyond the pale of civilised politics – a route inappropriate for European socialism. The repression and bloodshed in Romania in 1989 and the secession wars in Yugoslavia similarly situated these countries on the fringes of European civilisation for reformers elsewhere in the region.

Disciplining Transition and Democratic Peace

In the immediate aftermath of the fall of Communist regimes in late 1989, many in the West took the transformation in Eastern Europe as a symbol of the inevitable triumph of liberal democracy. The collapse of state socialism and later the end of the Soviet Union on 26 December 1991 fuelled imaginations of an Atlantic-centred world order founded on 'democratic peace'[147] among democratic nations unwilling to employ force against each other. Freedom worked, according to US president George Bush, 'through free markets, free speech, free elections, and the exercise of free will unhampered by the state'.[148] Leading Eastern European intellectuals vaunted the inevitability of liberal democracy. Adam Michnik spoke of a 'renaissance' of the region. The Hungarian philosopher Janos Kis counterposed liberal democracy to its alleged alternative,

---

[146] 'BCP Calls for Peaceful Transition to Democracy', *BTA*, 1 March 1990, FBIS-EEU-90–042, 1.
[147] Melvyn Leffler, 'Dreams of Freedom, Temptations of Power', in Engel, *Fall*, 133.
[148] Jeffrey Engel, '1989: An Introduction', in Engel, *Fall*, 26.

a 'Balkanisation' of the kind represented by Yugoslavia's descent into ethnic conflict and war.[149]

Yet this form of liberal democracy was hardly the only game in town around 1989: alternative conceptualisations of democracy flourished across the Eastern camp – from a reformed socialist version to direct democracy. Among the more participatory movements that blended underground culture, pacifism, environmentalism, and sometimes nationalism were the Orange Alternative or Freedom and Peace in Poland, the Peace Group for Dialogue in Hungary, the Independent Peace Association-Initiative for the Demilitarisation of Society in Czechoslovakia, the Lion Society in Ukraine, and the People for Peace Culture in Slovenia.[150] These alternatives within the opposition eventually lost out to their political elites' push for convergence with the West. They were eclipsed because international and local actors sought elite-managed change and indirect democracy: cure-all solutions to the populism, nationalism, and violence that they feared might erupt.

In the decades after 1989 leftist critics often claimed that the transformation of that year was a missed opportunity for progressive politics.[151] Indeed, the opposition had generated democratic imaginaries centred on self-management, workers' rights, and civic activism, which were correctives to what they saw as the limited representative potential of multiparty democracy or the alienating effects of Western modernity. However, most of the oppositionists participating in the roundtables were fearful of excessive democratic sentiment. Liberal-left elites in Solidarność dreaded the excessive religious, nationalist, and moralistic sentiments that the collapse of authoritarianism might release.[152] In Hungary the authors of the political settlement feared a return to the violence of 1956 without a managed process that kept radical anti-Communist forces on the political margins.[153] The South Korean president Roh Tae-woo warned Eastern European elites during his visit in late 1989 about 'violence and illegal demonstrations' as well as difficulties in 'maintaining law and order' because of the eruption of previously pent-up popular frustrations.[154] Organisations advocating direct democracy and radical change were sidelined and were often split by the difficult choices these pressures presented. The radical Polish Freedom and Peace movement, for example, divided between those who re-joined

---

[149] Isaac, 'Meanings', 297.   [150] Kenney, *Carnival*, 293–306.

[151] Nancy Fraser, 'Postcommunist Democratic Socialism?', in George Katsiaficas (ed.), *After the Fall: 1989 and the Future of Freedom* (London: Routledge, 2001), 200–202.

[152] Hella Dietz, *Polnischer Protest. Zur pragmatistischen Fundierung von Theorien sozialen Wandels* (Frankfurt am Main: Campus, 2015), 281–91.

[153] Mark, *Unfinished Revolution*, 5–6.   [154] 'No Tae-u Addresses Parliament', 80.

Solidarność to help shape negotiated change and became elected as MPs on this basis and others who wished to hold on to the movement's radical activism and internal pluralism in order to channel it towards new social issues; the latter mostly disappeared from the political scene.[155]

These regional processes of disciplining potential opposition had a counterpart in Western experts' and organisations' insistence on multi-party democracy, the free market, and the necessity of addressing the perils of an excessive political idealism in former socialist societies. Prominent Western intellectuals wrote about the dangers of populism from below, while criticizing the indecisiveness and moralizing stance of former dissents.[156] A policy booklet of the neoconservative Foreign Policy Research Institute, funded by the NED, warned about the resilience of 'utopian politics' in Eastern Europe, which it saw as rooted in Communist ideology as well as in the opposition to it. To counter this tendency, the study recommended the circulation of literature on classical liberalism and Anglo-American conservatism. The Sabre Foundation from Massachusetts, Laissez-Faire Books from New York, and the Atlas Economic Research Foundation from Virginia took on the task of neoliberal proselytism to what they considered the 'utopian wilderness' of the former socialist bloc.[157]

International organisations encouraged the disciplining of radicalism in what they branded 'transitional societies' in the former socialist camp, Latin America, or South Africa. At the Justice in Times of Transition (1992, Salzburg) and Dealing with the Past (1994, Cape Town) conferences, Eastern European dissidents, lawyers, and politicians along with Western scholars and Latin American and South African representatives discussed how to manage mobilisation from below mounting purportedly 'excessive' claims for political and social justice.[158] The events were sponsored by the German Marshall Fund of the United States, the NED, the Open Society Fund, and the Rockefeller Foundation. In Salzburg, András Sájo, legal advisor to the Hungarian president Árpád Göncz, insisted on the head of state's reluctance to sacrifice the rule of law in order to satisfy radical calls for trials against former Communist elites.[159] Adam Michnik rejected the disqualification from political and economic

---

[155] Kenney, *Carnival*, 89–90.
[156] Vladimir Tismaneanu, *Fantasies of Salvation: Democracy, Nationalism, and Myth in Post-communist Europe* (Princeton, NJ: Princeton University Press, 1998), 143–44.
[157] Vladimir Tismaneanu and Patrick Clawson, *Uprooting Leninism, Cultivating Liberty* (Lanham, MD: Foreign Policy Research Institute, 1992), 42–46.
[158] For the list of participants, see Arthur, 'How "Transitions"', 364–67.
[159] Mary Albon, 'Project on Justice in Times of Transition: Inaugural Meeting' (Salzburg, Austria, 7–10 March 1992), 10–11.

life of members of the party-state's top echelons through lustration. He feared that this would encourage the revenge fantasies of 'right-wing Bolshevism' and preferred 'letting a few bastards go unpunished rather than punishing huge numbers of innocents'.[160] Similarly, Alex Boraine, the founder of the Institute for Democratic Alternatives in South Africa (IDASA), dreaded the excessive activism of the African National Congress, the main anti-apartheid political organisation. In 1987, after a meeting between IDASA and African National Congress representatives in Dakar (sponsored by George Soros and the Ford Foundation), he argued that 'talking is better than expecting a state of escalating violence'.[161] By the early 1990s Boraine was a central figure in the articulation of 'truth for amnesty' as the path to reconciliation in South Africa. Just as Eastern European elites attempted to safeguard the democratic system that resulted from the roundtables, IDASA's solution was, in the words of Frederik van Zyl Slabbert, another of its founders, a response to 'one of the most daunting challenges ... protect[ing] the new political space created by negotiations from being used to contest the historical imbalances that precipitated negotiations in the first place'.[162]

The choice of Western-style parliamentary democracy was also an attempt to control what were considered to be disproportionate claims on democracy. Václav Klaus, the Czech prime minister from 1993 to 1998 and leader of the most influential party of the first post-socialist decade, the Civic Democratic Party, disparaged such options. He rejected calls for self-government – often meaning workers' councils in factories or decision making by local assemblies – which he thought endangered the peaceful transition. For him, popular democracy outside a party system would result 'not in freedom, the market and democracy, but in ... dependence on vaguely defined civic movements ... ambiguous utopian projects by intellectuals [and] new collectivisms'.[163]

Emphasis was placed on constitutional change from above rather than popular participation. Thus legal experts often played a central role in Eastern Europe's democratisation during the late 1980s and early 1990s.

[160] Ibid., 13.   [161] 'IDASA-ANC Talks Detailed', *Sunday Star*, 5 July 1987, 2.

[162] Quoted in Ian Taylor, 'South Africa's Transition to Democracy and the "Change Industry": A Case Study of IDASA', *Politikon: South African Journal of Political Studies*, 29/1 (2002), 44.

[163] Václav Klaus, speech at ODS tenth party conference, December 1999, quoted in Milan Znoj, 'Václav Havel, His Idea of Civil Society, and the Czech Liberal Tradition', in Michal Kopeček and Piotr Wciślik (eds.), *Thinking through Transition: Liberal Democracy, Authoritarian Pasts, and Intellectual History in East Central Europe after 1989* (Budapest: Central European University Press, 2015), 127.

The re-affirmation of the rule of law in the last decades of state socialism created the legal and political preconditions for negotiated, peaceful change. It expressed the centrality of belonging to a European space of 'civilised' politics that went beyond ideological antagonism and had foresworn repression.[164] In the GDR, the new head of the SED, entrusted with the task of recasting it as a democratic socialist entity in anticipation of the first free elections in 1990, was Gregor Gysi, one of the few trial lawyers in the country. In Poland, legal experts involved in overseeing the implementation of Martial Law supervised the first competitive elections in June 1989. In the Soviet Union, authors of the 1977 Constitution took part in joint Soviet–US programmes on the future of democracy and human rights in a post–Cold War world.[165] In May 1988 the Hungarian constitution was revised by the sociologist of law Kálmán Kulcsár, then deputy general secretary of the Academy of Sciences, who was responsible for coordinating the efforts of a number of other jurists from the University of Budapest.[166] Among them was László Sólyom, who a year later participated on the side of the opposition at the roundtable talks. In 1990 he was elected president of Hungary's newly established Constitutional Court – a similar institution, the Constitutional Tribunal, had been created in 1982 in Poland.

Following the post-1945 West German model, constitutional courts were considered essential instruments for transition to democracy, signalling the East's embrace of the (Western) European rule of law.[167] In Hungary the 1989 structural and legal transformation of the state had 'already been made by the Constitutional Court before the constituency had any say at all'.[168] A similar situation existed in Poland and Czechoslovakia, where complaints were heard about a government by unelected judges rather than representatives of electorates.[169] This focus on constitutional expertise at the expense of popular participation further frustrated important sections of the electorate in Eastern Europe, who

---

[164] Paul Blokker, 'Building Democracy by Legal Means: The East-Central European Experience' (paper presented at 'Revolution from Within. Experts, Managers and Technocrats in the Long Lawyers, Human Rights and Democratisation in Eastern Europe', Jena, 14–15 June 2018), 5.

[165] Ned Richardson-Little, 'Lawyers, Human Rights, and Democratization in Eastern Europe' (paper, 'Revolution from Within. Experts, Managers and Technocrats in the Long Lawyers, Human Rights and Democratisation in Eastern Europe', Jena, 14–15 June 2018), 10–11.

[166] Árpád Klimó, *Hungary since 1945* (London: Routledge, 2018), 34.

[167] Wojciech Sadurski, *Rights before Courts. A Study of Constitutional Courts in Postcommunist States of Central and Eastern Europe* (Dordrecht: Springer, 2008), 28.

[168] Klimó, *Hungary*, 53.

[169] Jacques Rupnik, 'The Post-Totalitarian Blues', *Journal of Democracy*, 6/2 (1995), 65.

became increasingly detached from the decision-making process. The promulgation of new constitutions, as in Romania and Bulgaria in 1991, did not mean more democratic participation. This led to disappointment among the wider population, who witnessed parliamentarians often engaging in sterile debates rather than issuing the legislation necessary for bringing sense in the chaos of early regime change.[170]

After the mass demonstrations in Prague, Leipzig, Budapest, Sofia, and Bucharest in 1989, the initial revolutionary enthusiasm soon gave way to significant political demobilisation. Top-down negotiations between party reformists and the opposition tried to control input from below. Such a disconnect between the new polities and their electorates affected popular participation in elections. In Poland only 63 per cent of registered voters went to the polls for the first semi-free elections.[171] The trend continued at the first free local elections of May 1990 when fewer than half of the registered voters participated. In Hungary only 33 per cent of eligible voters took part in the run-off parliamentary elections of April 1990.[172]

By 1991 political actors who were not prepared to work within the new liberal democratic structures were swept away in elections or lost their popularity. Gorbachev's talk of democratic socialism lost its appeal as the economy worsened.[173] He was eclipsed by a surging Boris Yeltsin – since June of that year the president of the Russian Soviet Federative Socialist Republic – who embodied the new politics that rejected the Soviet tradition. He had resigned from the CPSU in 1990, allied with economists advocating radical economic reform, and crafted for himself an image as a strong national leader above party politics. In Czechoslovakia Alexander Dubček, the former leader of the Prague Spring, despite his popularity during the Velvet Revolution, was not backed for the presidency by the Civic Forum, the main political force that had issued from the opposition. His opponents instead promoted Václav Havel as the real

---

[170] Venelin Ganev, *Preying on the State: The Transformation of Bulgaria after 1989* (Ithaca, NY: Cornell University Press, 2007), 132.

[171] Gregory Domber, 'Skepticism and Stability: Reevaluating US Policy during Poland's Democratic Transformation in 1989', *Journal of Cold War Studies*, 13/3 (Summer 2011), 81–82.

[172] John Hibbing and Samuel Patterson, 'A Democratic Legislature in the Making the Historic Hungarian Elections of 1990', *Comparative Political Studies*, 24/2 (1992), 430–54. There were exceptions: in Czechoslovakia, 96 per cent of the electorate voted in June 1990. In Romania and Bulgaria, the high levels of electoral participation during the elections in the early 1990s were due to the intense polarisation between the ruling parties and opposition forces.

[173] Brown, *Gorbachev Factor*, 271.

inheritor of the anti-Communist struggle.[174] The initial popular enthusiasm for democratic socialism and a mixed economy was diverted by liberals into a completely new polity that broke with the legacy of 1968. Dubček was elected chairman of the Czechoslovak parliament, but socialism with a human face lost out.

Projects of grassroots democracy were also unsuccessful in gaining prominence in the post-1989 political landscape. In East Germany the New Forum, which advocated direct citizen participation in politics, failed to advance an alternative to liberal democracy. It had been the most influential civic actor in the protests in the GDR. It aimed to preserve what was recoverable in socialist values and organisation and to create room for their renewal. It did not want East Germany to become an appendage of the Federal Republic. The widespread appeal of West German chancellor Helmut Kohl's promises of the 'blooming landscapes' that unification would usher in – combined with the New Forum's inability to find political allies in the democratic elections of 1990 – pushed this vision to the margins of German politics.[175]

The promise of Western prosperity, intrinsic to transition-minded elites' justification for the swift leap to free-market and multiparty pluralism, made Eastern Europeans suspicious of what could easily be coded as an outdated radicalism in times of severe recession. Polish constitutionalist Wiktor Osiatynski remarked in 1991 that people themselves 'are even throwing away the beliefs, including equality and social justice that led them to fight communism'.[176] Early governments of former socialist countries considered broader citizen participation in politics incompatible with the rapid transformation of state and economy. In Hungary the leftist dissident István Eörsi lambasted the implementation of such Western-mediated templates premised on discouraging popular participation. In 1991 he proclaimed that 'history has not yet pronounced the last word on direct democracy'. He scolded the opposition for its centrist politics: 'We should have proclaimed a social and ideological alternative much more forcefully to appeal to those voters who have been disoriented or indifferent in the absence of socialist and social democratic parties'.[177] Though he

---

[174] James Krapfl, *Revolution with a Human Face: Politics, Culture, and Community in Czechoslovakia, 1989–1992* (Ithaca, NY: Cornell University Press, 2013), 99.

[175] Konrad Jarausch, *The Rush to German Unity* (Oxford: Oxford University Press, 1994) and Gareth Dale, *The East German Revolution of 1989 and Popular Protest in East Germany* (Manchester: Manchester University Press, 2007).

[176] Osiatynski, 'Revolutions', 825.

[177] Ferenc Laczó, 'Five Faces of Post-Dissident Hungarian Liberalism: A Study in Agendas, Concepts, and Ambiguities', in Kopeček and Wciślik, *Thinking through Transition*, 55–56.

wrote in the opposition's most influential magazine *Beszélő*, Eörsi was an isolated voice because transitional elites were already firmly committed to Western-style, representative, capitalist democracy. The same year Andre Gunder Frank, one of the important theoreticians of dependency and world system analysis, warned about the loss of the civil democracy gained through social mobilisations in and around 1989 in Eastern Europe. He saw the new party system as stifling 'all the New, Civic, and other Forum movements in the GDR, Czechoslovakia, and Hungary', implicitly fuelling democratic deficits and inequalities just as had happened in Latin America.[178]

The elite-led transformation created feelings of alienation from such changes among a part of the population. The symbol of '1989' as the moment of Communism's collapse hid deep social and economic divisions within Eastern European societies caused by the obliteration of the socialist welfare system through policies that either minimised the state or captured its assets through corruption.[179] Such a disconnect between political parties and their electorates only deepened into the 2000s.[180] A gap continued to exist between international representations of these states as consolidated democracies and EU members and the perceptions of citizens, among whom significant numbers did not consider 1989 to have been an unambiguously positive turning point in their lives.[181]

Democracy Templates and the Spectre of Authoritarianism

Eastern Europe after 1989 bore the marks of the so-called 'democracy industry' created by the United States and the EC during the last decade of the Cold War. Democracy promotion signalled that the West had taken on a global mission that tied the spread of liberalism to European and North American foreign policies.[182] Initially these programmes concentrated on Latin America and Eastern Europe, but they were soon expanded to Sub-Saharan Africa, which experienced its own departures from local forms of dictatorial rule (see Chapter 5). After 1989, the US

[178] Andre Gunder Frank, 'No Escape from the Laws of World Economics', *Review of African Political Economy*, 18/50 (1991), 30–31.
[179] On the various structural weaknesses of post-socialist states see Dorothee Bohle and Béla Greskovits, *Capitalist Diversity on Europe's Periphery* (Ithaca, NY: Cornell University Press, 2012).
[180] Béla Greskovits, 'The Hollowing and Backsliding of Democracy in East Central Europe', *Global Policy*, 6/Supplement 1 (2015), 28–37.
[181] Padraic Kenney, *The Burdens of Freedom: Eastern Europe since 1989* (London: Zed Books, 2006), 1–13.
[182] Michael Cox, John Ikenberry, and Takashi Inoguchi (eds.), *American Democracy Promotion: Impulses, Strategies, and Impacts* (Oxford: Oxford University Press, 2000).

assistance that had been previously channelled through institutions such as the National Endowment for Democracy evolved into the Support for East European Democracy. The aid consisted of a yearly average of 360 million dollars for the region between 1989 and 1994, in addition to large-scale financial support for economic and political reforms in Russia.[183] The former socialist space was the main target of assistance at the expense of other regions of the world experiencing similar transformations. The focus of this aid was on economic restructuring, trade investment, and business development rather than democracy building and strengthening civil society.[184] US democracy promotion came with a template for system building, namely, the transition paradigm, which was first designed for Latin American post-authoritarian societies. It was founded on the core assumptions that dictatorships inevitably moved towards multiparty democracy in three stages (opening, breakthrough, and consolidation) by way of free elections regardless of underlying local conditions – and by modifying existing institutions rather than through the creation of an altogether new polity.[185] Critics on the left labelled this blueprint as a 'low intensity democracy' that relied on former elites and technocrats rather than popular participation.[186] For them it was deliberately designed to marginalise other visions during the transition from dictatorship.

Since the incorporation of Southern Europe into the EC in the wake of the collapse of right-wing dictatorships there, the EC also increasingly came to see itself as a promoter of democracy alongside economic integration.[187] By the time of the Maastricht Treaty of 1992, democracy and human rights were incorporated into the primary law of what was now the European Union (EU). Stable institutions, democracy, rule of

---

[183] Steven Hook, 'Inconsistent US Efforts to Promote Democracy Abroad', in Peter Schraeder (ed.), *Exporting Democracy: Rhetoric vs. Reality* (Boulder, CO: Lynne Rienner, 2002), 114; Sarah Mendelson and John Glenn, *The Power and Limits of NGOs: A Critical Look at Building Democracy in Eastern Europe and Eurasia* (New York: Columbia University Press, 2002); and Janine Wedel, *Collision and Collusion: The Strange Case of Western Aid to Eastern Europe 1989–1998* (New York: St. Martin's, 1998).

[184] Miller et al., *Democratisation in the Arab World*, 200.

[185] Thomas Carothers, 'The End of the Transition Paradigm', *Journal of Democracy*, 13/1 (2002), 6–9.

[186] Barry Gills and Joel Rocamora, 'Low Intensity Democracy', *Third World Quarterly*, 13/3 (1992), 501–23.

[187] Tom Buchanan, 'Human Rights, the Memory of War and the Making of a "European" Identity, 1945–1975', in Martin Conway and Kiran Klaus Patel (eds.), *Europeanisation in the Twentieth Century. Historical Approaches* (Basingstoke: Palgrave Macmillan, 2010), 166; Helene Sjursen, 'Enlargement and Identity: Studying Reasons', in Haakon Ikonomou, Aurélie Andry, and Rebekka Byberg (eds.), *European Enlargement across Rounds and Beyond Borders* (New York: Routledge, 2017), 57–74.

law, and human rights became the political preconditions – defined in the so-called 'Copenhagen criteria' of 1993 – for the East's accession, criteria that Southern European states had not had to face during their earlier transitions. In 1989, what was formerly the EC took on the task of coordinating international aid to Poland and Hungary – the so-called PHARE Programme – later extended to include the former Soviet Union under the TACIS Programme. However, the European Parliament insisted on adding a special 'democracy' line into the general budget only in 1992.[188] The aid for free-market reform dwarfed Brussels's democracy assistance. From 1990 to 1996 only 1 per cent of all PHARE funds were allocated to building civil society in former socialist countries. Only in the second half of the 1990s did EU's democracy talk go beyond the symbolic.

Political reform aimed at expanding pluralism, the rule of law, and civic participation conditioned European economic assistance. Because of the bloody repression of anti-government protests in the summer of 1990, Romania was excluded from the PHARE Programme until January 1991.[189] Two years later Romania signed its Association Agreement with the EU. The officials in Brussels designed a system of rewards for post-socialist governments that complied with accession requirements, while assistance was withheld in cases of dissent. Such a strategy was effective because local political forces considered the benefits of EU accession greater than those resulting from resisting conditionality. Such post-1989 alignment required a high level of intrusion by the EU in domestic affairs as well as little deliberation in adopting the legislation necessary for membership. Across the former socialist space the set of laws required for EU accession (the *acquis communautaire*) often passed without any parliamentary deliberation. In Hungary 152 of the 180 laws adopted were not subject to any debate whatsoever.

The harmonisation of domestic and EU legislation constituted an outsourcing of democratisation: a process that local elites, still doubting whether their own populations had in fact a genuine fondness for liberal democracy, found beneficial. A Western-controlled process made democracy appear, at least for a time, inevitable, modern, and incontestable. Representatives from EU member states were placed in Eastern European administrations as advisers in their respective fields of expertise. Such supervision of reform was accomplished also through the

[188] Gorm Olsen, 'The European Union: An Ad Hoc Policy with a Low Priority', in Schraeder, *Exporting Democracy*, 135–36.
[189] Roxana Radu, 'After a Violent Revolution: Romanian Democratisation in the Early 1990s', *Central European Journal of International and Security Studies*, 7/1 (2013), 1–21.

Brussels-sponsored Technical Assistance Information Exchange Office.[190] In the late 1990s the consolidation of democracy in Eastern Europe was the outcome of an unprecedented transfer of norms and expertise from the EU that was seldom accountable to electorates. This democracy deficit of European integration would have a lasting effect on local societies: consensus was the outcome of conditionality and not the result of dialogue between social and political groups in acceding ex-Communist states. The outsourcing of reform was often viewed as protection against explosions of nationalism – and any contestation from below was quickly labelled populism.[191]

Despite the peaceful character of post-1989 transformations and extensive Western assistance, the fear of a return to authoritarianism lasted throughout the 1990s. The political tribulations of the ex-Soviet space confirmed such anxieties. Between 1992 and 1996 the Russian government received the third largest volume of bilateral US aid (more than 2.1 billion dollars) along with substantial packages from other countries, particularly Germany, and billions more in multilateral assistance. However, ongoing major economic collapse and displacement in Russia irreparably damaged democratic reforms within a society already shaken by the severe recession of the Gorbachev years.[192] Many Russians now associated democratisation with chaos. Models of authoritarian capitalist transition widely discussed already during the final years of the Soviet Union, gained traction. The journalist Vadim Nifontov boiled down the sentiments of many liberals and parts of the Russian public in the early 1990s, claiming that the policies implemented in Chile by the dictator Augusto Pinochet now seemed a much better alternative to the Russian present: 'While Chile is blossoming, we march into the anus of history. This means we have to learn from their experience'.[193]

The 'Formula Pinochet', meaning reforms implemented through authoritarian rule, turned into the method of choice to keep economic liberalism afloat by un-democratic means. Even Western observers, such as the Radio Free Europe broadcaster George Urban, argued that an illiberal Russia was allegedly more suited to the nation's culture. In

---

[190] Frank Schimmelfenning and Ulrich Sedelmeier, 'Conceptualizing the Europeanisation of Central and Eastern Europe', in Schimmelfenning and Sedelmeier (eds.), *The Europeanisation of Central and Eastern Europe* (Ithaca, NY: Cornell University Press, 2005), 1–11.

[191] Ivan Krastev, *The Inflexibility Trap: Frustrated Societies, Weak States and Democracy* (Sofia: Centre for Liberal Strategies, 2002), 15–16 and 29.

[192] Stephen Kotkin, *Armageddon Averted: The Soviet Collapse 1970–2000* (Oxford: Oxford University Press, 2001), 119.

[193] Vadim Nifontov, 'Augusto Pinočet i ego rol'v russkoj istorii', 11 December 2006, www.apn.ru/%20publications/article11121.htm.

1993 Yeltsin disbanded parliament by decree and shelled the building when the nationalist and Communist opposition threatened to topple him using violence. The lasting consequence of this constitutional crisis was that the Russian legislative branch was reduced to a façade.[194] The campaign for the 1996 presidential elections was a successful attempt to enshrine liberal economic reforms in Russia with undemocratic methods – and the culmination of Pinochet's public celebration in the country.[195] The spectre of Latin American dictatorship in former social-ist countries was a popular theme during the 1990s. Scholars underlined the two regions' traditions of military rule, oligarchic order, and popu-lism – and feared their return in both regions.[196] A case often invoked was Argentina's Juan Perón, who symbolised presidentialism, corporat-ism, and one-party rule.[197]

Such a 'Peronist' took power in Minsk in 1994, when Alexander Lukashenko won the presidential elections on an anti-systemic platform. The dénouement in Belarus showed that democratisation was far from being inevitable. Lukashenko rejected Western political models that were popular amongst other Eastern European elites. He embraced the suc-cess story of Soviet modernisation in Belarus. He consolidated legitimacy by claiming to protect the people from the chaos of democratisation and shock therapy associated by many Belarusians with poverty, lack of food, and corruption.[198] The opposition represented by the Belarusian Popu-lar Front, which guided the country to post-Soviet independence, failed to articulate a programme of social transformation. It advocated a pre-Soviet Belarusians identity that excluded large sections of society that were not anti-Russian. Lukashenko's opposition to liberalism and his exploitation of popular frustration with capitalism foreshadowed illiberal rule in Russia and parts of Central Europe.[199]

Even in those countries that became model democracies for the first two decades after 1989, such fears of illiberal outcomes were never far away. It seemed for a while as if even Poland, the epicentre of the

---

[194] David Satter, 'When Russian Democracy Died', *Wall Street Journal*, 20 September 2018, www.hudson.org/research/14582-when-russian-democracy-died.

[195] Rupprecht, 'Formula Pinochet', 183–84.

[196] Adam Przeworski, 'The "East" Becomes the "South"? The "Autumn of the People" and the Future of Eastern Europe', *Political Science and Politics*, 24/1 (March 1991), 23.

[197] Tismaneanu, *Fantasies of Salvation*, 48.

[198] Paulina Pospieszna, *Democracy Assistance from the Third Wave: Polish Engagement in Belarus and Ukraine* (Pittsburgh: University of Pittsburgh Press, 2014), 4–5.

[199] Lukashenko's creation of government-organized NGOs (GONGOs), in parallel with repressive legislation directed against independent associations (branded as carriers of foreign interests) was later emulated by Vladimir Putin, Viktor Orbán, and Jarosław Kaczyński.

democratic '1989' moment, might succumb to an illiberal solution. During Lech Wałęsa's presidential term from 1991 to 1995, the former leader of Solidarność was in constant conflict with the parliament, the Sejm, as he sought enhanced constitutional powers. He tried to control the Polish General Staff and sought special powers in order to bypass the Sejm in the implementation of economic policies.[200] At the time the former dissident Karol Modzelewski tellingly wrote that 'the authoritarian threat hanging over post-communist Europe concentrates primarily around the presidency; one sees this not only in Moscow and Minsk, but also in Warsaw'.[201] Liberal commentators long spoke of Lukashenko as 'Europe's last dictator'; such talk largely disappeared with the rise of neo-authoritarianism across the region from 2010.

Emerging Democracies and Liberal Internationalism

Domestically, the democratic turn in Eastern Europe was considered a reintegration into 'normal' continental politics and into a world liberated from Cold War ideological and military divides. Yet in the early 1990s Eastern European politicians still imagined a democratic Europe and world that was not necessarily dominated by its Western side. They drew on the internationalist outlook of the pre-1989 East-West grassroots militant networks of human rights, environmental, and peace movements. Echoing the democratic imaginations of these alternative groups, which often were not liberal, some leaders argued for a more egalitarian Europe in which former socialist countries did not necessarily have to converge with Western political, economic, and security models.[202] Immediately after 1989, Václav Havel and Jiří Dienstbier, Czechoslovakia's first non-Communist foreign minister until 1992, continued the 'Helsinki from below' movement that advocated demilitarisation and imagined the Conference for Security and Cooperation in Europe (CSCE) as the democratic egalitarian intergovernmental organisation that would bring all states from the Atlantic to the Urals together to work collectively and equitably on security and democratisation.

The disappearance of the Warsaw Pact and the CMEA – the economic association of bloc countries – a move opposed by ex-Communist authorities in Bulgaria and in Romania, combined with the lure of EU and NATO accession, hastened the demise of such visions, however.

---

[200] Miller et al., *Democratisation in the Arab World*, 197.
[201] Karol Modzelewski, *Quelle voie après le communisme?* (Paris: Éditions de l'Aube, 1995), 169.
[202] Zsuzsa Gille, 'Is there a Global Postsocialist Condition?', *Global Society*, 24/1 (2010), 29.

The Prague Appeal of the Czechoslovak opposition Charta 77, which in 1985 had called for the dissolution of NATO and the Warsaw Pact, and the withdrawal of foreign troops, as the basis for a united Europe, was forgotten, especially against the background of the wars in the former Yugoslavia and the instability of the ex-Soviet space. A new orthodoxy was embraced by dissidents-turned-politicians: the idea that their countries' foreign policy was inevitably premised on their integration into a Western-dominated Euro-Atlantic space in which the EU and NATO became the ultimate guarantors of democracy. This shift during the 1990s fatally undermined earlier visions of the CSCE as a forum for continental convergence, which had been based on a greater egalitarianism and collectivism rooted in the processes of Europeanisation of the late Cold War.[203] Like the alternative democracy movements of the 1980s, these alternative international visions of democratisation were sidelined.

Post-socialist elites considered the adoption of democracy essential to their being recognised as European partners by the West. They came to focus on the EU, NATO, and liberal internationalism in part because they dreaded their own political re-peripheralisation. Former dissidents warned about the danger that geographical borders would become civilisational ramparts. Adam Michnik feared that the Oder-Neisse border between Germany and Poland would turn into 'a European Rio Grande' delimiting 'different levels of development',[204] turning former socialist countries into low-tier democracies in Europe and rendering them vulnerable to the return of dictatorship. Such marginalisation could be avoided if Eastern Europeans proved to be at the forefront of post–Cold War democracy offensives. Prague, a former centre of the international Communist movement, became the home of (often anti-Communist) opposition groups from Vietnam, Iraq, Cuba, and Myanmar.[205] During the first Gulf War in 1991 the former socialist countries pledged support for sanctions and military intervention against Saddam Hussein despite the negative impacts on their economies – Iraq was an important oil supplier for Bulgaria, Romania, and Hungary.[206]

---

[203] Szulecki, 'Heretical Geopolitics', 34; David Cadier, 'Après le retour à l'Europe: les politiques étrangères des pays d'Europe central', *Politique Étrangère*, 3 (Automne 2012), 573–84.

[204] Magda Papuzinska, 'Poland – Europe's Mexico?', *Gazeta Wyborcza*, 4 June 1990, FBIS-EEU-90–112, 76.

[205] 'Foreign Dissidents Begin to Operate in Prague', *FBIS Editorial Report*, 11 September 1995, FBIS-EEU-95–192, 9–10.

[206] On Eastern European foreign policy and realpolitik, see Zhong Yang, 'The Fallen Wall and Its Aftermath: Impact of Regime Change upon Foreign Policy Behaviour in Six East European Countries', *East European Quarterly*, 28/2 (1994), 235–57.

Yet the international circulation of democracy after 1989 was not solely a Western-driven process. Interactions remained among semi-peripheries, continuing the tradition of the last decades of the Cold War. New democracies from Latin America, East Asia, and Eastern Europe tried to work to support each other's democratisation during the 1990s. At the United Nations, post-authoritarian states from the South started a movement of emerging democracies that aimed to strengthen their negotiating position in relation to international organisations such as the IMF and the World Bank, donors and what were termed 'old democracies' (i.e. Western states). This process had begun on the international stage in 1988, as post-dictatorial authorities in Manila organised the International Conference of Newly Restored Democracies, which gathered together Latin America and Southern European delegates.

The wave of regime changes across the world in the following four years created circumstances for broadening this initiative. The second conference of 'new or restored democracies' was in Managua in 1994.[207] Fifty-two countries – twenty-two from Eastern Europe and the former Soviet Union, eighteen from Latin America and the Caribbean, seven from Africa, and five from Asia – attended the gathering. Two issues came into focus. Political stability was tied to free markets, but the latter were also seen as potentially disruptive for democratisation. Participants emphasised interdependence and solidarity to ease the burden of exiting dictatorship.[208] These two conferences in the South proposed an alternative conception of democratisation less beholden to the West that did not disregard collective rights or social justice in favour of market reforms, and criticised IMF and World Bank conditionality for its politically destabilising effects.[209] Eastern European representatives were cautious about the more radical critiques voiced by speakers from Latin America or Africa against Western democracies or institutions such as the IMF. On one hand, they embraced the idea of a UN developmental fund to help emerging democracies with reforms. On the other, they did not endorse interventions such as that of the Beninese representative who

---

[207] UN General Assembly, 49th Session, 15 November 1994, A/49/236, Annexes I and II, 3–4.
[208] Petru Dumitru, 'The History and Evolution of the New or Restored Democracies Movement', https://csrdar.org/content/resource/history-and-evolution-new-or-restored-democracies-movement.
[209] For criticism of Latin American and African representatives, see UN General Assembly, 49th Session, 79th Meeting, 7 December 1994, A/49/PV.79, 15–25 and UN General Assembly, 49th Session, 80th Meeting, 7 December 1994, A/49/PV.80, 1–26.

insisted that 'democracy was not an end in itself', for it depended on respective ability of states to bring about welfare and social justice.[210]

By the end of the decade the movement that had started as collaboration among post-dictatorial (semi-)peripheries critical of a Western consensus had morphed, with the active involvement of Eastern Europeans, into the institutionalisation of a Western-dominated idea of global liberal peace. At the third gathering of emerging democracies in Bucharest in 1997, the Romanian minister of foreign affairs, Adrian Severin, one of the authors of Romania's first market reforms in 1990/91, abandoned talk of alternative democratic forms and collective solidarity to embrace a Washington Consensus language of technocracy and good governance that could be applied everywhere with minimal local variation. He argued that concepts such as 'functioning democracy, institutional improvement and good governance' unified North and South, East and West.[211] The language of what acerbic observers termed the 'democracy industry' and Western conditionality was quickly entrenched in the official self-representations of newly created Eastern European democracies. In 2000, in Warsaw, under the coordination of the outgoing Clinton administration, the World Forum on Democracy assembled representatives from 107 countries. It proclaimed a new vision for the twenty-first century: liberal democracy was the exemplary form of governance and democracy promotion was hardwired to international relations.[212] Eastern Europe's democratisation had helped pave the way to the orthodoxy of irrepressible markets and democratic liberalism as engines for post–Cold War history.

[210] Intervention Mr. Mongbe (Benin), UN General Assembly, 49th Session, 79th Meeting, 7 December 1994, A/49/PV.79, 24.
[211] Both quoted in Dumitru, 'History', 10 and 11.
[212] Peter Schraeder, 'Promoting an International Community of Democracies', in Schraeder, *Exporting Democracy*, 1.

3.   Europeanisation

In the spring of 1989 a group of formerly senior, but marginalised, members of the Romanian Politburo mounted a campaign against their leader Nicolae Ceauşescu. They argued that he had taken their country 'out of Europe' and now refused to follow the lead set by reformist Communists to their west who had embraced the project of European reconciliation embodied in the so-called Helsinki Process. They rejected the country's turn towards the Global South in the 1970s: Romania had been classed as a 'Latin American country' for the purposes of joining the G77 group of developing nations in 1976, had developed close political and economic ties with Africa, and had sought to free itself from the grip of Western financial institutions in the 1980s by devoting a substantial share of its national income to paying off debts– with disastrous social consequences. In their so-called Letter of Six – regarded as one of the founding documents of the Romanian revolution – they declared, 'Romania is and remains a European country and as such must advance along with the Helsinki process and not turn against it. You [Nicolae Ceauşescu] ... cannot remove Romania to Africa'.[1]

For the exiled Romanian dissident Ion Vianu, writing in the tamizdat (a journal 'published abroad') *Agora*, Ceauşescu's rule represented a '"tropical despotism" transplanted by some miracle into this Carpathian-Danubian space'.[2] During the Romanian Revolution in December 1989 rumours circulated that so-called 'Arab terrorists' were fighting to protect the crumbling regime. Such accusations provoked strenuous rebuttals from Syria, Libya, and the PLO, who advised their citizens and compatriots in Romania to lie low until the fighting was

---

[1] This was an open letter sent to Ceauşescu by six party veterans who denounced his excesses, his economic policies, and the deterioration of Romania's international status. For the English text, see https://chnm.gmu.edu/1989/items/show/698. For details Vladimir Tismaneanu, *Stalinism for All Seasons: A Political History of Romanian Communism* (Berkeley: University of California Press, 2003), 227–29.

[2] Ion Vianu, 'O interpretare a României de azi', *Agora*, 1/2 (1988), 63–78 [text written in Vale de Leâo, Portugal, in August 1987].

over.[3] The truth of such allegations has never been proved and is perhaps not the point: the rumours hit home because they presented a now despised leader as a violent Oriental despot whose overthrow would guarantee Romania's reorientation to the West. In the years after the Revolution a campaign against black marketeers in Bucharest mainly targeted foreign students, particularly Arab and African ones.[4]

The revolutions of 1989 both at the time and since were celebrated as the return of the region 'to Europe'. The collapse of state socialism enabled the reinstatement of the region in its supposed natural home, denied to it by authoritarian leaders and Soviet occupation. At the 1990 Eurovision contest, the Italian singer Toto Cutugno won with 'Together: 1992'. It began 'Insieme, unite, unite Europe!' – and was popular across Eastern Europe.[5] To a certain extent, this had been the sort of language used by dissidents, who, alongside Western European conservatives, saw transformation as the recovery of half of Europe from the 'grip of the Orient'. Yet – as the above example shows – it was just as often reform-minded Communists who sold the idea of Europe as the way for their countries to re-join the modern world. As Gyula Horn, one of the most important reformists within the Hungarian Communist party, put it in March 1989: 'The nation is in the midst of a search for the truth ... These answers represent a choice between catching up with the civilised countries, or becoming irremediably banished to the peripheries of world developments ... In the 1940s we broke with the democratic traditions of European civilisation, adopting in its stead an anachronistic Byzantine-like style and practice [which] removed the country from the vanguard of world development'.[6] The idea of Europe was as much the work of an elite sphere as it was the rallying call of the dissident 'from below'.[7] For some outsiders this rediscovery was understood not as the inevitable reconstitution of a naturalised civilisational space that had been torn asunder by the Cold War, but rather as the production of new forms of borders, and of cultural and economic

---

[3] Telegramă nr. 025072, 29 December 1989/20:15, MAE-Libia, 550/1989, 19.

[4] For example, Mihai Ionescu 'Şoc: 200 oameni ai legii descind în lumea interlopă', *Adevărul*, 12 July 1991, 1 and 5.

[5] Marilena Zaroulia, '"Sharing the Moment": Europe, Affect, and Utopian Performatives in the Eurovision Song Contest', in Karen Fricker and Milija Gluhovic (eds.), *Performing the 'New' Europe. Studies in International Performance* (London: Palgrave Macmillan, 2013), 31–52.

[6] Gyula Horn, 'Your Weary Eyes on Europe Be Cast', *Március Tizenötödike*, 15 March 1989, 5.

[7] For an examination of this in the GDR, see Jana Wuestenhagen, 'Communist Europeanism: A Case Study of the GDR', in Dieter Gosewinkel (ed.), *Anti-liberal Europe. A Neglected Story of Europeanisation* (Oxford: Berghahn Books, 2015), 166.

exclusion based on Europe's imperial past. Some African observers in the late 1980s and early 1990s interpreted the collapse of state socialism in Eastern Europe not as an onwards march to openness and globalisation. Rather, the idea of 'fortress Europe'[8] – a term last widely used in defence of Nazi Europe towards the end of the Second World War – was now repurposed by economists and politicians to express their 'Afropessimist' anxieties that an East-West reconciliation would inevitably come at the expense of North-South links.[9] Some feared a united Europe would reinforce previously dominant colonial attitudes that had never truly been questioned. According to Abdulrahman Mohamed Babu, a Zanzibari left nationalist, 'when he [Gorbachev] made that fateful speech in Finland … in which he called for a "common European home", shock waves went through the radical "Third World". Our experience of a common European home forged by the pre–World War One "Great Powers" – Britain, Germany, France, Tsarist Russia and the Austro-Hungarian Empire – is not exactly pleasant'.[10] Europe, they feared, would be closed off to African goods, people, and ideas.

In August 1990 the president of the United Nations General Assembly, the Nigerian Joseph Garba, noted the emergence of this new equation. The changes in Eastern Europe would, he feared, leave Africa 'with the proverbial "short end of the stick"'. Drawing on a Swahili proverb, he noted, 'When two elephants fight, the grass suffers, and when the same elephants make love, the grass also suffers'.[11] According to Algerian intellectual Zaki Laïdî, writing in 1990, this convergence was termed *l'autocentrage du Nord* – the 'self-centering of the North': for him, the collapse of state socialism in Europe constituted a knitting together of neocolonial threads.[12] Seemingly abandoned by a half of Europe that had once supported their struggles for independence and their calls for a new economic order, they rather saw in this moment the affirmation of an essentially white continent allied to the Washington Consensus, with a

---

[8] See also its widespread use in those parts of the Balkans that did not accede to the EU: 'The Schengen Wall is now stronger than the Berlin Wall once was and has been turning Europe into a fortress': Goran Svilanović, 'The Schengen Fortress EU', *Danas*, 16 May 2006.

[9] Boutros Boutros-Ghali, 'The Marginalisation of Africa', in Nikolaos A. Stavrou (ed.), *Mediterranean Security at the Crossroads: A Reader* (Durham, NC: Duke University Press, 1999), 21–34.

[10] Abdulrahman Mohamed Babu, 'A New Europe: Consequences for Tanzania', *Review of African Political Economy*, 18/50 (1991), 75.

[11] Joseph N. Garba, 'Changing East-West Relations and Their Implications for Africa' (lecture, Carter Center, Atlanta, GA, 9 April 1990). Thanks to Kim Christiaens for this reference.

[12] François Constantin and Bernard Contamin, 'Perspectives africaines et bouleversements internationaux', *Politique Africaine*, 39 (October 1990), 56.

'single market' built around a revived sense of hard civilisational (and racialised) boundaries. Such a new constellation would inevitably hit Africa hard, many argued. One senior Kenyan politician remarked that for many in the West, 'Eastern Europe is a pretty girl, and Africa a shabby woman ... everyone is already tired of Africa'.[13]

These non-European views on '1989' take us beyond a celebratory narrative of a 'return to Europe'. They demonstrate that the so-called Europeanisation was not only a process of regional rediscovery but also a re-negotiation of Eastern Europe's position in a wider geopolitical context. The big offer of integration that Western political and economic institutions made to the East around 1989 entailed the jettisoning of many of the internationalist paradigms and linkages that had existed under late socialism. Thus, it is too simplistic to see '1989' solely as a journey from insularity to openness. '1989' was the culmination of a process that simultaneously questioned one set of borders that had divided Europe, whilst hiding new forms of boundary making necessary to produce a coherent European space based on complex assemblages of race, civilisational hierarchy, culture, and economics.[14] Hans-Dieter Klee, the director of the Africa Department of the West German public international broadcaster *Deutsche Welle*, wondered in 1989: 'is the concern of African countries justified? ... That it will become a fortress Europe, reaching from Portugal to Warsaw, maybe even to the Urals?'[15]

These observations also show that there were multiple understandings of what constituted the new Europe. Yet over the last few decades a particular narrative of Europeanisation has come to dominate: most of this literature found itself aligned with the memory politics of the EU, which presented itself as the embodiment and protector of a new

---

[13] B. A. Kiplagat, permanent secretary, Ministry of Foreign Affairs, cited in *Zambia Daily Mail*, 14 March 1990.

[14] Daniela Vicherat Mattar, 'Did Walls Really Come Down?', in Marc Silberman, Karen E. Till, and Janet Ward (eds.), *Walls, Borders, Boundaries: Spatial and Cultural Practices in Europe* (New York: Berghahn Books, 2012), 77–94. EU-sponsored memory initiatives celebrated East-West mobility: for example, the 1989 'pan-European picnic' memorial project was supported with this narrative of a 'borderless Europe' in mind. EC 2014, European Heritage, '2014 Panel Report' (Brussels: European Commission, 2014). On the role of 'fortress Europe' talk in the those countries outside the EU in the Balkans, see Tanja Petrović, 'Images of Europe and the Process of the West Balkans Countries' Association to the European Union', in Olga Gyarfasova and Karin Liebhart (eds.), *Constructing and Communicating Europe* (Zürich: LIT, 2014), 123–24; Tanja Petrović (ed.), *Mirroring Europe. Ideas of Europe and Europeanisation in Balkan Societies* (Leiden: Brill, 2014). On the sense of loss, see Ljubica Spaskovska, 'The "Children of Crisis". Making Sense of (Post)socialism and the End of Yugoslavia', *East European Politics and Societies and Cultures*, 31/3 (2017), 506–9.

[15] Hans-Dieter Klee, *Changes in Germany and Eastern Europe – Implications for Africa?* (Berlin: Deutsche Afrika-Stiftung, 1990), 5.

democratic, market- and rights-driven Europe that had triumphed over Southern European fascism and Eastern European Communism.[16] This somewhat provincial story of 1989 was used to reinforce the notion that Europe was a special zone of democracy, economic progress, and civilisation capable of peaceful change based on European traditions and notions of progress – ones that often excluded any references to Europe's own imperial past or contemporary global relationships.[17] Yet beyond the self-congratulatory narratives of post-1989 Europeanisation there have always been multiple conceptions of Europe, but often too little attention is paid to those that were politically sidelined.[18] The fissuring in understandings of exactly who it was that represented the true Europe since 2010 also had its roots in these multiple histories of conceptualising the continent.[19]

Such a shift in narration alters the role that Eastern Europe is accorded in the history of '1989'. No longer is it simply a region brought out of an insular backwardness into Western-led globalisation; rather, its actors and elites become active producers of new boundaries, inclusions, and exclusions. The rethinking of Europeanness in the 1970s and 1980s ought not be understood only as the recovery of something lost in the early Cold War: rather, it might also be seen as a contested process of recasting Europe's relationship with Africa and Asia as the hopes surrounding decolonisation faded. It was a coproduction between the East and West of the continent, once various elites on both sides of the Iron Curtain began to re-orient culturally and politically from North-South links to those running East-West. Alternative visions of Europe, based on the values of postcolonialism or non-alignment, were replaced by much more politically and culturally bounded senses of the continent.[20]

---

[16] On the subsidiary role accorded to Eastern Europe in this history, see Peter Pichler, 'A "Handmade" Historiographical Myth: The "East" and Eastern Europe in the Historiography of European Integration, 1968 to the Present', *History*, 103/356 (2018), 518–19.

[17] Gurminder K. Bhambra and John Narayan, 'Introduction. Colonial Histories and the Postcolonial Present of European Cosmopolitanism', in Bhambra and Narayan (eds.), *European Cosmopolitanism. Colonial Histories and Postcolonial Societies* (Abingdon: Routledge 2017), 2–3.

[18] Ulrike v. Hirschhausen and Klaus Kiran Patel, 'Europeanisation in History: An Introduction', in Martin Conway and Klaus Kiran Patel (eds.), *Europeanisation in the Twentieth Century. Historical Approaches* (Basingstoke: Palgrave Macmillan, 2010), 3–4; O. Woever, 'Conflicts of Vision, Visions of Conflict', in O. Woever, P. Lemaitre, and E. Tromer (eds.), *European Polyphony: Perspectives beyond East-West Confrontation* (London: Macmillan), 186–224.

[19] Gosewinkel, *Anti-liberal Europe*, 12.

[20] Giuliano Garavini, *After Empires: European Integration, Decolonisation, and the Challenge from the Global South, 1957–1986* (Oxford: Oxford University Press, 2012), 259–61.

Eastern Europeans helped create this vision, being the foremost producers of the idea of a historically based high civilisational European unity,
and reviving a particular regional tradition of being a bulwark against the
encroachment of Eastern ideas and peoples. Such ideas would contribute
to the cultural identity and political roles of what would soon after
1989 become the EU.

The Early Cold War: A Divided Europe

In the immediate postwar period, as the continent divided politically,
very different visions of Europe emerged. Western countries barred
sensitive goods from being exported to Comecon countries, thus restrict-
ing East-West trade and severing former economic linkages. Eastern
European states severely restricted the mobility of their populations to
the West, a legacy of the Soviet 'socialism in one country' ideology, and
out of fears of a possible labour shortage.[21] In the first years of the Cold
War travel remained very limited for most in the Eastern Bloc. Only
twenty-two thousand Poles were allowed to travel abroad; of those,
twelve thousand five hundred went to socialist countries and two thousand went to capitalist countries on business trips as 'state employees'.
According to the official figures, there were only fifty-two 'private trips'
from Poland across the Iron Curtain in 1954: mobility had decreased at
least one thousand-fold since the interwar period.[22]

As the Iron Curtain became a reality, elites on both halves of a divided
continent looked southwards. The Western European project that would
eventually become the European Community and then Union did not
initially reach out to Eastern Europe, but rather considered the terms on
which African states might be integrated – in a project referred to as
'Eurafrica'.[23] The European Economic Community (EEC) as it emerged
in the late 1950s was embedded in the needs of Western European states
to maintain trade links with and the flow of raw materials from their
colonies as they gained their independence. Eastern European states, to
varying degrees, looked South too. Cut off from the West, postwar decolonisation in Asia and Africa offered Communist leaders the possibility of
integration into a wider world that was committed to anti-imperialist

---

[21] Tara Zahra, 'Travel Agents on Trial: Policing Mobility in East Central Europe,
1889–1989', *Past & Present*, 223/1 (2014), 161–93.
[22] Dariusz Stola, 'Opening a Non-exit State: The Passport Policy of Communist Poland,
1949–1980', *East European Politics and Societies and Cultures*, 29/1 (2015), 98.
[23] Peo Hansen and Stefan Jonsson, *Eurafrica: The Untold History of European Integration and
Colonialism* (London: Bloomsbury Academic, 2015).

politics and adopting non-capitalist development.[24] Citizens in the Eastern Bloc were encouraged to consider themselves part of a now rapidly expanding global 'socialist camp' beyond Europe.[25]

Yet this did not mean the negation of the idea of Europe – indeed, throughout the postwar period many interlocutors assumed the existence of a continuous cultural European territory – albeit one whose true essence and form could be claimed by their own side. Conservatives from West Germany to Spain bemoaned the division of the continent, presenting themselves as the true Europeans: an area east of the Iron Curtain was deemed 'enslaved Europe', captured by a brutal 'Oriental Bolshevism'.[26] Eastern European Communist elites, by contrast, saw in Western Europe the remnants of fascism and imperialism; their systems in the East were, by contrast, embodiments of the true progressive traditions of European civilisation.[27] They even presented Sovietisation as the true Europeanisation.[28]

Some Communist intellectuals, particularly in South-Eastern Europe, began to rethink Europe's place in the world. This not only was due to postwar progressive efforts to rethink the civilisational hierarchies deemed responsible for the horrors of fascism and the Second World War, but also was a response to the rapid decolonisation of countries in Africa and Asia. At the United Nations, for instance, experts from Bulgaria, Romania, and the Soviet Union took part in the United Nations Educational, Scientific and Cultural Organisation's (UNESCO) Major Project on the Mutual Appreciation of Eastern and Western Cultural Value, launched in 1957 as a response to the Bandung Conference. Eastern European intellectuals in attendance argued that Europe

---

[24] Sedef Arat-Koç 'Contesting or Affirming "Europe"? European Enlargement, Aspirations for "Europeanness" and New Identities in the Margins of Europe', *Journal of Contemporary European Studies*, 18/2 (2010), 163.

[25] James Mark and Péter Apor, 'Socialism Goes Global: Decolonisation and the Making of a New Culture of Internationalism in Socialist Hungary 1956–1989', *Journal of Modern History*, 87 (2015), 852–91.

[26] Robert Moeller, *War Stories. The Search for a Usable Past in the Federal Republic of Germany* (Berkeley: University of California Press, 2003); Rosario Forlenza, 'The Politics of the Abendland: Christian Democracy and the Idea of Europe after the Second World War', *Contemporary European History*, 26/2 (2017), 261–86; James Mark, 'The Spanish Analogy: Imagining the Future in State Socialist Hungary 1948–1989', *Contemporary European History*, 26/4 (November 2017), 603–4.

[27] Greg Castillo, 'East as True West: Redeeming Bourgeois Culture, from Socialist Realism to Ostalgie', *Kritika: Explorations in Russian and Eurasian History*, 9/4 (2008), 747–68.

[28] Tarik Cyril Amar, 'Sovietisation as Civilizing Mission in the West', in Balazs Apor, Peter Apor, and E. A. Rees (eds.), *The Sovietisation of Eastern Europe: New Perspectives on the Postwar Period* (Washington, DC: New Academia, 2008), 29–46.

had to purge itself of the sense of itself as a universal culture,[29] and took part in the writing of new world histories that were supposed to inspire a more equitable appreciation of the world's different cultures. In the late 1950s, as the Soviets reached out to southern Asia, their leader Khrushchev called for equality between civilisations.[30] Chinese and Vietnamese Communists subsequently accused him of revisionist humanism and an abandonment of anti-imperialism and class struggle. Yet for the smaller countries of Eastern Europe, this language of civilisational equality was attractive because they sought recognition for their role in the constitution of European civilisation too.[31]

Helsinki – Re-bordering Europe?

These divided visions of what constituted Europe, and competing claims of different blocs to represent its true essence, began to dissolve only from the early 1970s. At an international level, 'Europe talk' intensified, spurred on in part by the so-called 'Helsinki Process', an intergovernmental initiative that sought to guarantee European security and a respect for freedoms and rights as well as to encourage cultural and scientific cooperation across the continent. This has often been viewed as a Western-instigated initiative that would eventually help to liberate Eastern European countries from the Soviet grip; in fact bloc countries played a major role in establishing this process, one that allowed them greater freedom of manoeuvre from Moscow.[32] From the mid-1960s Eastern European leaders intensified their calls for a summit on European security. This led, eventually, to the involvement of thirty-five states (the European countries plus the United States and Canada) in a three-year process that resulted in the Helsinki Conference in 1975.

---

[29] Documents of the Fourth Regional Conference of the European National Commissions for UNESCO (Sofia, 25–30 June 1962), 14–15.

[30] Hanna Jansen, 'Internationalizing the *thaw*: Soviet orientalists and the contested politics of spiritual solidarity in Asia 1954–1959', in James Mark, Artemy Kalinovsky, and Steffi Marung (eds.), *Alternative Globalizations: Eastern Europe and the Postcolonial World* (Bloomington: Indiana University Press, 2020); Paul Betts, 'Humanity's New Heritage: Unesco and the Rewriting of World History', *Past & Present*, 228/1 (2015), 249–85.

[31] Bogdan C. Iacob, 'South-East by Global South: The Balkans, UNESCO and the Cold War', in Mark et al., *Alternative Globalizations*.

[32] On the Eastern European origins of the Helsinki Process, see Laurien Crump, *The Warsaw Pact Reconsidered: International Relations in Eastern Europe, 1955–1969* (London: Routledge, 2015), 290, 296; Nicolas Badalassi and Sarah B. Snyder (eds.), *The CSCE and the End of the Cold War: Diplomacy, Societies and Human Rights, 1972–1990* (Oxford: Berghahn, 2018).

There had been earlier attempts at overcoming such divides from the late 1960s. Initiatives for town twinning, or new East-West collaborations between historians, heritage specialists, or architects, increasingly worked with the idea of a common European culture.[33] Nevertheless, the Helsinki Process, which lasted from the early 1970s until the end of the Cold War, gave this cultural shift towards the imagining of a less fractured European future much greater political weight. Helsinki had initially appeared to entrench the status quo: the treaty recognised the reality of a politically divided Europe, and respected the borders of the socialist states in the East so that their security and sovereignty were guaranteed. Yet over the longer term it opened up new possibilities for cooperation: Helsinki and its follow-up conferences were also premised on the idea that Europe possessed a historical or cultural unity – and one that needed, after the divisions of the previous decades, to have its loosened threads woven together again. Moreover, it heralded a shift away from the Global South on the part of both Western and Eastern Europeans. The European Community abandoned the Eurafrica idea and paid less attention to North-South trade and began to lay a greater emphasis on East-West integration.[34] Many Western European states came to imagine Europe as a zone of human rights, free markets, and political moderation into which the East might eventually be incorporated.

The notion of a 'European culture' provided a language through which those on both sides of an otherwise still deep ideological divide could find common understandings, and which might eventually underpin the relaxation of political tensions. Eastern European states were often at the forefront of such initiatives, viewing the process as an opportunity to place their often marginalised cultures at the centre of the continent's identity. In 1977, during the Commission on Security and Cooperation in Europe (CSCE) talks that had followed on from the Helsinki Accords, Yugoslavia proposed 'a year of cultural cooperation' among participating states that aimed at educating European peoples about the cultural heritage of other countries, including the production of joint TV programmes and travelling exhibitions. Yugoslav representatives insisted that projects must address the 'mutual interrelations and influences among European cultures; the cultures of smaller countries, national

---

[33] Michael Falser and Wilfried Lipp (eds.), *A Future for Our Past: The 40th Anniversary of European Architectural Heritage Year (1975–2015)* (Berlin: Hendrik Bäßler Verlag, 2015).

[34] Enzo R. Grilli, *The European Community and the Developing Countries* (Cambridge: Cambridge University Press, 1993), 331.

minorities and ethnic groups; [and] the interrelations between European and non-European cultures'.[35]

As part of the CSCE process socialist states gave their citizens greater mobility. Considering travel integral to building peace in Europe, they enabled travel across the Warsaw Pact countries in the so-called Borders for Peace programme from the early 1970s.[36] Restrictions on travel to the West were loosened too, but practice was highly variable. Yugoslavia had long re-opened its borders; almost half a million Yugoslavs moved for work to Western Europe in the 1970s. Whereas only fifty thousand Polish citizens had travelled privately to Western European countries annually in the late 1960s, their number increased tenfold after 1971. The guide book *Europe on $100*, published throughout the 1970s, helped these new tourists to find their ways around a re-discovered Western Europe. Hungarians, from 1967, could visit Western countries every three years – if they held sufficient hard currency. In the 1980s the Helsinki Process led to even greater possibilities for travel and family reunion in most Eastern European states. Soviet and East German citizens, however, were largely left out: to travel to the West they still required complicated permissions and authorisations and reports from their work brigade, the Communist Youth, or the local trade union, which assessed their trustworthiness and political loyalty.[37]

The intergovernmental Helsinki Process eventually helped spark pan-European activism from below. Environmental, peace, feminist, gay and lesbian, and human rights campaigns across the Iron Curtain imagined an open, non-aligned, demilitarised continent as an alternative to what they saw as neoconservative politics, an increasingly self-centred Europe, and the authoritarianism of state socialism.[38] In 1985 Eastern dissident groups such as Freedom and Peace in Poland and Charta 77 in Czechoslovakia, together with the Western European Nuclear Disarmament, called for the dissolution of NATO and the Warsaw Pact, the withdrawal

---

[35] CSCE/BM/10, 2, November 1977 (CSCE/OSCE Archive, Prague).

[36] Mark Keck-Szajbel, 'The Politics of Travel and the Creation of a European Society', *Global Society*, 24 (2010), 37–38.

[37] Vladimir Zubok, 'Introduction', in Patryk Babiracki and Kenyon Zimmer (eds.), *Cold War Crossings: International Travel and Exchange across the Soviet Bloc* (College Station: Texas A&M University Press, 2014), 2.

[38] Padraic Kenney, *A Carnival of Revolution: Central Europe 1989* (Princeton, NJ: Princeton University Press, 2002), 102–13; Kacper Szulecki, 'Hijacked Ideas Human Rights, Peace, and Environmentalism in Czechoslovak and Polish Dissident Discourses', *East European Politics and Societies*, 25/2 (2011), 272–95; Lukasz Szulc, *Transnational Homosexuals in Communist Poland. Cross-Border Flows in Gay and Lesbian Magazines* (Cham: Palgrave Macmillan, 2018).

of foreign troops, and the creation of a united Europe.[39] A year later peace movements from Poland, the GDR, Hungary, the Soviet Union, West Germany, Switzerland, France, the Netherlands, and Italy met in Budapest following a two-year round of dialogue to build 'continental solidarity'.[40] Additionally drawing on the need for pan-European cooperation following the nuclear plant accident at Chernobyl some four months earlier, they called on politicians involved in the CSCE process to bring an end to the continental divide symbolised by the postwar settlement in Yalta. They collectively issued the Giving Real Life to Helsinki Accords memorandum, which was made public a day before the CSCE meeting in Vienna in November 1986. Such groups, too, played vital roles in re-imagining a united Europe.

Although the calls to return to Europe are often attributed to oppositional voices, they was equally the preserve of those Communist elites who wished to see greater economic integration with the West – and to drag their countries away from what was seen as an excessive socialist internationalism. Already by the early 1970s, many leaders were beset by doubts about their relationship with those more radical anti-colonial economic and political projects of the South.[41] Yugoslavia's elites were becoming ever more critical of the increasingly narrow boundaries of the Non-Aligned Movement, particularly as Cuba, which accentuated anti-Western and pro-Soviet positions within the Movement, became increasingly dominant.[42] In 1967 the Slovenian journalist Jurij Gustinčič argued that Yugoslavia's rightful place was no longer with Asia or Africa; the Belgrade editor-in-chief of the Yugoslav party weekly *Komunist* Gavro Altman emphasised that a 'return to Europe' was a natural extension of the growing dominance of European economic links. The support of African and Asian countries was losing its importance, he argued, because sovereignty no longer needed to be defended in an era of détente.[43] While an alliance with the South and the turn towards Europe were seldom considered to be incompatible, it became possible for a

---

[39] Piotr Żuk, 'Anti-military Protests and Campaigns against Nuclear Power Plants: The Peace Movement in the Shadow of the Warsaw Pact in Poland in the 1980s', *Journal of Contemporary Central and Eastern Europe*, 25/3 (2017), 370.

[40] Kacper Szulecki, 'Heretical Geopolitics of Central Europe. Dissidents Intellectuals and an Alternative European Order', *Geoforum*, 65 (2015), 32.

[41] Konstantin Kilibarda, 'Non-aligned Geographies in the Balkans: Space, Race and Image in the Construction of New "European" Foreign Policies', in Abhinava Kumar and Derek Maisonville (eds.), *Security beyond the Discipline: Emerging Dialogues on Global Politics* (Toronto: York Centre for International and Security Studies, 2010), 41.

[42] BCA, *Family Collection – Legacy of Koča Popović and Lepa Perović*, 'Izlaganje predsednika Tita na sednici Izvršnog biroa, održanoj 22.III.1972. na Brionima'.

[43] Odjek, Sarajevo, No. 7, 1–15, April 1972.

liberal wing in the Yugoslav Party to articulate a stronger pro-European orientation. Only very late, in 1988–89, did they finally give up on this principle, moving closer to the EC.[44]

Elites in some Eastern Bloc countries articulated a much narrower notion of a specific and special European cultural zone to which they felt themselves to belong, which would help prepare the ground for the re-emergence of the idea of 'Central Europe'. By the early 1980s the Hungarian and Polish governments promoted a 'common European heritage'. Hungary campaigned to use UNESCO and a European 'Cultural Forum', coordinated initially through Budapest, to encourage cultural cooperation.[45] At this CSCE-sponsored initiative held in the Hungarian capital in the autumn of 1985, the Hungarian minister of culture Béla Köpeczi celebrated the idea of a 'cultural identity of Europe' that would 'improve the conditions of peaceful co-existence in this continent'. Unlike Yugoslav representatives, Köpeczi provided a far more bounded sense of European civilisation: 'Europe possesses a cultural heritage … ['which'] defines a specific intellectual quality – the European character'.[46] High European culture was especially important for the East: Czechoslovak elites promoted the development of education in pan-European modern literature, whilst the Hungarian delegation advocated the expansion of artistic training, festivals, and productions and the promotion of less studied languages across the continent.[47] Art exchanges, classical music, and film festivals dominated the Helsinki-inspired inter-bloc cultural traffic of the 1980s. Soviet and Eastern European elites' claims to be protectors of high European culture, often explicitly directed against the influence of supposedly shallow US popular culture, prefigured the post-Communist claims of conservatives that their nations were the true defenders of European civilisation.

---

[44] Benedetto Zaccaria, 'Under the Shadow of the Soviet Union: The EEC, Yugoslavia and the Cold War in the Long 1970s', in Svetozar Rajak et al. (eds.), *The Balkans in the Cold War* (London: Palgrave Macmillan, 2017), 253.

[45] Hungary advocated cultural exchange in the areas of radio programming, concerts and TV films – including more coproductions. CSCE/CFB.48, 6 November 1985. See also Johannes Sizoo and Rudolph Th. Jurrjens, *CSCE Decision-Making: The Madrid Experience* (The Hague: Martinus Nijhoff, 1984), 100. Also see 'The Concluding Document of the Madrid Meeting 1980 of Representatives of the Participating States of the Conference on Security and Co-operation in Europe, Held on the Basis of the Provisions of the Final Act Relating to the Follow-Up to the Conference' (Madrid, 1983), www.osce.org/mc/40871?download=true.

[46] Béla Köpeczi Speech, Opening of the CSCE Budapest Cultural Forum, 16 October 1985, Cultural Forum CSCE CFB 10–11 1985.

[47] CSCE/CFB. 10–11; CSCE/CFB. 48, 6.

An Anti-colonial Europe: Critiquing Helsinki

The Helsinki Process was not only the origin of a more *bordered* continent; it also helped to establish a political space within which very different visions of Europe were articulated. Not all socialists welcomed such new visions, viewing them as surrendering to a Western imperial project in which the re-assertion of a culturally distinct continent, the distancing of the non-European world, and the confinement of Eastern Europe to the status of periphery were all connected. Some Eastern European elites chose instead to reinterpret the meaning of Helsinki in order to argue for a 'progressive' or 'anti-colonial' Europe. The process represented *their* victory: *they* had forced Western powers to accept peaceful coexistence and recognise the sovereignty of Eastern European nations. Milan Matouš, the deputy director of the Czechoslovak Communist Party's Institute of Marxism-Leninism, believed that Helsinki represented if not a Waterloo, at least an Austerlitz for 'the most militant reactionary forces of imperialism' and that it would force 'reactionary' regimes and 'imperialists' from Western Europe to respect human rights.[48] Some hoped that the Helsinki Process and East-West reconciliation would hasten the end of colonialism and apartheid in Southern Africa. A reduction of the ideological heat in Europe had helped to undermine the legitimacy of the authoritarian regime in Portugal, which had claimed to be a bulwark against the expansion of Communism. Its collapse led to the end of Portuguese colonialism in Africa. Robert Mugabe in Zimbabwe and the African National Congress (ANC) in South Africa saw reconciliation within Europe as a softening of febrile Western European anti-Communism, which had sustained a dislike of leftist anti-colonial movements and progressive politics in independent African nations.[49]

Cultural initiatives supported such alternative visions of the continent and its new role in a world without western European Empire. In 1977, in response to the Helsinki Final Act, a European Festival of Friendship was held in Bucharest. Organised to coincide with the follow-up CSCE/ Helsinki meeting in Belgrade, all the socialist countries were present: the Soviet Union with the 250-person Academic State Opera and Ballet from Kiev; Bulgaria, Hungary, and Yugoslavia with folklore ensembles; the GDR with the Berlin String Quartet; Poland with two singers; and Czechoslovakia with the Prague Madrigalists ensemble. Such a combination of high- and low-brow culture was not unusual for socialist states'

---

[48] Milan Matouš, 'In the Costume of Humanists', *Mladá fronta*, 4 May 1977.
[49] This attitude shifted by 1989, when leftist intellectuals in Africa see East-West reconciliation as the reconstitution of the colonial global North. See Chapter 5.

self-representation: folk music and folklore embodied their claims to represent popular tradition, whilst the high cultural programme served to make their classical European heritage available to the masses.

Such cultural events were supposed to offer an alternative to emerging Western conceptions of a united continent. Based around peace, cultural equality, the rejection of neocolonialism, and the equality of European nations, they took their cue from internationalist visions of the New International Economic Order that the Global South had promoted (see Chapter 1). Mircea Malița, a former director of the international organisations section of the Romanian Ministry of Foreign Affairs and at the time personal advisor of Nicolae Ceaușescu, supported calls for a new cultural international order as part of the New International Economic Order, which meant, among other things, an essentialised understanding of the equality of world cultures. He backed his argument by invoking the Cultural Charter of Africa from 1976 stating that 'small and ignored cultures have maybe earned greater merit because they were able to preserve, despite a scarcity of means, the unity of their peoples and guided them through history'. Claims of European superiority were groundless because 'who can say before an African mask that its author did not reach the heights of artistic sensibility and of the profound exploration of the human soul?'[50] UNESCO's postwar call for the world to recognise the equality of different civilisations had opened up spaces in which peripheral European countries could assert their own worth as one of many important centres of European cultural development. This approach enabled Balkan intellectuals to situate their region as the 'true Europe' whose heterogeneity and liminality could now be celebrated as providing the continent's true values in a post-imperial world in which civilisational equality and syncretism had to be central.[51]

A less bordered, in-between, even 'postcolonial' vision found a powerful expression with the emergence of the idea of 'Mediterranean Europe' in the 1970s. This political imaginary transcended the political divides of Cold War Europe and brought together Romania, Yugoslavia, Bulgaria, Greece, Portugal, and Spain as semi-peripheral areas facing similar issues of underdevelopment outside the continent's North-Western economic core. At Helsinki these countries had argued that they be classified as 'European developing countries'. Such status, if permitted, would have granted them trade exceptions, aid, and preferential economic deals. Such a notion also articulated an opposition to the Northern

---

[50] Mircea Malița, 'Dimensiunea culturală a noii ordini economice internaționale', *Revista Comisie Naționale a RSR pentru UNESCO*, 19/1–2 (1977), 29–35.

[51] Iacob, 'South-East by Global South'.

'capitalist' EEC and aimed to offer an alternative to a Westernizing core-periphery Europe, rather identifying the continent with non-alignment and détente.[52] It signalled that elites in these countries advocated for the existence of an intermediate space between East and West, North and South that connected the continent to the postcolonial world. This idea of a progressive and socialist Mediterranean Europe was far less bordered than its Helsinki equivalent: it sought to incorporate forces in the Arab World – most notably Gaddafi's Libya, socialist Algeria, Morocco, and Tunisia – as part of a zone of economic cooperation, reviving, in a far more limited form, the earlier idea of Eurafrica.[53]

Western European politicians were suspicious of such 'Mediterranean passions'. For them, Southern Europe was becoming the continent's 'Third World', especially against the backdrop of the weakening of détente from the late 1970s onwards.[54] It looked as if an irresponsible 'militant Mediterraneanism' was now affecting major polities. The latter had in their view abandoned a commitment to a European space that should properly be defined by political moderation and free market capitalism. During the 1980s many initiators of the project of Mediterranean cooperation ceased to argue for their 'developing' status and reined in their advocacy of a Euro-Mediterranean area that linked Europe organically to North Africa or Western Asia. Spain, Greece, and Portugal began instead to call for integration within a Brussels-centred Europe, while elites in Romania, Yugoslavia, and Bulgaria gradually lost their appetite for 'in-betweenness' in the context of crippling economic crisis and the need for Western assistance. Over the coming decades the Mediterranean as a zone for an expanded Europe would be replaced by the idea of this space as the marker of a civilisational divide, a barrier to migrants and a threat to geopolitical stability that needed to be secured.[55] In 1994 the first UN general secretary from Africa, Boutros Boutros-Ghali, saw the Mediterranean as *the* key space in which the intensification

---

[52] Sofia Papastamkou, 'Greece between Europe and the Mediterranean, 1981–1986. The Israeli-Palestinian Conflict and the Greek-Libyan Relations as Case Studies', *Journal of European Integration History*, 21/1 (2015), 49–69.

[53] See, for instance, Elena Calandri, Daniele Caviglia, and Antonio Varsori, (eds.), *Détente in Cold War Europe: Politics and Diplomacy in the Mediterranean and the Middle East* (London: I.B. Tauris, 2015). When Spain joined the EC in 1986, it made significant efforts to bring the 'Mediterranean question' to the attention of Brussels. See Paul Kennedy, *The Spanish Socialist Party and the Modernisation of Spain* (Manchester: Manchester University Press, 2013), 120.

[54] Pierre Hassner, 'L'avenir des alliances en Europe', *Revue française de science politique*, 26/6 (1976), 1029–1053, 1049; Pierre Hassner, 'L'avenir prévisible des deux alliances en Europe', *Le Monde diplomatique*, June 1977, 8.

[55] Liliana Suárez-Navaz, 'Introduction', in *Rebordering the Mediterranean. Boundaries and Citizenship in Southern Europe* (Oxford: Berghahn Books 2004), 1–20.

of the global divide between North and South would be felt. According to him, a new Iron Curtain had descended across the Mediterranean, dividing Europe from Africa.[56]

A Prehistory of Fortress Europe: Civilisational Bordering in Late Socialism

The Helsinki Process had opened up a vast political and cultural space to rethink what Europe meant beyond the divides of the early Cold War, and many took this opportunity in order to make sense of, or proselytise for, their own visions of the region's future. Europe was a debate, never a static idea: there were many different conceptions of where Europe ended, what its core characteristics were, and what political projects a rhetoric of continental unity might address. The idea of Europe was powerful in Eastern Europe during the last decades of the Cold War in part because it had its uses for both Communists and the opposition as they each sought to make sense of the future of their countries and region: on one side, Soviet general secretary Mikhail Gorbachev came to argue for a 'common European home', whilst reformist Communists in Hungary, Yugoslavia, and elsewhere came to criticise their more conservative colleagues and claim their own right to lead their countries back to 'European civilisation'; on the other side, dissidents across Hungary, Poland, and Czechoslovakia justified their struggle against dictatorship and 'Soviet colonisation' through the appeal to their being 'European' or even 'Central European'.

Postcolonial or internationalist ideas of Europe lost their relevance. Definitions of Europe as a civilisational space with clearly defined cultural borders became dominant instead.[57] These notions foreshadowed Samuel Huntington's influential but much criticised 1993 book on *The Clash of Civilizations*; the prominent US political scientist argued that, in a post–Cold War world, culture had come to matter more than politics or national identity in defining the divides of the contemporary world. Such a sense of civilisational difference had already developed in Eastern Europe through the 1970s and 1980s. The revival of Europe as a distinct

---

[56] Boutros Boutros-Ghali, 'The Marginalisation of Africa', in W. C. Olson (ed.), *The Theory and Practice of International Relations*, 9th ed. (Englewood Cliffs, NJ: Prentice Hall, 1999), 24–25.

[57] On the fragility of Eastern European 'anti-colonialism' and its rapid 'melting away', see Imre, 'Whiteness', 84. She argues that the absence of a real extra-European colonial experience meant that imperialism happened only 'through fantasy' – thus a deep anti-colonial critique that would hold in political culture, and the 'white guilt' necessary to sustain it, did not develop.

zone of progress, civilisation, and advanced economic and political organisation led Communist elites and societies to revive and rework, in new settings, older representations of difference and exclusion – most notably in the ways they related to African or Islamic civilisations. This produced a vision of Europe that was sold to the West in late socialism and, in so doing, played a vital role in a broader re-imagining of the frontiers of a post–Cold War Europe. From this perspective, new forms of European bordering were not the result of the revolutions but were constitutive of them, having gained strength long before 1989.

Many political leaders during the last decades of socialism appealed rhetorically to an idea of Europe that could still be socialist and was still 'in-between' the West and a wider anti-imperialist or socialist world, the best known invocation of which was offered by the last Soviet leader, Mikhail Gorbachev. The rhetoric of a 'Common European Home', a phrase already used by Brezhnev during his 1981 visit to Bonn, and by Gorbachev in London in 1984, replaced the theory of two ideologically opposed camps that had divided Europe. Like many late Communist elites, he saw a new Europe not as a politically integrated unit but as separate nations – evoked by the reference to different 'rooms' in his Common Home analogy – which were nevertheless united in a broader European civilizational space. Already before the fall of the Berlin Wall, Gorbachev mused about a re-united Europe:

Contemplating the vistas of this long-suffering continent and also thinking about the common roots of the multifaceted but essentially collective European civilisation, I came to realise more and more how artificial the confrontation between the blocs is after all ... and how much the Iron Curtain is out of date ... The idea of a common European home most of all suggests a degree of unity, even if the countries belong to different social systems and opposing political-military alliances.[58]

For Gorbachev, Europeanisation was not the same as Westernisation, and the vision of a common civilizational space was not necessarily synonymous with liberal democracy and capitalism. His so-called 'New Thinking' in foreign policy still had an anti-American thrust, contained within broadly socialist categories, albeit ones that were ill-defined and shifting.[59] The attraction of these Europeanising visions to some late

---

[58] Quoted after Mary Kaldor, Gerard Holden, and Richard A. Falk (eds.), *The New Detente: Rethinking East-West Relations* (London: Verso, 1989), 36.

[59] Helmut Altrichter, *Russland 1989. Der Untergang des sowjetischen Imperiums* (München: C.H. Beck, 2009), 327–28; Dietrich Beyrau, 'Das sowjetische Modell. Über Fiktionen zu den Realitäten', in Peter Hübner, Christoph Kleßmann, and Klaus Tenfelde (eds.), *Arbeiter im Staatssozialismus. Ideologischer Anspruch und soziale Wirklichkeit* (Wien: Böhlau, 2005), 47–70; Archie Brown, 'Did Gorbachev as General Secretary Become a

Communist elites lay precisely in the hope that they would advance the cause of socialism across the continent. Gorbachev himself had long experienced genuinely popular leftisms in Europe. He was imbued with the idealist socialism of the Soviet 1960s generation, had seen the genuine reformism of the Prague Spring at close hand, and had experienced Italian Eurocommunism and the overwhelming popularity of Enrico Berlinguer. He had close links with the leading representatives of the Socialist International such as Willy Brandt and Pierre Mauroy;[60] and he had seen the collapse of Southern European dictatorships usher in popular left-wing governments.[61]

Leftist Western European leaders, such as Spanish prime minister Felipe González, who became one of Gorbachev's closest political friends, worked together with reform Communists in the late 1980s with the hope too that new alliances enabled by the end of Europe's political divides would strengthen the cause of European socialism in the 1990s.[62] Thus, even in the late 1980s, Gorbachev was able to sustain an earlier idealised version of socialist internationalism. It is in this context that Gorbachev's faith in the possibility of a socialist Europe, freely chosen, becomes more comprehensible. Some reformist elites in Eastern Europe aligned themselves with Gorbachev's hopes for a unified Europe based on socialist principles. In July 1989 the West German weekly *Der Spiegel* interviewed the leading Hungarian reforming Communist Imre Pozsgay, who had just outflanked hardliners in the party and taken up the reins of a transition process: 'I am a firm advocate of European culture and of Hungary's return to Europe', he stated. To the interviewer's question 'A farewell to Asia, a return to Europe?' Pozsgay replied, 'I cannot conceive of European culture ... without the idea of socialism'. Choosing not to reject the interviewer's association of socialism with Asiatic backwardness, he nevertheless articulated the idea that Europe could still be associated with left-wing politics.[63]

For Gorbachev the idea of a 'Common European Home' was not necessarily exclusionary in civilisational terms. He used it as a vague and capacious category that signalled a Western orientation that could nevertheless include all the peoples of the Soviet Union, including

Social Democrat?', *Europe-Asia Studies*, 65/2 (2013), 198–220. See the revival of such an idea in 2010 under Medvedev, in the Valdai Club, now termed the Alliance of Europe: www.karaganov.ru/docs/Karaganov_valdaj_eng.pdf.

[60] Michail Gorbatschow, *Erinnerungen* (Berlin: Siedler, 1995), 80, 147, 247, 759–61, 988; Archie Brown, *The Gorbachev Factor* (Oxford: Oxford University Press, 1995), 116.

[61] Gorbatschow, *Erinnerungen*, 752, 760–67.   [62] Mark, 'Spanish Analogy', 615.

[63] *Der Spiegel*, 3 July 1989, 119. In the end, 'Europe talk' became immensely useful to those who wished to dismantle the Communist system. Communists' claim to represent the 'true Europe' gave space in late socialism for others to contest their right truly to do so.

Muslims. Indeed, many Central Asian national elites within the Soviet Union were content with a version of the story that seemed to include them in a wider universal or even Eurasian civilization.[64] Nevertheless, such talk also gave political space to those who articulated a more exclusionary European identity. For a strain of an increasingly popular Russian nationalism, the Soviet Union had imprisoned Russia in an unwanted Asian and African embrace.[65] Sergej Soldatov, a prominent Russian dissident from Narva, in exchanges with Estonian nationalists developed an anti-imperialist democratic nationalism in which the end of a Third Worldist nationalism was tied to a decolonisation of the Soviet Union, and, with it, a programme for the reorientation of Russia to Europe. In his 'Letter to Russian patriots', he wrote from his Mordovia prison cell in March 1978: "It is a critical juncture in the fate of the Russian nation; our people are tired of utopianism and the lack of humanism. They demand the creation of a Russian national state up to the Urals, with a call to Russians to resettle there, and with Siberia and the Far East as condominiums, internationally administered through the United Nations."[66]

Soldatov called for a liberal, democratic, and decidedly European Russian nationalism that would complete Peter the Great's westernisation of Russia. Each Russian, he suggested, should spend at least a couple of months of their lives in Europe. Moscow should give up its 'Third World adventurism', and the Soviet Union itself should undergo a 'decolonisation': all republics and territories with a non-Russian majority should be granted independence after referenda. Eventually, an ethnically homogenised Russia should join the EC and integrate into the world economy. Some of Soldatov's visions were progressive: he wanted his country to demilitarise, decentralise, exit from its isolation from the West, and develop reliable rule of law and an ecological consciousness. But he also combined them with decidedly conservative ideas, calling for a revival of Christianity as basis of a European identity, mass pilgrimage to Jerusalem to restore Orthodox faith in Russia – and the return of women to a traditional role within the family.

---

[64] Diana T. Kudaibergenova, 'The Use and Abuse of Postcolonial Discourses in Post-independent Kazakhstan', *Europe-Asia Studies* 68/5 (2016), 917–35.

[65] On the slow rise of Russian nationalism from the 1950s, see Geoffrey Hosking, *Rulers and Victims: The Russians in the Soviet Union* (Cambridge, MA: Belknap, 2006); Vladislav Zubok, *Zhivago's Children: The Last Russian Intelligentsia* (Cambridge, MA: Belknap, 2009); Mark Bassin, *The Gumilev Mystique: Biopolitics, Eurasianism, and the Construction of Community in Modern Russia* (Ithaca, NY: Cornell University Press, 2016); Mark R. Beissinger, *Nationalist Mobilisation and the Collapse of the Soviet State* (Princeton, NJ: Princeton University, 2002); Yitzhak M. Brudny, *Reinventing Russia: Russian Nationalism and the Soviet State, 1953–1991* (Cambridge, MA: Harvard University Press, 1998).

[66] Distributed in Samizdat and also in the West: Russkaja Mysl, 27 September 1979, Archiv der Forschungsstelle Osteuropa, Bremen, Samizdat-Sammlung Abteilung Sowjetunion und Nachfolgestaaten.

For some Russian nationalists the idea that the Soviet Union was also an Asian power – a notion that was promoted and popular in an earlier era of postwar decolonisation – had little relevance.[67] For a brief moment they abandoned their commitment to a broader imperial identity and embraced the idea of a European future. Seeing the Caucasus and Central Asia as the Union's unwanted 'Third World', they believed an independent Russia would prosper without them. The late 1970s migration of those ethnic Russians who had once developed the Soviet periphery back to the Russian Republic was thus welcomed, whilst non-white migration from the Soviet periphery to the Russian industrial centres was seen by some as a threat. New discourses on racial hierarchy based on skin colour (as opposed to simple ethnicity) became ever more pronounced.[68] Racist attacks against non-white foreigners, such as African students, became more common in the 1980s.[69]

The rhetoric of a 'return to Europe' only occasionally made explicit any racializing intentions in its desire to realign with Western Europe – late socialist societies did not in general have a well-developed vocabulary to think through questions of race. Thus, we find such reflections for the most part through the observations of those directly affected by these attitudes. The Azeri Gamid Cherishchi, a Soviet Muslim living in Lithuania, wrote in the local newspaper *Soglássije* on 30 November 1989: 'Those who preach the idea of a common European home just want to replace a confrontation between East and West with a confrontation between North and South ... The idea of a "common European home" will fail because such a home will force a fissure across the Soviet Union, and this will not happen without tragedies'. He argued that it was necessary to preserve the integrity of the Soviet Union to protect the integration of Muslims. For some African students in the Soviet Union, too, Gorbachev's talk of 'universal values', 'entering world civilisation', and 'gaining normality through rejoining Europe' meant Eurocentrism, a categorising by skin colour, and the marginalisation of their continent.[70] Sometimes, however, the nature of the exclusion in the revival of Russians' rediscovered Europeanness was made explicit: a *Pravda*

---

[67] Hanna Jansen, 'Internationalizing the Thaw'.
[68] Jeff Sahadeo, '"Black Snouts Go Home": Migration and Race in Late Soviet Leningrad and Moscow', *Journal of Modern History*, 88/4 (2016), 797–826.
[69] Tobias Rupprecht, 'Gestrandetes Flaggschiff: Die Moskauer Universität der Völkerfreundschaft', *Osteuropa*, 1 (2010), 95–114.
[70] Nikolay Zakharov, *Race and Racism in Russia* (Houndmills: Palgrave Macmillan, 2015), 2.

headline in the late 1980s declared: 'We are Africans in a European home'.[71] Such framings pointed to the abandonment of an earlier internationalism which, although possessing its own developmental and (unspoken) racial hierarchies, nevertheless embraced the possibility of exchange, hybridity, and advancement for the South – now Africa was imagined as a space that was only near insofar as an internationalist socialism had enabled the dark continent to 'infect' Russia, dilute its civilisation, and hence wrench it from its true destiny in 'civilised Europe'.

This idea of Russia as fundamentally European had faded by the mid-1990s. Those who had imagined a post-imperial Russia as a normal European country lost ground to those who claimed that the West was humiliating their state, creating economic and political turmoil, and preventing Russia from fulfilling a great power mission within a broader Eurasian space. As early as 1992 the liberal presidential adviser Sergey Stankevich had remarked that Eurasianism was already 'knocking at the door' of the Foreign Ministry.[72] The new Russian elites did not feel that the West recognised them as equal partners. One journalist poignantly articulated this reversal in 1993: 'Is there anything more disgusting and insulting than saying that your own people "somehow does not live up to", somehow does not conform to global (understood as Western) standards?'[73] Some Russian liberals who had previously supported the idea of a 'Common European Home' now joined nationalists of various shades in embracing an alternative Eurasian course. In March 1996 the lower house of the parliament, the State Duma, dominated by nationalist and Communist parties, voted to make legally binding the 1991 Referendum, when 70 per cent of Russian voters supported the preservation of the Soviet Union.[74] Foreshadowing the Kremlin's later anti-liberal internationalism, a new geopolitical narrative fashioned the West into a symbol of cosmopolitan and globalizing forces that had shattered the great power status that Russians had felt itself to possess through the Soviet Union, and now endangered the very being of the Russian nation.[75] Over the course of the 1990s the Eurasian camp was a

---

[71] Quoted in Charles Quist-Adade, 'From Paternalism to Ethnocentrism: Images of Africa in Gorbachev's Russia', *Race and Class*, 46/4 (2005), 88.

[72] Iver Neumann, *Russia and the Idea of Europe: A Study in Identity and International Relations* (London: Routledge, 1996), 181.

[73] Anatoliy Utkin quoted in Neumann, *Russia*, 191.

[74] Yitzhak Brudny, *Reinventing Russia: Russian Nationalism and the Soviet State, 1953–1991* (Cambridge, MA: Harvard University Press, 1998), 259.

[75] Iver Neumann, *Uses of the Other* (Minneapolis: University of Minnesota Press, 1998), 169.

kaleidoscope of positions rooted in disillusionment with or rejection of the early years of liberal democratic experimentation. It developed many shades: from a hard version, often constructed on anti-Semitic, xenophobic, and even racist bases, that emphasised the uniqueness of the Russian nation and culture; to less bordered versions that drew on Gorbachev's 'Common European Home' and saw Eurasianism encapsulating a broader, fairer Europe from Lisbon to Vladivostok – one in which Russia fulfilled its historical and geopolitical role of bridging and negotiating between Europe and Asia.

Other visions of Europe had greater staying power. Oppositional movements in the Western borderlands of the Eastern Bloc had, from the early 1980s, articulated a more circumscribed version of Europeanness, adopting an identity as 'Central Europeans'. It was sometimes an argument for a tightly defined zone – commonly consisting of only Poland, Czechoslovakia, and Hungary – which, given its historical traditions, briefly interrupted by Communism, should be considered more Western than the West, with which it naturally belonged and would thus, free from political constraints, organically re-join. Such understandings had partly emerged in the response to the failures to establish 'socialism with a human face' in 1968: in the work of the Czech philosopher Karel Kosík and the novelist Milan Kundera this became understood as the tragic suppression of a region imbued with the potential to humanise socialism by an alien eastern Soviet tyranny.[76] One of the most well-known formulations was made by Hungarian Jenő Szűcs's in his famous essay on the three historical regions of Europe. Written in the wake of the suppression of the Solidarność Trade Union in Poland with the imposition of Martial Law, when writers often retreated from politics into cultural work,[77] Szűcs wrote a history that not only explored the distinction between Eastern Europe and Western Europe, but also made the case for a third historical region, Central Europe, where Hungary, together with historical Bohemia and the Polish Commonwealth, belonged. Published unofficially in 1981 and officially in 1983, and in time translated into English, French, German, Italian, Polish, Slovak, Czech, and Romanian,[78] Szűcs's piece implied not only that this newly formulated 'Central Europe' had been ripped away from its natural

---

[76] Balázs Trencsényi, 'Central Europe', in Diana Mishkova and Balázs Trencsényi (eds.), *European Regions and Boundaries. A Conceptual History* (Oxford: Berghahn, 2017), 175.
[77] Rafal Grupinski, 'Schwierigkeiten mit der Mitte Europas', in Hans-Peter Burmeister et al. (eds.), *Mitteleuropa Traum oder Trauma?* (Bremen: Edition Temmen, 1988), 51–64.
[78] Tomasz Kamusella, 'Central Europe in the Distorting Mirror of Maps, Languages and Ideas', *Polish Review*, 57/1 (2012), 68.

Western orientation by a Soviet (Russian)-led Eastern Europe, but that its future belonged with the West.[79]

In this way, 'Central Europe' was also conceptualised as a cultural defence against a so-called Asiatic despotism brought into Europe by the 'Soviet occupier'.[80] It described a zone distinct from the 'imperial' centre, leading some Soviet intellectuals to admit to the fact that they represented an empire, a concept that was previously absent from their discourse.[81] As one oppositional Polish journalist put it in 1988, 'The post-Stalinist crisis within the system [Soviet Union] has brought to the surface the anti-centrist aspirations of many nations, which have become increasingly aware that "Soviet internationalism" is only an elegant way of describing age-old, great Russian colonialism aimed at dominating the nations of Asia, Transcaucasia, the Baltic States, the Crimea, and Central Europe. The tragedy of the Soviet Union is that it has realised too late that the era of colonialism is well and truly over'.[82] Such narratives reconceptualised the West not merely as an obvious partner in matters of economic and political cooperation – as many contemporaneous party intellectuals would also like to claim – but also as a natural political or cultural model for newly defined 'Central European' societies to follow.

The concept of 'Central Europe' also marked the region's divergence from a non-European socialist world.[83] In Romania, for instance, the fight against socialist dictatorship was also an expulsion of a 'Third World' from Europe: here the leader Nicolae Ceaușescu had turned away from the West in the 1980s and maintained much closer relationships with African and Arab leaders than his equivalents in surrounding bloc countries. The exiled dissident Ion Vianu thus argued that Romania had become Haiti – now used a symbol for contemporary poverty and misrule rather than remembered as a site of the first nationalist anti-colonial revolution. Rejecting Ceaușescu's claim in the 1970s that

---

[79] Jenő Szűcs, 'The Three Historical Regions of Europe: An Outline', *Acta Historica Academiae Scientiarum Hungariae* 29 (1983), 131–84.

[80] Wolf Lepenies, *The Seduction of Culture in German History* (Princeton, NJ: Princeton University Press, 2006), 178–85.

[81] Jessie Labov, 'A Russian Encounter with the Myth of Central Europe' (paper presented at 'Contours of Legitimacy in Central Europe: New Approaches in Graduate Studies', European Studies Centre, St. Antony's College, Oxford, 1988).

[82] 'Armenia and the Polish Opposition Press', *Polish Independent Press Review*, no. 4, 18 May 1988, HU OSA 300–55–9 Box 1: 4 [quote from an article titled 'Colonialism in a Trap'].

[83] See Diana Mishkova, Bo Strath, and Balázs Trencsényi, 'Regional History as a "Challenge" to National Frameworks of Historiography: The Case of Central, Southeast, and Northern Europe', in Matthias Middell and Luis Roura (eds.), *Transnational Challenges to National History Writing* (New York: Palgrave Macmillan, 2013), 292–93.

Romania had developed like a Latin American country, Vianu argued that the country's 'silent majority' wanted to join a Western Europe – that was imagined not as multicultural but as white:

Many Romanian and foreign pundits argue that Romania today resembles an African country more than a European one. Which are the visible elements of the joining of the 'Third World', of the world of the 'South'? The disorganisation of public life, the administration's inability to maintain its activity at the level of one from the Old Continent; the state of roads, the squalor in the streets ... empty stores; the generalised practice of graft; the police's arbitrariness; here are the features that remind me of Haiti ... It is significant that the Despot [Ceauşescu] feels at home in Africa. This can be proven through his frequent visits to these regions ... the massive presence in Bucharest of African students, in short, a certain desire that Romania should play a role on the Afro-Asian stage to which we are not tied by any tradition or inspiration. [by contrast] ... there is another, different society in Romania. There are intellectuals ... who rightfully claim to belong to the best of European tradition. There is ... the adherence of some large sections of the masses to European values and culture. In the most natural way and with no snobbery, the Romanian wants to be 'Western'. S/he seeks European comfort, s/he is interested in what is happening in Germany, France, [or] England. When s/he emigrates, his steps take him/her there [into the West] ... Romanians with Western ideals are some sort of *silent majority* in today's Romania ... the potential stratum from whom one day an organised and radical contestation of the present state of things can come about'.[84]

For such writers, the struggle against socialism required the expulsion of colour brought about by an alien importation of socialist internationalism. The Polish dramatist Sławomir Mrożek, who had been a committed Stalinist in the 1950s, and written of the region's closeness to the Global South in the 1960s, wrote an imagined letter to the United Nations in the mid-1980s, mockingly claiming that Eastern Europeans need to 'black up' in order to be taken seriously, and that their cause was undermined by virtue of their whiteness:

I should like to report, that the Poles are also negros, as they are whites. By virtue of our rights to independence. If the dear organisation was disturbed by the colour of our skin, or if some kind of difficulty surfaces in this regard, then we can repaint ourselves. To this end we ask the dear organisation to supply us with black Kiwi-branded shoe polish. It's not our fault we are white. This was just how it came to be ... We don't ask for the polish for free. For every kilo we receive, we can send in exchange a tonne of red varnish.[85]

[84] Vianu, "O interpretare a României de azi," 76–7.
[85] Sławomir Mrożek, 'To the Deeply Revered United Nations', reproduced in *A Dél-Afrikai Magyar Egyesület Lapja* 4/2 (June 1986), 12.

Mrożek's satire resentfully appealed to a West that he imagined might respond more favourably to the language of racial oppression in the Global South than to their own suppression under Communism. Such discourses re-established the importance of racialised hierarchy in public speech, speaking of their sense of being 'lesser whites' on a predominantly white continent, whose status had been further eroded because of their being 'blackened by socialism'. Only through the struggle against Communism could Eastern European societies expel colour so as to become full members of European civilisation.[86] This rhetoric would return in the 2010s with the rise of populism and the perceived threat that Muslim migration posed to a region imagined as the protector of white Europe.

The concept of Central Europe also became directed against these countries' smaller near neighbours. In aiming to construct a new regional identity based on a natural cultural affinity with the West, elites were trying to smooth their pathway, ahead of other neighbouring states, back into the European fold. For them, Balkan countries to the south stood outside this Central European imaginary, positioned as not wholly European. Some Southeastern European intellectuals, in turn, were quick to assert that they were equally European, or critiqued 'Central Europe' as a parochial reading of Europeanness that did not allow for the idea of synthesis, liminality, or transregional influences in its understandings of how Europe had come to be. Moreover, in deploying it, they argued, Central Europeans sought to peripheralise the regions to their east and south by claiming the right to have a first attempt at European integration for those who boasted of their natural affinities with the West.[87] Nevertheless, the idea was taken up by intellectuals from countries to the east and south of the initial geocultural site of its production: in Slovenia and in Croatia, the term was used by those who wished to escape Yugoslavia and non-alignment;[88] in Romania, groups in multiethnic western-facing Timişoara employed it to counter the persisting influence of 'neo-Communists' in Bucharest.[89] Despite this variation, all were primarily concerned to steer the region towards Western modernity.

---

[86] Paul Betts, James Mark, Idesbald Goddeeris, and Kim Christiaens, 'Race, Socialism and Solidarity: Anti-Apartheid in Eastern Europe', in Robert Skinner and Anna Konieczna (eds.), *A Global History of Anti-Apartheid 'Forward to Freedom' in South Africa* (London: Palgrave, 2019), 178.

[87] Conférence Internationale des Balkanologues, Belgrade, 7–8 September 1982 (Belgrade: Académie Serbe des Sciences et des Arts, Institut des Etudes Balkaniques, 1984); Bogdan C. Iacob, 'Balkan Counter-circulation: Internationalizing Area Studies from the Periphery during the Cold War', in Matthias Middell (ed.), *Handbook of Transregional Studies* (London: Routledge, 2018), 29–37.

[88] Balázs Trencsényi et al., *Political Thought in East Central Europe. Volume II: Negotiating Modernity in the 'Short Twentieth Century' and Beyond Part II: 1968–2018* (Oxford: Oxford University Press, 2018), 134.

[89] Trencsényi, 'Central Europe', 180.

The expansion of Western political structures to the East was not a natural result of the end of the Cold War; a consensus that the West had a responsibility to reach eastwards was an argument that had to be won. Many intellectuals on both sides of the dissolving Iron Curtain were in fact reluctant to embrace a Western 'civilizing mission' in Eastern Europe, or were critical of assuming that a natural convergence of the East westwards would occur. Some Western foreign policy analysts argued that in contrast with the post-1945 period, when crises in Europe had been more effectively contained, a new expansion after would likely trigger serious political instability.[90] Voices were heard in both Germanys who were opposed to integration. For some West German conservatives the Iron Curtain had become a permanent fixture whose removal threatened a stable continent and a prosperous West. In his novel *The Wall Jumper*, Peter Schneider argued that Wessis ('West Germans') had become comfortable with a divided Europe and divided Germany, and saw the Berlin Wall not as a Schandmauer ('Wall of Shame') as they had in the 1960s – but, rather, a mirror in which they saw their own supposed superiority. According to his novel, the Wall 'shrank to ... a group therapy absorption with the self: for Germans in the West, the Wall became the mirror which told them, day by day, who was the fairest of them all'.[91] On the other side of this mirror, a hard-line GDR elite in the last years of the regime did not embrace Gorbachev's Europeanism, either: they believed that they had to protect the true progressive heritage of Europe and still regarded the EC as an extension of Nazi visions for Europe.[92] This could be found in the radical East German political opposition, too: panoramic photos of the demonstrations in Leipzig and elsewhere in Eastern Germany in the late 1980s show numerous posters equating a united Germany with Nazi slogans such as 'Heim ins Reich' or stating, 'Wiedersehen ja, – Wiedervereinigung nein' ('Seeing one another again, yes – reunification, no'). For them, two Germanys was a preferable outcome, even after the demise of the one-party state.

For some Poles, Hungarians, or Czechoslovaks, 'Central Europe' was a defence against the encroaching values of the West, as much as it was a marker of distance from the Soviet Empire. The Hungarian writer György Konrád, one of the initiators of the debate around the concept,

---

[90] See, e.g., the writings of US foreign policy analyst Richard Ullman: Tamara Resler, 'The United States and Central Europe: Principles and Pragmatism in the Evolving Partnership', in Zlatko Šabič and Petr Drulák (eds.), *Regional and International Relations of Central Europe* (New York: Palgrave Macmillan, 2012), 149.

[91] Peter Schneider, *The Wall Jumper* (London: Pantheon Books, 1985), 12.

[92] Wuestenhagen, 'Communist Europeanism', 167.

viewed it as a cultural defence in light of the Western governments' too easy accommodation with state socialist regimes after détente and Helsinki, and a reminder of the West's abandonment of the region to secure peace at the end of the Second World War.[93] Thus some of the Polish opposition in the mid-1980s had argued for a 'Central-Eastern European Community' with a 'joint economy and common passport', distinct from both East and West, and protecting itself against both, to maintain freedom, peace, and prosperity in the region.[94] In this sense, the concept of Central Europe could as readily articulate distinctiveness from the West as be used to naturalise the region's westerly direction of travel.

Nevertheless, the idea that 'Central Europe' represented an alternative to the West fell by the wayside. The notion that it was rather an organic part of Western Europe was effectively sold to international audiences, playing the card of Western responsibility for enabling the region's suffering under 'totalitarianism', and helping to reactivate long-held Western desires to 'rescue the East' from Communism. The concept became integral to charm offensives from former bloc countries that sought an expansion of European structures and institutions eastwards after 1989. Only a month after the Velvet Revolution in Prague, the former Czechoslovak dissident and now president Václav Havel declared to the Polish parliament:

There is before us the real historic chance to fill with something meaningful the great political vacuum that appeared in Central Europe after the break-up of the Habsburg Empire. We have the chance to transfer Central Europe from a phenomenon that has so far been historical and spiritual into a political one. We have the chance to take a string of European countries that until recently were colonised by the Soviets and that today are attempting the kind of friendship with the nations of the Soviet Union which would be founded on equal rights, and transform them into a definite special body, which would approach Western Europe not as a poor dissident or a helpless, searching amnestied prisoner, but as someone who has something to offer.[95]

In February 1991 this conception was given political form through the so-called Visegrád Group, made up initially of Czechoslovakia and Poland. Named after the medieval congress that had brought together John I of Bohemia, Charles I of Hungary, and Casimir III of Poland in 1335, it mobilised an idea of Central Europe as marking the limits of the civilised West. Directed at Western organisations and countries, it sought

---

[93] Trencsényi et al., *Political Thought*, 134.

[94] Wojtek Wojskowy, 'The Europe of the Future', *Niepodleglosc* 26 (February 1984) in RAD Polish Samizdat/1B, HU OSA 300–55–9 Box 2, 3.

[95] Václav Havel Speech to the Polish Sejm and Senate, 21 January 1990.

to insulate the reputation of the region from the chaos of the post–Yugoslav Wars and from the collapsing post-Communist Russian economy.[96] Such arguments were particularly important for joining NATO – which was considered for a time more important than EU accession as it guaranteed regional security through collective defence. Havel argued that membership was appropriate for Central European countries but not for Russia, 'a huge Euro-Asian Empire' whose 'only relationship with NATO can and will be that of a separate entity'.[97] Without a NATO ending at the Russian border, it was argued, these smaller countries would be more vulnerable to malevolent foreign influence. Without the ideological shield of Central Europe, Westerners could more easily revert to stereotypes of the distant Eastern other, in ways that might undermine their attempts at rapid integration.[98] The British intellectual Timothy Garton-Ash, in an appeal on behalf of Central Europe in October 1991 at the EC's Maastricht summit, argued: 'Though we should do our utmost to promote democracy in the new Russia, this should not obscure the more immediate and manageable challenge of Central Europe ... Historically and culturally, Poland, Hungary, and Czechoslovakia belong to Europe. A Europe that contains Crete but not Bohemia, Lisbon but not Warsaw, is historical nonsense'.[99]

The US Clinton administration followed suit in the mid-1990s and began to refer to a region called 'Central Europe', which was a natural fit for the expansion of Western influence. From 1994 NATO enlargement became a serious proposition. Richard Holbrooke, who negotiated the Dayton Accords during the Yugoslav Wars, led the process to expand NATO into this region, seeing it as a launching pad for further expansion to the east. As one author put it, 'Central Europe had become not so much an object of US foreign policy but an instrument of it'.[100] Madeleine Albright, who was born in Prague and whose family had left Communist Czechoslovakia in 1948, became President Clinton's US

---

[96] On the Europe-Balkan dichotomy in Slovenia and the idea of Europe, see, e.g., Bojan Baskar, 'Within or Without? Changing Attitudes towards the Balkans in Slovenia', *Ethnologica Balkanica*, 7 (2003), 195–206; Mitja Velikonja, *EUROSIS – A Critique of the New Eurocentrism* (Ljubljana: Peace Institute, 2005); Cirila Toplak, 'Evropska Ideja v Slovenski Politični Misli', *Teorija in Praksa*, 39 (2002), 579–87.

[97] Merje Kuus, *Geopolitics Reframed: Security and Identity in Europe's Eastern Enlargement* (London: Palgrave Macmillan, 2007), 52.

[98] Zlatko Šabič and P. Drulák, introduction to *Regional and International Relations of Central Europe*, 6. It also became employed as a self-descriptor by Croatian and Slovenian elites as they sought to distance themselves from Belgrade as new post-Yugoslav nation-states.

[99] Timothy Garton Ash, Michael Mertes, and Dominique Moisi, 'Let the East Europeans In!', *New York Review of Books*, 24 October 1991, 19.

[100] Resler, 'United States', 155.

ambassador at the UN (1993–97) and then secretary of state (1997–2001); she insisted on the term 'Central Europe', arguing that the term 'East European' was more fitting for the Baltic states, Ukraine, Belarus, and European Russia.[101] The State Department divided the post-Communist states into an Office of North-Central European Affairs (Czech Republic, Hungary, Poland, Romania, Slovakia, Slovenia, and, after 2005, Bulgaria) and an Office of South-Central European Affairs (Yugoslavia's successor countries and Albania) and added three additional offices for the ex-Soviet space.[102]

For some in the EC the concept of Central Europe offered the possibility of a part of the former bloc, insulated from the nationalism and political volatility in Yugoslavia or the Soviet Union, undergoing reform. At the end of 1989, the British prime minister John Major and the French president Jacques Delors discussed with their Polish and Hungarian counterparts the possibility of granting associate status within the EC. The idea was officially acknowledged at the EC foreign ministers' meeting in Dublin in January 1990. A year later the Visegrád countries had signed their association agreements, a moment that institutionalised EC's 'multi-tier approach' to the East. While Bulgaria and Romania eventually followed the same path as Central Europe, already in 1992, at the European Council summit in Lisbon, the European Commission admitted that it was 'not interested in the new independent states of the former Soviet Union'.[103] The Baltic countries however became part of the proactive approach to enlargement: the same year they were moved from the TACIS assistance programme that had targeted the Soviet space to PHARE, created initially for what became the Central European Visegrád group. The EU's endorsement of narratives of differentiated Europeanness was obvious in the nature of its commitment to these two programmes: during their first eight-year cycles, PHARE allocated more than twice the aid disbursed under TACIS. The former targeted infrastructural projects, economic reforms, and democratisation, while the latter focused primarily on nuclear safety and the environment.[104] The EU had clearly transformed into policy narratives its assumptions

---

[101] She had written a dissertation on the crushing of Czechoslovak reform socialism in 1968. Her deputy, Strobe Talbott, was also a specialist on the region, having translated Nikita Khrushchev's memoirs into English in his university days.

[102] Resler, 'United States', 147.

[103] Commission paper titled 'Europe and the Challenge of Enlargement', quoted in George Georgiadis, '"Differentiation by Design" as a Determinant of Convergence: Comparing Early EU Selection Policies in Central and Eastern Europe and the Commonwealth of Independent States', *Southeast European and Black Sea Studies*, 8/4 (2008), 409.

[104] Ibid., 417–18.

about the differentiated nature of the various Easts' proximity to the West: Central Europeans were champions of economic transition and Western convergence, while most of the states that used to be part of the Soviet Union or Yugoslavia became, first and foremost, objects of geopolitical securitisation. The EU's subsequent Neighbourhood Policy (2004) continued this strategy of locking entire regions of the continent, beyond Central Europe, into perpetual Europeanisation with a seemingly ever-receding promise of joining the European project.[105]

Eastern Europe, a Buffer against Islam?

Alongside Iberia, parts of Eastern Europe had the longest engagement with the Islamic world on the continent. Through the presence of domestic Muslim minorities and entanglement with the Ottoman Empire for over half a millennium, the idea of Islam – whether in times of conflict or of coexistence – played a formative role in the construction of a specifically Eastern European identity. In the last decades of state socialism Islam was once again mobilised in the cause of self-definition, increasingly constructed as a distinctive civilisational zone against which a new idea of Europe could be defined. Such visions that distanced and bordered civilisations from one another had, to some extent, been tempered under state socialism until the 1970s. For much of the postwar period historic Muslim communities both in South-Eastern Europe and Central Asia, despite periods of discrimination, had experienced at least a partial integration into European socialist projects in the context of global decolonisation.[106] In both Soviet Central Asia and Yugoslavia, for instance, not only had mosques proliferated, but high-ranking Communist Muslims were seen as vital instruments for the propagation of anti-imperialist or non-aligned internationalism.[107] Political elites from Muslim communities were

---

[105] Christoffer Kølvraa, 'Limits of Attraction: The EU's Eastern Border and the European Neighbourhood Policy', *East European Politics and Societies and Cultures*, 31/1 (2017), 22.

[106] Ben Fowkes and Bülent Gökay, 'Unholy Alliance: Muslims and Communists – An Introduction', *Journal of Communist Studies and Transition Politics*, 25/1 (2009), 1–31.

[107] Brenna Miller, 'The Islamic Religious Community in Socialist Yugoslavia's International Relations Program (1950s and 1960s)' (paper presented at '(Re)thinking Yugoslav Internationalism', University of Graz, 30 September – 1 October 2016). On not dismissing the revolutionary potential of Islamic movements, see Michael Kemper, 'Propaganda for the East, Scholarship for the West. Soviet Strategies at the 1960 International Congress of Orientalists in Moscow', in Artemy Kalinovsky and Martin Kemper (eds.), *Reassessing Orientalism: Interlocking Orientologies during the Cold War* (Routledge, 2015). On the relationship between NAM and Yugoslav Orientalist debates, see Armina Omerika, 'Competing National Orientalisms: The Cases of Belgrade and Sarajevo', also in Kalinovsky and Kemper, 169.

employed as political intermediaries – often as diplomats – with North African and Middle Eastern states – and cultural and religious leaders used to sell the idea that the Communist project protected minorities and their religious beliefs.[108] Political imaginaries such as Mediterranean Europe – which we explored above – appeared to offer the possibility of collective identities that stretched across Christian/Islamic divides, linking countries rather by a sense of peripherality, or a common socialist politics in ways that helped to undercut cultural or religious differences.

Amongst certain Eastern European countries – especially within an anti-imperialist older generation – this attempt to reconcile Arab/Islamic socialism with European socialist culture continued well into the 1980s, drawing on long histories of cultural exchange. Whilst new nationalist elites within both Communist parties and opposition forces began to use these images to revive an earlier anti-Islamism for their own political purposes, they promoted more moderate visions of difference that still offered the possibility of cross-cultural understanding, particularly as they sought to create popular support for the growing economic links with the Middle East. The Green Book – the foundational text of Gaddafi's anti-imperialist Islamic Revolution in Libya – was widely distributed in Hungarian schools.[109] In 1987 the Hungarian government agreed to build the country's first Islamic Centre, with the assistance of the Islamic World League, at the site of the Buda Mausoleum of Gul Baba, one of the Turkish leaders who had captured the city in 1541.[110] This rapprochement with Islam even included new ultra-religious regimes: photographic exhibitions of post-revolutionary life in Iran organised in Budapest's cultural centres aimed to play down the idea of cultural difference.[111] In many smaller Eastern European countries the Iranian Revolution had to be taken seriously as they needed Iranian oil – the Soviets wished to decrease bloc countries' reliance on their supplies, and the winter of 1979 had seen energy shortages across the

---

[108] Brenna Miller, 'Faith and Nation: Politicians, Intellectuals, and the Official Recognition of a Muslim Nation in Tito's Yugoslavia', in Theodora Dragostinova and Yana Hashamova (eds.), *Beyond Mosque, Church, and State: Alternative Narratives of the Nation in the Balkans* (Budapest: Central European University Press, 2016), 129–50. Some resented this instrumentalisation of their religion in the name of internationalism.

[109] Eszter Szakács, 'Propaganda, Mon Amour. An Arab "World" through Hungarian Publications (1957–1989)', *Mezosfera*, May 2018, http://mezosfera.org/propaganda-mon-amour/.

[110] 'Miklos Interviewed about Islamic Center', *Magyar Hírlap*, 16 September 1987, 3. Three decades later the Orbán-led FIDESZ government, seeking to forge links with the illiberal Erdogan, would use this site to promote a Hungarian-Turkish (illiberal) reconciliation.

[111] 'Iráni Kiállítás', *Népszabadság*, 24 September 1985.

region. In time much Iranian oil would also be (illegally) re-exported for hard currency to pay off debts. Many Eastern European Communist regimes highlighted the purportedly anti-imperialist nature of the changes in Iran after 1979 as they justified closer economic links: in the five years after the Islamic Revolution, GDR trade with Iran increased tenfold and Hungary's fourfold.[112] In Czechoslovakia, one propagandist argued that although Khomeini had said the Koran would be the highest law, there would be no 'return to the Middle Ages', as the Western press implied: there was a modern interpretation of the Koran and the Iranian Revolution would be 'unique' in the Moslem world.[113] The Albanian leader Enver Hoxha initially had high hopes for the Iranian Revolution's long-term anti-imperialist and Marxist potential.[114] As Hungarian industry sought its share of the post-revolutionary economic spoils in the pharmaceutical and agricultural sectors,[115] so these countries promoted histories of European–Near East cultural exchange. In a manner that prefigured Viktor Orbán's later recovery of Hungary's Turkic and Asian roots in the 2010s, the Hungarian Communist vice-president Rezső Trautmann argued in the early 1980s that the European continent owed its culture to Iran, a reference to tenth-century scholars whose discoveries had laid the foundations for subsequent European scientific progress.[116]

This demonstration of brotherhood with the Muslim world was driven less and less by a sense of solidarity: rather, it was a cultural politics that emerged from a realpolitik driven by the need for energy resources.[117] This was soon complemented by increasingly prominent representations of the Islamic world as a distinct region defined by its radicalised, unstable, and often violent politics. The idea of such civilisation units, defined by distinct cultural or religious practice, became increasingly

---

[112] 'Iran-Iraq Seeking to expand Barter Trade with Eastern Europe', B-wire, 20 September 1984, HU OSA 300–40–1–Box 717. The Iranians valued Eastern Europe's willingness to engage in barter trade (against OPEC rules), as hard currency reserves had been drained by the war with Iraq.

[113] Václav Jilek, *Radio Hvezda*, 15 February 1979.

[114] Piro Rexhepi, 'Unmapping Islam in Eastern Europe. Periodisation and Muslim Subjectivities in the Balkans', in Irene Kacandes and Yuliya Komska (eds.), *Eastern Europe Unmapped. Beyond Borders and Peripheries* (Oxford: Berghahn, 2017), 63.

[115] On support, see HU OSA 300-50-1-Box 556; HU OSA 300-40-1-Box 717; RFE Hungarian Report, 'Hungarian Tender Wins UNIDO Contract to Build Iranian Factory'.

[116] HU OSA 300–40–1–Box 860.

[117] On the shift from solidarity to economics with the Middle East, see Szakács, 'Propaganda, Mon Amour'. On the ambivalence towards the 'excessive radicalism' of the Palestinian Liberation Organisation, see György Makai, *Today's Questions: What Are Arabs Fighting For?* (Budapest: Kossuth, 1971).

current among rising political elites. Earlier ideas of an anti-colonial or less bordered Europe were now challenged by a new politics in which bloc countries revived their role as civilisational buffer on behalf of the whole of Europe. We should note that it was not only Europe where this was happening. To the east ideas of a culturally distinct Islamic world or Turkic civilisation were also being constructed.[118]

In the wake of the Iranian Islamic Revolution of 1979 the question of whether European socialism and Islam were compatible came to the fore. The Soviets feared that their version of secular Islamic modernity that they had tried to export over the previous decades was now in crisis.[119] Islamists were also a threat as the new bearers of revolutionary desire in the Global South that now had little to do with socialism. The Romanian minister of foreign affairs, Ştefan Andrei, longtime chair of the International Section of the Party's Central Committee, recounted a discussion with Ceauşescu about the revolutionary potential of Islam: 'We believed that Islam was the only religion that is spreading across the world, especially in Africa and Asia. In particular, it attracts poor populations in developing countries. Communism does not fascinate these people [anymore]'.[120] Although Ceauşescu had had the political acumen to send Romanian Muslims to Tehran to facilitate economic cooperation immediately after the Islamic Revolution, he nevertheless responded to the growing politicisation of conservative traditionalist Islam with alacrity.[121] Reviving a centuries-long discourse of uncivilised threats from a violent East now retooled for the Helsinki era's focus on 'European security', in 1980 he argued that unless the Afghan conflict was resolved soon, 'there is the danger that ... Islamic countries, which are quite numerous, will intensify sending forces either directly or in the guise of volunteers. These are a billion strong and they are fanatics.

---

[118] During the 1980s, politicians and intellectuals (excluding the left) in Turkey promoted an Islamic-centred projection of their civilisation, which subsequently brought them closer to other Arab and Muslim countries in what was termed the Turkish-Islamic synthesis: Bogdan C. Iacob, 'Together but Apart: Balkan Historians, the Global South, and UNESCO's *History of Humanity* 1978–1989', *East Central Europe*, 45/2–3 (2018), 270. During the 1990s, this trend was softened as Turkish elites balanced it with affirmations of Europeanness designed for Turkey's possible accession to the EU.

[119] Timothy Nunan, 'Getting Reacquainted with the "Muslims of the USSR": Staging Soviet Islam in Turkey and Iran, 1978–1982', *Ab Imperio*, 4 (2011), 133–71, 138.

[120] *I se spunea Machiavelli. Ştefan Andrei în dialog cu Lavinia Betea* (Bucureşti: Adevărul, 2011), 211.

[121] Zachary T. Irwin, 'The Fate of Islam in the Balkans: A Comparison of Four State Policies', in Pedro Ramet (ed.), *Religion and Nationalism in Soviet and East European Politics* (Durham, NC: Duke University Press, 1989), 403.

A long term war can be the result'.[122] As a result of the Afghan intervention, ideas of an 'Islamic world' were also defined in opposition to European Communism. The Saudi-based Muslim World League presented the Soviets as just another type of European colonialists, and the league called for a cultural boycott of Soviet Central Asia.[123]

Political Islam was increasingly considered antithetical to the Bloc's socialist development. With this rise of radical pan-Islamism, the codification of corporal punishment, and the consolidation of radical regimes, the Eastern European press came to represent the Islamic world – particularly Libya, Egypt, and Iran – as violent, culturally intolerant, premodern areas, untempered in their politics, and reverting to a religious fundamentalism that the socialist pan-Arabism of the decolonisation era had promised to end. This was contrasted with a Europe that had, since the Second World War, learnt how to build a peaceful moderate modernity despite ideological difference.[124] Europe increasingly became a zone of distinct cultural and political practice to which Communists allied themselves. The threat of Islamist terrorism in Eastern Europe, particularly after attacks on Syrian students in Bucharest in 1985, reinforced this attitude.[125] There was much greater vigilance on the part of security services, who cooperated across the Eastern Bloc in order to deal with this growing danger.[126] Communist authorities sometimes saw in Arab students potentially threatening bearers of this ideology within their own societies: Moscow feared the influence of the Muslim Brotherhood on Egyptian students,[127] whilst the Securitate sensed a 'predisposition to terrorism' amongst Arab students in Romania, and turned fellow students into informers in order to gauge the influence of Al

---

[122] 'Stenograma şedinţei Comitetului Politic Executiv al CC al PCR, 12.01.1980', ANIC, Fond CC al PCR, Cancelarie, 2/1980, 5.

[123] 'Muslim League Official Urges Tashkent Conference Boycott', Rabat MAP, 7 August 1980. 'Muslim League Leader Condemns USSR "Occupation"', Riyadh SPA, 27 December 1981.

[124] 'A testi fenyítések újbóli bevezetése az iszlám országokban', *Módszertani Füzetek*, March 1986, 62.

[125] Andra-Octavia Drăghiciu, 'Between "Totalitarianism" and "Terrorism." An Introductory Study about the "Arab" Students in the Romanian Socialist Republic (1974–1989)', *Caietele CNSAS*, 4/1–2 (2013), 329.

[126] Jordan Baev, 'Infiltration of Non-European Terrorist Groups in Europe and Antiterrorist Responses in Western and Eastern Europe (1969–1991)', in Siddik Ekici (ed.), *Counterterrorism in Diverse Communities* (Amsterdam: IOS Press, 2011), 60.

[127] Constantin Katsakioris, 'Soviet Lessons for Arab Modernisation: Soviet Educational Aid to Arab Countries after 1956', *Journal of Modern European History*, 8/1 (2010), 102–3.

Fatah, the Muslim Brotherhood, and the Palestinian Liberation Front.[128]

The 1980s saw a revival of the idea of the struggle for a *Christian* Europe that had been rent asunder by a barbarous anti-religious Communism. This is normally understood to be in the main a dissident discourse: '1989' was a revolt against secularism led in part by churches – whether Protestants in the GDR, Catholics in Poland, or the reformed church in Romania – whose role confirmed the end of Communism as the rebirth of a pan-Christian continent.[129] As recent research has shown, this stark dichotomy is too simple: national Communists were already turning to national religious traditions, and the Polish Pope John Paul II, who enjoyed widespread popularity across Catholic countries of Eastern Europe, targeted his message of a new European community of Christian nations as much at receptive reforming Communists as at society at large.[130] When we view this Christian revivalism through the lens of Islam, then the involvement of both Communist regimes and oppositional groups becomes readily apparent in certain bloc countries. In Poland the regime in fact provided space for anti-Iranian protest. Fearing the destabilising effects of the radical Islamic Revolution, it supported the rights of the US diplomats taken hostage in the Tehran embassy in 1979–1981 and allowed church congregations to pray for them – although they clamped down on a live demonstration in support of the captives in front of the Iranian Mission in Warsaw.[131] This helped provide space for the opposition: the leading dissident Jacek Kuroń organised letters of support, as did intellectuals in Łódź. In Hungary, Communists too were defining Europe as a Christian buffer against Islam. In June 1987, when the Spanish king Juan Carlos visited Budapest, he was taken to the sites at which Spanish troops had fought in the liberation of Buda from the Turks in 1686 – invoking a notion of a shared past for two of Europe's borderland nations that had each taken on their responsibility for defending the continent's Christian heritage against Islam.[132] Years before 1989, both Communists and oppositions were aligning with the defence of a Christian Europe.

---

[128] Drăghiciu, 'Between "Totalitarianism"', 328.

[129] Gerhard Rein (ed.), *Die Protestantische Revolution, 1987–1990* (Berlin: Wichern-Verlag, 1990).

[130] On the links between reforming Communists and new narratives of Europe as a Christian family of nations, see Agata Šústová Drelová, 'A Cultural History of Catholic Nationalism in Slovakia, 1985–1993' (PhD thesis, University of Exeter, 2015), esp. chap. 2.

[131] 'Eastern European people Support US in Iran Crisis', RFE Report, no date, HU OSA 300–50–1; BBC World Service, Tim Sebastian Report, 14 December 1979.

[132] 'Használjuk ki az együttmüködés tartalékait', *Magyar Hírlap*, 1 July 1987.

The threat of a newly empowered and transnational radical Islam meant that socialist elites in countries with substantial Muslim minorities – notably in Bulgaria, Yugoslavia, and the Soviet Union – increasingly feared the cultural and religious distinctiveness of such communities. This was particularly the case in Bulgaria, where the regime's national Communism had placed a revival of the country's ancient European heritage at the forefront of its cultural politics since the early 1980s. Here Muslims had experienced intermittent persecution since the turn to a more national Communism in 1956, but in the 1980s this discrimination rapidly intensified. Against the background of a purported failure to integrate, the state targeted its Turkish community in the south of the country and in 1984–85, in the so-called Revival Process, attempted to force a change of their names to Bulgarian forms, deprive them of the right to be educated in their own language, and convert them forcibly to Eastern Orthodoxy. This would lead to the forced migration of 350,000 Turks in 1989.

This emerging self-identity was seemingly endangered by Muslim communities that by their very presence on Bulgarian soil subverted such Europeanness and represented a security risk in the context of renewed political tensions and a growing fear of transnational Islam: by the late 1980s, Bulgarian Muslims took part in Koran reading competitions in Iran, studying to be imams in Tashkent, Damascus, and Cairo, and set up student exchanges with Afghanistan.[133] In response, some Bulgarian historians argued that these communities were, historically, not really Islamic at all; rather they were originally Bulgarian people who had been subject to forced Islamisation by the Ottoman Empire.[134] This policy was itself a reaction to newly assertive cultural-historical policies emanating from Istanbul, which asserted that the Ottoman Empire had been a 'commonwealth of nations', one that had acculturated Christian people into a superior imperial culture. This narrative was tied to Turkish scholars' claims that the Ottoman Empire was a civilisational project on a par with the European ones. Therefore, this Bulgarian state policy was simply reversing a historical process of cultural colonialisation. It re-Europeanised Bulgarians who had supposedly been 'civilisationally led astray' under the so-called Turkish yoke.[135]

---

[133] 'Islamic Religion in Bulgaria', Sofia BTA, 20 June 1989.

[134] It should be noted that significant parts of the cultural elite refused to endorse this policy in their research and writings.

[135] Antonina Zhelyazkova, 'Islamisation in the Balkans as a Historiographical Problem: The Southeast-European Perspective', in Fikret Adanir and Suraiya Faroqhi (eds.), *The Ottomans and the Balkans. A Discussion of Historiography* (Leiden: Brill, 2002), 223–66; and Nikolay Antov, 'Emergence and Historical Development of Muslim Communities

Yugoslavia did not experience the stark nationalising Communism of Bulgaria until the 1980s, and in many ways had sought to provide support for its Islamic minority. The Central Committee of the League of Communists of Bosnia and Herzegovina had in fact recognised Bosnian Muslims as an 'ethnically separate group' in 1968, and the 1971 constitution had offered the community national – but secular – status.[136] Yet from the late 1970s Communist authorities became concerned about the rise of an Islamic identity in Bosnia, supported by the growth of institutions of Muslim solidarity, rising support for Islamic education, and translations of foreign Islamic texts – which was being placed above Yugoslav or class affiliations.[137] Yugoslav federal elites began to criticise religious leaders, such as the Mufti of Belgrade, who were starting to use more explicitly religious modes of address and encourage everyday Islamic practices such as the banning of pork. Serb intellectuals with nationalist leanings also feared that Bosnian Moslems were looking to 'Arabic-Turkish-Persian culture', which was providing a new foundation for a new cultural, religious, and non-socialist heritage.[138] The growth of pan-Islamic networks was also a threat: the institutions of Yugoslavia's four-million-strong Muslim communities were increasingly financed from Saudi Arabia, Libya, and Iraq, and over three thousand Yugoslav Muslims made their pilgrimage to Mecca each year.[139] Students from Yugoslavia travelled to Islamist universities in much larger numbers, bringing Salafism back to the region.[140]

The important role that Bosnian Muslims had played in their non-aligned outreach to North Africa and the Middle East was used against them, as they were returning in increasing numbers as pan-Islamists after

---

in the Ottoman Balkans: Historical and Historiographical Remarks', in Dragostinova and Hashamova, *Beyond Mosque, Church, and State*, 42–56.

[136] Brenna Miller, 'Between Faith and Nation: Defining Bosnian Muslims in Tito's Yugoslavia, 1945–1980' (PhD thesis, Ohio State University, 2018). See also Iva Lucic, *In Namen der Nation: Der politische Aufwertungsprozess der Muslime im sozialistichen Jugoslawien 1956–1971* (Wiesbaden: Harrassowitz Verlag, 2018).

[137] Slobodan Stankovic, 'Croatian Muslims Urged to Resist Pan-Islamism', *Vjesnik*, 29 January 1981, 12; Harun Karčić, 'Globalisation and Islam in Bosnia: Foreign Influences and Their Effects', *Totalitarian Movements and Political Religions*, 11/2 (2010), 151–66.

[138] Dr. Vojislav Seselj, *Danas*, 22 August 1982, 26–27.

[139] Slobodan Stanković, 'Islamic Revival in Yugoslavia Hailed', RAD Background Report/ 67 (Yugoslavia), 26 April 1984. The Second International Islamic Congress in January 1984 demanded an Islamic way of life everywhere and was seen as a threat to Yugoslav unity.

[140] Nathalie Clayer, 'The Muslims in Southeastern Europe: From Ottoman Subjects to European Citizens', Roberto Tottoli (ed.), *Routledge Handbook of Islam in the West* (London: Routledge 2015), 80.

studying the Koran in the Middle East or working in the oil fields in Libya.[141] In the widely publicised 1983 'Sarajevo Process', Alija Izetbegović, who became the first president of an independent Republic of Bosnia and Herzegovina in 1992, was placed on trial for 'hostile propaganda' and sentenced to fourteen years in prison.[142] At the trial, aligning himself with the new pan-Islamism, he rejected those opportunities that had been offered to Yugoslav Muslims in the national non-aligned project, seeing them as betokening the instrumentalisation of his religion.[143] At the same time Serbian nationalists were promoting the idea of civilisational clashes in the context of new struggles over the future of Yugoslavia, which would provide the basis for Milošević's anti-Muslim policies in the Bosnian War.[144] The political scientist Miroljub Jevtić opined in *Komunist* in 1986 that, unlike Catholic, Orthodox, or Buddhist culture, Islam was incompatible with Communism. The World Muslim Congress and World Muslim League were profoundly anti-Communist, he claimed: they saw the Soviet Union as a colonial power 'enslaving 50 million Muslims', and had established a centre for anti-Communist propaganda to distribute to Muslims from Communist countries.[145]

Against this background, the notion of socialist Eastern Europe as a Christian continent's bulwark against Islam was being revived. Just as in Bulgaria in the 1980s, Serbian and Croatian nationalists under Communism tried to place Islam beyond their borders. They claimed that Yugoslavia's Muslims – most particularly in Bosnia – were superficially Islamicised Slavs rather than a genuine ethnic group in its own right.[146] Such arguments would later also be used to provide ideological justification for annexing Herzegovina to Croatia in the

---

[141] HU OSA 300–10–3 Box 44. RFE-RL Background Report, Slobodan Stankovic, 'Yugoslav Communists against Khomeini's Ideology of Pan-Islamism'. These links would survive after 1989, in Iran's involvement in the Bosnian War.

[142] For the manifesto, see Alija Izetbegović, *The Islamic Declaration: A Programme for the Islamisation of Muslims and the Muslim Peoples* (Sarajevo, 1990), http://profkaminskis readings.yolasite.com/resources/Alija%20Izetbegovic-%20The%20Islamic-Declaration %20%281990%29.pdf.

[143] Izetbegović claimed he was influenced by the Iranian revolution's call to pan-Islamism and had discovered the Muslim Brotherhood through Sudanese, Lebanese, Saudi, Kuwaiti, and Egyptian students studying in Yugoslavia. Sarajevo District Court, Court Decision No.K212/83, 1983, Archives of the Federation of Bosnia and Herzegovina, File 61, quoted in Rexhepi, 'Unmapping Islam'.

[144] Omerika, 'Competing National Orientalisms', 164.

[145] *Komunist* (Belgrade), 12 September 1986.

[146] Jasna Dragović-Soso, *'Saviours of the Nation': Serbia's Intellectual Opposition and the Revival of Nationalism* (Montreal: McGill-Queen's University Press, 2003), chap. 2; Bojan Aleksov, 'Perceptions of Islamisation in the Serbian National Discourse', *Southeast European and Black Sea Studies*, 5/1 (2005), 117–18.

early 1990s.[147] At the same time nationalist elites were successful at instrumentalising the fear of their own Muslims – however inauthentic their community might be – being radicalised by pan-Islamism. One interview project in Yugoslavia in 1989 noted the rise of the fear of pan-Islamism and its relationship to a revived discourse of European belonging and defence: 'Albanian Muslims and Bosnian Muslims are in this together ... They have big families in order to swamp Serbia and Yugoslavia with Muslims, and turn Yugoslavia into a Muslim republic. They want to see a Khomeini in charge here. But Belgrade is not their final goal. They will continue to advance until they have taken Vienna, Berlin, Paris, London – all the great cities of Europe. Unless they are – stopped'.[148] It has been argued that Islam quickly replaced the Communist threat as Europe's constitutive other after 1989.[149] Yet Communist elites had themselves already been constructing the idea of a civilisationally bordered Europe against Islam in the last decades of the Cold War. This was not new of course: Eastern Europe had a long tradition of engagement with Islam, and nationalist movements, particularly in South-Eastern Europe, had defined themselves in their struggle against the 'Ottoman yoke' since the nineteenth century.[150]

In the early years of socialism, which coincided with decolonisation and anti-imperialism across the Arab World, such antagonisms were tempered but never fully went away. In the last decades of the Cold War, these religious oppositions returned with a vengeance. Older pre-1945 notions of a struggle against an Ottoman legacy that had been a fundamental source of backwardness and had wrenched part of Eastern Europe from Western-style modernisation returned.[151] Eastern Europeans' experience in de-Ottomanisation before the socialist period was re-purposed in order to situate the region in a continental struggle to defend Europeanness from a resurgent Islamic offensive. Such ideas

---

[147] Nada Kisić-Kolanović, 'Envisioning the "Other" East: Bosnia-Herzegovina, Muslims, and Modernisation in the Ustaša State', in Rory Yeomans (ed.), *The Utopia of Terror: Life and Death in Wartime Croatia* (Rochester, NY: University of Rochester Press, 2015), 188–216.

[148] Sabrina Ramet, 'Islam in Yugoslavia Today', *Religion, State and Society*, 18/3 (1990), 226–35.

[149] Michael Wintle, 'Islam as Europe's "Other" in the Long Term: Some Discontinuities', *History*, 101/344 (2016), 42–61.

[150] Roumen Daskalov and Alexander Vezenkov, 'Introduction', in Daskalov and Vezenkov (eds.), *Entangled Histories of the Balkans Volume Three: Shared Pasts, Disputed Legacies* (Leiden: Brill, 2015), 6–7.

[151] Alexander Vezenkov and Tchavdar Marinov, 'The Concept of National Revival in Balkan Historiographies', in Daskalov and Vezenkov, *Entangled Histories of the Balkans*, 406–62.

would go on to play a major role in Eastern European realignments and identities in the post–Cold War period.

After 1989: 'Fortress Europe'?

In a speech given at a conference on the evolving African–Eastern European relationship in May 1990, the German historian of Africa Franz Nuscheler noted that the changes in Eastern Europe had led to a turning away from the Global South across the continent. As the Berlin Wall was coming down, he noted, 'mental and physical walls towards the "Third World" are being built up ... the German-German and Eurocentric self-indulgent introspection displaced news from the "Third World" in the media'.[152] The capacity of Europeans to 'render solidarity' to global racial issues was ending, he argued: 'Europe is in ... the "Third World" is out'.[153] In his hometown of Duisburg, he noted, an 'either-or' attitude was developing: 'Third World' groups were now 'fighting an uphill battle', particularly amongst churches, which now preferred to reach out to the East. Hospitals too were seeking new partner institutions in Poland and GDR rather than in the 'Global South'.[154] Poland, Hungary, and Romania were being recognised as 'developing countries' by the OECD, and inward investment was diverted from Africa to them.

New racialised 'regimes of mobility' also became apparent: North-South borders were erected just as hopes for freer East-West travel opened up across Europe. The number of African students in the Soviet Union had peaked in 1989;[155] hundreds of thousands of migrant workers from Vietnam, Mozambique, Cuba, and elsewhere worked across the GDR, Hungary, and Czechoslovakia. Many Africans, Asians, and Latin Americans had come to study, train, and work across the socialist bloc from the 1960s: whilst non-Western foreigners were on occasion targeted for racial abuse, they just as often were seen as evidence of a new proud global role for socialist countries. By the 1980s, as popular support for the Eastern Bloc project in the 'Third World' declined, acts of open

---

[152] Speech by Prof. Dr F. Nuscheler, at a seminar: 'What Are the Possibilities for Africa Resulting from the Process of Political and Economic Change in Germany and Eastern Europe?' (7–8 May 1990, Bonn), 13.

[153] Ibid., 12.   [154] Ibid., 14–15.

[155] In 1989, there were 23,809 African students in the Soviet Union, only 17,819 in the United States and 7,975 in the United Kingdom. Katsakioris, 'Soviet Lessons'. By 1989 the number of foreign students in Romania, many of whom came from Arab countries, was approaching the previous peak of 1982: Valentin Maier, 'Foreign Students Enrolled in the Medicine and Pharmacy Higher Education in Romania (1975–1989)', *Clujul Medical*, 89/2 (2016), 307–12.

discrimination and violence against students and labour migrants from the South increased markedly.[156] Akin to debates on 'welfare queens' in the United States, the question of whether labour migrants, alongside indigenous minorities such as the Roma, should have access to the generosity of the socialist welfare state became a key concern.[157] This led to a rising tolerance for racializing discourses that targeted immigrant communities.[158]

Many labour migrants were sent home in 1989, as they became the representatives of a now demonised socialist internationalism.[159] As many as eighty thousand contract workers from Vietnam, Angola, Mozambique, and Cuba were forced to leave during the collapse of the GDR, lest they settle in a re-united Germany. Attacks against Roma and Vietnamese exponentially increased in Czechoslovakia, leading to a public condemnation from Charta 77 and the Czechoslovak Helsinki Committee, who declared that such violence contradicted the ideals of their democratic revolution.[160] The situation worsened to the extent that the Czechoslovak government decided to expel thirty-seven thousand Vietnamese labour migrants.[161] Tens of thousands of Chinese migrants had been able to come to Eastern Europe, thanks to visa-free travel to Hungary, especially after the suppression of the Tiananmen Square protests. From 1992 their entry was barred.[162] Racially distinctive others seemed to have little place in post-socialist imaginations of Europeanness. This development was not lost on the

[156] On African students' experiences of racism in the late socialist period, see Grazia Scarfò Ghellab and Kamal Mellakh (eds.), *Étudier à l'Est. Expériences de diplômés africains* (Paris: Karthala, 2015), 117. Sahadeo, 'Black Snouts Go Home'; Maxim Matusevich, 'Probing the Limits of Internationalism: African Students Confront Soviet Ritual', *Anthropology of East Europe Review*, 27/2 (Fall 2009), 28–30; Maxim Matusevich, 'Testing the Limits of Soviet Internationalism. African Students in the Soviet Union', in Philip E. Muehlenbeck (ed.), *Race, Ethnicity and the Cold War* (Nashville: Vanderbilt University Press, 2012), 155–59.

[157] James Mark and Bálint Tolmár, 'From Heroes Square to the Textile Factory: Encountering Cuba in Socialist Hungary 1959–1990' (forthcoming).

[158] 'The Vietnamese Communities in Central and Eastern Europe', special issue of *Central and Eastern European Migration Review*, 4/1 (June 2015), www.ceemr.uw.edu.pl/sites/default/files/CEEMR_Vol_4_No_1.pdf. See also www.publicseminar.org/2016/03/the-communist-roots-of-anti-refugee-sentiment/#.VvGEc2SyOkp.

[159] Mark and Tolmár, 'From Heroes Square'.

[160] Intervention of Mr. Slaby (Czechoslovakia), UN General Assembly, 44th Session, Third Committee, 9th Meeting, 16 October 1989, A/C.3/44/SR.9, 16; David Crowe, *A History of the Gypsies of Eastern Europe and Russia* (New York: St. Martin's Griffin, 1994), 64–65.

[161] Liz Fekete and Frances Webber, *Inside Racist Europe* (London: Institute of Race Relations, 1994), 42.

[162] Pál Nyíri, 'Chinese Migration to Eastern Europe', *International Migration*, 41/3 (2003), 243.

Global South: one of Algeria's representatives at the UN complained in 1990 that 'racism and xenophobia against migrant workers was in the increase in many host countries, particularly in Europe'.[163] Jan Martenson, the UN under-secretary general for human rights, offered a sobering view of the global wave of democratisation symbolised by '1989': though it had brought about 'amazing changes', it had also triggered 'a resurgence of racial hatred, intolerance, and discrimination'.[164]

Whilst the labour-based North-South mobilities of late socialism were closed down, 1989 marked a shift in the expectations for East to West European population movements. Such possibilities did not start in 1989 – and they had their limits afterwards. Without the comfort of the Iron Curtain, Western governments increased restrictions, fearing large-scale immigration from an economically collapsing East. Between the end of Communist rule in the GDR and the unification of Germany, a growing concern in Bonn was how to avoid a mass migration of East Germans to the West and how to halt the flow of migrants from Poland and beyond.[165] Despite the dissident imaginary that celebrated the fall of the Wall and the possibility of East-West freedom of movement, '1989' in fact led to a less liberal travel environment for some Eastern Europeans.[166] The former oppositionist Bronisław Geremek cautioned in 1990 that a new Berlin Wall was possible if Eastern Europeans were not accepted by the West and allowed to join the European fold.[167] The Romanian dissident Mircea Dinescu expressed similar anxieties, stating that the European common home could prove 'a caravan that we, those from the East, will hopelessly chase' with no chance to board.[168] Western Europe would have to invest speedily in the East so as to enable former socialist states to become 'organic partners in the new cooperation system' lest Eastern European citizens flood across to the West: 'If capital does not quickly flow East, then labor will move West. No new wall can stop them. Millions of people will try to cross to the other side of the "golden curtain" if their countries are to be left out of the

---

[163] Intervention of Miss Boumaiza (Algeria), UN General Assembly, 45th Session, Third Committee, Eighth Meeting, 16 October 1990, A/C.3/45/SR.8, 3.

[164] Intervention of Mr. Martenson, UN General Assembly, 45th Session, Third Committee, Third Meeting, 8 October 1990, A/C.3/45/SR.3, 15.

[165] Keck-Szajbel, 'Politics of Travel', 47–48.   [166] Ibid., 50.

[167] 'Solidarity's Geremek Fears New "Berlin Wall"', *Neues Deutschland*, 20 September 1990, FBIS-EEU-90-183, 24–25.

[168] Mircea Dinescu, 'În căutarea timpului pierdut', *Agora*, 3/2 (1990), 172.

co-prosperity area'.[169] Nevertheless, the naturalisation of the idea of East-West mobility was most evident in the seeming absurdity of its initial denial – and confidence in its inevitable establishment.

In 1992, the signing of the Maastricht Treaty – which founded the EU and deepened integration – enabled much easier migration across Western European countries, whilst also tightening border controls and visa regulations for those outside, including citizens of countries from the former socialist world. The largest single East-West European movement of the 1990s was in fact enacted under the rubric of refugee policy rather than personal or labour migration. Around six hundred thousand Bosnians – over 80 per cent of them Muslims – resettled across Europe between 1992 and 1995, following their violent displacement in the war that accompanied the breakup of Yugoslavia.[170] Unlike later panics over Islamic mobility, these refugees in fact prompted scant objection. Many countries had experienced Yugoslav labour migration in the 1970s and 1980s; Bosnian Muslims were secular and seen as fellow Europeans, on 'Europe's doorstep', and in need of rescue as violence escalated quickly. Moreover, there was a widespread view in the early stages of the conflict that it would be over in a few months, that it was just a temporary crisis, and that all of the refugees would be able to return. Yet this was a brief moment of 'openness' produced by a sense of emergency: it was in the early 1990s that fears of uncontrolled migration began to shape political discourse in European countries previously little concerned about these issues.[171] As the numbers of immigrants, and with them the number of violent and in several cases lethal attacks on foreigners, rose dramatically in reunited Germany, the Bundestag considerably tightened the rules for asylum seekers in December 1992.

Many Eastern European countries, while expecting freer mobility for their citizens to the West, simultaneously increased control of migration from outside Europe. From the early 1990s Central European states were being used as a buffer against refugees and migrants coming into Western Europe.[172] Such countries needed to demonstrate their effective

---

[169] Mihály Simai, 'The Emerging New Market Economies and the Evolving New Democracies in Central and Eastern Europe', in Üner Kirdar (ed.), *Change: Threat or Opportunity to Human Progress? Volume 1: Political Change* (New York: United Nations, 1992), 236.

[170] Marko Valenta and Sabrina Ramet (eds.), *The Bosnian Diaspora: Integration in Transnational Communities* (Farnham: Ashgate, 2011), 4.

[171] Sarah Collinson, 'Visa Requirements, Carrier Sanctions, "Safe Third Countries" and "Readmission": The Development of an Asylum "Buffer Zone" in Europe', *Transactions of the Institute of British Geographers*, 21/1 (1996), 76–90.

[172] Fekete and Webber, *Inside Racist Europe*, 33.

role as a territorial cordon for non-European immigration to enable freer mobility with the West. Their governments – following cultural patterns established under late socialism – acquiesced with little difficulty in the emergence of a new post–Cold War system for the control of migration from the East and South, in which mobility was increasingly perceived as an issue of security, rather than one based on humanitarian concerns.[173] Hungary refused the entry of one million people through its territory in 1992; Germany effectively outsourced its Eastern border work to Poland around the same time.[174] The idea of 'safe passage' for refugees created a chain reaction of border controls going back eastwards.[175] This won popular support: in a 1993 poll, 73 per cent of Poles disapproved of such economic migration from outside Europe.[176] In the late 1990s the EU began to prioritise 'Third World' countries as buffer zones and to tie development aid to repatriation of unwanted migrants in the West.[177] Eastern European states aligned themselves with this outsourcing and strengthening of European bordering work: in Poland the 1997 Aliens Act introduced a more stringent procedure for the granting of refugee status. It introduced two terms, 'safe country of origin' and 'safe third country', ensuring that it was possible to eliminate applicants coming from countries defined as less dangerous.[178] Yet whilst the part of Eastern Europe that had acceded to the EU came to see itself more as a strict border policeman in relation to the Middle East and Africa, it nevertheless did not act along these lines everywhere, taking on the mission as a bridgehead for Western values, bringing a 'civilizing mission' further to the East into the civilisationally less distinct post-Soviet space.[179]

[173] Jef Huysmans, The European Union and the Securitisation of Migration', *Journal of Common Market Studies*, 38/5 (December 2000), esp. 763–64.

[174] Milada Anna Vachudova, 'Eastern Europe as Gatekeeper: The Immigration and Asylum Policies of an Enlarging European Union', in Peter Andreas and Timothy Snyder (eds.), *The Wall around the West: State Borders and Immigration Controls in North America and Europe* (Lanham, MD: Rowman & Littlefield, 2000); Fekete and Webber, *Inside Racist Europe*, chap. 2.

[175] Vachudova, 'Eastern Europe as Gatekeeper', 161.

[176] Sławomir Łodziński, 'Foreigners in Poland. Selected Issues in Poland's Migrational Policy 1989–1998', *Polish Sociological Review*, 126 (1999), 311.

[177] Liz Fekete, *A Suitable Enemy: Racism, Migration and Islamophobia in Europe* (London: Pluto Books, 2009), 24–25.

[178] Łodziński, 'Foreigners in Poland', 307.

[179] On the central role of Poland here, see Steffi Marung, 'Moving Borders and Competing Civilizing Missions. Germany, Poland, and Ukraine in the Context of the EU's Eastern Enlargement', in Marc Silberman, Karen E. Till, and Janet Ward Walls, (eds.), *Borders, Boundaries Spatial and Cultural Practices in Europe* (New York: Berghahn, 2012); *Die wandernde Grenze. Die EU, Polen und der globale Wandel politischer Räume, 1990–2010* (Göttingen: Vandenhoeck & Ruprecht, 2013).

Protecting the continent from Islam – a feature of nationalist politics of the region even under late socialism – continued to have significant political valence after 1989. Market economies brought greater banking interests from the Middle East. The persecution of Muslims in Bosnia during the Yugoslav Wars attracted Islamic relief organisations across South-Eastern Europe. These developments would prompt new anxieties about the influence of radical Islam, most notably around the claim of Saudi organisations that Bulgarian, Albanian, or Bosnian Muslims needed to rediscover rejected local traditions, which, according to the representatives of these bodies, had been corrupted by totalitarian Communism.[180] Believers in South-Eastern Europe felt pressure to present themselves as moderate (and sometimes secular) European Muslims unconnected to radical global currents. The idea of an anti-Islamic defence of Europe found its most extreme form in Serbian nationalism, where such rhetoric was used to justify genocide committed against Muslim communities during the wars of the Yugoslav dissolution.[181] Once Islam came to replace Communism as the West's hegemonic Other – particularly after the 11 September attacks on the United States in 2001 – the EU came to see policing of its borders as an issue of securitisation against a potentially threatening cultural-religious force.[182] Eastern European elites who were looking to Westernise readily accepted their region's status as an important civilisational and religious buffer to provide security for the continent as a whole.

This defence of a culturally and religiously defined Europe became central again in 2015 in the context of the migrant and refugee crises– the arrival of over one million people in Europe from countries such as Syria, Iraq, Afghanistan, and Eritrea. The language used to justify such bordered European mobilities had seldom been explicitly presented in racial terms in the first fifteen years after the end of state socialism. Rather, such mobility had been viewed as the natural expression of a seemingly obvious cultural or civilisational unity enabled by the end of the Cold War that, with the promise of EU accession, was taken for granted as a natural end point by their

---

[180] Kristen Ghodsee, *Muslim Lives in Eastern Europe: Gender, Ethnicity, and the Transformation of Islam in Postsocialist Bulgaria* (Princeton, NJ: Princeton University Press, 2010), 136–39.
[181] Rexhepi, 'Unmapping Islam', 65.
[182] Piro Rexhepi, 'Mainstreaming Islamophobia: The Politics of European Enlargement and the Balkan Crime-Terror Nexus', *East European Quarterly*, 43/2–3 (2015), 189–214.

Western European allies, too. Such work was an (often unspoken) assertion of their identity as white Europeans who defended the continent's borders and thus proved their worthiness in the European project. This is not to say that there were not racializing discourses from the West that targeted the East: some intellectuals in Western Europe argued that Easterners had been 'orientalised' by their experience of an Asiatic socialism. In Western Germany, for instance, East Germanness was sometimes associated with blackness – 'east Elbe Negroes', who needed to be colonised and improved, as one journalist from *Die Welt* sarcastically put it.[183] Nevertheless, such attitudes never erased the strong expectation that Easterners would be accepted as fully European.

Debates about race and mobility returned to the mainstream in the 2010s after both unwelcoming receptions for Eastern European immigrants in Western Europe, and the EU insistence on refugee resettlement in the East too. Populist elites turned away from what they saw as a liberal Western project that promoted multiculturalism and opened up their countries' borders. The migration crisis after 2015 brought back the motif of the East on the ramparts of fortress Europe. Such discourses readily lent themselves to the proposition that the region was the only one capable of defending a 'white Europe'. As the EU and Western capitals called for the settlement of such refugees, East European populists invoked the region's historical experience of defending the continent from the dictates of Western liberalism in a manner that echoed the claims of Communist elites during the last decade of the Cold War.

Conclusion

Volkmar Köhler, the parliamentary state secretary at the Ministry for Economic Cooperation in Bonn, saw 1989 as the final death knell of the idea of 'Eurafrica'.[184] This idea had been first considered in the interwar period and then became popular in the era of high decolonisation: that Western Europe, under the conditions of a divided continent, would look south, bringing their former African colonies into a

---

[183] Anke Pinkert, '"Postcolonial Legacies": The Rhetoric of Race in the East/West German National Identity Debate of the Late 1990s', *Journal of the Midwest Modern Language Association*, 35/2 (2002), 13–32. See the controversy over Luise Endlich's *NeuLand: ganz einfache Geschichten* (Frankfurt am Main: Fischer-Taschenbuch, 2000).

[184] Volkmar Köhler, 'European House or Third World: Are We Forgetting Development Policy?', in Üner Kirdar (ed.), *Change: Threat or Opportunity for Human Progress*, vol. 1 (New York: United Nations Publications, 1992), 212–13.

close economic and political partnership with the emerging European Community. Likewise, in the face of Cold War divisions and economic exclusion, Eastern Europe too had looked to the Global South for new political economic and cultural partnerships. From the early 1970s, however, the relaxation of Cold War tensions enabled growing linkages between East and West. Continental identity was now increasingly based on profitable East-West economic integration and the re-establishment of a notion of a bordered European civilisation.

Many histories of late twentieth-century Europeanisation give a Western-centric account of the expansion of the European project. Yet visions of this new Europe were produced as much in the East as in the West during the last decades of the Cold War. The Helsinki Process – which laid the foundations for East-West détente – had been initiated in the East; reforming Communists, alongside dissidents, were active participants in the redefinition, and later the rejection of earlier cultural linkages with the Global South. A decade before the Fall, Balkan states started abandoning visions of the continent that organically connected it across the Mediterranean, whilst states now defined as Central European defined themselves through, variously, a revalorised whiteness, on the idea of a separate European civilisational canon, or on distancing themselves from Bolshevism and Islam in the East and Africa to the South. These more firmly bordered imaginaries – whether 'Helsinki Europe' or, later, 'Central Europe' or the 'Common European Home' became immensely influential not only within the region but also in the shaping of a broader Western imaginary, confirming this shift from North-South to East-West links that had begun in the 1970s.

These late Cold War conceptions of Europe – and the role of Eastern Europe in it – have also informed debates on the civilisational, economic, or cultural frontiers of the region after 1989. They accelerated this East-West reorientation and North-South bordering, as those excluded from the new Europe – most notably from Africa – soon observed. But the idea of the region as a civilisational and racialised buffer against the East, which was already there in the 1970s and 1980s, was readily incorporated into the EC/EU-led re-bordering of the continent after the western half of the continent lost the comfort of the protection from the East that the Iron Curtain had readily supplied. The idea of Central Europe, with its exclusionary core based around anti-Russianness and anti-Islam, became a key driver of a broader re-imagining of Europe and was picked up by Western elites in their quest to remake the continent with a border moved further eastwards. Former Communist states came to play roles as both EU proselytizers and gatekeepers of the Eastern boundaries of a post–Cold War Europe. Yet, many Eastern European actors never fully accepted that the West was really able to protect their bordered Europe. Through the 1990s and 2000s the claim survived that only the East – through its historical suffering – knew the depth of the commitment necessary to defend their idea of Europe. These beliefs gained new traction during the migrant crisis from 2015.

4.   Self-Determination

Many participants in the revolutions of 1989 saw the collapse of state socialism as the culmination of a struggle for national self-determination. Forms of anti-Soviet anti-imperialism, sometimes connected to an earlier struggle against the Russian Empire, had long been common amongst dissidents in the region. As early as 1982 Adam Michnik had written about the 'goal of self-determination' from his prison cell in Warsaw's Białołęka internment camp: 'Reflection on analogous endeavours from some eighty years ago can create an intellectual bridge between the era of our ancestors and now, when it is our turn to strive for independence'.[1] Western anti-Communist conservatives concurred: as the Cold War heated up again, US president Ronald Reagan in 1983 labelled the Soviet Union an 'evil empire'. It was now a widespread view that the Soviet state was a continuation of an imperial Russia that, due to its consolidation by the Bolsheviks, had been spared the fate of the Ottoman, Habsburg, and German empires after the First World War.

With glasnost and the crumbling of Communist rule in the late 1980s, notions of living through the final stages of a long-term process of European imperial disintegration entered the political mainstream.[2] This re-assertion of national self-determinations drove anti-Soviet and pro-democracy movements in Eastern Europe, but it also led to the dissolution of large multinational polities: the Soviet Union, Czechoslovakia, and Yugoslavia all disappeared in the years after 1989 and were replaced by more ethnically homogeneous nation-states.[3] Eurasia underwent a similarly dramatic reconfiguration of its political space as large parts of Africa and South East Asia had a couple of decades earlier.

---

[1] Michal Kopeček, 'Human Rights Facing a National Past. Dissident "Civic Patriotism" and the Return of History in East Central Europe, 1968–1989', *Geschichte und Gesellschaft* 38/4 (2012), 573–602, 573.

[2] The internationally renowned Polish travel writer Ryszard Kapuściński called his 1993 volume about the Soviet Union *Imperium* (Warszawa: Czytelnik, 1993).

[3] Rogers Brubaker, *Nationalism Reframed: Nationhood and the National Question in the New Europe* (Cambridge: Cambridge University Press, 2010), 3.

In the years after 1989, Eastern European intellectuals drew on post-colonial theory to make sense of their experience of Soviet oppression and subsequent liberation between 1989 and 1991, particularly in Poland and the Baltic states.[4] Unlike in the West and South, Eastern postcolonialism was neither leftist nor internationalist. Conservatives invoked the language of anti-imperialism to demonise Communists and portray them as Soviet collaborators, who had survived the 1989 transitions.[5] This right-wing postcolonialism was more commonly a confirmation of nationalist victim stories. There was virtually no interest in connecting Soviet and Eastern European experiences to global twentieth-century histories of imperial disintegration in the Global South – approaches that were still associated with an earlier socialist-era internationalism or an unwelcome Western leftism.[6] Eastern European histories of self-determination tended to be enclosed within more limited boundaries; in these, the end of state socialism and the achievement of liberation were seen as the final culmination of a series of national – or sometimes regional – struggles.

The history of 'self-determination', however, was a global one from the beginning, and Eastern Europe and the Soviet Union were part of it. One of the most powerful and contentious political principles of the twentieth century, 'self-determination', linked the region in multiple ways with states and movements around the world. The origins of the concept lay in the post–First World War era. US president Woodrow Wilson had bestowed a name upon a principle with roots in Enlightenment and Marxist thought in his Fourteen Points speech on 8 January 1918, which would eventually help establish the self-determining nation-state as the dominant political form worldwide.[7] Afro-Asian liberation movements looked to Eastern Europe in the interwar period for inspiration on how to

---

[4] Violeta Kelertas (ed.), *Baltic Postcolonialism* (Amsterdam: Rodopi, 2006); Steven Tötösy De Zepetnek, 'Configurations of Postcoloniality and National Identity: Inbetween Peripherality and Narratives of Change', *The Comparatist* 23 (May 1999), 89. On the region as 'doubly postcolonial' – the object of both Soviet imperialism and Western 'peripheralizing capitalism' – see Dorota Kołodziejczyk and Cristina Şandru, 'Introduction: On Colonialism, Communism and East-Central Europe – Some Reflections', *Journal of Postcolonial Writing*, 48/2 (2012), 115.

[5] Adam Kola, 'A Prehistory of Postcolonialism in Socialist Poland', in James Mark, Artemy Kalinovsky, and Steffi Marung (eds.), *Alternative Globalizations: Eastern Europe and the Postcolonial World* (Bloomington: Indiana University Press, 2020).

[6] Diana T. Kudaibergenova, 'The Use and Abuse of Postcolonial Discourses in Post-independent Kazakhstan', *Europe-Asia Studies*, 68/5 (2016), 917–35.

[7] Uriel Abulof, 'We the Peoples? The Strange Demise of Self-Determination', *European Journal of International Relations*, 22/3 (2015), 536–65; Erez Manela, *The Wilsonian Moment: Self-Determination and the Origins of Anticolonial Nationalism* (Oxford: Oxford University Press, 2007).

overcome imperial rule. Indeed, the very term 'decolonisation' was first used in English in the 1930s to connect the already-achieved independence of states in Eastern Europe with an argument about the inevitability of the liberation of nations in Africa and Asia in the near future.[8] However, Wilson's idealism notwithstanding, the United States did not challenge the legitimacy of Western European colonial rule after the First World War. The more radical Leninist concept of self-determination did, and it offered an alternative that continued to have salience in the aftermath of the Second World War.[9]

Through the twentieth century Eastern Europe drew on both the liberal and the leftist conceptions of 'self-determination'. The enthusiasm for the Wilsonian idea in the interwar period was followed by its suppression by German and Soviet troops from the late 1930s, but also a brief period of independent statehood for some nations, under Nazi control, during the Second World War. The era of high decolonisation and self-determination in the Global South from the 1950s brought debates about self-determination back to Eastern Europe once again. The 1960s represented the first moment in history when nations dominated globally; this helped revive an anti-colonial language in the bloc, too. Self-determination could as readily serve as an anti-Soviet discourse deployed by critics of Communist regimes as be used by those same regimes to express support for movements battling Western European Empires.[10] Whether in Yugoslavia or in Czechoslovakia, domestic calls in the late 1960s for the greater autonomy of nations within federations – changes that would eventually lead to the breakup of these countries after the collapse of state socialism – echoed this widespread appeal to the nation as driver of change too.

In the more ethnically homogeneous nation-states of the former Soviet Bloc, the Europeanisation and liberalisation of national elites facilitated the taming of radicals and the branding of anti-imperialist violence as uncivilised or non-European. But ethnically and religiously intermixed federations like the Soviet Union and Yugoslavia were undermined by notions of 'self-determination' in which ethnically defined nationalisms

---

[8] Stuart Ward, 'The European Provenance of Decolonization', *Past and Present* 230/1 (2016), 227–60.

[9] Richard Falk, 'Self-Determination under International Law: The Coherence of Doctrine versus the Incoherence of Experience', in Wolfgang F. Danspeckgruber (ed.), *The Self-Determination of Peoples: Community, Nation, and State in an Interdependent World* (Boulder, CO: Lynne Rienner, 2002), 41.

[10] James Mark and Quinn Slobodian, 'Eastern Europe in the Global History of Decolonisation', in Martin Thomas and Andrew Thompson (eds.), *The Oxford Handbook of the Ends of Empire* (Oxford: Oxford University Press, 2018), 361-2.

filled the ideological void left by the fall of socialism. Memories of the violent struggle for statehood during the Second World War, sometimes further legitimised by the sight of the violent struggle against Western European Empires from the 1950s to the 1970s, were part of the explanation for interethnic violence where more radical notions of 'self-determination' unleashed tensions that a fragmenting authoritarian order could not suppress. The ensuing violence in Yugoslavia and parts of the southern Soviet periphery meant that the end of socialism was not so much a democratic awakening as an era of disintegration, chaos, and decline.

The collapse of state socialism was an important moment in both regional and wider histories of self-determination. It was not only anti-Communists, for example, Poland and the Baltic states who viewed the end of one-party rule and the withdrawal of Soviet troops as their 'national liberation'. At least for a short time, nationalist Russian elites at the centre of the Soviet system saw the collapse of 'their Empire' as both their own liberation from the burdens of rule and the chance to construct a more ethnically homogenous nation. '1989' also represented a wider re-invigoration of the principle of self-determination; the independence of Eastern European nations within federations – as Yugoslavia, Czechoslovakia, and the Soviet Union collapsed – inspired other movements in Western Europe and beyond.

The Rise of Anti-colonial Self-Determination

Claims to the right to self-determination and sovereignty were not just a question for the opposition under Communism. Socialist states in Eastern Europe had themselves long mobilised this rhetoric at home and abroad, and it would later be appropriated by dissidents who fought for freedom from Soviet 'occupation' or from 'unjust federations'. During much of the Cold War, the Soviet Union played a leading role in establishing the principle and then the right to self-determination in international law.[11] By defending African and Asian countries' sovereignty, the Eastern Bloc and Yugoslavia declared their solidarity with the decolonising world. Yet many Third World leaders suspected that the Soviet Union was simply using the rhetoric of self-determination for

---

[11] Bill Bowring, 'Positivism versus Self-Determination: The Contradictions of Soviet International Law', in Susan Marks (ed.), *International Law on the Left: Re-examining Marxist Legacies* (Cambridge: Cambridge University Press, 2008), 133–68. See also Frederic L. Kirgis, 'Degrees of Self-Determination in the United Nations Era', *American Journal of International Law*, 88/2 (1994), 304–10.

geopolitical advantage, embracing its form but hollowing out its substance.[12] The idea that the Soviet Union was not an enabler of self-determination but rather its destroyer gathered pace in the 1950s. Delegates at the 1955 Bandung conference, which brought together representatives of the nascent Non-Aligned Movement (NAM), drew parallels between Western colonialism and Soviet oppression in Eastern Europe. One of the most vocal was the Ceylonese prime minister John Kotelawala, who emphasised that there was little that distinguished the Soviet from the British imperialists: 'If we are united in our opposition to colonialism, should it not be our duty openly to declare our opposition to Soviet colonialism as much as to Western imperialism?'[13]

The use of the Soviet Army to suppress the 1956 Hungarian Uprising reinforced such sentiments. In 1957 a Chinese delegate from Taiwan made the case at the UN for the necessity of a broader definition of anti-colonialism, demanding that the world pay attention to 'new-style colonies' such as the Soviet ones, where 'foreign troops [had] suppressed the aspirations of the peoples'.[14] Such views would serve as one of the main ideological building blocks of the NAM, which initially defined itself against such Soviet control. Indeed, it was representatives of some of the future non-aligned states who exposed Soviet hypocrisy regarding this question during the debates at the UN on the 1960 Declaration on the Granting of Independence to Colonial Countries and Peoples. They managed to push through the Afro-Asian draft – against the narrower Soviet one – ensuring that 'colonialism in all its forms and manifestations' was condemned.[15]

The acceleration of decolonisation in the late 1950s lent further credence to a language of liberation that exiles from Eastern Europe turned against the Soviet Union. In this vein the journalist Heinz Frentzel, a refugee from East Germany, paraphrased the British prime minister Harold Macmillan, who had declared that the United Kingdom would not stand in the way of the independence movements moving across Africa. 'The great wind of change that is blowing through the southern

---

[12] Mark R. Beissinger, 'Self-Determination as a Technology of Imperialism: The Soviet and Russian Experiences', *Ethnopolitics*, 14/5 (2015), 479–87, 482.

[13] Luwam Dirar, 'Rethinking the Concept of Colonialism in Bandung and Its African Union Aftermath', in Luis Eslava, Michael Fakhri, and Vasuki Nesiah (eds.), *Bandung, Global History, and International Law: Critical Pasts and Pending Futures* (Cambridge: Cambridge University Press, 2017), 358.

[14] Roland Burke, *Decolonisation and the Evolution of International Human Rights* (Philadelphia: University of Pennsylvania Press, 2010), 47.

[15] 'Declaration on the Granting of Independence to Colonial Countries and Peoples, Adopted by General Assembly Resolution 1514 (XV) of 14 December 1960', www.un.org/en/decolonisation/declaration.shtml.

half of the world has swept away the last remnants of colonialism and has let loose the right to self-determination', Frentzel declared in a radio speech from West Berlin briefly after the erection of the Wall, 'it will not be possible for the people of our continent to remain under Communist dominance and withhold these rights in the long run'.[16] In the 1950s and 1960s, members of the anti-Communist Assembly of Captive European Nations displayed posters and billboards close to the UN Headquarters in New York that drew attention to the ongoing 'Soviet imperialism'.[17] Numerous dissident exile groups living in Western Europe, the United States, Canada, or Australia couched their demands for secession and democratisation in the language of self-determination. Slovenian dissident émigré communities launched the journal *Slovenian Freedom* in Munich in 1964.[18] Combining their lawful political activism with violence and terrorism, Croatian far-right militants urged the UN to endorse the creation of a 'free and independent Croatian state' against 'Yugoslavian violence and imperialism'.[19] Croatian nationalists in Australia complained in a pamphlet about the pusillanimous conduct of their exiled political leaders while 'in the African Continent, actual freedom has been achieved by practically all the negro tribes whose structure has hardly any national characteristics'.[20]

The vocabulary of anti-imperialist self-determination was also commonly used by minorities within multiethnic socialist federations in Eastern Europe. The language of socialist internationalism pervaded the political rhetoric of Armenians who struggled for more national sovereignty in the Soviet Union.[21] Within Yugoslavia, Albanian nationalists in Kosovo persistently used the language of anti-imperialism and self-determination to challenge what they perceived as their status as

---

[16] Nicholas J. Schlosser, *Cold War on the Airwaves. The Radio Propaganda War against East Germany* (Urbana: University of Illinois Press, 2015), 151.

[17] Martin Nekola, 'The Assembly of Captive European Nations: A Transnational Organisation and a Tool of Anti-Communist Propaganda', in Luc van Dongen, Stephanie Roulin, and Giles Scott-Smith (eds.), *Transnational Anti-Communism and the Cold War: Agents, Activities, and Networks* (Basingstoke: Palgrave Macmillan, 2014), 103.

[18] Jure Ramšak, '"Neodvisna Slovenija do konca leta 1964!" Kritika položaja Slovenije v Jugoslaviji in zgodnje ideje o samostojnosti', in Mitja Ferenc, Jurij Hadalin, and Blaž Babič (eds.), *Osamosvojitev 1991: država in demokracija na Slovenskem v zgodovinskih razsežnostih* (Ljubljana: Univerza v Ljubljani, 2011), 197-207.

[19] 'Freedom for Croatia', n.d., United Nations Archive, Secretary-General Kurt Waldheim (1972–1981), S-0904-0051-04.

[20] Mate Nikola Tokić, 'The End of "Historical-Ideological Bedazzlement": Cold War Politics and Émigré Croatian Separatist Violence, 1950–1980', *Social Science History*, 36/3 (2012), 421–45.

[21] Maike Lehmann, 'Apricot Socialism: The National Past, the Soviet Project, and the Imagining of Community in Late Soviet Armenia', *Slavic Review*, 74/1 (2015), 9–31.

second-class citizens. In November 1968, hundreds of protesters took to the streets of the Kosovan regional capital Prishtina, chanting slogans of 'self-determination', 'We want a republic', 'We want a university', and 'Down with colonialism'.[22] Calls for national self-determination were intertwined with demands for social and economic prosperity in 'an economy free of colonial characteristics'.[23]

Socialist states continued supporting the right to self-determination on the international stage nonetheless. The 1960 UN Declaration was a source on inspiration that many eastern bloc regimes thought they could harness to their own ends. The Polish legal scholar Franciszek Przetacznik later described the declaration as 'one of the most important living documents that has come out of the United Nations in the entire course of its life', because it affirmed that 'all peoples have the right to self-determination, by virtue of which they should determine their political status and freely pursue their economic, social and cultural advancement'.[24] In its wake, states from the Eastern Bloc and the Global South were at the forefront of the global promotion of rights – particularly to combat racial and religious discrimination and threats to national sovereignty. They supported the 1965 International Convention on the Elimination of All Forms of Racial Discrimination as well as the two International Covenants, on Economic, Social and Cultural Rights and on Civil and Political Rights, which both included the same wording: 'All peoples have the right of self-determination. By virtue of that right they freely determine their political status and freely pursue their economic, social and cultural development'. GDR experts then used this principle as a legal justification for the existence of two separate German states.[25]

Yet by establishing such rights as an accepted part of international law – a strategy that was designed to shame Western capitalism and colonialism – socialist states created norms that later disrupted their

---

[22] Mary Motes, *Kosova, Kosovo: Prelude to War 1966–1999* (Homestead, FL: Redline, 1999), 103–4; Sabrina P. Ramet, *Nationalism and Federalism in Yugoslavia, 1962–1991* (Bloomington: Indiana University Press, 1992), 296; Dennison I. Rusinow, *Yugoslavia: Oblique Insights and Observations* (Pittsburgh: University of Pittsburgh Press, 2008), 267.

[23] Gazmend Zajmi, 'Kosova's Constitutional Position in the Former Yugoslavia', in Ger Duijzings, Dušan Janjić, and Shkëlzen Maliqi (eds.), *Kosovo-Kosova: Confrontation or Coexistence* (Nijmegen: Peace Research Centre and Political Cultural Centre, 1996), 95–103.

[24] Franciszek Przetacznik, 'The Socialist Concept of Protection of Human Rights', *Social Research*, 38/2 (1971), 337–61, 344.

[25] Eberhard Poppe, 'Self-Determination of the Germans and the Enforcement of Human Rights in the German Democratic Republic', in *Self-Determination and Human Rights: 1968 Results in the Two German States* (Berlin: Committee for the Protection of Human Rights, 1968), 11-30.

own authority. The Soviet Union was often attacked for using different legal and political standards at home and abroad – 'Guinea Bissau could become independent but Latvia could not'.[26] In the context of détente, human rights and national sovereignty were included in the 1975 Helsinki Accords and the Conference for Security and Cooperation in Europe (CSCE) and became important pillars of East-West security.[27] The Eastern Bloc states had initially viewed the Helsinki agreement as a victory: it had ensured Western recognition for their previously contested borders and thus guaranteed their right to sovereignty in a politically divided Europe. The accords' protection of other types of rights – notably to free assembly and expression – according to the norms of the UN covenants did not initially appear to threaten states that claimed to be the true bearers of these ideals. Over the next decade, however, dissident groups, and the transnational networks of human rights advocates that supported them, made effective appeals to these legal frameworks to carve out spaces that became crucial for the expression of opposition, and developed arguments about sovereignty directed against the Soviet Union.[28] By the 1980s ideas about self-determination in Eastern Europe had become much less internationalist and focussed on an anti-Communist struggle of the nation against Soviet 'colonial domination' instead.

This transformation was also an unintended consequence of the adoption of nationalist politics within the official Communist sphere that had been designed to shore up party rule. Eastern European states had turned inward to build more nationalistic cultures at home, which were increasingly stripped of the internationalism that had bound together Eastern European nationalisms and those of the Global South in the 1950s and 1960s. The 2,050th anniversary of the first Dacian state in Romania and the 1,300th anniversary of Bulgarian statehood in 1981 captured this shift. Partially inspired by the 1971 celebration of the 2,500th anniversary of the founding of the Persian Empire in Persepolis, these festivities were underpinned by a strong sense of cultural nationalism. Such a turn to a nationalist Communism was often instigated from within parts of the

[26] Lauri Mälksoo, 'The Soviet Approach to the Right of Peoples to Self-Determination: Russia's Farewell to *jus publicum europaeum*', *Journal of the History of International Law*, 19/2 (2017), 200–218.

[27] Steven L. B. Jensen, *The Making of International Human Rights: The 1960s, Decolonization, and the Reconstruction of Global Values* (New York: Cambridge University Press, 2016), 217–18, 235.

[28] Ned Richardson-Little, 'Dictatorship and Dissent: Human Rights in East Germany in the 1970s', in Jan Eckel and Samuel Moyn (eds.), *The Breakthrough: Human Rights in the 1970s* (Philadelphia: University of Pennsylvania Press, 2013), 49–67.

nomenklatura: in Bulgaria, it was Lydmila Zhivkova, daughter of party boss Todor Zhivkov, who most actively promoted an ethnically defined Bulgarian national culture at home and abroad.[29]

The official nationalism of late socialism was often based on a revival of imperialist national identities. Polish Communists looked backed to the Polish-Lithuanian Commonwealth; elites in Belgrade celebrated the medieval Kingdom of Serbia; and GDR leaders embraced the Prussian past. The reconstruction of Nikolaiviertel, a quarter in central Berlin with panel buildings designed to appear medieval, as well as the re-erection of a statue of Frederick the Great on Unter den Linden in 1980 were emblematic of this rediscovery of the national past. In the Soviet Union Slavic nationalism became ever more acceptable and encompassed large parts of the Soviet Communist Party and especially the Army and the secret services. A radical nationalist and anti-Semitic organisation, Pamyat ('Memory'), grew from groups with an interest in Slavic folk history and culture.[30] The opposition's use of a much less internationalist, nationally focussed argument about sovereignty was thus not an alternative language but part of a nationalist turn that included the regimes that they sought to combat.

The language of 'empire' and 'national liberation' was also revived in the West in the early 1980s. West German diplomats now framed the reunification of the German nation as an act of 'free self-determination' – a formulation that would be later invoked when it eventually occurred: 'It was the declared political aim of the Federal Republic of Germany to work for a state of peace in Europe in which the German nation could regain its unity through free self-determination'.[31] Reagan's description of the Soviet Union as an 'evil empire' brought together

---

[29] There were two other initiatives: the exhibition of ancient Thracian gold, which opened in Vienna in March 1975, and the movement known as the Banner of Peace, a UNESCO-sponsored international assembly of children (1979). See Irina Gigova, 'The Feeble Charm of National(ist) Communism: Intellectuals and Cultural Politics in Zhivkov's Bulgaria', in Theodora Dragostinova and Yana Hashamova (eds.), *Beyond Mosque, Church, and State: Alternative Narratives of the Nation in the Balkans* (Budapest: Central European University Press, 2016), 151–77; Ivanka Nedeva Atanasova, 'Lyudmila Zhivkova and the Paradox of Ideology and Identity in Communist Bulgaria', *East European Politics and Societies*, 18/2 (2004), 278–315; Ivan Elenkov, '"The Second Golden Age": Historicisation of Official Culture in the Context of Bulgaria's 1,300th Anniversary Celebrations (1976–1981)', *Critique & Humanism*, 23/1 (2007), 31–58.

[30] Nikolaj Mitrochin, *Die 'Russische Partei'. Die Bewegung der russischen Nationalisten in der UdSSR 1953–1985* (Stuttgart: Ibidem-Verlag, 2014).

[31] United Nations General Assembly, 38th Session, Third Committee, 11th Meeting, 11 October 1985, A/C.3/40/SR.11, 4. The General Assembly allocates to the Third Committee agenda items relating to a range of social, humanitarian affairs and human rights issues.

anti-totalitarianism and anti-colonialism and was immediately popular with conservatives around the world. The issue of the Baltic states, whose annexation by the Soviet Union had never been recognised by the West, came to the fore again. US diplomats at the UN, even more than their more cautious West European colleagues, insisted that the right to self-determination implied 'periodic and genuine elections' and that therefore many people not living under formal colonial rule were only nominally independent because they lived under Communist regimes, like Latvia, Estonia, and Lithuania.[32] To many elites in the newly independent countries, to national liberation movements in Namibia, South Africa, or Palestine, and to the regimes in the socialist bloc, self-determination was still primarily about winning freedom from colonial domination and having the right to choose their own economic, social, and political system and their own path of development.[33] In the West, however, dominant voices now asserted that authentic self-determination was only truly exercised in states that had liberal multiparty democracy.

Opposition movements on the western fringes of the Eastern Bloc from the 1960s had identified with leftist anti-colonial internationalism, which had provided them with a new language for dissent that was tolerated as a form of official discourse, yet also contained within it the possibility of meaningful critique.[34] Both anti-Communists who wished to cast off Soviet control and leftist critics of Communist authoritarianism had taken inspiration from the postwar decolonisation of Africa and Asia and its socialist liberation movements. Left-wing Polish '68ers' such as Jacek Kuroń or Karol Modzelewski, who would later play leading roles in Solidarność, decried the bureaucratic turn in Polish socialism by invoking the commonalities with their radical compatriots in the South. The popular books about Third World despots and their court hangers-on by the journalist and travel writer Ryszard Kapuściński were often read as allegories of the Polish Communist regime.[35] At the same time, conservative exile groups and oppositionists hoped that the collapse of European empires in Africa would prove to be a prelude to the end for

---

[32] United Nations General Assembly, 38th Session, Third Committee, 11th Meeting, 15 October 1985, A/C.3/40/SR.11, 7–8.

[33] United Nations General Assembly, 38th Session, Third Committee, 8th Meeting, 11 October 1985, A/C.3/40/SR.8,13.

[34] On this, see also James Mark and Péter Apor, 'Socialism Goes Global: Decolonization and the Making of a New Culture of Internationalism in Socialist Hungary 1956–1989', *Journal of Modern History* 87/4 (2015), 870–78.

[35] Readers found equivalences between Polish first secretary Edward Gierek and Ethiopian emperor Haile Selassie in Ryszard Kapuściński, *Emperor: Downfall of an Autocrat* (London: Quartet Books, 1983). Kapuściński denied that he intended such a connection.

Soviet control of Eastern Europe.[36] Many such radicals were connected culturally across the Iron Curtain, despite limited mobility, and spoke an anti-colonial language shared by a younger European generation to express dissatisfaction with the political status quo – be it the colonisation of Europe by both the United States and Soviet Union or the excessive centralisation of political power.[37]

Against the backdrop of regime attempts to draw on nationalism, and the flourishing in the 1980s of a Western conservative anti-imperialism, various Eastern European oppositional movements revived the anti-colonial language of the 1960s. Yet they had stripped it of an earlier leftist Third Worldist internationalism – an ideology they now associated only with the hollowed-out rhetoric of their own socialist systems. Many older dissidents across the European socialist world soon forgot that their initial experiences of opposition had been moulded through such global connections and forged through their support of fellow anti-imperialists such as Cuban revolutionaries and the Vietcong. For the most part they now understood themselves to belong solely to national or regional struggles for sovereignty and democratisation against an Eastern authoritarianism. Mainstream voices in Solidarność, for instance, presented the trade union movement as part of a national tradition of resistance against centuries-old invaders, whether Prussian, Austrian, German, Russian, or Soviet. An increasingly assertive nationalism, devoid of socialist anti-imperialist rhetoric, and often explicitly anti-socialist, predominated in oppositional circles. For the most part African and Asian postcolonial movements' attempts to shake off Western dominance had little purchase on oppositional movements in the Eastern Bloc, who sought to escape their region's own subservient geopolitical status through a 'return to Europe'.

The Eastern European had for the most part distanced themselves from the global left. The internationally most widely supported oppositional movement of the 1980s – South Africa's anti-apartheid movement – had few supporters in the region. Solidarność could not bring itself to lend wholehearted support to the struggle of the African National Congress (ANC), despite the commonalities evident in their struggles as trade unions fighting for workers' rights. This hesitation on the part of Solidarność was both because the later decolonisation struggles in Africa were supported by the Warsaw Communist elite, and because right-wing Poles in exile in South Africa gave generously to support Solidarność's

---

[36] Mark and Slobodian, 'Eastern Europe', 361.
[37] James Mark and Anna von der Goltz, 'Encounters', in Robert Gildea, James Mark, and Anette Warring (eds.), *Europe's 1968: Voices of Revolt* (Oxford: Oxford University Press, 2013), 131–63.

anti-Communism. Moreover, the leadership of the ANC had defended the crackdown against the Polish opposition – as it had done for 1956 in Hungary and 1968 in Czechoslovakia – and then compared Solidarność with the Pinochet forces in Chile that aimed to overthrow Allende.[38] This rift had consequences after 1989: after the fall of the Berlin Wall, Hungary, Poland, and Czechoslovakia immediately renewed trade and diplomatic links with South Africa, which was still under white minority rule, breaching international sanctions, outraging the ANC and causing concern at the UN.[39] When confronted with his refusal to criticise the oppression suffered by the black majority in South Africa, the Hungarian conservative prime minister Joszef Antall only replied, 'When did the international community ever protest at the treatment of the Hungarian minority in Transylvania?'[40] All that remained after 1989 of decolonisation-era anti-imperialist solidarity in mainstream Eastern European politics were stories of national victimhood.

Yet new forms of anti-imperialist internationalism did emerge, based around a common anti-Soviet struggle. The Soviet invasion of Afghanistan in 1979 was of particular importance in reviving the idea of the Soviet Union as an empire, not only among anti-Communists but also within the Western left, across the Global South, and for a wider range of oppositional movements in Eastern Europe.[41] The Soviet Union claimed their presence was justified as they were there not only to protect the internal politics of Afghanistan from Western interference and imperialism, but also to ensure the future of a vision of socialist developmentalism and postcolonial territorial sovereignty.[42] Among its Eastern European allies, the Soviet Union received the most support from Bulgaria, Czechoslovakia, and East Germany, who laid the blame for Afghanistan's predicament at the door of the United States, its 'imperialist allies', and China – Radio East Berlin warned of a danger that Afghanistan might become a new Chile and a bastion of imperialism right on the Soviet frontier.[43] Fidel Castro, head of the NAM at the time, refused to criticise the Soviet support for the Afghan Communist

---

[38] Kim Christiaens and Idesbald Goddeeris, 'Competing Solidarities? Solidarność and the Global South during the 1980s', in Mark et al., *Alternative Globalizations*.

[39] Paul Hockenos and Jane Hunter, 'Pretoria Gold', *Australian Left Review*, 1/121 (1990), 16–19.

[40] Ibid., 18.

[41] 'Resolution ES-6/2', Security Council Report, www.securitycouncilreport.org/atf/cf/% 7B65BFCF9B-6D27-4E9C-8CD3-CF6E4FF96FF9%7D/Afgh%20ARESES6%202.pdf.

[42] Timothy Nunan, *Humanitarian Invasion: Global Development in Cold War Afghanistan* (Cambridge: Cambridge University Press, 2016).

[43] William F. Robinson, 'Afghanistan: The East European Reaction', *Radio Free Europe (Research)*, 22 January 1980, 3.

government. Yet condemnation was widespread. West European Communists were highly critical of the military intervention,[44] and Yugoslavia took the opportunity to re-assert NAM leadership and condemn the invasion of a fellow non-aligned state, the second in the course of that same year (Kampuchea being the first): 'bitterly critical'[45] of the Soviet intervention, Yugoslav officials stuck to the official non-aligned line, denouncing a 'witches' brew of great-power rivalry' and the great powers' unwillingness to establish relations of equality with small and medium-sized states.[46] A UN resolution that appealed to all states 'to respect the sovereignty, territorial integrity, political independence and non-aligned character of Afghanistan' was passed thanks to the initiative of non-aligned nations.

Afghan resistance against the Soviet Army also contributed to the strengthening of a new form of anti-imperialist internationalism in parts of the European socialist world. In Poland, the underground press constantly depicted the war in Afghanistan as a fight against a common enemy. The story of a 'Polish Mujahedeen' was used to mobilise opposition at home: the Polish exile activist Lech Zondek had left Australia to fight in Afghanistan and had been killed there in 1985.[47] The year after, an independent Poland-Afghanistan society was founded, and Radosław Sikorski, at the time a student in Oxford and later Polish foreign minister (2007–14), travelled to Afghanistan to report on the struggles for a Polish and international readership.[48] Later in 1986 the left-wing Peace and Freedom movement within Solidarność raised 130,000 zloty for medical aid for Afghan refugees. They also produced Afghan-fighter-themed postage stamps for Solidarność's mail system and in February 1987 gathered in Cracow to publicly protest against the torture of prisoners in Afghanistan.[49]

---

[44] Kevin Devlin, 'Boffa on Soviet Imperialism', *Radio Free Europe (Research)*, 18 February 1980; Zdenko Antic, 'Manuel Azcarate Blames Soviet Intervention in Afghanistan', *Radio Free Europe (Research)*, 25 July 1980.
[45] 'The Non-Aligned Foreign Ministers Meeting New Delhi 9–13 February 1981', *Foreign Policy Document No. 91* (London: International Section Research Department, August 1981), para. 19.
[46] Robinson, 'Afghanistan', 10.
[47] An incomplete bibliography of the contents shows that war in Afghanistan was discussed 400 times in 1985 and 300 times in the first half of 1986. HU OSA 300–55–9 Box 1 (OSA Archive, Budapest) 'Afghanistan: Polish Views and Hopes', RFE Press Review, 26 February 1987, 5–9.
[48] Radosław Sikorski, *Dust of the Saints: A Journey to Herat in Time of War* (London: Chatto & Windus, 1989).
[49] 'Opinion polls Radio Free Europe'; 'Afghanistan: Polish Views', Open Society Archive, HU OSA 300-6-2, 5–9.

Many liberal and conservative anti-Communists did see the withdrawal of Soviet troops and the collapse of Communist states as a moment of national liberation. This was echoed outside Europe too: Afghan representatives at the UN, recognising the commonalities in their former anti-Soviet struggles, repeatedly commended Eastern European states for surviving 'decades of pain and suffering' before achieving 'complete independence and democracy'.[50] Not all Eastern Europeans involved in the transformation of their region embraced this rhetoric, however: reform Communists, for example, preferred the rhetoric of transition (see Chapter 2), which allowed them to see themselves as responsible shepherds of their nations towards a more civilised future. Indeed, by the mid-1990s it was clear that such anti-imperialist rhetoric would be turned against those former Communists who survived in the new system: the idea that the pre-1989 era was one of Soviet occupation was used to demonise them as local collaborators in a wider imperial system. Fears that self-determination could be reversed did not go away overnight in 1989: many Eastern European nations' experience of the abrogation of national independence during the Second World War after only a short period of self-rule demonstrated that self-determination was reversible. Many feared a revival in Russian great power imperialism: it was for this reason that some Eastern European states pushed for membership in the military security system of NATO, as a priority over joining the EC, in order to preserve their newfound independence.[51]

The Soviet Withdrawal

It was not only from the smaller states on the western edge of the bloc that this critique of Soviet Empire came: a strain of Russian nationalism adopted this language too.[52] Russian nationalists around 1989 also compared an ostensible exploitation of 'Mother Russia' by the Soviet

---

[50] UN General Assembly, Afghan Delegation, 49th Session, 79th Meeting, 7 December 1994, A/49/PV.79, 8.

[51] Havel said in an interview with a German newspaper in 1995: 'Being accepted into NATO is indeed more urgent for us than being accepted into the European Union. No one knows what the further developments in Russia will be like and whether we will not experience unpleasant surprises there. Now the time is really ripe to seriously negotiate about our membership in NATO'. See Merje Kuus, *Geopolitics Reframed: Security and Identity in Europe's Eastern Enlargement* (London: Palgrave Macmillan, 2007), 46.

[52] Helmut Altrichter, *Russland 1989. Der Untergang des sowjetischen Imperiums* (München: C.H. Beck, 2009), 213–305.

Union with the repressions of the Mongol Empire.[53] And many elites in post-Soviet Russia who had sought the breakup of the Soviet Union spoke of the 'collapse of an empire'.[54] 'The Soviet Union could not exist without a notion of empire', Boris Yeltsin recalled in his memoirs, 'the empire, however, was inconceivable without military force'.[55] Such anti-imperial thinking from the centre of the 'empire' itself, quite similarly to developments in the final years of the British and French Empires in the 1950s and 1960s, was crucial in enabling '1989': large parts of the Soviet metropolitan elite in the late 1980s had lost their will to maintain and pay for Communist states across Europe and the Global South. Without much pressure from without, the Moscow elites charted the withdrawal from the 'Third World' from 1988, from Central and Eastern Europe from 1989, and eventually even from much of its own non-Russian periphery in 1991.

While this collapse of the Soviet Union was not a historically necessary outcome, intimations of an imperial-like retreat had been discernible from as early as the 1970s. These changes, too, were embedded in a global context: an idealistic notion of internationalism was giving way to more sober, pragmatic assessments of policies towards the Global South. A sense of solidarity with anti-colonial liberation struggles faded during the 1970s and the 1980s, as development aid came under attack as either self-serving, or well-meaning but counterproductive.[56] In Latin America leftist intellectuals had identified with Asian and African postcolonial societies during 1960s' *tercermundismo* – an identification that lost its appeal from the late 1970s. The People's Republic of China recalibrated its socialist development aid after Mao's death in 1976 and slowly turned to the pragmatism that would characterise Chinese Third World politics of the post–Cold War era. The Soviet Union was part of this global shift from socialist idealist 'Third Worldism' to political pragmatism: during détente, the Kremlin expanded its 'imperial' reach in the 1970s, but behind a public socialist rhetoric there now often stood collaborations with military regimes in strategically useful countries such as South Yemen, Ethiopia, Peru, or Syria, rather than idealistic support for liberation movements and anti-colonial governments. Indeed, developing countries in the Global South increasingly complained about a

---

[53] Ibid., 37.

[54] Egor Gaidar, *Gibel' Imperii: Uroki Dlja Sovremennoj Rossii* (Moskva: Rosspen, 2006).

[55] Boris Jelzin, *Mitternachtstagebuch. Meine Jahre im Kreml* (Berlin: Propyläen Verlag, 2000), 41.

[56] Brigitte Erler, *Tödliche Hilfe. Bericht von meiner letzten Dienstreise in Sachen Entwicklungshilfe* (Freiburg: Dreisam-Verlag, 1985).

relationship with the Soviet Union that amounted to 'a sort of socialist colonialism'.[57]

It was at the western borders of the Moscow-led bloc that authoritarian rule first started to crumble in 1989. Within two years, Eastern European Communist parties would lose their power and the Soviet Union would itself disintegrate. Democratisation was the result of, not the trigger for, this retreat of what many now saw as the last European empire of the twentieth century. At the moment when Gorbachev had taken over in the Kremlin four years earlier, national democratic movements in Eastern Europe as well as human rights activists in the Soviet Union were being firmly held at bay by authoritarian political rulers.[58] It was an impulse from Moscow, an act of voluntary withdrawal from imperial-style dominance, that allowed popular movements to regain influence in the periphery and that rendered viable their assertive claims to national independence.

Ironically, the withdrawal of Soviet control during perestroika, which led to the end of state socialism in Europe, had begun as an attempt to revive socialist ideology.[59] In the late Soviet Union under Leonid Brezhnev's and Yuri Andropov's leadership, the capacity to enact authoritarian control had often been more important than the belief in the socialist cause. In Poland, the Soviets had acclaimed the rule of a nationalist military leader, General Wojciech Jaruzelski – who suppressed Solidarność. The Soviet Union had also abandoned earlier socialist economic visions abroad: in the case of Vietnam, for example, the Kremlin terminated its support of failed industrialisation projects and suggested an adjustment to world market demands instead.[60] Gorbachev, by contrast, referred to an idealised notion of Leninism in both foreign and domestic politics and often used the old Prague Spring catchphrase of 'socialism with a human face'. His worldview was also informed by an early encounter with Nehru's political philosophy during his student years in

---

[57] Svetlana Savranskaya, 'Gorbachev and the Third World', in Artemy Kalinovsky and Sergey Radchenko (eds.), *The End of the Cold War and The Third World: New Perspectives on Regional Conflict* (London: Routledge, 2011), 23.

[58] Robert Brier, 'Entangled Protest: Dissent and the Transnational History of the 1970s and 1980s', in Robert Brier (ed.), *Transnational Approaches to the History of Dissent in Eastern Europe and the Soviet Union* (Osnabrück: Fibre, 2013), 25; Stephen Kotkin, *Uncivil Society. 1989 and the Implosion of the Communist Establishment* (New York: Random House, 2009), 122–23.

[59] Stephen Kotkin, *Armageddon Averted. The Soviet Collapse 1970–2000* (New York: Oxford University Press, 2008), 29–30; Michail Gorbatschow, *Perestroika. Die zweite Russische Revolution* (München: Droemer Knaur 1987), 27–29, 207–9.

[60] Tuong Vu, *Vietnam's Communist Revolution. The Power and Limits of Ideology* (New York: Cambridge University Press, 2017), 158–64.

the 1950s and by Italian and French Eurocommunism, which he got to know during his many trips to Western Europe in the 1960s and 1970s. Many Soviet citizens of Gorbachev's generation shared with their Western contemporaries an idealistic notion of global socialism and the decolonisation heroes of their youth. This distinguished Gorbachev's worldview from the often cynical pragmatism of the older generation, and the anti-Communism of the younger ones.[61]

Clinging to their idealised version of a socialist internationalism that predated the period of late Soviet imperial-like pragmatism, Gorbachev and his foreign policy advisors Anatoly Chernyaev and Alexander Yakovlev reinforced links with those believed to be true socialists and ended ties with pro-Soviet dictators. They increased their support for leftists such as the Nicaraguan Sandinistas,[62] while they saw the repressive Derg regime as 'embarrassing' for the Soviet Union and pushed for a 'perestroika' of the Ethiopian Marxist-Leninist regime.[63] In the West they reached out to leading representatives of the Socialist International as Willy Brandt and Pierre Mauroy. Gorbachev became a close friend of Felipe González, the head of the Spanish Socialist Workers' Party, and he admired the Swedish socialist Olof Palme.[64] In Europe he warned party diehards who refused reforms, such as Erich Honecker, that 'those who are late will be punished by life itself'.[65] In early 1989, after the death or retirement of a whole generation of Soviet hardliners, Gorbachev ordered the withdrawal of Soviet troops from Afghanistan and later that year from most of Eastern Europe.[66]

The Soviet retreat from Eastern Europe and the Third World was accompanied by the emergence of a specific Russian nationalism that – at least for a few vital years – celebrated the notion of a Russian nation stripped of any imperial pretentions. Many literati, painters, and musicians had turned to the countryside and folk traditions, and the devastating effects of Soviet modernity on rural life. No longer did this bring

---

[61] Michail Gorbatschow, *Erinnerungen* (Berlin: Siedler, 1995), 80, 147, 247, 759–61, 988; Archie Brown, *The Gorbachev Factor* (New York: Oxford University Press, 1995), 116.
[62] Gorbatschow, *Perestroika*, 221–46.
[63] Radoslav Yordanov, *The Soviet Union and the Horn of Africa during the Cold War* (Lanham, MD: Lexington Books, 2016), esp. 217–54.
[64] Gorbatschow, *Erinnerungen*, 752, 760–67.
[65] For the contested history of the quote, which has since become a German idiom, see Christoph Bock, 'Gorbatschow hat den berühmten Satz nie gesagt', *Die Welt*, 6 October 2014.
[66] By early 1988 most of those who had been voting members of the Politburo at the time of the invasion had either died or been retired, including Brezhnev, Kosygin, Suslov, Andropov, Chernenko, and Ustinov. See Richard A. Falk, 'The Afghan Settlement and the Future of World Politics', in Amin Saikal and William Maley (eds.), *The Soviet Withdrawal from Afghanistan* (Cambridge: Cambridge University Press, 1989), 144.

them into conflict with the Communist authorities. While moderate socialists or social democrats like Andrej Sakharov were still heavily repressed, anti-socialist and often anti-Semitic Slavic nationalist dissenters like Igor Shafarevich had been tolerated even before perestroika. The authors who produced so-called Russian village prose were usually themselves members of the official Soviet Writers Association. They often articulated their anti-modernism in terms of an anti-Western rhetoric that was adaptable to Soviet state ideology. During perestroika, some of these writers, Vasily Belov and Valentin Rasputin among them, became politicised and turned into outspoken right-wingers. Rasputin, one of the most popular Russian novelists at the time, addressed the Soviet People's Congress in early 1989 and, in a philippic against moral decline and Western pluralism, suggested that Russia leave the Union.[67] From his US exile, the Slavophile dissident Aleksandr Solzhenitsyn, too, suggested the creation of a Union of only the Slavic parts of the country.[68]

For a brief moment Russian nationalists stood at the forefront of an anti-imperial front because they shared the idea that the peripheries were a financial burden for the centre and because they associated the Soviet 'empire' with the socialism they detested. The corrosive effect of the traumatic Afghanistan War had been chipping away at many Soviet citizens' desire for imperial adventures. Economic decline, combined with the new opportunities to give voice to extreme discontent, led many during perestroika to inveigh against the spending of 'Russian money' in the 'Third World'. An old Soviet internationalist complained in 1991: 'I speak of the foreign debt, the lack of food, infant mortality, the political repressions in many Latin American countries, and the answer is: "Enough of feeding these wogs. They are ungrateful cattle. Remember Indonesia – we fed them, fed them; Egypt, we fed them, fed them, and then they all showed us their arses" ... All these opponents of mine had the same solid conviction: the lack of sausage at our shop counters is to be blamed on the Cubans, the Vietnamese, the Ethiopians and all the other scum from the "Third World"'.[69]

This re-emergence of Russian nationalism went in parallel with similar global developments from the 1970s. In the East and West economic decline and the emergence of an environmental awareness had ended an uncritical belief in human progress and in the predictability of industrial

---

[67] Altrichter, *Russland 1989*, 37.
[68] Vera Tolz, 'Conflicting "Homeland Myths" and Nation-State Building in Postcommunist Russia', *Slavic Review* 57/2 (1998), 267–94.
[69] Aleksandr Snitko, 'Skol'ko stoit naša sovest' v Latinskoj Amerike? Zametki ešče bolee neravnodušnye', *Latinskaja Amerika* 4 (1991), 38–44.

modernity. A return to local traditions and national myths had been visible in culture and the arts in the West at the same time. In the Soviet Union, such an ethnically defined nationalism and re-discovered religion filled the spiritual void left by a dwindling belief in Marxism. Their anti-Westernism notwithstanding, some of these Russian nationalists were actually influenced by Western conservative authors such as Knut Hamsun; the 'Russian Party', an informal group of nationalists from the 1970s, had built up contacts with political writers of the Western New Right such as Alain de Benoist. And based on their anti-Western, anti-capitalist ethnic nationalism, some Russian nationalists also found intellectual kinship in 'Third World' anti-imperial nationalism. Alexander Prokhanov, the editor of the early 1990s' most popular right-wing newspaper *Den*, had begun his career as *Pravda* correspondent in Cambodia, Angola, Ethiopia, and Nicaragua and had written several novels set in these countries. Vladimir Zhirinovski, head of the ultra-nationalist Liberal Democratic Party from 1991, was an alumnus of the Moscow Afro-Asian institute. Sergej Kurginjan, founder of the nationalist group Essence of Time, had some influence on the Communist Party and secret service elite with his particular ideology, a heterodox mixture of Communism, Christianity, and anti-Western 'Third World' nationalism.[70] Alexander Dugin and many of his disciples not only were well versed in the writings of Western neo-fascist authors but also had an intellectual background in orientalist studies; some took Iran as inspiration for their Russian Muslim nationalism. These connections would seem to have been recognised abroad: Ayatollah Khomeini sent his only ever message to a foreign leader to Gorbachev in January 1989, suggesting that Russia become a Muslim Republic so as to replace a crumbling Communist ideology.[71]

The interconnectedness of the Soviet camp was one of the determining factors for both the swift changes in the Eastern European countries and their rapid emulation among Soviet republics on the Western fringes.[72] Once Gorbachev had consolidated his power, the highly centralised decision-making processes of Soviet foreign policy allowed him to pursue his idealistic idea that freeing states from the Kremlin's control would liberate them to opt for reformed socialism and more amicable relations

---

[70] Walter Laqueur, *Black Hundreds: The Rise of the Extreme Right in Russia* (New York: HarperCollins, 1993), 181.

[71] 'Study Islam, Khomeini Suggests to Gorbachev', *New York Times*, 5 January 1989.

[72] Mark Kramer, 'The Dynamics of Diffusion in the Soviet Bloc and the Impact on Regime Survival', in Martin Dimitrov (ed.), *Why Communism Did Not Collapse: Understanding Authoritarian Regime Resilience in Asia and Europe* (Cambridge: Cambridge University Press, 2013), 180.

with Moscow. Soviet policies towards the Eastern European satellite states wavered between pressure for change and fears of destabilisation. The 'Sinatra Doctrine', announced by his foreign affairs spokesman Gennadi Gerasimov in Helsinki in October 1989, enabled the states of the Soviet Bloc to 'do it their way'. The reformers of perestroika initially foresaw multiple freely chosen paths to a reformed socialism. But the end of Communist rule in Eastern Europe immediately emboldened those who challenged the Soviet regime from within.

The political liberalisation under Gorbachev in the late 1980s had allowed nationalist sentiments to re-emerge. In the Baltics, in Armenia, and to a lesser extent in Georgia, Moldova, and Ukraine, anti-Soviet national sentiment had never gone away, and independence movements quickly developed from below. Many Central Asian intellectuals had actively participated in Soviet 'Third World' campaigns of the 1950s and 1960s, which had been designed to show that the Soviet cultural and economic model could provide areas formerly marginalised within empires with meaningful development. Yet by the 1980s, as the promises of development for the Soviet Union's southern periphery faded, the same anti-colonial language was turned back against the Soviet state by ever more nationally assertive Central Asian elites. Although they remained reluctant to leave, they increasingly questioned the Soviet claim to stand for equality and anti-colonialism and began to characterise the Soviet Union itself as an imperial power that had confined their region to the periphery, akin to the 'Third World' in the global system.[73] Societies now warmed to the nationalism of their political elites, which by 1990 had replaced socialism as a source of political legitimacy.[74]

Eastern European independence movements, profiting from the close links between the former socialist sister states, actively carried their message into the Soviet Union itself. Poland was the most active in promoting itself as a role model of transition for Soviet republics and helped to inspire a reinvigorated nationalism in the Baltics, in Belarus, Ukraine, and Moldova.[75] The Polish opposition kept a close eye in 1988 on demonstrations of anti-Sovietism in Armenia and in Central Asia. Polish tourists and organisations smuggled pro-independence literature into the Soviet Union, and Polish television was an important

---

[73] Artemy Kalinovsky, 'Writing the Soviet South', in Mark et al., *Alternative Globalizations*.
[74] Artemy Kalinovsky, *Laboratory of Socialist Development: Cold War Politics and Decolonization in Soviet Tajikistan* (Ithaca, NY: Cornell University Press, 2018), 219–43.
[75] Kotkin, *Uncivil Society*, 138–39.

source of information during the independence struggles in Latvia and Lithuania. Solidarność developed particularly close ties with pro-independence groups in Ukraine and Lithuania: political leaders in Vilnius declared their 'readiness to follow Poland's own path away from Communism'.[76] And in the Donbass striking coal miners took their inspiration from the Polish trade union movement.[77] Other East European reformers, however, likewise met with success in presenting themselves as role models. Estonian elites, for instance, called for a 'Hungarian model'; and the post-Ceaușescu Romanian government stoked pan-Romanian nationalist sentiment in the Soviet republic of Moldova.[78]

Encouraged by the drive for cultural autonomy and independence in the Baltic states, movements such as Rastokhez ('Revival') in Tajikistan and Birlik ('Unity') in Uzbekistan self-consciously modelled themselves on popular front movements like the Lithuanian Sajudis and received assistance from them in their political work, as activists in the Baltic states helped them produce newspapers that local government printers refused to print.[79] Yet in the Central Asian republics, populations voted to remain part of a reformed Union. Here, Eastern Europe's '1989' had the reverse effect: Communist Party bosses such as Nursultan Nazarbaev in Kazakhstan or Islam Karimov in Uzbekistan looked askance at the democratic awakening in the western borderlands of the Soviet Union and sought to preserve their power by managing independence from above and rebranding themselves as nationalist leaders.

In most parts of the former Soviet Union, these major ideological and political shifts unfolded in a remarkably peaceful manner. With the brief exception of a violent interference on the part of Soviet forces against the Lithuanian independence movement in Vilnius in early 1991, Moscow was not prepared to use violence to maintain control. Only in those areas with unresolved minority issues where republican borders were challenged by competing states at the periphery did long-lasting violence erupt: Armenians and Azeris fought over the protection of the Armenian minority in Nagorno Karabakh; and in Tajikistan, ethnic tensions and

---

[76] Mark Kramer, 'The Collapse of East European Communism and the Repercussions within the Soviet Union (Part 1)', *Journal of Cold War Studies*, 5/4 (2003), 178–256, 204–12.

[77] Ibid., 216–37.   [78] Ibid., 238–42.

[79] Isaac Scarborough, 'From February to February and from Ru ba Ru to Rastokhez: Political Mobilisation in Late Soviet Tajikistan (1989–1990)', *Cahiers d'Asie centrale*, 26 (2016), 143–71; Sabine Freizer 'Central Asian Fragmented Civil Society: Communal and Neoliberal Forms in Tajikistan and Uzbekistan', in Marlies Glasius, David Lewis, and Hakan Seckinelgin (eds.), *Exploring Civil Society: Political and Cultural Contexts* (Abingdon: Routledge, 2011), 117–19.

popular economic discontent eventually led to civil war.[80] But Moscow was an arbiter, not the instigator of violence in these conflicts. Unlike in Yugoslavia the centre allowed the periphery to secede and was not prepared to defend its own geopolitical interests, and those of its own dominant ethnic group, in the seceding republics.

An ideological struggle within the Soviet political elite had profoundly eroded the power of the 'imperial' centre. Gorbachev, who stood for the preservation of a democratically overhauled Soviet Union, was severely weakened by a failed August 1991 putsch attempt by more conservative political and secret service figures who stood for an ill-defined return to an earlier status quo. The destabilisation of the centre emboldened the 'peripheral' elites. Yeltsin, whose courageous intervention against the putschists crucially contributed to their surrender, actively hollowed out Soviet political structures to the benefit of those of the Russian Republic, over which he presided. In December Yeltsin met with the leaders of the Ukrainian and Belorussian republics in a state dacha in the Belovezha Forest near the Polish border, where they declared the creation of a Commonwealth of Independent States (CIS) and the dissolution of the Soviet Union. The leaders of the remaining republics as well as the international community soon recognised the breakup of the Soviet Union into fifteen new states – Vladimir Putin would later call the dissolution a major geopolitical disaster of the twentieth century.[81]

Peace or Violence

In September 1989, between the first elections in Poland and the fall of the Berlin Wall, the last Cold War summit of the Non-Aligned Movement took place in Belgrade. The Yugoslav hosts assumed a victorious demeanour: the dissolution of the blocs, one of the proclaimed aims of the movement in which Yugoslavia had played a key role, was on the horizon. Two years earlier the UN Medal of Peace Prize had been awarded to the Yugoslav Year of Peace Committee, which coincided with the celebrations to mark the birth of the five billionth world citizen in Zagreb, Yugoslavia. The UN secretary general Javier Pérez de Cuéllar

---

[80] Scarborough, 'From February to February', 147.

[81] A more dramatic and distorting popular translation of Putin's 2005 comment, which mostly addressed the fate of millions of ethnic Russians in now independent republics, spoke of 'the greatest geopolitical catastrophe of the twentieth century'.

expressed hope that baby Matej's generation would be a generation of peace.[82] However, ongoing economic decline and inter-republic tensions soon led to a constitutional crisis. The ensuing escalation of violence in 1991 took most Yugoslavs and foreign observers by surprise, not least the thousands of foreign tourists on the Adriatic coast. The most open and prosperous of the socialist states and the one closest to achieving European integration, swiftly succumbed to internecine violence and multiple conflicts that would persist until 1999. In contrast to much of Eastern Europe, arguments for self-determination were used here in the name of national homogenisation and violent secession. The Yugoslav experience of '1989' was thus a very different one. When asked about the fall of the Berlin Wall, a citizen of besieged Sarajevo allegedly said that, while on the one hand, it had been a good thing, on the other, the Wall had unfortunately 'crumbled down upon our heads'.[83]

Contemporaries struggled to make sense of the violence in Yugoslavia – how had Croatia, Bosnia, and Kosovo, previously part of a Western-facing seemingly Europeanising state, succumbed to such barbarous violence? After all, two other federations, the Soviet Union and Czechoslovakia, had also collapsed.[84] Yet Tajikistan, the Baltics and the Caucasus aside, they had dissolved with remarkably little conflict. Although elites were central to the dissolution process in all three countries, only in the Yugoslav case, empowered by a de facto confederal system, were they enabled to demand border changes and embrace violence as a means to achieving their projects of self-determination.[85] Even in countries with significant national minorities, such as Bulgaria and Romania, minority parties were deradicalised after 1989 by being co-opted into pro-Western opposition fronts and later involved in state government structures at the national level.[86] It was striking that many contemporaries avoided such comparisons: other Eastern European elites sought to distance themselves from the Yugoslav experience of

---

[82] 'UN Secretary-General Welcomes Five Billionth Inhabitant of the World'; 'Perez de Cuellar Awards Year of Peace Medal to Grlickov', n.d. United Nations Archive, Secretary-General Javier Perez de Cuellar (1982–1991), S-1022-0033-09.

[83] Quoted after Igor Štiks, '"The Berlin Wall Crumbled Down upon Our Heads!": 1989 and Violence in the Former Socialist Multinational Federations', *Global Society*, 24/1 (2010), 91–110.

[84] On the history of nationalism and victimhood in Czechoslovakia, see Mary Heimann, *Czechoslovakia: The State That Failed* (New Haven, CT: Yale University Press, 2009).

[85] Valerie Bunce, *Subversive Institutions: The Design and the Destruction of Socialism and the State* (Cambridge: Cambridge University Press, 1999), 112.

[86] Bogdan C. Iacob, 'A Transition to What and Whose Democracy? 1990 in Bulgaria and Romania', in Joachim von Puttkamer and Włodzimierz Borodziej (eds.), *From Revolution to Uncertainty: The Year 1990 in Central and Eastern Europe* (London: Routledge, 2019), 117–41.

war and secession for fear of being associated with it in the eyes of the West. Some suggested it was more meaningful to explain violence by comparing formerly non-aligned Yugoslavia not with the former Eastern Bloc, but rather with the many outbreaks of communal, interethnic, and religious violence in the non-aligned world that marked the immediate post-1989 era. In fact, to many in the Global South it was Yugoslavia, not the peacefully transitioning Poland or Hungary, that most resembled their own ethnically and religiously divided societies.[87] In India and Yugoslavia, the two founding members of the Non-Aligned Movement, a decades-long political consensus of secular nationalism dissolved as the Cold War was nearing its end and socialism was losing its legitimating force. In 1992 Hindu militants tore down the Ayodhya mosque in the Indian state of Uttar Pradesh, unleashing a spiral of violence and the proliferation of a Hindu nationalist movement around the Bharatya Janata Party (BJP). For educated and secular Indians, the integrity of Yugoslavia in the face of rising nationalist challenges was thus of grave concern – primarily because they feared the rise of religious nationalism in their own country.[88]

The explosion of ethnic and religious nationalism as a replacement for a socialist ideology that provided less and less political legitimacy and violent inter-communal strife based on it were at the heart of many similar conflicts around the world. In Algeria, another former close partner for Yugoslavia, violent riots in 1988 discredited the socialism of the revolutionary post-independence period and provided a space for the consolidation of religious fundamentalists.[89] An Islamist electoral victory in Algeria in 1991 then provoked a coup against them, which unleashed a ten-year civil war. The violence against civilians in Algeria was comparable to that during the Yugoslav dissolution wars and, as in the Yugoslav case, an economic crisis coupled with political liberalisation and the introduction of multiparty elections provided the impetus for conservative anti-regime mobilisation and intra-communal violence. Rwanda, another non-aligned state whose even more destructive civil war (1990–4) overlapped with the Yugoslav conflicts, came to dominate

[87] Daniel Chirot, 'Problematic Analogies and Forgotten Details of 1989', *East European Politics and Societies and Cultures*, 28/4 (2014), 657–63.
[88] Misha Glenny, *McMafia* (London: Vintage, 2009), 158.
[89] Gilles Kepel, *Jihad: The Trail of Political Islam* (Cambridge, MA: Harvard University Press, 2002), 159-84.

world media headlines for the same reasons as Bosnia-Herzegovina, the most heterogeneous of the Yugoslav federal units: genocide, United Nations peacekeeping missions, and international criminal tribunals. Although not directly related, both cases demonstrated that a complex and often fragile ethnic balance under an authoritarian system could quickly unravel with tragic consequences at the first attempt at changing the status quo. Both Bosnia and Rwanda – albeit at different scales – became examples of how idealised territorial aspirations of an ethnically pure nation-state could set the stage for genocide.[90]

Why was Yugoslavia different from Eastern Europe and similar to religious and ethnic violence in the Global South? Or, as a historian of Yugoslavia asked, reflecting on the role of leadership in preserving peace during the disintegration, 'Where Was the Serbian Havel?'[91] If before 1989 Yugoslavia was different from countries in the Soviet-dominated Eastern Bloc that surrounded it, it was because of its closer links as a non-aligned country to *both* Western Europe and the Global South, and the greater active popular support for the local variant of market socialism. Centrifugal forces had gained force within its federal system in late socialism, but there was scant appetite for a breakup of the federation up until 1990. The country's elites and many of its citizens were still attached to the idea of Yugoslavia, its independence and prestige abroad, the personality of Tito, and the democratic aspects of multinational pluralism and workers' self-management.[92] Indeed, in the late 1980s Yugoslavia seemed set fair for a Western-facing European future: federal elites in Belgrade embraced the prospect of progressive liberalisation and eventual accession to the EC/EU – as the only viable framework, they thought, for the democratisation and preservation of the federation.[93] Moreover, the federal government espoused a 'dialogue on the basis of a multi-party system', with a self-proclaimed direction at federal level set 'towards a modern state with a market economy and

---

[90] William B. Wood, 'Geographic Aspects of Genocide: A Comparison of Bosnia and Rwanda', *Transactions of the Institute of British Geographers*, 26/1 (2001), 57–75, 57.

[91] Nick Miller, 'Where Was the Serbian Havel?', in Vladimir Tismaneanu and Bogdan C. Iacob (eds.), *The End and the Beginning: The Revolutions of 1989 and the Resurgence of History* (Budapest: Central European University Press, 2012), 363–379.

[92] Susan L. Woodward, *Balkan Tragedy – Chaos and Dissolution after the Cold War* (Washington, DC: Brookings Institution, 1995), 144.

[93] Tanjug, 'Vklučuvanje vo evropskite procesi i integracii' (Joining the European Processes and Integrations), *Nova Makedonija*, 27 March 1991.

political pluralism'.[94] With the hope that Europeanisation would obviate the need for independence and secession, a broadly defined liberal platform was embraced by an array of pan-Yugoslav civic movements and newly emerging political parties.[95]

Whilst initially there was little support for the breakup of the state and the narrow interpretation of the right to self-determination, other forces pushed in that direction. First, the Yugoslav constitution – and the federal construction it underpinned – had enabled the mobilisation of radicalised nationalist elites at the level of the individual republics that made up Yugoslavia. Second, with the escalation of violence, some Western elites came to view the Balkans as a liminal space that was not fully European and where self-determination was the only reasonable response to now essentialised notions of Balkan violence and entrenched ethnic enmity that were revived with great rapidity in the early 1990s. Responding to the crisis, the EC took it upon itself to act as arbiter in self-determination. Reviving mechanisms derived from an earlier era of European imperial disintegration,[96] all the while trying to impose minority protection standards, it brought a particular legal and political understanding of self-determination to European soil.

The rise of an ethnically defined radical nationalism had happened everywhere in Eastern Europe too, but in Yugoslavia these forces were given space to grow within an ethno-territorial framework. Whereas Western-looking elites elsewhere in the ethnically more homogeneous and politically centralised Central European countries effectively disciplined their transition and kept out radical nationalists, such an option was less viable in multiethnic Yugoslavia with its complex, confederal-like structure. Instead, it was the nationalist forces incubated in late socialism, and radicalised from the late 1980s, who came to play the decisive roles in determining the country's future. Westernising pro-European elites who wished to temper extreme manifestations of nationalism were based mostly in Belgrade – and the federal centre they represented was losing power. Far more inward-looking elites in the different republics

---

[94] 'Secretary-General's Meeting with the Federal Secretary for Foreign Affairs of the Socialist Federal Republic of Yugoslavia Held in the United Nations Headquarters on Thursday', 26 April 1990, United Nations Archive, Secretary-General Javier Perez de Cuellar (1982–1991), S-1024-0097-06, 3.

[95] Ljubica Spaskovska, 'Landscapes of Resistance, Hope and Loss: Yugoslav Supra-Nationalism and Anti-Nationalism', in Bojan Bilić and Vesna Janković (eds.), *Resisting the Evil: [Post] Yugoslav Anti-war Contention* (Baden-Baden: Nomos, 2012), 37–62.

[96] 'Opinion No. 3 of the Arbitration Commission of the Peace Conference on Yugoslavia, Paris, 11 January 1992', in Snežana Trifunovska, *Yugoslavia through Documents: From Its Creation to Its Dissolution* (Dordrecht: Martinus Nijhoff, 1994), 479–80. For a full explanation, see 58.

within Yugoslavia had seen their influence increase under late socialism. All efforts to enact reform at federal level, initiate a federal referendum on the survival of Yugoslavia, or hold federal elections were readily undermined by the republics' leaderships, in particular those of Serbia, Slovenia and Croatia. This was despite the fact that public opinion surveys demonstrated popular enthusiasm for the reform programme of the federal government and the preservation of some sort of a Yugoslav union.[97]

A particular understanding of the right to national or ethnic self-determination in Yugoslavia's final two decades lay at the origins of the ethnic violence of the 1990s. Towards the end of an era of global decol-onisation marked by assertive claims to self-determination, Yugoslavia's last federal constitution from 1974 institutionalised the Marxist-Leninist notion of the withering away of the state and introduced decentralisation and thus more power for constituent republics that claimed a right to greater autonomy as nations defined by ethnic belonging. Similar aspects of such a 'national federalism'[98] were institutionalised on paper in all of the three socialist federations, but unlike in Czechoslovakia or the Soviet Union, in the case of Yugoslavia the federation itself was in fact progres-sively weakened through constitutional reform. After the death of Yugo-slavia's wartime leader and president Josip Broz Tito in 1980, a complex and increasingly inefficient rotating collective presidency stood at the helm of the country. In the absence of a strong centre, the constituent republics were granted many attributes of independent statehood. Slo-venia, Croatia, Bosnia, Serbia, Montenegro, and Macedonia all had their own parliaments, their own governments, their own central banks, and even their own commissions for foreign relations.[99] Federal decision making was thus rendered more difficult, since a type of minority veto was given to all federal units – and even to the two autonomous provinces of Kosovo and Vojvodina within Serbia. The federal system, and with it the Yugoslav economy, was further destabilised in the 1980s when the International Monetary Fund (IMF) began to insist on strengthening the competences of federal financial authorities at the centre. Republican

---

[97] Ljiljana Baćević et al., *Jugoslavija na kriznoj prekretnici* (Beograd: Institut društvenih nauka / Centar za politikološka istraživanja i javno mnenje, 1991), 301–23.
[98] Bunce, *Subversive Institutions*, 110–17.
[99] Mitja Žagar, 'The Collapse of the Yugoslav Federation and the Viability of Asymmetrical Federalism', in Sergio Ortino, Mitja Žagar, and Vojtech Mastny (eds.), *The Changing Faces of Federalism: Institutional Reconfiguration in Europe from East to West* (Manchester: Manchester University Press, 2005), 118; *Ustav Socijalističke Federativne Republike Jugoslavije – Stručno objašnjenje / The Constitution of the Socialist Federal Republic of Yugoslavia – Expert interpretation* (Belgrade: Institute for Political Studies, 1975).

leaderships saw these changes as a threat to their sovereignty. They allied against the federal government and vetoed various bills that were meant to reform the economic system, integrate a pan-Yugoslav market, and facilitate debt repayment.[100]

Yugoslavia was not the only country where ethnic majorities developed a strong sense of their own victimhood and enacted discriminatory citizenship laws. These could also be seen in the Baltic states where, as in Serbia and Croatia, post-Communist identities were built around the sense of the suffering nation – which saw itself as having endured foreign occupation, de-nationalisation, and what was, controversially, called 'genocide'. In Estonia and Latvia restrictive citizenship laws were enacted that targeted the Russian-speaking minority, now seen as representatives of the former occupying power.[101] In both the Baltics and the Balkans national narratives harked back to the Second World War, to the interwar period, and to unfulfilled dreams of national self-determination. Moreover, both Serb and Croat nationalism cultivated an acute sense of victimhood – nations of 'victims without allies'[102] – that helped further fuel the ensuing violence. However, it was only in the Balkans that other unique factors contributed to a distinctly different violent outcome. Only here was there a destabilising federal structure that decentralised power, and a dominant national group that was prepared to invade; the Baltics, by contrast, were compact centralised states with a neighbour, Russia, that did not countenance intervention to protect its ethnic kin.

---

[100] Gale Stokes, *The Walls Came Tumbling Down: The Collapse of Communism in Eastern Europe* (New York: Oxford University Press, 1993), 226; Susan L. Woodward, *Balkan Tragedy: Chaos and Dissolution after the Cold War* (Washington, DC: Brookings Institution, 1995), esp. 82–113.

[101] Dovile Budryte, *Taming Nationalism? Political Community Building in the Post-Soviet Baltic States* (London: Ashgate, 2005). See also Vello Pettai, 'Estonia and Latvia: International Influences on Citizenship and Minority Integration', in Jan Zielonka and Alex Pravda (eds.), *Democratic Consolidation in Eastern Europe, Volume 2: International and Transnational Factors* (Oxford: Oxford University Press, 2001), 257–80; Brubaker, *Nationalism Reframed.*

[102] Mate Nikola Tokić, 'The End of "Historical-Ideological Bedazzlement": Cold War Politics and Émigré Croatian Separatist Violence, 1950–1980', *Social Science History* 36/3 (2012), 421–45, 423. The narrative of victimhood and imposed guilt was present among Serbian oppositional/dissident intellectuals in the 1970s and 1980s: in an interview for a Swiss weekly in 1980, Serbian nationalist novelist and politician Dobrica Ćosić spoke of a 'feeling of historical guilt in the Serbian people' instilled by Comintern ideology, adding that 'the Serbian people, like any other people, should be allowed to live out their own identity'. Slobodan Stankovic, 'New Intellectual Dissident Journal in Yugoslavia?', *Radio Free Europe (Research)*, 28 October 1980, 3. For an analysis of the intellectual realm in the 1980s, see Jasna Dragović-Soso, *'Saviours of the Nation' – Serbia's Intellectual Opposition and the Revival of Nationalism* (London: Hurst & Company, 2002).

In the late 1980s the nationalist mobilisation that fed into the eventual unravelling of elite political consensus was led by members of these republican establishments, first in Serbia and Slovenia and later in Croatia.[103] The power that had grown in the republics' capitals since the 1970s gave space and political power to inward-looking nationalist elites. Former Communist leaders such as Slobodan Milošević in Serbia and Franjo Tuđman in Croatia turned into self-styled defenders of the national cause. Initially drawing on the language of Yugoslav socialist egalitarianism, elites in Serbia were able to translate labour unrest into an act of nationalist mobilisation in the late 1980s.[104] The Serbian elite then couched its new pan-Serbian nationalism in collective and ethnic terms. By contrast, Czechoslovak president Havel, head of a federation himself and aware of the destructive power of ethnic nationalism, framed his pleas in terms of individual rights and freedoms during the dissolution of his country in 1992–93. Serbian politicians, for their part, exalted the rights of their nation. For the majority of Serbs it was *national* self-determination that should have been applied irrespective of Yugoslavia's internal administrative boundaries between its constituent republics: more than a quarter of Yugoslavia's Serbs lived outside of Serbia – 580,000 in Croatia and 1.4 million in Bosnia. By 1990, in addition to the right to self-determination inscribed in the Yugoslav constitution Serbian nationalists could also draw on the recent unification of Germany to make their case. Germany's Unification Treaty offered a new interpretation of the concept by framing the re-unification as 'free self-determination'.[105] The argument that the Serb nation should not be

---

[103] Dejan Jović, *Yugoslavia: A State That Withered Away* (West Lafayette, IN: Purdue University Press, 2009).

[104] Goran Musić, '"They Came as Workers and Left as Serbs": The Role of Rakovica's Blue-Collar Workers in Serbian Social Mobilisations of the Late 1980s', in Rory Archer, Igor Duda, and Paul Stubbs (eds.), *Social Inequalities and Discontent in Yugoslav Socialism* (London: Routledge, 2016), 132–54; Veljko Vujačić, *Nationalism, Myth, and the State in Russia and Serbia: Antecedents of the Dissolution of the Soviet Union and Yugoslavia* (Cambridge: Cambridge University Press, 2015). For a detailed account of the 'antibureaucratic revolution', grassroots mobilisation in the late 1980s, and the role of industrial workers and other non-state actors in the events of 1988, see Nebojša Vladisavljević, *Serbia's Antibureaucratic Revolution: Milošević, the Fall of Communism and Nationalist Mobilisation* (Basingstoke: Palgrave Macmillan, 2008).

[105] 'The Federal Republic of Germany and the German Democratic Republic, resolved to achieve in free self-determination the unity of Germany in peace and freedom as an equal partner in the community of nations'. See 'The Unification Treaty between the FRG and the GDR (Berlin, 31 August 1990)', Centre Virtuel de la Connaissance sur l'Europe (CVCE), www.cvce.eu/content/publication/1997/10/13/2c391661-db4e-42e5-84f7-bd86108c0b9c/publishable_en.pdf.

divided while the Germans were allowed to unite resonated with many at the time.[106]

Whereas the federal government in Belgrade advocated a liberal European direction for the country, republic-based Communist parties and elites generally embraced ethno-nationalist politics to mobilise their local electorates as they remade themselves for a post-Communist era. These views prevailed in the republics in part because the federal centre was losing influence. Also, crucially, the first multiparty elections after Communism were held only at the level of the republics, which further reinforced the legitimacy of their elites. Campaigning on nationalist platforms, they hid or refashioned their own Communist-era biographies. Without elections at the federal level, it was easy for nationalist leaders in the republics to stigmatise such federal elite figures as the left-liberal prime minister Ante Marković and foreign minister Budimir Lončar as illegitimate representatives of an old, crumbling Communist order. Had federal elections been held, or had they preceded the republic-level ones, it is likely that Yugoslavia would have avoided a civil war – and would perhaps have developed a political system and voting patterns similar to that of India, with local nationalists dominant at the local level and a federally oriented party winning at the centre.[107] Whereas other elites in Eastern Europe accepted Western prescriptions for deradicalisation, both Milošević and Tuđman sabotaged all domestic and foreign EC- and US-sponsored attempts at avoiding conflict and finding a new federal or confederal settlement. The media under the control of the nationalist governments played a crucial role in stoking nationalist sentiment and stigmatising minority communities, labelling individuals and entire nations as traitors and foreign hirelings to promote a new consensus around exclusionary ethno-religious nation building.[108]

Nationalist elites in Belgrade and Zagreb even turned against their own more moderate ethnic compatriots who disagreed with the politics of exclusive nationalist homogenisation. It was they, in collaboration with local actors and newly formed paramilitaries in Bosnia, who deliberately

---

[106] The History of Yugoslavia (West Lafayette, IN: Purdue University Press, 2019), 291.

[107] Robert M. Hayden, *Blueprints for a House Divided – The Constitutional Logic of the Yugoslav Conflicts* (Ann Arbor: University of Michigan Press, 2000), 28.

[108] On the role of the media in inciting ethnic antagonism, see Kemal Kurspahić, *Prime Time Crime: Balkan Media in War and Peace* (Washington, DC: US Institute of Peace Press, 2003); Svetlana Slapšak (ed.), *The War Started at Maksimir: Hate Speech in the Media* (Belgrade: Media Center, 1997); Mirjana Vojvodić (ed.), *Not in My Name* (Niš: Center for Civic Initiative, 2008).

imported and instigated violence in areas with high levels of ethnic coexistence.[109] Their radicalisation came in different ways; for Croat elites, the return of émigré leaders enmeshed in cultures of radical violence was paramount; Serbian elites in Belgrade, by contrast, were first radicalised by Serbian minorities outside Serbia itself.

At a mass gathering on 28 June 1989 to commemorate the six hundredth anniversary of the Battle of Kosovo against the Ottomans, Slobodan Milošević used the memory of 1389 to underline that Serbia had always stood at the vanguard of a broader struggle to protect Europe:

Six centuries ago, Serbia heroically defended itself in the field of Kosovo, but it also defended Europe. Serbia was at that time the bastion that defended the European culture, religion, and European society in general. Therefore today it appears not only unjust but even unhistorical and completely absurd to talk about Serbia's belonging to Europe. Serbia has always been a part of Europe now just as much as it was in the past, of course, in its own way, but in a way that in the historical sense never deprived it of dignity.[110]

In this he drew on the growing tendency to construct these civilisations as distinct and in need of protection from others, rejecting the rhetoric of equality and liminality of cultures that had had enjoyed greater visibility in the Balkans in the decolonisation era – as we saw in Chapter 3. Already in the early 1980s Muslims in South-Eastern Europe were increasingly portrayed by nationalists as excessively radical and with ideological ties that placed them outside the body of the socialist nation – the greatest violence was in Bulgaria, but there were emerging tensions in Yugoslavia too. Such images would have a profound effect on how Serbian Communists-turned-nationalists in particular came to view Bosnia's Muslim population after 1989. Both Tuđman and Milošević appealed to the values of Christianity, Europe, and 'civilisation' and shared a strategy of heightening a constructed opposition between Christianity and Islam, and between modernity and fundamentalism.[111] Portrayed as remnants of Ottoman colonisation, Bosnia's generally secular Muslim Slavic community became a target for the Serbian extreme right and could be easily stigmatised and framed as the ultimate foreign Other. Intellectuals also played a role in producing official government propaganda that sought to stoke fear and resentment: some who were affiliated

---

[109] Chip Gagnon, *The Myth of Ethnic War: Serbia and Croatia in the 1990s* (Ithaca, NY: Cornell University Press, 2004).

[110] Slobodan Milošević's St. Vitus Day Speech, Gazimestan, 28 June 1989, www.slobodan-milosevic.org/spch-kosovo1989.htm See also Michael A. Sells, *The Bridge Betrayed: Religion and Genocide in Bosnia* (Berkeley: University of California Press, 1998), 122.

[111] Arne Johan Vetlesen, *Evil and Human Agency: Understanding Collective Evildoing* (Cambridge: Cambridge University Press, 2005), 153–4.

with the Serbian Academy of Sciences and the University of Belgrade wrote about the continuity of the Croatian genocidal threat towards Serbs,[112] or the imminent menace to Europe posed by Muslims and Islam as a purportedly totalitarian religion.[113] This sense of difference also fostered tensions with other minorities in other republics, such as Slovenia and Macedonia, where discriminatory citizenship laws were enacted in order to exclude ethnic Others from citizenship in emerging illiberal nation-states.[114]

In the 1990s, Croatia, Bosnia, and Kosovo became battlegrounds for the worst violence in Europe since the end of the Second World War; this would lead in turn to the establishment of the first international tribunal since the Nuremberg and Tokyo trials. It was the most ethnically mixed areas in the countryside that suffered the most: Bosnia became notorious for the 'ethnic cleansing' of its Muslim population. The 1995 Srebrenica genocide saw the massacre of over 8,000 Muslim Bosnians were massacred by the Bosnian Serb Army. Overall around 140,000 people lost their lives in the various conflicts, which also produced around 4 million refugees and internally displaced persons. Yet the eruption of violence was actively opposed and resisted by a majority of citizens, especially in urban areas. Popular grassroots support for armed conflict was almost non-existent at the beginning of Yugoslavia's dissolution. Serbia, for instance, witnessed one of the biggest campaigns of draft resistance in modern history – 85 to 90 per cent of the young men in Belgrade who were called up to fight in Bosnia refused to serve, and around two hundred thousand mostly young people left the country.[115]

At the same time the return of diaspora communities who espoused violence significantly contributed to the escalation of the conflict. Croatian returnees in particular proved influential. An estimated twelve thousand Croatian anti-Communists, amongst them many former Nazi collaborators, had found political asylum in West Germany after the Second World War.[116] An additional twenty to forty thousand had moved to the United States, Canada, Australia, and – with the help of Croatian Franciscan priests in Rome – Argentina and Uruguay. Some of them had harboured ideas of a violent struggle for national independence – ideas that had never been popular in the Croatian

---

[112] Dragović-Soso, 'Saviours of the Nation', 111.   [113] Sells, The Bridge Betrayed, 121.
[114] Jo Shaw and Igor Štiks (eds.), Citizenship after Yugoslavia (London: Routledge, 2012).
[115] See Gagnon, The Myth of Ethnic War; John B. Allcock, 'Rural-Urban Differences and the Break-Up of Yugoslavia', Recherches, 6/1–2 (2002), 101–25.
[116] Mate Nikola Tokić, 'Landscapes of Conflict: Unity and Disunity in Post–Second World War Croatian Émigré Separatism', Journal European Review of History: Revue européenne d'histoire, 16/5 (2009), 739–53.

republic until the dissolution of Yugoslavia. Committing from the 1950s numerous terrorist attacks against Yugoslav institutions and assassinations of its diplomats these groups saw the end of Communism as a moment of opportunity for the realisation of a 'Greater Croatia' along the lines of its Second World War borders, incorporating all of Bosnia-Herzegovina and parts of Serbia. Throughout the 1960s and 1970s, few terrorist political groups were more active than those supporting the destruction of socialist Yugoslavia and the establishment of an independent Croatian state: over a ten-year period, Croatian terrorists had averaged one act of political violence every five weeks, including more than fifty assassinations or assassination attempts, forty bombings of public buildings and monuments, and two aircraft hijackings.[117] The Croatian National Resistance, a terrorist organisation founded by exiles in Francoist Spain, had set a clear agenda for themselves: 'Our attitude is clear: Destroy Yugoslavia! Destroy it together with the Russians and the Americans, with the communists, the non-communists and the anti-communists; destroy it with anyone willing to do the same! Destroy it with the dialectics of words and dynamite, but destroy it unconditionally, because if there is one country which does not have the right to survive, that country is Yugoslavia'.[118] West Germany, which became the organisational centre of militant Croatian activism, was where most of these terrorist attacks were committed.[119] Although there were strongly nationalist exile groups among Yugoslavia's other nations – Slovene, Albanian, Serbian, Macedonian – none of these ever embraced violence and terrorism to anywhere near the same degree as the Croatian émigrés had done.

Theirs was an ideology of militant, chauvinist nationalism couched in a rhetoric of liberation, self-determination, and independence. Once in Germany, Spain, or Latin America, no efforts were made to deradicalise these groups. The era of decolonisation and liberation movements re-activated a violent imaginary, and some Croat nationalists came to sympathise with the Irish Republican Army (IRA) in the 1970s, building on the Ustaša's friendly relations with the Irish republicanism during the Second World War. For this reason official Yugoslav media often acted

---

[117] Ibid., 739.

[118] Ivica Lučić, 'Mi Hrvati srušit ćemo svaku Jugoslaviju!', *Večernji list*, 6 April 2013, www.vecernji.hr/vijesti/mi-hrvati-srusit-cemo-svaku-jugoslaviju-534860; Nir Arielli, *From Byron to bin Laden: A History of Foreign War Volunteers* (Harvard University Press, 2017). See Tokić, 'Landscapes of Conflict', 740.

[119] Dennis Pluchinsky, 'Political Terrorism in Western Europe: Some Themes and Variations', in Yonah Alexander and Kenneth Myers (eds.), *Terrorism in Europe* (London: Routledge, 1982/2015).

as the lone voice in Europe siding with the British Army during the 'Troubles' in Northern Ireland.[120] Although former émigrés tend to portray their struggle as democratic, it was in fact based on a narrow, authoritarian vision of national sovereignty and statehood without minorities.[121] After 1989 members of such exile groups, some of whom openly endorsed the pro-Nazi Ustaša regime during World War II, returned to Yugoslavia and joined the ruling Croat Democratic Union (HDZ).[122] Some of the most prominent émigré returnees were Gojko Šušak, a Canadian Croat who was appointed Minister of Emigration and then Minister of Defence between 1991 and 1998; and the top Croatian military commander Ante Gotovina, who brought with him military experience from the French Foreign Legion.[123] A radicalised Croatian state now started to discriminate against its Serbian minority.

The transformation of the Serbian elite was somewhat different – here, the trajectory of radicalisation and violence was generally from the Yugoslav periphery to the centre, in particular in the case of Kosovo. While radical groups among Serbs in Croatia were already a product of the radicalisation in Serbia itself, the Serb minority in Kosovo, and later in Croatia, called for protection from Belgrade in response to alleged discrimination by Albanians and Croats. Notwithstanding persistent grievances among some Serbian intellectuals and politicians about the 1974 Yugoslav constitution that effectively gave sovereignty to the two autonomous provinces of Vojvodina and Kosovo on Serbia's territory, Serbian minorities in Kosovo and Croatia began to mobilise in the late 1980s and demand the abolition of Kosovo's autonomy and the restoration of the political and judicial powers of Serbia over its provinces. The alleged exodus of Serbs from Kosovo came to occupy a central place in political debates after the 1981 riots in which Kosovo Albanians had called for greater autonomy for their region. Over the course of the 1980s the migration of Kosovan Serbs back to Serbia proper and the supposedly 'conscious decision on the part of Albanians to reproduce rapidly in order to change the demographic picture of Kosovo'[124]

---

[120] Richard West, *Tito and the Rise and Fall of Yugoslavia* (London: Faber and Faber, 2009).

[121] Paul Hockenos, *Homeland Calling: Exile Patriotism & the Balkan Wars* (Ithaca, NY: Cornell University Press, 2003), 68.

[122] Michael Mann, *The Dark Side of Democracy: Explaining Ethnic Cleansing* (Cambridge: Cambridge University Press, 2005), 353–81.

[123] Nir Arielli, *From Byron to bin Laden: A History of Foreign War Volunteers* (Cambridge, MA: Harvard University Press, 2017); see also: 'Gotovina et al. (IT-06–90)', ICTY, www.icty.org/en/case/gotovina/4.

[124] Momčilo Pavlović, 'Kosovo under Autonomy, 1974– 1990', in Charles W. Ingrao and Thomas Allan Emmert (eds.), *Confronting the Yugoslav Controversies: A Scholars' Initiative* (West Lafayette, IN: Purdue University Press, 2009), 48–82.

featured prominently in the Serbian nationalist discourse of demographic threat. It fed into the already widespread media and public discourse that portrayed the Serbian nation as a victim and under threat from Albanians and a political Islam.

The radicalisation of the Serbian minority in Croatia gave further justification for that part of the Serbian elite back in Belgrade who argued for the necessity of violence to defend their ethnic compatriots. After Tuđman's electoral victory in 1990, the nationalist HDZ had demoted the status of Serbs in Croatia from nation to minority and started campaigning for Croatia's independence. In reaction, a Serb assembly was established within Croatia: it became the ruling body of the self-proclaimed Republic of Serbian Krajina (RSK). Croatian political culture radicalised too, often invoking the Nazi-allied Independent State of Croatia as its precursor; the 'šahovnica', the chequered shield used by the Croatian government during the Second World War, was restored as Croatia's national symbol. Amongst the Serbian minority, painful memories of persecution resurfaced; their fears were then instrumentalised by the Serbian state in turn as a justification for armed intervention to support the RSK. With the support of Belgrade, the extremist wing in the Serb Democratic Party of Croatia sidelined more moderate voices among the Serbian community in Croatia.[125] Indeed, the victory of the hardliners within the Serb Party of Croatia was not based on wider popular support.[126]

The war in Bosnia (1992–5) was seen by many who fought in it as a conflict defined religion-based ethnic identities, along the lines of global civilisational frontlines. This drew in international financial support and volunteers, expanding the conflict beyond a collapsing Yugoslavia. Mujahideen fighters, including Afghanistan veterans, flocked from various Muslim countries to fight on the side of the Bosnian army and 'their besieged Muslim brethren', and in the summer of 1993 a separate unit, the El Mujahed, was established as part of the Bosnian Army.[127] Foreign mercenaries also participated amongst their opponents: Ukrainians, Russians, Greeks, and Romanians fought on the Serbian side while returning

---

[125] Richard Caplan, *Europe and the Recognition of New States in Yugoslavia* (Cambridge: Cambridge University Press, 2005), 114–19.

[126] Nina Caspersen, *Contested Nationalism: Serb Elite Rivalry in Croatia and Bosnia in the 1990s* (New York: Berghahn Books, 2010).

[127] Jennifer Mustapha, 'The Mujahideen in Bosnia: The Foreign Fighter as Cosmopolitan Citizen and/or Terrorist', *Citizenship Studies*, 17/6–7 (2013), 742–55; Jeanine de Roy van Zuijdewijn and Edwin Bakker, 'Returning Western Foreign Fighters: The Case of Afghanistan, Bosnia and Somalia' (International Centre for Counter-Terrorism – The Hague Background Note, June 2014), www.icct.nl/download/file/ICCT-De-Roy-van-Zuijdewijn-Bakker-Returning-Western-Foreign-Fighters-June-2014.pdf.

Croat émigrés and French, British, American, Dutch, Irish, and German mercenaries and volunteers fought with the Croat forces in both Croatia and Bosnia.[128] Their presence further inflamed the tensions and brought wider ideological, cultural, and religious conflicts into the heart of the Yugoslav Wars. Moreover, some of these Islamist fighters stayed on after the war as naturalised Bosnian citizens and continued to propagate fundamentalist beliefs; others became implicated in terrorist activity in the West.[129]

The violent dissolution of Yugoslavia was not only an internal affair of competing nationalisms: the international community also played a central role in legitimating the idea of self-determination. In just a few years the positive Westernising image of Yugoslavia had been shattered. Robert D. Kaplan, a US foreign policy expert, espoused a thesis of alleged 'ancient ethnic hatreds' in his controversial 1993 book *Balkan Ghosts* and argued that ethnic conflict was endemic to the region, which he had qualified as 'a Third World region within Europe'.[130] As the conflict spread into Bosnia in 1992, the former Yugoslav region came to be seen as a space where the usual rules of conflict management and minority protection did not apply, and enabling self-determination came to be seen as the only reasonable response to the crisis of a region where violence supposedly could not be stopped. Reductionist visions of backwardness and the inevitability of conflict that revived longer-term Western stereotypes of the Balkans quickly took hold.[131] Even internal briefing reports within the United Nations drew upon essentialised notions of cultural and civilisational difference.[132] It was often assumed that Yugoslavia existed in a liminal place between Europe and a Global South that stood beyond the realm of safe peaceful continental politics

---

[128] See Nir Arielli, 'In Search of Meaning: Foreign Volunteers in the Croatian Armed Forces, 1991–95', *Contemporary European History*, 21/1 (2012), 1–17; Rob Krott, *Save the Last Bullet for Yourself: A Soldier of Fortune in the Balkans and Somalia* (Havertown: Casemate Books, 2008).

[129] Frazer Egerton, *Jihad in the West: The Rise of Militant Salafism* (Cambridge: Cambridge University Press, 2011), 124.

[130] Robert Kaplan, 'Europe's Third World', *Atlantic*, July 1989, www.theatlantic.com/past/docs/unbound/flashbks/balkans/kaplanf.htm.

[131] For this attitude, see Robert Kaplan, *Balkan Ghosts* (New York: Piacador, 1993); Eugene Michail, 'Western Attitudes to War in the Balkans and the Shifting Meanings of Violence, 1912–91', *Journal of Contemporary History* 47/2 (2012), 239.

[132] 'The battle lines are reminiscent of the old discords between the Catholics of the Austro-Hungarian Empire and the Orthodox and Muslim peoples of the Ottoman Empire, and between areas belonging to the Latin and Byzantine traditions respectively'. Francesc Vendrell, 'Yugoslavia: Some Current Issues (Confidential)', 2 March 1989, United Nations Archive, Secretary-General Javier Perez de Cuellar (1982–1991), S-1024-0097-06, 3.

that had developed since 1945. The Yugoslav Wars were seen as a violent throwback within a new world order – thus Western elites sometimes came to overcompensate, supporting self-determination as supposedly inevitable and without alternative, and ignoring the exclusionary ethnic (and violent) politics of those who claimed to be the 'good' democratic forces. When Croatian elites lobbied for independence in 1989–90 they were viewed as extreme; following Serbian military intervention in 1991–92, both Croatian and Slovenian nationalist politicians effectively utilised the language of democracy and Europeanisation – concealing their internal undemocratic practices against minorities – in order to present their nationalist projects to an international audience as the only reasonable solution in a region that otherwise was disposed to violent barbarism. It is worth noting that the Western equation of violence and un-civilisation in South-Eastern Europe was stronger in the early 1990s than over the previous century: the first Balkan war in the early twentieth century received a sympathetic hearing as a struggle of Christians against the Turks, and was supposedly comprehensible due to Ottoman atrocities; the violence of the Second World War was sometimes judged as part of a much larger conflict born out of an ideological clash between fascism and anti-fascism or between the Axis and the Allies.

Despite these reductionist visions, there were important Western defenders of the idea of Yugoslavia as late as 1991. The United States pursued its policy of prioritising stability for the Yugoslav federal government well into that year: James Baker, US secretary of state, visited Belgrade in June and extended support to the federal reformist prime minister Ante Marković for the preservation of Yugoslavia. In an international context where the US presidential race was under way at the same time as the EC was negotiating its further integration, many in the West pinned their hopes on Marković for a future for Yugo-slavia.[133] What some of them saw as his 'far-reaching economic *pere-stroika*'[134] included many reforms which were initially perceived as painful and accepted with a lot of reservations, but proved highly effective within a year. However, like that of Gorbachev, Marković's vision of reformed federalist socialism was not shared by conservatives and other factions within the Yugoslav Communist party, who were

---

[133] Stokes, *The Walls Came Tumbling Down*, 240.

[134] Michael Palairet, 'The Inter-regional Struggle for Resources and the Fall of Yugoslavia', in Lenard J. Cohen and Jasna Dragović-Soso (eds.), *State Collapse in South-eastern Europe: New Perspectives on Yugoslavia's Disintegration* (West Lafayette, IN: Purdue University Press, 2008), 233.

more interested in the retention of power and for that purpose decided to sympathise with or overtly exploit nationalist rhetoric. Until as late as September 1991 the federal presidency was conducting negotiation talks with the EC in Brussels.[135] Marković himself, in fear for his safety, during his last months in office in Belgrade – before he resigned at the end of December 1991 – was guarded by Marines loaned out by the US ambassador.[136]

But by late 1991, as violence escalated and the Yugoslav federal institutions had ceased to function, the EC took on a more proactive role. When it established the Peace Conference for Yugoslavia and the quasi-judicial Arbitration Commission in August 1991, a definitive breakup was still not on the cards. Indeed, just a few months earlier the EC had promised substantial financial support and an immediate start to talks for an associate membership if a political/constitutional settlement among the republics could be reached.[137] However, as the crisis escalated, the EC issued in December 1991 the Declaration on the Guidelines on the Recognition of New States in Eastern Europe and in the Soviet Union, paving the way for the recognition of the independence of those Yugoslav republics that sought recognition without the agreement of Serbia.[138] The EC also initiated the Badinter Arbitration Commission, composed of five Western European constitutional judges that invoked legal rulings from mid-century decolonisation. Indeed, it discarded the Yugoslav constitution's postulates on self-determination – which were, in any case, contradictory, as they allowed each nation the choice to secede, whilst also requiring consensus for border changes – and instead searched in international law for a precedent. Not only were frontier changes through armed conflict on European soil seen as something that had been long relegated to history, but also Western governments lacked the legal and political vocabulary to make sense of and deal with the complexity of the

---

[135] Omer Karabeg, 'Vasil Tupurkovski: Raspad je bio neminovan, ali ne i rat' (The Dissolution Was Unavoidable, but Not the War – Interview), *Radio Free Europe*, www.slobodnaevropa.org/content/article/1045340.html.

[136] Mark Thompson, *A Paper House: The Ending of Yugoslavia* (London: Vintage, 1992).

[137] 'Evropa ne dozvoluva raspaganje na Jugoslavija' (Europe Will Not Allow the Disintegration of Yugoslavia), *Nova Makedonija*, 17 April 1991; 'EZ ke ja pomogne edinstvena Jugoslavija' (The EC Will Support Unitary Yugoslavia), *Nova Makedonija*, 7 June 1991; 'Evropskata banka e za edinstvena Jugoslavija' (The European Bank Is for Unitary Yugoslavia), *Nova Makedonija*, 22 June 1991.

[138] Malgosia Fitzmaurice, 'Badinter Commission (for the Former Yugoslavia)', in *Max Planck Encyclopedia of Public International Law*, http://opil.ouplaw.com/view/10.1093/law:epil/9780199231690/law-9780199231690-e13.

Yugoslav crisis. Thus they looked back to the dissolution of Western European Empires: Yugoslavia became the first country outside of the Global South where a legal principle (*uti possidetis*) was applied that 'upgraded former administrative delimitations, established during the colonial period, to international frontiers'.[139] Its original purpose had been to prevent the stability of new states being endangered by fratricidal struggles provoked by the changing of frontiers following the withdrawal of an administering power. However, in the case of Yugoslavia, this represented a novel, unprecedented extension: a central principle of self-determination had moved from the Global South northwards.[140] Techniques and a legal vocabulary drawn from the period of high decolonisation were used to legitimise the dissolution of a state on the European continent. The Commission originally issued ten opinions, the first of which stated that Yugoslavia no longer met the criteria of a state under international law as its essential government organs had become powerless. Opinion Number 8 from 4 July 1992 stated that the dissolution was complete and the Socialist Federal Republic of Yugoslavia no longer existed.

The Yugoslav crisis was the first exercise in conflict management for a European Community on the way to greater political integration and a newfound geopolitical confidence. Whether subnational forms of self-determination were legal and to be encouraged was a central question for the community in this period. However, the lack of a unified European policy that culminated in Germany's unilateral pushing for recognition of Croatia's and Slovenia's independence – despite the fact that Croatia did not fulfil the EC criteria for statehood – was perceived as sending mixed signals to the different political forces in the country and exacerbating the crisis. The international community was divided on the issue: the EC proceeded with the recognition of the two Westernmost and predominantly Catholic Yugoslav republics against the advice of its own chief negotiator Lord Carrington, the UN secretary-general, and the United States. This undermined Europe's credibility as a neutral mediator, and

---

[139] *Case Concerning the Frontier Dispute (Burkina Faso v Republic of Mali)* [1986] ICJ Rep 554 para 23, as cited in Christian Walter, Antje von Ungern-Sternberg, and Kavus Abushov (eds.), *Self-Determination and Secession in International Law* (Oxford: Oxford University Press, 2014), 2.

[140] Snežana Trifunovska, *Yugoslavia through Documents: From Its Creation to Its Dissolution* (Dordrecht: Martinus Nijhoff, 1994); Daniel Bethlehem and Marc Weller (eds.), *The Yugoslav Crisis in International Law* (Cambridge: Cambridge University Press, 1997).

it provided a pretext for the Serbian delegation to withdraw from the negotiations.[141]

Germany's and the EC's recognition of Slovenia and Croatia in December 1991 and January 1992 remains an unresolved controversy,[142] although in some cases the responsibility that this decision has been thought to bear for the violent conflict has been overstated.[143] Indeed, the conflict had erupted much earlier. However, it was in the case of Bosnia that the connection between EC recognition and the explosion of armed conflict was strongest.[144] Germany's and the EC's selective recognition of Croatia disregarded the republic's serious violations of minority rights and Tuđman's territorial ambitions in Bosnia. This was at a time when the Badinter Commission ruled that only Macedonia and Slovenia satisfied the criteria for recognition. The European response to the Yugoslav crisis established a new pattern of collective recognition as a tool in political conflict management, where such acknowledgement was made dependent upon a catalogue of criteria of legitimate statehood.[145] Drawing upon traditionally strong ties to Croatia through the ethnic Croatian diaspora in Germany and responding to the first waves of refugees, Germany stressed what it called 'its moral duty to help other nations coming out of an era of Communism'.[146] Helmut Kohl's reaction to the voices of condemnation coming from Britain, France, and the United States illustrated this newfound international role and diplomatic assertiveness post-reunification: 'We won't let ourselves be lectured by others who have hardly raised a finger to support the reform process in Eastern Europe'.[147]

---

[141] Annemarie Peen Rodt and Stefan Wolff, 'EU Conflict Management in Bosnia and Herzegovina and Macedonia', in Richard G. Whitman and Stefan Wolff (eds.), *The European Union as a Global Conflict Manager* (London: Routledge, 2012), 138–41.

[142] Charles W. Ingrao and Thomas Allan Emmert (eds.), *Confronting the Yugoslav Controversies: A Scholars' Initiative* (West Lafayette, IN: Purdue University Press, 2009), 166–67. See also Steven L. Burg and Paul S. Shoup, *The War in Bosnia-Herzegovina: Ethnic Conflict and International Intervention* (New York: M. E. Sharpe, 1999); Beverly Crawford, 'German Foreign Policy and European Political Cooperation: The Diplomatic Recognition of Croatia in 1991', *German Politics & Society*, 13/2 (35) (1995), 1–34; Susan Woodward, 'The Political Economy of Ethno-Nationalism in Yugoslavia', *Socialist Register* 39 (2003), 73–92.

[143] Caplan, *Europe and the Recognition of New States in Yugoslavia*, 97.   [144] Ibid.,120.

[145] Christian Walter and Antje von Ungern-Sternberg, 'Introduction', in Walter, von Ungern-Sternberg, and Abushov, *Self-Determination and Secession in International Law*, 7. See also Stefan Oeter, 'The Role of Recognition and Non-recognition with Regard to Secession' in the same volume.

[146] Rodt and Wolff, 'EU Conflict Management', 140.

[147] Josip Glaurdić, *The Hour of Europe: Western Powers and the Breakup of Yugoslavia* (New Haven, CT: Yale University Press, 2011), 273.

Washington did not extend such recognition to Slovenia, Croatia, and Bosnia-Herzegovina until April 1992. As a senior official at the White House remarked at the time, 'We have felt that for the United States to have proceeded with selective recognition – that is, of Croatia or Slovenia – before now would not have served the purpose of containing and ending the conflict'.[148] The American dilemma surrounding secession underpinned by national self-determination was similarly reflected in President Bush Senior's speech in 1991 before Ukraine's independence referendum, where he warned against 'suicidal nationalism': 'And yet freedom is not the same as independence. Americans will not support those who seek independence in order to replace a far-off tyranny with a local despotism. They will not aid those who promote a suicidal nationalism based upon ethnic hatred'.[149] US President Bill Clinton's dismissal of Europe as 'incompetent' in the handling of the Yugoslav crisis meant that in the end a more decisive involvement of the UN and especially of the United States and NATO was needed to supplant Brussels's role and put an end to the conflict in 1995. The intervention in Kosovo four years later to stop the conflict between Serbian forces and Kosovar Albanians was built on the memory of failure in the early 1990s – the 'not another Bosnia' lesson was crucial in ensuring the western military response.[150]

The disintegration of Yugoslavia acted as a warning: it caused varying degrees of concern and anxiety about possible similar outcomes elsewhere in the post-socialist world. Western policy makers were primarily concerned with stability. 'Don't break up Yugoslavia because people in the Soviet Union will use it as a model', warned a State Department official.[151] According to the German diplomat Gerhard Almer, in the first half of 1991 the foreign minister of the Federal Republic of Germany Hans-Dietrich Genscher often saw events in Yugoslavia through Soviet lenses: 'Well, Yugoslavia disintegrating is a bad example for Soviet disintegration, and this was bad for us since we needed a Soviet Union capable of action because we needed to get a deal with them on our unity'.[152] Russia's post-Soviet leaders also recognised many of their own countries' issues through the Yugoslav mirror and feared a similarly

---

[148] David Binder, 'US Recognizes 3 Yugoslav Republics as Independent', *New York Times*, 8 April 1992.

[149] 'After the Summit: Excerpts from Bush's Ukraine Speech: Working "for the Good of Both of Us"', *New York Times*, 2 August 1991.

[150] Oliver Daddow, '"Tony's War?" Blair, Kosovo and the Interventionist Impulse in British Foreign Policy', *International Affairs*, 85/3 (2009), 547–60. See also Bill Clinton, *My Life* (London: Arrow, 2005), 849; Richard Caplan, 'International Diplomacy and the Crisis in Kosovo', *International Affairs*, 74/4 (1998), 745–61.

[151] Glaurdić, *Hour of Europe*, 175.   [152] Ibid., 160.

violent scenario in the post-Soviet realm. 'The Yugoslav experience was very important for us', Yeltsin recalled in his memoirs; after all, the country had been 'formed after the model of the Soviet Union ... [and] Yugoslavia's problems began as a chain reaction to the events in the Soviet Union'.[153] The liberal foreign minister Andrei Kozyrev in particular was haunted by nightmares about ethnic strife in the post-Soviet space. He often invoked the Yugoslav tragedy on his numerous trips to conflict areas, and it seems to some effect: in Transnistria he calmed down an angry crowd of Slavic women who had been incited by the Russian nationalist Rutskoi, asking whether they wanted to send their sons to a civil war.[154] In China, pundits argued that China's weakened state capacity put the country at risk of disintegrating, just as Yugoslavia had: 'If we were permitted to take another step here and speculate on the worst case scenario, it seems possible that once the "political strong man" at the centre (for example, Deng Xiaoping) passes away, a situation like that in Yugoslavia after the death of Tito could take place in China ... We could go from economic disintegration to political fragmentation, and, in the end, fall into national disintegration'.[155]

In the immediate aftermath of 1989, conflicts escalated in Transnistria, Nagorno Karabakh, South Ossetia, Abkhazia, Chechnya, and the Fergana Valley.[156] As in Yugoslavia, nationalist conflicts in the Caucasus at the end of the Soviet Union were exacerbated by the complex administrative solutions of the 'national question' stemming from socialist federalist principles and the Leninist understanding of self-determination. Elsewhere in the post-Soviet space, as in Croatia, significant transnational diaspora communities that adopted terrorism as an acceptable political strategy were a crucial factor in provoking conflict and violence, especially in the case of Armenia.[157] This reinvigoration of ethnic separatisms persisted long into the post-socialist era. Both the Autonomous Province of Kosovo in Yugoslavia and the Nagorno Karabakh Autonomous Region in Azerbaijan are cases in point, as militant groups and elites saw an opportunity for different territorial/ethnonational arrangements once the tectonic shifts unleashed by the events

---

[153] Boris Jelzin, *Mitternachtstagebuch. Meine Jahre im Kreml* (Berlin: Ullstein, 2001), 178.
[154] Alfred Koch and Petr Aven, *Gaidar's Revolution: The Inside Account of the Economic Transformation of Russia* (New York: I.B. Tauris, 2015), 251.
[155] As cited in Joseph Fewsmith, *China since Tiananmen: The Politics of Transition* (New York: Cambridge University Press, 2008), 135.
[156] Fred Halliday, 'Third World Socialism. 1989 and After', in George Lawson et al. (eds.), *The Global 1989. Continuity and Change in World Politics* (Cambridge: Cambridge University Press, 2010), 112–34, 132.
[157] Tokić, 'Landscapes of Conflict', 740.

around 1989 opened up sites for the use of violence and even ethnic cleansing as tools for implementing a different understanding of self-determination.

Reverberations of Eastern European Self-Determination

The revival of minority nationalisms did not stop at the former Iron Curtain. In May 1989 all major Belgian parties agreed on the political isolation of the right-wing populist nationalist Flemish party Vlaams Belang, whose support was growing. Separatists in northern Italy founded the Lega Nord in December 1989. The vocabulary of 1989 was also used by South Tyrol activists in their demands for the 're-unification' of Tyrol and chants at manifestations: 'Wir sind ein Volk' ('We are one people'). 'If peoples in Central and Eastern Europe stand up', declared the separatist movement, 'then the nations of Western Europe should become more aware of their own sovereignty as well'. Placards were seen at demonstrations contrasting Roland Riz, the leader of the South Tyrolian People's Party who was seen as too moderate, with the more radical anti-Soviet Russian president: 'We exchange Riz for Yeltsin'.[158] In Spain, Prime Minister Felipe González, confronted with Catalan and Basque separatism, was well aware of the contagiousness of this reinvigorated nationalism from the East. More than any other Western political figure, he encouraged Gorbachev to keep the Soviet Union together. Spain, alongside Romania, Slovakia, and China, later refused to recognise the independence of Kosovo.[159]

Eastern European self-determination nevertheless became both part and catalyst of what would become a European and a global trend. The independence of the Baltic states was mobilised by those Catalan nationalists who argued for pro-independence positions in the 1990s, which in turn led to the Catalan Parliament articulating its right to self-determination. With the revival of the Catalan cause in the 2010s, 1989 was remembered again: the Via Catalana ('Catalan Way') human chain protest of 2013 drew inspiration from the Baltic Chain of 23 August 1989 when two million people joined hands across Estonia, Latvia, and Lithuania to demonstrate for their independence. The Catalan as well as the Scottish and the Quebec cases have important parallels with the former state socialist processes of secession in terms of

---

[158] 'Tiroler Einheitskundgebung am Brenner. Wenige aber hartnäckige Befürworter der Selbstbestimmung', *Neue Zürcher Zeitung*, 16 September 1991.
[159] Gorbatschow, *Erinnerungen*, 763.

the institutional frameworks that provided for regional autonomy or different degrees of devolution and decentralisation. Considering that Catalan and Basque demands for self-determination had been at the centre of the struggle against Franco's dictatorship, the Spanish Constitution of 1978 provided for a decentralised organisation of the post-Franco state and recognised the right of 'nationalities and regions' to autonomy.[160] Later, Catalan nationalism also drew inspiration from the former Yugoslav republics, in particular from Slovenia, where Catalan separatism found more support, from both the general population and political parties. Overall, the various struggles for independence in Eastern Europe were seen by Catalan nationalists as the best model to achieve a peaceful independence that is also recognised by the international community.

Slovenia featured in Catalan debates as a Central European country, where a referendum that was initially not recognised by either the federal authorities or Europe nevertheless led to successful independence within the European family – after hostilities initiated by the central power were overcome.[161] The violence of the Yugoslav disintegration also became an inspiration for extremely violent right-wing white nationalists across the world. The ethnic cleansing of European Muslims by Serbia in the 1990s was invoked by mass murderers in their manifestos, where they railed against the NATO intervention designed to protect 'Muslim Kosovo' in 1999 against a country defending white Christian civilisation and celebrated the nineteenth-century violent struggle against the Ottoman Empire.[162]

Conclusion

The end of European state socialism was a crucial moment in the twentieth-century global history of self-determination. The narratives

---

[160] Xavier Cuadras Morató (ed.), *Catalonia: A New Independent State in Europe? A Debate on Secession within the European Union* (London: Routledge, 2016), 9.

[161] 'Les claus de la independència d'Eslovènia: similituds i diferències amb Catalunya. La via eslovena s'ha presentat en els últims dies com una opció per aplicar a Catalunya', *Nació*, 11 October 2007; '¿Qué es la vía eslovena a la independencia a la que apunta Puigdemont?', *El Diario*, 10 October 2017.

[162] See the manifestos of the far-right terrorist responsible for the mass murder on Utøya, Norway, in 2011 and of the gunman in the mosque attacks in Christchurch, New Zealand, in March 2019: he played a song honouring Radovan Karadžić (the Bosnian Serb leader found guilty of genocide in Srebrenica) before shooting with weapons inscribed with the names of fighters against the Ottoman Empire. Maja Zivanovic, 'New Zealand Gunman "Inspired by Balkan Nationalists"', 15 March, 2019, Balkan Insight, https://balkaninsight.com/2019/03/15/new-zealand-mosque-gunman-inspired-by-balkan-nationalists/.

created in the aftermath of 1989 remained mostly national in focus and revolved around heroic myths of various countries' liberations. Yet the processes that led to the withdrawal of Soviet control in Eastern Europe and the partly violent collapse of multiethnic federations in the region were connected to manifestations of self-determination elsewhere. The reinvigoration of the language of self-determination in the 1960s was rooted in decolonisation in Africa and Asia and in the institutionalisation of human rights at the international level through the United Nations. These developments provided movements, on both the left and the right of politics, with a language in which to couch their demands. Marxist renewal movements and conservative anti-Communists alike, both at home and in exile, saw themselves as part of a wider anti-imperialist struggle in ways that commonly linked anti-Sovietism to the struggles of Cuba or Vietnam against the US. Noting that Africa was now liberated from the Empire, diasporas called for the liberation of Croatia from the Yugoslav federation and the Baltic states from the Soviet Union. Anti-Communist organisations such as the Assembly of Captive European Nations campaigned for liberation from 'red imperialism'. In the early 1980s, the Soviet invasion of Afghanistan revived the notion of the Soviet Union as an imperial power and rekindled narratives that conflated state socialism with colonialism.

In Eastern Europe, solidarity with the Global South eventually lost its potency. By the last decades of the Cold War, the framing of self-determination in the region became less internationalist and focussed on the national struggle. Yet claims to sovereignty were not just a question of an oppositional rhetoric; socialist states themselves long mobilised this language at home and abroad, and, from the 1970s, began to assert a form of ethnic nationalism to legitimise themselves. Ultimately, attempts by elites to capture nationalism for socialism only strengthened demands for freedom from Soviet 'occupation'. Moreover, the idea of self-determination came as much from the centre as from the periphery of the bloc. Gorbachev put an end to Soviet geopolitical over-reach and began the process of retreat from the Global South, and then Eastern Europe. Russian nationalists increasingly clamoured for their liberation from the burdens of maintaining the Soviet Union and its 'Empire'.

On the fringes of the Soviet-dominated socialist world and in the Balkans, sovereignty and self-determination became associated with the right to secession from federations. In the case of dissolutions of Czechoslovakia and (most of) the Soviet Union, this occurred with a remarkable absence of conflict. Yet in Yugoslavia, a combination of a weakening federation, the return of radical diaspora, nationalising elites, and an international community that legitimated secession, contributed to the spread of conflict and the break-up of the country. The violent dissolution of Yugoslavia sparked fears of a similar scenario in the Soviet Union. The international community, including the US, attempted to limit the application of self-determination, first through supporting the status quo and only later by endorsing territorial, but not ethno-national, secession. Nevertheless, self-determination remained a potent concept in the region; by the 2010s, populism entered the political mainstream, and, with it, the language of liberation from the alleged neocolonial tutelage of Brussels or the Euro-Atlantic Empire, as we shall see in Chapter 6.

5.   Reverberations

On 21 December 1989 Nicolae Ceaușescu returned from a state visit to Iran. In an attempt to build a bulwark against the contagious effects of the transformations under way in other socialist countries, he had explored the establishment of a developmental bank to obviate Western interference and had pleased his hosts by placing a wreath on the tomb of the recently deceased Ayatollah Khomeini. At home rumours spread that he had also sought, and was given, assistance from the Revolutionary Guards to quell the mass demonstrations that had erupted against him in the Romanian town of Timișoara. Four days later a swiftly established military tribunal charged Ceaușescu and his wife Elena with embezzlement and an alleged genocide during the protests. Both were condemned to death within an hour, and a firing squad executed them immediately. Parts of the military and middle echelons of the Communist Party organised this coup d'état behind the scenes. They had the show trial and execution filmed and shown to audiences in Romania and the West, to discourage possible resistance from Ceaușescu loyalists and hence cement their own power grab. The footage of the couple's mock trial and their dead bodies in a courtyard quickly circulated around the world.[1]

Ceaușescu had developed close links with statesmen in many different countries since the 1970s, and the spectre of his demise was commonly invoked in the following months. To other authoritarian leaders, his cruel end served as a warning. Fearing a demonstration effect, the broadcasting of the Ceaușescus' execution was blocked in countries from Albania to Zaire.[2] Chinese media did not broadcast the footage either, but behind the scenes Deng Xiaoping showed a videotape recording to other leading figures within the Chinese Communist Party in a successful attempt to convince them to postpone the lifting of martial law after the Tiananmen

[1] Telegramă nr. 061854, 31 October 1989, MAE-Iran 463/1989, 49.
[2] Vicky Randall, 'The Media and Democratisation in the Third World', *Third World Quarterly*, 14/3 (1993), 638.

incident in June. Pointing at Ceauşescu's dead body, Deng allegedly said, 'We'll be like this if we don't carry out reforms and bring about benefits for the people'.[3] Three units of the People's Liberation Army were deployed around trouble spots in Beijing, while the Politburo discussed countermeasures to contain spillover from Eastern Europe.[4] In Cuba, at around the same time, the authorities deported the correspondent of Radio Prague, who had predicted that Fidel Castro would soon suffer the same fate as the Romanian dictator.[5]

Democratically inclined protesters and other opponents of authoritarian rulers took their cue from Ceauşescu's end as well: in May 1989 Joaquim Alberto Chissano, then president of Mozambique, had been one of the last world leaders to meet Ceauşescu in Bucharest. The deprivation and authoritarianism he had witnessed in Romania reinforced his belief in the need to pursue democratisation and market reforms back home.[6] In South Africa the anti-apartheid newspaper the *Sowetan* warned: 'Whilst it is difficult to celebrate the death of any leader, the execution of Ceauşescu and his wife must further the spirit of democracy... the message is clear to all world leaders, including South Africans. History is on the side of the masses who are tired of dictatorship and oppression'.[7] In Zaire the longtime one-party-state dictator Mobutu Sese Seko fatally underestimated this shockwave created by the collapse of the regimes from the East. In January 1990 he had declared that 'perestroika does not concern the people of Zaire'; but in over five thousand petitions his opponents denounced the regime. In March leading Foreign Ministry civil servants demanded that Mobutu dissolve the state party, convoke a national conference, and resign from all functions – or he would experience 'the same fate as that of President

---

[3] John W. Garver, *China's Quest: The History of the Foreign Relations of the People's Republic of China* (Oxford: Oxford University Press, 2016), 512; Péter Vámos, 'The Tiananmen Square "Incident" in China and the East Central European Revolutions', in Wolfgang Mueller, Michael Gehler, and Arnold Suppan (eds.), *The Revolutions of 1989: A Handbook* (Vienna: Austrian Academy of Sciences Press, 2014), 107.

[4] Czeslaw Tubilewicz, '1989 in Sino-East Central European Relations Revisited', in Frank Columbus (ed.), *Central and Eastern Europe in Transition* (Commack, NY: Nova Science, 2001), 153.

[5] Hannes Bahrmann, *Abschied vom Mythos. Sechs Jahrzehnte kubanische Revolution, Eine kritische Bilanz* (Berlin: CH. Links Verlag, 2016), 115.

[6] A Mozambican TV report about Chissano's visit condemned 'the very disadvantageous cooperation' with Romania and called for pragmatic economic relations with socialist countries. Yet a level of fascination with Ceauşescu remained, and his repayment of foreign debt was described as 'an economic miracle'. Telegramă nr. 047696, 25 May 1989, 90 and Telegramă nr. 047693, 24 May 1989, 87 in MAE-Mozambic 608/1989.

[7] Editorial, *Sowetan*, 27 December 1989, 6; Douglas G. Anglin, 'Southern African Responses to Eastern European Developments', *Journal of Modern African Studies*, 28/3 (1990), 434.

Ceauşescu of Romania'.[8] In due course Mobutu was forced to legalise oppositional parties, after the United States, having propped him up for decades as an anti-Communist ally, withdrew its political and financial assistance on the grounds of a manifest lack of 'good governance', and in so doing invoked Romania, too: 'Why bankroll Africa's Ceauşescus?'[9]

The enormous geopolitical shifts around the world in the aftermath of Eastern Europe's '1989' had their roots in Moscow's imperial retreat. The end of the Cold War, the lack of political and financial aid from the Soviet Union, and the massive erosion to the political legitimacy that had derived from socialism had momentous repercussions, particularly in Africa and Latin America. The imagery of the crumbling Berlin Wall and mass demonstrations across Eastern Europe came to symbolise that change. 1989 represented the peaceful triumph of liberal democratic popular movements that inspired others in their revolt against authoritarian regimes.[10] The reactions to Ceauşescu's execution, however, illustrate that Eastern Europe's 1989 had a variety of impacts in different regions. As opposed to the widespread image of largely isolated countries, Eastern European socialist states, and strongmen like Ceauşescu, had been closely linked with many countries of the Global South and East Asia. Authoritarian leaders there did not simply give way to liberal democracy; some took the end of state socialism in Eastern Europe as a warning and successfully adapted their political systems to the geopolitics of the post–Cold War world.

1989 as a New Global Script

Over the course of the 1990s Eastern Europe's transformation came to be construed as a powerful global script, emblematic of a new type of world that was turning away from revolutionary violence, abandoning the bipolarity of the Cold War, and embracing peaceful market-based democratic change. Of all the world regions beyond Eastern Europe, Africa was to feel the most profound impact. On the one hand, this derived from the networks created by an earlier socialist

---

[8] 'Mémorandum adressé au Président-fondateur du MPR, président de la République du Zaïre par les agents et fonctionnaires du département des Affaires étrangères', quoted in Mwayila Tshiyembe, 'L'autopsie de l'échec de la transition démocratique en Afrique à la lumière de la théorie desconjonctures politiques fluids', *Présence Africaine*, 157 (1998), 76.

[9] 'Why Bankroll Africa's Ceausescu?', *New York Times*, 21 April 1990.

[10] Julia Sonnevend, *Stories without Borders. The Berlin Wall and the Making of a Global Iconic Event* (New York: Oxford University Press, 2016).

internationalism. Many of the continent's states in the late 1980s were ruled by authoritarian regimes. While some, such as Mobutu's Zaire, were staunchly anti-Communist, most of the others maintained some form of socialist rule. Several ruling parties were part of the family of Communist and workers' parties, such as those in Angola, Benin, Ethiopia, Guinea-Bissau, Mozambique, and the Republic of Congo. Many more had been closely linked to the socialist camp through decades of developmental, educational, technical, and military aid, although support from the European socialist camp had been in decline for some time. These numerous connections meant that both the economic reforms of the late 1980s and the eventual fall of regimes in Eastern Europe were closely observed. On the other hand, the transformation of Eastern Europe was instrumentalised by Western institutions and governments, which employed the experience of democratic market-based transition to pressurise African governments into reform. Although democracy talk was indeed invigorated, its effects across the continent were very mixed.

Some democratic reformist movements in Africa had already started before the changes behind the Berlin Wall; one could speak of a co-emergence of oppositional 'democracy talk' in Africa and Eastern Europe. The language of dissidence was powerful in that it appeared to embody a new common anti-authoritarian consensus – promoted also in the West – that overcame the seemingly stale left-right divisions of the Cold War.[11] Eastern Europe's '1989' accelerated this phenomenon, and democracy movements in Africa invoked its message.[12] Voices across Africa saw the collapse of the socialist bloc and then of the Soviet Union as a fundamental challenge for their continent. Meteorological metaphors abounded in Africa, too: 'Like a cyclone, the wind of freedom kept blowing, uprooting everything in its path', observed the journal *Présence Africaine*, an intellectual mouthpiece of Francophone Africa.[13] In December 1989 the outspoken chairman of the Zambia Congress of Trade Unions warned the nation that events in Eastern Europe would not spare Africa and urged reconsideration of the merits of a return to

[11] Kim Christiaens and Idesbald Goddeeris, 'Competing Solidarities? Solidarność and the Global South during the 1980s', in James Mark, Steffi Marung, and Artemy M. Kalinovsky (eds.), *Alternative Globalizations: Eastern Europe and the Postcolonial World* (Bloomington: Indiana University Press, 2002).

[12] Karuti Kanyinga, 'Limitations of Political Liberalisation: Parties and Electoral Politics in Kenya', in Walter Oyugi, Peter Wantande, and C. Odhiambo-Mbai (eds.), *The Politics of Transition in Kenya: From Kanu to NARC* (Nairobi: Heinrich Böll Foundation, 2003), 104.

[13] Laoukissam Feckoua, 'The Changing World: A Glance at the International Geopolitical Evolution since 1989', *Présence Africaine*, 153 (1996), 18.

multiparty politics. If the 'owners of socialism', he declared, 'have abandoned the one-party state, who are the Africans to continue with it?'[14] The 1990 Africa Leadership Forum conference focussed on the implications for Africa of changes in Eastern Europe and attracted some fifty political leaders from across the continent.[15]

One of the most immediate effects of 1989 was a sense of a crisis of legitimacy for many African elites. In the months that followed the fall of socialist governments in Eastern Europe, at least gestures were made towards multiparty rule.[16] Between February 1990 and August 1991 the authoritarian leaders of Benin, Gabon, Congo, Mali, Togo, Niger, and Zaire faced the demands of pro-democracy forces such as students, church leaders, and trade unions, and convened national conferences – with echoes of Eastern Europe's roundtables. During this same period, opposition groups in the Central African Republic, Cameroon, Madagascar, Burkina Faso, Mauritania, and later Chad mobilised campaigns to press their demands for national conferences to reform their political systems.[17] Marxism-Leninism was abandoned as official state ideology by ideologically flexible leaders in Angola, Mozambique, Congo-Brazzaville, Cape Verde, Guinea-Bissau, Benin, Zambia, Mali, and Madagascar.[18] Certainly, some dictators felt their position threatened after the collapse of one-party states in Eastern Europe. The leaders of the People's Movement for the Liberation of Angola (MPLA) feared they would not be able to lead their transition and began to move their savings to Portugal, causing a small real estate boom in Lisbon.[19] President Omar Bongo of Gabon noted a 'wind from the East that is shaking the coconut trees'.[20] Before long his party relinquished its monopoly of political power, and he legalised a political opposition.

---

[14] Frederick Chiluba, *Times of Zambia*, 31 December 1989 quoted in Anglin, 'Southern African Responses', 442.

[15] Ulf Engel, 'Africa's "1989"', in Ulf Engel, Frank Hadler, and Matthias Middell (eds.), *1989 in a Global Perspective* (Leipzig: Leipziger Universitätsverlag, 2015), 331–48; Francis Fukuyama, *The End of History and the Last Man* (New York: Penguin, 2012), 35; Jorge Braga de Macedo, Foy Colm, and Charles Oman (eds.), *Development Is Back* (Paris: OECD Development Studies, 2002), 270.

[16] Samuel Decalo, 'The Process, Prospects and Constraints of Democratisation in Africa', *African Affairs*, 91/362 (1992), 7–35.

[17] Pearl T. Robinson, 'The National Conference Phenomenon in Francophone Africa', *Comparative Studies in Society and History*, 36/3 (1994), 576.

[18] Richard Banégas, 'Tropical Democracy', in Jacques Rupnik (ed.), *1989 as a Political World Event. Democracy, Europe and the New International System in the Age of Globalisation* (London: Routledge, 2007), 101–10.

[19] Ricardo Soares De Oliveira, *Magnificent and Beggar Land: Angola since the Civil War* (London: Hurst, 2015), 14.

[20] Statement made in April 1990, quoted in Eric Packham, *Africa in War and Peace* (New York: Nova Science, 2004), 209.

Mozambique's president Chissano felt that 'this Marxism story is beginning to decidedly create problems for us'. Emulating Eastern European democratisation in 1990, he turned the one-party regime of Soviet-inspired and supported Frente de Libertação de Moçambique (Frelimo) into a multiparty model.[21]

Although the changes in Eastern Europe further invigorated democracy talk, actual democratisation was limited. Indeed, some rulers even invoked the idea of 'African Gorbachevs' to suggest the necessity of benevolent dictators who, without the constraints of participatory democracy, would ensure the necessary 'substantial social machine and support' for economic reform.[22] Others understood 'democracy talk' as a phenomenon inspired by the collapse of Communism, which African leaders nevertheless should have to perform only symbolically in order to obtain Western backing. One African minister at the Franco-African Summit of June 1990 was reported as stating that, 'If it is necessary to move towards greater liberty in order to get aid, promising to do so commits one to nothing'.[23] Some, such as Muammar Gaddafi in Libya, held on to their own version of socialism, but increasingly distanced themselves from an earlier era of Eastern Bloc internationalism. Several other former Soviet allies, such as the MPLA in Angola, shelved socialism, but maintained their one-party systems, re-labelling themselves as nationalists and embracing only nominal forms of democracy.

Mengistu's Ethiopia, which had received varying levels of Soviet support since the mid-1970s, found in early 1990 that its special relationship had ended: all Soviet advisors and previously generous allocations of heavy weaponry were withdrawn, and Moscow signalled that a special relationship would be replaced by a 'more business-like' one.[24] Mengistu felt abandoned and removed the Marxist trappings of his party and leadership, renaming the Workers Party of Ethiopia the Democratic Unity Party. When, in 1991, the Soviet military mission returned home, youths seized the opportunity to topple the bronze statue of

---

[21] *Expresso* (Lisbon), 12 May 1990; Joaquim Chissano: 'Democrat among the Despots', *Independent*, 23 October 2007, www.independent.co.uk/news/world/africa/joaquim-chissano-democrat-among-the-despots-397608.html.

[22] Olivier Roy, 'The Arab Four Seasons. When an Excess of Religion Leads to Political Secularisation', in Rupnik, *1989 as a Political World Event*, 114.

[23] J. Coleman Kitchen and Jean-Paul Paddack, 'The 1990 Franco-African Summit' (Washington, DC: Center for Strategic and International Studies, 30 August 1990), 2, CSIS Africa Notes, https://csis-prod.s3.amazonaws.com/s3fs-public/legacy_files/files/publication/anotes_0890.pdf.

[24] Radoslav Yordanov, *The Soviet Union and the Horn of Africa during the Cold War* (Lanham, MD: Lexington Books, 2016), 246–47.

Lenin in the capital.[25] Yet this symbolic act was no portent of liberal democracy, either: the opposition forces who took over from the socialist military junta that had ruled Ethiopia between 1974 and 1987 were Marxists and ethno-nationalists who now shelved Communist iconography but maintained their parties' vertical political control. Eventually, only a handful of African states actually travelled the whole road to liberal democracy in the 1990s, amongst them Botswana, Gambia, Mauritius, Namibia, and Senegal.[26] Yet the changes in the East were nevertheless important: they provided a language that African oppositional movements could use against autocrats, especially those whose IMF programmes had led to savage cuts in social services, currency devaluations, and slashed government salaries and positions, which had affected the urban middle classes.

One of the most significant reverberations of Eastern Europe's 1989 was felt in Southern Africa. Superpower rapprochement allowed for a settlement of the war in what became Namibia as both Cuba and South Africa withdrew their troops. Within the now ruling South West Africa People's Organisation (SWAPO), moderate forces gained the upper hand over the Marxist wing. Perestroika rendered increasingly implausible the South African apartheid regime's self-justification through invoking a fear of 'red terror'. The collapse of the Soviet Union eventually weakened the hand of the radicals in the anti-apartheid opposition, and soothed the fearful fantasies of whites that black suffrage would usher in a Moscow-directed Communist dictatorship.[27] Hence, it helped erode the Manichean opposition that had sustained both apartheid and anti-apartheid in the late Cold War, opening up the possibility for compromise and an end to the last decolonisation struggle in Africa. No longer fearing the pro-Moscow strand within the African National Congress (ANC), the United States urged the South African government to end the ban on the organisation and release Nelson Mandela from prison.[28] The political turn in countries that had once provided refuge

---

[25] Gebru Tareke, *The Ethiopian Revolution* (New Haven, CT: Yale University Press, 2009), 308; K. Somerville, 'Sub-Saharan Africa', in Alex Pravda (ed.), *Yearbook of Soviet Foreign Relations* (London: Tauris, 1991), 218.

[26] Francis Fukuyama, *The End of History and the Last Man* (New York: Penguin, 2012), 35.

[27] Chris Saunders, 'The Ending of the Cold War and Southern Africa', in Artemy Kalinovsky and Sergey Radchenko (eds.), *The End of the Cold War and the Third World: New Perspectives of Regional Conflict* (London: Routledge, 2011), 270; Rob Nixon, 'The Collapse of the Communist-Anticommunist Condominium: The Repercussions for South Africa', *Social Text*, 31/32 (1992), 235–51. Even the reaction to Nelson Mandela's release from prison in February 1991 was muted in the Soviet Union.

[28] Chris Saunders, '"1989" and Southern Africa', in Engel, Hadler, and Middell, *1989 in a Global Perspective*, 349–61.

for the ANC and South African Communist Party exiles now gave a boost to forces across Southern Africa who argued for political pluralism, catalysing democratisation processes that had already begun in countries such as Mozambique and Zambia before 1989.

Instrumentalising 1989: The West and New Forms of Political Conditionality

'1989' was also vital for Africa as its message was mediated through Western institutions and governments. Very rapidly the story of the Eastern European transformation was absorbed into the idea of an ongoing mission of the West. It served to confirm the superiority of the Western model and could be used to normalise the idea that democratic governance and market economy represented the only viable future. Such stories were used to enforce what was becoming known as 'conditionality': the tying of aid or economic investment to the enactment of a very specific form of political-economic transition. In the 1970s many states had been spared such pressures in the wide-ranging economic pacts between the European Community (EC) and African countries – the so-called Lomé Agreements. These had provided over three billion dollars to African countries (mainly former colonies) and preferential access for some goods to the European market. With the assertive politics of the New International Economic Order in the background, the fear of another oil shock, and European concerns about losing access to raw materials, African regimes were able to resist any European moves to enforce conditionality. Lomé became seen as the embodiment of a progressive agreement between the Global North and the Global South.[29] This absence of conditionality was not to last.

By the mid-1980s an increasingly Western-dominated International Monetary Fund (IMF) used conditionality behind loans to enforce market-based state structural adjustment to economies outside the West.[30] The withdrawal of support to Africa from the Communist bloc from the early 1980s further accelerated this pressure: after being

---

[29] Guia Migani, 'The EEC and the Challenge of ACP States' Industrialisation, 1972–1975', in Christian Grabas and Alexander Nützenadel (eds.), *Industrial Policy in Europe after 1945: Wealth, Power and Economic Development in the Cold War* (London: Palgrave Macmillan, 2014), 256–76.

[30] Alexander Kentikelenis and Sarah Babb, 'The Making of Global Neoliberalism: Norm Substitution and the Clandestine Politics of International Institutional Change' (paper presented at 'Global Neoliberalisms: Lost and Found in Translation', British Academy, 7 June 2018). See also Susan Woodward, *Balkan Tragedy: Chaos and Dissolution after the Cold War* (Washington, DC: Brookings Institution Press, 1995).

rejected for Comecon membership, and failing to obtain Eastern European financial assistance in 1983, Mozambique was forced by the middle of the decade to turn to the IMF.[31] Such was the case in Ghana too, where leaders of the military regime that took power in 1981 – the so-called Provisional National Defence Council – failed in their pleas for bloc assistance: Zaya Yeebo, a former PNDC secretary, commented, 'I thought we could go to the Soviet Union and the Scandinavian countries for help rather than the IMF. Only later did I realize that the Soviets were either unwilling or unable to help us'.[32] He then noted that in the early 1980s the IMF was not concerned about supporting fledgling authoritarians, as long as they reformed their economies. These disciplining strategies could be particularly powerful in regions such as Eastern Europe or Africa where countries were indebted or in need of outside investment – which gave outside private banks or international institutions greater leverage.

In the early 1980s, the IMF and the World Bank had remained agnostic about the type of political system that would best deliver economic reform. They were prohibited from intervention in political affairs and usually had no qualms about collaborating with authoritarian states. Poland under Martial Law, Jerry Rawlings's Ghana, and Pinochet's Chile were seen as more effective in the implementation of economic reform against social pushback.[33] Yet this was changing by later in the decade. As Eastern European reformers debated whether development was possible without democracy, so did international institutions: a 1989 World Bank Report for the first time articulated the idea that structural adjustment required the overhaul of entire political frameworks.[34] These developments were inspired by debates over political reform in Latin America and governance in Africa. Nevertheless, it was the collapse of the Eastern Bloc that gave such an approach to political conditionality a global impetus. State socialism's implosion confirmed ideas about the unsustainability of the 'big state'. The attacks

---

[31] John Loxley, 'The IMF, the World Bank and Sub-Saharan Africa: Policies and Politics', in Kjell J. Havenik (ed.), *The IMF and the World Bank in Africa. Conditionality, Impact and Alternatives* (Uppsala: Scandinavian Institute of African Studies, 1987), 59.

[32] Kwame Akonor, *Africa and IMF Conditionality: The Unevenness of Compliance, 1983–2000* (London: Routledge, 2006), 41.

[33] See Chapter 1. See also Nicolas Guilhot, *The Democracy Makers: Human Rights and International Order* (New York: Columbia University Press, 2005), 189.

[34] World Bank Report, 1989. On the shift to conditionality with rights in EU-African relations, see Guia Migani, 'Lomé and the North-South Relations (1975–1984): From the "New International Economic Order" to a New Conditionality', in Claudia Hiepel (ed.), *Europe in a Globalising World: Global Challenges and European Responses in the 'Long' 1970s* (Baden-Baden: Nomos, 2014), 143–44.

against overstaffed and underperforming governments also took on cultural overtones. In both the Global South and Eastern Europe, socialist governments were presented as foreign forms of governance, considered to have perverted local political traditions and autochthonous institutions.[35] The form of the transformation in Eastern Europe became the new mantra of important international institutions and donors: for instance, new guidelines from the US Agency for International Development in March 1991 stated that democratisation would now be placed on an 'equal footing' with performance in economic reform in determining the recipients of US foreign aid.[36] This new political conditionality was particularly forcefully imposed in Africa.

Western European capital had begun shifting from Africa to the new economic opportunities opening up in Eastern Europe from the 1970s.[37] The more Europe integrated economically, the smaller the percentage of Europe's trade came to be with the Third World. This trend accelerated in the 1980s: many African states were mired in debt, and foreign private investment in the whole continent dwindled from 2.3 billion dollars in 1982 to 500 million in 1986.[38] This outflow of capital increased again with the collapse of state socialism and the creation of the European Bank for Reconstruction and Development in 1991, which supported private sector development in the East with an initial investment of more than seven billion dollars.[39] The direct economic impact of the collapse of state socialism in terms of trade was actually quite limited; never more than 5 per cent of African exports had gone to Eastern Europe, and usually much less. Rather, what affected Africa was the diversion of finance and investment, which hit middle-income African states particularly hard. In August 1990, the Nigerian Joseph Garba, then president of the United Nations General Assembly, noted the emergence of this new equation: 'It is no secret that as Eastern Europeans open up to embrace democratic principles, they have instantly become the favourites to

---

[35] On the cultural definition of the World Bank's concept of 'good governance', see Guilhot, *Democracy Makers*, 219–20.

[36] Decalo, 'Process, Prospects', 23.

[37] Oladeji Ojo, 'Introduction', in Ojo (ed.), *Africa and Europe. The Changing Economic Relationship* (London: Zed Books, 1996), 7. Also see Oladeji Ojo and Christopher Stevens, 'Recent Changes in the Former Soviet Union and Eastern Europe: Opportunities and Challenges for Africa', in Ojo, *Africa and Europe*, 133, 141–42.

[38] Ivan T. Berend, *An Economic History of Twentieth-Century Europe* (Cambridge: Cambridge University Press, 2006), 270.

[39] Africa Research Bulletin, Economics Series, June 1990, in Decalo, 'Process, Prospects', 19–20.

receive Western aid and assistance which have never so freely been given to African countries'.[40]

The redirected capital flows strengthened Western Europe's position. As African states now had to compete more forcefully with other opportunities available to Western European capital, Western leaders could exert more pressure on African governments to reform politically and respect human rights in exchange for aid, investment, or continued military protection.[41] The French president François Mitterrand used precisely these arguments in order to suggest that Africa needed to follow the example of Eastern European democratisation. Otherwise the continent stood little chance of maintaining inward investment, which was now being diverted to a competitor region: 'It is important for us to talk about democracy ... it is a universal principle which recently emerged among the peoples of Central Europe ... In the space of a few weeks, governments once considered strong, were overthrown ... It was the revolution of the people, the most important since the French Revolution of 1789, and it is going to continue ... The event that convulsed Eastern Europe have led to questions amongst you ... You are worried that capital might be diverted away from Africa. France does its duty [but] ... unless we are able to restore confidence, it is difficult to hope private capital will come'.[42] Conferences were organised to instruct African leaders in the Eastern European transformation: democratic rights, good stewardship and effective governance were now key to ensure international investment.[43] Lynda Chalker, the United Kingdom's minister for overseas development, echoed this point at one such meeting in May 1990: 'I know that many people in Africa fear that Eastern Europe may prove an irresistible magnet for assistance and investment which the West has hitherto given to Africa ... It is therefore in the interests of African governments to ensure that they take steps in parallel to maintain and enhance the political and economic attractiveness of their own countries as candidates for investment'.[44]

---

[40] Quoted in Fatima Nduka-Eze, *Joe Garba's Legacy: Thirty-Two Selected Speeches and Lectures* (New York: Xlibris Corporation, 2012), 355.

[41] Decalo, 'Process, Prospects', 19–20.

[42] Opening Address of President François Mitterrand at the Conference of Heads of State of France and Africa, La Baule, 20 June 1990.

[43] Olusegun Obasanjo and Hans d'Orville (eds.), *The Impact of Europe in 1992 on West Africa: Papers from a Conference Held in Brussels, Belgium, Apr. 21–23, 1989* (New York: C. Russak, 1990); Eboe Hutchful, 'Eastern Europe: Consequences for Africa', *Review of African Political Economy*, 18/50 (1991), 51–59.

[44] Lynda Chalker, 'South Africa and Europe – The Way Ahead', Speech at a South African Foundation conference, 22 May 1990, *South Africa International*, 21 (July 1990), 1–7.

Many African leaders resented being asked to accept forms of democracy based on regionally specific changes in Eastern Europe.[45] The twenty-sixth summit of the Organisation for African Unity declared that countries had the right to 'determine, in all sovereignty, their system of democracy on the basis of their sociocultural values, taking into account the realities of each [country]'.[46] Nevertheless, as the Cold War ended there was consensus that aspects of the realignment that the Eastern European collapse heralded were necessary – state socialism was exhausted, and the much cited 'wind of change' might have a vital cleansing effect on African dictatorships where poor leadership had held back development. As in Eastern Europe, the argument was increasingly made that democratic input was a necessary prerequisite for effective development because the 'less participatory political systems have become in Africa, the more politically decadent and economically backward they have tended to become'.[47]

However, the debate on democracy was not supposed to become 'an unabashed celebration of liberalism', to quote the Tanzanian law professor Issa Shivji. He, along with others, argued that the re-imagining of politics in various countries on the continent should be rooted in local historical experiences, thus avoiding what he saw as the unconditional adoption of Western models by Africans.[48] It was in this context that the G-15, a grouping of leading developing nations from the Global South aiming to revive the North-South cooperation that the United States had marginalised in the 1980s, was initiated. It was hoped that such renegotiation of the terms of engagement would alleviate the new imbalances that the collapse of Communism and East-West reconciliation exacerbated.[49]

Within a few years these new norms based on *political* conditionality would be embedded in fresh agreements between the EU and African states. In the Lomé Convention IV (1995), substantial space was allotted

---

[45] Boutros Boutros-Ghali, 'The Marginalisation of Africa', in Nikolaos A Stavrou (ed.), *Mediterranean Security at the Crossroads: A Reader* (Durham, NC: Duke University Press, 1999), 29.

[46] 'Declaration on the Political and Socio-economic Situation in Africa and the Fundamental Changes Taking Place in the World', Twenty-Sixth Ordinary Session of the Assembly of the Organisation of African Unity, Addis Ababa, Ethiopia, from 9–11 July 1990, AHG/Decl.1 (XXVI) 1990, 4 https://archive.au.int/collect/auassemb/import/English/AHG%20Decl%201%20XXVI_E.pdf.

[47] Roy, 'Arab Four Seasons', 114.

[48] Issa G. Shivji, 'The Democracy Debate in Africa: Tanzania', *Review of African Political Economy*, 18/50 (1991), 80.

[49] Kripa Sridharan, 'G-15 and South-South Cooperation: Promise and Performance', *Third World Quarterly*, 19/3 (1998), 358–60.

to ensuring the twin goals of economic adjustment and human rights and democratic accountability necessary to ensure attractive environments for foreign investment. Yet, a political conditionality model that was created for the states in the European East had the potential to be deeply damaging in the far more fragile states of Sub-Saharan Africa.[50]

'Taming' the Left

Eastern Europe's '1989' and the subsequent collapse of the Soviet Union had a profound impact across the spectrum of the political left around the world. State socialism, the only existing systemic alternative to capitalism, had failed spectacularly in the region where it had first taken state power. Most of the few remaining champions of Soviet-style Communism lost not only an important source of income but also their belief in revolutions as successful vehicles for political change. But '1989' had just as great an impact on those leftists who had long distanced themselves from Eastern European Communism. Violent revolution all but disappeared from the arsenal of leftist strategies for political change. The end of European state socialism catalysed ongoing processes of deradicalisation and instigated a fundamental rethinking amongst both social democrats and various radical left groups. The failures of not only state planning but also market socialism helped embed a new consensus over capitalist market economy and democratic change amongst a reforming left from Latin America and Western Europe to Southern Africa and South Asia. This message of an accommodation with a capitalist world order was powerful because it also came from a region that had until 1989 defined itself against the imperialism of the West.

This was the culmination of a long-term deradicalisation of the left from the heights of a global anti-imperialist struggle to its return to the fold of Western liberalism. In the aftermath of decolonisation, many Western European and Latin American leftists, including moderate social democrats, had embraced Third World liberation movements and more radical forms of democracy. The Swedish prime minister Olof Palme had been an advocate for Castro's Cuba and a sharp critic of US foreign policy. In the United Kingdom, Gordon Brown and Jack Straw, future Labour prime minister and home secretary, had rallied in solidarity with the Chilean socialism of Salvador Allende. Young social democrats and left Catholics had travelled to Cambodia, Central America,

---

[50] Daniel C. Bach, 'Europe-Afrique: le régionalisme sans co-prospérité', *Politique Africaine*, 49 (1993), 31–46.

North Korea, and Yugoslavia in search of viable non-Soviet types of socialism.[51] The 1970s and 1980s witnessed a creeping disillusionment with such regimes. But parts of the West European and Japanese post-1968 left still sought to emulate the Chinese Cultural Revolution with Communist splinter groups and party cells; when China changed tack in the late 1970s, they turned to Enver Hoxha's Albania as their final socialist utopia. In the 1980s many such activists in West Germany joined the nascent Green Party, which profited from their experience with disciplined party work. With the disappearance of the Second World, they reached an accommodation with liberalism and moderate politics. After 1989, many of the former young Maoists and Hoxhaists formed the more pragmatic and – at least in this respect in continuity with their earlier political stance – Moscow-critical wing of the party.

The practices of peaceful dissidence and the spectacle of the negoti-ated dismantling of what had appeared monolithic systems further dele-gitimised revolution as a method for political transformation. For parts of the West German radical left, work with Eastern European dissidents – most notably with Solidarność in Poland – provided powerful educations in incremental and non-confrontational anti-authoritarianism.[52] Former 68ers were frequently impressed by the maturity of Eastern European struggle, contrasting it to their own earlier dreams of utopia. Here was a progressive democratic movement with which they could identify, and whose practices confirmed the rightness of their abandonment of what now seemed an excessive idealism. The Mexican public intellectual and former student activist Enrique Krauze, on a trip to Prague in late 1989, felt reminded of his youthful protests in 1968, but commended the more responsible nature of the East European revolution: 'We [the Mexican 68ers] attained next to nothing because we wanted to change everything, from the police chief to the world capitalist system … As opposed to us, the young Czechs of 1989 understand that civic liberty is not a pure

---

[51] Bernd Rother, 'Die SPD und El Salvador 1979 bis 1985. Linke Politik im atlantischen Dreieck von Bundesrepublik, Zentralamerika und USA', *Vierteljahreshefte für Zeitgeschichte*, 1 (2019), 645–83; Benedetto Zaccaria, 'Learning from Yugoslavia? Western Europe and the Myth of Self-Management (1968–1975)', in Michel Christian, Sandrine Kott, and Ondrej Matejka (eds.), *Planning in Cold War Europe: Competition, Cooperation, Circulations (1950s–1970s)* (Berlin: De Gruyter, 2018), 213–36; Peter Fröberg Idling, *Pol Pots leende* (Skönlitterär dokumentär, Atlas Förlag, 2006); Luise Rinser, *Nordkoreanisches Reisetagebuch* (Frankfurt am Main: Fischer-Taschenbuch-Verlag, 1981).

[52] James Mark and Anna von der Goltz, 'Encounters', in Robert Gildea, James Mark, and Anette Warring (eds.), *Europe's 1968: Voices of Revolt* (Oxford: Oxford University Press, 2013), 155–59; Gerd Koenen, *Das Rote Jahrzehnt. Unsere Kleine Deutsche Kulturrevolution, 1967–1977* (Köln: Kiepenheuer & Witsch, 2001).

outbreak or a never-ending ecstasy, but a flow which at every turn constructs and limits its cause. There was no provocation, and there was no violence'.[53]

The overwhelming majority of the global left after 1989 no longer saw revolutions and one-party rule as part of civilised modern politics. This was not a trend that began with the Eastern European events. Eurocommunists in Southern Europe in the late 1970s or various regional Indian Communist parties in the 1980s were already coming to terms with multiparty liberal democracy. The left in urban Latin America had long been critical of the bureaucratic authoritarianism of Eastern European socialism. Former *dependencia* theorists and leftist opponents of military dictatorships in South America had distanced themselves from violent resistance and had begun advocating negotiations with military dictators about a return to democracy in the 1980s.[54] But Eastern Europe further reinforced this new direction of travel and had profound demonstration effects as it provided several models of reform from within authoritarian one-party regimes and pacted transitions with the former authoritarian leaders.

These ideas attracted most interest in states with their own versions of one-party regimes or long dominant parties that had come under attack. Mexican critics of the decades-long one-party rule of the Partido Revolucionario Institucional (PRI) in the late 1980s were demanding its democratisation from within and had high hopes for its new leader Carlos Salinas. The parallel reforms in the Soviet Union reminded Mexicans of the 1920s when both their political systems had been created: inspired by Gorbachev, some Mexican pundits thus demanded a 'PRIstroika' or a 'Salinastroika' of the country's political institutions.[55] Representatives of Eastern Europe's 1989 were invited by former leftists to speak of their experiences, which were used to show the journey from radical leftist to a responsible, moderated, and accommodating politics. In the summer of 1990 Octavio Paz, that year's Nobel Prize laureate and one of many Latin American leftists turned liberal, hosted some fifty intellectuals from Eastern Europe and Latin America to discuss, live on Mexican TV, the consequences of Eastern Europe's abandonment of one-party rule for Mexico. The intellectual magazine *Vuelta* titled a

---

[53] Enrique Krauze, 'Diario de Praga', *Vuelta* 1 (1990), 17–21.
[54] Carlos Castañeda, *Utopia Unarmed. The Latin American Left after the Cold War* (New York: Penguin Random House, 1993), 240–41.
[55] Russell Bartley and Sylvia Erickson Bartley, *Eclipse of the Assassins. The C.I.A., Imperial Politics, and the Slaying of Mexican Journalist Manuel Buendía* (Madison: University of Wisconsin Press, 2015), 63; 'Mexicans Hoping for Salinastroika', *New York Times*, 5 January 1989.

special issue 'Cheers to Poland' and invited Adam Michnik as well as several Polish philosophers and poets to contribute.[56]

The sight of Eastern European Communists making their compact with liberal democracy was a powerful one for the left in South Africa, too. Amongst radical opponents of apartheid, the events in Eastern Europe helped erode their reservations regarding 'bourgeois' democracy as a purported entry point for neo-imperialism: a multiparty system became could now be considered as a progressive alternative. Moderate leftists invoked 1989 in their attempt to marginalise the more radical confrontational voices within the ANC. The Institute for Democratic Alternatives in South Africa (IDASA), founded in 1986 with support from George Soros and US companies, was designed to promote a non-radical transformation for South Africa. In March 1990 an editorial in the organisation's magazine underlined the main lesson that they thought 1989 offered: 'Contrary to the impression created by dramatic TV coverage of the incidents of mass protest action, it has been discipline, restraint, tolerance and even sophistication of the process of democratisation, which have been impressive in most cases'.[57] An IDASA delegation to Eastern Europe in April 1992, whose trip was co-organised by the liberal German Naumann Foundation and funded by Soros and the Ford Foundation, noted the elite-guided nature of the transition and concluded that 'there are many lessons that South Africa can learn from Germany, Czechoslovakia and Hungary and elsewhere; economic development and progress must go hand in hand with political change'.[58] Their recipes for change reinforced calls by IDASA leader Alex Boraine that the ANC should move 'beyond being a liberation movement to becoming a normal political party'.[59] For some on the South African left, this was moderation taken too far: radical critics of negotiated transitions demanded public protest and street politics to bring down the regime.[60] South African Communist periodicals often referred to this as the 'Leipzig option', named after the mass protests in that city in

---

[56] *Vuelta* 166 (1990); Tobias Rupprecht, *Soviet Internationalism after Stalin: Interaction and Exchange between the USSR and Latin America during the Cold War* (Cambridge: Cambridge University Press, 2015), 291.

[57] John Barrat, 'Eastern Europe: Too Soon to Tell', *Democracy in Action*, March 1990, 12.

[58] Charlene Smith, 'Eastern Europe Wrestling with Too Much History', *Democracy in Action*, April 1992, 1–6.

[59] Ian Taylor, 'South Africa's Transition to Democracy and the "Change Industry": A Case Study of IDASA', *Politikon: South African Journal of Political Studies*, 29/1 (2002), 31–48; Alex Boraine, 'Strong Hearts and Cool Heads Needed', *Democracy in Action*, March 1990, 2.

[60] Ulf Engel, 'Africa's "1989"', in Engel, Hadler, and Middell, *1989 in a Global Perspective*, 358.

autumn 1989 that were crucial in smashing the legitimacy of the SED in East Germany.[61]

Violent Cold War radicalism were tamed by 1989, too. Leftist terrorist groups such as the West German Red Army Faction, the Japanese Red Army, the Uyghur East Turkestan People's Revolutionary Party, the Italian Red Brigades, the Kurdistan Workers' Party (PKK), and the Irish Republican Army had continued to be active in the 1980s. After the collapse of the Eastern Bloc, whose secret services occasionally supported them, they either disbanded or downplayed their Marxist ideology and anti-colonial rhetoric. The urban guerrilla in South America, which had inspired many of them, disappeared too, with the return of democracy there. Rural guerrillas, once linked with anti-imperialist networks from Algeria to Vietnam, either disbanded or sunk into battles over drug money.[62]

The trend of an accelerated deradicalisation of the global left after 1989 did not mean that all hopes for socialism were abandoned. Indian Communist parties actually gained electoral support in the 1990s. A minority of Marxist dissidents across the former Eastern Bloc, from Rudolf Bahro in Germany to Roy Medvedev in Russia, saw the dismantling of the one-party state as an opportunity to create a democratic socialism.[63] And in South Africa in 1989, Joe Slovo, the general secretary and leading theorist of the South African Communist Party, wrote 'Has Socialism Failed?', a text that became one of the defining statements of the Communist left in the last years of apartheid. Slovo, who came from a Lithuanian Jewish family that had immigrated to South Africa in the 1930s, argued that the Communists had to resist any call to violence or the lure of an authoritarian one-party state to achieve their objectives. Only multiparty democracy, he insisted, would do: 'Our party's programme holds firmly to a post-apartheid state which will guarantee all citizens the basic rights and freedoms of organisation, speech, thought, press, movement, residence, conscience and religion; full trade union rights for all workers including the right to strike, and one person one vote in free and democratic elections. These freedoms constitute the very essence of our national liberation and socialist objectives and they clearly

---

[61] Jeremy Cronin, 'The Boat, the Tap and the Leipzig Way', *African Communist*, 130 (1992).

[62] Aldo Marchesi, *Latin America's Radical Left. Rebellion and Cold War in the Global 1960s* (Cambridge: Cambridge University Press, 2017).

[63] Roy Medvedev, 'Politics after the Coup', *New Left Review* 189 (1991), 104; Rudolf Bahro, 'Gastrede auf dem SED/PDS-Parteitag am 16. Dezember 1989', in Lothar Hornbogen et al. (eds.), *Außerordentlicher Parteitag der SED/PDS. Protokoll der Beratungen am 8./9. und 16./17. Dezember 1989 in Berlin* (Dietz: Berlin, 1999).

imply political pluralism'.[64] Nevertheless, Slovo held on to a faith in the future possibilities of socialism for South Africa: 'Socialism certainly produced a Stalin and a Ceauşescu, but it also produced a Lenin and a Gorbachev. Despite the distortions at the top, the nobility of socialism's basic objectives inspired millions upon millions to devote themselves selflessly to building it on the ground'.[65]

'1989' also reduced the space available on the left for alternative economic thinking. Leftists across the Americas, South Asia, and Europe took the collapse of the Eastern Bloc as the final proof that not only state planning but also market socialism had failed – and that there was no systemic alternative to global capitalism. Not only did it delegitimise other Marxist projects, but also more moderate forms of mixed economy in the West and the South. In India, for example, 1989 happened against the backdrop of the collapse of the Nehruvian consensus, based around economic planning, secularism, and anti-imperialism. Socialism, enshrined in the country's constitution, had been losing traction in the 1980s; two weeks after the fall of the Berlin Wall, the long-ruling Congress Party that embodied these principles lost its absolute majority in the general elections. In 1991 Congress took the collapse of Soviet Union, its longtime supporter, as a warning sign and a major argument to push through the deregulation and opening up of the Indian economy. The political class now embraced capitalist markets and entrepreneurship; government intervention in commercial decisions was greatly reduced; IMF credits came with the conditionality of structural adjustment with world markets.[66]

While socialism was abandoned in all but name at the federal level, Communist parties remained powerful in some Indian states. For the Communist Party of India (Marxist) (CPI(M)) in West Bengal, economic liberalisation unexpectedly shored up their continued rule. States could now set up industries and attract foreign capital without federal control. 'Marxism is a science … not a dogma', declared the Politburo member Buddhadeb Bhattacharya to justify his deals with various corporations that had stimulated economic growth, '[it] will have to keep pace with changing times'.[67] The party leadership now pointed at the fate

---

[64] Joe Slovo, 'Has Socialism Failed?', *Cape Times*, 16 May 1990, FBIS-AFR-90-122-S, 21. See also his call for Communist parties to accelerate their democratisation after the resignation of Gorbachev in summer 1991: Patrick Laurence, 'Democracy the Lesson of the Soviet Coup- Slovo', *Star*, 26 August 1991, 6.

[65] Slovo, 'Has Socialism Failed?'

[66] Nivedita Menon and Aditya Nigam, *Power and Contestation: India since 1989* (London: Zed Books, 2007), 5.

[67] Ibid., 107.

of the Soviet command economy and argued that even China and Vietnam were now having to invite private capital for development. They also began reining in trade union militancy. Critics later lamented that such policies of 'dialectical marketism' pursued by the CPI(M)-led Left Front government made them 'virtually indistinguishable from those of other parties committed to the neoliberal agenda'.[68]

As in the case of Indian socialists and Communists, an acceptance of the constraints of global capitalism amongst the West European and Latin American left had begun in the decade before 1989. But the collapse of state socialism in the East accelerated such processes, as it confirmed that a future for any kind of market socialism was neither likely nor desirable. Chilean socialists who had been exiles in the GDR during the years of the military dictatorship, for example, upon their return had no wish to implement centralised planning as they had experienced it in their daily lives in a socialist country and thus accepted the continued liberal economic policies of the new democratic government.[69] 'Politics is no longer a battle between the state and the market', mused a young Tony Blair in 1991 in *Marxism Today*, the theoretical journal of the British Communist Party, 'all fixed points on the landscape have changed. There are no safe havens of political doctrine. Everything and anything can be thought or rethought. We start again. Yet there is an irony. Even as events in the East unfold, the potential for advance by socialist and social democratic parties has not been greater for many decades'.[70] This advance came with the embracing of markets and individual responsibility by the tamed social democratic left in Western Europe. By the end of the decade after 1989, Tony Blair's New Labour in the United Kingdom and Gerhard Schröder's SPD in Germany were elected on platforms of a 'Third Way' or *Neue Mitte* ('new centre') committing the left to an accommodation with neoliberal economics and support for armed liberal interventionism.

Interventionism and the '1989' Myth

The '1989' myth – that the world was converging on liberal market democracy – was powerful in large part because it had been constructed and promoted in Western Europe and North America. Understood by

---

[68] Ibid., 105.

[69] Jadwiga Pieper Mooney, 'East Germany: Chilean Exile and the Politics of Solidarity in the Cold War', in Kim Christiaens, Idesbald Goddeeris, and Magaly Rodríguez García (eds.), *European Solidarity with Chile 1970s–1980s* (Frankfurt am Main: Peter Lang, 2014), 275–300.

[70] Tony Blair, 'Forging a New Agenda', *Marxism Today*, 10 (1991), 32–34.

both the right and a deradicalised left as a victory over dictatorship, and a confirmation of the political and moral rightness of liberal democracy and the market economy, it became central to the constitution of the very idea of the West in the post–Cold War world. Whilst '1989' was often celebrated less within Eastern Europe, it became an important part of the memory politics of the EU, which presented itself as the embodiment and protector of a democratic 'third' way that triumphed over Southern European fascism and Eastern European Communism. From this perspective, '1989' was a crucial staging post on the journey to the reconstitution of Europe under the guidance of the West. The Nobel Committee employed exactly this narrative when it awarded its 2012 Peace Prize to the EU.[71]

'1989' was also narrated as year zero in a self-congratulatory story of the victory of market-capitalism and the spread of a 'democratic peace'. In the 1990s the US presidents George H. W. Bush and Bill Clinton referred to the idea that a newly interconnected world economy would reduce the pressures that had formerly led to conflict and convince authoritarian states to see the advantages of democracy.[72] Western organisations that had been founded to support Eastern European oppositions in the 1980s expanded their work to cover new democracy promotion programmes. First they turned to authoritarian leaders that had remained in the formerly Communist Europe, then to dictators in the wider world. The post-1989 democracy promotion activities of Western organisations in Eastern Europe produced in the second half of the 1990s a revolutionary template that was exported during the 2000s across Eurasia and later in North Africa. It centred on the idea of toppling authoritarian leaders by the fostering of opposition forces and civic mobilisation.

Western organisations such as the National Endowment for Democracy and the Open Society Foundation employed modern marketing practices during the elections that unseated governments led by successors of the former Communist parties in Romania (1996), Bulgaria (1997), Slovakia (1998), and Croatia (1999). The template acquired a revolutionary aura in Serbia, after a combination of massive popular protests and electoral success led to the toppling of

---

[71] Wilfred Loth, *Building Europe: A History of European Unification* (Berlin: De Gruyter, 2015), 433.

[72] Melvyn Leffler, 'Dreams of Freedom, Temptations of Power', in Jeffrey Engel (ed.), *The Fall of the Berlin Wall: The Revolutionary Legacy of 1989* (Oxford: Oxford University Press, 2012), 133.

Slobodan Milošević.[73] Just as in Bucharest, Sofia, Bratislava, and Zagreb, democracy-promotion organisations focused on pre-existing local civil society organisations in Belgrade as essential actors for tilting elections against (neo-)authoritarian leaders. The US government gave assistance to the Serbian anti-Milošević student movement Otpor! ('Resistance!') and the Democratic Opposition of Serbia to the tune of 10 million dollars in 1999 and 31 million in 2000.[74]

Serbia set an example for the coming Colour Revolutions in the former Soviet space: Georgia (2003), Ukraine (2004), Kyrgyzstan (2005) – as well as for the Arab Spring in Tunisia and Egypt (2011).[75] With Western financial support, Otpor! activists became traveling consultants on non-violent political tactics. They exported know-how based on electoral campaigning and promoted books by the US political scientist Gene Sharp about peaceful change from dictatorship to democracy across Eurasia and North Africa.[76] The Otpor! activist Aleksandar Marić described his promotion of political marketing to the Ukrainian youth opposition: 'We trained them in how to set up an organisation, how to open local chapters, how to create a 'brand', how to create a logo, symbols, and key messages'.[77] The initial success of the Colour Revolutions consolidated the notion, amongst local activists and Western supporters alike, that democratic change could be created with outside help at a very rapid tempo.[78] The speed of the collapse of socialist regimes in Eastern Europe as well as the success of the 'bulldozer revolution' in Belgrade (called this on account of the demonstrators' storming of the national TV station with heavy machinery) fuelled the belief in the possibility of forcibly creating democracy rather than seeing it as the outcome of a long, meandering evolutionary process.[79] The Colour Revolutions transformed 1989 into a globally exported idea that

---

[73] Gerald Sussman and Sascha Krader, 'Template Revolutions: Marketing US Regime Change in Eastern Europe', *Westminster Papers in Communication and Culture*, 5/3 (2008), 91–112.

[74] Jon Bacher, 'Video Review: Bringing Down a Dictator', *Peace Magazine*, 18/3 (2002), 28.

[75] Asiem El Difraoui, 'No "Facebook Revolution" – But an Egyptian Youth We Know Little About', in Muriel Asseburg (ed.), *Protest, Revolt and Regime Change in the Arab World* (Berlin: German Institute for International and Security Affairs, 2011), 18.

[76] Lucan Way, 'The Real Causes of the Coloured Revolutions', *Journal of Democracy*, 19/3 (July 2008), 55–69.

[77] Sussman and Krader, 'Template Revolutions', 103.

[78] Barbara Falk calls this misreading of 1989 a belief in the 'elixir of speed'. Barbara Falk, 'From Berlin to Baghdad: Learning the "Wrong" Lessons from the Collapse of Communism', in George Lawson et al. (eds.), *The Global 1989. Continuity and Change in World Politics* (Cambridge: Cambridge University Press, 2011), 255–57.

[79] Sussman and Krader, 'Template Revolutions', 104.

advocated nonviolent revolutions implemented by way of professional activism funded through democracy-promotion programmes.

By the early 2000s a less multilaterally inclined variant of the 'liberal-interventionist' school dominated US foreign policy. Under President George W. Bush, influential advisors reached back to the late Cold War to make sense of their new civilisational mission for the public. Following the attacks of 11 September 2001, Bush declared the anniversary of the fall of the Berlin Wall to be 'World Freedom Day': 'Like ... the defeat of totalitarianism in Central and Eastern Europe ... freedom will triumph in this war against terrorism'.[80] If the resolve of late Cold War struggles could be revived, then 'freedom' could be brought to the Middle East. When, in April 2003, following the invasion of Iraq, the statue of Saddam Hussein was torn down, the US secretary of defence Donald Rumsfeld remarked: 'Watching them ... one cannot help but think of the fall of the Berlin Wall and the collapse of the Iron Curtain'.[81] The so-called 'neo-conservatives' in Washington now saw the Middle East as a site to extend the export of liberal democracy to those revolutionary autocrats whom they regarded as hangovers from the Cold War. The collapse of socialist regimes in Eastern Europe had contributed to the entrenchment of authoritarian regimes such as Saddam's in Iraq or Gaddafi's in Libya. The demise of their former supporters and the rapid weakening of the Non-Aligned Movement isolated these regimes. Middle Eastern dictators, after 1989, resolved to entrench their rule by crushing any movements for liberalisation. Absent from the 'neocon' rhetoric was the fact that, unlike in Eastern Europe or Southern Africa, such secular and protectionist authoritarian dictators had the backing of some of the urban and educated middle classes who feared the rise of political Islam under democratic rule.[82]

Eastern Europeans and the Export of the Revolutionary Idea

Eastern European elites in the 1990s and 2000s often participated in this 'export' of the ideals of 1989. As their countries joined Western political and military institutions, so they adapted themselves to such ways of reading the end of European state socialism, and started to play roles in democracy export initiatives. At home, memories and interpretation of the meanings of 1989 in Eastern Europe were often the source of

---

[80] Leffler, 'Dreams of Freedom', 134.   [81] Ibid., 134.
[82] Roy, 'Arab Four Seasons', 113.

fractious political division.[83] On the world stage, however, regional elites could celebrate Eastern Europe's contribution to the global development of democracy. They founded institutes to spread the regional experience of a peaceful, negotiated transition worldwide.

In the early 1990s, it was through work to support the transition from apartheid in South Africa and with Cuban dissidents that Eastern European liberals refined this new role. In the 1980s Eastern European oppositions had in fact distanced themselves from the anti-apartheid struggle. With the notable exception of East Germany, dissidents had associated Nelson Mandela and the ANC with socialism, and support for the anti-apartheid cause with the official anti-imperialist rhetoric of their own despised regimes. In 1990 voices in the South African anti-apartheid opposition had feared that a new 'reactionary' post-socialist Eastern Europe would abandon them, and the prospect of early trade deals with the apartheid regime in Pretoria appeared to confirm these fears.[84] Accusations that Hungary and Romania were secretly attempting to 'circumvent economic sanctions' against the apartheid regime were made at the Commission on Human Rights at the UN.[85]

But increasingly the story was re-scripted: in the early 1990s the cause of Eastern Europeans and South Africans was rediscovered as a common struggle against authoritarianism. In June 1991 the United Nations' Special Committee Against Apartheid co-sponsored in Prague a conference of Eastern European politicians in cooperation with the Association of West European Parliamentarians for Action Against Apartheid. The meeting aimed to offer lessons in democratisation from Eastern Europe to Southern Africa. The event was opened by the then chairman of the Czechoslovak Federal Assembly, the former reform Communist leader Alexander Dubček. He insisted that the model to be followed in South Africa was that of the Velvet Revolution, namely, peaceful, negotiated change. Employing the language of the Prague Spring in 1968, he

---

[83] James Mark, Muriel Blaive, Adam Hudek, Anna Saunders, and Stanisław Tyszka, '1989 after 1989: Remembering the End of State Socialism in East-Central Europe', in Michal Kopeček and Piotr Wciślik (eds.), *Thinking through Transition: Liberal Democracy, Authoritarian Pasts, and Intellectual History in East Central Europe after 1989* (Budapest: Central European University Press, 2015), 463–503.

[84] Paul Betts, James Mark, Idesbald Goddeeris, and Kim Christiaens 'Race, Socialism and Solidarity: Anti-Apartheid in Eastern Europe', in Robert Skinner and Anna Konieczna (eds.), *Global History of Anti-apartheid: Forward to Freedom in South Africa* (New York: Palgrave, 2019), 174–5.

[85] Representative of the Pan-Africanist Congress of Azania Commission on Human Rights (ECOSOC), 46th Session, 10th Meeting, 5 February 1990, E/CN.A/1990/SR.10, 21.

underlined the imperatives of justice and legality for economic development, and added that 'understanding and dialogue without confrontation must be reached not only between Whites and Blacks, but also among Blacks in South Africa'.[86] Other participants were not so enthusiastic about the impact of changes in the former socialist bloc on South Africa. Ibrahim Gambari, the chairman of the Special Committee Against Apartheid, reminded the audience about socialist countries' support for the struggle against racism. However, he added that 'with the turn to truly democratic forms of government … it was hoped that Eastern Europeans would continue to stand in the forefront of the solidarity movement'.[87] Participants in the Polish roundtable were later invited to South Africa to share their experiences of negotiation.[88]

In the 1990s, in a reversal of its role as safe home for leftist exiles and international socialist organisations during the Cold War, Prague was the most active Eastern European centre for the promotion of the liberal values of 1989. In the Prague Castle, President Václav Havel met with leading Chinese dissidents and with the Dalai Lama. He also invited Palestinians, who were seeking support for a Middle East peace conference, to hold this meeting with the government of Israel in Prague. Yet, as the Czechoslovak government did not wish to fund its president's global ambitions, the process began secretly in Norway instead, and the agreements would eventually become known as the Oslo Accords.[89] Havel nominated Burma's leading dissident Aung San Suu Kyi for the Nobel Peace Prize – a move that was undermined by the discovery that the Prague-based arms firm Omnipol had been supplying weapons to the military junta she was opposing. Before 1989 it was from Prague's airport that socialist elites had flown to Havana, and Czechoslovakia was Cuba's named economic coordinator on behalf of the Eastern Bloc. Following the Velvet Revolution it became the site of the most active anti-Castro movement in the region, receiving Cuban refugees in 1990, supporting movements in Florida and elsewhere that sought to topple Castro's regime, condemning Cuban human rights violations at the UN, and

---

[86] 'Report on the International Conference on Eastern Europe and Southern Africa: Supporting Democracy and Development, Prague, 13–15 June 1991', UN General Assembly, 46th Session, Special Committee against Apartheid, 1991, A/AC.115/L.682, 5.

[87] Ibid., 8–9.

[88] Padraic Kenney, 'Electromagnetic Forces and Radio Waves or Does Transnational History Really Happen?', in Robert Brier (ed.), *Entangled Protest: Transnational Approaches to the History of Dissent in Eastern Europe and the Soviet Union* (Osnabrück: Fibre, 2013), 50.

[89] Michael Zantovsky, Havel: A Life (London: Atlantic Books, 2014), 344.

opposing the softening of EU relations with Castro.[90] Havel was the founding president of the Comité Internacional para la Democracia en Cuba (CIDC), through which he worked with the conservative Spanish prime minister José María Aznar and the first post-dictatorial Chilean president Patricio Aylwin to promote system change. On the fifteenth anniversary of the fall of the Berlin Wall, the CIDC organised a celebration in Miami for exiled Cubans that featured Czech rock bands. In Latin America Havel was widely seen as the face of Eastern Europe's democratic revolutions. Violeta Chamorra, leader of Nicaragua's own post-1989 transition from socialism, called him 'a brother in defeating with the vote the long night of oppression'.[91] As the 1990s wore on, however, Havel would increasingly receive criticism that he had abandoned his late Cold War insistence on a programme for human rights in general for a more narrowly defined anti-Communist crusade.

Such Eastern European interventions were most powerful when aligned with a broader Western project of exporting democracy and market reform. Interpreting the assistance of Western anti-Communists during the Cold War for Eastern Europe's liberation as a source of moral obligation, and viewing support for democracy as an important demonstration of their newly cemented Western identity, many other Eastern European elites backed US-led anti-Communist and anti-authoritarian interventions. In 2003, Polish elites and society overwhelmingly supported their country's participation in the US-led intervention in Iraq. Their assistance was understood domestically both as a show of gratitude for US backing during the Cold War, and as an obligation not to abandon nations to dictatorship, as they had been after the Second World War.[92] Indeed, many former dissidents, from Adam Michnik to Václav Havel and Liu Xiaobo (the 'Chinese Sakharov'), spoke out in favour of the Iraq War.[93] The anticipated success of the invasion and the transition from dictatorship revived their own memories of transformation. The Eastern European transition was now presented as a relevant source of instruction for US foreign policy and for military elites planning post-invasion political and economic reconstruction. In April

---

[90] 'Foro internacional mixto Europa-Estados Unidos-Exilio Cubano pide clara y firme condena de la tiranía castrista', *Miami Herald*, 8 April 2008.

[91] Jay Nordlinger, 'Solidarity, Exemplified. The Amazing Story of the Czechs and the Cubans', *National Review*, 14 March 2005.

[92] Maria Mälksoo, *The Politics of Becoming European. A Study of Polish and Baltic Post–Cold War security imaginaries* (London: Routledge, 2010), 125, 128–130.

[93] Mark McDonald, 'An Inside Look at China's Most Famous Political Prisoner', *New York Times*, 23 July 2012, https://rendezvous.blogs.nytimes.com/2012/07/23/an-inside-look-at-chinas-most-famous-political-prisoner/.

2003 Leszek Balcerowicz, who had twice been Poland's deputy prime minister, and as finance minister the prime exponent of its shock therapy programme, argued in Washington that Iraq's predicament was no more challenging than the situation that had faced Eastern Europe in 1989, and that Eastern European and Baltic countries could play an important role in transmitting what they had learnt about the rapid privatisation that would in all likelihood follow the invasion. The Russian liberal economist and former finance minister Yegor Gaidar shared his expertise from the Russian privatisation and deregulation programmes for the transformation of Iraq as well. And in September that year fourteen (former) finance ministers and central bank chiefs from Eastern Europe, among them Gaidar and the Pole Marek Belka, met in Baghdad to help plan the post-invasion economy.[94]

This interest was again revived during the so-called Arab Awakening from 2008 onwards.[95] Although unifying commemorations twenty years after state socialism's fall were impossible at home, foreign policy and economic elites began to 'market' their experience of revolution abroad.[96] In their outreach to the Arab world they could re-imagine what Western liberals had once denigrated as merely their 'catch up' or 'rectifying' revolutions, the memory of which was proving politically divisive and hence unusable at home, as events of global significance.[97] As holder of the EU presidency in the second half of 2011, Poland led initiatives for the promotion of international support for democratisation in North Africa and the Near East, the EU's so-called southern neighbourhood.[98] The Polish foreign minister Radosław Sikorski argued that given the absence of a colonial history and their own

---

[94] 'Economic Shock Therapy – A Prescription for the Middle East?', American Enterprise Institute, www.aei.org/events/2003/04/15/economic-shock-therapy–a-prescription-for-the-middle-east/; Leszek Balcerowicz, 'Economic Reform. Lessons for Post-Saddam Iraq from Post-Soviet Europe' (working paper, American Enterprise Institute, 24 March 2005); 'Ein "Balcerowicz-Plan" für den irakischen Wiederaufbau. Was der Irak von Polen lernen kann', *Neue Zürcher Zeitung*, 14 June 2005; Oksana Yablokova and Catherine Belton, 'Gaidar Invited to Shock, Awe Iraq', *Moscow Times*, 9 March 2003.

[95] Robert Springborg, 'Whither the Arab Spring? 1989 or 1848?', *International Spectator*, 46/3 (2011), 5–12; Barbara Falk, 'Reflections on the Revolutions in Europe. Lessons for the Middle East and the Arab Spring', in Friederike Kind-Kovács and Jessie Labov (eds.), *Samizdat, Tamizdat, and Beyond. Transnational Media During and After Socialism* (Oxford: Berghahn, 2013), 281–315.

[96] See, for example, the conference in Tallinn directed at Arab reformers held in 2011: G. Jones and G. Baczynska, 'Solidarity in the Arab Spring', Reuters, June 2011.

[97] Mark et al., ''1989 after 1989', 498–99.

[98] See the Report of Poland's EU presidency, http://pl2011.eu/sites/default/files/users/shared/spotkania_i_wydarzenia/raportue_eng_final.pdf.

experience of dictatorship, Eastern Europeans would be more readily listened to than Western advisors:

We sponsored a documentary in Arabic on the Polish democratic transition on Al Jazeera. We sent Lech Walesa to Tunisia to tell them how we did it. I was the first EU foreign minister in Benghazi, when Qaddafi was still fighting. And meeting with the then Provisional National Council made me realise that the challenges that these societies face are identical to what we in Central Europe faced two decades ago. For example, are you going to have a unitary state or a federation? What is the role of organised religion in your country going to be? Do you amend the existing constitution, or do you write a new one? Do you want a Presidential or a parliamentary system? What do you do about the personnel of the old regime, meaning secret policemen but also judges, teachers, bureaucrats, diplomats, all of whom got tainted in some way? What do you do about the archives of the old regime? These usually contain explosive material about large swathes of a society that can make or break careers. Do you destroy them, lock them up, make them accessible to the public? How do you write a media law in a democracy, and how do you grant broadcasting licences so that oligarchs don't dominate the airwaves? In various countries in the post-Soviet world, these issues were dealt with differently, and so people in the Middle East today can see what decisions lead to what results. That is why some of these countries think of us as role models. We are more comparable to them than the United States. And they are more willing to take lessons from us than from their former colonial masters or from countries with strong ties to their former dictators. Poland is true to herself when we play the role of a beacon of international solidarity on democratisation. This is what the majority of Poland's developmental assistance is devoted to. We've created a Polish Foundation for International Solidarity. And during our presidency of the EU, we initiated the creation of the European Endowment for Democracy, consciously modelled on its U.S. counterpart.[99]

Other Eastern Europeans, too, offered lessons for the Middle East: Hungary shared its experience with the problem of the accountability of former elites of toppled authoritarian regimes.[100] The Bulgarian government organised an international workshop on transitional justice and conferences to transfer their experience of transformation, offering specific help with the drafting of constitutions and the establishment of new political parties. Pointing to the peaceful, civilised, and negotiated nature of their transitions, Eastern Europeans argued against large-scale purges, and advocated the preservation of expertise from the previous regime.[101]

[99] 'The Polish Model: A Conversation with Radek Sikorski', *Foreign Affairs*, 92/3 (2013), 75.
[100] Éva Ladányi and Erzsébet N. Rózsa, 'Hungary and the Arab Spring', 5 August 2014, 12, www.grotius.hu/doc/pub/TKYIUP/2014-08-05_ladanyi_n.rozsa_hungary-and-the-arab-spring.pdf.
[101] Sara Jones, 'Cross-border Collaboration and the Construction of Memory Narratives in Europe', in Tea Sindbæk Andersen and Barbara Törnquist-Plewa (eds.), *The Twentieth*

The Stasi Prison Memorial Berlin-Hohenschönhausen established partnerships with the Tunisian and Egyptian governments as well as with civil rights activists from these two countries. Arguing that democracy required that the injustices of the previous regimes be remembered, its director Hubertus Knabe called on the Tunisian authorities 'to do everything possible to ensure that the files of the state security service are retained'.[102]

From around 2012, these celebratory political imaginaries that linked waves of democratisation in Eastern Europe to those in North Africa receded. As the hopes of democratisation in the Arab World subsided, Western countries began supporting strongmen in the region, and democracy itself came under pressure from new populist authoritarians in Eastern Europe. Parallels were used as much to explain the disappointments of the Arab Spring as to inspire: a Rand Corporation book from 2012 invoked the violent, dark side of 1989 – notably the similarity between Ben Ali's and Ceaușescu's regimes, and the violence that followed each, in order to explain the post-dictatorial quagmire in countries such as Tunisia or Egypt.[103] And it was clear that Eastern European actors had internationalised the ambiguous representations of their own post-dictatorial transformations: Knabe argued that North Africans should avoid the mistake that Eastern Europeans had made, and should therefore ban former ruling parties.[104] By the mid-2010s the idea that Eastern Europe represented a model of democratisation that had global relevance no longer received much support either at home or abroad.

From Cuba to China: Rejecting '1989'

Peaceful negotiated regime change in Eastern Europe was central to the Western-curated script of global democratic revolution that would underpin a new liberal international order. This triumphalist and often teleological narrative was not without its discontents: prominent intellectuals from the Global South warned of the rejuvenation of Western imperialism and called for new forms of democracy rooted in local historical contexts rather than international liberal templates. Countries

Century in European Memory: Transcultural Mediation and Reception (Leiden: Brill, 2017), 49.

[102] Ibid., 44.

[103] 'Eastern Europe and the Post-Soviet Space', in Laurel E. Miller, Jeffrey Martini, F. Stephen Larrabee, Angel Rabasa, Stephanie Pezard, Julie E. Taylor and Tewodaj Mengistu, *Democratisation in the Arab World: Prospects and Lessons from Around the Globe* (Santa Monica, CA: Rand Corporation, 2012), 213–14.

[104] Jones, 'Cross-border Collaboration', 48.

in the non-European parts of the socialist world, with their similar political systems and histories of ideological, economic, and cultural interaction, were often amongst the most affected. While authoritarian socialist regimes in Africa shelved Marxism (but not necessarily one-party rule), socialist regimes in East Asia and Cuba took the developments in the Soviet Union and Eastern Europe of the late 1980s as a warning, and a source of instruction on how to avoid the mistakes of socialist leaders that had led to their demise. This learning process in fact preceded 1989: in the cases of Vietnam, Laos, Cambodia, North Korea, and Cuba dating back to the beginning of perestroika in the Soviet Union from 1985, in the Chinese case even to the late 1970s. Reform impulses were taken up from Eastern Europe by political leaders and their opponents alike, but any Soviet or Eastern European–inspired mobilisation against existing regimes faced violent retaliation in all of these countries. As a result, no non-European Communist one-party state, with the exception of Mongolia, underwent substantial democratic political reforms.

Most Westerners saw the collapse of the socialist bloc and later of the Soviet Union as a triumph of liberalism. For many Africans, it was a fundamental challenge for their continent. And for those on the anti-imperialist left, particularly from an older revolutionary decolonisation generation, this was not a change for the better. As Abdulrahman Mohamed Babu, a Zanzibari nationalist and former Maoist, argued,

December 1989 will certainly go on record as one of the most decisive turning points in history since the end of World War II. Its significance must not be seen from the point of view of the cold war's so-called 'numbers game', but in terms of Europe returning to its pre–World War One imperial menace – the Europe which has done so much damage to the rest of the world in conquest, slavery, colonisation, settlerism, distortion and diversion of our national histories, through the massive devastation of world wars, the depletion of our resources, and the endangering of the world's environment.[105]

For him, a politically divided Europe had previously given African countries the ability to play both sides, and to obtain from the East support for their claims for economic justice in the world economy. Indeed, in the 1980s, some in East Africa had argued for Eastern European or Chinese market socialism as an alternative to IMF structural adjustment programmes. Babu drew on a specific phenomenon of the early 1990s, namely, 'Afro-pessimism': the idea that the eventual unification of Europe, coming on top of the withdrawal of Soviet support in

[105] Abdulrahman Mohamed Babu, 'A New Europe. Consequences for Tanzania', *Review of African Political Economy*, 18/50 (1991), 75.

the region, would mean only a strengthening of the influence of the 'West', and further marginalisation of Africa in the world economy. For part of the African left, the Eastern European collapse was a hammer blow for the possibilities of an alternative postcolonial modernity. Moreover, Hungarian and Polish elites now appeared to be aligning with apartheid South Africa, which itself had spotted a new investment opportunity in the region as a springboard for economic expansion across Europe. 'Our experience with Europe is bad enough' Babu argued, and with a right-wing Europe, it is bloody. Not only the lives of millions of people of African descent living in Europe are at stake; the continent itself is at risk. Already Hungary, Poland, and East Germany are changing their position in favour of South Africa whose interests are diametrically opposed to Africa's interests'.[106]

State socialism's collapse combined with an acceleration of western-led globalisation endangered the very idea and reality of a 'Third World' as well as the doctrine of non-alignment. Developing countries that opposed the new convergence with the liberal West were left with few geopolitical alternatives. Even the *Wall Street Journal* remarked in August 1990 upon the danger that the United Nations would be used by 'newly united superpowers ... for their own purposes, ignoring "Third World" concerns'.[107] Critical voices feared the advent of a new world order dominated by capitalism with novel inequalities, and social conflicts. As Fernando Collor de Mello, president of Brazil, put it in July 1991, 'The end of the world's ideological division has not signified an era of peace and prosperity but has led to the emergence of a great empire, the Empire of the North, absolutely rich, which controls the most advanced forces of knowledge'.[108] Amady Aly Dieng, professor of economy at the University in Dakar and central figure of pan-Africanism, argued that the disintegration of the socialist camp and the Gulf War signalled 'the symphony of a new world hegemony'.[109]

Such criticisms of an unconditional triumphalism stemming from the collapse of Communism were accompanied by sober reassessments of democratic options in Africa. Some argued that aspects of this realignment that the Eastern European collapse heralded were in fact necessary. Others, as shown above, argued that the newfound enthusiasm for debating democracy should focus on identifying original, locally grounded,

---

[106] Ibid., 76.   [107] Quoted in Hutchful, 'Eastern Europe', 54.
[108] Quoted in Reg Whitaker, 'Security and Intelligence in the Post–Cold War World', *Socialist Register,* 28 (1992), 111.
[109] Amady Aly Dieng, 'L'Afrique noire après la chute du Mur de Berlin', *Présence Africaine,* 153 (1996), 189.

democratic political forms. They doubted that the multiparty Western type of democracy would prove more responsive to the needs or wishes of the majority of Africa's population than the one-party and military dictatorships had been.[110]

Such an argument sometimes functioned as an excuse for authoritarian leaders to preserve their rule. In conversations with the Romanian ambassador in Beijing, after the Chinese Communist Party's crackdown against protesters in Tiananmen Square and across the country, Somali and Rwandan diplomats expressed their solidarity with the Chinese leadership, which they saw as guarantor of their own independence. Their invocation of socialism and 'democratic forms specifically African, which are foreign, in large measure, to the concepts typical of bourgeois Western liberalism' were meant to prop up 'the vision of a unique party and leadership in power'.[111] Nevertheless, some of the intellectuals who expressed similar misgivings about the Western script of the irrepressible march of liberalism genuinely hoped that 1989 might usher in democratic rule based on local structures rather than on civil or military bureaucracies modelled on foreign blueprints.[112] Such critiques were strikingly similar to those formulated by isolated former dissidents in Eastern Europe disenchanted with what they perceived in the early 1990s as the uncritical embrace of Western models of governance and statehood. For instance, in Hungary the left-winger István Eörsi lambasted in the main opposition journal *Beszélő* the post-1989 elites' reluctance to risk going down untraveled political roads and their opting for a simple imitation of the West. He also echoed the fears of some African intellectuals that former socialist countries had become 'new markets, cheap labor, and political support' for the West 'in its undeclared global war against the "Third World"'.[113]

In East Asia and Cuba, the fall of the Eastern European socialist regimes, as opposed to the events in the Soviet Union, had relatively little direct political impact. Thanks to the local roots of their socialist

---

[110] Adotey Bing, 'Salim A. Salim on the OAU and the African Agenda', *Review of African Political Economy*, 18/50 (1991), 67.

[111] Telegramă nr. 016071, 07 July 1989, MAE-China, Situaţia internă volum III, 214/1989, 2.

[112] For example, the left-wing historian of Africa Basil Davidson declared in an interview in 1990 that 'if these grand solutions from outside haven't worked – and the "Eastern" ones have collapsed even more completely than the "Western" ones – then surely there may be scope for saying that the Africans, out of their own history ... can find their own solutions'. Basil Davidson and Barry Munslow, 'The Crisis of the Nation-State in Africa', *Review of African Political Economy*, 7/49 (1990), 21.

[113] Ferenc Laczó, 'Five Faces of Post-Dissident Hungarian Liberalism: A Study in Agendas, Concepts, and Ambiguities', in Kopeček and Wciślik, *Thinking through Transition*, 57.

systems, which had not been imposed from abroad as in large parts of Europe, they enjoyed more legitimacy and stability, which allowed the regimes to cope better with the drop in financial aid and withdrawal of trade partners during their geopolitical reorientation. But the stories and the imagery of 1989 provided various lessons for designers of economic reform plans and oppositional groups – as well as for political figures determined to stave off a similar transformation. While Gorbachev's economic rethinking had an impact everywhere in the socialist world, local interpretations and implications were diverse. The regimes in North Korea and Cuba saw them as just another reform within the socialist system. Like early perestroika, their parallel initiatives included tighter labour disciplining and an intensification of ideological agitation. But in contrast to Gorbachev's plans for the Soviet Union, they also meant an expansion of government control over the economy. Cuba banned free trade in farming produce in 1986;[114] North Korea reduced the licence for such markets to one day a month.[115]

Both Fidel Castro and Kim Il-Sung reacted harshly to any political reform impulses that might threaten their authority. In reaction to perestroika, North Korea soon withdrew all its students from the Soviet Union; hundreds of them were sent to East Germany instead (from where they were quickly removed, the day after the Wall came down, and dispatched to labour camps as a pre-emptive measure against dissent among the population).[116] While the North Korean regime instigated the creation of a few joint ventures with Japan and Western Europe, heir apparent Kim Jong Il prepared high officials for imminent 'temporary difficulties' in 1986, demanding absolute loyalty to the North Korean interpretation of socialism in a talk called 'Some Problems Arising in "Chuch'e" Ideological Education': 'The fundamental superiority of a socialist system over a capitalist system must not be viewed from the perspective of that which is more advantageous from the standpoint of developing the economy'.[117]

In reaction to perestroika, Fidel Castro initiated his programme of 'rectificación', which he announced at a Communist Party Congress

---

[114] Carmelo Mesa-Lago, 'Efectos económicos en Cuba del derrumbe del socialismo en la Unión Soviética y Europa Oriental', *Estudios Internacionales*, 26/103 (1993), 341–414.

[115] Hy-Sang Lee, 'North Korea's Closed Economy. The Hidden Opening', *Asian Survey*, 28/12 (1988), 1269.

[116] David Hawk, *The Hidden Gulag. The Lives and Voices of 'Those Who Are Sent to the Mountains'* (Washington, DC: US Committee for Human Rights in North Korea, 2012), 25.

[117] Hajime Izumi, 'North Korea and the Changes in Eastern Europe', *Korean Studies*, 16 (1992), 4.

speech in December 1986, and which prepared the country for an intensification of the ideological struggle.[118] 'Rectification' in Cuba echoed some of Gorbachev's early initiatives, but, as in North Korea, the economy was further centralised. Once the reforms in the Soviet Union proved ever more comprehensive, the Cuban regime came under increasing pressure from its own population to emulate them; the Spanish translation of Gorbachev's book *Perestroika* was sold out after only a couple of days.[119] But the regime pushed back. Possible perestroika-inspired opponents to the Castro brothers from within the apparatus faced the harshest consequences.

Many Cuban technocrats and military elites who had studied in the Soviet Union, or had contacts with Soviets in Africa, were open to Gorbachev-style reforms within the system. The popular general Arnaldo Ochoa, member of the Central Committee of the Cuban Communist Party, had been trained at a military academy in Moscow, spoke fluent Russian, and was well connected and highly regarded among the Soviet elite. 'The world is changing', he told his old friend and brother-in-arms Raúl Castro, 'we cannot keep isolating ourselves evermore'.[120] Before long, in June 1989, Ochoa, who was widely respected amongst Cubans for his military feats in Congo, Angola, and Ethiopia, was indicted for drug smuggling and high treason. In a June 1989 show trial, recordings of which were broadcast on Cuban TV, Ochoa and three other high-ranking militaries received the death penalty and were executed shortly thereafter – a warning signal to possible renegades and the population at large not to entertain any subversive ideas from Moscow.[121]

In South-East Asia, too, Gorbachev's slogan of *demokratizatsiya* ('democratisation') went unheard. But as links with Moscow and other Eastern Bloc capitals remained strong, so messages of economic reform circulated and found a place in local debates. Vietnam was politically and economically dependent on Moscow in the 1980s: even in early

---

[118] 'Discurso pronunciado por el comandante en jefe Fidel Castro Ruz, Primer Secretario del Comite Central del Partido Comunista de Cuba y Presidente de los consejos de estado y de ministros, en la clausura de la sesion diferida del Tercer Congreso del Partido Comunista de Cuba, en el teatro "Carlos Marx", el 2 de diciembre de 1986, año del xxx aniversario del desembarco del Granma', www.cuba.cu/gobierno/discursos/1986/esp/f021286e.html.

[119] Bahrmann, *Abschied vom Mythos*, 106.

[120] Stanislav Kázecký, 'La oposición interna en Cuba desde el triunfo de la Revolución en 1959 hasta 2006' (PhD diss., Univerzita Karlova v Praze, 2007), 55.

[121] Accusations of drug smuggling and the involvement of Cuban officials were not entirely trumped up, but it is very unlikely that these activities happened without the knowledge of the Castro brothers. Robert Pear, 'Cuban General and Three Others Executed for Sending Drugs to US', *New York Times*, 14 July 1989, www.nytimes.com/1989/07/14/world/cuban-general-and-three-others-executed-for-sending-drugs-to-us.html.

1989 there were still twenty-five thousand Soviet advisors in the country and many Vietnamese labour migrants in Eastern Europe.[122] Perestroika helped a faction led by the Vietnamese president Trường Chinh galvanise support for their ideas of market-oriented reform within the socialist system.[123] One of the slogans of the Vietnamese reforms, Đổi mới tư duy ('renovation of thinking'), echoed Gorbachev's novaya mysl' ('new thinking'), as did the Laotian Communist Party's reform programme chintanaakaan mai ('new thinking') that was announced at its 1986 Fourth Party Congress.[124] Both Communist countries now allowed a more decentralised economy driven by private capital. In Vietnam a cautious liberalisation of the economy had already been under way since 1979; an adaptation of its production to world market demands had actually been encouraged by the Soviet Union, which sought to decrease its financial obligations towards often failing industrialisation projects in the Global South.[125] After the death of the longtime party boss Lê Duẩn in 1986, a similar generational change took place as in the Kremlin, and the new party leader Nguyễn Văn Linh was able to push through the more radical reform programme Đổi Mới ('renovation') with reference to the changes under way in Moscow.[126] But while the impulse for reforms came from Moscow, their content was also inspired by regional neighbours, especially after the failure of perestroika became obvious. Like the East Asian Tigers and Indonesia, and also their geopolitical foe China, Vietnam and Laos combined authoritarian power with elements of a market economy.[127]

By the time the grand cascade of regime collapses in Eastern Europe began, the Vietnamese economy was already growing considerably, if from a very low level, helping cement the regime's legitimacy. The defeat of the Polish Communists in the 4 June election 1989 convinced

---

[122] Balász Szalontai, 'From Battlefield into Marketplace. The End of the Cold War in Indochina 1985–1989', in Kalinovsky and Radchenko, End of the Cold War, 165.

[123] Tuong Vu, Vietnam's Communist Revolution. The Power and Limits of Ideology (New York: Cambridge University Press, 2017), 24, 238, 246–47, 253.

[124] Jonathan Rigg, Living with Transition in Laos. Market Integration in South-East Asia (London: Routledge, 2005).

[125] Evgenija Bogatova, 'V'etnam. Put' k novoj khozjajstvennoj modeli', Kommunist, 3 (1990), 106–10.

[126] Wladimir Andreff, 'The Double Transition from Underdevelopment and from Socialism in Vietnam', Journal of Contemporary Asia, 23/4 (1993), 515–31; Jonathan London, 'Vietnam and the Making of Market-Leninism', Pacific Review, 22/3 (2009), 383–84.

[127] Jörn Dosch and Alexander L. Vuving, 'The Impact of China on Governance Structures in Vietnam' (discussion paper, Deutsches Institut für Entwicklungspolitik, 2008), 18.

Vietnamese elites that any political liberalisation was not in their interest – rather than congratulate Mazowiecki on his victory in the presidential elections, the Vietnamese Communist Party organised mass meetings to condemn Poland's 'counter-revolution'.[128] An interest in the Hungarian model of market socialism ended abruptly when the one-party regime was dismantled in Budapest.[129] And when, in March 1990, the liberal Politburo member Trần Xuân Bách started making speeches and publishing articles about a Vietnamese glasnost and an end to the monopoly of the Communist Party, he was sacked from the Central Committee. While reducing many links with Eastern Europe, the socialist states in Asia cultivated their relations with non-socialist Asian countries and with Cuba instead. The Vietnamese Communist Party leader Linh was received in Havana in April 1989; throughout the massive economic crisis of the 1990s, Vietnam continued to donate shiploads of rice to Cuba.[130] When Eastern European states established diplomatic relations with Seoul, North Korea, too, sought friends elsewhere: with much public fanfare. Kim Il-Sung received Iran's Ayatollah Khamenei in Pyongyang in May 1989, and, hoping to sell weapons and to obtain lucrative contracts for the reconstruction of Iran after its war with Iraq, supported Ayatollah Khomeini's fatwa against Salman Rushdie.[131]

China became an important trade and political partner for North Korea, Cuba, and Vietnam in the following years. The precondition for Vietnam's reconciliation with China was its withdrawal from Cambodia, which it left in 1989, together with Soviet and Eastern European advisors, after a ten-year occupation. In October 1991 nineteen states ended the twenty-year conflict over Cambodia in the Paris peace agreements. As its brother parties in South-East Asia, the formerly pro-Soviet Kampuchean People's Revolutionary Party remained in power, yet in the early 1990s changed its name to Cambodian People's Party, legalised oppositional parties, and allowed the former king Sihanouk to be reinstalled as nominal head of state.[132] Here, as everywhere else in South-East Asia, the initial reform impulse from perestroika, the events in Eastern Europe in 1989, and the disintegration of the Soviet Union

---

[128] Ronald J. Cima, 'Vietnam in 1989. Initiating the Post-Cambodia Period', *Asian Survey* 30/1 (1990), 88, 93.

[129] Dosch and Vuving, 'Impact of China', 26.

[130] Julie Marie Bunck, 'Marxism and the Market. Vietnam and Cuba in Transition' (working paper, Association for the Study of the Cuban Economy, 30 November 1996).

[131] Ayatollah Khamenei in the DPRK in 1989, www.youtube.com/watch?v=SXeuTGoYhcE.

[132] Viviane Frings, 'Cambodia after Decollectivisation (1989–1992)', *Journal of Contemporary Asia*, 24/1 (1994), 49–66.

two years later did not inspire a democratic awakening. In elite and popular perception, this was not always seen as a lost opportunity: many Vietnamese allegedly felt pity for the Russians, whose once powerful country collapsed and who then suffered from economic and political instability.[133]

In North Korea and Cuba economic policies remained essentially unchanged, but the authoritarian leaders drew markedly similar political lessons from Eastern Europe in 1989 as their South-East Asian counterparts. Very cautious moves towards political liberalisation in the years before were rescinded, their party hierarchies remained intact, and both attempted to isolate their populations from the sparks of rebellion emanating from Prague, Warsaw, East Berlin, and Moscow. A group of US scholars who visited Pyongyang in late 1989 noticed that North Korean regional specialists were 'abreast of every detail' of the changes in Eastern Europe and that the Soviet crisis created an acute sense of danger amongst the upper party echelons.[134] But geographical and linguistic distance helped them ward off any influence of the events on society at large, as did an all-encompassing censorship of the media. The authorities in Pyongyang also shut down the Soviet news bureaus in the country after they had published unfavourable articles about the North Korean regime. Discussions on a reunification of Korea were briefly rekindled, when the Soviet Union organised a meeting of the North Korean minister for reunification, Ho Dam, with the South Korean opposition leader Kim Yong-Sam in June 1989, but the talks produced few concrete results. Eventually, the German reunification based on a scrapping of socialism and a political annexation of the former socialist to the capitalist part was, unsurprisingly, not a source of inspiration for the North Korean leadership.[135]

The Cuban Communist Party, too, banned those Soviet publications that had begun to question the socialist project in 1989.[136] But many more links between the island and Eastern Europe meant that the events reverberated much more strongly in Cuba than in North Korea. A loosely organised dissident scene had been in existence in Cuba since

---

[133] Susan Bayly, 'Mapping Time, Living Space. The Moral Cartography of Renovation in Late-Socialist Vietnam', *Cambridge Anthropology*, 31/2 (2013), 60–84.

[134] Izumi, 'North Korea', 2.

[135] Kong Dan Oh, 'North Korea in 1989. Touched by Winds of Change?', *Asian Survey*, 30/1 (1990), 77; 'Khamenei, in North Korea, Attacks US', *AP News*, 4 May 1989; Rhee Sang-Woo, 'North Korea in 1990: Lonesome Struggle to Keep Chuch'e', *Asian Survey*, 31/1 (1991), 71–78.

[136] Peter Cross, 'Soviet Perestroika. The Cuban Effect', *Third World Quarterly*, 13/1 (1992), 143-58.

the 1960s, some of its members being explicitly anti-Communist, while others criticised the regime's human rights abuses from a Marxist perspective as a betrayal of the revolution.[137] Some of these dissidents were in touch with their counterparts in Eastern Europe. The philosopher Elizardo Sánchez, founder of the Comisión Cubana de Derechos Humanos y Reconciliación Nacional ('Cuban Commission for Human Rights and National Reconciliation'), had broken with Castro after reading *A Socialist Manifesto for Poland* by the Polish dissidents Jacek Kuroń and Karol Modzelewski in the late 1960s. He spent much of the 1970s and 1980s in prison, amongst other reasons for possessing a copy of this book, which was held to be 'enemy propaganda'.[138] By 1988 a small democratisation movement was being established, influenced not only by Eastern European dissidents, but also by the wave of democratisation in continental Latin America. From Europe, some of the Cuban dissidents took the idea of a civil society as a basis for a peaceful resistance to the totalitarian state, and as a result, rather than direct their activities against the regime, took on the task of promoting a civic education of the Cuban population. Other oppositionists were inspired more by the recent plebiscitary ousting of the Pinochet regime in Chile and demanded a referendum on the future of the Communist government in Cuba in their Declaración de La Habana de 1988 – which they were denied.[139]

In the spring of 1989 Gorbachev visited Cuba and received a rapturous welcome, from both the regime and its opponents. Fidel Castro and the entire Cuban Politburo received him at the airport with hugs and kisses. Half a million Cubans waved Soviet flags. Cuban state TV reported live with upbeat commentaries. Gorbachev signed a Treaty of Friendship and Cooperation with the government and assured Fidel Castro of the Soviet Union's ongoing assistance to the island.[140] Cuban dissidents nonetheless continued to pin their hopes on Gorbachev. During his visit twenty-one members of the Cuban Party of Human Rights were arrested after they had publicly welcomed Gorbachev and demanded perestroika and glasnost for Cuba as well. Roberto Bahamonde Massot, one of their number and dubbed by some of his supporters at the time 'our Boris Yeltsin', had been the first Cuban since the Revolution to dare to run as

---

[137] Ariel Hidalgo, *Disidencia. Segunda revolución cubana?* (Miami: Ediciones Universal, 1994).

[138] 'Maciej Stasiński, Jak towarzysze Jacek i Karol popsuli humor Fidelowi', *Gazeta Wyborcza*, 25 October 2014.

[139] Kázecký, 'La oposición', 51, 52.

[140] Mervyn Bain, 'Cuba–Soviet Relations in the Gorbachev Era', *Journal of Latin American Studies*, 37 (2005), 770.

an independent candidate in the 1989 local elections.[141] Demands for a Cuban glasnost were easily contained by the regime; Miami car drivers who in late 1989 sported bumper stickers about a 'Christmas in Havana'[142] discovered that they had begun cheering too soon. But the fall of the Berlin Wall and the Velvet Revolution in Prague in the autumn kept hopes for a wind of change alive amongst Cuban dissidents on the island. José Acosta Ferrer, who had created the Movimiento Pacifista Cubano Solidaridad y Paz ('Cuban Pacifist Movement Solidarity and Peace') earlier in 1989, remembered the impact that the events in Eastern Europe and especially Václav Havel's text on the *Power of the Powerless* had on him: 'Until that time, the question of whether I would leave [Cuba] or stay was in the air. But the fall of the Communist bloc and this book encouraged me to start the struggle'.[143]

To some in the Cuban opposition the peacefully negotiated transitions in Warsaw, Prague, and Budapest and the outburst of violence in Bucharest proved that solutions had to be found within the country, not from exile groups, and through dialogue with the Communist regime. Amongst those who suggested a roundtable solution along Polish lines was the Catholic civil rights activist Oswaldo Payá. This opening up of the opposition towards the Communist authorities on the island was vehemently opposed by exile organisations such as the Cuban American National Foundation.[144] The Cuban regime's own interpretation of Eastern Europe's 1989 was that admitting any sort of political pluralism would end with the overturning of the entire socialist system.[145] Towards their population they presented the events in Prague, Warsaw, and Berlin as a disaster, with harsh consequences for Eastern Europeans and the 'Third World', from which Cubans had to be protected. At a December 1989 rally for martyrs of his revolution, Fidel Castro castigated the Eastern European transition as a long-term strategy of the United States to undermine socialist states from within: 'Imperialism today invites the socialist countries in Europe to turn into recipients of its capital surpluses, and to join its pillaging of the countries of the "Third World" ... The capitalist powers are now much more interested in investing in Eastern Europe than in any other part of the planet. In the course of such historical events, what resources can the "Third World" still expect,

---

[141] Anna Husarka, 'Los derechos humanos', *Vuelta*, 168 (1990), 61.

[142] Susan Kaufman Purcell, 'Cuba's Cloudy Future', *Foreign Affairs*, 69/3 (1990), 113–30.

[143] 'José Daniel Ferrer, the Man behind Cuba's Largest Opposition Group', *Miami Herald*, 27 May 2006.

[144] Kázecký, 'La oposición', 58–59.   [145] Cross, 'Soviet Perestroika', 146

where thousands of millions of people still live under subhuman conditions?'[146]

Yet living conditions in Cuba after 1989 did not themselves improve. No less than 85 per cent of the island's trade had been with socialist states; much of its hard currency income had been earned by selling Soviet oil on the world market. Soviet aid, to the tune of a widely disputed number of billions of dollars a year, had been of the utmost importance to the Cuban regime. Official rhetoric about the Soviet leadership would thus remain largely positive until Soviet troops were withdrawn from the island in the summer of 1991. The Cuban regime saw this final rupture as a betrayal akin to that suffered during the Missile Crisis of 1962 because they had not been involved in the negotiations between Moscow and Washington, and their demand that the United States give up their military presence in Guantanamo had likewise been ignored. By that time it had also become obvious that large parts of the continued economic support from the Soviet Union promised to them no longer actually arrived on the island, which entered a painful 'special period' still led by a regime that resisted all pressure to embark upon political reform. Tourism was now encouraged and trade in dollars legalised, but these very cautious economic reforms were a far cry from those of Cuba's old and new political partner, China.

Market Socialism Re-imagined Beyond 1989

Hopes for democratisation in China ended the day that they were fulfilled in Poland and before any other Eastern European country did away with the rule of the Communist parties. Deng ordered the clearing of demonstrators from Tiananmen Square and the violent crushing of any public signs of dissent in the streets of Beijing and other Chinese cities. In the following weeks in July, thousands of protesters were arrested, often received death penalties, and were summarily executed. The leaders of the student movement fled to the countryside or abroad. Over the following years Eastern Europe, after the end of state socialism, would no longer be seen as one of several sources of inspiration for economic reform, but a threatening exemplar of destabilising reform that had led to the disastrous collapse. The initial interest in its socialist marketisation

---

[146] 'Discurso pronunciado por Fidel Castro Ruz, Presidente de la República Cuba, en el acto de despedida de duelo a nuestros internacionalistas caidos durante el cumplimiento de honrosas misiones militares y civiles, efectuado en el Cacahual, el 7 de diciembre de 1989, año 31 de la revolucion', www.cuba.cu/gobierno/discursos/1989/esp/f071289e.html.

turned into a cautionary tale of excessive political liberalisation. It was the changes in Poland and Hungary, not the Soviet Union, that were of immediate concern.[147] An internal Chinese party report in 1990 titled *Dong Ou ju bian ji shi* ('A Record of Drastic Change in Eastern Europe') saw the Polish Communist party as responsible for the changes that were sweeping the region.[148] It is notable that Chinese leaders identified in the former socialist countries of Eastern Europe a much closer approximation to their own situation than in Taiwan, South Korea, the Philippines, and Thailand, the non-socialist countries in the East Asian region that were also throwing off one-party states at the time. The Chinese crackdown on dissent also helped to prevent further change in the wider region, and Communist parties in Vietnam, Laos, and North Korea held on to political power. In much of Asia around 1989 economic policies changed more than political systems did. Democratisation was limited to Taiwan, South Korea, and the Philippines. Nevertheless, many countries from Indonesia to India abandoned their state developmentalist policies, deregulated their economies, and opened to the world market.[149]

The schism with the Soviet Union in the late 1950s had long prevented the Chinese Communist Party from any substantial exchange with reformers in Moscow. But from the beginning of Deng's reforms in 1978 it had looked to market socialism in Hungary, Yugoslavia, and Romania as a way to reinvigorate the Chinese socialist project.[150] Delegations were exchanged, some of them funded by George Soros, and the successes and shortcomings of Eastern European market socialism were duly noted. China had however lost interest by 1983, and instead drew many of its reform ideas from Japan and the East Asian Tigers. This early interest early interest in Eastern European marketisation created links that were revived as perestroika-driven reforms were initiated in Prague, Budapest, and Warsaw. Most Eastern European leaders travelled to Beijing in 1986 and 1987. The most important of these was the Hungarian General Secretary János Kádár: his visit was timed to coincide with the reform drive of the Thirteenth Congress of the Chinese Communist Party and was used by Deng as evidence of the benefits of the economic 'opening up' of

---

[147] M. E. Sarotte, 'China's Fear of Contagion. Tiananmen Square and the Power of the European Example', *Quarterly Journal: International Security*, 37/2 (2012), 167, 171–72.

[148] Ibid., 176.

[149] David Harvey, *A Brief History of Neoliberalism* (New York: Oxford University Press, 2005), 118.

[150] Péter Vámos, 'A Hungarian Model for China? Sino-Hungarian Relations in the Era of Economic Reforms, 1979–89', *Cold War History*, 18/3 (2018), 361–78.

socialist countries.[151] While Hungary was of interest on account of its economic reforms, Poland, on the other hand, was seen as providing instructive lessons as to how to maintain regime stability. In the 1980s Chinese leaders, obsessed with avoiding the emergence of an independent trade union, sent observers to Warsaw to learn how the Communist government had crushed Solidarność. 'If worse comes to worst', Deng remarked in 1986, 'we will impose military control just as the Polish are doing'.[152]

Yet it was not only China's political elites that were taking inspiration and receiving cautionary tales from Eastern Europe in the late 1980s. For the emergence of oppositional movements, most notably Poland's Solidarność, was also widely reported in the Chinese press – and widely read. A debate sprung up from 1986 amongst Chinese intellectuals on the applicability of the concept of 'civil society', which they, like the Cuban dissidents, had taken from Eastern Europe. The Chinese premier Li Peng later noted in his diary that he thought that the student protestors, who were becoming ever more vocal, were influenced mainly by the popular movements they saw in Poland, Hungary, Yugoslavia, and the Soviet Union.[153] And indeed when Gorbachev visited Beijing in May 1989 he was greeted enthusiastically by students, some of whom held posters with 'democracy' written in Cyrillic letters. The authorities decided to change the original programme of his visit and did not let him speak at Tiananmen Square. The curious fact that, for once, Russia was seen as a beacon of democracy, however, does not mean that Chinese notions of democracy were sparked only by Eastern Europe. Similarly to Africa and Latin America, anti-authoritarian and democratic sentiments had been on the rise in East Asia through the 1980s. The Korean and Philippine student movements and their contribution to the democratisation of their respective countries had an effect on Chinese students too. And Deng himself, who had needed social support in his own post-Mao succession struggle, had fostered a generation of youngsters with an egalitarian democratic idealism and an anti-bureaucratic and elitist stance. In the late 1980s they came increasingly into conflict

---

[151] 'Meeting with the Chinese Embassy's Leading Diplomats', 30 October 1987, HAHSS, 1.11.4, S-II/2/87, 245.

[152] Jeanne Wilson, 'The Polish Lesson. China and Poland 1980–1990', *Studies in Comparative Communism*, 3/4 (1990), 269; Jean-Philipp Béja, 'China and the End of Socialism in Europe. A Godsend for Beijing Communists', in Rupnik, *1989 as a Political World Event*, 214–15; Maurice Meisner, *The Deng Xiaoping Era. An Inquiry into the Fate of Chinese Socialism, 1978–1994* (New York: Hill & Wang, 1996), 455.

[153] Li Peng, *Liu si ri ji zhen xiang* (Xianggang: Ao ya chu ban you xian gong si, 2010), 85.

with those in power who profited from the new economic system but would be threatened by any kind of democratisation.[154]

The Chinese leadership accepted the fall of socialism in Eastern Europe: the new Romanian government was immediately recognised, and the Soviet August Putsch was called a strictly internal affair.[155] Yet they drew their lessons from the events for China itself. The Soviet Union's demise suggested that excessive criticism undermined faith in the party, and that democratisation would lead to social and economic chaos. Chinese media portrayed the democratisation in Eastern Europe with images of burnt party buildings, Communists subjected to political discrimination, economic decline, and waves of suicides.[156] Rather than offering inspiration for a democratisation of the political system, the most momentous consequence of the events in Eastern Europe was their empowerment of those within the Chinese Communist Party who advocated a further deregulation of the economy. After the crackdown at Tiananmen Square, the group around Deng had been sidelined by conservatives around Li Peng; economic liberalisation had been halted in June, and the liberal Zhao Ziyang was sacked. It was impressions from Eastern Europe in the autumn that turned the tide.

Chinese commentators in the official Communist Party newspaper had found the key problem that led to the upheaval in Poland and the loss of power of the Communist Party in an ailing economy.[157] And the interpretation of events in Romania made Chinese leaders nervous; they feared that unemployment and underemployment would lead to unrest among urban workers, who might eventually turn against them. As a result economic policy shifted: Li began to distance himself from the conservative agenda of inflation control, and money was pumped into the economy. Soon he announced his support for a coastal development strategy and rescinded his opposition to rural enterprises.[158] In 1992 Deng went on his famous 'Southern Tour', dared to openly attack the conservatives, and then got his 'socialist market economy' ratified by the Fourteenth Party Congress. The Chinese interpretation of Eastern

---

[154] Wang Hui, *China's New Order. Society, Politics, and Economy in Transition* (Cambridge, MA: Harvard University Press, 2003), 77.

[155] 'Yangzhuxi Lizongli fenbie zhidian zhuhe luomaniya xin lingdaoren' (President Yang and Premier Li Send Messages of Congratulations to New Leaders of Romania), *Renmin Ribao*, 28 December 1989.

[156] Czeslaw Tubilewicz, 'Chinese Press Coverage of Political and Economic Restructuring of East Central Europe', *Asian Survey*, 37/10 (1997), 937.

[157] Tang Deqiao, 'Bolan daxuan jieguo shuoming le shenme' ('What Shows from the Polish Election'), *Renmin Ribao* (People's Daily), 11 June 1989, 11.

[158] Barry Naughton, *Growing Out of the Plan. Chinese Economic Reform 1978–1993* (Cambridge: Cambridge University Press, 1995), 283.

Europe's 1989 thus played some role in forcing the changes that would lead to the huge economic boom of the 1990s and the acknowledgement by many hitherto critical voices of the ongoing rule of the Communist Party. As the average income rose fivefold from 1989 to 2006, more and more Chinese intellectuals were willing to accept or even support their government.[159]

Throughout the 1990s and 2000s the history of the fall of state socialism and especially of the disintegration of the Soviet Union was of great importance in China. Large numbers of research programmes and studies were instituted to ensure that Chinese Communists would not face a similar fate.[160] From 1992 to 2004 there were nearly a thousand articles published in domestic newspapers and magazines on the causes of the dissolution of the Soviet Union, and more than forty related monographs were published.[161] The Chinese press remained critical of the Eastern European political reform process – although it was often supportive of its market-oriented reforms – and it continued to play up the supposed violence of anti-Communist sentiment across the region.[162] The lessons of Gorbachev were widely taught across party and military schools to emphasise the need for party discipline. Jiang Zemin, general secretary of the Communist Party of China from 1989 to 2002, believed that the collapse was essentially a failure of elites to hold to socialist beliefs, and he blamed Gorbachev both for abandoning Marxism and for his passivity during crises. In 2006 the Central Commission for Discipline of the Chinese Communist Party launched an eight-part series of a TV play called *Ju An Si Wei* ('be aware of the difficulties and risks, even when we are enjoying stability and prosperity'). It was based on the historical lessons to be drawn from the alleged degeneration of the Communist Party of the Soviet Union – and enjoyed some popularity among the party leadership.[163] Xi Jinping commissioned yet another lengthy study of the Soviet Union from the policy research office in 2009; after he took office in 2012 cadres were required to watch a six-part documentary on the Soviet Union's collapse, featuring a US conspiracy to topple

---

[159] Joseph Fewsmith, *China since Tiananmen. From Deng Xiaoping to Hu Jintao* (Cambridge: Cambridge University Press, 2008), 2.

[160] Guan Guihai, 'The Influence of the Collapse of the Soviet Union on China's Political Choices', in Thomas Bernstein and Hua-Yu Li (eds.), *China Learns from the Soviet Union, 1949–Present* (Lanham, MD: Rowman & Littlefield, 2010), 506.

[161] Meng Yinghui, *Political Belief and the Soviet Revolution* (Beijing: China Social Sciences Press, 2005), 2.

[162] Czeslaw Tubilewicz, 'Chinese Press Coverage of Political and Economic Restructuring of East Central Europe', in *Asian Survey* 37/10 (1997), 927–43.

[163] Liu Ge, *Theoretical Literacy of the Top Leaders of the CPSU and the Rise and Fall of the Soviet Union* (Seattle: Current Affairs Press, 2016), 26.

Communism through the steady infiltration of subversive Western political ideas.[164]

For the dissidents and exiles who were defeated in 1989, Eastern Europe and its transition to democracy remained an important reference, too. While most intellectuals, shocked into silence by the colossal scale of regime violence, had no influence on political debates after June 1989, there were still discussions on how to evaluate the events in Eastern Europe. Some Chinese intellectuals of a liberal bent saw 1989 as the implementation of the very ideas that they had been fighting for themselves.[165] A couple of years later Ma Shaohua, a student leader from Xi'an, wrote a widely read book called *Dong'ou 1989–1993* ('Eastern Europe 1989–1993'). It echoed the triumphalist Western narrative of the early 1990s: Ma saw the drastic changes in Eastern Europe as a popular upheaval against repressive and privileged Communist elites. He enthusiastically celebrated the transition of Eastern European states from poor backwards dictatorships with state-run economies to economically thriving, freedom- and human-rights-respecting pro-Western polities. Socialism had failed, according to Ma, who avoided mentioning China directly, and would collapse everywhere else like the Berlin Wall.[166]

But the student and democratisation movement of the 1980s in China had not been limited to Westernisers. A New Left had emerged that was struggling for a democratic socialism and directed its criticism less against the rule of the Communist Party per se than against its turn to capitalism. A prominent representative of this strand was the literary scholar and Tiananmen activist Wang Hui. From his domestic exile in central China after 4 June, he participated prominently in an extended intellectual debate on the takeaways for China from the events of 1989. In a widely read 1994 article, published in English translation around the world and circulated illegally in China, he introduced the Western concept of 'neoliberalism' (*xin ziyouzhuyi*) as a derogatory term for capitalism.[167] His narrative of Eastern Europe's 1989 considerably diverges from Ma's: for Wang, '1989' had started in China as a socialist movement, which was then crushed by authoritarians in China and capitalists who, inspired by Tiananmen, dismantled socialism in Eastern

---

[164] Evan Osnos, 'Born Red. How Xi Jinping, an Unremarkable Provincial Administrator, Became China's Most Authoritarian Leader since Mao', *New Yorker*, 6 April 2015.

[165] Béja, 'China', 212–22.

[166] Ma Shaohua, *Dong'ou 1989–1993* (Xi'an: Sha'anxi Renmin Jiaoyu Chubanshe, 1993), 284.

[167] Wang Hui, 'Dangdai Zhongguo de Sixiang Zhuangkuang yu Xiandaixing Wenti' ['Contemporary Chinese Thought and the Question of Modernity'], *Tianya* 5 (1997).

Europe. In this view of the world, which echoes the narrative of some East German leftists in 1989, Western liberals, Chinese Westernisers, and the old Communist Party elite belonged in the same category of authoritarian neoliberals; the managed top-down privatisation of the Eastern European economy was seen as proof of the anti-democratic nature of consumerist neoliberalism.[168]

Many oppositional figures who had drawn upon Eastern European democratic dissidence in the 1980s disagreed entirely with this view: some of them actually invoked neoliberalism in the 1990s in their demands for the liberal democracy that, as in Milton Friedman's view, would follow the creation of a deregulated economy. Echoes of Eastern Europe's 1989 could still be heard occasionally amongst the few who dared to oppose the Communist governments in China and Cuba: the Charter 08, a manifesto of 303 Chinese intellectuals demanding a new constitution, free elections, separation of powers, and the dissolution of the still existing labour camps, modelled many of its demands and even its name on the Czechoslovak role model Charta 77. Liu Xiaobo, one of its most prominent activists, received the Homo Homini Prize from Václav Havel, whose work had been translated to Chinese in the early 2000s[169] – and continued to inspire dissidents in China and Cuba. When Havel died in 2011, the Cuban blogger Yoani Sanchez tweeted that '*The Power of the Powerless* helped me find my voice, to recognise myself as a civic being. Thank you, teacher!'[170] But the Communist leaders in Beijing and Havana had learned their lessons from Eastern Europe too. Liu died in prison in 2017, and Sanchez in another Twitter message acknowledged that 'Václav Havel had passed away and we barely started to walk the path he walked dozens of years ago :-('.[171]

Conclusion

The fall of the Berlin Wall and images of jubilant Germans have become the most powerful symbol for a liberal interpretation of 1989 as the demise of authoritarian Communism. For many Western Europeans, US leaders, and also newly Westernised East European political elites, such an interpretation of 1989 swiftly became integral to the very defin-ition and mission of the 'West' and was used as an argument to support liberal interventionism and democracy promotion, and to impose

---

[168] Wang, vii, 43, 100.   [169] Béja, 'China', 214.
[170] Yoani Sanchez, 'Reading Václav Havel in Havana', *Huffington Post*, 25 December 2011.
[171] http://cubanexilequarter.blogspot.com/2011/12/cuban-dissidents-on-passing-of-Václav.html.

political-economic conditionality, across the world. Until the failures of the Arab Spring, West's international role was framed as the reproduction of this foundational end of Cold War moment that had supposedly finally revealed the natural convergence of market and liberal democracy. Western financial institutions and politicians were able to use the example of the Eastern European transition to pressurise other countries – mostly in Africa – to deregulate and display the signs of good governance wherever they were in need of outside investment. Former liberal dissidents from Eastern Europe often aligned themselves with Western actors in new attempts to support them and to export their own models of democracy from the former Soviet republics to the Arab world to Latin America. 1989 also reshaped the West itself: the end of state socialism in the East helped to provide arguments that supported the liberalisation and deregulation of Western economies at home.

Yet Eastern Europe's 1989 and the collapse of the Soviet Union had further, more varied reverberations, providing a set of images and ideas that entered political cultures in manifold ways across the globe. Third-wave democratisation and marketisation, catalysed by Eastern Europe's 1989, was not simply a story of instrumentalisation by the West and then export to the rest. Eastern Europe had been a part of a socialist or non-aligned world, and it was perceived as outside the Western core of the world economy: thus there were linkages or senses of affinity across the 'socialist ecumene'[172] that linked the region to East Asia, Africa, or Latin America with very little Western mediation.[173] In China and South-East Asia, the Soviet and Eastern European collapse had a profound impact on the Communist parties that survived the end of the Cold War: these events were, and still are, read as a warning against excessive, irresponsible reform. Across Africa and Latin America, former Communists had to come to terms with the end of their idealised system. The democratisation of the Second World provided arguments for oppositional movements to rise up against their own authoritarian leaders and demand pluralism and liberal democracy – whilst also being used to discipline them into a reconciliation with moderate negotiated transitions and forsake 'excessive' revolutionary change. The power of 1989 lay in its

---

[172] Susan Bayly, 'Vietnamese Narratives of Tradition, Exchange and Friendship in the Worlds of the Global Socialist Ecumene', in Harry West and Parvathi Raman (eds.), *Enduring Socialism. Explorations of Revolution and Transformation, Restoration and Continuation* (Oxford: Berghahn, 2008), 125–47.

[173] Cornel Ban, 'Translation and Economic Ideas', in Jonathan Evans and Fruela Fernandez (eds.), *The Routledge Handbook of Translation and Politics* (London: Routledge, 2018), 48–63.

multiple re-workings through ideologically diverse networks across the world.

For at least two decades the idea of 1989 encapsulated a set of ideas that became significant to argue with or against across the world. In the 2010s, however, such resonances fell away. Whatever 1989 triumphalism carried over into the 1990s and 2000s vanished as the teleology of the Western-curated script of a liberal democratic march was proven painfully tone-deaf after 2008, with the disappointments of the Arab Spring or the successive revolutions in Ukraine, and in the face of the rise of populist and far-right parties across Europe. There followed disenchantment with exporting 1989-inspired democratic change in the former Soviet space and the Middle East – whether through military intervention or by way of the democracy industry. No longer were Eastern European politicians enamoured of exporting such a global vision based on a now contested transformation and new order. Populist politicians, most prominently the Hungarian leader Viktor Orbán and the Pole Jarosław Kaczyński, rejected liberalism by employing a rhetoric of political self-determination that often touched on the same notes as those articulated by the early critics outside Europe of post-1989 politics. They legitimised their authoritarian takeover of state structures in terms of the need to protect their respective nations from the alleged imperialistic policies of international organisations such as the EU, the IMF, and the World Bank, which once instrumentalised the Eastern European transition as part of a market democracy 'export industry'. Their criticisms of 1989 came along with its own alternative global imaginaries where the 'outsiders' of the post–Cold War world, primarily China and Russia, held the central place. These political forces sought a post-liberal and post-Western global order that has no uses for the liberal myths of 1989: indeed, for such rulers, this moment rather represented a catalyst for a series of calamitous historical events.

6.   A World without '1989'

A giant neon red heart adorned the Hrad, the Prague Castle and seat of the Czech president, in the autumn of 2002. Representatives of Bulgaria, Estonia, Latvia, Lithuania, Romania, Slovakia, and Slovenia had been invited to a NATO summit to start talks about their membership. Poland, Hungary, and the Czech Republic had already joined the Western alliance three years earlier. Addressing his international guests, Václav Havel called the pulsating heart a symbol of love, understanding, and decency. The installation, by the Czech artist Jiří David, marked the thirteenth anniversary of the end of state socialism and was a vivid illustration of how Eastern Europe's liberal elites saw 1989. The celebrations at the NATO summit presented the enlargement of the Western military alliance as the embodiment of the spirit of the 1968 Prague Spring and the natural consequence of Czechoslovakia's Velvet Revolution.[1] The symbolism drawn from 1989 was channelled into support for a military organisation that saw itself as a worldwide bastion of liberal democracy. Western participants at the NATO summit seemed certain that 1989 triggered, in the words of the former CIA director James Woolsey, the spread of democracy 'regardless of skin, colour or religion'.[2] Some intellectuals from the region were already more guarded: Adam Michnik noticed that there was no feeling of euphoria in the Czech capital and that the streets of Prague were deserted – with the exception of mostly young anti-NATO protesters.[3]

A decade after the Summit in Prague, the idea that 1989 should be celebrated as a moment of convergence with the liberal West was challenged with a vengeance. A populist counterrevolution from the margins, spearheaded by Viktor Orbán in Hungary and Jarosław Kaczyński in

---

[1] Timothy Garton Ash, 'Love, Peace and NATO', *Guardian*, 28 November 2002, www.theguardian.com/world/2002/nov/28/nato.comment.

[2] Merje Kuus, '"Love, Peace and NATO": Imperial Subject-Making in Central Europe', *Antipode*, 39/2 (2007), 269–90.

[3] Woolsey and Michnik quoted in Martin Simecka, 'The Havel Paradox', *Transitions Online*, 21 March 2003, www.tol.org/client/article/9130-the-havel-paradox.html.

Poland, glorified an illiberal vision of Europeanness that emphasised cultural divergence from the liberal West of the continent.[4] It rejected the basic teleology of post-socialism – that the East would inevitably converge with the West in a liberal democratic Europe – which had seemed unassailable only a few years earlier.[5]

Right- and left-wing populists – united in a new political imaginary that opposed the people to corrupt transitional elites – now extolled their own vision of the region and its place in the world. They fought for greater national sovereignty founded on a nebulous people's will that could be invoked in any and every context.[6] These ideological groups were no longer bound to the mystique of East-West convergence; instead, they viewed their region as the defender of the true Europe, the frontline of a growing pan-European ideological army that would protect whiteness, Christianity, and traditional gender roles against extra-European migrants and a decadent West. Western integration was now complemented by new alliances with China, Russia, or Turkey – not only in Poland, Hungary, or the Czech Republic, but also in the western Balkans, where disillusionment with the prospect of joining the EU opened up space for greater geopolitical competition.[7] This counter-revolution was met in turn with resistance both in former socialist countries and within the structures of the EU. '1989' remained a powerful mobilising symbol for politicians and civic groups committed to defending and developing democratic consensus around the institutions, laws, and values that populists became so eager to dismantle.

Towards the West? Ambiguous Convergence

Until the end of the 2000s the Eastern European political landscape was dominated by a consensus over the basics of post-socialist change: EU and NATO integration, free-market reform, the strengthening of the rule

---

[4] Anton Shekhovtsov, 'The No Longer Silent Counter-revolution', *Religion and Society in East and West*, 44/9–10 (2016), 10.

[5] Ivan Krastev, 'Eastern Europe's Illiberal Revolution', *Foreign Affairs*, May/June 2018, www.foreignaffairs.com/articles/hungary/2018-04-16/Eastern-europes-illiberal-revolution. See also 'In EU, There's an East-West Divide over Religious Minorities, Gay Marriage, National Identity', www.pewresearch.org/fact-tank/2018/10/29/east-west-divide-within-the-eu-on-issues-including-minorities-gay-marriage-and-national-identity/.

[6] Cas Mudde, 'The Populist Zeitgeist', *Government and Opposition*, 39/3 (2004), 543. For a summary of critiques of the concept 'populism', see Peter Baker, '"We Are the People": The Battle to Define Populism', *Guardian*, 10 January 2019, www.theguardian.com/news/2019/jan/10/we-the-people-the-battle-to-define-populism.

[7] Marina Mitrevska and Nano Ruzhin, 'Geopolitics of the Western Balkans: An Area of Geopolitical Competition of the Great Powers', *Contemporary Macedonian Defence*, 18/34 (2018), 21–35.

of law, and the promotion of minority rights. Europe seemed to have lost its 'East', as 'Central Europe' frequently replaced 'Eastern Europe' in official rhetoric, whilst Russia gradually took on the role of the 'other' beyond the European pale.[8] Even the Balkans, which had been associated with the Yugoslav Wars in the 1990s, were offered a route to Westernisation: in 1999, the EU created the Stability Pact for South-Eastern Europe, which outlined a pathway for the region towards liberal democratic norms and eventual EU accession. Degrees of Europeanness were defined by a nation's adherence to EU standards and regulations. After Bulgaria's and Romania's accession to the EU in 2007, officials in Brussels categorised the geography of the remaining not yet European states by introducing the term 'Western Balkans', which comprised the former Yugoslav republics plus Albania and Moldova.[9] It suggested a future with the West of the continent; yet, for this group promises of integration increasingly wore thin.

There were early post–Cold War hopes that Russia could be Westernised, too: the country was the recipient of massive economic aid from Western European states and the United States. The first post-Communist Russian president, Boris Yeltsin, imagined European convergence along the lines of Gorbachev's Common European Home. During the first half of the 1990s Andrei Kozyrev, his minister of foreign affairs, insisted that Russia had previously experienced distorted development that could be corrected only by way of the free market and political liberalism on the basis of a 'natural partnership' with Western countries.[10] The vehicle of this convergence was the Organisation for Security and Cooperation in Europe (OSCE), the institution created after the Helsinki Accords in 1975 – not the EU or NATO. It would assist Russia's internal transformation through the harmonisation of legislation with international standards in human rights and by aiding its transformation into a market economy.[11]

This faith in the convergence of Russia waned in the second half of the 1990s. The acceleration of EU and NATO enlargement plans up to Russia's Western borders made Moscow's focus on European

---

[8] Sorin Antohi, 'Habits of the Mind: Europe's Post-1989 Symbolic Geographies', in Sorin Antohi and Vladimir Tismaneanu (eds.), *Between Past and Future: The Revolutions of 1989 and Their Aftermath* (Budapest: Central European University Press, 2000), 61–77.

[9] Diana Mishkova, *Beyond Balkanism: The Scholarly Politics of Region Making* (London: Routledge, 2018), 212, 223–24.

[10] Andrei Tsygankov, 'Finding a Civilisational Idea: "West", "Eurasia", and "Euro-East" in Russia's Foreign Policy', *Geopolitics*, 12/3 (2007), 383.

[11] Vsevolod Samokhvalov, 'What Kind of "Other"? Identity and Russian–European Security Interaction in Eurasia', *Europe-Asia Studies*, 70/5 (2018), 799.

integration through cooperation within the OSCE superfluous, which took the wind out of the Westernisers' sails. In 1998 one highly influential Russian politician, Vyacheslav Nikonov, remarked on the deflating effects of this shift: 'The idea of Common European Home is now implemented without Russia's participation'.[12] Moreover, the economic and social turmoil of the 1990s alienated the local population from this Western turn. Ultranationalist forces as well as a resurgent Communist Party of the Russian Federation quickly became the main challengers to Boris Yeltsin. As Yeltsin grew more authoritarian and anti-liberal, the Kremlin's foreign policy turned towards Eurasianism. The latter was spearheaded by the former chief of foreign intelligence Yevgeni Primakov, who was prime minister between 1998 and 1999 and a spokesperson for a coalition of military industrialists, the army, and the security services. He advocated re-establishing the principle of Russia as great power between Europe and Asia and sought security within the Commonwealth of Independent States, an intergovernmental organisation of ten post-Soviet countries. Eurasianism became the platform for a broad coalition of Communists and nationalists across the political spectrum that opposed Russian liberals' emphasis on convergence with the West.[13] Western observers, too, increasingly saw Russia as a region that was civilisationally distinct from those other former Soviet Republics that were now, as independent nations, turning westwards. The managing director of the British advertising agency Saatchi & Saatchi, which had recently set up shop across the former Soviet Union, related in 2000 that 'Estonia is like a drive-through zoo where you can look out the window from the safety of your car. If you go to Russia or the Ukraine, you have to climb into the cage with the animals. Estonia provides an environment where it is possible to learn something and yet not get your feet dirty'.[14]

Vladimir Putin's ascension to power in 1999 briefly rekindled domestic and international hopes of having a Westerniser in the Kremlin. In this spirit an influential early biography dubbed Putin 'The German in the Kremlin'.[15] Despite noting his reluctance to criticise the Soviet past,

---

[12] Ibid., 802.

[13] Peter Katzenstein and Nicole Weygandt, 'Mapping Eurasia in an Open World: How the Insularity of Russia's Geopolitical and Civilisational Approaches Limits Its Foreign Policies', *Perspectives on Politics*, 15/2 (2017), 428–454 and Didier Chaudet, Florent Parmentier, and Benoît Pélopidas, *When Empire Meets Nationalism: Power Politics in the US and Russia* (Burlington, VT: Ashgate, 2009).

[14] Merje Kuus, *Geopolitics Reframed: Security and Identity in Europe's Eastern Enlargement* (London: Palgrave Macmillan, 2007), 105.

[15] Alexander Rahr, *Wladimir Putin: Der Deutsche im Kreml* (Tübingen: Universitas, 2000).

Western governments and many Russian liberals alike saw Putin initially as a bulwark against the return of Communists and guarantor of Russia's ongoing liberalisation and globalisation. In 2002 the president of the European Commission, Romano Prodi, proclaimed the EU's re-imagining of its neighbourhood, which comprised a 'ring of friends' surrounding it, 'from Morocco to Russia and the Black Sea', all of them to be included in 'a common market'.[16] To Prodi, as to many other Western observers, Putin's early talk of a united greater Europe from Lisbon to Vladivostok seemed reminiscent of Russia's Westernising vision of the late 1980s and early 1990s.

Similar hopes of convergence were entertained with regard to other post-Soviet republics. The Colour Revolutions in Georgia (2003), Ukraine (2005) and Kyrgyzstan (2005), were large-scale protests for the peaceful transformation of authoritarian, corrupt, pro-Russian governments and their countries' greater interaction with the EU. A sense of optimism was still palpable amongst local pro-Western elites as mass popular movements seemed to bring them closer to substantive representative democracy.[17] Memories of the 1989 era and the possibilities of Western integration were enthusiastically reignited in 2013 by the Maidan demonstrations in Ukraine. Countrywide protests against the incumbent pro-Putin president Viktor Yanukovych and his government were triggered by his decision not to sign Ukraine's association agreement with the EU, which symbolised for the demonstrators his administration's corruption and violations of human rights, which were understood to be expressions of his 'non-Europeanness'.[18] Yet while these protests led to another revolution and pro-EU parties taking power, Ukrainian democracy neither curbed the power of its oligarchs nor was able to create political stability. This was exacerbated by the Russian occupation of Crimea and Putin's support for separatists in eastern Ukraine.[19]

Rather than converge with the West, Russia developed an ambivalent relationship with the EU. Collaboration intensified in the guise of stronger energy ties with Germany, France, and Italy; competition

---

[16] Elena Korosteleva, 'Eastern Partnership and the Eurasian Union: Bringing "the Political" Back in the Eastern Region', *European Politics and Society*, 17/Supplement 1 'The Eurasian Project in Global Perspective' (2016), 67–68.

[17] Timothy Garton Ash, 'This Tale of Two Revolutions and Two Anniversaries May Yet Have a Twist', *Guardian*, 8 May 2008, www.theguardian.com/commentisfree/2008/may/08/1968theyearofrevolt.

[18] David Marples and Frederick Mills (eds.), *Ukraine's Euromaidan: Analyses of a Civil Revolution* (Stuttgart: Ibidem Press, 2015).

[19] Paul Quinn-Judge, 'The Revolution That Wasn't', *New York Review of Books*, 19 April 2018, www.nybooks.com/articles/2018/04/19/ukraine-revolution-that-wasnt/.

increased over the western borderlands of the former Soviet Union. While the West sought to teach Russia European democratic norms, Russia wanted to be acknowledged for its superior competence in security architecture and its civilisational role in what the political analyst Gleb Pavlovski branded as the 'Euro-East' region, that is, Ukraine, Moldova, Belarus, and Kazakhstan.[20] By 2003 Putin had begun to champion Russia's role as a great European power and criticised what he considered the EU's egoistic self-interest and manipulative policies in the post-socialist and post-Soviet space. Reacting to Western involvement in the so-called Colour Revolutions in Serbia, and then Ukraine, Georgia, and Central Asia, Putin defensively affirmed Russia's right to 'decide for itself the pace, terms and conditions of moving towards democracy'. The ex-Soviet states should adopt democratic models reflecting specific regional conditions, he argued.[21] The Russian leadership now firmly rejected the idea that the West was the sole signifier of the idea of Europe and democracy – drawing on much older civilisational claims, dating back to the nineteenth century, that Russia represented the true Europe.

The US secretary of state Hillary Clinton pushed a symbolic 'reset button' on Russian-West relations in 2009, in a futile attempt to return to the early post–Cold War scenario of Moscow's liberal apprenticeship. But a dramatic spike in oil revenues around 2010 consolidated Putin's power and his ability to project Russia's influence abroad.[22] In 2011 liberals around the world cheered on the Arab Spring and mass demonstrations in Russia that contested the validity of the recent parliamentary elections.[23] For a threatened Russian regime, this global and local popular unrest was a turning point and proof of the necessity of assertive countermeasures. The Kremlin developed its authoritarianism and appealed to traditional Russian culture at home, while simultaneously embracing the role of a global centre of alternative illiberal modernity.[24] Putin and various intellectuals with links to the regime began to construct a right-wing international founded on (ultra-)conservative values at odds

---

[20] Quoted in Tsygankov, 'Finding a Civilisational Idea', 382 and 393; Samokhvalov, 'What Kind of "Other"?', 807.

[21] Quoted in Tsygankov, 'Finding a Civilisational Idea', 385–86.

[22] Aviezer Tucker, 'Restoration and Convergence: Russia and China since 1989', in George Lawson, Chris Armbruster, and Michael Cox (eds.), *The Global 1989. Continuity and Change in World Politics* (Cambridge: Cambridge University Press, 2011), 174.

[23] Mischa Gabowitsch, *Protest in Putin's Russia* (Cambridge: Polity, 2017).

[24] Stephen Hanson, 'Plebiscitarian Patrimonialism in Putin's Russia', *Annals of the American Academy of Political and Social Science* 636/1 (2011), 32–68.

with the cosmopolitan liberal Europe that 1989 had served to mythologise.[25] Domestically, there was a drastic crackdown on opposition forces, pluralism, and independent civic organisations.

Signs of a similar divergence from the liberal script of 1989 could be observed in other parts of Eastern Europe from the 2000s as well, even if they had not yet become central to official political discourse. These attitudes within former socialist societies were partly reactions to the apparent impossibility of their ever escaping their designation and treatment as less developed European countries. Despite an expectation that the processes of accession would enable their recognition as full Europeans, different regions of Eastern Europe continued to be judged – and were often found wanting – according to their capacity for convergence with economic and political standards set by the EU. The Visegrád group countries (Czech Republic, Hungary, Poland, and Slovakia) scored the best grades on the score sheets of the transition paradigm. The rest of the former socialist region was considered a mélange of struggling countries that still had to prove to be 'willing and able' to adapt to EU norms.[26]

Eastern European elites internalised the idea of their countries as peripheral outposts of a Western civilising project. In 1994 Jüri Luik, Estonia's foreign minister, defined his country's geopolitical position in terms strongly reminiscent of influential US scholar Samuel Huntington's *Clash of Civilizations*: '[We are] at the frontier of democratic and free-market thinking'.[27] Such representations were rife across the region and became even more pronounced upon EU accession because one of its criteria was a country's ability to (in official terminology) 'securitise' its borders with non-EU countries, in effect creating civilisational frontiers. Countries that remained outside of EU borders were treated as if they were potential threats because of structural instability, limited democratic credentials, and, more generally, less developed societies. Being judged as not conforming to standards of liberal, market democracy set in Brussels sometimes consolidated Eastern European understandings of themselves as being placed by external forces on a civilisational hierarchy that sloped from West to East.[28]

---

[25] Brain Whitmore, 'Vladimir Putin, Conservative Icon', *Atlantic*, 20 December 2013, www.theatlantic.com/international/archive/2013/12/vladimir-putin-conservative-icon/282572/.

[26] Merje Kuus, 'Europe's Eastern Expansion and the Reinscription of Otherness in East-Central Europe', *Progress in Human Geography*, 28/4 (2004), 477.

[27] Kuus, *Geopolitics Reframed*, 55. Samuel Huntington's *The Clash of Civilizations* was very popular among Estonian politicians during the 1990s and the 2000s (ibid., 54 and 77).

[28] Sławomir Łodziński, 'Foreigners in Poland. Selected Issues in Poland's Migrational Policy 1989–1998', *Polish Sociological Review*, 126 (1999), 301–321 and Robert Stojanov, Oldřich Bureš, and Barbora Duží, 'Migration and Development Policies:

Voices from outside Europe began to imagine a reversed hierarchy – one that would feed a growing rejection of liberal Westernisation in later years. Commending the more enthusiastic support for the US-led invasion of Iraq in 2003 from the eastern half of the continent, the neoconservative US secretary of defence, Donald Rumsfeld, distinguished between 'new' and 'old' Europe.[29] For him Europe was divided into a weak, feminised West and the masculine East, hardened by historical suffering, the latter being capable of understanding the true nature of a democratic Western civilisation and the necessity of its military defence.[30] This narrative lionised Eastern European cultural and civilisational distinctiveness in a form that would later be mobilised politically to challenge the EU's right to define how to be European. It also marked an upswing in the US neoconservatives' promotion of the idea of Eastern Europe as the better half of the continent: a position that found its ultimate realisation in US president Donald Trump's fascination with Putin as a strong, masculine leader.

While the mainstream imaginary of Eastern European politicians continued to rely on a particular reading of 1989 as a moment that prefigured a path to a natural convergence with Western liberal democratic values and practices, Westernisation and the EU were always objects of criticism too. Some Eastern Europeans deplored a loss of folk culture, of the region's traditional products, farming, and traditional ways of life. In the 1990s Christian, conservative, and nationalist groups had expressed strong anxieties about the way in which a new European cosmopolitanism could weaken the bonds of the 'cultural nation'. Some even countered the liberal EU with the idea of an 'Orthodox Europe' that preserved the regional communality of traditions.[31] The elites' embrace of neoliberalism and their over-dependence on Western political models were criticised by some on the left as economic colonisation and re-peripheralisation. A 2000 IMF summit in Prague brought the alter-globalisation movement to Eastern Europe. These protests were joined by local left-wing intellectuals such as Karel Kosík and Jan Keller, who had had significant influence on pre-1989 dissident thought and

The State of Affairs before the 2015 European Migration Crises in the Czech Republic and Its Current Implications', *Communist and Post-Communist Studies*, 50/3 (2017), 169–81.

[29] Inga Grote, 'Donald Rumsfeld's Old and New Europe and the United States' Strategy to Destabilize the European Union', *Rivista di Studi Politici Internazionali*, 74/3 (2007), 347–56.

[30] Luiza Bialasiewicz and Claudio Minca, 'Old Europe, New Europe: For a Geopolitics of Translation', *Area*, 37/4 (2005), 365–72.

[31] Mishkova, *Beyond Balkanism*, 217–18.

galvanised local opposition to neoliberalism.[32] Some left-leaning intellectuals in Croatia and Slovenia thought that EU and NATO membership turned their countries into 'insignificant colonies on the periphery of the Euro-Atlantic Empire', which itself was in deep crisis.[33] Dušan Keber, member of the Slovenian Committee for the Defence of Human Rights in the late 1980s, summarised this sense of disillusionment with contemporary political realities: 'Was it necessary to throw out the baby with the dirty water of socialism? [Was it necessary] that we have forgotten about democracy the moment it became dependent on ourselves, that we did not set a vision about the kind of society and state we want to live in, that we have opened a hunt for national wealth, that we started dancing around the golden calf of neoliberalism?'[34]

Indeed, during the 2000s the left in Eastern Europe regained its voice by criticising inequalities of neoliberal development and the unaccountability of political elites. In Poland, a movement coalesced around the magazine *Krytyka Polityczna* (Political Critique, created in 2002). It aimed to recuperate the sense of experimentation and participatory politics that had been popular around 1989, invoking concepts of direct democracy and self-organisation that had been expounded by pre–Martial Law Solidarność or by dissidents such as Václav Havel or Jacek Kuroń.[35] Those on the radical left were often the first to foresee the rise of the radical right. In Hungary, Tamás Krausz, member of the Left Alternative, one of the organisations sidelined at the Hungarian roundtable, presciently warned in an open letter to then prime minister Ferenc Gyurcsány that if the left lost its social dimension, 'extreme right populism will be resurrected from its decades-long sleep'.[36] During the 1990s

---

[32] Stanislav Holubec, 'The Formation of the Czech Post-Communist Intellectual Left: Twenty Years of Seeking an Identity', in Michal Kopeček and Piotr Wciślik (eds.), *Thinking through Transition: Liberal Democracy, Authoritarian Pasts, and Intellectual History in East Central Europe after 1989* (Budapest: Central European University Press, 2015), 414.

[33] 'Boris Buden: Narodu koji je ostao bez svega ostaje još samo iluzija identiteta', www.glas-slavonije.hr/337535/11/Boris-Buden-Narodu-koji-je-ostao-bez-svega-ostaje-jos-samo-iluzija-identiteta.

[34] Dušan Keber, 'Čigava je obletnica JBTZ?', *Mladina* 22, 31 May 2013, www.mladina.si/144718/cigava-je-obletnica-jbtz/.

[35] Sławomir Sierakowski, 'Vaclav Havel's Fairy Tale', *New York Times*, 17 December 2013, www.nytimes.com/2013/12/18/opinion/sierakowski-vaclav-havels-fairy-tale.html?mtrref=www.google.ro&gwh=EC408601F1B0E27897B2ABE2A98B3D97&gwt=pay&assetType=opinion; Sławomir Sierakowski, 'Poland's Forgotten Dissident', *New York Times*, 30 May 2014, www.nytimes.com/2014/05/30/opinion/sierakowski-polands-forgotten-dissident.html?rref=collection%2Fcolumn%2Fslawomir-sierakowski.

[36] Ágnes Gagyi, 'The Non-post-communist Left in Hungary after 1989: Diverging Paths of Leftist Criticism, Civil Activism, and Radicalizing Constituency', in Kopeček and Wciślik, *Thinking through Transition*, 339.

the Slovenian philosopher and political activist Rastko Močnik argued that fascism would re-awaken 'from the Adriatic to Siberia' as a response to the region's subordinate postcolonial condition combined with a neoliberal capitalism that fuelled clientelism and corruption at home.[37]

Such critical voices from the right or the left remained isolated until the late 2000s. Most Eastern European elites still believed in the value of convergence with the West and viewed EU integration not primarily in terms of membership within political institutions and networks that would impact on citizens' economic and social conditions, but as part of an imagined cultural destiny in the West. Amongst a broader population, EU accession seemed to be an obvious outcome of its cultural-historical identity, and the West was expected to re-admit the region into its charmed circle after having failed to 'rescue' it from Communism. Critics of neoliberalism were policed out of the mainstream: dissent from those economic accession criteria that defined countries' ability to join the EU threatened isolation in Europe. Only after former Communist states had joined the EU in 2004 and 2007, and then faced the 2008 economic crisis, did post-socialist governments and the EU face much more powerful criticisms of the increased inequalities in post-1989 societies. The impact of conditionality diminished as Brussels did not have any clear mechanisms of accountability to apply to member states. This paved the way for the Eastern European elites' later illiberal deviations.

Who Is the True Europe? The Turn to Divergence

By the end of the 2000s the criticism of EU-centred Europeanisation began to enter the mainstream. It reflected the growing prominence of conservative thought in public debates about post-socialist politics and social transformations – a counter-reaction to the previous dominance of the liberal transitional consensus. Across Eastern Europe right-wing thinkers contested the values of technocratic rule and cosmopolitanism in post-accession polities. In some countries, such as Poland, Hungary, or Slovenia, these critiques developed into a full-blown rejection of what were now considered 'failed transitions'.[38] This ever-strengthening intellectual rejection of 1989's legacy provided the ideological background for the right-wing FIDESZ (Hungarian Civic Alliance, in power since 2010) and PiS (Law and Justice Party, in power 2005–7 and from 2015

---

[37] Rastko Močnik, *Koliko Fašizma?* (Zagreb: Arkzin, 1998), 65.

[38] Balázs Trencsényi et al., *Political Thought in East Central Europe. Volume II: Negotiating Modernity in the 'Short Twentieth Century' and Beyond Part II: 1968–2018* (Oxford: Oxford University Press, 2018), 281–94.

onwards) takeovers of their respective political systems. Yet this challenge did not arise only from one end of the political spectrum; alongside other populists on the right such as Boyko Borisov in Bulgaria, Kolinda Grabar-Kitarović in Croatia, Janez Janša in Slovenia, and Andrej Babiš in Czech Republic, there were those on the left, for example social democrats such as Robert Fico in Slovakia, Liviu Dragnea in Romania, and President Miloš Zeman in the Czech republic who also refused to be beholden to European liberal visions of their region's destiny.

What united these leaders from across the political spectrum was their re-imagining of the region's role in Europe and the world. No longer was the political, economic, and cultural Westernisation of the former socialist space deemed inevitable. Instead they claimed to defend the sovereignty of their nations against liberal politics that had engendered, variously, economic crisis, an undesired cosmopolitanism, demographic decline, and immorality, whilst also threatening ethnic purity and Christian values. Their solution was to call for an EU with less supranational governance and a greater range of powers for sovereign nations. These visions were not solely an Eastern European phenomenon – populist movements with similar agendas emerged across Western Europe, most notably in France and Italy, but also in Austria, Sweden, Netherlands, or Denmark. Radical right-wing leaders such as Matteo Salvini (the leader of the far-right party Lega Nord and Italian deputy prime minister) or Marine Le Pen (the leader of France's Rassemblement National [National Rally], the country's second largest political force) developed strong bonds with populists in the post-socialist space and together called for re-founding Europe. Other actors such as the ultra-conservative wing of the Republican Party in the United States, Vladimir Putin, Recep Tayyip Erdoğan's Turkey, and Communist China utilised and hence reinforced Eastern European conservative representations of their own distinctive Europeanness pitted against the liberal West. This global environment emboldened Eastern European political entrepreneurs to construct their countries and region as the embodiment of a vanguard that would lead a pan-continental defence of true European values against a decaying and noxious liberalism.

It was in large part the economic crisis of 2008 that severely weakened faith in the natural superiority of a Western developmental model. Even though in some countries recession was mild (Czech republic) or nonexistent (Poland), the global breakdown of neoliberal capitalism combined with local politics of austerity had a powerful effect across the region. For the challengers of the liberal model, the financial and economic crisis was a pivotal moment in world affairs that replaced 1989 in relative importance. For them the crash symbolised the West's decadence; it was the moment when the democracies that dominated the post–Cold War world lost out to countries that defied this political template. Moreover, such political forces advocated the idea of liberal democratic forms as alien to the needs of the region, whose development could best be constructed on the basis of non-Western democracy, embracing alternative political forms of government such as those existing in Russia, Turkey, Singapore, or China.

Released from the burden of having to conform that the processes of EU accession had required, populists on both the right and the left started treating liberalism as 'the god that failed', and their de-mystification of the West entered the political mainstream.[39] At the heart of the new criticisms was an understanding of the EU as a colonial power that in their view had systematically subverted their countries' sovereignty and had created severe inequalities, as only a select, well-off, cosmopolitan few had unconditionally benefited from integration. These increasingly mainstream interpretations –pioneered by FIDESZ in Hungary and PiS in Poland – presented previous adaptations to EU or IMF conditionality as designs to bypass proper national conversations over public policy. By 2018, with the election of Babiš and Zeman in parliamentary (2017) and presidential (2018) elections respectively in the Czech Republic, the whole of the Central European Visegrád grouping became a pressure group within the EU that presented the institutions in Brussels as encroaching on their people's sovereignty. The notion of Central Europe had long been capable of being instrumentalised as argument for either Westernisation against the East or the protection of the 'true Europe' against the dissolute West – as we saw in Chapter 3. Since 1989 it had been used to argue that such countries belonged in the bosom of the West; in the 2010s its earlier purpose was revived, albeit with a new ideology: 'Central Europe' became an 'anti-colonial' ideology, a repository for a traditionalist, ethnically defined and anti-liberal Europe.[40]

Those who supported Western liberalism were pilloried as representatives of transitional elites who had betrayed the true national interest. In Poland, Law and Justice talked about 'the Network', comprising former

---

[39] James Traub, 'The Regression of Viktor Orbán', *Foreign Policy*, 31 October 2015, https://foreignpolicy.com/2015/10/31/the-regression-of-viktor-orban-hungary-europe/.

[40] Seán Hanley and Milada Anna Vachudova, 'Understanding the Illiberal Turn: Democratic Backsliding in the Czech Republic', *East European Politics*, 34/3 (2018), 276–96; Stefano Braghiroli and Andrey Makarychev, 'Redefining Europe: Russia and the 2015 Refugee Crisis', *Geopolitics*, 23/4 (2017), 823–48; Andrea Schmidt, 'Friends Forever? The Role of the Visegrad Group and European Integration', *Politics in Central Europe*, 12/3 (2016), 113–40.

Communist party dignitaries, high-ranking representatives of the security apparatus, and former Solidarność activists, who in the past had been secret collaborators or party members.[41] In the Czech Republic Prime Minister Babiš railed against 'the matrix' and labelled the Velvet Revolution the result of a secret deal between Moscow, Czech Communists, and dissident elites to put Václav Havel in power.[42] The leader of the Social Democratic Party in Romania, Liviu Dragnea, employed the term 'parallel state' to define a nefarious hidden coalition between intelligence services, the judiciary, post-accession national elites, and Western politicians.[43]

These radical critiques of post-1989 establishments and a pro-Western consensus exploited real imbalances in the post-EU enlargement development of the region. For instance, in the Visegrád countries multinational companies controlled up to 80 per cent of productive assets, but employed only 30 per cent of the labour force; it was unclear whether the rest of the population directly benefited from this foreign investment. However, because of EU legislation concerning the common market and the free movement of goods and capital, Central European governments had little leverage to negotiate a better deal in the relationship with such multinationals.[44] Indeed, in the former socialist space, levels of social and economic inequality were still high, entire regions had been left out of the accession boom, and there were significant gaps between ruling parties' governmental agendas and their populations' expectations as to what they might hope to gain from EU membership. Discontent with aspects of economic dislocation caused by the disappearance of entire sectors of local economies, along with the social networks that had sustained them, fuelled much broader critiques of the entire transformation.[45] The social costs of 'transition' left deep scars in the public psyche, which was apparent in opinion polls about the pre-1989 past that consistently produced significant percentages of respondents gripped with a nostalgia for lost certainties. In 2009 the Pew Centre

---

[41] Andrzej Paczkowski, 'Twenty-Five Years "After": The Ambivalence of Settling Accounts with Communism: The Polish Case', in Vladimir Tismaneanu and Bogdan C. Iacob (eds.), *Remembrance, History, and Justice: Coming to Terms with Traumatic Pasts in Democratic Societies* (Budapest: Central European University Press, 2015), 251–52.

[42] Hanley and Vachudova, 'Understanding the Illiberal Turn', 286.

[43] 'Dragnea: NATO și EU au finanțat statul paralel', *Digi24*, 11 June 2018, www.digi24.ro/ stiri/actualitate/politica/dragnea-nato-si-ue-au-finantat-statul-paralel-944886.

[44] Laszlo Bruszt, 'Regional Normalisation and National Deviations: EU Integration and Transformations in Europe's Eastern Periphery', *Global Policy* 6/Supplement 1 (2015), 42.

[45] Ivan Krastev, *The Inflexibility Trap: Frustrated Societies, Weak States and Democracy* (Sofia: Centre for Liberal Strategies, 2002), 21.

reported that 72 per cent of Hungarians thought themselves to be poorer than they had been under Communism.[46] The accumulation of inequalities paired with social and economic dislocation led to the de-coupling of the link between democracy and prosperity.[47] Another Pew Centre study from 2017 showed that the support for democracy decreased significantly across the region, down to 47 per cent of the population in Poland, 48 per cent in Hungary, 39 per cent in Bulgaria, 34 per cent in Latvia, and 25 per cent in Serbia.[48]

Against such dislocation, parties such as FIDESZ, PiS, SMER (Direction-Social Democracy in Slovakia), PSD (Social Democratic Party in Romania), and GERB (Citizens for European Development of Bulgaria) radicalised themselves.[49] Populists' accession to power in Hungary and Poland was, ironically, rooted in the idea of 'civil society', one of the essential concepts used by Eastern European democrats to express the need for a social space to express a politics distinct from that of the Communist state and its elites, and which had played a major role in mobilising opposition in 1989. Now its practices were retooled to mobilise significant sections of the population into anti-democratic, ethno-nationalist civic organisations.[50] The epitome of this grassroots realignment from the right was the Civic Circles movement created by Viktor Orbán in 2002, after he had lost the elections of that year. It consisted of a network of associations, media, and groups who re-imagined the ethnic and religious community, Europe, and citizenship itself. In Hungary between 2006 and 2010, the populist opposition effectively branded the centre-left as an elite who did not bother to engage with the social sphere – an image made more plausible by a series of major corruption scandals. By contrast, both FIDESZ and the far-right Jobbik party bypassed state institutions and developed networks and associations from below as well as media outlets, which reinvented everyday lifestyles, holidays, symbols, and national heroes from a

---

[46] Pew Research Center, 'End of Communism Cheered but Now with More Reservations' (2009) www.pewglobal.org/2009/11/02/end-of-communism-cheered-but-now-with-more-reservations/.

[47] Irena Grudzińska-Gross, 'The Backsliding', *East European Politics and Societies and Cultures*, 28/4 (2014), 667–68.

[48] Antoaneta Dimitrova, 'The Uncertain Road to Sustainable Democracy: Elite Coalitions, Citizen Protests and the Prospects of Democracy in Central and Eastern Europe', *East European Politics*, 34/3 (2018), 265.

[49] Béla Greskovits, 'The Hollowing and Backsliding of Democracy in East Central Europe', *Global Policy* 6/Supplement 1 (2015), 28–37.

[50] Balázs Trencsényi, 'From Goulash-Communism to Goulash-Authoritarianism?', *Tr@nsit Online*, 2013, www.iwm.at/transit/transit-online/from-goulash-communism-to-goulash-authoritarianism/.

conservative perspective. Members of these grassroots movements were mobilised through participation in cultural, educational, charity, and leisure activities.[51] They provided the militancy essential to mobilise the popular vote.[52] Similarly, Poland's PiS has long relied on the nationalist-Catholic network built around Radio Maryja, a station created in 1991 that promoted xenophobia, Europhobia, and anti-Semitism,[53] while also harnessing the Catholic Church's mobilisation of parishioners against the gay community, divorce, abortion, contraception, and in vitro fertilisation.[54] In Poland the idea of a parallel, conservative society was mobilised in 2014, a year before PiS returned to power, when Jarosław Kaczyński rejected the results of the local elections and organised street protests, some of which turned violent.[55]

Once legitimised by their electoral victories, these politicians proclaimed the genesis of a new social contract, which they presented as the real revolution 'at the voting booth' as opposed to the 'elite conspiracy' of 1989. In their political rhetoric, Orbán, and others, dismissed the rule-of-law state that was built in the 1990s as one that had never belonged to 'the people'.[56] Aided by a network of partisan media outlets and a process of media capture underpinned by concentrated, non-transparent ownership with links to oligarchic networks, populists in the region eroded press freedom.[57] They were also deeply critical of the social impact of the shrunken state under the neoliberal policies of the first decades of transformation; rather, they implemented redistributive policies that sought to

---

[51] Béla Greskovits, 'Rebuilding the Hungarian Right through Civil Organisation and Contention: The Civic Circles Movement' (EUI Working Paper RSCAS 37, 2017), 4.

[52] Ibid., 13–14.

[53] Ireneusz Krzemiński, 'Radio Maryja and Fr. Rydzyk as a Creator of the National-Catholic Ideology', in Sabrina Ramet and Irena Borowik (eds.), *Religion, Politics, and Values in Poland: Continuity and Change since 1989* (New York: Palgrave Macmillan, 2017), 85–112.

[54] Anna Szwedand Katarzyna Zielińska, 'A War on Gender? The Roman Catholic Church's Discourse on Gender in Poland', in Ramet and Borowik (eds.), *Religion, Politics*, 113–36.

[55] 'Poland's Independence Turned Violent', *BBC News*, 11 November 2014, www.bbc.com/news/world-europe-30012830; 'Tens of Thousands of Poles Protest in Warsaw over Alleged Election Rigging', 13 December 2014, www.rt.com/news/214207-poland-protest-elections-rigged/.

[56] András Pap, *Democratic Decline in Hungary: Law and Society in an Illiberal Democracy* (London: Routledge, 2017), 39.

[57] Michael Abramowitz, *Democracy in Crisis: Freedom in the World 2018 Report* (New York: Freedom House, 2018); Alina Mungiu Pippidi, 'How Media and Politics Shape Each Other in the New Europe', in Karol Jakubowicz and Miklós Sükösd (eds.), *Finding the Right Place on the Map: Central and Eastern European Media Change in a Global Perspective* (Bristol: Intellect Books, 2008), 91. See also John Downey and Sabina Mihelj (eds.), *Central and Eastern European Media in Comparative Perspective: Politics Economy and Culture* (Farnham: Ashgate, 2012).

reaffirm the role of the state in the wider social and economic spheres. FIDESZ created a new system of 'national cooperation' in Hungary and combined a neoliberal tax regime with paternalist policies, family subsidies, and a push for the spread of state ownership over the economy.[58] Poland's Law and Justice Party focused on welfare measures that would revitalise the nation. In 2018 an Oxfam report listed the Polish state as one of the leaders in combating income inequality and child poverty.[59]

It is important to note that populist governments did not consider their radical critique of European integration incompatible with EU membership. For them, such an agenda was a necessary corrective against an association that was not, for them, a partnership but rather a designed-to-be-unending relationship between master and pupil.[60] Extracting as much financial support as possible from an EU they affected to despise could thus still be justified in terms of a project that sought to affirm sovereignty and create a more equal Europe. In Poland between 2012 and 2016, regional development funds to the tune of some 80 billion euros bankrolled a developmental boom, the main beneficiary of which was PiS. Hungary, a much smaller country, received close to 30 billion euros over the same period. For their leaders, Orbán and Kaczyński, these resources from Brussels were presented to their supporters as rectification for what they saw as inequalities accumulated during and after EU enlargement.[61] Such narrative of correcting imbalances between East and West seemed be confirmed by continuing high levels of support for the Union within countries where important parts of the electorates voted for populists. In Poland in 2018 an opinion poll showed that 92 per cent of the citizens were in favour of EU membership.[62] In Hungary only 14 per cent were against.[63]

---

[58] Wade Jacoby and Umut Korkut, 'Vulnerability and Economic Re-orientation: Rhetoric and in Reality in Hungary's "Chinese Opening"', *East European Politics and Societies and Cultures*, 30/3 (2016), 49.

[59] Joanna Berendt and Marc Santora, 'Poland Elections a Test for Governing Party's Populist Message', *New York Times*, 19 October 2018, www.nytimes.com/2018/10/19/world/europe/poland-election-law-and-justice.html.

[60] Michal Kopeček, 'Sovereignty, "Return to Europe" and Democratic Distrust in the East after 1989 in the Light of Brexit', *Central European History* 28/1 (2019), 75.

[61] Roger Cohen, 'How Democracy Became the Enemy', *New York* Times, 6 April 2018, www.nytimes.com/2018/04/06/opinion/sunday/orban-hungary-kaczynski-poland.html?action=click&module=Opinion&pgtype=Homepage.

[62] Dimitrova, 'Uncertain Road', 272.

[63] Radu Eremia, 'Guvernarea PSD-ALDE îi îndepărtează pe români de Uniunea Europeană. Unde se clasează România în topul creșterii euroscepticismului', *Adevarul*, 17 October 2018, https://adevarul.ro/news/politica/guvernarea-psd-alde-indeparteaza-romani-uniuneaeuropeana-claseaza-romania-topul-cresterii-euroscepticismului-1_5bc7653cdf52022f759a0b14/index.html.

This notion that Eastern Europeans would never be accepted as fully European was exploited by populist politicians who wished to distance their region from the liberal West. Immigration was a key issue: following the accession of Eastern European states from 2004, the West was perceived as remarkably inhospitable to Eastern European migrants.[64] Former socialist countries had been accepted into the organisation on condition that their citizens did not settle or work in other member states for a period of seven years. The only states that opened their labour markets immediately were Sweden, Ireland, and the United Kingdom. These debates, often acrimonious, confirmed the asymmetry of post-1989 Europeanisation. By the time that the ban on the movement of labour from the East was about to expire, a wave of xenophobic stereotypes arose in many of the countries of 'old' Europe in the expectation of yet another wave of migration. The idea that accession would lead to a full public acceptance of Easterners as Europeans was, at the very least, still waiting for its full realisation.

This sense of being denied their status as 'full Europeans' was further reinforced in the populists' mind-sets by Western reactions to the arrival in Europe of over one million people from predominantly Muslim countries such as Syria, Iraq, and Afghanistan during the so-called refugee crisis of 2015. The German chancellor Angela Merkel supported a 'welcome culture' to greet refugees. She later justified it to Hungarian prime minister Viktor Orbán in a manner that berated Easterners for a supposed failure to see their hypocrisy in enabling their own mobility but denying others – whilst simultaneously skating over the very real barriers that had surrounded Europe since the 1990s: 'I've lived behind a wall once in my life and have no desire to do so again'.[65] Brussels was perceived to be unduly hasty in its determining of refugee quotas; echoing similar reactions in the West, politicians and public opinion leaders in Eastern European member states often presented this as an unwanted imposition that compromised sovereignty and threatened national survival. A former Romanian minister of foreign affairs contrasted the West's negative treatment of Eastern European migrants with the warm welcome accorded to 'the wave of Syrians'. He warned that such double standards deepened Euroscepticism in an East that was traditionally

---

[64] Philipp Ther, *Europe since 1989: A History* (Princeton, NJ: Princeton University Press, 2016), 310–12.

[65] Quoted in Jeremy Cliffe, 'The Great Survivor. Angela Merkel's Last Stand', *New Statesman*, 27 June 2018, www.newstatesman.com/world/europe/2018/06/great-survivor-angela-merkel-s-last-stand.

enthusiastic about the European cause.[66] A former protester on the streets of East Germany compared the incoming refugees with the take-over of GDR's state and economy by Western Germans. The outcome for him was the same – the spectre of further marginalisation: 'I didn't risk my skin back then [in 1989] to become a third class citizen. First there are western Germans, then there are asylum seekers, then it's us'.[67]

Moreover, in such views Eastern European identities built around the powerful, important, and enduring image of national victimhood under Communist rule were seemingly endangered by new waves of war refugees whose victimisation seemed to have greater appeal to Western audiences. The Croatian intellectual Slavenka Drakulić noted that for conservatives 'the victims of Communism now have serious competitors: war refugees arriving from the Middle East and Africa'.[68] In this reading, the 'new victims, mostly Muslims arriving in frighteningly high numbers' did not trigger empathy among Eastern Europeans, who jealously defend their hard-won status as acknowledged European victims of totalitarianism. As Drakulić sarcastically put it, 'Are [they] expected to renounce their victimhood and national homogeneity in order to show solidarity?'[69]

It was not only that the West lost its allure as an unquestioned beacon of modernity, and that Western Europeans appeared unable to accept the Easterners as European equals; according to new populist movements, the powerful reach of Western liberalism represented a threat to the very strength and cohesion of white Christian Eastern European nations. At the heart of this anxiety was demography: Eastern Europe was the only world region to suffer population loss in the twenty-first century. For this Western liberalism was often deemed to be the culprit. Freedom of movement within the EU had enabled significant sections of the populations of former socialist countries to emigrate to the West, despite the initially inhospitable immigration politics aimed at Easterners.[70] In Romania since the late 1990s, at least a third of the labour force

---

[66] Teodor Baconschi, 'Islamofobia e o crimă?', Ziare.com, 10 September 2015, www.ziare.com/invazie-imigranti/romania/islamofobia-e-o-crima-1381641.

[67] Kartin Bennhold, 'One Legacy of Merkel? Angry East German Men Fueling the Far Right', New York Times, 5 November 2018, www.nytimes.com/2018/11/05/world/europe/merkel-east-germany-nationalists-populism.html.

[68] Slavenka Drakulić, 'Competing for Victimhood. Why Eastern Europe Says No to Refugees', Eurozine, 4 November 2015, www.eurozine.com/articles/2015-11-04-drakulic-en.html.

[69] Ibid.

[70] Belgian magazine Le Vif referred to a study of the Austrian Academy of Sciences that stated the population of the former socialist countries that joined the EU dropped on average by 7 per cent between 1990 and 2017: 'Le fossé démographique se creuse entre l'est et l'ouest de l'Europe', Le Vif, 22 June 2018, www.levif.be/actualite/international/le-fosse-demographique-se-creuse-entre-l-est-et-l-ouest-de-l-europe/article-normal-857547.html.

emigrated, and work abroad became a safety valve for the massive social dislocation that the post-Communist economy had brought.[71] During the first twenty-five years of post-socialism, 10 per cent of Bulgarians chose to work abroad.[72] In Hungary an opinion poll from 2016 showed that almost 50 per cent of all Hungarians between the ages of nineteen and thirty and one-third of those between thirty and forty wanted to leave their country.[73] Such an exodus, it was claimed, threatened both the productivity of the economy in the short term and the health of the nation in the future. Alongside this, liberal conceptions of gender relations threatened to extend eastwards and further undermine a conservative vision of family. Populists presented women's rights, abortion, or gay marriage as the result of the Western transfer of overly individualistic, amoral, and irreligious politics that likewise weakened the national body. Polish conservatives termed Western cosmopolitanism a liberal 'civilisation of death' because of its defence of the rights of LGBTQ communities and of abortion. Against this background, the populist imagination feared that the EU's insistence on migration quotas for refugees was another Western attempt to weaken nations whose ethnically dominant groups were already being eroded.

At the centre of this new political imagination was the defence of the white Christian nation in Eastern Europe against the attacks of the liberal West. The rural became valorised – in contrast with the cosmopolitan dissolute Westernised city – as the true embodiment and bulwark of the traditional values of the nation. Eastern European states sought to reverse demographic loss by adopting new approaches to population movement. Some sought – with little success – to bring back those who had left. In Bucharest a social democratic government proposed in 2018 a five-year period for Romanian citizens working abroad to decide whether they wished to remain outside of their country or to return home. Its initiator argued that 'at European level we must learn that, as one area gets poorer and another richer, at some point things break apart. There should be true social cohesion: one should not strengthen the West while leaving the rest of Europe for all sorts of reasons on the outside'.[74] In other cases, governments dealt with labour shortages by encouraging the migration of

---

[71] Cornel Ban, *Ruling Ideas: How Global Neoliberalism Goes Local* (Oxford: Oxford University Press, 2016), 69.

[72] Dace Dzenovska, 'Coherent Selves, Viable States: Eastern Europe and the "Migration/ Refugee Crisis"', *Slavic Review*, 76/2 (2017), 294.

[73] Árpád Klimó, *Hungary since 1945* (London: Routledge, 2018), 111.

[74] Quoted in 'Teodorovici vrea să limiteze dreptul la muncă al românilor în UE', *Euractiv. ro*, 27 November 2018, www.euractiv.ro/economic/teodorovici-vrea-sa-limiteze-dreptul-la-munca-al-romanilor-in-ue-12738.

European labour from further East, beyond the EU, or by recruiting ethnically, culturally or religiously familiar labour mainly drawn from less developed countries outside of Europe. In Poland, the problem was addressed by opening the borders in 2017 both to 'white' European Ukrainian skilled workers and, to a far lesser degree, to supposedly culturally familiar Catholic migrants from East Asia – most notably from the Philippines and Vietnam. Small numbers of North Koreans also work around Kraków: a result both of Cold War–era socialist links, and Pyongyang's policy of farming out workers in order to garner hard currency for the regime.[75] Despite PiS's strong anti-immigration rhetoric, Poland actually had the highest levels of immigration of any European country in 2017.[76] In Hungary, immigration was initially deemed out of the question to solve a dearth of labour: instead, FIDESZ government created a policy, dubbed by critics as the 'slave law', which allowed employers to increase the amount of overtime they could ask employees to work. This legislation brought the liberal-left and far right together in protest against this seemingly neocolonial compact between their government and large multinationals.[77]

From early 2018, however, exploiting the economic chaos brought about by the Maduro government in Caracas, and seeking to address these economic pressures, the government began secretly to encourage Catholic anti-Communist Venezuelans of Hungarian descent to immigrate.[78] Once the policy emerged and required public justification its advocates argued that whilst liberal migration regimes diluted the strength of the cultural nation, their policy achieved the opposite. It brought the diaspora home and hence strengthened the national body – a policy that, once focussed solely on ethnic Hungarians in the Carpathian basin, was now extended beyond Europe. Yet in various Eastern European countries this extra-European immigration created a second-class, dependent working force often relegated to the social margins.[79]

---

[75] 'What Are North Koreans Doing in Małopolska?', *Krakow Post*, 10 January 2018, www.krakowpost.com/18504/2018/01/north-korean-workers-malopolska-poland.

[76] Frey Lindsay, 'Ukrainian Immigrants Give the Polish Government an Out on Refugees', *Forbes*, 19 September 2018, www.forbes.com/sites/freylindsay/2018/09/19/ukrainian-immigrants-give-the-polish-government-an-out-on-refugees/#29327d9d4bb1.

[77] Valerie Hopkins, 'Hungary's "Slave Law" Unites Orban Opponents in Protest', *Financial Times*, 18 December 2018, www.ft.com/content/feeb9330-02be-11e9-99df-6183d3002ee1; in 2018, 17 per cent of the Ukrainian labour force worked abroad.

[78] Imre Fónai, 'Épp kitört az új migránspánik, mire kiderült: "csak" venezuelai magyarok költöztek a balatonőszödi üdülőbe', *Magyar Narancs*, 13 April 2018. https://magyarnarancs .hu/kismagyarorszag/epp-kitort-az-ujabb-migranspanik-mire-kiderult-csak-venezuelai-magyarok-koltoztek-a-balatonoszodi-udulobe-110578.

[79] Romania recruited from the Philippines, Nepal, Vietnam, India, Indonesia, and Thailand, especially for light and hotel industries or agriculture. On these workers' social exclusion, see

Populists often defined themselves as defenders of their nations from the supposedly deleterious effects of Western liberal gender politics on the Christian nation. As early as 2006 the Polish prime minister Jarosław Kaczyński proclaimed, referring to same-sex marriage and abortion, that Poland 'will demand full sovereignty in moral matters'.[80] When Jarosław Gowin was appointed minister of science and higher education in 2015, he announced his determination to withdraw 'gay and lesbian studies journals' from publication.[81] Gender studies courses in Hungarian higher education were effectively banned.[82] In September 2018 the Romanian social democratic government held a referendum that was triggered by lobbying from conservative civil associations that sought to change the constitutional definition of 'family' to describe it only as a relationship between 'man and woman' – in reality a constitutional ban on gay marriage.

For some months Bucharest became the centre of attention for a global network advocates of illiberal gender policies from Russia, US Christian right organisations such as the Liberty Council and the Alliance Defending Freedom, as well as public figures involved in similar referenda in Croatia or Slovakia.[83] This alliance came together under the umbrella of the World Congress of Families, an international forum that promotes the values of the Christian right. Tellingly, in the late 2010s its international congresses were all held in the region, in Tbilisi (2016), Budapest (2017), and Chişinău (2018).[84] Whilst the referendum failed due to a low turnout, the debates it provoked provided a telling illustration of how Eastern European governments, together with global anti-liberals, have managed to give new weight to an international anti-gay and anti-abortion agenda.

'România, căutată de angajaţii din şase ţări asiatice', *Digi24*, 30 July 2018, www.digi24.ro/ stiri/economie/companii/romania-cautata-de-angajatii-din-sase-tari-asiatice-972234.

[80] Kuus, *Geopolitics Reframed*, 66–67.

[81] Agnieszka Graff and Elżbieta Korolczuk, '"Worse Than Communism and Nazism Put Together": War on Gender in Poland', in Roman Kuhar and David Paternotte (eds.), *Anti-gender Campaigns in Europe: Mobilizing Against Equality* (New York: Rowman & Littlefield, 2017), 175–94; Agnieszka Graff, 'Report from the Gender Trenches: War against "Genderism" in Poland', *European Journal of Women's Studies*, 21/4 (2014), 431–442.

[82] 'The Orbán Regime Feels Threatened by Gender Studies', http://hungarianspectrum.org/ 2018/08/10/the-orban-regime-feels-threatened-by-gender-studies/.

[83] Vlad Viski, 'Bătălia pentru Europa de Est', *Adevărul*, 3 May 2018, https://adevarul.ro/ news/politica/batalia-europa-est-1_5aeae44adf52022f75890952/index.html.

[84] Quoted in Tom Porter, 'The Christian Right Is Looking to Putin's Russia to Save Christianity from the Godless West', *Newsweek*, 15 September 2018, www.newsweek .com/how-evangelicals-are-looking-putins-russia-save-christianity-godless-west-1115164.

In the 2010s the defence of the cultural nation also required, for populists, the prevention of Islamic settlement. This had not always been the case: during the 1990s, the region had received large numbers of Muslim migrants and with only limited disruption. The Czech Republic took in thousands from Bosnia, Ukraine, and Moldova; Poland welcomed Muslim Chechen refugees, and Hungary was the second largest recipient of refugees from former Yugoslavia.[85] This earlier Eastern European 'welcome culture' reflected both regional solidarities and the previous acceptance of liberal humanitarianism aimed at safeguarding populations that were on the very edge of Europe. By the 2010s this had changed: liberal humanitarianism was deemed a threat to ethnic and cultural homogeneity, while in the West too it was heavily contested; moreover, the refugees under discussion were marked as outsiders – neither white nor Christian, nor European.

Some argued that Eastern European states were not under any obligation to take refugees of non-European heritage as they had not held extra-European empires and hence, by contrast with states in the West of the continent, did not have contemporary responsibilities that stemmed from that historical experience.[86] A Czech ethnologist, Mnislav Zelený-Atapana, stated that 'Mrs Merkel and those like her are basically undertaking an artificial mixing of the races in which the white race will be gradually liquidated and we Europeans will become black or brown. This is a genocide against white people ... They started in the distant past the colonial division of the world and after World War Two began to reap the rotten fruit as they opened borders to people of former colonies. We, however, did not participate in [colonialism] and therefore we have no moral obligation to accept refugees'.[87] Others (mainly liberals) noted that these assertions deliberately left out earlier Eastern European migration to western European imperial settler colonialisms, socialist-era migration from Africa and Asia to the region, and the presence of the region's troops in destabilising conflicts in the Middle East that had helped to precipitate these migrations to begin with.[88]

---

[85] Lenka Bustikova and Petra Guasti, 'The Illiberal Turn or Swerve in Central Europe?', *Politics and Governance*, 5/4 (2017), 171.

[86] 'Interview with Gergely Pröhle, Former Ambassador of Hungary in Berlin', *Körber Stiftung*, May 2018, www.koerber-stiftung.de/en/topics/the-value-of-europe/contributions-2018/interview-proehle.

[87] Quoted in Imogen Tyler, 'The Hieroglyphics of the Border: Racial Stigma in Neoliberal Europe', *Ethnic and Racial Studies*, 41/10 (2018), 1789.

[88] Salman Sayyid, 'Islamophobia and the Europeanness of the Other Europe', *Patterns of Prejudice*, 52/5 (2018), 420–22.

In 2016, when the EU proposed quotas of refugees to be accommodated in each member state, Hungary, Slovakia, the Czech Republic, and then Romania opposed the decision. A year later the Hungarian and Slovak governments attacked the policy at the European Court of Justice, arguing that the quotas would attract new waves of immigration from non-European regions. The court upheld Brussels's policy and formally requested that the authorities in Budapest, Warsaw, and Prague comply with it; but they refused to do so.[89] Populists in these countries legitimised their stance by employing anti-Islamic historical narratives about the region's struggles against the Ottoman Empire. Anti-Arab representations from late socialism and the early 1990s, which associated Muslims with profiteering, backwardness, and terrorism, were revived. Eastern Europeans' opposition to quotas was shared by many other member states: anti-immigration and anti-refugee rhetoric was central to the Brexit vote and populist electoral progress during the European elections in 2014,[90] as well as in 2018 elections in Italy, Austria, the Netherlands, Sweden, and Germany. Several states within the EU provisionally suspended the free circulation of people out of fear of illegal immigration and terrorist attacks, meeting then with little opposition from the European Commission.[91]

For populists, the battle to keep out Muslim immigrants became a part of a wider campaign to define their nations' cultural superiority: against the resilient indeterminacy of the post-socialist space the West told them they lived in, their zealotry in the service of white, Christian, heterosexual Europeanness reversed the hierarchies of civilisational virtue.[92] Such anti-Islamic understandings of Europe came not only from the right: liberal feminists in Eastern Europe, too, saw Islamic migration as a threat to women's rights. They feared that Muslim conservatives might join forces with their own local Catholic or Orthodox ones to restrict women's freedoms. In Poland, the feminist intellectual Magdalena Środa compared Muslim attitudes towards women with the populists' anti-feminism: she saw them as natural allies who wished to control women's bodies; other critics took this idea further and branded them, using the acronym for the Polish populist party Law and Justice, PiSlamists.[93]

---

[89] Bustikova and Guasti, 'Illiberal Turn', 171–72.

[90] Cas Mudde, 'Local Shocks. The Far Right in the 2014 European Elections', *Eurozine*, 13 March 2015, www.eurozine.com/articles/2015-03-13-mudde-en.html.

[91] Stefano Braghiroli and Andrey Makarychev, 'Redefining Europe: Russia and the 2015 Refugee Crisis', *Geopolitics*, 23/4 (2017), 826.

[92] Ivan Kalmar, 'Islamophobia in the East of the European Union: An Introduction', *Patterns of Prejudice*, 52/5 (2018), 389–405.

[93] Monika Bobako, 'Semi-peripheral Islamophobias: The Political Diversity of Anti-Muslim Discourses in Poland', *Patterns of Prejudice*, 52/5 (2018), 455–56.

The image of the Jew was also crucial in this worldview. On one hand, drawing on many older anti-Semitic stereotypes, they were seen as the threatening carriers of liberal globalist contagion that encouraged immigration in order to ethnically and culturally weaken nations. This rhetoric was deployed in Hungarian prime minister Viktor Orbán's crusade against the (Jewish) US billionaire George Soros, who in the 1980s had helped to establish the networks that underpinned a global liberal transition template – as we explored in Chapter 2. The FIDESZ government's 'Stop Soros' initiatives restricted the ability of nongovernmental organisations to act in asylum cases; individuals or groups that helped illegal migrants to obtain the status to stay in Hungary were liable to prison terms.[94] For the conservative counterrevolution, Soros and the Open Society Foundations, two crucial actors in democracy promotion campaigns across the postsocialist space after 1989,[95] became symbols of the Western liberal threat against national homogeneity and foreign interference in domestic politics.[96] At the same time, the populists embraced the idea of protecting Jewish communities – but only so far as it enabled them to bolster anti-Muslim policies in the name of defending a conservative vision of Europe. For Orbán, Muslims were 'genetically' anti-Semitic; he co-opted the fear of anti-Jewish violence and the memory of the Holocaust into his narratives of whiteness under attack. Local anti-Semitism was not addressed, but the protection of nationals of Jewish descent was cynically employed to justify the rejection of Islamic and immigrant outsiders who would supposedly bring anti-Semitism with them.

Populist politicians from both the right and the left exploited fears of 'ethnic disappearance' triggered by the Eastern European exodus to the West. They crafted ideological agendas aimed at a putative defence of 'endangered nations' against labour shortages as well as so-called onslaughts of liberal gender politics and a 'Muslim invasion' that, they claimed, threatened their very civilisation. They went onto the offensive, employing the same arguments to assert their societies' cultural superiority against the West, countering perceived systematic marginalisation

---

[94] 'Hungary Passes Anti-immigrant "Stop Soros" Laws', *Guardian*, 20 June 2018, www.theguardian.com/world/2018/jun/20/hungary-passes-anti-immigrant-stop-soros-laws.

[95] Daniel Bessner, 'The Globalist: George Soros after the Open Society', *N+1*, 18 May 2018, https://nplusonemag.com/online-only/online-only/the-globalist/.

[96] This narrative was not limited to Eastern Europe. US president Donald Trump and the right wing of the Republican Party attacked Soros in similar fashion as he became a *bête noire* for populist mobilisation. Kenneth Vogel, Scott Shane, and Patrick Kingsley, 'How Vilification of George Soros Moved from the Fringes to the Mainstream', *New York Times*, 31 October 2018, www.nytimes.com/2018/10/31/us/politics/george-soros-bombs-trump.html?action=click&module=Top%20Stories&pgtype=Homepage.

within the EU. It also went further. For them, Eastern Europeans not only were defenders of their homeland, but were also required to act as a vanguard to sustain a broader vision of a Christian and conservative Europe. The lack of recognition of the East as fully European was now challenged by the claim that the West was feeble and decadent and that the EU's East was the 'true Europe' – the champion of the struggle for the continent's white, Christian soul.[97] Despite the rhetoric, this populist counterrevolution was in fact a much more pan-European – and internationalist – affair, bringing Eastern Europeans into new alliances with populists in Italy, France, Austria, and beyond.

A siege mentality fuelled these politicians' narratives, which justified building fences along EU frontiers, recruiting border militias, banning minarets, and constructing camps to contain migrants. For Orbán's ally Mária Schmidt, the Syrian refugee crisis was primarily part of a centuries-old campaign by Islamic forces seeking to 'occupy Europe', and she revived the idea of Hungary as symbolic and historical bulwark protecting European civilisation. A Romanian centre-right intellectual went further, suggesting that Western Europe needed to revive a 'beneficial colonialism' in Africa and the Middle East to save the white Christian East of the continent faced, he argued, with demographic decline and a new wave of Islamic migration.[98] The Czech president Zeman warned that the refugees were 'Muslim invaders' who would bring infectious diseases and could harbour 'sleeper cells' of Islamic terrorists.[99] A broader civilisational interpretation was advanced in Romania by the former dissident Ana Blandiana. In March 2016, the longtime president of the Civic Alliance, the most important NGO advocating anti-Communist memory and justice, declared that the crisis of Europe was similar to the fall of the Roman Empire. The continent was threatened by millions of immigrants carrying a 'cultural baggage' incompatible with democracy and therefore 'more dangerous than terrorism'. From her perspective, Islamophobia was the necessary reaction to the EU's 'bureaucratic and vegetative' politics.[100]

[97] See this argument for Poland in Lucy Mayblin, Aneta Piekut, and Gill Valentine, '"Other" Posts in "Other" Places: Poland through a Postcolonial Lens?', *Sociology*, 50/1 (2016), 70.

[98] Andrei Pleşu, 'Înapoi în colonii?', https://adevarul.ro/international/in-lume/Inapoi-coloniii-1_56f8ded65ab6550cb84ebb70/index.html.

[99] Tyler, 'Hieroglyphics of the Border', 1785.

[100] The statements were part of her acceptance speech upon receiving the title of Doctor Honoris Cause of University Babeş-Bolyai (a bilingual institution) in Cluj (a multicultural city): Despina Tudor, 'Ana Blandiana: "Epoca noastră seamănă izbitor cu cea de la finalul Imperiului Roman"', 24 March 2016, *Revista 22*, https://revista22.ro/70252912/ana-blandiana-epoca-noastr-seamn-izbitor-cu-cea-de-la-finalul-imperiului-roman.html; for a review of the Romanian reactions to the refugee

Populists claimed that the cause of a true Europe had been weakened to such an extent in the West that its political mainstream, incapable of understanding such crises, could no longer be relied upon. This had happened because most Western politicians and opinion leaders were still wracked by post-imperial guilt, hence unable to resist what Eastern Europeans saw as the cultural threat of Islamic migration. According to a former Romanian minister of foreign affairs, Teodor Baconschi, 'the cholera of political correctness … this moralizing political police, the eternal obsession of a West "guilty" about its past and compelled to repent' had generated the 'weakening of the Euro-American civilisation'.[101] Eastern Europeans, according to populist narratives, could immediately recognise such crises as their region had suffered to defend Europe in a way few Westerners could imagine.

For this reason this populist politics drew on a culture of right-wing national memory that emphasised their nations' sacrifice under Communist rule.[102] The West had not suffered comparably and this, it was argued, rendered it complacent when faced with threats to its civilisation.[103] Transnational conservative networks of politicians, activists, and institutions from former socialist countries successfully lobbied Brussels for an official EU acknowledgement that their suffering be accorded an equal weight in a 'common European memory'. As a consequence, they often sought to downplay the Western narrative of the 'uniqueness of the Holocaust': both because it threatened to undermine the appeal to the depth of their own suffering, and as the cosmopolitan memory culture it supported seemed to them shaped to undergird a Western liberal view of the world.[104] Once free of the requirements of

---

crisis, see Doru Pop, 'Misrepresentation of Muslims and Islamophobic Public Discourses in Recent Romanian Media Narratives', *Journal for the Study of Religions and Ideologies*, 44 (2016), 33–51.

[101] Baconschi, 'Islamofobia'.

[102] Grudzińska-Gross, 'Backsliding', 667; Laure Neumayer, *The Criminalisation of Communism in the European Political Space after the Cold War* (New York: Routledge, 2019).

[103] Zuzana Kepplová, 'Recycled Rhetoric. Could the Real Tragedy of Central Europe Please Stand Up?', *Visegrad Insight*, 10 July 2018, https://visegradinsight.eu/recycled-rhetoric/.

[104] Laure Neumayer, 'Integrating the Central European Past into a Common Narrative: The Mobilisations around the "Crimes of Communism" in the European Parliament', *Journal of Contemporary European Studies*, 23/3 (2015), 348 and 360. This criminalising discourse also led to a new nationalist non-cosmopolitan Putin-supported Russian Holocaust memory after the invasion of Crimea. Russian authorities presented themselves as defenders of moral values, whilst attacking 'Westernising' former socialist states such as Ukraine, the Baltics, and Poland: accusations that they had, by contrast, marginalised the memory of the Holocaust were used in Russia foreign policy discourse as evidence of these states' reactionary, fascist-like, politics. Isabel Sawkins, 'Russia's Nationalist Mobilisation of the Holocaust on the Screen: Khabensky's film

EU accession, which had pressured states to recognise, or accord more weight to, their involvement in the Holocaust or anti-Semitic repression, populists could develop collective memories that downplayed complicity and upgraded their own national martyrdom.[105] Such mobilisation over the recognition of suffering and survival laid the groundwork for the conservative cultural counterrevolution. For instance, in Poland PiS passed a law that carried a criminal punishment of up to three years for any statements arguing Poles' complicity in the Holocaust and Nazi concentration camps; later on, because of an international outcry, a new version of the bill was passed that removed the threat of a jail sentence but still considered a civil offence any claim deemed by the authorities to be defamatory towards Poland's role in the Second World War.[106]

At one time, during the Cold War, it had been Eastern European Communists who had claimed to be the defenders of the true Europe – for them, this had meant the protection of the continent from the return of fascism. Now their successors, of a very different ideological hue, drawing legitimacy from their own claims to have suffered protecting Europe from Communism, articulated a new defence of the continent imagined as a Christian cultural fortress, fenced off like an Asterix village, to paraphrase Czech prime minister Andrej Babiš's reference to the French comic about a village of Gauls that resist Roman occupation in 50 BC.[107] They took advantage of the increasing reliance on anti-immigration narratives in European politics.[108] Working with politicians such as Matteo Salvini or Sebastian Kurz (Austria's conservative prime minister), Orbán, Kaczyński, or Fico advocated a 'Marshall plan for Africa' that employed development assistance for the continent's countries as a mechanism for keeping potential migrants outside of Europe, thus preventing civilisational 'miscegenation'. Or as Babiš put it, 'They have their culture, we have our culture ... They have their values, but we want to keep [our] values'.[109]

Sobibor (2018)' (paper presented at 'A Crisis in "Coming to Terms with the Past"? At the Crossroads of Translation and Memory', London, February 2019); Laure Neumayer, 'Advocating for the Cause of the "Victims of Communism" in the European Political Space: Memory Entrepreneurs in Interstitial Fields', *Nationalities Papers*, 45/6 (2017), 992–1012.

[105] Maria Mälksoo, 'Criminalizing Communism: Transnational Mnemopolitics in Europe', *International Political Sociology* 8/1 (2014), 82–99.

[106] Damien Sharkov, 'Poland Makes Big U-Turn on Holocaust Death Camps Law', *Newsweek*, 27 June 2018, www.newsweek.com/poland-makes-big-u-turn-holocaust-death-camps-law-998071.

[107] Hanley and Vachudova, 'Understanding the Illiberal Turn', 282.

[108] Tyler, 'Hieroglyphics of the Border', 1786.

[109] Patrick Wintour, 'Migrants to Europe "Need to Go Home", Says Czech Prime Minister', *Guardian*, 25 October 2018, www.theguardian.com/world/2018/oct/25/europe-migrants-need-to-go-home-says-czech-prime-minister.

A central symbol in this struggle to forestall the dilution and breakdown of Europeanness was the call to re-Christianise the continent. Polish Catholics, partly reflecting their long-held sense of national messianism, were at the forefront of Eastern European attempts to encourage the placing of Christian values at the centre of European life. The Polish justice minister Zbigniew Ziobro vetoed the adoption of an annual report on the EU's Charter of Fundamental Rights arguing that the document did not mention the need to protect Christians and Jews against religious discrimination in the same way as it dealt with the protection of the rights of LGBTQ persons, children of immigrants, or women.[110] In 2017 the Polish prime minister Beata Szydło offered to take the statue of the late Polish-born Pope John Paul II from a site in Brittany where it had been removed owing to its display of religious symbolism in public – which the French state bans.[111] The year after, the leader of the Polish parliament Stanisław Karczewski warned the Viennese to take seriously their historical role in protecting Christian Europe from the Ottomans – arguing for the erection of statues of the Polish King John III Sobieski, who had led the fight in the Battle of Vienna in 1683 and turned the tide of Ottoman expansion into Europe. Due to its suffering under dictatorships and occupations, often filtered through a religious frame of martyrdom, Eastern Europe had the weight of experience necessary to understand what it took to protect Christian Europe.

A Croat Catholic priest, who publicly discouraged his parishioners from providing food and drink to refugees, argued that 'for 500 years, Croatia was the bulwark of Christianity and a defender of Europe from Islamic heresy. Let's continue this tradition and protect Europe from the invasion of illegal Islamic migration'.[112] From this viewpoint Europe could still provide assistance to other ethnicities – but only if they were Christians. While protesting against Muslim immigration, the Hungarian government provided assistance for Christians in Iraq, Syria and Lebanon to restore their homes and churches as well as scholarships for young members of

---

[110] 'Poland's Justice Minister Vetoes EU Fundamental Rights Report', *Radio Poland*, 12 October 2018, www.thenews.pl/1/10/Artykul/386868,Poland.

[111] www.catholicherald.co.uk/news/2017/11/06/polish-pm-offers-to-save-john-paul-ii-statue-after-french-court-orders-removal-of-cross/. Szydło said: 'Our great Pole, a great European, is a symbol of a Christian, united Europe. The dictate of political correctness – secularisation of the state – makes room for values which are alien to our culture, which leads to terrorising Europeans in their everyday life'.

[112] Mersiha Gadzo, "Solidarity, Understanding, Humanity" Welcome Refugees in Bosnia', *Al Jazeera*, www.aljazeera.com/news/europe/2018/10/understanding-humanity-refugees-bosnia-181004100937794.html.

Christian families who had suffered persecution.[113] Hungarian officials complained that the international community failed to recognise the atrocities committed against Christian communities as genocide. According to Orbán, who created a state secretariat for 'Aiding Persecuted Christians', countries in the EU only had an obligation to accept those refugees who fitted their particular understandings of what belonging to European civilisation entailed – such as Syrian Christians.[114]

The anti-immigration mantra peddled by populist parties in former socialist EU member states stood in contrast to more inclusive attitudes in some countries that had been part of the former Yugoslavia. In these Balkan states, a tradition of cultural hybridity and in-betweenness, coupled with a still more intense desire for European integration, led to quite different reactions to the refugee crisis. Countries such as Serbia, Macedonia, Montenegro, or, outside the ex-Yugoslav space, Albania, had their own recent histories of displacement. They were also still in the process of negotiating EU accession for which Brussels developed more demanding conditions than East Central Europe had experienced.[115] Showing willingness to conform to EU plans for the migration crisis was thus seen as constituting a step forwards in this torturous process. Serbia and Albania for instance expressed their readiness to accept a quota of refugees as part of a continent-wide solution.[116] The refugees who on their way to the EU ended up being stuck in Macedonia, Serbia, or Bosnia-Herzegovina, received support from NGOs and civic initiatives, and there was generally a much more positive public response. This was particularly the case in Bosnia-Herzegovina, where many still harboured memories of their own wartime sufferings and their lives as Muslim refugees during the Yugoslav conflicts of the 1990s.[117] Peter Van der Auweraert, the Western

[113] 'Schmidt: Western Countries Want to "Civilize" Central Europe in a Colonial Fashion', *Hungary Today*, 18 October 2018, https://hungarytoday.hu/schmidt-western-countries-want-to-civilize-central-europe-in-a-colonial-fashion/.

[114] Ibid.

[115] Frank Schimmelfennig and Ulrich Sedelmeier, 'The Europeanisation of Eastern Europe: The External Incentives Model Revisited' (paper presented at the Jean Monnet Fellowship @25 Alumni Conference, Florence, 22–23 June 2017), 10–11, www.eui.eu/Documents/RSCAS/JMF-25-Presentation/Schimmelfennig-Sedelmeier-External-Incentives-Revisited-JMF.pdf.

[116] Neil Buckley, 'Serbia's PM Says Country Willing to Take Its Share of Refugees', *Financial Times*, 25 February 2016, www.ft.com/content/dedb7f5a-daf4-11e5-a72f-1e7744c66818; 'Albania Willing to Take in Migrants Docked in Italy', *Transitions Online*, 27 August 2018, www.tol.org/client/article/27917-albania-italy-migrants-refugees-quotas-crisis-eu.html.

[117] 'Bosnian War Veteran Turns His Cafe into Free Kitchen for Migrants', *Guardian*, 15 August 2018, www.theguardian.com/world/2018/aug/15/bosnian-war-veteran-turns-his-cafe-into-free-kitchen-for-migrants; 'Blocked in the Balkans: The Refugees

Balkans coordinator for the International Organisation for Migration, voiced his admiration for the reactions of Bosnian citizens: 'whether they are poor, middle-class, rich, whether they are Serbs, Croats or Bosniak; the overwhelming majority responded with solidarity, understanding and humanity'.[118] There were exceptions: the Serbian leader of the Bosnian entity of the Republic of Srpska stated that the refugee crisis was not a humanitarian issue but a plot of a 'hidden Sarajevo structure' that wanted to settle the Syrian, Afghan, and other, primarily Muslim, migrants in order to boost the numbers of the Bosniak Muslim majority.[119]

The conservative fashioning of 'the East' as the anti-liberal 'true Europe' generated substantial resistance both within the countries where it took shape and from EU institutions and leaders in Brussels. Anti-immigration rhetoric, illiberal gender politics, and the authoritarian turn was also rejected by sections of post-socialist societies and by some politicians. In Poland the Civic Platform (PO), led by Donald Tusk, the prime minister between 2007 and 2014, responded to the attempt of the Law and Justice Party to create an illiberal democracy by presenting itself as a defender of the liberal European idea. During the local elections in October 2018, the PO's successful mayoral candidate for Warsaw, Rafal Trzaskowski, presented the elections as a last ditch attempt to keep the city (and the country) on the path it had taken since 1989: 'The future of the city is at stake … one of the most tolerant, open and ambitious cities in Europe'.[120] PiS's poor results in the main cities during local elections was the result of very significant anti-conservative urban mobilisation around opposition to the populist vision of the future. For instance, PiS's attempt in 2016 to completely ban abortion was met with fierce and massive resistance from anti-conservative civic groups who organised the so-called 'Black Protests' (around a hundred thousand people joined) to force legislators to withdraw the law. Two years later a new ultra-restrictive law against abortion was introduced into Parliament and again was met with steadfast civic resistance.[121]

That Europe Won't Allow In', *Guardian*, 8 August 2017, www.theguardian.com/world/2017/aug/08/eu-refugees-serbia-afghanistan-taliban.

[118] Gadzo, 'Solidarity, Understanding'.

[119] 'Dodik: RS Will Not Allow Migrants in RS', *N1*, http://ba.n1info.com/a261807/English/NEWS/Dodik-RS-will-not-allow-migrants-in-RS.html.

[120] Joanna Berendt and Marc Santora, 'Poland Elections a Test for Governing Party's Populist Message', *New York Times*, 19 October 2018, www.nytimes.com/2018/10/19/world/europe/poland-election-law-and-justice.html.

[121] Anna Koper and Marcin Gootting, 'Thousands Join "Black Friday" Marches against Polish Abortion Restrictions', Reuters, 23 March 2018, www.reuters.com/article/us-poland-abortion/thousands-join-black-friday-marches-against-polish-abortion-restrictions-idUSKBN1GZ2LP.

Similarly, in Romania the majority of the population refused to participate in the referendum against same-sex marriage: a low turnout ensured
its result was invalid. Dan Barna, the president of the centrist party Save
Romania Union (USR), characterised this populist failure as a sign that
Romanians 'refused to take steps backwards' and that the country
remained 'a European and tolerant nation'.[122]

Attempts of centrist parties to adopt anti-refugee policies often
weakened them, diluting their own support whilst opening up greater
space to the right and far right. In 2017 in Slovakia the centre-left SMER
party tried to outbid the country's radical right on the topic, whilst
managing only to strengthen them. The same year in the Czech republic
Social Democrats lost 70 per cent of their support because of their
adoption of an anti-refugee agenda.[123] Such developments had echoes
in the West of the continent, where mainstream parties who adopted
strong anti-immigration narratives sometimes ended up losing their main
partisan base and legitimizing the far right. In 2018 the Christian Social
Union failed to win their usual absolute majority of the seats in the
Bavarian parliament and facilitated the far-right Alternative for
Germany's entrance into the legislature.[124]

The EU itself began to pursue a more militant approach in order to
forestall Eastern Europe's divergence. Keen to bolster political forces
that opposed the populist wave, the Polish liberal Donald Tusk was re-
elected in 2017 as European Council president – even though then Polish
prime minister, Beata Szydło, a PiS member, rejected his nomination.[125]
Similar symbolic backing emerged for Romanian president Klaus Iohannis, a defender of EU democratic norms against the Social Democratic
Party's attempts to dismantle the rule of law.[126] Yet the EU's ability to
prevent Eastern European divergence towards authoritarianism
remained limited as it lacked appropriate supra-national strategies and

---

[122] 'Barna: Referendumul nu a fost validat de cetățenii României. România refuză să facă
pași înapoi', *Adevărul*, 7 October 2018, https://adevarul.ro/news/politica/barna-
referendumul-nu-fost-validat-cetatenii-romaniei-romania-refuza-faca-pasi-inapoi-1_
5bba4be7df52022f754532a6/index.html.

[123] Bustikova and Guasti, 'Illiberal Turn', 172.

[124] Dan Hough, 'Bavaria's Christian Social Union Party's Campaign Strategy Flopped',
Washington Post, 15 October 2018, www.washingtonpost.com/news/monkey-cage/wp/
2018/10/15/bavarias-christian-social-union-partys-campaign-strategy-flopped-heres-what-
this-means-for-germany-and-europe/?utm_term=.0b436a779fda.

[125] Wojciech Przybylski, 'Can Poland's Backsliding Be Stopped?', *Journal of Democracy*,
29/3 (2018), 57–58.

[126] 'Klaus Iohannis Has Support in Brussels to Become President of the European Council
in 2019', *Business Review*, 2 March 2018, http://business-review.eu/news/klaus-iohannis-
has-support-in-brussels-to-become-President-of-the-european-council-in-2019-media-
159807.

legal instruments. It had only started adding enforcement mechanisms to prevent illiberal backsliding for the later EU accession of Romania and Bulgaria; thus the governments of these two states could be disciplined in a way that Hungary and Poland could not. In 2012 Brussels was faced with two attempts to flout the rule of law and European legislation in Hungary and Romania. In the first case, it failed to bring into line the FIDESZ government, which, despite being condemned by the European Court of Justice, could not be penalised politically for its infringements. By contrast, then Romanian prime minister Victor Ponta was successfully pressured into conforming to Brussels's demands to row back on his legislative abuses.[127] The difference consisted first and foremost in the fact that for Romania (and Bulgaria) the EU maintained a post-accession instrument of accountability through the cooperation and verification mechanism (CVM). It periodically assessed the progress made in these countries in the fight against corruption and organised crime as well as in judicial reform. The European Commission linked breaches in the rule of law to continued CVM monitoring, while some member states tied it to Sofia's and Bucharest's prospective membership in the Schengen space (where internal border controls had been abolished). Negative CVM reports also had the function of 'naming and shaming', and thereby affecting the legitimacy of targeted governments.[128]

In spite of the CVM, Brussels still had to rely on pro-EU affinities in Bulgaria and Romania in order to keep politicians in line. In Budapest such an option was not available due to the local popularity of Viktor Orbán's commitment to a wholesale transformation of the post-socialist state and society as a final overcoming of Communism.[129] These new fault lines, a return of an East-West divide in Europe, were on full display in September 2018, when the European Parliament passed a report condemning the breach of the rule of law in Hungary. This triggered the so-called 'nuclear option', Article 7 of the EU Treaty, which, if passed in a parliamentary vote, meant that some of Hungary's

---

[127] Jan-Werner Müller, 'Should the EU Protect Democracy and the Rule of Law Inside Member States?', *European Law Journal*, 21/2 (2015), 141–60.

[128] Antoaneta Dimitrova and Aron Buzogány, 'Post-Accession Policy-Making in Bulgaria and Romania: Can Non-state Actors Use EU Rules to Promote Better Governance?', *Journal of Common Market Studies*, 52/1 (2014), 139–56.

[129] Ulrich Sedelmeier, 'Anchoring Democracy from Above? The European Union and Democratic Backsliding in Hungary and Romania after Accession', *Journal of Common Market Studies*, 52/1 (2014), 105–21; Venelin Ganev, '"Soft Decisionism" in Bulgaria', *Journal of Democracy*, 29/3 (2018), 91–103; Vlad Perju, 'Cazul UE împotriva României – Ce urmează după Raportul MCV', *Contributors.ro*, 16 November 2018, www.contributors.ro/editorial/cazul-ue-impotriva-romaniei-%E2%80%93-ce-urmeaza -dupa-raportul-mcv/.

membership rights would have been suspended. The balloting demonstrated the weakness of the EU, an institution established mainly to foster economic integration rather than rights, in protecting its liberal and democratic values. The majority of delegates from former socialist countries voted against the report condemning Hungary's illiberal turn. The new political elites in Eastern Europe had rejected their status of apprentice within the EU system and were now committed to carving out a new role for themselves and their populist agenda in a re-imagined Europe.[130]

Beyond the EU: Post-socialist Global Trajectories

The end of an uncritical naturalisation of Eastern European convergence with a liberal West was not only a matter of regional self-definition from within: it was supported by powers across the world from Vladimir Putin's Russia to the US right, Western European conservatives and ultra-nationalists, Communist China, and Recep Tayyip Erdoğan's Turkey. All of these players sought to conscript Eastern European elites to embrace a vision of Europe and the West consistent with their own populist or autocratic projects. Equally, Eastern European political actors considered such relationships beneficial as they provided international support for their nascent political movements and rejection of the post-1989 liberal consensus. In these new global mappings, networks between Beijing, Moscow, and Ankara represent a post-Western multipolar order founded on the idea of a community of sovereign states each with its specific ideological profile unencumbered by liberal democratic exigencies. Through such relationships, Eastern European populists began to re-imagine their region's place in a broader world beyond Western-style politics, EU conditionality, and the Euro-Atlantic space. This opening to alternative symbolic, economic, and political geographies was rooted in the ambivalences of the post-1989 'return to Europe'. Populists in states that had joined the EU sought allies for their political programmes centred on affirming sovereignty against Brussels and Western capitalism, thus ensuring limited external interference in their domestic neo-authoritarian politics. In South-Eastern European

---

[130] The term 'nuclear option' was coined by former President of the European Commission, José Manuel Barroso. One scholar has argued that Article 7 is more 'a kind of *moral quarantine*, not an actual intervention' against a member state that breached EU fundamental values. Müller, 'Should the EU Protect Democracy?', 144–45. Also, Péter Krekó, 'The Vote on the Sargentini Report: Good News for Europe, Bad News for Orbán, no News for Hungary', 21 September 2018, *Heinrich Böll Stiftung*, https://eu.boell.org/en/2018/09/21/vote-sargentini-report-good-news-europe-bad-news-orban-no-news-hungary.

countries which had not yet acceded to the EU, the limbo of a seemingly never-ending Europeanisation further confirmed their in-betweenness within post–Cold War hierarchies; this created the space for other actors to exert influence, such as Russia, China, or Turkey.

Eastern Europe's populists were not met with unanimous disapproval outside the region. Their opposition to admitting refugees, their advocacy of conservative gender roles, their Islamophobia and their extolling of the governance of strong men were supported and encouraged by a range of political and intellectual figures in the West – and even in anti-Uyghur populist movements in China. Yet rather than admitting common Eastern and Western connections to explain the revival of anti-liberalism, some Western liberals preferred to deploy earlier discourses that emphasise an 'infection' from the East, rejecting ideas of convergence in order to contain ideological spillover from Budapest, Warsaw, or even worse Moscow.[131] At a conference in London, former US secretary of state Hillary Clinton thus called upon 'the EU and the people of Europe [to] resist the backsliding we are seeing in the East'.[132] Such rhetoric re-peripheralised the post-socialist space, in the process glossing over the communalities in the pan-European rise of the right rooted in anti-immigration rhetoric and Islamophobia.

Although Western liberals attempted to promote an image of a specifically illiberal Eastern 'infection' that threatened the stability of the European project, drawing on a much longer term history of Western fears of Eastern backwardness or barbarism, Eastern European cultural and political conservatism was in fact part of a much broader phenomenon that extended from Western Europe to North America, the Middle East, and East Asia. Some disgruntled Westerners encouraged Eastern European populists to see themselves as culturally superior to a feminised Western Europe, reanimating Donald Rumsfeld's distinction between 'new' versus 'old' Europe. Remarkably, this stereotype drew on tropes about the 'decadent' and 'imperialist' West dating from the socialist period. During his trip to Warsaw in July 2017, US President Donald Trump insisted that Poland, 'the soul of Europe', was an example of 'the will to defend our civilisation' from the enemies of the West coming 'from inside or out, from

[131] Beppe Severgnini, 'Italy's Government Is Looking East. Or Is It Heading There?', 9 October 2018, *New York Times*, www.nytimes.com/2018/10/09/opinion/italy-europe-east-west.html; André Liebich, 'Central Europe and the Refugees', *Tr@nsit Online*, 2 November 2015, www.iwm.at/read-listen-watch/transit-online/central-europe-refugees/.

[132] Haroon Siddique, 'Hillary Clinton Criticises Tory MEPs over Failure to Censure Hungary', *Guardian*, 9 October 2018, www.theguardian.com/us-news/2018/oct/09/hillary-clinton-criticises-tory-meps-over-failure-to-censure-hungary.

the South or the East, that threaten ... the bonds of culture, faith and tradition that make us who we are'.[133]

Western conservatives and far-right politicians exalted the merits of Eastern European strongmen because of their willingness to defend Christian values and ethnic homogeneity in Europe.[134] For politicians such as Matteo Salvini or Donald Trump, Viktor Orbán is a model to emulate.[135] For representatives of UK's Conservative Party, especially Brexit hardliners, the authoritarians in Eastern Europe were useful allies for their offensive against the EU.[136] Western European populists turned East to legitimise their own projects as part of new alliances to defend the 'true Europe'. As Marine Le Pen put it: 'We are the enlightened guardians of the national spirit and defenders of the interests of the peoples of Europe. An opposition force that embodies an alternative to the globalised, technocratic and anti-democratic Europe of Brussels ... We have chosen another Europe'.[137] In early 2019 the Italian deputy prime minister Matteo Salvini called for a Warsaw-Rome Axis to build an anti-immigrant conservative Europe.[138]

The populist wave in East and West has thrived on the weakened sense of mission among EU officials and member states, who have lost their appetite for enlargement, preferring to focus instead on policies that quarantine the EU from spaces deemed unready for integration. The European neighbourhood policy (ENP) was launched in the mid-2000s, founded on a civilising drive to expand the Union and its values from Brussels to the fringes of the continent and beyond. Angela Merkel articulated this idea at the twenty-fifth anniversary of the fall of the Berlin Wall: 'We have the power to shape. We can turn things to the good: That

---

[133] 'Remarks by President Trump to the People of Poland', 6 July 2017, www.whitehouse .gov/briefings-statements/remarks-President-trump-people-poland/.

[134] PiS MP Dominik Tarczyński received in September 2018 a Phyllis Schlafly Eagle Award due to his 'work on behalf of freedom in Europe'. Alongside him were the anti-Islamic blogger Pamela Geller and antifeminist 'race realist' Stefan Molyneux.

[135] On the Orbán-Salvini alliance, see Hegedüs, Daniel, 'The Great Orbán-Salvini Hack', Visegrád Insight, 14 September 2018, https://visegradinsight.eu/the-great-orban-salvini-hack/; Heather Conley and Charles Gati, 'Trump Loves a Strongman, So of Course He Fawns over Hungary's Viktor Orbán', Washington Post, 25 May 2018, www.washington post.com/outlook/trump-loves-a-strongman-so-of-course-he-fawns-over-hungarys-viktor-orban/2018/05/25/a10bff28-5f64-11e8-a4a4-c070ef53f315_story.html?utm_term=.ce80 ec961b24.

[136] Anne Applebaum called them 'useful idiots' for FIDESZ and PiS: 'How Orbán Duped the Brexiteers', Spectator, 22 September 2018, www.spectator.co.uk/2018/09/how-orban-duped-the-brexiteers/.

[137] Braghiroli and Makarychev, 'Redefining Europe', 839.

[138] Angela Giuffrida, 'Matteo Salvini Says Italy and Poland Could Build New Europe', Guardian, 8 January 2019, www.theguardian.com/world/2019/jan/09/matteo-salvini-says-italy-and-poland-could-build-new-europe.

is the message of the fall of the Wall. At this time, this [message] is aimed at Ukraine, Syria, Iraq and many other regions of the world. The fall of the Wall showed us that dreams can come true'.[139] Yet the prospect of accession became increasingly distant for countries from the former Soviet space or the Western Balkans (Croatia's accession in 2013 bucked the trend).[140] The EU's 'neighbourhood' policies have often taken the form of negative assessments of the Europeanness of ENP's target countries. Under pressure from increased migration and the populist resurgence, the ENP led to a situation in which 'neighbours' were deemed either to be security threats, or potential partners in policing EU's borders.[141]

In this context, the ENP transformed into a process of accession with no end in sight for South-Eastern European non–member states. In the ex-Yugoslav space the receding prospect of EU enlargement affected the drive for reforms. Or, as the Macedonian foreign minister Nikola Dimitrov put it: 'It is like being locked in a waiting room with no exit'. Despite the fact that EU officials, such as Johannes Hahn, the commissioner in charge of enlargement, called for 'finish[ing] the work of 1989' in the Balkans,[142] few in Brussels believed that this was a feasible goal. The sense of waiting and irresolvable liminality opened up South-Eastern Europe as a battlefield in the new conflict between other powers seeking influence, and the EU. Since coming under the sway of Recep Tayyip Erdoğan, Turkey has steadily expanded its political, cultural and economic foothold in what the EU calls the Western Balkans. Its trade with the region ballooned from 364 million euros in 2002 to 2.5 billion in 2016. The government was involved in development aid and the organisation of major infrastructure projects and has opened universities and restored mosques, while encouraging Turkish businesses to invest in the region.[143] Along the way, Erdoğan's authoritarianism carried over into the former Yugoslav space in the form of either arrests of his political opponents in

---

[139] 'Angela Merkel: "Fall of Wall Showed Us Dreams Come True"', *Financial Times*, 10 November 2014, www.ft.com/content/72c821d0-682f-11e4-bcd5-00144feabdc0.

[140] Elena Korosteleva, Tom Casier, and Richard Whitman, 'Building a Stronger Eastern Partnership: Towards an EaP 2.0' (working paper, Global Europe Centre, University of Kent GEC policy paper, 2014).

[141] Christoffer Kølvraa, 'Limits of Attraction: The EU's Eastern Border and the European Neighbourhood Policy', *East European Politics and Societies and Cultures*, 31/1 (2017), 14.

[142] Both quoted in Steven Erlanger, 'In a New Cold War With Russia, Balkans Become a Testing Ground', *New York Times*, 11 April 2018, www.nytimes.com/2018/04/10/world/europe/european-union-balkans.html.

[143] Zia Weise, 'Turkey's Balkan Comeback', *Politico*, 17 May 2018, www.politico.eu/article/turkey-western-balkans-comeback-european-union-recep-tayyip-erdogan/.

Kosovo or as a model for local politicians hampered by the checks and balances of liberal democracy (such as Aleksandar Vučić, the president of Serbia).[144]

Russia, too, became increasingly involved in the Western Balkans, adopting an active strategy to undermine Western influence in the region or covertly to tip the balance in elections and referenda. It was the main culprit for unsuccessful destabilisation efforts such as the coup in Montenegro in 2016 and the failed Euro-Atlantic integration referendum in Macedonia in 2018.[145] It also sponsored parties which promoted its message: the small pro-Russian United Macedonia party, for instance, refers to NATO as the 'Fourth Reich' and calls for a 'radical shift' in Macedonian foreign policy through joining the Russian-led Eurasian Economic Union.[146] Serbia, Russia's closest partner in the Balkans, became an observer at the Russian-led Collective Security Treaty Organisation military alliance in 2013.[147]

As the dynamics within the ex-Yugoslav space suggest, it was Vladimir Putin who offered the most powerful vision of an alternative future. The confluence between right-wing populism in East and West was reinforced by Putin's vigorous global projection of his regime's values and influence. He constructed an alternative geopolitical imaginary which emphasised Moscow's role as leader of a newly defined space that challenged the idea that smaller states in Eastern Europe were simply an extension of the West. His own vision of regional integration, the Eurasian Economic Union (EEU) was designed after the EU and aimed at an expansion of common spaces of security and business cooperation

[144] Some have argued that Ankara does not see its presence in the Western Balkans as a counterbalance to or not mutually exclusive with the region's EU integration. See Asli Aydintasbas, 'From Myth to Reality: How to Understand Turkey's Role in the Western Balkans', *European Council on Foreign Relations*, www.ecfr.eu/publications/summary/from_myth_to_reality_how_to_understand_turkeys_role_in_the_western_balkans.

[145] Srdjan Darmanović, 'The Never-Boring Balkans: The Elections of 2016', *Journal of Democracy* 28/1 (2017), 116–28; Simon Tisdall, 'Result of Macedonia's Referendum Is Another Victory for Russia', *Guardian*, 1 October 2018, www.theguardian.com/world/2018/oct/01/result-of-macedonia-referendum-is-another-victory-for-russia; Macedonia has been an accession candidate for EU membership since 2005. Both NATO membership and EU accession talks were repeatedly blocked due to the dispute with Greece over the country's name 'Macedonia'. In 2018 the two countries achieved a historic deal and settled on the name of Republic of North Macedonia.

[146] 'Proglas na Edinstvena Makedonija za radikalen presvrt vo makedonskata politika – členstvo vo Evroaziskata Ekonomska Unija i strateško partnerstvo so Rusija', *Edinstvena Makedonija* [United Macedonia], 6, http://edinstvenamakedonija.mk/wp-content/uploads/2018/06/proglas-edinstvena-makedonija.pdf.

[147] Matthias Bieri, 'The Western Balkans between Europe and Russia', *CSS Analyses in Security Policy* 170 (2015), 2, www.research-collection.ethz.ch/bitstream/handle/20.500.11850/99131/eth-47456-01.pdf?sequence=1&isAllowed=y.

in the former Soviet sphere of influence.[148] In the aftermath of the Maidan protests in the Ukraine in 2013, the annexation of Crimea, and the war in eastern Ukraine, the EEU turned into a vehicle for Putin to assert the idea that Europe itself could be multipolar, and could have more than one ideological flavour.[149] In the early 2000s Putin had called Western-facing European integration the 'historic choice' for Russia; by 2010s he called the EU 'lesser Europe', and Eastern Europe an 'under-Europe'[150] that the Kremlin promised to liberate from Brussels tutelage. Divergence had reached its apex.

After the refugee crisis from 2015, the Kremlin was presented with an opportunity to take a broader role in Europe: Putin assisted the consolidation of a form of masculine authoritarian politics as an alternative to a supposedly feminised West. He delivered an anti-liberal message to Eastern Europeans by combining topics such as immigration, gender politics, and Christianity with the lure of economic deals free from EU strict regulations and controls. His political advisers took advantage of the new global trend towards this type of rule. Dmitry Peskov, the Kremlin's long-serving spokesman, best characterised his practice: 'There's a demand in the world for special, sovereign leaders, for decisive ones … Putin's Russia was the starting point'.[151] In East and West, this leadership model caught on. In continuation of the Republican Party's right-wing praise of Eastern Europe's traditionalism and geopolitical virility, Pat Buchanan commended Putin as a conservative icon, who fought a 'cultural war' against 'militant secularism, abortion, gay marriage, pornography, promiscuity and against the Hollywood panoply'.[152] Similarly, the prominent Republican Rudy Giuliani admired Putin for the Crimean invasion.[153] In Europe, several key figures within far-right parties such as the Rassemblement National in France or the Alternative for Germany expressed their admiration for Putin, too.[154] In Slovakia and Hungary in the late 2010s, Putin was more popular than major

---

[148] Vladimir Putin quoted in Korosteleva, 'Eastern Partnership', 68.

[149] Richard Sakwa, 'How the Eurasian Elites Envisage the Role of the EEU in Global Perspective', *European Politics and Society*, 17/Supplement, 'The Eurasian Project in Global Perspective' (2016), 11.

[150] Braghiroli and Makarychev, 'Redefining Europe', 840.

[151] Anton Troianovski, 'Branding Putin: How the Kremlin Turned the Russian President into a Global Icon', *Washington Post*, 12 July 2018, www.washingtonpost.com/graphics/2018/world/putin-brand/?utm_term=.90db5831a456.

[152] Tamás Csillag and Iván Szelényi, 'Drifting from Liberal Democracy: Traditionalist/Neo-conservative Ideology of Managed Illiberal Democratic Capitalism in Post-communist Europe', *Intersections*, 1/1 (2013), 38.

[153] Ibid., 39.

[154] Andreas Umland, 'Post-Soviet Neo-Eurasianism, the Putin System, and the Contemporary European Extreme Right', *Perspectives on Politics*, 15/2 (2017), 469.

Western leaders such as Trump, Merkel, and Macron. In Prague, it was reported that Putin T-shirts sold better than those of Albert Einstein and Marilyn Monroe.[155]

Putin and his government were now the standard bearers of the new conservative and traditionalist offensive against the EU's 'cosmopolitan' policies. Echoing his counterparts in Eastern Europe, Putin claimed to be engaged in a bid to save his own earlier version of Europe, from Lisbon to Vladivostok, from what he considered the debilitating effects of liberal tolerance, political correctness, and cultural fragmentation. Eurasianism was for his inner circle an ideology that underpinned Russia's geopolitical revival by offering a model alternative to 1989's 'return to Europe': the integration of the continent's diverse peoples, civilisations, and traditions through respecting sovereign democracy and ideological difference.[156] They also argued that Eurasianism could extend beyond the limits of the former Soviet space by connecting Russia's and Europe's nationalist elites.[157] In Eastern Europe, Hungary's Orbán and Czech President Zeman hearkened to Eurasianism's siren call, rhetorically embracing the Russian alternative, extolling its political, economic, and even cultural possibilities. In Zeman's case, his commitment went as far as endorsing a memory politics that no longer relied on the cardinal motif of pre-1989 anti-Communist opposition: the idea of the Soviets as imperialists in Eastern Europe. He refused to take part in the commemoration of the fiftieth anniversary of the 1968 invasion of Czechoslovakia by Soviet-led troops from the socialist bloc.[158]

The Kremlin's international influence was also exercised in its claim to be defending Christianity in general, and Orthodoxy in particular. The theme of Eastern Christianity as a civilisational commonwealth alternative to the West had been a resilient motif in the critiques of the post-1989 liberal consensus. The Russian Orthodox Church's ability to tap into such a rich resource of identity politics became crucial for the articulation of regional imaginations that reject the idea of convergence with the West. Moreover, its open support, domestically and internationally, for the Kremlin's policies reinforced Putin's image as defender of traditional values at home and abroad. In October 2018, the geopolitical game behind Russia's religious politics burst on to the international

---

[155] Troianovski, 'Branding Putin'.
[156] Marlène Laruelle, *Russian Eurasianism: An Ideology of Empire* (Baltimore: Johns Hopkins University Press, 2012), 129–31.
[157] Umland, 'Post-Soviet Neo-Eurasianism', 467.
[158] Siegfried Mortkowitz, 'Czech President under Fire for Skipping Prague Spring Commemoration', *Politico*, 21 August 2018, www.politico.eu/article/Miloš-zeman-skips-prague-spring-commemoration/.

scene when the Orthodox Church's Istanbul-based leader, Patriarch Bartholomew, decided to grant Ukraine's Church its independence from Russia. Russian Church officials argued that by supporting Ukraine's bid for an independent Church, Istanbul put Orthodox unity at risk.[159] The Russian Patriarch proclaimed that 'we cannot maintain relations with this church [in Istanbul] because it is [currently] in a state of schism'.[160] The rejection of the Ecumenical Patriarchate signalled Moscow's willingness to effectively take on the role of 'third Rome'. This is the idea that Moscow succeeded Rome and Byzantium as the authentic centre of Christianity and the Roman Empire: it has periodically been revived to assert Russia's claim to represent the true Europe, and by Putin as a cultural politics designed to ward off the intervention of any outside authority within Russia's 'near abroad' as well as to re-assert the leadership of Moscow over Orthodox Europe.

The significant role of China in Eastern European politics and economy in particular provided a new way of imagining the region's relationship with the broader world. After 1989 former socialist states engaged with China but relations did not amount to a strategic alternative. The financial and economic crisis from 2008 changed this: for populists, the crash symbolised the decadence of Western democracy. In 2010, the new FIDESZ government in Hungary announced a *keleti nyitás*, or 'opening to the East'. Against a feeling of cultural alienation from the European project, and a deep anxiety about the economic sclerosis of the European economic model, Orbán argued that the authoritarian capitalist models of Singapore, China, and Central Asia could be attractive models for his country. In a speech given to the National Association of Entrepreneurs and Employers on 26 July 2012, he argued that power needed to be centralised in Hungary – a natural state of affairs, he contended, for a 'half-Asian nation'.[161] His minister of national economy György Matolcsy then spoke of genetic closeness and 'kinship' with the Far East.[162] These instances were part and parcel of a broader shift to a cultural 'Eurasianism', the revival of nationalist Turanic ideologies in

---

[159] Gabby Deutch, 'Ukraine's Spiritual Split from Russia Could Trigger a Global Schism', *Atlantic*, 11 October 2018, www.theatlantic.com/international/archive/2018/10/ukraine-orthodox-church-independence-russia/571333/.

[160] 'Biserica ortodoxă a Rusiei rupe legăturile cu Patriarhatul Constantinopolului', *Hotnews*, 15 October 2018, http://m.hotnews.ro/stire/22759232.

[161] Chris Moreh, 'The Asianisation of National Fantasies in Hungary: A Critical Analysis of Political Discourse', *International Journal of Cultural Studies*, 13 March 2015, http://ics.sagepub.com/content/early/2015/03/12/1367877915573781.refs.

[162] Ibid. He referred to the red dots found on both Japanese and Hungarian babies, claiming this proved a genetic connection.

which Hungarians' supposed origins, and natural cultural sphere, resided in Central and East Asia.[163]

This recasting of geopolitics came from East Asia too. By 2012, under President Xi Jinping, the image of Eastern Europe was reimagined in China in ways that did not coincide with the EU's understanding of European geopolitics. The Chinese government placed great emphasis on what they call 'discourse power', a term they derived from French philosopher Michel Foucault, which in this context was viewed as the capacity to change and control the language of the spatial organisation of global economy as a form of soft power.[164] So-called 'Europe 1' generally consisted of the more economically developed western parts of the EU, 'Europe 2' became the target of Beijing's '16+1 initiative' to develop a new relationship with a historically and culturally familiar former Communist Europe, covering issues such as investment, trade, culture, and education. The group includes eleven EU countries – Bulgaria, Croatia, the Czech Republic, Estonia, Hungary, Latvia, Lithuania, Poland, Romania, Slovakia, and Slovenia – and five non-EU countries from the Balkans – Albania, Bosnia and Herzegovina, Macedonia, Montenegro, and Serbia. Again, the Visegrád group led the way because the bulk of Chinese investment and economic presence was in Poland, Czech Republic, Hungary, and Slovakia (though significant infrastructural projects existed also in Serbia and Romania).[165] Beijing focussed on non-hierarchical 'people-to-people' contacts with Eastern European actors: they established a complex environment of mutual socialisation for policy-makers and civil servants at all levels of government as well as scholars, think-tankers, political parties, youth organisations, sportsmen/women, artists, journalists, and entrepreneurs.[166]

The interaction was on both sides expressed as a form of bilateral friendship, and drew on language recognisable from the pre-1989 socialist era in its references to past experiences of exploitation by the West.

[163] For an account of the rise of this phenomenon in both far-right politics and everyday life, see Emel Akçalı and Umut Korkut, 'Geographical Metanarratives in East-Central Europe: Neo-Turanism in Hungary', *Eurasian Geography and Economics*, 53/5 (2012), 596–614; Emel Akçali, 'Hungary', in Pelin Ayan Musil and Juraj Mahfoud (eds.), *Public Portrayal of Turkey in Visegrad Countries* (Anglo-American University, 2013), 48–50.

[164] Nadine Godehardt, 'Constructing Global Connectivity: The European Politics of China's Belt & Road Initiative' (paper presented at Eastern Europe – Global Area – Annual Conference of GWZO and EEGA, University of Leipzig, July 2018).

[165] Eric Maurice, 'China's 16+1 Foray into Central and Eastern Europe', 26 June 2017, *euobserver,* https://euobserver.com/eu-china/138347.

[166] Anastas Vangeli, 'Global China and Symbolic Power: The Case of 16 + 1 Cooperation', *Journal of Contemporary China*, 27/113 (2018), 675–76.

Eastern European leaders relying on an (often anti-colonial) nationalism for legitimacy were quick to take their cue from this approach. Miloš Zeman, during his 2015 visit to Beijing, explained that the two states were brought together by similar experiences of 'one hundred years of humiliation', as the Czech Republic had been caught between Russia and Germany while its post-1989 governments were 'very submissive to the pressure from the US and from the EU'.[167] Chinese officials couched the relationship in terms of emancipation and 'mutual benefit': terms such as 'win-win cooperation 'and 'common destiny' were used.

The manner in which Beijing selected Central and Eastern European countries as part of its maritime and land routes within the Belt and Road Initiative – the project of creating a global role for China[168] – rejected the fundamental principle of post-1989 geography: the re-imagining of the former socialist space according to 'slopes' of Europeanness, a developmental hierarchy that ran West to East and was at the core of much EU thinking. Furthermore, the lure of FDI and loans from China countered the hegemonic pull of the West. Despite the strategic partnership between China and the EU, voices in Brussels were quick to lambast the 16+1 initiative as Beijing's way of infringing on the 'one Europe policy' and even as an attempt to restore the Berlin Wall by splitting former socialist states off from the rest of Europe.[169]

However, for many Eastern Europeans engagement with China was not seen as incompatible with EU membership. In fact, it was a reaffirmation of their sovereignty and agency as Europeans in a changing global environment. In 2010 Orbán argued that Hungary 'was sailing under the Western flag, but in the world economy an Eastern wind blows'.[170] Serbian president Aleksandar Vučić (often accused of having a bent for authoritarian politics) described the future Belgrade-Budapest high-speed rail project (initially set to begin in 2014, but subsequently postponed for 2017 and 2019), a 'real game-changer', in terms of both its

---

[167] Bartosz Kowalski, 'China's Foreign Policy towards Central and Eastern Europe: The 16 +1 Format in the South–South Cooperation Perspective. Cases of the Czech Republic and Hungary', *Cambridge Journal of Eurasian Studies*, 1 (2017), 7.

[168] Nadine Godehardt, 'No End of History: A Chinese Alternative Concept of International Order?' (Berlin: Stiftung Wissenschaft und Politik Research Paper, 2/2016), 6. https://nbn-resolving.org/urn:nbn:de:0168-ssoar-461135.

[169] Vangeli, 'Global China', 682. Also Anastas Vangeli, 'China's Engagement with the Sixteen Countries of Central, East and Southeast Europe under the Belt and Road Initiative', *China and World Economy*, 25/5 (2017), 104–5.

[170] Quoted in Wade Jacoby and Umut Korkut, 'Vulnerability and Economic Re-orientation: Rhetoric and in Reality in Hungary's "Chinese Opening"', *East European Politics and Societies and Cultures*, 30/3 (2016), 500.

economic impact and 'our EU path [and] ... closeness to Central and Western Europe'.[171]

The burgeoning relationships of former socialist countries with China served to further underline the sense that Eastern Europe was no longer only Western-facing. The region would best benefit, it was argued, from the geopolitical instrumentalisation of the region's global in-betweenness *between* East and West. As a way of enticing Chinese investors aiming to gain access to Western markets, several Eastern European countries leveraged the affinities arising from their once having been part of a common Eurasian socialist world that stretched from Berlin to Beijing, and vied for the status of 'China's bridge to Europe'.[172] The leadership of the Communist Party of China encouraged this newfound sense of agency by inserting Eastern and Central European states into their post-2008 imaginary of a 'Global South'[173] that had yet to overcome the negative effects of neoliberal globalisation and aspired to relinquish its peripheral status in relation to the West. Echoing similar pronouncements from the Kremlin, Beijing described its presence as compensation for EU failures in the region.[174] In his turn, Viktor Orbán presented Hungary's 'global opening'[175] and particularly relations with China to be a crucial facet of FIDESZ's emancipation of the country from neoliberalism as well as from EU and IMF imposed 'debt slavery'.[176] In 2014, he even contrasted 'a few developed countries [which] have been continuously lecturing most of the world on human rights, democracy,

[171] Dragan Pavlićević, '"China Threat" and "China Opportunity"': Politics of Dreams and Fears in China-Central and Eastern European Relations', *Journal of Contemporary China*, 27/113 (2018), 693.

[172] Richard Turcsanyi, 'Is the Czech Republic China's New "Bridge to Europe"?', *Diplomat*, 12 September 2015, http://thediplomat.com/2015/09/is-the-czech-republic-chinas-new-bridge-to-europe/.

[173] In April 2012, Premier Wen Jiabao, at the inaugural 16+1 summit in Poland, described the new partnership as 'go[ing] forward hand in hand', a phrase used mainly for relations with developing countries in Africa. In 2015 Xi Jinping characterized Chinese–Eastern European cooperation as 'a new path of development of relations between China and traditional friends, introducing innovations to the practice of relations between China and Europe, establishing a new platform for South-South cooperation, which has the characteristics appropriate for North-South cooperation'. Both quotes in Kowalski, 'China's Foreign Policy', 5–6.

[174] Jeanne Wilson, 'The Eurasian Economic Union and China's Silk Road: Implications for the Russian–Chinese Relationship', *European Politics and Society*, 17/Supplement 1, 'The Eurasian Project in Global Perspective' (2016), 113–32.

[175] James Mark and Péter Apor, 'Socialism Goes Global: Decolonisation and the Making of a New Culture of Internationalism in Socialist Hungary, 1956–1989', *Journal of Modern History*, 87/4 (2015), 891.

[176] Jacoby and Korkut, 'Vulnerability and Economic Re-orientation', 500 and 505.

development, and the market economy' with China's emphasis on the fact that 'everyone has the right to their own social structure, culture, approach, and values'.[177] At times, pre-1989 links were used to legitimate and provide a sense of historical continuity for these new alliances: during Xi Jinping's visit to Serbia in 2016, the Serbian president Tomislav Nikolić gifted him a framed photograph of his father Xi Zhongxun attending the 1986 congress of the Yugoslav League of Communists in Belgrade as part of the Chinese delegation.[178]

Conclusion

'Europe, not Moscow' was one of the chants in support of the Central European University (CEU) in Budapest in 2017 and 2018. Yet the protesters shouted in vain as concerted attacks from the FIDESZ government continued. In December 2018, the university, a powerful symbol of 1989-inspired liberal cosmopolitanism created by George Soros in 1993, announced its retreat to a new campus in Vienna.[179] The decision marked the end of an era. An institution conceived to facilitate open societies in Eastern Europe was forced into retreat from the former socialist space. This political shift, however, was long in the making. During the past thirty years, many Eastern Europeans had not conformed to the narratives of inevitable convergence that were shared by Westerners and their own liberal elites. While liberals promoted the story of '1989' as a staging post on the road to the East's inevitable Westernisation, many post-socialist politicians had refused this hegemonic but seemingly alien reading of their nations' histories very early on. In the first decades after the end of Communism, few memorials or public spaces in capital cities had been named after the transformations of that year. The liberal narrative was never entirely pervasive in the East. Thirty years later, it had become marginalised.

Already at the time of the twentieth anniversary of the end of state socialism, a fragmentation of the views of 1989 and a contestation of the

---

[177] Aron Suba, 'Betting on the Eastern Model: The Cooperation between Hungary and China Is More about Politics Than Economics', 11 April 2018, http://visegradinsight.eu/betting-on-the-Eastern-model/.

[178] 'Nikolić poklonio Si Đinpingu fotografiju, danas dobija orden', *N1*, 18 June 2016, http://rs.n1info.com/Vesti/a169734/Nikolic-poklonio-Si-Djinpingu-fotografiju.html.

[179] 'CEU to Open Vienna Campus for US Degrees in 2019; University Determined to Uphold Academic Freedom' (Central European University), www.ceu.edu/article/2018-10-25/ceu-open-vienna-campus-us-degrees-2019-university-determined-uphold-academic; Sean Coughlan, 'How a University Became a Battle for Europe's Identity', *BBC News*, 3 May 2017, www.bbc.co.uk/news/business-39780546.

legitimacy of the post-socialist order had come into full view.[180] Eastern European populists had little use for stories of liberal democratic convergence and instead turned to sanitised national histories embedded in past Golden Ages. Victimhood founded on national suffering inflicted by Soviet and Communist repression was connected to traditions of interwar statehood and were used to confirm the ethnically defined European identity of their societies. The references to these pre-1945 national entities, as opposed to the liberal 1989 narratives, linked modern polities to decidedly non-liberal traditions such as anti-Semitism, fascism, discrimination against minorities, and the absence of democratic institutions and political cultures. For many Eastern European conservatives, 1939 superseded 1989 because it symbolised both national martyrdom and the non-Western, non-liberal roots of their national and Christian European identity.

Yet 1989 did not totally disappear from the symbolic political repertoires of Eastern Europeans. During the 2010s, it was revived as a symbol of liberal and Western-facing resistance against new populisms and of the unfulfilled hopes of substantial democratic transformation across the region. Bulgarian demonstrators chose 10 November, the day of the toppling of the Communist leader Todor Zhivkov in 1989, for their 'March of Justice' protest that called for governmental accountability and the defence of pluralism in 2013.[181] In Bucharest, protesters against local social democrats' attempts to dismantle the rule of law identified with the civil disobedience and revolt that had been the basis for the revolution against Nicolae Ceaușescu and the challenge against the early political hegemony of the National Salvation Front in 1990.[182] In December 2018, an announcement calling for street protests against the amnesty of those sentenced in corruption cases proclaimed: 'In December 1989, 1,116 people died for freedom ... Now, after twenty-nine years, their struggle risks becoming futile ... During Romania's darkest days they believed in freedom. Do you?'[183] In Poland, before the PiS electoral victory in 2015, left-wing critics interpreted anti-establishment demonstrations as a revival of pre-roundtable civic

---

[180] Ferenc Laczó and Joanna Wawrzyniak, 'Memories of 1989 in Europe between Hope, Dismay, and Neglect', *East European Politics and Societies and Cultures*, 31/3 (2017), 431.

[181] Tom Junes, 'Students Take Bulgaria's Protests to the Next Level. Can They Break the Political Stalemate?', *Tr@nsit Online* (2013), www.iwm.at/read-listen-watch/transit-online/students-take-bulgarias-protests-to-the-next-level-why-the-student-protests-could-break-the-political-stalemate/.

[182] Marius Stan and Vladimir Tismaneanu, 'Democracy under Siege in Romania', *Politico*, 21 August 2018, www.politico.eu/article/protest-piata-victoriei-bucharest-democracy-under-siege-in-romania/.

[183] www.hotnews.ro/stiri-esential-22880728-protest-piata-victoriei-1-116-oameni-murit-decembrie-pentru-libertate-nu-pentru-amnistia-ticalosilor.htm.

mobilisation in 1989.[184] The protests in 2017 and 2018 against the elimination of the separation of powers in government and anti-abortion legislation indicated the determination of Polish liberals to defend core aspects of the post-socialist Polish order. In Slovakia, the outrage over the assassination of a journalist drew in March 2018 massive crowds into street demonstrations to denounce the corruption sponsored by the ruling party SMER.[185] Symbols of the Velvet Revolution were employed while representatives of the Public Against Violence, the leading opposition movement in the country in 1989, revived their political participation.[186] In Serbia, the tens of thousands who opposed the autocratic rule of President Aleksandar Vučić invoked the legacy of the Bulldozer Revolution, an offspring of 1989's peaceful transformation: just as in 2000, protesters blew whistles, a symbol of revolt since the period when Slobodan Milošević held power in the 1990s.[187]

However, the challenge in the streets to the populist counterrevolution did not yet generate political alternatives or significantly rally liberal forces at the polls. These non-ideological movements were less driven by clear-cut political projects as they were expressions of the desire to hold governments accountable and to prevent the authoritarian takeover of institutions.[188] In the late 2010s in the Czech republic, Slovakia, Poland, Romania, and Hungary issues such as corruption, political participation, and responsible governance re-took centre stage and challenged populists' capture of public discourse.[189] The idea of convergence with the liberal democratic West that 1989 represented was transformed into a symbol of resistance to newly hegemonic imaginings of cultural divergence, ethnocentric difference, and populist politics.

---

[184] Jakub Dymek, 'A New Solidarity for the New Poland', *Dissent*, 5 May 2014, www.dissentmagazine.org/blog/polands-children-of-tina.

[185] Zuzana Hudáková, 'Czech/o/Slovak Democracy: 30 Years in the Making', *Eurozine*, 20 April 2018, www.eurozine.com/czechoslovak-democracy-30-years-making/.

[186] Shaun Walker, 'Slovakia: Thousands Protest against Business-as-Usual under New Leaders', *Guardian*, 6 April 2018; Michaela Terenzani, 'We Want a Decent Slovakia, People Chanted in Squares', *Slovak Spectator*, 16 November 2018, https://spectator.sme.sk/c/20963805/we-want-a-decent-slovakia-people-chanted-in-squares.html.

[187] 'Serbia: Thousands Rally in Fourth Week of Anti-government Protests', *Guardian*, 30 December 2018, www.theguardian.com/world/2018/dec/30/serbia-thousands-rally-in-fourth-week-of-anti-government-protests.

[188] Ivan Krastev, 'The Global Politics of Protest', *IWM Post* 113 (Spring/Summer 2014), 4.

[189] Ivan Krastev, 'Why Viktor Orbán and His Allies Won't Win the EU Elections', *Guardian*, 20 March 2019, www.theguardian.com/commentisfree/2019/mar/20/viktor-orban-eu-elections-rightwing-populists-immigration.

Bibliography

Primary Sources

Archiv der Forschungsstelle Osteuropa, Bremen

Samizdat-Sammlung Abteilung Ostmitteleuropa
Samizdat-Sammlung Abteilung Sowjetunion und Nachfolgestaaten

Arhivele Naționale Istorice Centrale, Bucharest (ANIC)

Comitetul Central al Partidului Comunist Român, Cancelarie, 2/1980–47/
1989

CSCE/OSCE Archive, Prague (CSCE)

Bm:10; CSCE CFB 10–11 1985; CSCE/CFB.48, 6 November 1985

Foreign Broadcast Information Services, Reston, VA (FBIS)

AFR-90-122-S
EEU-93-104
EEU-87-190
EEU-89-061
EEU-90-056
EEU-90-183
EEU-89-230
EEU-89-106
EEU-90-042
EEU-90-112
EEU-95-192

IMF Archive, Washington, DC (IMF-EUR)

Box 38-2, Poland: Economic Reform: 1981–1987
Box 38-3, Poland: Economic Reform since 1980–1984

Ministerul Afacerilor Externe, Bucharest (MAE)

Algeria: 27: 1989
China: Situația internă volum I: 212: 1989
China: Situația internă volum II: 213: 1989
China: Situația internă volum III: 214: 1989
Iran: 463: 1989
Libia: 550: 1989
Mozambic: 608: 1989

Open Society Archivum, Budapest (HU OSA)

300-2-5; 300-8-3; 300-40-1; 300-40-2; 300-50-1; 300-55-9; 300-55-9;
300-10-3; 300-55-9; 300-6-2

UN Archives, New York

Secretary-General Kurt Waldheim (1972–1981), S-0904-0051-04
Secretary-General Javier Pérez de Cuéllar (1982–1991), S-1022-0033-09;
S-1024-0097-06

UNESCO Archives, Paris

European National Commission

United Nations Digital Library (https://digitallibrary.un.org/)

ECOSOC, Commission on Human Rights, 46th Session, 1990: 8th Meeting,
A/C.3/45/SR.8; 10th Meeting, E/CN.A/SR.10.
UN General Assembly, 38th Session, Third Committee, 8th Meeting, 1985,
A/C.3/40/SR.8; 11th Meeting, 1985, A/C.3/40/SR.11.
UN General Assembly, 44th Session, Third Committee, 9th Meeting, 1989,
A/C.3/44/SR.9.
UN General Assembly, 45th Session, Third Committee, 1990: 3rd Meeting,
A/C.3/45/SR.3; 8th Meeting, A/C.3/45/SR.8 .
UN General Assembly, 46th Session, Special Committee against Apartheid,
1991, A/AC.115/L.682.
UN General Assembly, 49th Session, 1994: 79th Meeting, A/49/PV.79;
80th meeting, A/49/PV.80; A/49/236, Annexes I and II.

UN Office, Geneva (UNOG)

Economic Commission for Europe ECE Box 011 ECLA 121
Proceedings of the United Nations Conference on Trade and Development
UNCTAD Division for Trade with Socialist Countries

Newspapers and Magazines

Belgium

EUObserver

Bosnia and Herzegovina

Odjek

Bulgaria

Sofia BTA

China

Renmin Ribao

Croatia

Nacional
Večernji list
Vjesnik

France

Libération

Germany

Die Welt
Der Spiegel
Frankfurter Allgemeine Zeitung
Mitteldeutsche Zeitung
Neues Deutschland
Tagesspiegel

Hungary

Budapest Beacon
Hungarian Exporter
Hungary Today
Magyar Hirlap
Népszabadság

North Macedonia

Nova Makedonija

Morocco

Rabat MAP

Poland

Gazeta Wyborcza
Krakow Post
Merkuryusz Krakowski i Światowy

Portugal

Expresso

Romania

Adevărul
Euractiv.ro
HotNews.ro
Wall-Street
Ziare.com

Russia

Moscow Times
Nezavisimaya gazeta

Saudi Arabia

Riyadh SPA

Serbia

Danas
Komunist

Slovakia

Slovak Spectator

Slovenia

Mladina

South Africa

Democracy in Action
Sowetan

Spain

El Diario

Switzerland

Neue Zürcher Zeitung

United Kingdom

Financial Times
Guardian

Independent
Star
Sunday Star

United States

Atlantic
Forbes
Foreign Policy
Huffington Post
Miami Herald
National Review
New Yorker
New York Review of Books
New York Times
Wall Street Journal
Washington Post

Venezuela

Nacional

Zambia

Zambia Daily Mail

Television and Radio

Al Jazeera – Qatar
Digi24 – Romania
Johannesburg Television Service – South Africa

Radio Hvezda – Czech Republic
Radio Poland – Poland
RT (Russia Today) – Russia

Official Documents

Documents of the Fourth Regional Conference of the European National Commissions for UNESCO, Sofia, 25–30 June 1962.

EC 2014, European Heritage, '2014 Panel Report' (Brussels: European Commission, 2014).

Final Document – Declaration, 9th Summit Conference of Heads of State or Government of the Non-Aligned Movement, Belgrade, 4–7 September 1989, 87–90.

Human Development Report 1990 (New York: United Nations Development Programme, 1990).

Inhaltlicher Bericht über Vortrag und Diskussion mit Professor G. Izik-Hedri am 15. Dezember 1981 am IPW / Bericht über ein Gespräch von Genossin Prof. Izik-Hedri beim Forschungsinstitut des Ministeriums für Außenhandel am 16. Dezember 1981. Bundesarchiv BArch DC 204/61.

The Non-Aligned Foreign Ministers Meeting New Delhi 9–13 February 1981, Foreign Policy Document No. 91 (London: International Section Research Department, August 1981).

World Bank Report, 1989.

Speeches

Castro, Fidel, 'Comments on Czechoslovakia – Speech 24 August 1968', https:// marxists.org/history/cuba/archive/castro/1968/08/24.html.

'Discurso pronunciado por el comandante en jefe Fidel Castro Ruz, Primer Secretario del Comite Central del Partido Comunista de Cuba y Presidente de los consejos de estado y de ministros, en la clausura de la sesion diferida del Tercer Congreso del Partido Comunista de Cuba, en el teatro "Carlos Marx", el 2 de diciembre de 1986, año del xxx aniversario del desembarco del Granma', www.cuba.cu/gobierno/discursos/1986/esp/f021286e.html.

'Discurso pronunciado por Fidel Castro Ruz, Presidente de la República Cuba, en el acto de despedida de duelo a nuestros internacionalistas caidos durante el cumplimiento de honrosas misiones militares y civiles, efectuado en el Cacahual, el 7 de diciembre de 1989, año 31 de la revolucion', www.cuba.cu/gobierno/discursos/1989/esp/f071289e.html.

Chalker, Lynda, 'South Africa and Europe – The Way Ahead', Speech at the South African Foundation Conference, 22 May 1990, South Africa International, 21 (July 1990), 1–7.

Clinton, William J., 'Remarks at the Signing Ceremony for the Supplemental Agreements to the North American Free Trade Agreement', 14 September 1993, www.govinfo.gov/app/details/PPP-1993-book2/PPP-1993-book2-doc-pg1485-2.

Havel, Václav, Speech to the Polish Sejm and Senate, 21 January 1990, www.researchgate.net/publication/313440087_President_Vaclav_Havel's_Speech_to_the_Polish_Sejm_and_Senate_January_21_1990.

Klaus, Václav, Speech at the World Economic Forum, Davos, January 1990.

Milošević, Slobodan, 'St. Vitus Day Speech, Gazimestan, 28 June 1989', www.slobodan-milosevic.org/spch-kosovo1989.htm.

Mitterrand, François, Opening Address at the Conference of Heads of State of France and Africa, La Baule, 20 June 1990.

Nuscheler, F., 'What Are the Possibilities for Africa Resulting from the Process of Political and Economic Change in Germany and Eastern Europe?', Bonn, 7–8 May 1990.

Tito, Josip Broz, 'Izlaganje predsednika Tita na sednici Izvršnog biroa, održanoj 22.III.1972. na Brionima', BCA, Family Collection – Legacy of Koča Popović and Lepa Perović.

Trump, Donald, 'Remarks by President Trump to the People of Poland', 6 July 2017, www.whitehouse.gov/briefings-statements/remarks-President-trump-people-poland/.

Secondary Sources

Abramowitz, Michael, *Democracy in Crisis: Freedom in the World 2018 Report* (New York: Freedom House, 2018).

Abulof, Uriel, 'We the Peoples? The Strange Demise of Self-Determination', *European Journal of International Relations*, 22/3 (2015), 536–65.

Adelman, Jeremy and Margarita Fajardo, 'Between Capitalism and Democracy: A Study in the Political Economy of Ideas in Latin America, 1968–1980', *Latin American Research Review*, 51/3 (2016), 3–22.

Amar, Tarik Cyril, 'Sovietisation as Civilizing Mission in the West', in Balazs Apor, Peter Apor, and E. A. Rees (eds.), *The Sovietisation of Eastern Europe: New Perspectives on the Postwar Period* (Washington, DC: New Academia, 2008), 29–46.

Akçalı, Emel, 'Hungary', in Pelin Ayan Musil and Juraj Mahfoud (eds.), *Public Portrayal of Turkey in Visegrad Countries* (Prague: Anglo-American University, 2013), 37–60.

Akçalı, Emel and Umut Korkut, 'Geographical Metanarratives in East-Central Europe: Neo-Turanism in Hungary', *Eurasian Geography and Economics*, 53/5 (2012), 596–614.

Akonor, Kwame, *Africa and IMF Conditionality: The Unevenness of Compliance, 1983–2000* (London: Routledge, 2006).

Alamgir, Alena and Christina Schwenkel, 'From Socialist Assistance to National Self-Interest: Vietnamese Labor Migration into CMEA Countries', in James Mark, Artemy Kalinovsky, and Steffi Marung (eds.), *Alternative Globalizations: Eastern Europe and the Postcolonial World* (Bloomington: Indiana University Press, 2020).

'Albania Willing to Take in Migrants Docked in Italy', *Transitions Online*, 27 August 2018, www.tol.org/client/article/27917-albania-italy-migrants-refugees-quotas-crisis-eu.html.

Albon, Mary, 'Project on Justice in Times of Transition: Inaugural Meeting' (Salzburg, Austria, 7–10 March 1992), 1–19, www.pjtt.org/.

Aleksov, Bojan, 'Perceptions of Islamisation in the Serbian National Discourse', *Southeast European and Black Sea Studies*, 5/1 (2005), 113–127.

Aligică, Paul Dragoş and Anthony John Evans, *The Neoliberal Revolution in Eastern Europe. Economic Ideas in the Transition from Communism* (Cheltenham: Edward Elgar, 2009).

Altrichter, Helmut, *Russland 1989. Der Untergang des sowjetischen Imperiums* (München: C.H. Beck, 2009).

Andreff, Wladimir, 'The Double Transition from Underdevelopment and from Socialism in Vietnam', *Journal of Contemporary Asia*, 23/4 (1993), 515–31.

Anglin, Douglas G., 'Southern African Responses to Eastern European Developments', *Journal of Modern African Studies*, 28/3 (1990), 431–55.

Antohi, Sorin, 'Habits of the Mind: Europe's Post-1989 Symbolic Geographies', in Sorin Antohi and Vladimir Tismaneanu (eds.), *Between Past and Future: The Revolutions of 1989 and Their Aftermath* (Budapest: Central European University Press, 2000), 61–77.

Antov, Nikolay, 'Emergence and Historical Development of Muslim Communities in the Ottoman Balkans: Historical and Historiographical Remarks', in Theodora Dragostinova and Yana Hashamova (eds.), *Beyond Mosque, Church, and State: Alternative Narratives of the Nation in the Balkans* (Budapest: Central European University Press, 2016), 42–56.

Apor, Péter and James Mark, 'Mobilizing Generation: The Idea of 1968 in Hungary', in Anna von der Goltz (ed.) *'Talkin' 'bout My Generation': Conflicts of Generation Building and Europe's '1968'* (Göttingen: Wallstein Verlag, 2011).

'Solidarity: Homefront, Closeness, Need', in James Mark and Paul Betts (eds.), *Socialism Goes Global: Cold War Connections between the 'Second' and 'Third Worlds'*, vol. 1 (Oxford: Oxford University Press, forthcoming).

Applebaum, Anne, 'How Orbán Duped the Brexiteers', *Spectator*, 22 September 2018, www.spectator.co.uk/2018/09/how-orban-duped-the-brexiteers/.

Arat-Koç, Sedef, 'Contesting or Affirming "Europe"? European Enlargement, Aspirations for "Europeanness" and New Identities in the Margins of Europe', *Journal of Contemporary European Studies*, 18/2 (2010), 181–91.

Arielli, Nir, *From Byron to bin Laden: A History of Foreign War Volunteers* (Cambridge, MA: Harvard University Press, 2017).

'In Search of Meaning: Foreign Volunteers in the Croatian Armed Forces, 1991–95', *Contemporary European History*, 21/1 (2012), 1–17.

Arthur, Paige, 'How "Transitions" Reshaped Human Rights: A Conceptual History of Transitional Justice', *Human Rights Quarterly*, 31/2 (2009), 321–67.

Aschmann, Birgit, 'The Reliable Ally. Germany Supports Spain's European Integration Efforts 1957–1967', *Journal of European Integration History*, 7/1 (2011), 37–51.

'Ask Not from Whom the AK-47s Flow', *Economist*, www.economist.com/europe/2016/04/16/ask-not-from-whom-the-ak-47s-flow.

Åslund, Anders, *How Capitalism Was Built. The Transformation of Central and Eastern Europe, Russia, the Caucasus, and Central Asia* (Cambridge: Cambridge University Press, 2013).

Åslund, Anders and Simeon Djankov, *The Great Rebirth. Lessons from the Victory of Capitalism over Communism* (Washington, DC: Peterson Institute for International Economics, 2014).

Aspaturian, Vernon, Jiri Valenta, and David Burke (eds.), *Eurocommunism between East and West* (Bloomington: Indiana University Press, 1980).

Atanasova, Ivanka Nedeva, 'Lyudmila Zhivkova and the Paradox of Ideology and Identity in Communist Bulgaria', *East European Politics and Societies*, 18/2 (2004), 278–315.

Ausch, Sándor, *Theory and Practice of Cmea Cooperation* (Budapest: Akadémiai Kiadó, 1972).

'Ayatollah Khamenei in the DPRK in 1989', www.youtube.com/watch?v=SXeuTGoYhcE.

Aydintasbas, Asli, 'From Myth to Reality: How to Understand Turkey's Role in the Western Balkans' (European Council on Foreign Relations, 13 March 2019), www.ecfr.eu/publications/summary/from_myth_to_reality_how_to_understand_turkeys_role_in_the_western_balkans.

Babu, Abdulrahman Mohamed, 'A New Europe: Consequences for Tanzania', *Review of African Political Economy*, 18/50 (1991), 75–78.

Baćević, Ljiljana, et al. *Jugoslavija na kriznoj prekretnici* (Beograd: Institut društvenih nauka / Centar za politikološka istraživanja i javno mnenje, 1991).

Bach, Daniel C., 'Europe-Afrique: le régionalisme sans co-prospérité', *Politique Africaine*, 49 (1993), 31–46.

Bacher, Jon, 'Video Review: Bringing Down a Dictator', *Peace Magazine*, 18/3 (2002), 28.

Badalassi, Nicolas and Sarah B. Snyder (eds.), *The CSCE and the End of the Cold War: Diplomacy, Societies and Human Rights, 1972–1990* (Oxford: Berghahn, 2018).

Baer, Werner and Joseph Love, 'Introduction', in Werner Baer and Joseph Love (eds), *Liberalisation and Its Consequences. A Comparative Perspective on Latin America and Eastern Europe* (Cheltenham: Elgar, 2000), 1–11.

Baev, Jordan, 'Infiltration of Non-European Terrorist Groups in Europe and Antiterrorist Responses in Western and Eastern Europe (1969–1991)', in Siddik Ekici (ed.), *Counterterrorism in Diverse Communities* (Amsterdam: IOS Press, 2011), 58–74.

Bahrmann, Hannes, *Abschied vom Mythos. Sechs Jahrzehnte kubanische Revolution, Eine kritische Bilanz* (Berlin: CH. Links Verlag, 2016).

Bahro, Rudolf, 'Gastrede auf dem SED/PDS-Parteitag am 16. Dezember 1989', in Lothar Hornbogen et al. (eds.), *Außerordentlicher Parteitag der SED/PDS. Protokoll der Beratungen am 8./9. und 16./17. Dezember 1989 in Berlin* (Dietz: Berlin, 1999).

Bain, Mervyn, 'Cuba–Soviet Relations in the Gorbachev Era', *Journal of Latin American Studies*, 37 (2005), 769–91.

Baker, Catherine, *Race and the Yugoslav Region: Postsocialist, Post-conflict, Postcolonial?* (Manchester: Manchester University Press, 2018).

Balcerowicz, Leszek, 'Economic Reform. Lessons for Post-Saddam Iraq from Post-Soviet Europe', American Enterprise Institute working paper, 24 March 2005.

Post-Communist Transition. Some Lessons (London: Institute of Economic Affairs, 2002).

Socialism, Capitalism and Transformation (Budapest: Central European University Press, 1996).

Ban, Cornel, 'Neoliberalism in Translation. Economic Ideas and Reforms in Spain and Romania' (Ph.D. diss., University of Maryland College Park, 2011).

Ruling Ideas: How Global Neoliberalism Goes Local (Oxford: Oxford University Press, 2016).

'Sovereign Debt, Austerity, and Regime Change. The Case of Nicolae Ceaușescu's Romania', *East European Politics and Societies*, 26/4 (2012), 743–76.

'Translation and Economic Ideas', in Jonathan Evans and Fruela Fernandez (eds.), *The Routledge Handbook of Translation and Politics* (London: Routledge, 2018), 48–63.

Banégas, Richard, 'Tropical Democracy', in Jacques Rupnik (ed.), *1989 as a Political World Event. Democracy, Europe and the New International System in the Age of Globalisation* (London: Routledge, 2007), 101–10.

Bánki, Erika, 'Nemzetközi tapasztalok. A testi fenyítések újbóli bevezetése az iszlám országokban', *Módszertani Füzetek* (March 1986), 62–64.

Bartley, Russell and Sylvia Erickson Bartley, *Eclipse of the Assassins. The C.I.A., Imperial Politics, and the Slaying of Mexican Journalist Manuel Buendía* (Madison: University of Wisconsin Press, 2015).

Baskar, Bojan, 'Within or Without? Changing Attitudes towards the Balkans in Slovenia', *Ethnologica Balkanica*, 7 (2003), 195–206.

Basosi, Duccio, 'An Economic Lens on Global Transformations. The Foreign Debt Crisis of the 1980s in the Soviet Bloc and Latin America', in Piotr H. Kosicki and Kyrill Kunakhovich (eds.), *The Legacy of 1989: Continuity and Discontinuity in a Quarter-Century of Global Revolution* (forthcoming).

Bassin, Mark, *The Gumilev Mystique: Biopolitics, Eurasianism, and the Construction of Community in Modern Russia* (Ithaca, NY: Cornell University Press, 2016).

Bayly, Susan, 'Mapping Time, Living Space. The Moral Cartography of Renovation in Late-Socialist Vietnam', *Cambridge Anthropology*, 31/2 (2013), 60–84.

'Vietnamese Narratives of Tradition, Exchange and Friendship in the Worlds of the Global Socialist Ecumene', in Harry West and Parvathi Raman (eds.), *Enduring Socialism. Explorations of Revolution and Transformation, Restoration and Continuation* (Oxford: Berghahn, 2008), 125–47.

Beissinger, Mark R., *Nationalist Mobilisation and the Collapse of the Soviet State* (Princeton, NJ: Princeton University Press, 2002).

'Self-Determination as a Technology of Imperialism: The Soviet and Russian Experiences', *Ethnopolitics*, 14/5 (2015), 479–487.

Béja, Jean-Philipp, 'China and the End of Socialism in Europe: A Godsend for Beijing Communists', in Jacques Rupnik (ed.), *1989 as a Political World Event: Democracy, Europe and the New International System in the Age of Globalisation* (New York: Routledge, 2013), 212–22.

Bekus, Nelly, *Struggle over Identity: The Official and the Alternative 'Belarusianness'* (Budapest: Central European University Press, 2010).

Benedicto, Ainhoa Ruiz and Pere Brunet, 'Building Walls: Fear and Securitization in the European Union' (2018). www.tni.org/files/publication-down loads/building_walls_-_full_report_-_english.pdf.

Berend, Ivan T., *An Economic History of Twentieth-Century Europe* (Cambridge: Cambridge University Press, 2006).

'Global Financial Architecture and East Central Europe Before and After 1989', in Ulf Engel, Frank Hadler, and Matthias Middell (eds.), *1989 in a Global Perspective* (Leipzig: Leipziger Universitätsverlag, 2015), 49–62.

History in My Life: A Memoir of Three Eras (Budapest: Central European University Press, 2009).

Berman, Harold, 'Joint Ventures between United States Firms and Soviet Economic Organizations', *Maryland Journal of International Law* 1 (1976), 139–53.

Berrios, Ruben, 'The Political Economy of East-South Relations', *Journal of Peace Research*, 20/3 (1983), 239–52.

Bessner, Daniel, 'The Globalist: George Soros after the Open Society', *N+1*, 18 June 2018, https://nplusonemag.com/online-only/online-only/the-globalist/.

Bethlehem, Daniel and Marc Weller (eds.), *The Yugoslav Crisis in International Law* (Cambridge: Cambridge University Press, 1997).

Betts, Paul, James Mark, Idesbald Goddeeris, and Kim Christiaens, 'Race, Socialism and Solidarity: Anti-Apartheid in Eastern Europe', in Robert Skinner and Anna Konieczna (eds.), *A Global History of Anti-Apartheid: 'Forward to Freedom' in South Africa* (Cham: Palgrave Macmillan, 2019), 151–200.

Beyrau, Dietrich, 'Das sowjetische Modell. Über Fiktionen zu den Realitäten', in Peter Hübner, Christoph Kleßmann, and Klaus Tenfelde (eds.), *Arbeiter im Staatssozialismus. Ideologischer Anspruch und soziale Wirklichkeit* (Wien: Böhlau, 2005), 47–70.

Bhambra, Gurminder K. and John Narayan, 'Introduction. Colonial Histories and the Postcolonial Present of European Cosmopolitanism', in Gurminder K. Bhambra and John Narayan (eds.), *European Cosmopolitanism. Colonial Histories and Postcolonial Societies* (Abingdon: Routledge, 2017), 1–13.

Bialasiewicz, Luiza and Claudio Minca, 'Old Europe, New Europe: For a Geopolitics of Translation', *Area*, 37/4 (2005), 365–72.

Bieri, Matthias, 'The Western Balkans between Europe and Russia', *CSS Analyses in Security Policy*, 170 (2015), www.research-collection.ethz.ch/bitstream/handle/20.500.11850/99131/eth-47456-01.pdf?sequence=1&isAllowed=y.

Bing, Adotey, 'Salim A. Salim on the OAU and the African Agenda', *Review of African Political Economy*, 18/50 (1991), 60–69.

Blair, Tony, 'Forging a New Agenda', *Marxism Today*, 10 (1991), 32–34.

Bléjer, Mario I. and Fabrizio Coricelli, *The Making of Economic Reform in Eastern Europe: Conversations with Leading Reformers in Poland, Hungary, and the Czech Republic* (Cheltenham: Edward Elgar, 1995).

Blokker, Paul, 'Building Democracy by Legal Means: The East-Central European Experience' (paper presented at 'Revolution from Within. Experts, Managers and Technocrats in the Long Lawyers, Human Rights and Democratisation in Eastern Europe', Jena, 14–15 June 2018).

Boatcă, Manuela, 'Semi-peripheries in the World-System: Reflecting Eastern European and Latin American Experiences', *Journal of World-Systems Research*, 12/2 (2006), 321–46.

Bobako, Monika, 'Semi-peripheral Islamophobias: The Political Diversity of Anti-Muslim Discourses in Poland', *Patterns of Prejudice*, 52/5 (2018), 448–60.

Bockman, Johanna, 'The Long Road to 1989. Neoclassical Economics, Alternative Socialisms, and the Advent of Neoliberalism', *Radical History Review*, 112 (2012), 9–42.

Markets in the Name of Socialism. The Left-Wing Origins of Neoliberalism (Stanford, CA: Stanford University Press, 2011).

'The 1980s Debt Crisis Revisited: The Second and Third Worlds as Creditors' (manuscript).

'Scientific Community in a Divided World. Economists, Planning, and Research Priority during the Cold War', *Comparative Studies in Society and History*, 50 (2008), 581–613.

'Socialist Globalisation against Capitalist Neocolonialism: The Economic Ideas behind the New International Economic Order', *Humanity*, 6/1 (2015), 109–28.

Bogatova, E., 'V'etnamskaja model' dviženija k konvertiruemosti nacional'noj valjuty', *Voprosy Ekonomiki*, 9 (1990), 69–75.

'V'etnam. Put' k novoj khozjajstvennoj modeli', *Kommunist*, 3 (1990), 106–10.

Bohle, Dorothee, *Europas neue Peripherie. Polens Transformation und transnationale Integration* (Münster: Westfälisches Dampfboot, 2002).

Bohle, Dorothee and Béla Greskovits, *Capitalist Diversity on Europe's Periphery* (Ithaca, NY: Cornell University Press, 2012).

'Boris Buden: Narodu koji je ostao bez svega ostaje još samo iluzija identiteta', www.glas-slavonije.hr/337535/11/Boris-Buden-Narodu-koji-je-ostao-bez-svega-ostaje-jos-samo-iluzija-identiteta.

Boutros-Ghali, Boutros, 'The Marginalisation of Africa', in Nikolaos A. Stavrou (ed.), *Mediterranean Security at the Crossroads: A Reader* (Durham, NC: Duke University Press, 1999), 21–34.

Bowring, Bill, 'Positivism versus Self-Determination: The Contradictions of Soviet International Law', in Susan Marks (ed.), *International Law on the Left: Re-examining Marxist Legacies* (Cambridge: Cambridge University Press, 2008), 133–68.

Bradley, Mark, 'Human Rights and Communism', in Silvio Pons and Stephen Smith (eds.), *The Cambridge History of Communism. Volume 1: World Revolution and Socialism in One Country 1917–1941* (Cambridge: Cambridge University Press, 2017), 151–77.

Braghiroli, Stefano and Andrey Makarychev, 'Redefining Europe: Russia and the 2015 Refugee Crisis', *Geopolitics*, 23/4 (2017), 823–48.

Bren, Paulina and Mary Neuburger, 'Introduction', in Bren and Neuburger (eds.), *Communism Unwrapped. Consumption in Cold War Eastern Europe* (New York: Oxford University Press, 2012), 3–19.

Brier, Robert, 'Broadening the Cultural History of the Cold War: The Emergence of the Polish Workers' Defence Committee and the Rise of Human Rights', *Journal of Cold War Studies*, 15/4 (2013), 104–27.

'Entangled Protest. Dissent and the Transnational History of the 1970s and 1980s', in Brier (ed.), *Transnational Approaches to the History of Dissent in Eastern Europe and the Soviet Union* (Osnabrück: Fibre, 2013), 11–43.

'Poland's Solidarity as a Contested Symbol of the Cold War: Transatlantic Debates after the Polish Crisis', in Kiran Patel and Kenneth Weisbrode (eds.), *European Integration and the Atlantic Community in the 1980s* (Cambridge: Cambridge University Press, 2013), 83–104.

Bright, Christopher, 'Neither Dictatorships nor Double Standards: The Reagan Administration's Approach to Human Rights', *World Affairs*, 153/2 (1990), 51–80.

Brown, Archie, 'Did Gorbachev as General Secretary Become a Social Democrat?', *Europe-Asia Studies*, 65/2 (2013), 198–220.

The Gorbachev Factor (Oxford: Oxford University Press, 1995).

Brubaker, Rogers, *Nationalism Reframed: Nationhood and the National Question in the New Europe* (Cambridge: Cambridge University Press, 2010).

Brucan, Silviu, *Generaţia irosită* (Bucureşti: Editurile Univers & Calistrat Hogaş, 1992).

Piaţă şi democraţie (Bucureşti: Editura ştiintifică, 1990).

World Socialism at the Crossroads (New York: Praeger, 1987).

Brudny, Yitzhak M., *Reinventing Russia: Russian Nationalism and the Soviet State, 1953–1991* (Cambridge, MA: Harvard University Press, 1998).

Bruszt, Laszlo, 'Regional Normalisation and National Deviations: EU Integration and Transformations in Europe's Eastern Periphery', *Global Policy* 6/ Supplement, 1 (2015), 38–45.

Buchanan, Tom, 'Human Rights, the Memory of War and the Making of a "European" Identity, 1945–1975', in Martin Conway and Kiran Klaus Patel (eds.), *Europeanisation in the Twentieth Century. Historical Approaches* (Basingstoke: Palgrave Macmillan, 2010), 157–71.

Budryte, Dovile, *Taming Nationalism? Political Community Building in the Post-Soviet Baltic States* (London: Ashgate, 2005).

Bunce, Valerie, *Subversive Institutions: The Design and the Destruction of Socialism and the State* (Cambridge: Cambridge University Press, 1999).

Bunck, Julie Marie, 'Marxism and the Market. Vietnam and Cuba in Transition' (working paper, Association for the Study of the Cuban Economy, 30 November 1996).

Burg, Steven L. and Paul S. Shoup, *The War in Bosnia-Herzegovina: Ethnic Conflict and International Intervention* (New York: M. E. Sharpe, 1999).

Burke, Roland, *Decolonisation and the Evolution of International Human Rights* (Philadelphia: University of Pennsylvania Press, 2010).

Bustikova, Lenka and Petra Guasti, 'The Illiberal Turn or Swerve in Central Europe?', *Politics and Governance*, 5/4 (2017), 166–76.

Cadier, David, 'Après le retour à l'Europe: les politiques étrangères des pays d'Europe central', *Politique Étrangère* 3 (Automne 2012), 573–84.

Calandri, Elena, Daniele Caviglia, and Antonio Varsori (eds.), *Détente in Cold War Europe: Politics and Diplomacy in the Mediterranean and the Middle East* (London: I.B. Tauris, 2015).

Caldwell, Bruce and Leonidas Montes, 'Friedrich Hayek and His Visits to Chile', *Journal of Austrian Economics*, 28/3 (2015), 261–309.

Calic, Marie-Janine, The History of Yugoslavia (West Lafayette, IN: Purdue University Press, 2019).

Calori, Anna, 'Making Transition, Remaking Workers. Market and Privatisation Reforms in Bosnia and Herzegovina: The Case of Energoinvest (1988–2008)' (PhD thesis, University of Exeter, 2019).

Caplan, Richard, *Europe and the Recognition of New States in Yugoslavia* (Cambridge: Cambridge University Press, 2005).

'International Diplomacy and the Crisis in Kosovo', *International Affairs*, 74/4 (1998), 745–61.

Carothers, Thomas, *Aiding Democracy Abroad: The Learning Curve* (Washington, DC: Carnegie Endowment for International Peace, 1999).

'The End of the Transition Paradigm', *Journal of Democracy*, 13/1 (2002), 5–21.

Caspersen, Nina, *Contested Nationalism: Serb Elite Rivalry in Croatia and Bosnia in the 1990s* (New York: Berghahn Books, 2010).

Castañeda, Carlos, *Utopia Unarmed. The Latin American Left after the Cold War* (New York: Penguin Random House, 1993).

Castillo, Greg, 'East as True West: Redeeming Bourgeois Culture, from Socialist Realism to Ostalgie', *Kritika: Explorations in Russian and Eurasian History*, 9/4 (2008), 747–68.

Cemović, Momčilo, *Zašto, kako i koliko smo se zadužili? Kreditni odnosi Jugoslavije sa inostranstvom* (Beograd: Institut za unapredenje robnog prometa, 1985).

'CEU to Open Vienna Campus for US Degrees in 2019; University Determined to Uphold Academic Freedom' (Central European University), www.ceu.edu/article/2018-10-25/ceu-open-vienna-campus-us-degrees-2019-university-determined-uphold-academic.

Chari, Sharad and Katherine Verdery, 'Thinking between the Posts. Postcolonialism, Postsocialism, and Ethnography after the Cold War', *Comparative Studies in Society and History*, 51/1 (2009), 6–34.

Chaudet, Didier, Florent Parmentier, and Benoît Pélopidas, *When Empire Meets Nationalism: Power Politics in the US and Russia* (Burlington, VT: Ashgate, 2009).

Chen, Zhong Zhong, 'Defying Moscow: East German-Chinese Relations during the Andropov-Chernenko Interregnum, 1982–1985', *Cold War History*, 14/2 (2014), 259–80.

'Defying Moscow, Engaging Beijing: The German Democratic Republic's Relations with the People's Republic of China, 1980–1989' (PhD diss., London School of Economics, 2014).

Chirot, Daniel, 'Problematic Analogies and Forgotten Details of 1989', *East European Politics and Societies and Cultures*, 28/4 (2014), 657–63.

Christiaens, Kim, 'Europe at the Crossroads of Three Worlds: Alternative Histories and Connections of European Solidarity with the Third World, 1950s–80s', *European Review of History: Revue européenne d'histoire*, 24/6 (2017), 932–54.

Christiaens, Kim and Idesbald Goddeeris, 'Competing Solidarities? Solidarność and the Global South during the 1980s', in James Mark, Steffi Marung, and Artemy M. Kalinovsky (eds.), *Alternative Globalizations: Eastern Europe and the Postcolonial World* (Bloomington: Indiana University Press, 2020).

Christiaens, Kim, James Mark, and José M. Faraldo, 'Entangled Transitions: Eastern and Southern European Convergence or Alternative Europes? 1960s–2000s', *Contemporary European History*, 26/4 (2017), 577–99.

Christian, Michel, Sandrine Kott, and Ondrej Matejka (eds.), *Planning in Cold War Europe. Competition, Cooperation, Circulations (1950s–1970s)* (Berlin: De Gruyter Oldenbourg, 2018).

Christofferson, Michael Scott, *French Intellectuals against the Left* (New York: Berghahn Books, 2004).

Cima, Ronald J., 'Vietnam in 1989. Initiating the Post-Cambodia Period', *Asian Survey*, 30/1 (1990), 88–95.

Claudio, Lisandro E., 'Memories of the Anti-Marcos Movement: The Left and the Mnemonic Dynamics of the Post-authoritarian Philippines', *South East Asia Research*, 18/1 (2010), 33–66.

Clayer, Nathalie, 'The Muslims in South-Eastern Europe: From Ottoman Subjects to European Citizens', in Roberto Tottoli (ed.), *Routledge Handbook of Islam in the West* (London: Routledge 2015), 70–84.

Cliffe, Jeremy, 'The Great Survivor. Angela Merkel's Last Stand', *New Statesman*, 27 June 2018, www.newstatesman.com/world/europe/2018/06/great-survivor-angela-merkel-s-last-stand.

Cliffe, Lionel, and David Seddon, 'Africa in a New World Order', *Review of African Political Economy*, 18/50 (1991), 3–11.

Clinton, Bill, *My Life* (London: Arrow, 2005).

Clover, Joshua, *1989: Bob Dylan Didn't Have This to Sing About* (Berkeley: University of California Press, 2009).

Collinson, Sarah, 'Visa Requirements, Carrier Sanctions, "Safe Third Countries" and "Readmission": The Development of an Asylum "Buffer Zone" in Europe', *Transactions of the Institute of British Geographers*, 21/1 (1996), 76–90.

'The Concluding Document of the Madrid Meeting 1980 of Representatives of the Participating States of the Conference on Security and Co-operation in Europe, Held on the Basis of the Provisions of the Final Act Relating to the Follow-Up to the Conference' (Madrid, 1983), www.osce.org/mc/40871?download=true.

Conférence Internationale des Balkanologues, Belgrade, 7–8 September 1982 (Belgrade: Académie Serbe des Sciences et des Arts, Institut des Etudes Balkaniques, 1984).

Constantin, François, and Bernard Contamin, 'Perspectives africaines et bouleversements internationaux', *Politique Africaine*, 39 (October 1990), 55–67.

Coughlan, Sean, 'How a University Became a Battle for Europe's Identity', *BBC News*, 3 May 2017, www.bbc.co.uk/news/business-39780546.

Cox, Michael, John Ikenberry, and Takashi Inoguchi (eds.), *American Democracy Promotion: Impulses, Strategies, and Impacts* (Oxford: Oxford University Press, 2000).

Crawford, Beverly, 'German Foreign Policy and European Political Cooperation: The Diplomatic Recognition of Croatia in 1991', *German Politics & Society*, 13/2 (35) (1995), 1–34.

Cronin, Jeremy, 'The Boat, the Tap and the Leipzig Way', *African Communist*, 130 (1992), 41–54.

Cross, Peter, 'Soviet *Perestroika*: The Cuban Effect', *Third World Quarterly*, 13/1 (1992), 143–58.

Crowe, David, *A History of the Gypsies of Eastern Europe and Russia* (New York: St. Martin's Griffin, 1994).

Crump, Laurien, *The Warsaw Pact Reconsidered: International Relations in Eastern Europe, 1955–1969* (London: Routledge, 2015).

Cruz, Rodolfo, 'New Directions in Soviet Policy towards Latin America', *Journal of Latin American Studies*, 21/1 (1989), 1–22.

Csaba, László, *Eastern Europe in the World Economy* (Cambridge: Cambridge University Press, 1990).

Csillag, Tamás, and Iván Szelényi, 'Drifting from Liberal Democracy: Traditionalist/Neo-conservative Ideology of Managed Illiberal Democratic Capitalism in Post-communist Europe', *Intersections*, 1/1 (2013), 18–48.

Daddow, Oliver, '"Tony's War?" Blair, Kosovo and the Interventionist Impulse in British Foreign Policy', *International Affairs*, 85/3 (2009), 547–560.

Dahrendorf, Ralf, *Reflections on the Revolution in Europe: In a Letter Intended to Have Been Sent to a Gentleman in Warsaw, 1990* (London: Chatto & Windus, 1990).

'Straddling Theory and Practice', 4 April 1989, http://globetrotter.berkeley .edu/conversations/Elberg/Dahrendorf/dahrendorf0.html.

Dale, Gareth, *Between State Capitalism and Globalisation. The Collapse of the East German Economy* (Bern: Peter Lang, 2004).

The East German Revolution of 1989 and Popular Protest in East Germany (Manchester: Manchester University Press, 2007).

Darmanović, Srdjan, 'The Never-Boring Balkans: The Elections of 2016', *Journal of Democracy* 28/1 (2017), 116–28.

'Darowizny dla europosjkiego centrum solidarnosci. Jest juz numer konta do wpłat' (Donations for the European Solidarity Centre. There Is Already an Account Number for Deposits), *Portal Miasta Gdańska*, 31 January 2019, www.gdansk.pl/wiadomosci/darowizny-dla-europosjkiego-centrum-solidar nosci-jest-juz-numer-konta,a,136983#.XFGai2w5bzc.facebook.

Daskalov, Roumen and Alexander Vezenkov, 'Introduction', in Daskalov and Vezenkov (eds.), *Entangled Histories of the Balkans Volume Three: Shared Pasts, Disputed Legacies* (Leiden: Brill, 2015), 1–9.

Daudin, Guillaume, Matthias Morys, and Kevin O'Rourke, 'Europe and Globalisation 1870–1914', in Stephen N. Broadberry and Kevin H. O'Rourke (eds.), *Unifying the European Experience: An Economic History of Modern Europe* (Cambridge: Cambridge University Press, 2010), 5–29.

Davidson, Basil and Barry Munslow, 'The Crisis of the Nation-State in Africa', *Review of African Political Economy*, 7/49 (1990), 9–21.

Decalo, Samuel, 'The Process, Prospects and Constraints of Democratisation in Africa', *African Affairs*, 91 (1992), 7–35.

'Declaration of Principles', XVIII Congress of the Socialist International, 20–22 June 1989, www.socialistinternational.org/viewArticle.cfm?ArticlePageID= 984.

'Declaration on the Granting of Independence to Colonial Countries and Peoples, Adopted by General Assembly Resolution 1514 (XV) of 14 December 1960', United Nations, www.un.org/en/decolonisation/declaration.shtml.

'Declaration on the Political and Socio-economic Situation in Africa and the Fundamental Changes Taking Place in the World', Twenty-Sixth Ordinary Session of the Assembly of the Organisation of African Unity, Addis Ababa, Ethiopia, 9–11 July 1990, AHG/Decl.1 (XXVI) 1990, https://archive.au.int/collect/auassemb/import/English/AHG%20Decl%201%20XXVI_E.pdf.

De Macedo, Jorge Braga, Foy Colm, and Charles Oman (eds.), *Development Is Back* (Paris: OECD Development Studies, 2002).

De Oliveira, Ricardo Soares, *Magnificent and Beggar Land: Angola since the Civil War* (London: Hurst, 2015).

Deutch, Gabby, 'Ukraine's Spiritual Split from Russia Could Trigger a Global Schism', *Atlantic*, 11 October 2018, www.theatlantic.com/international/archive/2018/10/ukraine-orthodox-church-independence-russia/571333/.

De Zepetnek, Steven Tötösy, 'Configurations of Postcoloniality and National Identity: Inbetween Peripherality and Narratives of Change', *Comparatist*, 23 (May 1999), 89–110.

Dieng, Amady Aly, 'L'Afrique noire après la chute du Mur de Berlin', *Présence Africaine*, 153 (1996), 189–93.

Dietz, Hella, *Polnischer Protest. Zur pragmatistischen Fundierung von Theorien sozialen Wandels* (Frankfurt am Main: Campus, 2015).

Dimant, Jeff and Scott Gardner, 'In EU, There's an East-West Divide over Religious Minorities, Gay Marriage, National Identity', www.pewresearch.org/fact-tank/2018/10/29/east-west-divide-within-the-eu-on-issues-including-minorities-gay-marriage-and-national-identity/.

Dimitrov, Martin, 'Understanding Communist Collapse and Resilience', in Martin Dimitrov (ed.), *Why Communism Did Not Collapse: Understanding Authoritarian Regime Resilience in Asia and Europe* (Cambridge: Cambridge University Press, 2013), 3–39.

Dimitrov, Vesselin, *Bulgaria: The Uneven Transition* (London: Routledge, 2008).

Dimitrova, Antoaneta, 'The Uncertain Road to Sustainable Democracy: Elite Coalitions, Citizen Protests and the Prospects of Democracy in Central and Eastern Europe', *East European Politics*, 34/3 (2018), 257–75.

Dimitrova, Antoaneta and Aron Buzogány, 'Post-accession Policy-Making in Bulgaria and Romania: Can Non-state Actors Use EU Rules to Promote Better Governance?', *Journal of Common Market Studies*, 52/1 (2014), 139–56.

Dinescu, Mircea, 'În căutarea timpului pierdut', *Agora*, 3/2 (1990), 168–72.

Dirar, Luwam, 'Rethinking the Concept of Colonialism in Bandung and Its African Union Aftermath', in Luis Eslava, Michael Fakhri, and Vasuki Nesiah (eds.), *Bandung, Global History, and International Law: Critical Pasts and Pending Futures* (Cambridge: Cambridge University Press, 2017), 355–66.

Dobozi, István, 'Patterns, Factors and Prospects of East-South Economic Relations', in Pawel Bożyk (ed.), *Global Challenges and East European Responses* (Warsaw: Polish Scientific Publishers, 1988), 326–49.

'Dodik: RS Will Not Allow Migrants in RS', *N1*, http://ba.n1info.com/a261807/English/NEWS/Dodik-RS-will-not-allow-migrants-in-RS.html.

Domber, Gregory, 'The AFL-CIO, The Reagan Administration and Solidarność', *Polish Review* 52/3 (2007), 277–304.

'Skepticism and Stability: Reevaluating US Policy during Poland's Democratic Transformation in 1989', *Journal of Cold War Studies*, 13/3 (Summer 2011), 52–82.

Dosch, Jörn and Alexander L. Vuving, 'The Impact of China on Governance Structures in Vietnam' (discussion paper, Deutsches Institut für Entwicklungspolitik, 2008).

Downey, John, and Sabina Mihelj (eds.), *Central and Eastern European Media in Comparative Perspective: Politics Economy and Culture* (Farnham: Ashgate, 2012).

Drăghiciu, Andra-Octavia, 'Between "Totalitarianism" and "Terrorism". An Introductory Study about the "Arab" Students in the Romanian Socialist Republic (1974–1989)', *Caietele CNSAS*, 4/1–2 (2013), 323–34.

'Dragnea: NATO şi EU au finanţat statul paralel', *Digi24*, 11 June 2018, www.digi24.ro/stiri/actualitate/politica/dragnea-nato-si-ue-au-finantat-statul-paralel-944886.

Dragović-Soso, Jasna, *'Saviours of the Nation': Serbia's Intellectual Opposition and the Revival of Nationalism* (Montreal: McGill-Queen's University Press, 2003).

Drahokoupil, Jan, *Globalisation and the State in Central and Eastern Europe* (London: Routledge, 2009).

Drakulić, Slavenka, 'Competing for Victimhood. Why Eastern Europe Says No to Refugees', *Eurozine*, 4 November 2015, www.eurozine.com/articles/2015-11-04-drakulic-en.html.

Drelová, Agata Šústová, 'A Cultural History of Catholic Nationalism in Slovakia, 1985–1993' (PhD thesis, University of Exeter, 2015).

Duda, Igor, 'Adriatic for All: Summer Holidays in Croatia', in Breda Luthar and Maruša Pušnik (eds.), *Remembering Utopia: The Culture of Everyday Life in Socialist Yugoslavia* (Washington, DC: New Academia Publishing, 2010), 289–311.

Dufner, Georg 'Chile als Partner, Exempel und Prüfstein. Deutsch-deutsche Außenpolitik und Systemkonkurrenz in Lateinamerika', *Vierteljahreshefte für Zeitgeschichte*, 4 (2013), 513–49.

Dumitru, Petru, 'The History and Evolution of the New or Restored Democracies Movement', https://csrdar.org/content/resource/history-and-evolution-new-or-restored-democracies-movement.

Dymek, Jakub, 'A New Solidarity for the New Poland', *Dissent*, 5 May 2014, www.dissentmagazine.org/blog/polands-children-of-tina.

Dzenovska, Dace, 'Coherent Selves, Viable States: Eastern Europe and the "Migration/Refugee Crisis"', *Slavic Review* 76/2 (2017), 297–306.

Dzielski, Mirosław, *Duch nadchodzącego czasu, 1–2* (Wrocław: Wektory, 1985).

'Potrzeba twórczego antykomunizmu', *13 Grudnia* 11 (1987), 7–8.

Eckel, Jan and Samuel Moyn (eds.), *The Breakthrough of Human Rights in the 1970s* (Philadelphia: University of Pennsylvania Press, 2014).

'Economic Shock Therapy – A Prescription for the Middle East?' (American Enterprise Institute, 15 April 2003), www.aei.org/events/2003/04/15/eco nomic-shock-therapy-a-prescription-for-the-middle-east/.

Egerton, Frazer, *Jihad in the West: The Rise of Militant Salafism* (Cambridge: Cambridge University Press, 2011).

Ekiert, Grzegorz and Jan Kubik, *Rebellious Civil Society: Popular Protest and Democratic Consolidation in Poland, 1989–1993* (Ann Arbor: University of Michigan Press, 2001).

El Difraoui, Asiem, 'No "Facebook Revolution" – But an Egyptian Youth We Know Little About', in Muriel Asseburg (ed.), *Protest, Revolt and Regime Change in the Arab World* (Berlin: German Institute for International and Security Affairs, 2011), 18–20.

Elenkov, Ivan, '"The Second Golden Age": Historicisation of Official Culture in the Context of Bulgaria's 1,300th Anniversary Celebrations (1976–1981)', *Critique & Humanism*, 23/1 (2007), 31–58.

Endlich, Luise, *NeuLand: ganz einfache Geschichten* (Frankfurt am Main: Fischer-Taschenbuch, 2000).

Engel, Jeffrey, '1989: An Introduction to an International History', in Jeffrey Engel (ed.), *The Fall of the Berlin Wall: The Revolutionary Legacy of 1989* (Oxford: Oxford University Press, 2012), 1–30.

Engel, Ulf, 'Africa's "1989"', in Ulf Engel, Frank Hadler, and Matthias Middell (eds.), *1989 in a Global Perspective* (Leipzig: Leipziger Universitätsverlag, 2015), 331–48.

English, Robert, 'Ideas and the End of the Cold War: Rethinking Intellectual and Political Change', in Silvio Pons and Federico Romero (eds.), *Reinterpreting the End of the Cold War: Issues, Interpretations, Periodisations* (London: Frank Cass, 2005), 116–36.

Erler, Brigitte, *Tödliche Hilfe. Bericht von meiner letzten Dienstreise in Sachen Entwicklungshilfe* (Freiburg: Dreisam-Verlag 1985).

Fábián, Katalin (ed.), *Globalization. Perspectives from Central and Eastern Europe* (Bingley: Emerald, 2007).

Fabry, Adam, 'The Origins of Neoliberalism in Late "Socialist" Hungary. The Case of the Financial Research Institute and "Turnabout and Reform"', *Capital & Class*, 42/1 (2017), 77–107.

Falk, Barbara, *Dilemmas of Dissidence in East-Central Europe: Citizen Intellectuals and Philosopher Kings* (Budapest: Central European University Press, 2003).

'From Berlin to Baghdad: Learning the "Wrong" Lessons from the Collapse of Communism', in George Lawson et al. (eds.), *The Global 1989. Continuity and Change in World Politics* (Cambridge: Cambridge University Press, 2011), 243–70.

'Reflections on the Revolutions in Europe. Lessons for the Middle East and the Arab Spring', in Friederike Kind-Kovács and Jessie Labov (eds.), *Samizdat, Tamizdat, and Beyond. Transnational Media during and after Socialism* (Oxford: Berghahn, 2013), 281–315.

Falk, Richard, 'The Afghan Settlement and the Future of World Politics', in Amin Saikal and William Maley (eds.), *The Soviet Withdrawal from Afghanistan* (Cambridge: Cambridge University Press, 1989), 142–60.

'Self-Determination under International Law: The Coherence of Doctrine versus the Incoherence of Experience', in Wolfgang F. Danspeckgruber (ed.), *The Self-Determination of Peoples: Community, Nation, and State in an Interdependent World* (Boulder, CO: Lynne Rienner, 2002), 31–66.

Falkenheim Meyer, Peggy, 'Gorbachev and Post-Gorbachev Policy toward the Korean Peninsula. The Impact of Changing Russian Perceptions', *Asian Survey*, 32/8 (1992), 757–72.

Falser, Michael and Wilfried Lipp (eds.), *A Future for Our Past: The 40th Anniversary of European Architectural Heritage Year (1975–2015)* (Berlin: Hendrik Bäßler Verlag, 2015).

Feckoua, Laoukissam, 'The Changing World: A Glance at the International Geo-political Evolution since 1989', *Présence Africaine*, 153 (1996), 5–28.

Fekete, Liz, *A Suitable Enemy: Racism, Migration and Islamophobia in Europe* (London: Pluto Books, 2009).

Fekete, Liz and Frances Webber, *Inside Racist Europe* (London: Institute of Race Relations, 1994).

Fewsmith, Joseph, *China since Tiananmen: The Politics of Transition* (New York: Cambridge University Press, 2008).

Fischer, Karin, 'The Influence of Neoliberals in Chile before, during, and after Pinochet', in Dieter Plehwe and Philip Mirowski (eds.), *The Road from Mont Pèlerin. The Making of the Neoliberal Thought Collective* (Cambridge, MA: Harvard University Press), 305–46.

Fitzmaurice, Malgosia, 'Badinter Commission (for the Former Yugoslavia)', in *Max Planck Encyclopedia of Public International Law*, http://opil.ouplaw.com/view/10.1093/law:epil/9780199231690/law-9780199231690-e13.

Fónai, Imre, 'Épp kitört az új migránspánik, mire kiderült: "csak" venezuelai magyarok költöztek a balatonőszödi üdülőbe', *Magyar Narancs*, 13 April 2018, https://magyarnarancs.hu/kismagyarorszag/epp-kitort-az-ujabb-migranspanik-mire-kider ult-csak-venezuelai-magyarok-koltoztek-a-balatonoszodi-udulobe-110578.

Foot, Rosemary, 'The Cold War and Human Rights', in Melvyn Leffler and Odd Arne Westad (eds.), *The Cambridge History of the Cold War. Volume III Endings* (Cambridge: Cambridge University Press, 2010), 445–65.

Forlenza, Rosario, 'The Politics of the Abendland: Christian Democracy and the Idea of Europe after the Second World War', *Contemporary European History*, 26/2 (2017), 261–86.

Fowkes, Ben and Bülent Gökay, 'Unholy Alliance: Muslims and Communists – An Introduction', *Journal of Communist Studies and Transition Politics*, 25/1 (2009), 1–31.

Frank, Andre Gunder *Crisis: In the World Economy* (New York: Holmes and Meier, 1980).

'Long Live Transideological Enterprise! The Socialist Economies in the Capitalist International Division of Labor and West-East-South Economic Relations', *Review (Fernand Braudel Center)*, 1/1 (1977), 91–140.

'No Escape from the Laws of World Economics', *Review of African Political Economy*, 18/50 (1991), 21–32.

'Nothing New in the East: No New World Order', *Social Justice*, 19/1 (1992), 34–59.

Fraser, Nancy, 'Postcommunist Democratic Socialism?', in George Katsiaficas (ed.), *After the Fall: 1989 and the Future of Freedom* (London: Routledge, 2001), 200–202.

Freizer, Sabine, 'Central Asian Fragmented Civil Society: Communal and Neoliberal Forms in Tajikistan and Uzbekistan', in Marlies Glasius, David Lewis, and Hakan Seckinelgin (eds.), *Exploring Civil Society: Political and Cultural Contexts* (Abingdon: Routledge, 2011), 130–40.

Frings, Viviane, 'Cambodia after Decollectivisation (1989–1992)', *Journal of Contemporary Asia*, 24/1 (1994), 49–66.

Fröberg Idling, Peter, *Pol Pots leende* (Skönlitterär dokumentär, Atlas Förlag, 2006).

Fukuyama, Francis, *The End of History and the Last Man* (New York: Penguin, 2012).

Gabowitsch, Mischa, *Protest in Putin's Russia* (Cambridge: Polity, 2017).

Gagnon, Chip, *The Myth of Ethnic War* (Ithaca, NY: Cornell University Press, 2004).

Gagyi, Ágnes, 'The Non-post-communist Left in Hungary after 1989: Diverging Paths of Leftist Criticism, Civil Activism, and Radicalizing Constituency', in Michal Kopeček and Piotr Wciślik (eds.), *Thinking through Transition: Liberal Democracy, Authoritarian Pasts, and Intellectual History in East Central Europe after 1989* (Budapest: Central European Univrsity Press, 2015), 335–70.

Gaidar, Yegor, *Days of Defeat and Victory* (Seattle: University of Washington Press, 1999).

Gibel' Imperii: Uroki Dlja Sovremennoj Rossii (Moskva: Rosspen, 2006).

Gallagher, Tom, *Theft of a Nation: Romania since Communism* (London: Hurst, 2006).

Ganev, Venelin I., *Preying on the State. The Transformation of Bulgaria after 1989* (Ithaca, NY: Cornell University Press, 2007).

'"Soft Decisionism" in Bulgaria', *Journal of Democracy*, 29/3 (2018), 91–103.

Garavini, Giuliano, *After Empires: European Integration, Decolonisation, and the Challenge from the Global South, 1957–1986* (Oxford: Oxford University Press, 2012).

Garba, Joseph N., 'Changing East-West Relations and Their Implications for Africa' (lecture, Carter Center, Atlanta, GA, 9 April 1990).

Garver, John W., *China's Quest: The History of the Foreign Relations of the People's Republic of China* (Oxford: Oxford University Press, 2016).

Ge, Liu, *Theoretical Literacy of the Top Leaders of the CPSU and the Rise and Fall of the Soviet Union* (Seattle: Current Affairs Press, 2016).

Georgiadis, George, '"Differentiation by Design" as a Determinant of Convergence: Comparing Early EU Selection Policies in Central and Eastern Europe and the Commonwealth of Independent States', *Southeast European and Black Sea Studies*, 8/4 (2008), 399–429.

Germuska, Pál, 'Failed Eastern Integration and a Partly Successful Opening Up to the West: The Economic Re-orientation of Hungary during the 1970s', *European Review of History*, 21/2 (2014), 271–91.

Gewirtz, Julian, *Unlikely Partners. Chinese Reformers, Western Economists, and the Making of Global China* (Cambridge, MA: Harvard University Press, 2017).

Ghellab, Grazia Scarfò, Monique de Saint Martin, and Kamal Mellakh (eds.), *Étudier à l'Est. Expériences de diplômés africains* (Paris: Karthala, 2015).

Ghodsee, Kristen, *Muslim Lives in Eastern Europe: Gender, Ethnicity, and the Transformation of Islam in Postsocialist Bulgaria* (Princeton, NJ: Princeton University Press, 2010).

Gigova, Irina, 'The Feeble Charm of National(ist) Communism: Intellectuals and Cultural Politics in Zhivkov's Bulgaria', in Theodora Dragostinova and Yana Hashamova (eds.), *Beyond Mosque, Church, and State: Alternative Narratives of the Nation in the Balkans* (Budapest: Central European University Press, 2016), 151–77.

Gille, Zsuzsa, 'Is There a Global Postsocialist Condition?', *Global Society*, 24/1 (2010), 9–30.

Gilley, Bruce, 'Deng Xiaoping and His Successors', in William Joseph (ed.), *Politics in China: An Introduction* (Oxford: Oxford University Press, 2010), 103–25.

Gills, Barry and Joel Rocamora, 'Low Intensity Democracy', *Third World Quarterly*, 13/3 (1992), 501–23.

Gills, Barry, Joel Rocamora, and Richard Wilson (eds.), *Low Intensity Democracy: Political Power in the New World Order* (London: Pluto Press, 1994).

Gilman, Nils, 'The New International Economic Order: A Reintroduction', *Humanity*, 6/1 (2015), 1–16.

Girvan, Norman, 'Economic Nationalists v. Multinational Corporations: Revolutionary or Evolutionary Change?', in Carl Widstrand (ed.), *Multinational Firms in Africa* (Dakar/Uppsala: African Institute for Economic Development and Planning/Scandinavian Institute of African Studies, 1975), 25–56.

Glaurdić, Josip, *The Hour of Europe: Western Powers and the Breakup of Yugoslavia* (New Haven, CT: Yale University Press, 2011).

Glenny, Misha, *McMafia* (London: Vintage, 2009).

Gnoinska, Margaret, '"Socialist Friends Should Help Each Other in Crises": Sino-Polish Relations within the Cold War Dynamics, 1980–1987', *Cold War History*, 17/2 (2017), 143–59.

Godehardt, Nadine, 'Constructing Global Connectivity: The European Politics of China's Belt & Road Initiative' (paper presented at Eastern Europe – Global Area – Annual Conference of GWZO and EEGA, University of Leipzig, July 2018).

'No End of History: A Chinese Alternative Concept of International Order?' (Berlin: Stiftung Wissenschaft und Politik Research Paper, 2/2016), https://nbn-resolving.org/urn:nbn:de:0168-ssoar-461135.

Gorbatschow, Michail, *Erinnerungen* (Berlin: Siedler, 1995).

Perestroika. Die zweite Russische Revolution (München: Droemer Knaur, 1987).

Gorz, André, *Le socialisme difficile* (Paris: Seuil, 1967).

'Gotovina et al. (IT-06–90)', *ICTY*, www.icty.org/en/case/gotovina/4.

Gowan, Peter, 'Neo-liberal Theory and Practice for Eastern Europe', *New Left Review*, 213/1 (1995), 3–60.

Graff, Agnieszka, 'Report from the Gender Trenches: War against "Genderism" in Poland', *European Journal of Women's Studies*, 21/4 (2014), 431–42.

Graff, Agnieszka and Elżbieta Korolczuk, '"Worse Than Communism and Nazism Put Together": War on Gender in Poland', in Roman Kuhar and David Paternotte (eds.), *Anti-gender Campaigns in Europe: Mobilizing Against Equality* (New York: Rowman & Littlefield, 2017), 175–94.

Grandin, Greg, 'The Instruction of Great Catastrophe: Truth Commissions, National History, and State Formation in Argentina, Chile, and Guatemala', *American Historical Review*, 110/1 (2005), 46–67.

Greskovits, Béla, 'The Hollowing and Backsliding of Democracy in East Central Europe', *Global Policy*, 6/Supplement 1 (2015), 28–37.

'Rebuilding the Hungarian Right through Civil Organisation and Contention: The Civic Circles Movement' (EUI Working Paper RSCAS 37, 2017).

Grilli, Enzo R., *The European Community and the Developing Countries* (Cambridge: Cambridge University Press, 1993).

Grosescu, Raluca, *Les communistes dans l'après communisme: Trajectoires de conversion politique de la nomenklatura roumaine après 1989* (Paris: Michel Houdiard Éditeur, 2012).

Grote, Inga, 'Donald Rumsfeld's Old and New Europe and the United States' Strategy to Destabilize the European Union', *Rivista di Studi Politici Internazionali*, 74/3 (2007), 347–56.

Grudzińska-Gross, Irena, 'The Backsliding', *East European Politics and Societies and Cultures*, 28/4 (2014), 664–68.

Grupinski, Rafal, 'Schwierigkeiten mit der Mitte Europas', in Hans-Peter Burmeister et al. (eds.), *Mitteleuropa—Traum oder Trauma?* (Bremen: Edition Temmen, 1988), 51–64.

Grzybowski, K., 'Socialist Countries in GATT', *American Journal of Comparative Law*, 4 (1980), 539–54.

Guihai, Guan, 'The Influence of the Collapse of the Soviet Union on China's Political Choices', in Thomas Bernstein and Hua-Yu Li (eds.), *China Learns from the Soviet Union, 1949–Present* (Lanham, MD: Rowman & Littlefield, 2010), 505–16.

Guilhot, Nicolas, *The Democracy Makers: Human Rights and International Order* (New York: Columbia University Press, 2005).

'A Network of Influential Friendships: The Fondation Pour Une Entraide Intellectuelle Européenne and East–West Cultural Dialogue, 1957–1991', *Minerva*, 44 (2006), 379–409.

'Une vocation philanthropique: George Soros, les sciences sociales et la régulation du marché mondial', *Actes de la recherche en sciences sociales*, 151–152/1 (2004), 36–48.

'Long Live Transideological Enterprise! The Socialist Economies in the Capitalist International Division of Labor and West-East-South Economic Relations', *Review (Fernand Braudel Center)*, 1/1 (1977), 91–140.

Gutman, Patrick, 'Tripartite Industrial Cooperation and Third Countries', in Christopher T. Saunders (ed.), *East-West-South: Economic Interactions between Three Worlds* (London: Macmillan, 1981), 337–64.

Gvishiani, D., *Organisation and Management. A Sociological Analysis of Western Theories* (Moscow: Progress, 1972).

Habermas, Jürgen, 'What Does Socialism Mean Today? The Rectifying Revolution and the Need for New Thinking on the Left', *New Left Review*, 183 (1990), 3–21.

Hall, Richard Andrew, 'Theories of Collective Action and Revolution: Evidence from the Romanian Transition of December 1989', *Europe-Asia Studies*, 52/6 (2000), 1069–93.

Halliday, Fred, 'Third World Socialism. 1989 and After', in George Lawson et al. (eds.), *The Global 1989. Continuity and Change in World Politics* (Cambridge: Cambridge University Press, 2010), 112–34.

Hamburg, Roger, 'Soviet Foreign Policy toward Different Audiences and with Conflicting Premises: The Case of Nicaragua', *Conflict Quarterly*, 9/1 (Winter 1989), 5–19.

Hanley, Eric, 'Cadre Capitalism in Hungary and Poland. Property Accumulation among Communist-Era Elites', *East European Politics and Societies*, 14/1 (1999), 143–78.

Hanley, Seán and Milada Anna Vachudova, 'Understanding the Illiberal Turn: Democratic Backsliding in the Czech Republic', *East European Politics*, 34/3 (2018), 276–96.

Hansen, Peo and Stefan Jonsson, *Eurafrica: The Untold History of European Integration and Colonialism* (London: Bloomsbury Academic, 2015).

Hanson, Stephen, 'Plebiscitarian Patrimonialism in Putin's Russia', *Annals of the American Academy of Political and Social Science*, 636/1 (2011), 32–68.

Harrison, Lawrence E., *Underdevelopment Is a State of Mind: the Latin American Case* (Cambridge, MA: Center for International Affairs, Harvard University and University Press of America, 1985).

Harvey, David, *A Brief History of Neoliberalism* (New York: Oxford University Press, 2005).

Hassner, Pierre, 'L'avenir des alliances en Europe', *Revue française de science politique*, 26/6 (1976), 1029–53.

'L'avenir prévisible des deux alliances en Europe', *Le Monde diplomatique*, June 1977, 8.

Havel, Václav, "Preface" in Joerg Forbrig and Pavol Demeš (eds.), *Reclaiming Democracy: Civil Society and Electoral Change in Central and Eastern Europe* (Washington DC: German Marshall Fund of the United States, 2007), 7–8.

Hawk, David, *The Hidden Gulag. The Lives and Voices of 'Those Who Are Sent to the Mountains'* (Washington, DC: US Committee for Human Rights in North Korea, 2012).

Hayden, Robert M., *Blueprints for a House Divided – The Constitutional Logic of the Yugoslav Conflicts* (Ann Arbor: University of Michigan Press, 2000).

Hayek, Friedrich, *The Road to Serfdom* (London: Routledge 1944).

Hegedüs, Daniel, 'The Great Orbán-Salvini Hack', *Visegrád Insight*, 14 September 2018, https://visegradinsight.eu/the-great-orban-salvini-hack/.

Heimann, Mary, *Czechoslovakia: The State That Failed* (New Haven, CT: Yale University Press, 2009).

Helleiner, G. K., *The IMF and Africa in the 1980s: Essays in International Finance* (Princeton, NJ: Princeton University Press, 1983).

Hibbing, John and Samuel Patterson, 'A Democratic Legislature in the Making the Historic Hungarian Elections of 1990', *Comparative Political Studies*, 24/2 (1992), 430–54.

Hidalgo, Ariel, *Disidencia. Segunda revolución cubana?* (Miami: Ediciones Universal, 1994).

Hîncu, Adela, 'Managing Culture, Locating Consent: The Sociology of Mass Culture in Socialist Romania, 1960s–1970s', *Revista Română de Sociologie*, 1–2 (2017), 3–14.

Hirschhausen, Ulrike v. and Klaus Kiran Patel, 'Europeanisation in History: An Introduction', in Martin Conway and Klaus Kiran Patel (eds.), *Europeanisation in the Twentieth Century. Historical Approaches* (London: Palgrave Macmillan, 2010), 1–18.

Hockenos, Paul, *Homeland Calling: Exile Patriotism & the Balkan Wars* (Ithaca, NY: Cornell University Press, 2003).

Hockenos, Paul and Jane Hunter, 'Pretoria Gold', *Australian Left Review*, 1/121 (1990), 16–19.

Hoffman, David E., *The Oligarchs. Wealth and Power in the New Russia* (New York: Public Affairs, 2002).

Högselius, Per, *Red Gas: Russia and the Origins of European Energy Dependence* (New York: Palgrave Macmillan, 2013).

Holubec, Stanislav, 'The Formation of the Czech Post-communist Intellectual Left: Twenty Years of Seeking an Identity', in Michal Kopeček and Piotr Wciślik (eds.), *Thinking through Transition: Liberal Democracy, Authoritarian Pasts, and Intellectual History in East Central Europe after 1989* (Budapest: Central European University Press, 2015), 397–430.

Hook, Steven, 'Inconsistent US Efforts to Promote Democracy Abroad', in Peter Schraeder (ed.), *Exporting Democracy: Rhetoric vs. Reality* (Boulder, CO: Lynne Rienner, 2002), 109–28.

Horvath, Robert, '"The Solzhenitsyn Effect": East European Dissidents and the Demise of the Revolutionary Privilege', *Human Rights Quarterly*, 29/4 (2007), 879–907.

Hosking, Geoffrey, *Rulers and Victims: The Russians in the Soviet Union* (Cambridge, MA: Belknap, 2006).

Hough, Jerry, 'The Evolving Soviet Debate on Latin America', *Latin American Research Review*, 16/1 (1981), 124–143.

Hudáková, Zuzana, 'Czech/o/Slovak Democracy: 30 Years in the Making', *Eurozine*, 20 April 2018, www.eurozine.com/czechoslovak-democracy-30-years-making/.

Huntington, Samuel, *The Clash of Civilizations* (New York: Simon & Shuster, 1996).
  The Third Wave: Democratization in the Late Twentieth Century (Norman: University of Oklahoma Press, 1993).

Husarka, Anna, 'Los derechos humanos', *Vuelta*, 168 (1990), 61–62.

Hutchful, Eboe, 'Eastern Europe: Consequences for Africa', *Review of African Political Economy*, 18/50 (1991), 51–59.

Huysmans, Jef, 'The European Union and the Securitisation of Migration', *Journal of Common Market Studies*, 38/5 (December 2000), 751–77.

Iacob, Bogdan C., 'Balkan Counter-circulation: Internationalizing Area Studies from the Periphery during the Cold War', in Matthias Middell (ed.), *Handbook of Transregional Studies* (London: Routledge, 2018), 29–37.

'South-East by Global South: The Balkans, UNESCO and the Cold War', in James Mark, Artemy Kalinovsky, and Steffi Marung (eds.), *Alternative Globalizations: Eastern Europe and the Postcolonial World* (Bloomington: Indiana University Press, 2020).

'Together but Apart: Balkan Historians, the Global South, and UNESCO's *History of Humanity* 1978–1989', *East Central Europe*, 45/2–3 (2018), 245–78.

'Transition to What and Whose Democracy? 1990 in Bulgaria and Romania', in Joachim von Puttkamer and Włodzimierz Borodziej (eds.), *From Revolution to Uncertainty: The Year 1990 in Central and Eastern Europe* (London: Routledge, 2019), 117–41.

Iliescu, Ion, *Revoluţie şi reformă* (Bucureşti: Editura Enciclopedică, 1994).

Imre, Anikó, 'Whiteness in Post-socialist Eastern Europe: The Time of the Gypsies, the End of Race', in Alfred J. Lopez (ed.), *Postcolonial Whiteness: A Critical Reader on Race and Empire* (Albany: State University of New York Press, 2005), 79–102.

Ingrao, Charles W. and Thomas Allan Emmert (eds.), *Confronting the Yugoslav Controversies: A Scholars' Initiative* (West Lafayette, IN: Purdue University Press, 2009).

'Interview with Gergely Pröhle, Former Ambassador of Hungary in Berlin', *Körber Stiftung*, May 2018, www.koerber-stiftung.de/en/topics/the-value-of-europe/contributions-2018/interview-proehle.

Iriye, Akira, Petra Goedde, and William Hitchcock, *The Human Rights Revolution: An International History* (Oxford: Oxford University Press, 2012).

Irwin, Douglas I., 'The Nixon Shock after Forty Years: The Import Surcharge Revisited', *World Trade Review*, 12/1 (2013), 29–56.

Irwin, Zachary T., 'The Fate of Islam in the Balkans: A Comparison of Four State Policies', in Pedro Ramet (ed.), *Religion and Nationalism in Soviet and East European Politics* (Durham, NC: Duke University Press, 1989), 378–409.

Isaac, Jeffrey, 'The Meanings of 1989', *Social Research*, 63/2 (1996), 291–344.

I se spunea Machiavelli. Ştefan Andrei în dialog cu Lavinia Betea (Bucureşti: Adevărul, 2011).

Izetbegović, Alija, *The Islamic Declaration: A Programme for the Islamisation of Muslims and the Muslim Peoples* (Sarajevo, 1990), www.angelfire.com/dc/mbooks/Alija-Izetbegovic-Islamic-Declaration-1990-Azam-dot-com.pdf.

Izumi, Hajime, 'North Korea and the Changes in Eastern Europe', *Korean Studies* 16 (1992), 1–12.

Jacoby, Wade and Umut Korkut, 'Vulnerability and Economic Re-orientation: Rhetoric and in Reality in Hungary's "Chinese Opening"', *East European Politics and Societies and Cultures*, 30/3 (2016), 496–518.

Jakubowski, Jerzy, *Przedsiebiorstwa w Handlu Miedzynarodowym. Problematyka prawna* (Warsaw, 1970).

James, Harold, *International Monetary Cooperation since Bretton Woods* (Oxford: Oxford University Press, 1996).

Jansen, Hanna, 'Internationalizing the Thaw: Soviet Orientalists and the Contested Politics of Spiritual Solidarity in Asia 1954–1959', in James Mark, Artemy Kalinovsky, and Steffi Marung (eds.), *Alternative Globalizations: Eastern Europe and the Postcolonial World* (Bloomington: Indiana University Press, 2020).

Jarausch, Konrad H., 'People Power? Towards a Historical Explanation of 1989', in Vladimir Tismaneanu and Bogdan C. Iacob (eds.), *The Revolutions of 1989 and the Resurgence of History* (Budapest: Central European Press, 2012), 109–25.

The Rush to German Unity (Oxford: Oxford University Press, 1994).

Jasińska-Kania, Aleksandra, 'National Stereotypes and Economic Cooperation: Images of Korea in Poland' (paper presented at 'Korean and Korean Business Interests in Central Europe and CIS Countries', Seoul National University, August 1997).

Jeffery, Renée, *Transitions to Democracy: Amnesties, Accountability, and Human Rights* (Philadelphia: University of Pennsylvania Press, 2014).

Jelzin, Boris, *Mitternachtstagebuch. Meine Jahre im Kreml* (Berlin: Propyläen Verlag, 2000).

Jensen, Steven L. B., *The Making of International Human Rights: The 1960s, Decolonization, and the Reconstruction of Global Values* (New York: Cambridge University Press, 2016).

Jones, Sara, 'Cross-border Collaboration and the Construction of Memory Narratives in Europe', in Tea Sindbæk Andersen and Barbara Törnquist-Plewa (eds.), *The Twentieth Century in European Memory: Transcultural Mediation and Reception* (Leiden: Brill, 2017), 27–55.

Jović, Dejan, *Yugoslavia: A State That Withered Away* (West Lafayette, IN: Purdue University Press, 2009).

Junes, Tom, 'Students Take Bulgaria's Protests to the Next Level. Can They Break the Political Stalemate?', *Tr@nsit Online* (2013), www.iwm.at/read-listen-watch/transit-online/students-take-bulgarias-protests-to-the-next-level-why-the-student-protests-could-break-the-political-stalemate/.

Jurkat, Kathrin, '"I'm both a Worker and a Shareholder". Workers' Narratives and Property Transformations, Continuity and Change in Post-socialist Bosnia and Serbia', *Südosteuropa*, 4 (2017), 654–78.

Kádár, János, *A fejlett szocialista társadalom építésének utján* (Budapest: Kossuth, 1975).

Kagarlitsky, Boris, *The Disintegration of the Monolith* (London: Verso, 1992).

Kaldor, Mary, Gerard Holden, and Richard A. Falk (eds.), *The New Detente: Rethinking East-West Relations* (London: Verso, 1989).

Kalinovsky, Artemy, *Laboratory of Socialist Development: Cold War Politics and Decolonization in Soviet Tajikistan* (Ithaca, NY: Cornell University Press, 2018).

'Writing the Soviet South', in James Mark, Artemy Kalinovsky, and Steffi Marung (eds.), *Alternative Globalizations: Eastern Europe and the Postcolonial World* (Bloomington: Indiana University Press, 2020).

Kalmar, Ivan, 'Islamophobia in the East of the European Union: An Introduction', *Patterns of Prejudice*, 52/5 (2018), 389–405.

Kamusella, Tomasz, 'Central Europe in the Distorting Mirror of Maps, Languages and Ideas', *Polish Review*, 57/1 (2012), 33–94.

Kansikas, Suvi, 'Acknowledging Economic Realities. The CMEA Policy Change vis-à-vis the European Community 1970–3', *European Review of History*, 21/2 (2014), 311–28.

Kanyinga, Karuti, 'Limitations of Political Liberalisation: Parties and Electoral Politics in Kenya', in Walter Oyugi, Peter Wanyande, and C. Odhiambo-Mbai (eds.), *The Politics of Transition in Kenya: From Kanu to NARC* (Nairobi: Heinrich Böll Foundation, 2003), 96–127.

Kaplan, Robert, *Balkan Ghosts* (New York: Piacador, 1993).

Kapuściński, Ryszard, *Emperor: Downfall of an Autocrat* (London: Quartet Books, 1983).

Imperium (Warszawa: Czytelnik, 1993).

Karčić, Harun, 'Globalisation and Islam in Bosnia: Foreign Influences and Their Effects', *Totalitarian Movements and Political Religions*, 11/2 (2010), 151–66.

Karkova, Nikolay R. and Zhivka Valiavicharska, 'Rethinking East-European Socialism: Notes toward an Anticapitalist Decolonial Methodology', *Interventions*, 20/6 (2018), 785–813.

Katsakioris, Constantin, 'Soviet Lessons for Arab Modernisation: Soviet Educational Aid to Arab Countries after 1956', *Journal of Modern European History*, 8/1 (2010), 85–106.

Katzenstein, Peter and Nicole Weygandt, 'Mapping Eurasia in an Open World: How the Insularity of Russia's Geopolitical and Civilisational Approaches Limits Its Foreign Policies', *Perspectives on Politics*, 15/2 (2017), 428–54.

Kaufman Purcell, Susan, 'Cuba's Cloudy Future', *Foreign Affairs*, 69/3 (Summer 1990), 113–30.

Kázecký, Stanislav, 'La oposición interna en Cuba desde el triunfo de la Revolución en 1959 hasta 2006' (PhD diss., Univerzita Karlova v Praze, 2007).

Keber, Dušan, 'Čigava je obletnica JBTZ?', *Mladina* 22, 31 May 2013, www.mladina.si/144718/cigava-je-obletnica-jbtz/.

Keck-Szajbel, Mark, 'The Politics of Travel and the Creation of a European Society', *Global Society*, 24 (2010), 31–50.

Kelertas, Violeta (ed.), *Baltic Postcolonialism* (Amsterdam: Rodopi, 2006).

Kemper, Michael, 'Propaganda for the East, Scholarship for the West. Soviet Strategies at the 1960 International Congress of Orientalists in Moscow', in Artemy Kalinovsky and Martin Kemper (eds.), *Reassessing Orientalism: Interlocking Orientologies during the Cold War* (London: Routledge, 2015), 170–210.

Kennedy, Paul, *The Spanish Socialist Party and the Modernisation of Spain* (Manchester: Manchester University Press, 2013).

Kenney, Padraic, *The Burdens of Freedom: Eastern Europe since 1989* (London: Zed Books, 2006).

A Carnival of Revolution. Central Europe 1989 (Princeton, NJ: Princeton University Press, 2002).

'Electromagnetic Forces and Radio Waves or Does Transnational History Really Happen?', in Robert Brier (ed.), *Entangled Protest: Transnational Approaches to the History of Dissent in Eastern Europe and the Soviet Union* (Osnabrück: Fibre, 2013), 43–52.

Kentikelenis, Alexander and Sarah Babb, 'The Making of Global Neoliberalism: Norm Substitution and the Clandestine Politics of International Institutional Change' (paper presented at 'Global Neoliberalisms: Lost and Found in Translation', British Academy, 7 June 2018).

Kepel, Gilles, *Jihad: The Trail of Political Islam* (Cambridge, MA: Harvard University Press, 2002).

Keys, Barbara, *Reclaiming American Virtue: The Human Rights Revolution of the 1970s* (Cambridge, MA: Harvard University Press, 2014).

Kilibarda, Konstantin, 'Non-aligned Geographies in the Balkans: Space, Race and Image in the Construction of New "European" Foreign Policies', in Abhinava Kumar and Derek Maisonville (eds.), *Security beyond the Discipline: Emerging Dialogues on Global Politics* (Toronto: York Centre for International and Security Studies, 2010), 27–57.

Kisić-Kolanović, Nada, 'Envisioning the "Other" East: Bosnia-Herzegovina, Muslims, and Modernisation in the Ustaša State', in Rory Yeomans (ed.), *The Utopia of Terror: Life and Death in Wartime Croatia* (Rochester, NY: University of Rochester Press, 2015), 188–216.

Kitchen, J. Coleman and Jean-Paul Paddack, 'The 1990 Franco-African Summit', *CSIS Africa Notes*, no. 115 (30 August 1990), https://csis-prod.s3.amazonaws.com/s3fs-public/legacy_files/files/publication/anotes_0890.pdf.

Klee, Hans-Dieter, *Changes in Germany and Eastern Europe – Implications for Africa?* (Berlin: Deutsche Afrika-Stiftung, 1990).

Klein, Naomi, *The Shock Doctrine. The Rise of Disaster Capitalism* (London: Penguin, 2007).

Klimó, Árpád, *Hungary since 1945* (London: Routledge, 2018).

Koch, Alfred and Petr Aven, *Gaidar's Revolution: The Inside Account of the Economic Transformation of Russia* (New York: I.B. Tauris, 2015).

Koenen, Gerd, *Das Rote Jahrzehnt. Unsere Kleine Deutsche Kulturrevolution, 1967–1977* (Köln: Kiepenheuer & Witsch, 2001).

Köhler, Volkmar, 'European House or Third World: Are We Forgetting Development Policy?' in Üner Kirdar (ed.), *Change: Threat or Opportunity for Human Progress*, vol. 1 (New York: United Nations Publications, 1992), 212–24.

Kola, Adam, 'A Prehistory of Postcolonialism in Socialist Poland', in James Mark, Artemy Kalinovsky, and Steffi Marung (eds.), *Alternative Globalizations: Eastern Europe and the Postcolonial World* (Bloomington: Indiana University Press, 2020).

Kołodziejczyk, Dorota and Cristina Şandru, 'Introduction: On Colonialism, Communism and East-Central Europe – Some Reflections', *Journal of Postcolonial Writing*, 48/2 (2012), 113–16.

Kølvraa, Christoffer, 'Limits of Attraction: The EU's Eastern Border and the European Neighbourhood Policy', *East European Politics and Societies and Cultures*, 31/1 (2017), 11–25.

Kopátsy, Sándor, 'A magyar privatizácio sajátos vonásai', *Mozgó Világ*, 1 (1993), 23–28.

'Új világrend felé. Vissza és előre ötven évet', *Társadalmi Szemle*, 5 (1992), 13–23.

Kopeček, Michal (ed.), *Expertní kořeny postsocialismu: Československo sedmdesátých až devadesátých let* (Prague: Argo, 2019).

'From Scientific Social Management to Neoliberal Governmentality? Czechoslovak Sociology and Social Research on the Way from Authoritarianism to Liberal Democracy, 1969–1989', *Stan Rzeczy*, 13 (2017), 171–96.

'Human Rights Facing a National Past. Dissident "Civic Patriotism" and the Return of History in East Central Europe, 1968–1989', *Geschichte und Gesellschaft*, 38/4 (2012), 573–602.

'The Socialist Conception of Human Rights and Its Dissident Critique. East Central Europe 1960s–1980s', *East Central Europe* (forthcoming).

'Sovereignty, "Return to Europe" and Democratic Distrust in the East after 1989 in the Light of Brexit', *Central European History*, 28/1 (2019), 73–76.

Kornai, János, *By Force of Thought. Irregular Memoirs of an Intellectual Journey* (Cambridge, MA: MIT Press, 2006).

The Road to a Free Economy. Shifting from a Socialist System (New York: Norton, 1990).

Kornetis, Kostis, 'Introduction: The End of a Parable? Unsettling the Transitology Model in the Age of Crisis', *Historein*, 15/1 (2015), 5–12.

Korosteleva, Elena, 'Eastern Partnership and the Eurasian Union: Bringing "the Political" Back in the Eastern Region', *European Politics and Society*, 17/ Supplement 1 'The Eurasian Project in Global Perspective' (2016), 67–81.

Korosteleva, Elena, Tom Casier, and Richard Whitman, 'Building a Stronger Eastern Partnership: Towards an EaP 2.0' (working paper, Global Europe Centre, University of Kent GEC policy paper, 2014).

Kotkin, Stephen, *Armageddon Averted: The Soviet Collapse 1970–2000* (Oxford: Oxford University Press, 2001).

'The Kiss of Debt. The East Bloc Goes Borrowing', in Niall Ferguson et al. (eds.), *Shock of the Global. The 1970s in Perspective* (Cambridge, MA: Harvard University Press, 2010), 80–93.

Uncivil Society: 1989 and the Implosion of the Communist Establishment (New York: Modern Library 2009).

Kovács, János Mátyás, 'Importing Spiritual Capital. East-West Encounters and Capitalist Cultures in Eastern Europe after 1989', in Peter Berger and Gordon Redding (eds.), *The Hidden Form of Capital. Spiritual Influences in Societal Progress* (London: Anthem Press, 2010), 133–69.

Kovács, János Mátyás and Violetta Zentai, 'Prologue', in Kovács and Zentai (eds.), *Capitalism from Outside? Economic Cultures in Eastern Europe after 1989* (Budapest: Central European University Press, 2012), 1–14.

Kowalski, Bartosz, 'China's Foreign Policy towards Central and Eastern Europe: The 16+1 Format in the South–South Cooperation Perspective. Cases of the

Czech Republic and Hungary', *Cambridge Journal of Eurasian Studies*, 1 (2017), www.veruscript.com/CJES/publications/china-s-foreign-policy-towards-the-cee-countries/?journalSlug=cambridge-journal-of-eurasian-studies.

Kramer, Mark, 'The Collapse of East European Communism and the Repercussions within the Soviet Union (Part 1)', *Journal of Cold War Studies*, 5/4 (2003), 178–256.

'The Decline in Soviet Arms Transfers to the Third World, 1986–1991', in Artemy Kalinovsky and Sergey Radchenko (eds.), *The End of the Cold War and The Third World: New Perspectives on Regional Conflict* (Abingdon: Routledge, 2011), 46–100.

'The Dynamics of Diffusion in the Soviet Bloc and the Impact on Regime Survival', in Martin K. Dimitrov (ed.), *Why Communism Did Not Collapse. Understanding Authoritarian Regime Resilience in Asia and Europe* (New York: Cambridge University Press, 2013), 149–81.

Krapfl, James, *Revolution with a Human Face: Politics, Culture, and Community in Czechoslovakia, 1989–1992* (Ithaca, NY: Cornell University Press, 2013).

Krastev, Ivan, *After Europe* (Philadelphia: University of Pennsylvania Press, 2017).

'The Global Politics of Protest', *IWM Post*, 113 (Spring/Summer 2014), 3–4.

The Inflexibility Trap: Frustrated Societies, Weak States and Democracy (Sofia: Centre for Liberal Strategies, 2002).

Krauze, Enrique, 'Diario de Praga', *Vuelta* 1 (1990), 17–21.

Krekó, Péter, 'The Vote on the Sargentini Report: Good News for Europe, Bad News for Orbán, No News for Hungary', *Heinrich Böll Stiftung*, 21 September 2018, https://eu.boell.org/en/2018/09/21/vote-sargentini-report-good-news-europe-bad-news-orban-no-news-hungary.

Krepp, Stella, 'A View from the South. The Falklands/Malvinas and Latin America', *Journal of Transatlantic Studies*, 15/4 (2017), 348–65.

Krzemiński, Ireneusz, 'Radio Maryja and Fr. Rydzyk as a Creator of the National-Catholic Ideology', in Sabrina Ramet and Irena Borowik (eds.), *Religion, Politics, and Values in Poland: Continuity and Change since 1989* (New York: Palgrave Macmillan, 2017), 85–112.

Kudaibergenova, Diana, 'The Use and Abuse of Postcolonial Discourses in Post-independent Kazakhstan', *Europe-Asia Studies*, 68/5 (2016), 917–35.

Kukliński, Antoni, 'The Geography of New Europe', *GeoJournal*, 30/4 (1993), 459–60.

Kuroń, Jacek and Krystyna Aytoun, 'Reflections on a Program of Action', *Polish Review*, 22/3 (1977), 51–69.

Kurspahić, Kemal, *Prime Time Crime: Balkan Media in War and Peace* (Washington, DC: US Institute of Peace Press, 2003).

Kuus, Merje, 'Europe's Eastern Expansion and the Reinscription of Otherness in East-Central Europe', *Progress in Human Geography*, 28/4 (2004), 472–89.

Geopolitics Reframed: Security and Identity in Europe's Eastern Enlargement (London: Palgrave Macmillan, 2007).

'"Love, Peace and NATO": Imperial Subject-Making in Central Europe', *Antipode*, 39/2 (2007), 269–90.

Labov, Jessie, 'A Russian Encounter with the Myth of Central Europe' (paper presented at 'Contours of Legitimacy in Central Europe: New Approaches in Graduate Studies', European Studies Centre, St. Antony's College, Oxford, 1988).

Laczó, Ferenc, 'Five Faces of Post-dissident Hungarian Liberalism: A Study in Agendas, Concepts, and Ambiguities', in Michal Kopeček and Piotr Wciślik (eds.), *Thinking through Transition: Liberal Democracy, Authoritarian Pasts, and Intellectual History in East Central Europe after 1989* (Budapest: Central European University Press, 2015), 39–72.

Laczó, Ferenc and Joanna Wawrzyniak, 'Memories of 1989 in Europe between Hope, Dismay, and Neglect', *East European Politics and Societies and Cultures*, 31/3 (2017), 431–38.

Ladányi, Éva and Erzsébet N. Rózsa, 'Hungary and the Arab Spring', 5 August 2014, www.grotius.hu/doc/pub/TKYIUP/2014-08-05_ladanyi_n.rozsa_hungary-and-the-arab-spring.pdf.

Laruelle, Marlène, *Russian Eurasianism: An Ideology of Empire* (Baltimore: Johns Hopkins University Press, 2012).

Laqueur, Walter, *Black Hundreds: The Rise of the Extreme Right in Russia* (New York: HarperCollins, 1993).

Lavelle, Ashley, *The Death of Social Democracy. Political Consequences in the 21st Century* (Aldershot: Ashgate, 2008).

Lebow, Katherine, Małgorzata Mazurek, and Joanna Wawrzyniak, 'Making Modern Social Science: The Global Imagination in East Central and Southeastern Europe after Versailles', *Contemporary European History*, 28/2 (2019), 137–42.

Lee, Hy-Sang, 'North Korea's Closed Economy. The Hidden Opening', *Asian Survey*, 28/12 (1988), 1264–79.

Leffler, Melvyn, 'Dreams of Freedom, Temptations of Power', in Jeffrey Engel (ed.), *The Fall of the Berlin Wall: The Revolutionary Legacy of 1989* (Oxford: Oxford University Press, 2012), 132–61.

'Le fossé démographique se creuse entre l'est et l'ouest de l'Europe', *Le Vif*, 22 June 2018, www.levif.be/actualite/international/le-fosse-demographique-se-creuse-entre-l-est-et-l-ouest-de-l-europe/article-normal-857547.html.

LeftEast Platform, www.criticatac.ro/lefteast/about/.

Lehmann, Maike, 'Apricot Socialism: The National Past, the Soviet Project, and the Imagining of Community in Late Soviet Armenia', *Slavic Review*, 74/1 (2015), 9–31.

Leonov, N., E. Fediakova, and J. Fermandois, 'El general Nikolai Leonov en el CEP', *Estudios Públicos* 73 (1999), 65–102.

Lepenies, Wolf, *The Seduction of Culture in German History* (Princeton, NJ: Princeton University Press, 2006).

'"Letter of Six," Making the History of 1989: Primary Sources', https://chnm.gmu.edu/1989/items/show/698.

Lévesque, Jacques, *The Enigma of 1989: The USSR and the Liberation of Eastern Europe* (Berkeley: University of California Press, 1997).

Li Peng, *Liu si ri ji zhen xiang* (Xianggang: Ao ya chu ban you xian gong si, 2010).

Liebich, André, 'Central Europe and the Refugees', *Tr@nsit Online*, 2 November 2015, www.iwm.at/read-listen-watch/transit-online/central-europe-refugees/.

Linz, Juan and Alfred Stepan, *Democratic Transitions and Consolidation: Eastern Europe, Southern Europe and Latin America* (Baltimore: Johns Hopkins University Press, 1996).

Łodziński, Sławomir, 'Foreigners in Poland. Selected Issues in Poland's Migrational Policy 1989–1998', *Polish Sociological Review*, 126 (1999), 301–21.

London, Jonathan, 'Vietnam and the Making of Market-Leninism', *Pacific Review*, 22/3 (2009), 375–99.

Lorenzini, Sara, 'Comecon and the South in the Years of Détente: A Study on East–South Economic Relations', *European Review of History*, 21/2 (2014), 183–99.

 'Globalising Ostpolitik', *Cold War History*, 9/2 (2009), 223–42.

Loth, Wilfred, *Building Europe: A History of European Unification* (Berlin: De Gruyter, 2015).

Loxley, John, 'The IMF, the World Bank and Sub-Saharan Africa: Policies and Politics', in Kjell J. Havenik (ed.), *The IMF and the World Bank in Africa. Conditionality, Impact and Alternatives* (Uppsala: Scandinavian Institute of African Studies, 1987), 47–63.

Lucic, Iva, *In Namen der Nation: Der politische Aufwertungsprozess der Muslime im sozialistischen Jugoslawien 1956–1971* (Wiesbaden: Harrassowitz Verlag, 2018).

Ludlow, Piers (ed.), *European Integration and the Cold War Ostpolitik–Westpolitik, 1965–1973* (London: Routledge, 2007).

Luif, Paul, 'Embargoes in East-West Trade and the European Neutrals: The Case of Austria', *Current Research on Peace and Violence*, 7/4 (1984), 221–28.

Ma Shaohua, *Dongou [Eastern Europe] 1989–1993* (Xi'an: Sha'anxi Renmin Jiaoyu Chubanshe, 1993).

Maier, Charles, 'What Have We Learned', *Contemporary European History*, 18/3 (2009), 253–69.

Maier, Valentin, 'Foreign Students Enrolled in the Medicine and Pharmacy Higher Education in Romania (1975–1989)', *Clujul Medical*, 89/2 (2016), 307–12.

Makai, György, *Today's Questions: What Are Arabs Fighting For?* (Budapest: Kossuth, 1971).

Malița, Mircea, 'Dimensiunea culturală a noii ordini economice internaționale', *Revista Comisie Naționale a RSR pentru UNESCO*, 19/1–2 (1977), 29–35.

Mälksoo, Lauri, 'The Soviet Approach to the Right of Peoples to Self-determination: Russia's Farewell to *jus publicum europaeum*', *Journal of the History of International Law*, 19/2 (2017), 200–218.

Mälksoo, Maria, 'Criminalizing Communism: Transnational Mnemopolitics in Europe', *International Political Sociology*, 8/1 (2014), 82–99.

 The Politics of Becoming European. A Study of Polish and Baltic Post-Cold War Security Imaginaries (London: Routledge, 2010).

Mandela, Nelson and Mandla Langa, *Dare Not Linger: The Presidential Years* (London: Macmillan, 2017).

Manela, Erez, *The Wilsonian Moment: Self-Determination and the Origins of Anticolonial Nationalism* (Oxford: Oxford University Press, 2007).

Mann, Michael, *The Dark Side of Democracy: Explaining Ethnic Cleansing* (Cambridge: Cambridge University Press, 2005).

Marchesi, Aldo, *Latin America's Radical Left. Rebellion and Cold War in the Global 1960s* (Cambridge: Cambridge University Press, 2017).

Mark, James, '"The Spanish Analogy": Imagining the Future in State Socialist Hungary, 1948–1989', *Contemporary European History*, 26/4 (2017), 600–620.

The Unfinished Revolution. Making Sense of the Communist Past in Central-Eastern Europe (New Haven, CT: Yale University Press, 2010).

Mark, James and Péter Apor, 'Socialism Goes Global: Decolonisation and the Making of a New Culture of Internationalism in Socialist Hungary, 1956–1989', *Journal of Modern History*, 87/4 (2015), 852–91.

Mark, James, Péter Apor, Radina Vučetić, and Piotr Osęka, '"We Are with You, Vietnam": Transnational Solidarities in Socialist Hungary, Poland and Yugoslavia', *Journal of Contemporary History*, 50/3 (2015), 439–64.

Mark, James and Yakov Feygin, 'The Soviet Union, Eastern Europe and Alternative Visions of a Global Economy 1950s–1980s', in James Mark, Artemy Kalinovsky, and Steffi Marung (eds.), *Alternative Globalizations: Eastern Europe and the Postcolonial World* (Bloomington: Indiana University Press, 2020).

Mark, James, Artemy Kalinovsky, and Steffi Marung (eds.), 'Introduction – Alternative Globalizations: Eastern Europe and the Postcolonial World', in Mark, Kalinovsky, and Marung (eds.), *Alternative Globalizations: Eastern Europe and the Postcolonial World* (Bloomington: Indiana University Press, 2020).

Mark, James, Anna Saunders, Muriel Blaive, Adam Hudek, and Stanislaw Tyszka, '1989 after 1989: Remembering the end of State Socialism in East-Central Europe', in Michal Kopecek and Piotr Wciślik (eds.), *Thinking through Transition: Liberal Democracy, Authoritarian Pasts, and Intellectual History in East Central Europe after 1989* (Budapest/New York: Central European Press, 2015), 463–503.

Mark, James and Quinn Slobodian, 'Eastern Europe in the Global History of Decolonisation', in Martin Thomas and Andrew Thompson (eds.), *The Oxford Handbook of the Ends of Empire* (Oxford: Oxford University Press, 2018), 351–72.

Mark, James and Bálint Tolmár, 'From Heroes Square to the Textile Factory: Encountering Cuba in Socialist Hungary 1959–1990' (forthcoming).

Mark, James and Anna von der Goltz, 'Encounters', in Robert Gildea, James Mark, and Anette Warring (eds.), *Europe's 1968: Voices of Revolt* (Oxford: Oxford University Press, 2013), 132–63.

Marples, David and Frederick Mills (eds.), *Ukraine's Euromaidan: Analyses of a Civil Revolution* (Stuttgart: Ibidem Press, 2015).

Marung, Steffi, *Die wandernde Grenze. Die EU, Polen und der globale Wandel politischer Räume, 1990–2010* (Göttingen: Vandenhoeck & Ruprecht, 2013).

'Moving Borders and Competing Civilizing Missions. Germany, Poland and Ukraine in the Context of the EU's Eastern Enlargement', in Marc

Silberman, Karen E. Till, and Janet Ward (eds.), *Walls, Borders, Boundaries Spatial and Cultural Practices in Europe* (New York: Berghahn, 2012), 131–51.

Matusevich, Maxim, 'Probing the Limits of Internationalism: African Students Confront Soviet Ritual', *Anthropology of East Europe Review*, 27/2 (2009), 19–39.

'Testing the Limits of Soviet Internationalism. African Students in the Soviet Union', in Philip E. Muehlenbeck (ed.), *Race, Ethnicity and the Cold War* (Nashville: Vanderbilt University Press, 2012), 145–65.

Maxwell, Kenneth, 'Portugal's Revolution of the Carnations, 1974–75' in Adam Roberts and Timothy Garton-Ash (eds.), *Civil Resistance and Power Politics* (Oxford: Oxford University Press, 2009), 144–61.

Mayblin, Lucy, Aneta Piekut, and Gill Valentine, "Other" Posts in "Other" Places: Poland through a Postcolonial Lens?' *Sociology*, 50/1 (2016), 60–76.

Mazower, Mark, *Governing the World: The History of an Idea, 1815 to the Present* (New York: Penguin, 2013).

Medvedev, Roy, 'Politics after the Coup', *New Left Review* 189 (1991), 91–109.

Meisner, Maurice, *The Deng Xiaoping Era. An Inquiry Into the Fate of Chinese Socialism, 1978–1994* (New York: Hill & Wang, 1996).

Melenciu, Sorin, 'Klaus Iohannis Has Support in Brussels to Become President of the European Council in 2019', *Business Review*, 2 March 2018, http://business-review.eu/news/klaus-iohannis-has-support-in-brussels-to-become-President-of-the-european-council-in-2019-media-159807.

Mendelson, Sarah and John Glenn, *The Power and Limits of NGOs: A Critical Look at Building Democracy in Eastern Europe and Eurasia* (New York: Columbia University Press, 2002).

Menon, Nivedita and Aditya Nigam, *Power and Contestation: India since 1989* (London: Zed Books, 2007).

Mesa-Lago, Carmelo, 'Efectos económicos en Cuba del derrumbe del socialismo en la Unión Soviética y Europa Oriental', *Estudios Internacionales*, 26/103 (1993), 341–414.

Michail, Eugene, 'Western Attitudes to War in the Balkans and the Shifting Meanings of Violence, 1912–91', *Journal of Contemporary History*, 47/2 (2012), 219–39.

Michnik, Adam, *Letters from Freedom. Post–Cold War Realities and Perspectives* (Berkeley: University of California Press, 1998).

Letters from Prison and Other Essays (Berkeley: University of California Press, 1985).

Migani, Guia, 'The EEC and the Challenge of ACP States' Industrialisation, 1972–1975', in Christian Grabas and Alexander Nützenadel (eds.), *Industrial Policy in Europe after 1945: Wealth, Power and Economic Development in the Cold War* (London: Palgrave Macmillan, 2014), 256–76.

'Lomé and the North-South Relations (1975–1984): From the "New International Economic Order" to a New Conditionality', in Claudia Hiepel (ed.), *Europe in a Globalising World: Global Challenges and European Responses in the 'Long' 1970s* (Baden-Baden: Nomos, 2014), 123–45.

Migranjan, A., 'Avtoritarizm – mechta dlja nas', *Latinskaja Amerika*, 1 (1990), 44–50.

Mihailović, S., et al., *Deca krize: Omladina Jugoslavije krajem osamdesetih* (Beograd: Institut društvenih nauka/Centar za politikološka istraživanja i javno mnenje, 1990).

Miller, Brenna, 'Between Faith and Nation: Defining Bosnian Muslims in Tito's Yugoslavia, 1945–1980' (PhD thesis, Ohio State University, 2018).

'Faith and Nation: Politicians, Intellectuals and the Official Recognition of a Muslim Nation in Tito's Yugoslavia', in Theodora Dragostinova and Yana Hashamova (eds.), *Beyond Mosque, Church, and State: Alternative Narratives of the Nation in the Balkans* (Budapest: Central European University Press, 2016), 129–50.

'The Islamic Religious Community in Socialist Yugoslavia's International Relations Program (1950s and 1960s)' (paper presented at '(Re)thinking Yugoslav Internationalism', University of Graz, 30 September–1 October 2016).

Miller, Chris, *The Struggle to Save the Soviet Economy: Mikhail Gorbachev and the Collapse of the USSR* (Chapel Hill: University of North Carolina Press, 2016).

Miller, Laurel, Jeffrey Martini, Stephen Larrabee, Angel Rabasa, Stephanie Pezard, Julie Taylor, and Tewodaj Mengistu, *Democratisation in the Arab World: Prospects and Lessons from Around the Globe* (Santa Monica, CA: Rand Corporation, 2012).

Miller, Nick, 'Where Was the Serbian Havel?', in Vladimir Tismaneanu and Bogdan C. Iacob (eds.), *The End and the Beginning: The Revolutions of 1989 and the Resurgence of History* (Budapest: Central European University Press, 2012), 363–79.

Mink, Georges and Jean-Charles Szurek, *La grande conversion: Le destin des communistes en Europe de l'Est* (Paris: Seuil, 1999).

Mishkova, Diana, *Beyond Balkanism: The Scholarly Politics of Region Making* (London: Routledge, 2018).

Mishkova, Diana, Bo Strath, and Balázs Trencsényi, 'Regional History as a "Challenge" to National Frameworks of Historiography: The Case of Central, Southeast, and Northern Europe', in Matthias Middell and Luis Roura (eds.), *Transnational Challenges to National History Writing* (New York: Palgrave Macmillan, 2013), 257–314.

Mitrevska, Marina and Nano Ruzhin, 'Geopolitics of the Western Balkans: An Area of Geopolitical Competition of the Great Powers', *Contemporary Macedonian Defence*, 18/34 (2018), 21–35.

Mitrochin, Nikolaj, *Die 'Russische Partei'. Die Bewegung der russischen Nationalisten in der UdSSR 1953–1985* (Stuttgart: Ibidem-Verlag, 2014).

Mitrovits, Miklós, 'From the Idea of Self-Management to Capitalism. The Characteristics of the Polish Transformation Process', *Debatte. Journal of Contemporary Central and Eastern Europe* 18/2 (2010), 163–84.

Močnik, Rastko, *Koliko Fašizma?* (Zagreb: Arkzin, 1998).

Modzelewski, Karol, *Quelle voie après le communisme?* (Paris: Éditions de l'Aube, 1995).

Moeller, Robert, *War Stories: The Search for a Usable Past in the Federal Republic of Germany* (Berkeley: University of California Press, 2003).

Mong, Attila, *Kádár hitele. A magyar államadósság története 1956–1990* (Budapest: Libri, 2012).

Morató, Xavier Cuadras (ed.), *Catalonia: A New Independent State in Europe? A Debate on Secession within the European Union* (London: Routledge, 2016).

Moreh, Chris, 'The Asianisation of National Fantasies in Hungary: A Critical Analysis of Political Discourse', *International Journal of Cultural Studies*, 13 March 2015, http://ics.sagepub.com/content/early/2015/03/12/1367877915573781.refs.

Mortkowitz, Siegfried, 'Czech President under Fire for Skipping Prague Spring Commemoration', *Politico*, 21 August 2018, www.politico.eu/article/Miloš-zeman-skips-prague-spring-commemoration/.

Motes, Mary, *Kosova, Kosovo: Prelude to War 1966–1999* (Homestead, FL: Redline, 1999).

Mrożek, Sławomir, 'To the Deeply Revered United Nations', reproduced in *A Dél-Afrikai Magyar Egyesület Lapja*, 4/2 (June 1986), 12.

Ucieczka na poludnie (Warsaw: Iskry, 1961).

Mudde, Cas, 'Local Shocks. The Far Right in the 2014 European Elections', *Eurozine*, 13 March 2015, www.eurozine.com/articles/2015-03-13-mudde-en.html.

'The Populist Zeitgeist', *Government and Opposition*, 39/3 (2004), 541–63.

Müller, Jan-Werner, 'Should the EU Protect Democracy and the Rule of Law inside Member States?', *European Law Journal*, 21/2 (2015), 141–60.

Müller, Martin, 'In Search of the Global East: Thinking between North and South', *Geopolitics* (2018), www.tandfonline.com/doi/full/10.1080/14650045.2018.1477757.

Murgescu, Bogdan, *România și Europa. Acumularea decalajelor economice (1500–2010)* (București: Polirom, 2010).

Murgescu, Costin (ed.), *Criza economică mondială* (București: Editura științifică, 1986).

Musić, Goran, '"They Came as Workers and Left as Serbs": The Role of Rakovica's Blue-Collar Workers in Serbian Social Mobilisations of the late 1980s', in Rory Archer, Igor Duda, and Paul Stubbs (eds.), *Social Inequalities and Discontent in Yugoslav Socialism* (London: Routledge, 2016), 132–54.

Mustapha, Jennifer, 'The Mujahideen in Bosnia: The Foreign Fighter as Cosmopolitan Citizen and/or Terrorist', *Citizenship Studies*, 17/6–7 (2013), 742–55.

Naughton, Barry, *Growing Out of the Plan. Chinese Economic Reform 1978–1993* (Cambridge: Cambridge University Press, 1995).

Nduka-Eze, Fatima, *Joe Garba's Legacy: Thirty-Two Selected Speeches and Lectures* (New York: Xlibris Corporation, 2012).

Nekola, Martin, 'The Assembly of Captive European Nations: A Transnational Organisation and a Tool of Anti-communist Propaganda', in Luc van Dongen, Stephanie Roulin, and Giles Scott-Smith (eds.), *Transnational Anti-communism and the Cold War: Agents, Activities, and Networks* (Basingstoke: Palgrave Macmillan, 2014), 96–112.

Neumann, Iver, *Russia and the Idea of Europe: A Study in Identity and International Relations* (London: Routledge, 1996).

Uses of the Other (Minneapolis: University of Minnesota Press, 1998).

Neumayer, Laure, 'Advocating for the Cause of the "Victims of Communism" in the European Political Space: Memory Entrepreneurs in Interstitial Fields', *Nationalities Papers*, 45/6 (2017), 992–1012.

The Criminalisation of Communism in the European Political Space after the Cold War (New York: Routledge, 2019).

'Integrating the Central European Past into a Common Narrative: The Mobilisations Around the "Crimes of Communism" in the European Parliament', *Journal of Contemporary European Studies*, 23/3 (2015), 344–63.

Nifontov, Vadim, 'Augusto Pinočet i ego rol' v russkoj istorii', 11 December 2006, www.apn.ru/%20publications/article11121.htm.

'Nikolić poklonio Si Đinpingu fotografiju, danas dobija orden', *N1*, 18 June 2016, http://rs.n1info.com/Vesti/a169734/Nikolic-poklonio-Si-Djinpingu-fotografiju.html.

Nunan, Timothy, 'Getting Reacquainted with the "Muslims of the USSR": Staging Soviet Islam in Turkey and Iran, 1978–1982', *Ab Imperio*, 4 (2011), 133–71.

Humanitarian Invasion: Global Development in Cold War Afghanistan (Cambridge: Cambridge University Press, 2016).

Nyíri, Pál, 'Chinese Migration to Eastern Europe', *International Migration*, 41/3 (1/2003), 239–65.

Obadic, Ivan, 'A Troubled Relationship: Yugoslavia and the European Economic Community in Détente', *European Review of History*, 21/2 (2014), 329–48.

Obasanjo, Olusegun and Hans d'Orville (eds.), *The Impact of Europe in 1992 on West Africa* (New York: C. Russak, 1990).

O'Donnell, Guillermo and Philippe Schmitter (eds.), *Transitions from Authoritarianism: Comparative Perspectives* (Baltimore: Johns Hopkins University Press, 1986).

Oh, Kong Dan, 'North Korea in 1989. Touched by Winds of Change?', *Asian Survey*, 30/1 (1990), 74–80.

Ojo, Oladeji, 'Introduction', in Ojo (ed.), *Africa and Europe. The Changing Economic Relationship* (London: Zed Books, 1996), 1–9.

Ojo, Oladeji and Christopher Stevens, 'Recent Changes in the Former Soviet Union and Eastern Europe: Opportunities and Challenges for Africa', in Oladeji Ojo (ed.), *Africa and Europe. The Changing Economic Relationship* (London: Zed Books, 1996), 141–142.

Olsen, Gorm, 'The European Union: An Ad Hoc Policy with a Low Priority', in Peter Schraeder (ed.), *Exporting Democracy: Rhetoric vs. Reality* (Boulder, CO: Lynne Rienner, 2002), 131–46.

Omerika, Armina, 'Competing National Orientalisms: The Cases of Belgrade and Sarajevo', in Artemy Kalinovsky and Martin Kemper, *Reassessing Orientalism: Interlocking Orientologies during the Cold War* (New York: Routledge, 2015), 153–69.

'Opyt Latinskoj Ameriki – na sluzhbu Rossii', *Latinskaja Amerika* 7/12 (1993).

'The Orbán Regime Feels Threatened by Gender Studies', *Hungarian Spectrum*, 10 August 2018, http://hungarianspectrum.org/2018/08/10/the-orban-regime-feels-threatened-by-gender-studies/.

Osiatynski, Wiktor, 'Revolutions in Eastern Europe', *University of Chicago Law Review*, 58/2 (1991), 823–58.

Ost, David, 'The Consequences of Postcommunism. Trade Unions in Eastern Europe's Future', *East European Politics and Societies*, 23/1 (2009), 14–19.

Defeat of Solidarity. Anger and Politics in Postcommunist Europe (Ithaca, NY: Cornell University Press, 2006).

Packham, Eric, *Africa in War and Peace* (New York: Nova Science, 2004).

Paczkowski, Andrzej, 'Twenty-Five Years "After": The Ambivalence of Settling Accounts with Communism: The Polish Case', in Vladimir Tismaneanu and Bogdan C. Iacob (eds.), *Remembrance, History, and Justice: Coming to Terms with Traumatic Pasts in Democratic Societies* (Budapest: Central European University Press, 2015), 239–55.

Palairet, Michael, 'The Inter-regional Struggle for Resources and the Fall of Yugoslavia', in Lenard J. Cohen and Jasna Dragović-Soso (eds.), *State Collapse in South-eastern Europe: New Perspectives on Yugoslavia's Disintegration* (West Lafayette, IN: Purdue University Press, 2008), 221–48.

Pap, András, *Democratic Decline in Hungary: Law and Society in an Illiberal Democracy* (London: Routledge, 2017).

Papastamkou, Sofia, 'Greece between Europe and the Mediterranean, 1981–1986. The Israeli-Palestinian Conflict and the Greek-Libyan Relations as Case Studies', *Journal of European Integration History*, 21/1 (2015), 49–69.

Pavlićević, Dragan, '"China Threat" and "China Opportunity": Politics of Dreams and Fears in China-Central and Eastern European Relations', *Journal of Contemporary China*, 27/113 (2018), 688–702.

Pavlović, Momčilo, 'Kosovo under Autonomy, 1974– 1990', in Charles W. Ingrao and Thomas Allan Emmert (eds.), *Confronting the Yugoslav Controversies: A Scholars' Initiative* (West Lafayette, IN: Purdue University Press, 2009), 48–82.

Peck, Jamie, *Offshore: Exploring the Worlds of Global Outsourcing* (Oxford: Oxford University Press, 2017).

Perczyński, Maciej, 'Global Determinants of East-South Relations', in Pawel Bożyk (ed.), *Global Challenges and East European Responses* (Warsaw: Polish Scientific Publishers, 1988), 309–25.

Perju, Vlad, 'Cazul UE împotriva României – Ce urmează după Raportul MCV', *Contributors.ro*, 16 November 2018, www.contributors.ro/editorial/cazul-ue-impotriva-romaniei-%E2%80%93-ce-urmeaza-dupa-raportul-mcv/.

Péteri, György, 'Introduction', in Péteri (ed.), *Imagining the West in Eastern Europe and the Soviet Union* (Pittsburgh: University of Pittsburgh Press, 2010), 1–12.

Petrescu, Cristina, *From Robin Hood to Don Quixote: Resistance and Dissent in Communist Romania* (București: Editura Enciclopedică, 2013).

Petrović, Tanja, 'Images of Europe and the Process of the West Balkans Countries' Association to the European Union', in Olga Gyarfasova and Karin Liebhart (eds.), *Constructing and Communicating Europe* (Zürich: LIT, 2014), 121–44.

(ed.), *Mirroring Europe. Ideas of Europe and Europeanisation in Balkan Societies* (Leiden: Brill, 2014).

Pettai, Vello, 'Estonia and Latvia: International Influences on Citizenship and Minority Integration', in Jan Zielonka and Alex Pravda (eds.), *Democratic Consolidation in Eastern Europe, Volume 2: International and Transnational Factors* (Oxford: Oxford University Press, 2001), 257–80.

Pew Research Center, 'End of Communism Cheered but Now with More Reservations' (2009). www.pewglobal.org/2009/11/02/end-of-communism-cheered-but-now-with-more-reservations/.

Pfaff, Steven, *Exit-Voice Dynamics and the Collapse of East Germany: The Crisis of Leninism and the Revolution of 1989* (Durham, NC: Duke University Press, 2006).

Pichler, Peter, 'A "Handmade" Historiographical Myth: The "East" and Eastern Europe in the Historiography of European Integration, 1968 to the Present', *History*, 103/356 (2018), 505–19.

Pieper Mooney, Jadwiga, 'East Germany: Chilean Exile and the Politics of Solidarity in the Cold War', in Kim Christiaens, Idesbald Goddeeris, and Magaly Rodríguez García (eds.), *European Solidarity with Chile 1970s–1980s* (Frankfurt am Main: Peter Lang, 2014), 275–300.

Pinkert, Anke, '"Postcolonial Legacies": The Rhetoric of Race in the East/West German National Identity Debate of the Late 1990s', *Journal of the Midwest Modern Language Association*, 35/2 (2002), 13–32.

Plamper, Jan, 'Foucault's Gulag', *Kritika: Explorations in Russian and Eurasian History*, 3/2 (2002), 255–80.

Pluchinsky, Dennis, 'Political Terrorism in Western Europe: Some Themes and Variations', in Yonah Alexander and Kenneth Myers (eds.), *Terrorism in Europe* (London: Routledge, 1982/2015), 40–78.

'Poland's Independence Turned Violent', *BBC News*, 11 November 2014, www.bbc.com/news/world-europe-30012830.

Pons, Silvio, *The Global Revolution. A History of International Communism 1917–1991* (Oxford: Oxford University Press, 2014).

'Western Communists, Mikhail Gorbachev and the 1989 Revolutions', *Contemporary European History*, 18/3 (2009), 349–62.

Pons, Silvio and Michele di Donato, 'Reform Communism', in Juliane Fürst, Silvio Pons, and Mark Selden (eds.), *The Cambridge History of Communism. Volume 3: Endgames? Late Communism in Global Perspective, 1968 to the Present* (Cambridge: Cambridge University Press, 2017), 178–202.

Pop, Doru, 'Misrepresentation of Muslims and Islamophobic Public Discourses in Recent Romanian Media Narratives', *Journal for the Study of Religions and Ideologies*, 44 (2016), 33–51.

Poppe, Eberhard, 'Self-Determination of the Germans and the Enforcement of Human Rights in the German Democratic Republic', in *Self-determination and Human Rights: 1968 Results in the Two German States* (Berlin: Committee for the Protection of Human Rights, 1968), 11–30.

Porter, Tom, 'The Christian Right Is Looking to Putin's Russia to Save Christianity from the Godless West', *Newsweek*, 15 September 2018, www.newsweek.com/how-evangelicals-are-looking-putins-russia-save-christianity-godless-west-1115164.

Pospieszna, Paulina, *Democracy Assistance from the Third Wave: Polish Engagement in Belarus and Ukraine* (Pittsburgh: University of Pittsburgh Press, 2014).

'Proglas na Edinstvena Makedonija za radikalen presvrt vo makedonskata politika – členstvo vo Evroaziskata Ekonomska Unija i strateško partnerstvo so Rusija', *Edinstvena Makedonija* [United Macedonia], http://edinstvenamakedonija.mk/wp-content/uploads/2018/06/proglas-edinstvena-makedonija.pdf.

Przetacznik, Franciszek, 'The Socialist Concept of Protection of Human Rights', *Social Research*, 38/2 (1971), 337–61.

Przeworski, Adam, *Democracy and the Market. Political and Economic Reforms in Eastern Europe and Latin America* (Cambridge: Cambridge University Press, 1991).

'The "East" Becomes the "South"? The "Autumn of the People" and the Future of Eastern Europe', *Political Science and Politics*, 24/1 (March 1991), 20–24.

Przybylski, Wojciech, 'Can Poland's Backsliding Be Stopped?', *Journal of Democracy*, 29/3 (2018), 52–64.

Pula, Besnik, *Globalization Under and After Socialism: The Evolution of Transnational Capital in Central and Eastern Europe* (Stanford, CA: Stanford University Press, 2018).

Půlpán, Karel, *Economic Development of Spain as Inspiration for the Czech Republic* (Stockholm: Institute of Economic Studies, 2001).

Quist-Adade, Charles, 'From Paternalism to Ethnocentrism: Images of Africa in Gorbachev's Russia', *Race and Class*, 46/4 (2005), 79–89.

Radchenko, Sergey, *Unwanted Visionaries: The Soviet Failure in Asia at the End of the Cold War* (Oxford: Oxford University Press, 2014).

Radu, Roxana, 'After a Violent Revolution: Romanian Democratisation in the Early 1990s', *Central European Journal of International and Security Studies*, 7/1 (2013), 1–21.

Rahr, Alexander, *Wladimir Putin: Der Deutsche im Kreml* (Tübingen: Universitas, 2000).

Rakowski, Mieczysław, *Dzienniki polityczne 1987–1990* (Warszawa: ISKRY, 2005).

Ramet, Sabrina, 'Islam in Yugoslavia Today', *Religion, State and Society*, 18/3 (1990), 226–35.

Nationalism and Federalism in Yugoslavia, 1962–1991 (Bloomington: Indiana University Press, 1992).

Ramšak, Jure, '"Neodvisna Slovenija do konca leta 1964!" Kritika položaja Slovenije v Jugoslaviji in zgodnje ideje o samostojnosti', in Mitja Ferenc, Jurij Hadalin, and Blaž Babič (eds.), *Osamosvojitev 1991: država in demokracija na Slovenskem v zgodovinskih razsežnostih'* (Ljubljana: Univerza v Ljubljani, 2011), 197–208.

Randall, Vicky, 'The Media and Democratisation in the Third World', *Third World Quarterly*, 14/3 (1993), 625–46.

Rein, Gerhard (ed.), *Die Protestantische Revolution, 1987–1990* (Berlin: Wichern-Verlag, 1990).

Renwick, Alan, 'Anti-political or Just Anti-communist? Varieties of Dissidence in East-Central Europe and Their Implications for the Development of Political Society', *East European Politics and Societies*, 20/2 (2006), 286–318.

'Report of Poland's EU Presidency', http://pl2011.eu/sites/default/files/users/shared/spotkania_i_wydarzenia/raportue_eng_final.pdf.

Resler, Tamara, 'The United States and Central Europe: Principles and Pragmatism in the Evolving Partnership', in Zlatko Šabič and Petr Drulák (eds.), *Regional and International Relations of Central Europe* (New York: Palgrave Macmillan, 2012), 145–61.

'Resolution ES-6/2', in *Security Council Report*, www.securitycouncilreport.org/atf/cf/%7B65BFCF9B-6D27-4E9C-8CD3-CF6E4FF96FF9%7D/Afgh%20ARESES6%202.pdf.

Rév, István, 'Parallel Autopsies', *Representations*, 49 (Winter 1995), 15–39.

Retroactive Justice: Prehistory of Post-communism (Stanford, CA: Stanford University Press, 2005).

Rexhepi, Piro, 'Mainstreaming Islamophobia: The Politics of European Enlargement and the Balkan Crime-Terror Nexus', *East European Quarterly*, 43/2–3 (2015), 189–214.

'Unmapping Islam in Eastern Europe. Periodisation and Muslim Subjectivities in the Balkans', in Irene Kacandes and Yuliya Komska (eds.), *Eastern Europe Unmapped. Beyond Borders and Peripheries* (Oxford: Berghahn, 2017), 53–78.

Richardson-Little, Ned, 'Dictatorship and Dissent: Human Rights in East Germany in the 1970s', in Jan Eckel and Samuel Moyn (eds.), *The Breakthrough: Human Rights in the 1970s* (Philadelphia: University of Pennsylvania Press, 2013), 49–67.

'The Failure of the Socialist Declaration of Human Rights: Ideology, Legitimacy, and Elite Defection at the End of State Socialism, 1981–1991', *East Central Europe* (forthcoming).

'Human Rights as Myth and History: Between the Revolutions of 1989 and the Arab Spring', *Journal of Contemporary Central and Eastern Europe*, 23/2–3 (2015), 151–66.

'Lawyers, Human Rights, and Democratization in Eastern Europe' (paper presented at 'Revolution from Within. Experts, Managers and Technocrats in the Long Lawyers, Human Rights and Democratisation in Eastern Europe', Jena, 14–15 June 2018).

Rigg, Jonathan, *Living with Transition in Laos. Market Integration in South-East Asia* (London: Routledge, 2005).

Rinser, Luise, *Nordkoreanisches Reisetagebuch* (Frankfurt am Main: Fischer-Taschenbuch-Verlag, 1981).

Robinson, Pearl T., 'The National Conference Phenomenon in Francophone Africa', *Comparative Studies in Society and History*, 36/3 (1994), 575–610.

Rodt, Annemarie Peen and Stefan Wolff, 'EU Conflict Management in Bosnia and Herzegovina and Macedonia', in Richard G. Whitman and Stefan Wolff (eds.), *The European Union as a Global Conflict Manager* (London: Routledge, 2012), 138–52.

Romano, Angela and Federico Romero, 'European Socialist Regimes Facing Globalisation and European Co-operation: Dilemmas and Responses. Introduction', *European Review of History*, 21/2 (2014), 157–64.

Rother, Bernd, 'Die SPD und El Salvador 1979 bis 1985. Linke Politik im atlantischen Dreieck von Bundesrepublik, Zentralamerika und USA', *Vierteljahreshefte für Zeitgeschichte*, 1 (2019), 645–68.

Roy, Olivier, 'The Arab Four Seasons. When an Excess of Religion Leads to Political Secularisation', in Jacques Rupnik (ed.), *1989 as a Political World Event. Democracy. Europe and the New International System in the Age of Globalisation* (London: Routledge, 2007), 111–26.

Rupnik, Jacques, 'The Post-Totalitarian Blues', *Journal of Democracy*, 6/2 (1995), 61–73.

'Totalitarianism Revisited', in John Keane (ed.), *Civil Society and the State: European Perspectives* (London: Verso, 1988), 263–89.

Rupprecht, Tobias, 'Formula Pinochet. Chilean Lessons for Russian Liberal Reformers during the Soviet Collapse, 1970–2000', *Journal of Contemporary History*, 51/1 (2016), 165–86.

'Gestrandetes Flaggschiff: Die Moskauer Universität der Völkerfreundschaft', *Osteuropa*, 1 (2010), 95–114.

Soviet Internationalism after Stalin: Interaction and Exchange between the USSR and Latin America during the Cold War (Cambridge: Cambridge University Press, 2015).

Rus, Alin, *Mineriadele: Între manipulare politică și solidaritate muncitorească* (București: Curtea Vehce, 2007).

Ryall, Julian, 'Polish Firms Employing North Korean "Slave Labourers" Benefit from EU Aid', *Telegraph*, 31 May 2016, www.telegraph.co.uk/news/2016/05/31/polish-firms-employing-north-korean-slave-labourers-benefit-from/.

Šabič, Zlatko and Petr Drulák, 'Introduction to "Central Europe"', in Šabič and Drulák (eds.), *Regional and International Relations of Central Europe* (New York: Palgrave Macmillan, 2012), 1–17.

Sachs, Jeffrey, *The End of Poverty. Economic Possibilities of Our Time* (New York: Penguin, 2006),

Poland's Jump to the Market Economy (Cambridge, MA: MIT Press, 1993).

Sadurski, Wojciech, *Rights before Courts. A Study of Constitutional Courts in Post-communist States of Central and Eastern Europe* (Dordrecht: Springer, 2008).

Sahadeo, Jeff, '"Black Snouts Go Home": Migration and Race in Late Soviet Leningrad and Moscow', *Journal of Modern History*, 88/4 (2016), 797–826.

Sakwa, Richard, 'How the Eurasian Elites Envisage the Role of the EEU in Global Perspective', *European Politics and Society*, 17/Supplement 1 (2016), 4–22.

Samokhvalov, Vsevolod, 'What Kind of "Other"? Identity and Russian–European Security Interaction in Eurasia', *Europe-Asia Studies*, 70/5 (2018), 791–813.

Sang-Woo, Rhee, 'North Korea in 1990: Lonesome Struggle to Keep Chuch'e', *Asian Survey*, 31/1 (1991), 71–78.

Sarotte, Mary Elise, 'China's Fear of Contagion. Tiananmen Square and the Power of the European Example', *Quarterly Journal: International Security*, 37/2 (2012), 156–82.

Collapse: The Accidental Opening of the Berlin Wall (New York: Basic Books, 2014).

1989: The Struggle to Create Post–Cold War Europe (Princeton, NJ: Princeton University Press, 2014).

Saunders, Chris, 'The Ending of the Cold War and Southern Africa', in Artemy Kalinovsky and Sergey Radchenko (eds.), *The End of the Cold War and the Third World: New Perspectives of Regional Conflict* (London: Routledge, 2011), 264–76.

'"1989" and Southern Africa', in Ulf Engel, Frank Hadler and Matthias Middell, (eds.), *1989 in a Global Perspective* (Leipzig: Leipziger Universitätsverlag, 2015), 349–61.

Savranskaya, Svetlana, 'Gorbachev and the Third World', in Artemy Kalinovsky and Sergey Radchenko (eds.), *The End of the Cold War and The Third World: New Perspectives on Regional Conflict* (London: Routledge, 2011), 21–45.

Sawkins, Isabel, 'Russia's Nationalist Mobilisation of the Holocaust on the Screen: Khabensky's film *Sobibor* (2018)' (paper presented at 'A Crisis in "Coming to Terms with the Past"? At the Crossroads of Translation and Memory', London, February 2019).

Saxer, Carl, 'Democratic Transition and Institutional Crafting: The South Korean Case', *Democratisation*, 10/2 (2003), 45–64.

Sayyid, Salman, 'Islamophobia and the Europeanness of the Other Europe', *Patterns of Prejudice*, 52/5 (2018), 420–35.

Scarborough, Isaac, 'From February to February and From Ru ba Ru to Rastokhez: Political Mobilisation in Late Soviet Tajikistan (1989–1990)', *Cahiers d'Asie centrale*, 26 (2016), 143–71.

Šćepanović, Vera and Dorothee Bohle, 'The Institutional Embeddedness of Transnational Corporations: Dependent Capitalism in Central and Eastern Europe', in Andreas Nölke and Christian May (eds.), *Handbook of the International Political Economy of the Corporation* (Northampton, MA: Edward Elgar, 2018), 152–66.

Schaefer, Bernd, 'Socialist Modernisation in Vietnam: The East German Approach, 1976–1989', in Quinn Slobodian (ed.), *Comrades of Color: East Germany in the Cold War World* (New York: Berghahn, 2015), 95–114.

Schimmelfennig, Frank and Ulrich Sedelmeier, 'Conceptualizing the Europeanisation of Central and Eastern Europe', in Schimmelfennig and Sedelmeier (eds.), *The Europeanisation of Central and Eastern Europe* (Ithaca, NY: Cornell University Press, 2005), 1–11.

'The Europeanisation of Eastern Europe: the External Incentives Model Revisited' (paper presented at the Jean Monnet Fellowship @25 Alumni Conference, Florence, 22–23 June 2017), www.eui.eu/Documents/RSCAS/JMF-25-Presentation/Schimmelfennig-Sedelmeier-External-Incentives-Revisited-JMF.pdf.

The Politics of European Union Enlargement: Theoretical Approaches (London: Routledge 2005).

Schlosser, Nicholas J., *Cold War on the Airwaves. The Radio Propaganda War against East Germany* (Urbana: University of Illinois Press, 2015).

Schmidt, Andrea, 'Friends Forever? The Role of the Visegrad Group and European Integration', *Politics in Central Europe*, 12/3 (2016), 113–40.

Schneider, Peter, *The Wall Jumper* (London: Pantheon Books, 1985).

Schraeder, Peter, 'Promoting an International Community of Democracies', in Schraeder (ed.), *Exporting Democracy: Rhetoric vs. Reality* (Boulder, CO: Lynne Rienner, 2002), 1–13.

Schwenkel, Christina, 'Rethinking Asian Mobilities. Socialist Migration and Post-socialist Repatriation of Vietnamese Contract Workers in East Germany', *Critical Asian Studies*, 46/2 (2014), 235–58.

Sedelmeier, Ulrich, 'Anchoring Democracy from Above? The European Union and Democratic Backsliding in Hungary and Romania after Accession', *Journal of Common Market Studies*, 52/1 (2014), 105–21.

Sells, Michael A., *The Bridge Betrayed: Religion and Genocide in Bosnia* (Berkeley: University of California Press, 1998).

Sharkov, Damien, 'Poland Makes Big U-Turn on Holocaust Death Camps Law', *Newsweek*, 27 June 2018, www.newsweek.com/poland-makes-big-u-turn-holocaust-death-camps-law-998071.

Shekhovtsov, Anton, 'The No Longer Silent Counter-revolution', *Religion and Society in East and West*, 44 (2016), 9–10.

Shivji, Issa G., 'The Democracy Debate in Africa: Tanzania', *Review of African Political Economy*, 18/50 (1991), 79–91.

Shmelev, Nikolaj, *Ekonomicheskie sviazi Vostok-Zapad. Problemy i vozmozhnosti* (Moscow: Mysl', 1976).

Shore, Marci, *The Taste of Ashes. The Afterlife of Totalitarianism in Eastern Europe* (New York: Random House, 2013).

Sikorski, Radosław, *Dust of the Saints: A Journey to Herat in Time of War* (London: Chatto & Windus, 1989).

Sikorski, Radosław, 'The Polish Model: A Conversation with Radek Sikorski', *Foreign Affairs*, 93/2 (May/June 2013).

Simai, Mihály, 'The Emerging New Market Economies and the Evolving New Democracies in Central and Eastern Europe', in Üner Kirdar (ed.), *Change: Threat or Opportunity to Human Progress? Volume 1: Political Change* (New York: United Nations, 1992), 225–48.

Sizoo, Johannes and Rudolph Th. Jurrjens, *CSCE Decision-Making: The Madrid Experience* (The Hague: Martinus Nijhoff, 1984).

Sjursen, Helene, 'Enlargement and Identity: Studying Reasons', in Haakon Ikonomou, Aurélie Andry, and Rebekka Byberg (eds.), *European Enlargement across Rounds and beyond Borders* (New York: Routledge, 2017), 57–74.

Slapšak, Svetlana (ed.), *The War Started at Maksimir: Hate Speech in the Media* (Belgrade: Media Center, 1997).

Slaughter, Joseph, 'Hijacking Human Rights: Neoliberalism, the New Historiography, and the End of the Third World', *Human Rights Quarterly*, 40/4 (2018), 735–75.

Slobodian, Quinn, 'China Is Not Far! Alternative Internationalism and the Tiananmen Square Massacre in East Germany's 1989', in Artemy Kalinovsky, James Mark, and Steffi Marung (eds.), *Alternative Globalizations: Eastern Europe and the Postcolonial World* (Bloomington: Indiana University Press, 2020).

Smith, Shane, 'North Korean Labor Camps in Siberia', *CNN*, 15 December 2011, https://edition.cnn.com/2011/12/15/world/asia/north-korean-labor-camps-in-siberia/index.html.

Snitko, Aleksandr, 'Skol'ko stoit naša sovest' v Latinskoj Amerike? Zametki ešče bolee neravnodušnye', *Latinskaja Amerika*, 4 (1991), 38–44.

Soboczynski, Adam, "The Communist Roots of Anti-Refugee Sentiment," *Public Seminar*, 22 March 2016, www.publicseminar.org/2016/03/the-communist-roots-of-anti-refugee-sentiment/#.VvGEc2SyOkp.

Solnick, Steven Lee, *Stealing the State: Control and Collapse in Soviet Institutions* (Cambridge, MA: Harvard University Press, 1998).

Somerville, K., 'Sub-Saharan Africa', in Alex Pravda (ed.), *Yearbook of Soviet Foreign Relations* (London: Tauris, 1991), 208–26.

Sommer, Vítězslav, 'Forecasting the Post-socialist Future: Prognostika in Late Socialist Czechoslovakia, 1970–1989', in Jenny Andersson and Eglė

Rindzevičiūtė (eds.), *The Struggle for the Long-Term in Transnational Science and Politics: Forging the Future* (New York: Routledge, 2015), 144–68.

Sonnevend, Julia, *Stories without Borders. The Berlin Wall and the Making of a Global Iconic Event* (New York: Oxford University Press, 2016).

Sosnowska, Anna, *Zrozumieć zacofanie. Spory historyków o Europę Wschodnią, 1947–1994* (Warszawa: Trio, 2004).

Spaskovska, Ljubica, 'The "Children of Crisis". Making Sense of (Post)socialism and the End of Yugoslavia', *East European Politics and Societies and Cultures*, 31/3, (2017), 500–517.

'Landscapes of Resistance, Hope and Loss: Yugoslav Supra-Nationalism and Anti-nationalism', in Bojan Bilić and Vesna Janković (eds.), *Resisting the Evil: [Post] Yugoslav Anti-war Contention* (Baden-Baden: Nomos, 2012), 37–62.

The Last Yugoslav Generation: The Rethinking of Youth Politics and Cultures in Late Socialism (Manchester: Manchester University Press, 2017).

'Společné prohlášení k situaci v Chile', *Informace o Chartě 77*, 10/7 (1987), 24–25, www.vons.cz/data/pdf/infoch/INFOCH_07_1987.pdf.

Spooner, Mary Helen, *The General's Slow Retreat: Chile after Pinochet* (Berkeley: University of California Press, 2011).

Springborg, Robert, 'Whither the Arab Spring? 1989 or 1848?', *International Spectator*, 46/3 (2011), 5–12.

Sridharan, Kripa, 'G-15 and South-South Cooperation: Promise and Performance', *Third World Quarterly*, 19/3 (1998), 357–73.

Stan, Marius and Vladimir Tismaneanu, 'Democracy under Siege in Romania', *Politico*, 21 August 2018, www.politico.eu/article/protest-piata-victoriei-bucharest-democracy-under-siege-in-romania/.

Stanciu, Cezar, 'Nicolae Ceaușescu and the Origins of Eurocommunism', *Communist and Post-Communist Studies*, 48/1 (2015), 83–95.

Staniszkis, Jadwiga, *The Dynamics of the Breakthrough in Eastern Europe* (Berkeley: University of California Press, 1991).

'"Political Capitalism" in Poland', *East European Politics and Societies*, 5/1 (1991), 127–141.

Steiner, André, 'The Globalisation Process and the Eastern Bloc Countries in the 1970s and 1980s', *European Review of History*, 21/2 (2014), 165–81.

Štiks, Igor, '"The Berlin Wall Crumbled Down upon Our Heads!": 1989 and Violence in the Former Socialist Multinational Federations', *Global Society*, 24/1 (2010), 91–110.

Štiks, Igor and Srećko Horvat (eds.), *Welcome to the Desert of Post-Socialism: Radical Politics After Yugoslavia* (London: Verso, 2015).

Štiks, Igor and Krunoslav Stojaković, 'Southeastern Europe's New Left', *Rosa Luxemburg Stiftung*, February 2019, www.rosalux.de/en/publikation/id/39943/#_ftn1.

Stojanov, Robert, Oldřich Bureš, and Barbora Duží, 'Migration and Development Policies: The State of Affairs before the 2015 European Migration Crises in the Czech Republic and Its Current Implications', *Communist and Post-communist Studies*, 50/3 (2017), 169–81.

Stokes, Gale, 'Purposes of the Past', in Vladimir Tismaneanu and Bogdan C. Iacob (eds.), *The End and the Beginning: The Revolutions of 1989 and the Resurgence of History* (Budapest: Central European University Press, 2012), 35–54.

The Walls Came Tumbling Down: The Collapse of Communism in Eastern Europe (New York: Oxford University Press, 1993).

Stola, Dariusz, 'Opening a Non-exit State: The Passport Policy of Communist Poland, 1949–1980', *East European Politics and Societies and Cultures*, 29/1 (2015), 96–119.

Stoner, Kathryn and Michael McFaul (eds.), *Transitions to Democracy: A Comparative Perspective* (Baltimore: Johns Hopkins University Press, 2013).

Storkmann, Klaus, *Geheime Solidarität: Militärbeziehungen und Militärhilfen der DDR in die 'Dritte Welt'* (Berlin: Christoph Links, 2012).

Stout, Jeffrey, 'Between Secularism and Theocracy. King, Michnik and the American Culture Wars', in Piotr Kosicki and Kyrill Kunakhovich (eds.), *The Legacy of 1989: Continuity and Discontinuity in a Quarter-Century of Global Revolution* (forthcoming).

Strauß, Franz-Josef, *Die Erinnerungen* (Berlin: Siedler, 1989).

Suarez, John, 'Cuban Dissidents on the Passing of Vaclav Havel', *Notes from the Cuban Exile Quarter*, 18 December 2011, http://cubanexilequarter.blogspot .com/2011/12/cuban-dissidents-on-passing-of-vaclav.html.

Suárez-Navaz, Liliana, 'Introduction', in *Rebordering the Mediterranean. Boundaries and Citizenship in Southern Europe* (Oxford: Berghahn Books 2004), 1–20.

Suba, Aron, 'Betting on the Eastern Model: The Cooperation between Hungary and China Is More about Politics Than Economics', 11 April 2018, http:// visegradinsight.eu/betting-on-the-Eastern-model/.

Sussman, Gerald and Sascha Krader, 'Template Revolutions: Marketing US Regime Change in Eastern Europe', *Westminster Papers in Communication and Culture*, 5/3 (2008), 91–112.

Szabó, Miklós, 'Egy tilalommal kevesebb, vagy egy elvtelenséggel több?', *Beszélő* 2/2 (1990), http://beszelo.c3.hu/print/2868.

Szacki, Jerzy, *Liberalism after Communism* (Budapest: Central European University Press, 1996).

Szakács, Eszter, 'Propaganda, Mon Amour. An Arab "World" through Hungarian Publications (1957–1989)', *Mezosfera*, May 2018, http://mezosfera.org/ propaganda-mon-amour/.

Szalontai, Balász, 'From Battlefield into Marketplace. The End of the Cold War in Indochina 1985–1989', in Artemy Kalinovsky and Sergey Radchenko (eds.), *The End of the Cold War and the Third World. New Perspectives on Regional Conflict* (New York: Routledge 2011), 155–72.

'The Path to the Establishment of Hungarian-South Korean Diplomatic Relations: The Soviet Bloc and the Republic of Korea, 1964–1987', *Cold War International History Project Bulletin*, 14/15 (2010), 87–103.

Szczerek, Ziemowit, 'New Separatisms: Or What Could Happen if the West Disappeared from Eastern Europe?', *New Eastern Europe* 3/4 (2018), http:// neweasterneurope.eu/2018/04/26/new-separatisms-happen-west-disappeared-eastern-europe/.

Szelényi, Iván, 'Eastern Europe in an Epoch of Transition: Toward a Socialist Mixed Economy?', in Victor Nee and David Stark (eds.), *Remaking the Economic Institutions of Socialism: China and Eastern Europe* (Stanford, CA: Stanford University Press, 1989), 208–32.

Szűcs, Jenő, 'The Three Historical Regions of Europe: An Outline', *Acta Historica Academiae Scientiarum Hungariae*, 29 (1983), 131–84.

Szulc, Lukasz, *Transnational Homosexuals in Communist Poland. Cross-Border Flows in Gay and Lesbian Magazines* (Cham: Palgrave Macmillan, 2018).

Szulecki, Kacper, 'Heretical Geopolitics of Central Europe. Dissidents Intellectuals and an Alternative European Order', *Geoforum*, 65 (2015), 25–36.

'Hijacked Ideas Human Rights, Peace, and Environmentalism in Czechoslovak and Polish Dissident Discourses', *East European Politics and Societies*, 25/2 (2011), 272–95.

Szwedand, Anna and Katarzyna Zielińska, 'A War on Gender? The Roman Catholic Church's Discourse on Gender in Poland', in Sabrina Ramet and Irena Borowik (eds.), *Religion, Politics, and Values in Poland: Continuity and Change since 1989* (New York: Palgrave Macmillan, 2017), 113–36.

Tareke, Gebru, *The Ethiopian Revolution* (New Haven, CT: Yale University Press, 2009).

Taubman, William and Svetlana Savranskaya, 'If a Wall Fell in Berlin and Moscow Hardly Noticed, Would It Still Make a Noise?', in Jeffrey Engel (ed.), *The Fall of the Berlin Wall: The Revolutionary Legacy of 1989* (Oxford: Oxford University Press, 2012), 69–92.

Taylor, Ian, 'South Africa's Transition to Democracy and the "Change Industry": A Case Study of IDASA', *Politikon: South African Journal of Political Studies*, 29/1 (2002), 31–48.

Taylor, Karin and Hannes Grandits, 'Tourism and the Making of Socialist Yugoslavia', in Karin Taylor and Hannes Grandits (eds.), *Yugoslavia's Sunny Side: A History of Tourism in Socialism (1950s–1980s)* (Budapest: Central European University Press, 2010), 1–32.

Ther, Philipp, *Die neue Ordnung auf dem alten Kontinent. Eine Geschichte des neoliberalen Europa* (Berlin: Suhrkamp, 2014).

Europe since 1989: A History (Princeton, NJ: Princeton University Press, 2016).

Thompson, Mark, *A Paper House: The Ending of Yugoslavia* (London: Vintage, 1992).

Tismaneanu, Vladimir, *The Devil in History: Communism, Fascism, and Some Lessons of the Twentieth Century* (Berkeley: University of California Press, 2012).

Fantasies of Salvation: Democracy, Nationalism and Myth in Post-communist Europe (Princeton, NJ: Princeton University Press, 1998).

'On Neo-conservatorism', 25 September 2009, https://tismaneanu.wordpress .com/2009/09/25/.

Stalinism for All Seasons: A Political History of Romanian Communism (Berkeley: University of California Press, 2003).

Tismaneanu, Vladimir and Patrick Clawson, *Uprooting Leninism, Cultivating Liberty* (Lanham, MD: Foreign Policy Research Institute, 1992).

Tismaneanu, Vladimir and Judith Shapiro, *Debates on the Future of Communism* (New York: Palgrave Macmillan, 1991).

Tőkés, Rudolf, *A harmadik magyar köztársaság születése* (Budapest: L'Harmattan, 2015).

Tokić, Mate Nikola, 'The End of "Historical-Ideological Bedazzlement": Cold War Politics and Émigré Croatian Separatist Violence, 1950–1980', *Social Science History*, 36/3 (2012), 421–45.

'Landscapes of Conflict: Unity and Disunity in Post–Second World War Croatian Émigré Separatism', *Journal European Review of History: Revue européenne d'histoire*, 16/5 (2009), 739–53.

Tolz, Vera, 'Conflicting "Homeland Myths" and Nation-State Building in Post-communist Russia', *Slavic Review*, 57/2 (1998), 267–94.

Toplak, Cirila, 'Evropska Ideja v Slovenski Politični Misli', *Teorija in Praksa*, 39 (2002), 579–87.

Török, Adam and Agnes Györffy, 'Ungarn in der Vorreiterrolle', in Jutta Günther and Dagmar Jaješniak-Quast (eds.), *Willkommene Investoren oder nationaler Ausverkauf? Ausländische Direktinvestitionen in Ostmitteleuropa im 20. Jahrhundert* (Berlin: Berliner Wissenschafts-Verlag, 2006), 253–74.

Travin, Dmitrij, 'Avtoritarnyj tormoz dlja "krasnogo kolesa"', *Zvezda*, 6 (1994), 125–35.

Trencsényi, Balázs, 'From Goulash-Communism to Goulash-Authoritarianism?', *Tr@nsit Online*, 2013, www.iwm.at/transit/transit-online/from-goulash-com munism-to-goulash-authoritarianism/.

Trencsényi, Balázs, Maciej Janowski, Monika Baár, Maria Falina, and Michal Kopeček, 'Introduction', in Trencsényi, Janowski, Baár, Falina, and Kopeček, *A History of Modern Political Thought in East Central Europe. Volume I: Negotiating Modernity in the 'Long Nineteenth Century'* (Oxford: Oxford University Press, 2018), 1–14.

Political Thought in East Central Europe. Volume II: Negotiating Modernity in the 'Short Twentieth Century' and Beyond Part II: 1968–2018 (Oxford: Oxford University Press, 2018).

Trifunovska, Snežana, *Yugoslavia through Documents: From Its Creation to Its Dissolution* (Dordrecht: Martinus Nijhoff, 1994).

Trutowski, Dominik, 'Poland and Spain "Entangled". Political Learning in Transitions to Democracy' (paper presented at 'Entangled Transitions: Between Eastern and Southern Europe 1960s–2014', University of Leuven, 2014).

Tshiyembe, Mwayila, 'L'autopsie de l'échec de la transition démocratique en Afrique à la lumière de la théorie desconjonctures politiques fluids', *Présence Africaine*, 157 (1998), 71–99.

Tsygankov, Andrei, 'Finding a Civilisational Idea: "West", "Eurasia", and "Euro-East", in Russia's Foreign Policy', *Geopolitics*, 12/3 (2007), 375–99.

Tubilewicz, Czeslaw, 'Chinese Press Coverage of Political and Economic Restructuring of East Central Europe', *Asian Survey*, 37/10 (1997), 927–43.

'1989 in Sino-East Central European Relations Revisited', in Frank Columbus (ed.), *Central and Eastern Europe in Transition* (Commack, NY: Nova Science, 2001), 21–48.

Tucker, Aviezer, 'Restoration and Convergence: Russia and China since 1989', in George Lawson, Chris Armbruster, and Michael Cox (eds.), *The Global 1989. Continuity and Change in World Politics* (Cambridge: Cambridge University Press, 2011), 157–78.

Tudor, Despina, 'Ana Blandiana: "Epoca noastră seamănă izbitor cu cea de la finalul Imperiului Roman"', 24 March 2016, *Revista 22*, https://revista22.ro/70252912/ana-blandiana-epoca-noastr-seamn-izbitor-cu-cea-de-la-finalul-imperiului-roman.html.

Tudoran, Dorin, 'Farmecul discret al democrației', *Agora*, 1/2 (1988), 1–18.

Turcsanyi, Richard, 'Is the Czech Republic China's New "Bridge to Europe"?', *The Diplomat*, 12 September 2015, http://thediplomat.com/2015/09/is-the-czech-republic-chinas-new-bridge-to-europe/.

Tyler, Imogen, 'The Hieroglyphics of the Border: Racial Stigma in Neoliberal Europe', *Ethnic and Racial Studies*, 41/10 (2018), 1783–1801.

Uhl, Petr, 'The Alternative Community as Revolutionary Avant-Garde', in Václav Havel et al., *The Power of the Powerless: Citizens against the State in Central-Eastern Europe* (London: Routledge, 2015), 188–97.

Umland, Andreas, 'Post-Soviet Neo-Eurasianism, the Putin System, and the Contemporary European Extreme Right', *Perspectives on Politics*, 15/2 (2017), 465–76.

'The Unification Treaty between the FRG and the GDR (Berlin, 31 August 1990)', Centre Virtuel de la Connaissance sur l'Europe (CVCE), www.cvce.eu/content/publication/1997/10/13/2c391661-db4e-42e5-84f7-bd86108c0b9c/publishable_en.pdf.

Ustav Socijalističke Federativne Republike Jugoslavije – Stručno objašnjenje/The Constitution of the Socialist Federal Republic of Yugoslavia – Expert Interpretation (Belgrade: Institute for Political Studies, 1975).

Vachudova, Milada Anna, 'Eastern Europe as Gatekeeper: The Immigration and Asylum Policies of an Enlarging European Union', in Peter Andreas and Timothy Snyder (eds.), *The Wall around the West: State Borders and Immigration Controls in North America and Europe* (Lanham, MD: Rowman & Littlefield, 2000), 153–71.

Valenta, Marko and Sabrina Ramet (eds.), *The Bosnian Diaspora: Integration in Transnational Communities* (Farnham: Ashgate, 2011).

Valiavicharska, Zhivka, 'How the Concept of Totalitarianism Appeared in Late Socialist Bulgaria: The Birth and Life of Zheliu Zhelev's Book *Fascism*', *Kritika: Explorations in Russian and Eurasian History*, 15/2 (2014), 303–34.

Vámos, Péter, 'A Hungarian Model for China? Sino-Hungarian Relations in the Era of Economic Reforms, 1979–89', *Cold War History*, 3/18 (2018), 361–78.

'The Tiananmen Square "Incident" in China and the East Central European Revolutions', in Wolfgang Mueller, Michael Gehler, and Arnold Suppan (eds.), *The Revolutions of 1989: A Handbook* (Vienna: Austrian Academy of Sciences Press, 2015), 93–111.

Vangeli, Anastas, 'China's Engagement with the Sixteen Countries of Central, East and Southeast Europe under the Belt and Road Initiative', *China and World Economy*, 25/5 (2017), 101–24.

'Global China and Symbolic Power: The Case of 16 + 1 Cooperation', *Journal of Contemporary China*, 27/113 (2018), 674–87.

van Vuuren, Hennie, *Apartheid, Guns and Money – A Tale of Profit* (Johannesburg: Jacana Media, 2017).

van Zuijdewijn, Jeanine de Roy, and Edwin Bakker, 'Returning Western Foreign Fighters: The Case of Afghanistan, Bosnia and Somalia' (International Centre for Counter-Terrorism – The Hague Background Note, June 2014), www.icct.nl/download/file/ICCT-De-Roy-van-Zuijdewijn-Bakker-Returning-Western-Foreign-Fighters-June-2014.pdf.

Varas, Augusto (ed.), *Soviet–Latin American Relations in the 1980s* (Boulder, CO: Westview, 1987).

Velikonja, Mitja, *EUROSIS – A Critique of the New Eurocentrism* (Ljubljana: Peace Institute, 2005).

Vetlesen, Arne Johan, *Evil and Human Agency: Understanding Collective Evildoing* (Cambridge: Cambridge University Press, 2005).

Vezenkov, Alexander and Tchavdar Marinov, 'The Concept of National Revival in Balkan Historiographies', in Roumen Daskalov and Alexander Vezenkov (eds.), *Entangled Histories of the Balkans Volume Three: Shared Pasts, Disputed Legacies* (Leiden: Brill, 2015), 406–62.

Vianu, Ion, 'O interpretare a României de azi', *Agora*, 1/2 (1988), 63–78.

Vicherat Mattar, Daniela, 'Did Walls Really Come Down?', in Marc Silberman, Karen E. Till, and Janet Ward (eds.), *Walls, Borders, Boundaries: Spatial and Cultural Practices in Europe* (New York: Berghahn Books, 2012), 77–94.

'The Vietnamese Communities in Central and Eastern Europe', special issue of *Central and Eastern European Migration Review*, 4/1 (2015), www.ceemr.uw.edu.pl/sites/default/files/CEEMR_Vol_4_No_1.pdf.

Vladisavljević, Nebojša, *Serbia's Antibureaucratic Revolution: Milošević, the Fall of Communism and Nationalist Mobilisation* (Basingstoke: Palgrave Macmillan, 2008).

Vojvodić, Mirjana (ed.), *Not in My Name* (Niš: Center for Civic Initiative, 2008).

Vu, Tuong, *Vietnam's Communist Revolution. The Power and Limits of Ideology* (New York: Cambridge University Press, 2017).

Vujačić, Veljko, *Nationalism, Myth, and the State in Russia and Serbia: Antecedents of the Dissolution of the Soviet Union and Yugoslavia* (Cambridge: Cambridge University Press, 2015).

Walter, Christian, Antje von Ungern-Sternberg, and Kavus Abushov (eds.), *Self-Determination and Secession in International Law* (Oxford: Oxford University Press, 2014).

Wang, Hui, *China's New Order. Society, Politics, and Economy in Transition* (Cambridge, MA: Harvard University Press, 2003).

'Dangdai Zhongguo de Sixiang Zhuangkuang yu Xiandaixing Wenti', *Tianya* 5 (1997), 133–50.

Ward, Stuart, 'The European Provenance of Decolonization', *Past and Present* 230/1 (2016), 227–60.

Way, Lucan, 'The Real Causes of the Coloured Revolutions', *Journal of Democracy*, 19/3 (July 2008), 55–69.

Wciślik, Piotr, 'Political Languages of Anti-solidarity: Mirosław Dzielski and the Differentia Specifica of Polish Neo-liberalism', in *Proceedings of the 16th International Conference on the History of Concepts, Bilbao, 29–31 August 2013*, 170–176, http://dx.doi.org/10.1387/conf.hcg2013.2.

Weapons of the Islamic State (London: Conflict and Armed Research, 2017), www.conflictarm.com/reports/weapons-of-the-islamic-state/.

Wedel, Janine, *Collision and Collusion: The Strange Case of Western Aid to Eastern Europe 1989–1998* (New York: St. Martin's, 1998).

Weise, Zia, 'Turkey's Balkan Comeback', *Politico*, 17 May 2018, www.politico.eu/article/turkey-western-balkans-comeback-european-union-recep-tayyip-erdogan/.

West, Richard, *Tito and the Rise and Fall of Yugoslavia* (London: Faber and Faber, 2009).

Westad, Odd Arne, 'Conclusion', in George Lawson et al. (eds.), *The Global 1989. Continuity and Change in World Politics* (Cambridge: Cambridge University Press, 2010), 271–80.

Whitaker, Reg, 'Security and Intelligence in the Post–Cold War World', *Socialist Register*, 28 (1992), 111–30.

Wilczynski, Jozef, *The Multinationals and East-West Relations: Towards Transideological Collaboration* (Boulder, CO: Westview, 1976).

Wilson, Jeanne, 'The Eurasian Economic Union and China's Silk Road: Implications for the Russian–Chinese Relationship', *European Politics and Society*, 17/Supplement 1, 'The Eurasian Project in Global Perspective' (2016), 113–32.

'"The Polish Lesson": China and Poland 1980–1990', *Studies in Comparative Communism*, 23/3–4 (1990), 259–79.

Wintle, Michael, 'Islam as Europe's "Other" in the Long Term: Some Discontinuities', *History*, 101/344 (2016), 42–61.

Woever, O., 'Conflicts of Vision, Visions of Conflict', in O. Woever, P. Lemaitre, and E. Tromer (eds.), *European Polyphony: Perspectives beyond East-West Confrontation* (London: Macmillan 1989), 186–224.

Wood, William B., 'Geographic Aspects of Genocide: A Comparison of Bosnia and Rwanda', *Transactions of the Institute of British Geographers*, 26/1 (2001), 57–75.

Woodward, Susan, *Balkan Tragedy. Chaos and Dissolution after the Cold War* (Washington, DC: Brookings Institute, 1995).

'The Political Economy of Ethno-Nationalism in Yugoslavia', *Socialist Register*, 39 (2003), 73–92.

Wuestenhagen, Jana, 'Communist Europeanism: A Case Study of the GDR', in Dieter Gosewinkel (ed.), *Anti-liberal Europe. A Neglected Story of Europeanisation* (Oxford: Berghahn Books, 2015), 157–78.

Wunschik, Tobias, *Knastware für den Klassenfeind. Häftlingsarbeit in der DDR, der Ost-West Handel und die Staatssicherheit 1970–1989* (Göttingen: Vandenhoeck & Ruprecht, 2014).

Yang, Zhong, 'The Fallen Wall and Its Aftermath: Impact of Regime Change upon Foreign Policy Behaviour in Six East European Countries', *East European Quarterly*, 28/2 (1994), 235–57.

Yinghui, Meng, *Political Belief and the Soviet Revolution* (Beijing: China Social Sciences Press, 2005).

Yordanov, Radoslav, *The Soviet Union and the Horn of Africa during the Cold War* (Lanham, MD: Lexington Books, 2016).

Zaccaria, Benedetto, 'Learning from Yugoslavia? Western Europe and the Myth of Self-Management (1968–1975)', in Michel Christian, Sandrine Kott, and Ondrej Matejka (eds.), *Planning in Cold War Europe: Competition, Cooperation, Circulations (1950s–1970s)* (Berlin: De Gruyter, 2018), 213–36.

'Under the Shadow of the Soviet Union: The EEC, Yugoslavia and the Cold War in the Long 1970s', in Svetozar Rajak et al. (eds.), *The Balkans in the Cold War* (London: Palgrave Macmillan, 2017), 239–59.

Žagar, Mitja, 'The Collapse of the Yugoslav Federation and the Viability of Asymmetrical Federalism', in Sergio Ortino, Mitja Žagar, and Vojtech Mastny (eds.), *The Changing Faces of Federalism: Institutional Reconfiguration in Europe from East to West* (Manchester: Manchester University Press, 2005), 107–33.

Záhořík, Jan, 'Czechoslovakia and Congo/Zaire under Mobutu, 1965–1980', *Canadian Journal of History*, 52/2 (2017), 290–314.

Zahra, Tara, 'Travel Agents on Trial: Policing Mobility in East Central Europe, 1889–1989', *Past & Present*, 223/1 (2014), 161–93.

Zajmi, Gazmend, 'Kosova's Constitutional Position in the Former Yugoslavia', in Ger Duijzings, Dušan Janjić, and Shkëlzen Maliqi (eds.), *Kosovo-Kosova: Confrontation or Coexistence* (Nijmegen: Peace Research Centre and Political Cultural Centre, 1996), 95–103.

Zakharov, Nikolay, *Race and Racism in Russia* (Houndmills: Palgrave Macmillan, 2015).

Zaroulia, Marilena, '"Sharing the Moment": Europe, Affect, and Utopian Performatives in the Eurovision Song Contest', in Karen Fricker and Milija Gluhovic (eds.), *Performing the 'New' Europe. Studies in International Performance* (London: Palgrave Macmillan, 2013), 31–52.

Zarycki, Tomasz, 'De-spatialisation and the Europeanisation of Late Communist Imaginary: The Intellectual Trajectory of Polish Geographer Antoni Kukliński' (paper presented at Revolution from Within: Experts, Managers and Technocrats in the Long Transformation of 1989, Jena, June 2018).

Zantovsky, Michael, *Havel: A Life* (London: Atlantic Books, 2014).

Zhelyazkova, Antonina, 'Islamisation in the Balkans as a Historiographical Problem: The Southeast-European Perspective', in Fikret Adanir and Suraiya Faroqhi (eds.), *The Ottomans and the Balkans. A Discussion of Historiography* (Leiden: Brill, 2002), 223–66.

Zivanović, Maja, 'New Zealand Mosque Gunman "Inspired by Balkan Nationalists"', *Balkan Insight*, 15 March 2019, https://balkaninsight.com/2019/03/15/new-zealand-mosque-gunman-inspired-by-balkan-nationalists/.

Znoj, Milan, 'Václav Havel, His Idea of Civil Society, and the Czech Liberal Tradition', in Michal Kopeček and Piotr Wciślik (eds.), *Thinking through Transition: Liberal Democracy, Authoritarian Pasts, and Intellectual History in East Central Europe after 1989* (Budapest: Central European University Press, 2015), 109–38.

Zubok, Vladislav, 'Introduction', in Patryk Babiracki and Kenyon Zimmer (eds.), *Cold War Crossings: International Travel and Exchange across the Soviet Bloc* (College Station: Texas A&M University Press, 2014), 1–13.

'The Soviet Union and China in the 1980s: Reconciliation and Divorce', *Cold War History*, 17/2 (2017), 121–41.

Zhivago's Children: The Last Russian Intelligentsia (Cambridge, MA: Belknap, 2009).

Żuk, Piotr, 'Anti-military Protests and Campaigns against Nuclear Power Plants: The Peace Movement in the Shadow of the Warsaw Pact in Poland in the 1980s', *Journal of Contemporary Central and Eastern Europe*, 25/3 (2017), 367–74.

Index

Note: Locators with an 'n' refers to footnotes, e.g. 298n64 refers to footnote 64 on p.298.